*History of Literature in Canada*

*European Studies in American Literature and Culture*

Edited by Reingard M. Nischik
(University of Constance)

# History of Literature in Canada

## English-Canadian and French-Canadian

Edited by
Reingard M. Nischik

CAMDEN HOUSE
Rochester, New York

First published 2008
by Camden House

Camden House is an imprint of Boydell & Brewer Inc.
668 Mt. Hope Avenue, Rochester, NY 14620, USA
www.camden-house.com
and of Boydell & Brewer Limited
PO Box 9, Woodbridge, Suffolk IP12 3DF, UK
www.boydellandbrewer.com

ISBN–13: 978–1–57113–359–5
ISBN–10: 1–57113–359–3

**Library of Congress Cataloging-in-Publication Data**

History of literature in Canada : English-Canadian and French-Canadian /
   edited by Reingard M. Nischik.
      p. cm. — (European studies in American literature and culture)
   Includes bibliographical references and index.
   ISBN-13: 978-1-57113-359-5 (alk. paper)
   ISBN-10: 1-57113-359-3 (alk. paper)
      1. Canadian literature — History and criticism.   2. French-Canadian
   literature — History and criticism.   3. National characteristics, Canadian,
   in literature.   4. Group identity — Canada.   I. Nischik, Reingard M.
   II. Title.   III. Series.

   PR9184.3.H56 2008
   810.9'—dc22

                                          2008025359


A catalogue record for this title is available from the British Library.

This publication is printed on acid-free paper.
Printed in the United States of America.

Any future survey of Canadian literature must include both French and English.

— Lorne Pierce, 1927

Canadians cannot agree what their meta-narrative is. . . . Where the impulse in the US is usually to define oneself as American, the Canadian, like a work of postmodern architecture, is always quoting his many sources. . . . If we can't be united we can't be disunited. . . . We survive by working with a low level of self-definition and national definition. We insist on staying multiple. . . . This disunity is our unity.

— Robert Kroetsch, 1985

"I assume you consider yourself a citizen of the world?" "No. I'm Canadian."

— Yann Martel in an interview, 2003

The time of the "two solitudes" that for too long described the character of this country is past. . . . Today's world demands that we learn to see beyond our wounds, beyond our differences for the good of all. . . . Every one of us rekindles in his own way the sense of belonging to this space that we all share, a space that contains the world.

— Michaëlle Jean, 2005

# Contents

# Acknowledgments

THIS UNDERTAKING IS INDEBTED to an earlier project involving Canadianists exclusively from Germany and Austria, the German-language *Kanadische Literaturgeschichte* (2005) published by Metzler in Stuttgart in its renowned series of literary histories. I coedited that book with German Canadianists Konrad Groß and Wolfgang Klooß. I decided early on to try and make the material available to the international English-speaking Canadian Studies community. Camden House saw the worth of such a project, yet did not wish to publish a mere translation of an earlier book. So I made a virtue of necessity and transformed this literary history into an even more ambitious transatlantic undertaking: Whereas some of the chapters of the *Kanadische Literaturgeschichte* appear here in English translation in a revised and updated form (the chapters by Dorothee Scholl, Fritz Peter Kirsch, Reingard M. Nischik, Ursula Mathis-Moser, Doris G. Eibl, Caroline Rosenthal, Martin Kuester, and Andrea Oberhuber), about half of the chapters were written from scratch by new German and, mainly, Canadian specialists, both English-Canadian and French-Canadian (the chapters by Eva Gruber, Iain M. Higgins, Guy Laflèche, Gwendolyn Davies, Tracy Ware, Julia Breitbach, Lorraine York, Marta Dvorak, Jerry Wasserman, Sherrill Grace, Anne Nothof, Nicholas Bradley, Georgiana Banita, and Gilles Dupuis). The book at hand is thus a transatlantic undertaking in which twelve German-language and eleven English-Canadian and French-Canadian scholars, twenty-three in all, joined forces.

During the long editorial process, I was repeatedly reminded that Canada is indeed a bilingual (actually multilingual) country. Two contributors from the Université de Montréal, for instance, produced their chapters for this book in French and then had them translated into English by Canadian translators. The new selection of contributors also rejuvenated the project, since this book intentionally combines senior, established, and young scholars. I find it particularly gratifying that the young scholars I invited to participate on account of their excellent earlier achievements rose to the occasion and produced highly competent chapters that fit in well with those written by their elders. (These young, emerging scholars are Eva Gruber, Georgiana Banita, and Julia Breitbach from the University of Constance, and Nicholas Bradley from the University of Victoria.)

Last, but not least, my statements of gratitude: I thank those kind collaborators who helped make this huge transatlantic venture possible, and within the planned time period. Oliver Schütze from Metzler, Stuttgart, gave the green light for this new undertaking to be published in the United States. My former coeditors Konrad Groß and Wolfgang Klooß preferred not to embark on this project, yet welcomed its realization. Some of the earlier contributors to the *Kanadische Literaturgeschichte* valiantly helped to produce English translations of their previously German-language chapters (Ursula Mathis-Moser, Doris G. Eibl, Martin Kuester). My teammates Emily Petermann, Julia Breitbach, and Georgiana Banita produced excellent first translations of other German-language chapters. Sherrill Grace from the University of British Columbia in Vancouver was helpful during the important stage of selecting Canadian contributors to this project. I thank all contributors for their hard work on their chapters and for bearing with me when, during the seemingly never-ending editorial process, I may have seemed overly tenacious and persistent. My doctoral students Julia Breitbach and Florian Freitag devoted their extraordinary editorial expertise, gained from our rewarding cooperation over several years, also to this project. Without my conscientious secretary Christine Schneider I probably would not have tackled one book after another, since without her reliable work at the PC my resolve might have faltered. Christina Duck Kannenberg helped in editing the manuscript — and along the way rekindled her interest in the literature of her native country. Anja Ging and Julia Sutter reliably and promptly helped with various aspects of the manuscript, Eva Gruber and Georgiana Banita did excellent critical reading at short notice. Ursula Mathis-Moser, Caroline Rosenthal, and Doris G. Eibl read my introductory chapter and made useful suggestions for change. Anja Ging, Emily Petermann, and Barbara Giehmann conscientiously produced the index. Last but not least, I would like to thank Jim Walker and his team at Camden House for their excellent cooperation.

Financial assistance for this publication was provided by the University of Constance's Center of Excellence, "Cultural Foundations of Integration," in the framework of the Excellence Initiative of the Federal and State governments of the Federal Republic of Germany. A subvention grant by the Gesellschaft für Kanada-Studien (Association of Canadian Studies in German-speaking Countries) is also gratefully acknowledged here.

R. N.
Constance, Germany, July 2008

# Introduction: Writing a History of Literature in Canada

*Reingard M. Nischik (University of Constance)*

> "Canadian" has been broadly used for whatever is native, or has been naturalized, or has a distinct bearing on the native — that is, on people, events, and writings which had their focus in our "environment," as Northrop Frye has put it. . . . That which is distinctly Canadian-French in language, thought, culture, and literary production has been left, in accord with their own wishes, to the French scholars of Québec. The time will come, one may hope, when it will be possible to have a French series of books paralleling our English ones — and translations in each of the languages — to facilitate a much-needed comparative study.
>
> Carl F. Klinck, introduction, volume 3
> of *Literary History of Canada* (2nd ed., 1976)

> Even if we assume smooth relations on the political level . . . another generation will probably pass before we see a healthy and mutual interchange between the two literatures. At the present time, English- and French-Canadian writing are best discussed separately.
>
> William Keith, introduction,
> *Canadian Literature in English* (1985)

## The Project in Brief

LITERATURE IN CANADA, particularly the booming cultural production from the 1960s onwards, has arrived at the center stage of world literature. Books by English-Canadian authors today make regular appearances on international bestseller lists, both through established writers such as Margaret Atwood (1939–) and Michael Ondaatje (1943–) and through new talents such as Yann Martel (1963–) and Madeleine Thien (1974–). Atwood, Ondaatje, and Martel, for instance, won the prestigious annual

Man Booker Prize in the space of just one decade.[1] "CanLit," the institutionalized canon of Canadian literature, has likewise developed into a staple of academic interest, pursued in Canadian Studies programs in Canada and around the world. At the same time, with the help of the Quiet Revolution (Révolution tranquille)[2] and a remarkable network of cultural institutions, French-Canadian literature has found its own voice in the North American and francophone worlds, a voice that, as the recent surge of transcultural *écriture migrante* in French Canada shows, further transforms the multicultural scope of literature in Canada. Esteemed for its high literary quality as well as for the different perspectives it provides on North American realities when compared to the literary tradition of the United States, literature in Canada has generated a wealth of scholarly critical responses representing, among others, postcolonial, multicultural, transcultural,[3] feminist, and eco-critical approaches.

It seemed high time, then, to provide a history of literature in Canada for the international market, a compendium that interweaves the various

---

[1] Ondaatje won the prize in 1992, Atwood in 2000, Martel in 2002. Due to a change in sponsorship the award, originally called the Booker Prize, was renamed the Man Booker Prize in 2002.

[2] The Quiet Revolution/Révolution tranquille, dating from roughly 1960 until 1966, was a period of rapid and sweeping change in Quebec society that followed the eighteen-year reign, known as "la grande noirceur," of conservative Union nationale Premier Maurice Duplessis. Duplessis had left the province industrialized but not modernized, and the Quebec people, ripe for change in 1960, elected Liberal Jean Lesage as their new premier. Among Lesage's vast reforms were the reformation of the Catholic Church-run education system, nationalizing Quebec's important hydroelectric industry, setting up the Quebec pension plan, universal health care, and establishing a new ministry for federal-provincial relations. The arts also flourished at this time, as the previously agrarian and church-controlled society became secularized and modernized. Although it involved no violent upheavals, the period of the Quiet Revolution truly revolutionized Quebec's social values, economy, and government.

[3] While I am aware of recent debates around the viability of "transculturalism" as an alternative concept to "multiculturalism" (especially in the writings of Wolfgang Welsch and Rocío G. Davis), I use the term in the sense conferred by Janice Kulyk Keefer's phrase "transcultural aesthetics," implying a kind of de-ethnicization and a cultural politics of inclusion rather than ghettoization. Keefer prefers to see Canadian culture in terms of a kaleidoscope rather than a mosaic; see Janice Kulyk Keefer, "From Mosaic to Kaleidoscope," *Books in Canada* 6 (1991): 13–16; and Keefer, "From Dialogue to Polylogue: Canadian Transcultural Writing During the Deluge," in *Difference and Community: Canadian and European Cultural Perspectives*, ed. Peter Easingwood, Konrad Groß, and Lynette Hunter (Amsterdam: Rodopi, 1996), 59–70.

threads making up this multifarious literature, rather than focusing on only one of the Canadian "literatures" or, as in the rare cases in which English-Canadian and French-Canadian literature have been brought together in one volume, clearly privileging one over the other. *History of Literature in Canada: English-Canadian and French-Canadian* traces literature produced in Canada over the centuries. Starting with the indigenous population's oral tradition, which reaches back some 20,000 years, it then turns to the development of French-Canadian and English-Canadian writing from colonial to contemporary times. While the volume conceives of Canada as a single though multifaceted culture, it accounts for the specific characteristics of English-Canadian and French-Canadian literatures, such as the vital role of the short story in English Canada or the chanson in French Canada. Yet it also pays special attention to Aboriginal literature and to the pronounced transcultural, ethnically diverse character of much contemporary Canadian literature, thus moving the debate about what constitutes literature in Canada clearly beyond the traditions of the two founding nations.

## Cultural Contexts, Editorial Principles

While its inclusive approach of encompassing all major cultural traditions of literature written in Canada is innovative, other traits of this book are less surprising, and intentionally so. With hardly an English-language literary history in existence that comprehensively covers both English-Canadian and French-Canadian literature,[4] a chronological, alternating treatment of both literatures according to genre, enriched by some chapters outside the generic framework, offered the clearest possible overview. Clarity and balance of structure are primary aims of this book,[5] which devotes equal attention to English-Canadian and French-Canadian literary cultures and allows for and encourages an immediate comparison between the two.

---

[4] Altogether, there are only three earlier examples, two of them dating from the 1920s, all of them mentioned below.

[5] In terms of structural balance, one might have aimed at an even larger symmetry by adding a chapter on the institutionalization of literature in English Canada, yet the sections titled "Politics and Literature between Nationalism and Internationalism" and "Sociopolitical and Cultural Developments from 1967 to the Present" deal with such issues, as do some of the chapters structured according to genre. Then too, French Canada is a special case also in this particular respect. One might also have added a chapter on popular music in English Canada to match the chapter on the chanson from French Canada, but the chanson comes much closer to poetry than much of the popular music from English Canada does. Thus the chanson had an impact on literary production in French Canada that has no counterpart on the English-Canadian scene.

Regarding the title of this book and its implications, the very terms "English-Canadian" and "French-Canadian" or even "Canadian" are contested terms in Canada. In the hope that this controversy excludes the name of the country itself, "Canada," this book is titled "History of Literature *in Canada*," not "History of *Canadian* Literature." As Frank Davey has shown in an article of 1997, there has been a long and more or less intense, sometimes open and sometimes covert cultural battle about such identifying terms in transcultural Canada. At the end of the nineteenth century, when academic study of Canadian literature began, there were no models for studying and theorizing a bilingual or multilingual national literature, and English-speaking Canada largely regarded itself, in Davey's words, as "a unilingually anglophone country, in which francophone culture was a minor phenomenon, something like Welsh in Britain."[6] Davey also points out that

> anglophone-Canadian literary institutions and their practices have by and large developed less in response to the general field of Canadian cultural conditions and more as adaptations of institutional structures already developed or concurrently developing in Britain and the US [the norm being that one nation has one official language and one national literature]. In this they have differed from many of our country's federal institutions, like Parliament, the legal system, the Canada Council, or The National Film Board, which have developed bilingual practices not found in similar British and American institutions. (Davey, " 'AND Quebec,' " 9)

Thus "Canadian Literature" has come to signify increasingly only "anglo-Canadian literature," whereas scholars from Quebec "renounced their rights to terms like 'Canada' or 'Canadien' at the very time that English-Canadians have implicitly staked exclusive claim to them."[7] In fact, Lucie Robert reported in 1991 that Quebec culture viewed itself as "québécoise" and no longer as "canadienne française."[8] As Davey points out, "English-Canadian"

---

[6] Frank Davey, " 'AND Quebec': Canadian Literature and Its Quebec Questions," *Canadian Poetry* 40 (Spring/Summer 1997): 6–26, here 10.

[7] Davey, " 'AND Quebec,' " 17. Such issues came to bear on the present project when a contributor from Quebec made it a precondition for his cooperation that the term "Canadian" should not appear in the book's title because it would slight Québécois literature.

[8] Davey, " 'AND Quebec,' " 7. Ever since the Quiet Revolution the term "québécois(e)" has been used to refer to Quebec culture after the 1960s, whereas "canadien(ne) français(e)" has come to refer to the time before the Quiet Revolution. Alternatively, "québécois(e)" is sometimes also used retroactively today to refer to Quebec culture both before and after the Quiet Revolution, for example in the *Histoire de la littérature québécoise* by Michel Biron, François Dumont, and Élisabeth

no longer seems to include anglophone Quebecers (7). There is thus an increasing separation between the terms "Canadian" (signifying English Canadian or Canada outside Quebec) and "québécois" (signifying from the province of Quebec, or only French Canadians from the nation of Quebec[9]). This territorialization of language and ethnicity (Quebec vs. "rest of [predominantly English-speaking] Canada") raises further problems, of course. What about literature from Quebec not written in French? What about literature written in French in a Canadian province other than Quebec?

Such complications present a tremendous challenge to the production of literary histories concerning Canada, which may partly explain why there have been relatively few. In particular, literary histories dealing with both English-Canadian and French-Canadian literature are few and far between, and pretending that there is no francophone Canada (or the other way round) is a frequently employed means of dealing with the challenge. If French-Canadian literature is included at all in literary histories written in English, it is usually done according to what Davey calls the "supplementary" or "peripheral" model: Only a small proportion of the book is devoted to French-Canadian literature in a token, condescending gesture.[10] Similarly, most literary histories written in French concentrate exclusively on French-Canadian literature, although due to a recent widening of the concept of "littérature québécoise" (see note 9), one finds literary histories

---

Nardout-Lafarge (Montreal: Boréal, 2007), 12. Francophones in Canada had used "canadien(ne)" to refer to themselves until the middle of the nineteenth century, after which the term was changed to "canadien(ne) français(e)," a practice that persisted until the current usage of the terms was established in the 1960s. As late as 1904, however, Camille Roy still employed "canadien(ne)" to exclusively refer to literature written in French in Canada ("La nationalisation de la littérature canadienne").

[9] See Davey, " 'AND Quebec' ": "What appears purposefully left ambiguous . . . is whether "québécois" denotes ethnicity and language or whether it is the adjectival form of the name of a Canadian province. . . . The view among francophone-Canadian critics that the literature of Quebec consists (or ought to consist) only of French-language writing became commonplace in the 1980s and '90s" (24, n. 1). This view, of course, has been contested by, among others, "transcultural" writers from Quebec such as Marco Micone, for whom "les Québécois n'[ont] pas que le français comme langue identitaire" (Micone, "Libre-opinion — Nous, les Québécois," *Le Devoir*, 28 November 2007). In their *Histoire de la littérature québécoise* (2007), Michel Biron, François Dumont, and Élisabeth Nardout-Lafarge also label anglophone texts written in Quebec as "québécois(e)."

[10] See, for instance, Elizabeth Waterston's *Survey: A Short History of Canadian Literature* (Toronto: Methuen, 1973), which includes only one chapter on Quebec.

that include texts written in English (but within Quebec), the most recent example being Biron, Dumont, and Nardout-Lafarge's 2007 *Histoire*.

The present project comes closer to what Davey calls the "bicultural" or "side by side" model. There are only three forerunners (two in English, one in French) and two realized examples (one in English, one in French) of this type of literary history so far. Archibald MacMechan's pioneering *Headwaters of Canadian Literature* (Toronto: McClelland & Stewart, 1924, repr. 1974) devotes two chapters to French-Canadian literature (90 pages) and two chapters to English-Canadian literature (135 pages), but its preface rightly stresses that the book is "emphatically a sketch, an outline, not a complete history of Canadian literature." Based on its title and table of contents, Lorne Pierce's *An Outline of Canadian Literature (French and English)* (Toronto: Ryerson, 1927) seems to take a balanced approach in its treatment of English-Canadian and French-Canadian literature, but upon closer scrutiny three-fourths of the book is devoted to English-Canadian literature, so that it actually verges on the supplementary model. More recently, W. H. New's *A History of Canadian Literature* (2nd ed. Montreal and Kingston: McGill-Queen's University Press, 2003), too, in its combined approach focuses considerably more on English-Canadian literature, although the book is to be commended for discussing English- and French-Canadian writing in an innovative way, being organized around selected thematic issues.

Édmond Lareau's *Histoire de la littérature canadienne* (Montreal: John Lovell, 1874, repr. 1990) is mainly structured according to fictional and nonfictional genres ("Poésie," "Histoire," "Romanciers et Nouvellistes," "Science," etc.). Lareau considers English- and French-Canadian literatures as "deux littératures distinctes" (ch. 2); yet this distinction is not reflected formally in the structure of his chapters, which often freely mix authors writing in French with those writing in English, devoting equal attention to both languages. Similar to New's *A History of Canadian Literature*, Clément Moisan's *L'âge de la littérature canadienne* (Montreal: HMH, 1969) is organized around thematic issues; Moisan's approach, however, is more balanced than New's, as it is his goal, as he states in the introduction, to "démontrer la parenté des deux littératures canadiennes." Similar to MacMechan, though, Moisan considers his work to be written from the superficial perspective of a "vol d'oiseau."

A further development of the "bicultural" model is the "coordination" model, where coordination takes the place of supplementarity in linking the literatures presented. As Davey comments, the coordination model "rests in part on the Quebec shift from *canadianité française* to *québécoisité*, and like that shift operates to exclude francophone-Canadian literature written outside Quebec" (19). The present project is related to these two models, yet it also differs from them in that it includes culturally hybrid literatures in Canada written in English and French by writers of non-English or non-French descent (see especially chapters 27 and 34) and in that it also includes texts in English and French written outside these languages' main "territories" in Canada — examples are Mordecai Richler (1931–2001) and Mavis Gallant (1922–) writing in English in Montreal and even in Paris as well as Andrée Lacelle (1947–) writing in French in Ottawa. Thus we can now add the "transcultural model (with literature written in English and French)" to Davey's earlier analytical differentiation.[11]

Under these circumstances, the subtitle "English-Canadian and French-Canadian" seemed the most appropriate, referring to the languages in which the literature presented is written. This choice, like any other, may have drawbacks, and some Québécois scholars might prefer other designations.[12] The subtitle, however, wholeheartedly keeps faith with Canadian writer and critic Robert Kroetsch's dictum "disunity is our unity."[13] In other words, this project, being fully aware of potential bicultural, multicultural, or "postnational" counterarguments, regards literature in Canada in the final analysis as a single though multifaceted whole, and considers the multicultural/transcultural strands of this literature an attractive cultural asset of Canada. With the distanced and perhaps somewhat privileged detachment of a non-Canadian observer from abroad trying to displace the ideological weight of identity debates Canada has been fraught with,[14] I hope that our attempt to present these literatures together in one book, in spite of all complexities, will be recognized as what it is meant to be — a taking stock and celebration of the diverse literatures written in Canada.

[11] Then too, the book at hand is, to my knowledge, only the second literary history of Canada by an American publisher. Ray Palmer Baker's *A History of English-Canadian Literature to the Confederation: In Relation to the Literature of Great Britain and the United States* (Cambridge, MA: Harvard University Press, 1920; repr. New York: Russell & Russell, 1968) curiously states in the preface that the book "may show the intellectual continuity of the English-speaking peoples and the fact that, in spite of their differences, they are unescapably one."

[12] One of the contributors from Quebec suggested the title "History of Literature in Canada: Canadian, French-Canadian, and Québécoise." He further commented on his suggestion: "Il dénote la particularité absolue des littératures au Canada, celle du Québec, de la nation québécoise, qui est par définition irréductible aux littératures (pluriel) de la nation canadienne. On n'y peut rien, puisque c'est la réalité. Votre sous-titre actuel correspond à une réalité qui date maintenant d'un demi-siècle. Le nouveau sous-titre que je propose s'imposera avant longtemps (de sorte que votre titre actuel serait vite un archaisme)" (email to the editor, 3 March 2008).

[13] Robert Kroetsch, "Disunity as Unity: A Canadian Strategy," in Kroetsch, *The Lovely Treachery of Words: Essays Selected and New* (Toronto: Oxford University Press, 1989), 21–33, here 20, 31.

[14] See Davey's summary from a Canadian perspective: "an impatience at a cultural situation that makes the name of one's country problematical — in need of qualification

Next to its openness to diverse cultures, another characteristic of the book at hand is that literary texts are viewed in their sociohistorical, political, and cultural contexts, including side glances at the strong neighboring influence of the United States and the transatlantic view toward Europe. In fact, Canada and its literatures' varying positions in a political and cultural constellation of nationalism, provincialism or regionalism, biculturalism, multiculturalism, transculturalism, continentalism (the relationship between Canada and the United States), and internationalism may be regarded as the threads connecting the chronologically sequenced sections in the book. Another editorial principle concerned conciseness, readability, and homogeneity of style, which we painstakingly encouraged in order to give this book a unified front in spite of the rather heterogeneous strands of literature it treats. Contributors were asked to focus their accounts and analyses largely on "canonical" texts where possible. If the main title of this book, *History of Literature in Canada*, also suggests a survey and discussion of individual books, this connotation is indeed welcome. At the same time, there are potential traps implied in the concept of the canon, especially in a "postnational" country like Canada. To the extent that some literary phenomena, such as the Canadian novel, have longer histories, they are treated at greater length than more recent developments such as multicultural and transcultural writing, where it would even be difficult to speak of one canon: As the chapter title "Canons of Diversity in Contemporary English-Canadian Literature" suggests, multicultural plurality itself challenges the very concept of the literary canon. All in all, however, the aim here is to present a literary history of writers and texts that have stood the test of time and seem prominent enough today to warrant further recognition in the foreseeable future. This approach, of course, tends to put younger, up-and-coming writers at a disadvantage. Let me explain, by way of example, the procedure with respect to the two short-story chapters I contributed to this book. Whereas the "canon" of the earlier modernist English-Canadian short story seems largely uncontroversial, the question of whom to include in the chapter on the contemporary English-Canadian short story was much more problematic, not least because the short story is such a vibrant genre in English-Canadian literature. In order to reduce subjectivity in the selection process, I surveyed ninety-two short-story anthologies, most of them published in Canada, noting which English-Canadian short-story writers are most frequently anthologized. My decisions on which individual writers and stories to discuss in these short-story

---

and supplement; an impatience at the linguistic and political difficulty of creating inclusively Canadian anthologies; a resentment that a straightforward Canadianness is not easily available" (Davey, " 'AND Quebec,' " 17).

chapters are thus based on multiple decisions by many short-story experts and editors about which English-Canadian short stories are most worthy of attention.

The authors of the individual chapters — specialists on their topics — were given leeway as to what writers and works to include in their overviews. I did intervene where I considered, for instance, that important authors were unjustly neglected. Of course, many choices are debatable and show the inevitable and legitimate amount of subjectivity involved in canon formation. Is it adequate, for instance, to elaborate on Ernest Buckler's novels but to mention Ethel Wilson's novels only in passing? (But then, her short stories are treated at greater length in another chapter.) Is Don McKay a more important poet than Anne Carson or Anne Michaels, as the space allotted to each of them here might suggest? Concerning French-Canadian literature, is it adequate to discuss the (French) works *about* the colony in as great detail as the embryonic literature emanating *from* New France? Do the former even belong in a history of literature *in* Canada? In any case, a literary history should involve compromise and a collaborative effort to relativize subjective choices and restrictions, allowing for discussion and negotiation in the ongoing process of canon formation. Such a work is by definition retrospective rather than meant to feel the pulse of contemporary writing as the book leaves the press. Who knows whether some of the new talents we appreciate and talk about today will still be around in, say, five or ten years' time? By including certain authors and not others, this book inevitably contributes to the formation of a canon, or canons, of literature in Canada. Some chapters do mention relatively young authors whose texts were published as late as 2007, placing their achievements within the larger field of writing in Canada. This, I believe, is how a literary history demonstrates the perpetually changing and adapting canons of a literature both established and young.

## Outline of This Volume:
## Literary Developments in Canada

After this introductory chapter, the book is divided into six parts, encompassing thirty-five chapters. Applying a wide conception of literature — which, for instance, also includes texts in the oral tradition and musical forms of lyrical texts — the book starts out at the very beginning in part 1 with a chapter titled "Aboriginal Oral Traditions" in Canada. This chapter stresses not only the distinctness of Aboriginal cultures (the Inuit and some one hundred other Aboriginal nations) and their communal, performative "orature" featuring trickster characters and other cultural heroes, but also justifies the specifically Canadian designation "First Nations" (where

Americans speak of "Native Americans"). The second chapter, "White
Writing before Canada, 1000–1600," features texts providing evidence of
the land as a contact zone of White European encounters with the indigenous Other. From the Old Norse sagas to sixteenth-century French and
English travelers' and explorers' reports, these texts display White
Eurocentric views of the newly "discovered" land and its indigenous
population.

## Colonial Writing in New France and British Canada

Part 2, "The Literature of New France, 1604–1760," discusses the French
colonial period. It is prefaced by a short chapter focusing on the sociohistorical and political context of the era. (Such contextualizing chapters are
also provided in each of the other parts of the book: chs. 3, 6, 11, 16, and
21; and other chapters, too, regularly refer to the sociohistorical context.)
Part 2 chronicles the tentative beginnings of French-language writing in
what would later become Canada, works mostly authored by Frenchmen
exploring or traveling this section of the North American continent. Their
texts often had a predominantly documentary, rather than aesthetic, function, with First Nations people frequently at the center of attention.
Exploration reports, travelogues, ethnographic writing, missionary reports,
letters, and historical works were the early text formats making up French
writing on New France. Colonial literature in the narrower sense of the
term, that is, literary texts fulfilling aesthetic demands, were few and far
between (yet see Lescarbot's "La deffaite des Sauvages Armouchiquois"
[1607] and Lahontan's *Dialogues avec un sauvage* [1703]). Although there
was by 1760 a French culture distinct from that of the mother country, no
developed literary scene existed in New France — the texts were often written with a pragmatic function, for special occasions, and often not preserved
for posterity. Most of the people in the colony were illiterate, "comedies . . . and other dangerous spectacles" were forbidden by the Catholic
clergy (as was the printing trade), and actors were often excommunicated.
In these adverse circumstances, writing in French developed slowly, mainly
in the areas of drama and poetry (prominent here is the writing by Marc
Lescarbot). As Guy Laflèche concludes: "This culture had no time to
develop a literature of its own. Only a few major works can be numbered
from a literary life that remained embryonic."

Part 3, "The Literature of British Canada, 1763–1867," explores the
English colonial period. Similarly to French-language writing in North
America, English-language writing in British North America first took the
form of pragmatically oriented exploration narratives of the West and the
North as well as settler accounts, often by female authors (such as Catharine
Parr Traill [1802–1899] and Susanna Moodie [1803–1885]), from Central

and Western Canada. Writing of a literary nature first began to flourish in the Canadian East, where (in Halifax) the first garrison theatricals, a printing press, and a newspaper were established. In the second half of the eighteenth century, after heavy immigration from the U.S. (especially British Loyalists around the time of American independence), a cultural infrastructure conducive to the growth of colonial literature began to develop in what was then called Upper Canada (today's Ontario) and Lower Canada (today's Quebec). With the prose narrative *The Clockmaker* (1836), Thomas Chandler Haliburton produced British North America's first international bestseller, a satire, as much fiction was at the time. The first novel written in North America was Frances Brooke's epistolary novel *The History of Emily Montague* (1769), set in Quebec in the late 1760s. Later English-Canadian novelists of importance, also female, found Quebec fascinating material for their fiction, too (for instance Julia Beckwith Hart [1796–1867]). Rosanna Leprohon's 1864 novel *Antoinette de Mirecourt* deals with the cultural conflicts between the British military and the resident French Canadians — and not surprisingly, it was soon also available in Quebec in French translation. William Kirby (1817–1906) and Gilbert Parker (1862–1932) also set novels in Quebec, yet back in the French-colonial period of New France (Kirby's *The Golden Dog*, first published in English in 1877, appeared in French translation in 1884). John Richardson's *Wacousta* (1832), Canada's first major gothic novel, is informed by Aboriginal history and is indebted to James Fenimore Cooper's American adventure novels of the frontier. In spite of the popularity of English-language fiction in British North America, poetry counts as the foremost genre of the period. English-language poetry was distributed even in Quebec City and Montreal. The long poem became a popular genre (for instance, Oliver Goldsmith Jr.'s *The Rising Village*, 1825). Although English-Canadian colonial literature maintained ties with British culture, writers in this period were already turning to the United States for publishing opportunities, which sometimes caused them to rewrite the settings of their works from Canadian to American.

French-Canadian writing of the period, in contrast, was much more self-reflective and to some extent more nationalistic. This self-reflection and nationalism arose largely in connection with the process of coming to terms with the loss of French Canada to the English in 1763 at the end of the Seven Years' War, codified in the signing of the Treaty of Paris, and the attempt to develop into a "société distincte" amidst anglophone majority cultures on the North American continent. It is not surprising, given this history, that French Canada's relation to its two colonial mother countries, France and England, has not been without regret or resentment. An important vehicle for such sentiments was the patriotic journalistic *littérature de combat*, often published in anglophone newspapers and journals. Other journalistic writing, which was fostered in its development by some thirty francophone journals, was the *littérature engagée*, which promoted the formation of a distinct French national identity in Canada. However, the continuing, moralistically motivated censorship of the Catholic Church and its clergy had a chilling effect on the development of French-Canadian literature, especially drama and the novel. Both genres were considered immoral, yet the clergy did promote the performance of classicist plays from France. In a style modeled on Molière, Marivaux, and Beaumarchais, Louis-Joseph Quesnel (1749–1809) produced a one-act play in which he condemned the English and his francophone compatriots who fell prey to the English way of life. The poetry of Michel Bibaud (1782–1857), too, followed French literary models, such as that of Nicolas Boileau (1636–1711). The Durham Report of 1839, which claimed that French Canadians were without history or literature and that the national character of Lower Canada "must be that of the British Empire," served to enhance an awareness among French Canadians of their colonized, if not inferior status. As Dorothee Scholl, the author of chapter 8 of this volume, writes: "Self-degradations constitute obsessive motifs in French-Canadian literature, pervading historiographical as well as literary texts and chansons." Yet at the same time the report also backfired and had a catalyzing effect on the development of French-Canadian literature under British rule. As French-Canadian literature opened itself — belatedly — to Romanticism and developed a consciousness of its own unique regional (and national) beauties and characteristics, French Canada increasingly aimed at a "national" identity, which it attempted to reconstruct from a more satisfying version of the past under French rule. Conservative values, such as the land, nature, the rural community, and French Canada's determination to survive inspired the creation of the *mythe du terroir* and the *roman du terroir* (the prototype for which was Patrice Lacombe's 1846 *La terre paternelle*). Oral folk literature, such as folk legends and songs, was seen as fundamental for French-Canadian culture, and the Club des anciens (founded in 1858) dedicated itself to the collection and publication of such texts. François-Xavier Garneau's three-volume *Histoire du Canada* (1845, 1846, 1848), written in a distinctive literary style, became a national inspiration, celebrating French culture and its traditions — even claiming French Canadians to be a chosen people (as the Puritans in Massachusetts had done). In a similar vein, Octave Crémazie (1827–1879) wrote passionate patriotic verse, celebrating French Canadians and denouncing English Canadians. The prominence of Adolphe-Basile Routhier's "chant national" "O Canada," composed in 1880 with lyrics in French, points to the relevance of songs for French Canada's literary tradition (see ch. 32, Mathis-Moser). The original French song also refers to French Canada's supposed missionary role in the world. Its adoption as Canada's official national anthem in 1980 — but in an English version — symbolizes English and French Canada's many entanglements since the onset of British rule.

## Literature from Confederation in 1867 until 1918

Part 4 is dedicated to the period from the establishment of the Dominion of Canada in 1867 until the end of the First World War. The chapters on English-Canadian and on French-Canadian cultural developments in this period focus on the issue of nation formation and cultural autonomy. English-Canadian writing sought a comprehensive Canadian identity by focusing on Canadian topics and settings in both traditional and popular literary forms (poetry and novels as well as historical and adventure romances and animal stories). The territorial completion of the nation, with province after province joining the Dominion, resulted in the Latin phrase "A mari usque ad mare" ("from sea to sea") becoming the national motto in 1906. Just as had been the case in the United States about one hundred years before, Canadian Confederation in 1876 effected a greater stress on the regional aspects of the vast country and its literature, with Quebec being among the frequent settings (for instance, in D. C. Scott's short-story cycle *In the Village of Viger*, published in Boston in 1896, or in Gilbert Parker's romances). Canadian writers found it difficult to publish their works in Canada, particularly until the early 1890s, in part due to the lack of international copyright between Canada, Britain, and the United States. Writers continued to look for publication in the United States or published some of their works at their own expense, as, for instance, did Isabella Valancy Crawford (1850–1877) and Susan Frances Harrison, whose stories also display a fascination with Quebec. The Confederation Poets (Charles G. D. Roberts [1860–1943], Archibald Lampman [1861–1899], Bliss Carman [1861–1929], D. C. Scott [1862–1947], and W. W. Campbell [1858–1918]), with their regionally oriented, clearly Canadian works, managed to achieve an international reputation, being published in Canadian, American, and British journals. Charles G. D. Roberts and Ernest Thompson Seton (1860–1946) brought Canadian short fiction to an international readership by means of their popular animal stories. In the early 1890s, the publishing situation in Canada improved with the introduction of new inexpensive paperback reprint editions, which soon became dominant. The novels of Robert Barr (1850–1912), Ralph Connor (1860–1937), Nellie McClung (1873–1951), and Robert Stead (1880–1959) thus were also financially successful. It was Lucy Maud Montgomery (1874–1942), however, who created the most famous character in Canadian literature in her *Anne of Green Gables* novel series, the namesake first volume of which appeared in 1908 and was soon translated into many languages. Pauline Johnson (1861–1913), of Mohawk and English parentage, Edith Eaton (aka Sui Sin Far, 1865–1914), of Chinese and English parentage, and Sara Jeannette Duncan (1861–1922), who lived the latter part of her life in India and included her experiences there in her writing, added multicultural flair to English-Canadian literature. Pauline Johnson stressed the predominance of the idea of Canadian unity at a time before multiculturalism became Canada's official policy later in the twentieth century, writing in 1903 that "White Race and Red are one if they are but Canadian born."

The French-Canadian literature of the pre–First World War period continued the trends of the previous period: a self-reflective, self-protective drive toward cultural autonomy; an attempt to define itself in contrast to France; a focus on the time-honored agriculturalist ideology of the Quebec elites (the *mythe du terroir*, manifesting itself in the *poésie du terroir* and particularly the *roman du terroir*); a focus on the oral folklore traditions in the service of the "nationalization" of French-Canadian literature; the continued strong influence of the Catholic Church on predominant values — which decided which books parish libraries and bookstores would stock and which plays, if any, would be performed; and finally, a continuing apparent irrelevance of female writers in a strongly conservative climate. Félicité Angers (1845–1924), who published several historical novels under the pseudonym Laure Conan (see *L'oublié*, 1900), is the first important female writer of literature mentioned in the chapters on French-Canadian literature. Louis Honoré Fréchette (1839–1908) published patriotic poetry, a collection of short prose texts (*La légende d'un peuple*, 1887), and successful plays that deal with the failed "Rebellions of the Patriots" of 1837–1838. Philippe Aubert de Gaspé's *Les anciens Canadiens* (1863), probably the most important French-Canadian novel of this period, is also oriented toward the past, dealing with the military conflict between the "Anglais" and the "Français" near the end of the Seven Years' War. Inspired by Sir Walter Scott's historical novels, the work distances itself from French classicist aesthetics and becomes "tout canadien par le style," as the author himself stressed, by including a rich repertoire of French-Canadian oral culture. Napoléon Bourassa's Acadian novel *Jacques et Marie: Souvenirs d'un peuple dispersé*, published in 1866, shows the fictional fashion of the time both in its historical theme (the "Great Upheaval," or expulsion of the Acadians, which began in 1755) and by resorting to oral traditions. This is true also of Louis Hémon's international bestseller *Maria Chapdelaine* (1914), a classical *roman du terroir*. It was not until around 1895, when the École littéraire de Montréal was founded, that antitraditional, future-oriented values became more influential. In the poetry of the best and best-known writer of the school, Émile Nelligan (1879–1941), national and traditionalist elements are absent. Nelligan was much more interested in form, and in that way was a linking figure with modernism.

## Modernism in English-Canadian and French-Canadian Literature

The first four parts of the book, concerned with Canada's cultural beginnings up until the end of the First World War and the coming of modernism, take up roughly one fourth of the book. The remaining two parts, 5 and 6, in turn, dealing with modernism in English and French Canada and the period from 1967 until the present, encompass so much material that an additional subdivision by genre was called for: Thus in part 5 parallel chapters survey poetry, the novel, the short story, and drama in the English-Canadian and French-Canadian contexts, again prefaced by a short historical overview concerning both sections. Part 5 traces the delayed struggle of English-Canadian and French-Canadian literature with the opposing tendencies of nationalism and internationalism, eventually opening up to modernism. The chapters on English Canada show this breakthrough with respect to all major genres, marking, for instance, the realist novel's displacement of the romance, which occurred in Canada later than in the United States or Great Britain, the gradual emergence of modernist fiction, and the increasingly international orientation of poetry.

The poetry chapter by Lorraine York revises the traditional account of modernism's sweeping advent on the Canadian poetry scene. It argues that Canadian modernism is a highly complex movement, a "fascinating amalgamation of Victorian, Romantic, decadent, aestheticist, *and* modernist practice." As was the case with other genres in both French and English Canada, so-called little magazines (such as *Preview* and *First Statement*) played a seminal role in the promotion of a truly indigenous poetry. They served as a platform for progressive literary exchange between avant-garde poets such as A. J. M. Smith (1902–1980), F. R. Scott (1899–1985), and A. M. Klein (1909–1972), who argued for a cosmopolitan and international modernism, and poets such as Louis Dudek (1918–2001), Irving Layton (1912–2006), and Kay Smith (1911–2004), who advocated a continentalist orientation of poetry in tune with North American realities.

Poetry, as in English Canada and the United States, was also a progressive vehicle of modernism in French Canada, leaving behind the rural tradition in French-Canadian literature. The agriculturalist orientation, out of tune with the growing urbanization and industrialization of the country, was called into question from the 1930s onwards and finally outgrown during the Révolution tranquille in the 1960s. A similar debate between two rivaling forces dominated post-First World War poetry in French Canada: between the regionalists, who wanted to focus on purely French-Canadian themes and settings, and the exoticists, who saw themselves in both a francophone and an international context. In the 1930s and 1940s, major innovations toward modernism with regard to both theme and style came from a generation of poets known as the Big Four (Hector de Saint-Denys Garneau [1912–1943], Alain Grandbois [1900–1975], Rina Lasnier [1915–1997], and Anne Hébert [1916–2000]). At that time, socio-critical voices could be found in poetry by authors such as Jean Narrache (1893–1970) and Clément Marchand (1912–), but on the whole these works could not compete with the socially critical anglophone poetry of the 1930s. In the

1940s and 1950s surrealism proved to be a driving force for the further development of the genre. With the foundation of the publishing house L'Hexagone in 1953, francophone poetry found a home. In the following years a multitude of publishing companies were indicative of Quebec's lively poetry scene, which in the 1960s actively participated in the promotion of the national cause: the establishment of an independent Quebec.

Female modernist poets were by no means as absent from poetry in Canada as a glance into standard literary histories might suggest. In French Canada, female authors such as Jovette-Alice Bernier (1900–1981), Simone Routier (1901–1987), and Éva Sénécal (1905–1988) had their breakthroughs as early as during the decade from the mid-1920s to the mid-1930s. On the English-Canadian side, P. K. Page (1916–), Dorothy Livesay (1909–1996), and lesser-known poets such as Louise Bowman (1882–1944) and Katherine Hale (1878–1956), who were among the first female practitioners of free verse, participated in the development of a specifically Canadian modernist poetry.

At a time when modernism had already gained ground in European and American literature, many Canadian authors willingly adhered to more conventional aesthetics. The *roman du terroir*, which saw major innovations in the 1930s (which are evident in Ringuet's *Trente arpents*, 1938) attests to a strong tradition of regional writing in a realist or naturalist manner, as does the English-Canadian prairie novel. Novels set in Canada's urban centers explore topics of social, political, and ethical concern, such as the harsh living conditions of Montreal's working class portrayed in Gabrielle Roy's *Bonheur d'occasion*, published in 1945, or the anti-Semitism that members of urban Jewish communities frequently encountered, prominent in works by Mordecai Richler and Norman Levine (1923–2005). Despite an initial predominance of realism, modernist influences are discernable in works by English-Canadian novelists such as Morley Callaghan (1903–1990) as well as in the francophone psychological novel. With the works of Ernest Buckler (1908–1984) and Sheila Watson (1909–1998), English-Canadian literature tied in with international modernist literature and foreshadowed postmodern practices. In francophone literature, a connection with the modernist aesthetics of the European and American avant-garde was established in 1965 and 1966 with the publication of texts by Jacques Godbout (1933–) and Réjean Ducharme (1941–).

The English-Canadian short story, its authors having begun to adopt modernist writing conventions in the 1920s, became Canada's strongest and most progressive literary genre next to English-Canadian poetry. The French-Canadian short story did not begin to undergo such an independent development until at least the 1940s; with regard to both form and content, its development mirrors that of the French-Canadian novel. The advance of modernism in the English-Canadian short story was closely associated with Raymond Knister (1899–1932), a prolific short-story writer, critic, and editor of the 1928 anthology *Canadian Short Stories*, which became a benchmark. In the late 1920s, the genre reached international standards with the works of Morley Callaghan. Like Knister, Callaghan concentrated on his protagonists' inner worlds rather than on external plot description, and his works attest to a well-developed repertoire of modernist writing techniques. Frederick Philip Grove (1879–1948) and Sinclair Ross (1908–1996), whose short stories display a combination of modernist and more traditional writing practices, stand for a less experimental branch of writing. With innovations introduced to the genre in the 1950s, female writers such as Ethel Wilson (1888–1980), Joyce Marshall (1913–2005), and Sheila Watson (1909–1998) made major contributions to the development of the English-Canadian short story.

In French Canada the short story had long been the favorite genre of female authors, whose keen interest in social problems, even if expressed in rather conventional ways, distinguished them from the majority of male francophone writers. Among the best-known French-Canadian short stories is Anne Hébert's "Le torrent" (1950). In the 1950s and 1960s, readers and critics alike interpreted the motif of the problematic mother-son relationship that Hébert's story explored, which also figured in francophone dramas and novels, as emblematic of the difficult situation of Quebec's population vis-à-vis independence or loyalty to Canada. In the 1960s the variety of aesthetic approaches multiplied with the publication of countless short stories, ranging from the socio-critical realism of André Major (1942–) and the magic realism of Claude Mathieu (1930–1985) to the macabre and fantastic writings of Michel Tremblay (1942–). Before the Révolution tranquille, formal aspects in many French-Canadian short stories bore witness to a vital oral culture. The radical break with the commitment to oral culture, which occurred in the late 1970s, made way for striking new innovations. Global political events such as the two world wars and the Great Depression had strengthened (separate) nationalist tendencies in English and French Canada, and had a direct impact on literature: After the modernist influences of the 1920s, literary production in English Canada was significantly slowed down in the 1930s by the Depression, leading to a delay in the publication of several works until after the Second World War and a growing sense of political urgency expressed in the texts that were published during the war. In contrast, the impact of the war on the French-Canadian literary scene was, astonishingly, rather positive. The temporary relocation of the French publishing industry from France to Canada during the war led to fresh impulses in French-Canadian literature, as can be seen with the psychological novel of the 1940s and 1950s, which was strongly influenced by French existentialism. In the following years, the francophone literary market experienced a tremendous upswing, due to the publication of both French classics and books that had formerly been censored by the Catholic Church.

Because of Quebec's religiously dominated institutional framework, French-Canadian drama, as previously mentioned, had gotten off to a hesitant start. In the 1930s, influences from Europe led to a modernization of the clerical theater with respect to both repertoire and performance practices. As a reaction to the internationalization of French-Canadian theater, many francophone authors advocated a "realistic" drama with a strong focus on topoi of French-Canadian identity construction, a tendency prominent in all genres of francophone literature in Canada at some point. Symbolic representations of French-Canadian identity and collective mentality were put on stage by distinguished playwrights such as Gratien Gélinas, with the *Fridolinades* (performed 1938–1947) and *Tit-Coq* (1950), and Marcel Dubé, with *Zone* (1953) and *Florence* (1958). In both English Canada and French Canada, theater became a major tool for criticizing and challenging the status quo. In English Canada, it was the Worker's Theatre, a manifestation of the Little Theatre movement, that first employed art as a political weapon. In French Canada, references to historical events or individual personalities were common practice during and after the Révolution tranquille, when theater addressed the "national" collective consciousness in order to critically educate the audience, and, especially in the case of feminist drama, to reform society. In the 1960s, measures implemented on recommendation of the Massey Report (a report on the national development of cultural institutions in arts, letters, and sciences, commissioned by the government and published in 1951) set off a cultural explosion in all literary fields by completing major processes of professionalization and institutionalization that had begun before the Second World War with the establishment of theater festivals such as the Dominion Drama Festival in Stratford and continued after the war with the founding of the first professional performance groups. In the 1940s, the Canadian Broadcasting Corporation became the first radio network to employ dramatists and performers in English Canada, a development that took hold in French Canada in the 1950s and subsequently produced new genres such as the "téléthéâtre." When the discussions surrounding Canada's centennial celebrations, marked by the 1967 World Exposition or "Expo 67" in Montreal, triggered a new national self-examination, Canadians could, for the first time, rely on their own cultural institutions to tell their stories.

## Literature from 1967 to the Present

Part 6 opens with a chapter titled "Sociopolitical and Cultural Developments from 1967 to the Present" in both English and French Canada and then returns to the organizational scheme of previous parts, namely according to genre. Yet in this part the lens is widened by special chapters titled "English-Canadian Literary Theory and Literary Criticism," "The

Institutionalization of Literature in Quebec," "Canons of Diversity in Contemporary English-Canadian Literature," "Literature of the First Nations, Inuit, and Métis," and "Transculturalism and *écritures migrantes*," plus a chapter called "Orality and the French-Canadian Chanson." The question of how to integrate Canada's ethnically diverse writing into a book largely structured according to the "English-Canadian" and "French-Canadian" dichotomy of its subtitle was thus handled here by devising separate chapters devoted to ethnic diversity in Canadian culture, yet also treating many significant diasporic authors in the generically structured chapters.

Canada's Elizabethan Age, or L'âge d'or, which is generally considered to have begun in 1967 and to have lasted into the late 1970s, was characterized by an explosive development of literature in all genres and by an intensive search for "national" identities, with both English-Canadian and Québécois literatures turning inward. In Quebec, the attempt to promote a "Québécité" was prominent in all literary genres, particularly during the 1960s and 1970s and up to the failure of the 1980 referendum on the question whether to pursue political independence. (This tended to result in neglect of the literature of Canadian francophone communities outside Quebec, which later experienced a similar literary renaissance.) In English Canada, as a reaction to growing Quebec nationalism and to the Massey Report, literary criticism in particular sought to identify, as Caroline Rosenthal states, "recurrent symbols, motifs, and themes in Canadian texts that were believed to not only reflect a certain literary tradition but to reveal a national character as well" (this was referred to as "thematic criticism"). More recently, however, increasing transcultural diversity has become one of the strongest and most fascinating characteristics of contemporary literature in Canada, with writers of many ethnic backgrounds entering the arena of English- and French-language literature in Canada. Many do so in negotiation with the two official Canadian languages from the perspective of another language that they owe to their heritage, whether it is of indigenous or foreign or mixed ethnicity (for instance Fred Wah). Prominent themes in such transcultural literature (written in either English or French) include the quest of an individual or an immigrant or indigenous community for cultural identity, as well as tensions between these individual and collective quests; the conflict between nostalgia for the homeland that has been lost or left behind and the longing to find a new Canadian — or even global — identity; a preoccupation with history and memory; and related issues of exile and culture shock. A conscious negotiation of otherness has also rendered ethnic writing a platform from which relations between concepts such as ethnicity and gender are reexamined. Rooted in the sociocultural patterns of ethnic communities is the portrayal of generational conflicts, especially strong in writing by Asian-Canadian women such as Joy Kogawa (1935–) and Madeleine

Thien. Recently, transcultural writing has tended to portray characters whose identity formation can be characterized as cosmopolitan and globalized, as is the case in the works of Trinidadian-Canadian author Dionne Brand (1953–), who writes in English, and of Asian-Canadian author Ying Chen (1961–), who writes in French.

Even though immigrants in the French-speaking parts of Canada share many concerns with immigrants in English-speaking Canada, the concept of transcultural literature (in French, *écriture migrante*) was established relatively late in Quebec, since during the 1960s and 1970s even minority writers were joining the strong nationalist strain in Québécois literature. This strong ideological orientation can most notably be found in French-Canadian drama, which staged almost exclusively Québécois themes and even adopted the Québécois sociolect *joual* as an acceptable language for theater productions, thereby largely isolating itself from an international reception. At the same time, English-language Canadian drama was also preoccupied with questions of identity, though in a less obvious way, as it revisited themes of regional Canadian history. After the failure of the 1980 independence referendum, French-language drama experienced a crisis of representation and turned toward metatheater to negotiate the new disorientation in Québécois culture. Opening up to an international repertoire of plays, Québécois drama finally joined English-language drama in its recent tendency to stage plays of international and transcultural concern, aided by a budding community of ethnic playwrights. Another specialty of Québécois drama can be seen in the frequent creative reworking of earlier material and the production of translations, adaptations, or tradaptations (a mixture of the two), as well as collages of canonized plays. English-language drama shows a preference for drama cycles and trilogies, and tends to depict cultural values by analyzing family structures as symptomatic of the national mentality and morals, a motif that had also been used in Québécois literature in general (for instance in Robert Gurik's play *Hamlet, Prince de Québec* [1968]; or Hébert's aforementioned 1950 short story "Le torrent").

The prominence of feminist writing in Quebec during the 1970s and 1980s can be seen not only in the fact that it found its way onto the stage even while Quebec was still in its intense nationalist phase, but also in its contribution to poetry and the novel format. Most distinctly in poetry, the concept of *écriture féminine* ("gendered women's writing") informed the publication of works by such authors as Nicole Brossard (1943–) and mingled to a high degree with theoretical considerations in the narrative mode of "fiction-theory." As the feminist movement grew less radical over time, feminist poetry gave way to the "poets of the intimate," who chose to explore female subjectivity in the personal sphere.

As was the case with drama, Québécois poetry in the 1960s and to some extent also in the 1970s showed a high degree of nationalist content, for example in the works of Gaston Miron (1928–1996), perhaps the most important representative of the "poésie du pays." Yet the 1970s also saw a new orientation of Québécois poetry toward France (especially French formalism and structuralism) and the United States (the American Counter-Culture movement and its desire for cultural liberation). The latter, continentalist connection is especially interesting, as English-Canadian poetry has almost never — and certainly not during the intense nationalist phase of the 1960s and 1970s — exhibited such a proximity to American culture, which has been felt to be a threat to English-Canadian identity. What English-Canadian and French-Canadian poetry had in common, however, was a playful, experimental aesthetic, which manifested itself in Quebec through the influence of dadaism, surrealism, and automatism, while English-language poets such as Christian Bök (1966–) and bpNichol (1944–1988) were influenced by the techniques of *oulipo*[15] and concrete poetry. Other currents that followed in English-language poetry were a fascination with extended forms, such as the long poem, and multigeneric forms, such as composite works including poetry, photographs, and historical accounts (for example, Michael Ondaatje's *The Collected Works of Billy the Kid* [1970]). Ondaatje also ushered in an interest in ethnicity. In English-Canadian poetry, in contrast to French-Canadian poetry, there is a tradition of nature poetry, such as that of Al Purdy (1918–2000). English-Canadian poetry is also characterized by pronounced regional traditions: West Coast poetry, for example, exhibits a stronger tendency toward radical poetic forms, as can be seen in works by Fred Wah (1939–) and Daphne Marlatt (1942–). Starting in the 1990s, after French-Canadian poetry outside Quebec had also experienced its local renaissances and was ready to go beyond nationalist issues, poetry in Quebec and throughout Canada discovered the themes of ecology and the environment in general.

The short story is the only literary genre that is notably more prominent in one of the two main literatures in Canada than in the other. The English-language short story rose to an extraordinary status within the Canadian literary landscape, featuring a wide range of themes and several brilliant writers such as Alice Munro (1931–) and Margaret Atwood. Within the format of the English-Canadian short story, the more conventional (neo)realist or modernist writing style has prevailed despite excursions into a postmodernist narrative style, and themes tend to be regionally topical, set against a rural or urban background. Owing to the high percentage of female writers active in the genre, specifically female themes

---

[15] A literary technique based on the approach by the French writers workshop Ouvroir de Littérature Potentielle, foregrounding the formal aspects of language — some works even going so far as to, for instance, completely omit the vowel "e" (Georges Perec's *La Disparition*, 1969).

such as gender discrimination, a concern with the domestic sphere, and mother-daughter relationships are prominent. Ethnic identity formation within the framework of the Canadian nation-state is a topic of intense interest that has been developed in the short-story format by writers such as Thomas King (1943–), Lee Maracle (1950–), Neil Bissoondath (1955–), Dionne Brand (1953–), and Austin Clarke (1934–).

Compared to the success of the English-language short story in Canada, the short prose narrative written in French has had to compete more with the French-language novel for public attention and remains largely over-shadowed by the longer prose form. A few characteristics of the French-Canadian variety of the genre can nevertheless be distinguished. The short story in Quebec and other French-speaking parts of the country has exhib-ited a stronger tendency toward postmodernism and metafictional strate-gies, as well as a more pronounced interest in the fantastic and in science fiction. Thematically coherent collections of stories are popular within Québécois literary production (exemplified in works by Anne Dandurand [1953–], Élise Turcotte [1957–], and Pierre Yergeau [1957–]), but are by no means restricted to French-Canadian literature — Margaret Laurence (1926–1987), Alice Munro, Mavis Gallant, Clark Blaise (1940–), Rohinton Mistry (1952–), and Margaret Atwood immediately come to mind as writ-ers who have published English-language short-story cycles during their careers. It remains to be seen whether the French-language short prose narrative will be able to further amplify its impact, bearing in mind that it began to develop later than the Canadian short story in English. On the other hand, the chanson and the *monologue québécois* are forms of artistic expression that have their home in Quebec. Both forms are performed orally, creatively crossing genre and media boundaries and enriching Canadian culture in a uniquely French-Canadian way.

The first North American novel, Frances Brooke's aforementioned *The History of Emily Montague* (1769), was written (and set) in Quebec, and the novel in general has received much more attention in Quebec than has the short story, experiencing a considerable flourishing from the 1960s onwards. Typically, during the 1960s and 1970s, the novel in Quebec was saturated with political thought (postcolonial and Marxist), but also devoted itself to an analysis of traditional family structures and of religion, which, in the form of Catholicism, still plays a crucial role in Quebec. In the novels of the 1980s, a feeling of nostalgia and the need for a cultural redefinition of the status quo can also be sensed, as novel writing largely turned away from ideology and began to deal with a kind of identity that was harder to define than the identity that was thematized during the nationalist phase, and was further complicated by an examination of the relations between the individual and society. Exponents of the French-Canadian feminist movement such as Nicole Brossard and Louky Bersianik (1930–) worked in the novel format as well, and, as was the case in poetry, the movement evolved toward less radical treatments of female desire and homoeroticism, and remains significant today. The examination of national identity in the Quebec novels of the 1980s and 1990s (for instance those by Jacques Poulin [1937–], who had begun in this vein as early as the 1960s) frequently concerns itself with American literature and culture, comparing national myths and situating Québécois identity in a larger North American context by means of fictional travels through the United States, which English-Canadian culture rather tries to set itself off from.

The English-language Canadian novel has displayed clearly different emphases since the 1960s. Frequently making use of irony, which Linda Hutcheon characterized as a typically "Canadian" literary attitude, the English-Canadian novel shows a strong tendency toward historiographic metafiction and the subgenres of the Bildungsroman and Künstlerroman, while settings range from rural to urban environments and have become increasingly international. The English-Canadian novel is partly characterized, as is the English-Canadian short story, by a strong regionalism that ranges from a depiction of the Eastern cities in works by Margaret Atwood and Mordecai Richler, to Vancouver in works by Audrey Thomas (1935–), to the Canadian Pacific Northwest in the novels of George Bowering (1935–), and to the prairies in those of Robert Kroetsch (1927–) and Aritha van Herk (1954–). Furthermore, the particularly English-Canadian genre of historiographic metafiction can be found in various gendered or ethnic variations, as in novels by Daphne Marlatt, Audrey Thomas, and Wayne Johnston (1958–). By the turn of the millenium, the English-language novel had moved beyond a treatment of predominantly Canadian themes and had set itself up as an international genre boasting a wide variety of topoi and writing styles.

Part 6 of this volume not only treats the development of literary genres, but also allows for a comparison of sociocultural developments such as the degree of institutionalization of literature. The process of institutionalization is particularly advanced in Quebec, and a separate chapter illustrates how it is intertwined with literature's frequent function of promoting a "national" character. With Montreal serving as the center of French-Canadian publishing and with research centers examining Québécois literature throughout the province, it is even suggested that the institutionalization of French-Canadian literature has reached a higher level than is justified by the actual literary output. Interestingly, though, while "Canadian Studies" programs — meaning the study of English-Canadian literature among other subjects of national interest like politics or economics — do exist in every large university in Canada, there are only a few programs on Québécois literature (for instance, at the Université du Québec à Trois Rivières and Université Laval) and its treatment is often embedded in French Studies programs. Conversely, the separate teaching of Québécois literature is a valued tradition in the francophone Cégep curricula (Collège d'enseignement général et professionnel, an institution comparable to a junior college).

The institutionalization of English-language literature in Canada has been achieved mainly through the establishment of Canadian Studies programs and through the efforts of Canadian Studies scholars, as well as through a vital publishing system including book series like the New Canadian Library, numerous anthologies, and several encyclopedias. For both literatures, the longevity of literary journals and the support by national institutions such as the Canada Council for the Arts have been crucial in the process of institutionalization. References to an increasing international orientation and reception of Canadian literature conclude most of the chapters of part 6, and the growing awareness of literature in Canada as a "postnational" conglomerate of literatures with different cultural traditions — this being regarded as cultural wealth rather than lack of homogeneity or identity — is an important development for all literatures in Canada.

# Ground Gained

Let me end this introductory chapter of a literary history on a history-conscious note. I have been involved in Canadian Studies since my time as a doctoral student at the University of Cologne in the late 1970s. I still remember the second annual conference of the Gesellschaft für Kanada-Studien (Association for Canadian Studies in German-speaking Countries) in 1978. While listening to a paper on Canadian literature delivered by a German scholar, I overheard two Canadians behind me asking each other in muffled tones why on earth Germans did not stick to their own literature, why they should devote their time to Canadian literature? Some years later, when *Gaining Ground: European Critics on Canadian Literature*, which I coedited with Robert Kroetsch in 1985, was reviewed by William French in *The Globe and Mail*, French, too, admitted surprise that anyone abroad was taking note of CanLit, considering that many Canadians did not. Of course, these anecdotes go back to the period when thematic criticism prevailed in Canada and Canadians were often self-reflective and inward-oriented.

In the meantime, much has changed. The present book, then, also testifies to the further recognition and the ground literature in Canada has gained in the past two or three decades. *History of Literature in Canada: English-Canadian and French-Canadian* wishes to contribute its small share to the further exploration as well as international recognition of this vibrant literature enriching world literature.

# I. Beginnings

# 1: Aboriginal Oral Traditions

*Eva Gruber (University of Constance)*

A S RENDERED IN THE HAU-DE-NO-SAU-NEE (Iroquois) creation story, the earth came into being when First Woman fell down from the sky world into the water world. In an attempt to break her fall, loons placed themselves beneath her, while the sea animals — duck, otter, beaver, serpent, toad, and muskrat — dived to the bottom of the sea for a piece of mud to create a place for her to land on. After several attempts they succeeded, and the little clump of earth on Great Turtle's back where First Woman safely landed began to grow and expand. Today, the earth still rests on Great Turtle's back.

While this and similar Aboriginal creation stories in their collaborative notion of creation clearly differ from the Western biblical creation account, they bear certain analogies to the early explorers' impressions and accounts upon encountering the North American continent, inasmuch as the land mass indeed appeared at first sight to surface from the vastness of the Atlantic Ocean. More importantly, however, such creation stories claim that North America's Native people originated in North America and have always lived there. They thus contest the Bering Strait Theory, which holds that North America's indigenous population migrated onto the continent from Asia via Alaska over a prehistoric land bridge approximately twenty thousand years ago. Instead, these narratives underline Aboriginal primacy and Native peoples' close and inseparable ties to the land which in their view they are meant to live on.

## Oral Tradition, "Oral Literature," and Orature

Long before Europeans first caught sight of the continent, what is now Canada was home to the Inuit and approximately one hundred different Aboriginal nations with diverse cultural traditions. There existed over fifty languages from originally ten linguistic stocks among Canada's Aboriginal people (with mainly the Algonquian languages still spoken widely today), with an eleventh group comprising six different dialects of Inuktitut, the language of the Inuit. Depending on factors such as their ecological contexts as well as economic and sociocultural patterns, the societies of the

Eastern Woodlands, Plains, Plateau, West Coast, Sub-Arctic, and Arctic developed distinct cultures and oral traditions, which express both their vast diversity and some common characteristics. Significantly, in contrast to written modes of documentation and transmission which characterize European cultures, among Canada's Aboriginal peoples a community's essential cultural knowledge, narratives, spiritual beliefs, principles, and history were usually passed on orally from one generation to the next. Although physical and graphic methods of documentation did exist in the form of petroglyphs and pictographs, birchbark scrolls, wampum belts, board plates, bundles of notched sticks, and, among the Inuit, picture knifing in snow, they have usually been considered mnemonic devices used in conjunction with the oral tradition, rather than as forms of writing.

The clear emphasis was thus on the spoken word, which already points to the intricacies of terminology that arise when discussing the oral tradition. If one takes into account the etymological roots of both of its components, the expression "oral literature" seems to be a contradiction in terms. Walter J. Ong refers to it as a "preposterous term . . . [which] reveals our inability to represent to our own minds a heritage of verbally organized materials except as a variant of writing" (1982, 11). Yet the expression may also be seen as a reverential and respectful recognition of the equal merit and sophistication of Aboriginal oral traditions. In their entirety, the latter comprise bodies of cultural expression and knowledge comparable to Western literatures, and they are in no way to be considered anachronistic, inferior, or as stages preceding the development of a "true" (that is, written) literature. One way out of this impasse is offered by the term "orature," first established by the Canadian linguist Tom McArthur to describe "the poetic, dramatic, and other oral genres and traditions of pre- or non-literate peoples, either before the invention of writing or in parts of the world that have maintained non-literate traditions intact" (McArthur 1992, 731). Even with this term, though, it is important to emphasize that the oral tradition has not come to an end with the advent of literacy. Such a notion, which in its exacerbated version is often referred to as the "doomed culture myth" (that is, the idea that European culture would eventually subsume Aboriginal cultures), has in the past frequently motivated European collectors of Aboriginal myths.

## Transcribing the Oral Traditions

The first to record the oral narratives of Canada's Aboriginal population in writing were explorers, travelers, and, most significantly and substantially, Jesuit missionaries, who in the seventeenth century collected examples of the oral narratives of the Aboriginal peoples east of the Georgian Bay and published them in the *Relations des Jésuites* (see ch. 4, Laflèche). Starting with Henry Rowe Schoolcraft, who served as an Indian agent among the Ojibway from 1812 to 1842, the nineteenth and first half of the twentieth century saw scholars from the newly forged disciplines of anthropology, ethnography, folklore studies, and linguistics recording Aboriginal stories and songs under the auspices of institutions such as the Canadian Institute, the Geological Survey of Canada, and the Royal Society of Canada, but also the Smithsonian Institution and the American Folklore Society. Documentary and scientific in focus, the verbatim renderings by researchers such as Franz Boas, John Swanton, Marius Barbeau, and Diamond Jenness in their literal translation and interlinear style are certainly more faithful to the actual performance than are many other transcriptions; however, they betray little or no interest in the narratives' literary qualities. The analyses frequently suggest inappropriate analogies and similarities, for instance, to Scandinavian and Greek mythologies, and on the whole the narratives remain rather inaccessible to a wider readership. Many less scientifically motivated collections that were geared to a general audience in turn truncated and distorted the oral narratives. They either exaggerated their allegedly "Indian" flavor to answer the sentimental and romantic tastes of the day, or tried to make them comply with Western notions of narrative and storytelling, likening them to fairy tales or simple fables and thus robbing them of their culturally specific characteristics.

Oral narratives in their synesthetic composition and use of reiteration were rhetorically perfected, well-organized performances, often offering distinct contextualized statements. Yet they were frequently stigmatized as simple, incoherent, even "primitive" or "childlike" by those who transcribed, translated, edited, and published them. Lacking the necessary linguistic and cultural competence, scholars interpreted and evaluated the narratives according to Western criteria. Readers likewise felt alienated, not only finding their expectations in terms of suspense, plot, and closure unanswered, but also confronted with unfamiliar elements such as open sexuality and violence, characters who are both human and animal, or physically impossible features and acts. Taken from their situational and functional context and heavily edited and sanitized — omitting the seemingly "useless" repetitions, "long-winded" beginning and ending formulas, complicated allegories, and material considered obscene and morally offensive — it is not surprising that the stories of Canada's Aboriginal peoples edited by European-Canadians appeared "bland and devoid of sense" to a Western readership (Johnston 1998, 103) simply because several vital features of the oral performances, such as modulation of voice, the effects of rhythm or onomatopoeia, gestures, and facial expression, were missing.

Rather than merely describing a different mode of transmission for essentially the same materials and purposes, the concept of oral tradition has several implications for style, content, and use, as well as for notions of authorship, textual stability, and permanence. In the Aboriginal oral traditions, stories are usually considered communal, with each performer entering the role of the teller without actually "claiming" the story for him- or herself. While there are personal stories that belong to a certain family or clan, or narratives and songs that are only to be performed by a select group of knowledgeable speakers, Western notions of individual authorship are alien to Aboriginal oral traditions. What is more, since oral performances are interactive, with the audience reacting to or even prompting the storyteller, not just the "ownership" of a particular text but the entire process of story-telling itself may be considered communal rather than individual. Most likely, the audience already knows the story, so that Aboriginal storytelling may be thought of in terms of musical performance, where the audience enjoys a particular rendering (with its vocal inflections, verbal innovations, omissions, and additions) rather than curiously awaiting developments in the plot (see Kroeber 2004, 2). Accordingly, from a Western perspective, Aboriginal oral narratives may appear rambling and episodic rather than structured around and building towards a singular climax (see van Toorn 2004, 25). For obvious reasons, the oral transmission of stories, speeches, and songs also has to place greater emphasis on memory than written tradi-tions do. Aboriginal oral narratives and performances therefore make use of techniques and rhetorical patterns to facilitate memorization, such as repeti-tion (which especially in a ceremonial context also serves to convey an accu-mulation of power), parallel phrasing, the phonetic effects of rhyming and rhythm, allusion, figurative and formulaic language, and underlining extra-textual features. While narratives passed on orally retain their basic structure and content, they leave far greater room for individual interpretations and changes than written documentation does. Often somewhat paratactic in style, open ended, and conceptualizing their elements in terms of both/and rather than either/or concepts, traditional Aboriginal stories furthermore tend to eschew establishing clear-cut causal connections or delivering a sin-gle unambiguous message. This "leaves more to listeners' imagination — they are not *told* what the relation of two events is; they are encouraged to imagine different possibilities and implications of the relationship" (Kroeber, 5). Through this flexibility, a particular story may be selected and adapted for a certain occasion or context, or a particular member of the community, so that no two performances have precisely the same meaning, and particu-lar performances may offer different readings depending on the listeners' own situations. Oral texts are both ancient and alive, then, and can be modified and adjusted with every telling, an aspect that also accounts for the transcultural integration of European and especially Christian elements into Aboriginal oral traditions from the seventeenth century onwards. This dynamic potential and vitality is lost to a large degree once the narratives are fixed in writing. Alerting readers to the danger of petrifaction inherent in the process of transcription, Anishinabe poet and critic Marie Annharte Baker (1942–) likens it to the fixatives used by entomologists in preserving specimens of rare insects (Baker 1994). Baker's analogy can be extended to a further problematic aspect: Just as rare insects are usually named after those who discovered them, the stories — for lack of a clearly attributable "authorship" or "copyright" — were often simply appropriated by those who collected, transcribed, and/or published them. While collections arising from early "collaborations" thus frequently did not sufficiently acknowledge the Aboriginal informants — providing such generic sources as "legend of the Ojibway" or "Iroquois prayer" — more recent works exemplify a truly cooperative representation of the oral tradition. Ethnomusicologist Wendy Wickwire, for instance, attempts to render Okanagan storyteller Harry Robinson's (1900–1990) narratives in a fashion faithful to the syntactic, phonetic, rhythmic, and verbal idiosyncrasies of Robinson's oral telling. The resulting volumes, *Write It on Your Heart: The Epic World of an Okanagan Storyteller* (1989) and *Nature Power: In the Spirit of an Okanagan Storyteller* (1992), convey much of the original flavor, power, and beauty of these stories. Furthermore, contemporary ethnographers and scholars such as Dell Hymes, Dennis Tedlock, and Karl Kroeber have suggested more culturally sensitive and respectful approaches to Aboriginal oral traditions, and consequently present readings and interpretations of oral narratives that sometimes differ substantially from those of earlier anthropologists and folklorists. Finally, our understanding of the importance and beauty of the oral traditions is increased by texts put together and published by Aboriginal people themselves. George Clutesi in 1967 published *Son of Raven, Son of Deer: Fables of the Tse-Shaht People*. Legends and myths of the Ojibway oral traditions are presented in Basil Johnston's *Ojibway Heritage* (1976) and *Tales the Elders Told* (1981), and Norval Morisseau's *Legends of My People, the Great Ojibway* (1975), while Kenneth B. Harris's *Visitors Who Never Left: The Origins of the People of Damelahamid* (1974) records a sequence of Ksan creation myths and origin stories from northern British Columbia.

These developments are paralleled with regard to the Inuit oral traditions: After initially being recorded exclusively by European researchers, they were later presented in Inuit-authored/-edited texts such as Zebedee Nungak and Eugene Arima's bilingual English-Inuktitut collection of Inuit legends *Stories from Povungnituk, Québec* (1969), *Tales from the Igloo* (1972, transcribed from the recordings of Copper Inuit elders by Maurice Metayer), and *How Kabloonat Became and Other Inuit Legends* (1974) by Mark Kalluak. Collections such as *We Don't Live in Snow Houses Now* (1976), edited by Susan Cowan, *Paper Stays Put: A Collection of Inuit Writing* (1980), edited by Robin Gedalof, and *Northern Voices: Inuit Writing in English* (1988), edited by Penny Petrone, include both Inuit oral traditions and contemporary writing. Among the most recent and most personal renderings of Aboriginal oral narratives are Saulteaux-Ojibwa Alexander Wolfe's *Earth Elder Stories: The Pinayzitt Path* (1988), Métis writers Maria Campbell's *Stories of the Road Allowance People*

(1995), and Warren Cariou's *Lake of the Prairies: A Story of Belonging* (2002), all of which (albeit all in differing fashion) recount and comment on their families' and communities' oral narratives.

As these examples indicate, despite all the drawbacks of transcriptions and the ensuing risks of appropriation, putting oral narratives into written form to many Aboriginal people today appears a necessary step. Cherokee-Greek writer Thomas King (1943–) gleefully recounts a Native storyteller's response to European-Canadian skepticism towards the Hau-de-nau-so-nee creation story rendered above: When a member of the audience asked what is below the turtle that carries the earth, the storyteller replied: "Another turtle. . . . And below that turtle? Another turtle. And below that? Another turtle. . . . So how many turtles are there? he wanted to know. The story-teller shrugged. No one knows for sure, she told him, but it's turtles all the way down" (King 2005, 91–92). Just as it takes an unbroken line of turtles for the world to stay in place, it takes an unbroken line of tellers for the oral tradition to survive, which makes the oral tradition an inherently precarious mode of transmission. Any oral narrative, song, or story merely lives in the potential of human beings to tell it, and thus is, as Basil Johnston (1929–) points out in an essay of the same title, always but "one generation from extinction" (Johnston 1998), disappearing with the last person able to remember and recite it. Consequently, much was lost through the diseases that decimated Aboriginal peoples (especially the smallpox epidemics along the Northwest coast) and through measures such as the so-called "Potlatch Law" (which until 1951 outlawed rituals and ceremonies central to many Aboriginal cultural traditions) and the compulsory training in residential schools. These schools — the last of which existed in Canada until the middle of the twentieth century — were located off-reserve and reduced Aboriginal children's contact with their family and community to a minimum. By promoting European-Canadian values and prohibiting Aboriginal children from speaking their Native language, they denied them access to their cultural heritage, effectively breaking the chain of oral cultural transmission. Thus, "erroneous as it was, the idea that cultures evolved from orality to literacy became a self-fulfilling prophecy because it was enforced through government policies" (van Toorn, 24). Since the oral traditions comprise the core of Aboriginal cultures and are closely tied to a nation's territory, these policies, in combination with the displacement from their homelands, have caused, according to Neal McLeod, an alienation of Canada's First Nations from their collective memory and have forced them into a kind of "internal exile" and "ideological diaspora." It would be a stark misconception to think of Aboriginal oral traditions only in terms of historic "artifacts," however; they are still passed on through continued performances, constantly renewing themselves in every telling. Yet in this as well as many other respects, the devastating impact of the colonial encounter remains an undeniable fact for Canada's Aboriginal peoples.

# "Genres" and Forms

While assessments such as Petrone's assertion that "the primary role of oral literature was utilitarian and functional rather than aesthetic" (1990, 4) may appear too sweeping, the oral tradition did and still does serve important purposes. Didactically it conveys the vital knowledge and skills for living in a particular area as well as teaching the community's social and religious norms and principles. It accounts for and commemorates a community's history, the events and traditions that shaped its cultural identity. It figures as a form of prayer or blessing, serving but also entertaining the audience. In addition to this functional diversity, traditional Aboriginal narratives often defy a clear categorization along generic or systematic lines. In the following overview, functional, thematic, and (at times hazy) generic aspects are combined in order to offer an encompassing picture of the texts, speeches, performances, and story cycles that comprise Aboriginal oral traditions.

Common to many oral narratives is a clear emphasis on the interrelation and interconnectedness of all things and beings, a holistic approach which shows in beginning formulas such as "All my relations," an invocation addressing not only humans but all parts of creation. Oral narratives and performances frequently do not clearly distinguish between what from a Western perspective is separated into the natural and supernatural, realistic and fantastic, animal and human (who in Aboriginal narratives frequently transform into each other), or the animate and inanimate parts of the world: Everything is considered alive and necessary. Many of the stories are marked by cyclical rather than linear notions of time, and while particular narratives may arise from a person's specific memories of his or her own lifetime, many stories recall events from what is generally referred to as "time immemorial," that is, so far back that, were it not for the oral tradition, they would no longer have a place in a community's collective memory.

Ceremonial performances, which as a form of ritual enactment are accorded particular sacredness and power, include elements such as song or chant, prayer, dance, and dramatic address. Sometimes restricted to a closed circle of initiates — the "keepers" of a particular story, song, or prayer — they are central elements in initiation, purification, blessing, healing, empowerment, and vision-seeking contexts, but also on occasions such as planting and harvesting, hunting, or preparing food, since religion in most Aboriginal cultures was/is not separate from everyday life but tends to permeate all aspects of it.

Oratory played an important role among Canada's Aboriginal peoples in diverse contexts, including personal honoring songs to praise and celebrate a person's accomplishments, in ceremonies and rituals, and in political speeches in council meetings or diplomatic negotiations. Eloquence and the power to persuade were held in high esteem, skills that figured both in the relations of the various nations with each other as well as in their dealings with Europeans. In the seventeenth century, in view of the supreme skill and coerciveness that the Aboriginals displayed, the Jesuit missionary Paul Lejeune observed in the Jesuit Relations: "There is no place in the world where Rhetoric is more powerful than in Canada . . . as the Captain is elected for his eloquence alone, and is obeyed in proportion to his use of it for they have no other law than his word" (1896–1901, V, 195). In the struggles between English and French colonizers over North America, numerous Aboriginal orators during the seventeenth and eighteenth centuries addressed European trading partners, government agencies, or missionaries in such an impressive manner (see Petrone, 27–34). Two of the most outstanding orators in the eighteenth century were the Ottawa war chief Pontiac (1720–1769), whose vision of a Native confederacy allied to the French inspired the revolt of 1763–1764, and the Iroquois Thayendanegea (Joseph Brant, 1742–1807), who acted as a spokesman for the Mohawk loyalists.

In the wider field of narrative, creation stories that account for the origin of the world and its people are present in all Aboriginal cultures. Many of them either follow the "earth diver" pattern exemplified in the aforementioned Hau-de-no-sau-nee version, in which various animals help to create the earth in its original state or after a great flood, or belong to the so-called "emergence" stories, in which the first people emerge into the present world from a previous place. Characteristically, many of these creation stories describe what is less an ad hoc creation *ex nihilo* than an evolutionary process of transformation from the mythological shape of the world to its present stage, facilitated by several agents rather than one authoritative creator. Origin and culture myths — that is, genealogical and explicatory narratives that account for particular characteristics of the landscape, the wildlife, and the universe, or for the existence of particular traditions, rules, or social structures — reflect but also perpetuate an Aboriginal culture's specific metaphysical worldview, and thus contribute to the survival of a nation's cultural identity. Like creation stories, they may be situated partly in the realm of the fantastic, but they are also frequently clearly linked to a concrete area. Rather than merely providing the setting or stage for a plot, place in Aboriginal oral narratives becomes central to the understanding of the narrative itself, with events being mapped and documented in and amidst a nation's specific territories and geographic features. Aboriginal identity derives from a sense of place, and it is the oral tradition that, as Cruikshank points out, "anchors history to place" (413). This links the oral narratives of an Aboriginal nation's past to contemporary land claims, as Canada's Aboriginal peoples increasingly struggle for the recognition of narratives preserved in the oral tradition as legitimate representations of their history, to be accorded equal standing as Western chronicles. Ron Hamilton recounts the historiographic aspects of the Nuu-cha-nulth oral tradition: "At home, when people bring this kind of story up they always preface it with 'li ax misshlaa yaa mis, yuk wii mitas,' which means, this story which comes from our old people which we will now call in English 'history'" (in Young-Ing 1996, 159). Moreover, among the Plains tribes there is the tradition of so-called winter counts, symbolic graphic renderings on buffalo hide, which trace a year's important events in linear fashion. Since the oral narrative accounts are not self-evident or easily accessible and do not present exact dates — and also taking into account that they may change with varying contexts, performers, and motivations — Canadian courts, in a Eurocentric manner, tended to dismiss them as inadequate on the grounds that they provided insufficient "evidence." Yet in a landmark decision in 1997 the Supreme Court ruled that the Gitskan Wet'suwet'en oral traditions were to be considered equal to written documents.

Trickster characters and culture heroes appear in the narrative traditions of nearly all Aboriginal cultures, albeit in different shapes. While Coyote is certainly the best known and most common, in other regions tricksters take the shape of Raven (especially along the Northwest coast), Badger, Mink, Hare, Nanabozho (among the Ojibway), Old Man (on the Plains), Weesakedjak (among the Saulteaux and Cree), and Glooscap (among the Mi'kmaq of Nova Scotia), to name but a few. Disrupting academic definitions or analytic categorizations, the trickster is not only a shape-shifter who can transform from male to female or from human to animal; s/he is also a curious mixture of culture hero and fool. While s/he is governed by tremendous appetites, particularly for food and sex, the trickster's irresponsible and selfish ploys often turn out to be beneficial to humanity by creating or changing important features of the world (which is why these tales often overlap with creation and origin myths, making a clear categorization impossible). The trickster is therefore both divine creator (or transformer) and a very earthly glutton and blunderer; and while s/he is not truly malevolent but rather child-like and impulsive, his/her jealous, amoral, and antisocial behavior clearly challenges established rules and existing orders. The trickster has often inspired comparisons to the picaresque heroes of European literatures and to mythical figures such as the Greek Hermes or the Nordic Loki; on the other hand, the overtly sexual and scatological aspects and the earthy humor of trickster stories, as well as the inconsistent or even contradictory traits of trickster characters, may be perplexing or even disturbing to a Western audience.

First of all evoking laughter, trickster stories also teach, mostly by bad example. Where the trickster errs, the audience learns; where s/he breaks norms and rules, the audience recognizes their relevance and meaningfulness; and where the trickster's selfishness gets him/her into trouble, the audience realizes the importance of altruistic behavior within a community.

Trickster stories in their permitted disrespect thus simultaneously reinforce rules and boundaries, yet also allow for their imaginative testing and transgression, a characteristic that through the aforementioned flexibility and openness might be said to mark the oral tradition as a whole. As Kroeber points out, changes in the performance of an oral text can be considered a form of negotiating a community's values and practices, a "way of 'debating' solutions to practical personal, social, and political contemporary problems" (2). Rather than presenting binding laws in a dogmatic fashion, storytelling was and continues to be a "means by which Native Americans sustained and strengthened, through continual self-reflexive reassessments, the effectiveness of their cultures in a world sacred because vital — never static nor dependably stable, yet therefore hospitable to beings capable of self-transformation and self-renewal" (7).

# The Power of the Word

Storytelling as it is conceived of within the oral tradition is therefore not to be mistaken for trivial amusement (although this may also be one of its intended effects). For Aboriginal cultures it has traditionally been the most important cultural activity, which encompasses aspects that in Western traditions are institutionalized in schools, councils, laws and courts, churches, and archives. Consequently, within the oral tradition a far greater significance and power is attributed to the spoken word itself. For most Native cultures, "the *word* carried the power to create, to make things happen — medicine to heal, plants to grow, animals to be caught, and human beings to enter the spiritual world" (Petrone, 10). Instead of considering language and narrative as representational, words in Aboriginal oral cultures are thought of as presentational (see Einhorn 2000, 119); that is, they intrinsically carry the power to create or change reality (which is also one of the reasons for restricting the performance of particular stories to special occasions or seasons). Thus the Okanagan writer, culture worker, and storyteller Maria Campbell (1940–) explains: "When we are studying oral tradition, . . . the old people always say *payatick*, which means 'careful.' Think before you speak; words have power. The words and the story have work to do" (in Gingell 2004, 191–92). One of the most important tasks of word and story within the oral tradition is to bestow, sustain, and strengthen Aboriginal cultural identity and community — an aspect which makes immediately apparent the continued relevance of the oral tradition. Oral traditions today maintain their continuity even while they absorb new influences and adjust to the conditions of being Native, Inuit, or Métis in twenty-first-century Canada. They are now complemented (not replaced) by Canadian Aboriginal authors' writing, and in turn strongly influence written works. Texts such as Cree author Tomson Highway's plays,

Thomas King's novel *Green Grass, Running Water* (1993), and Chippewa writer Lenore Keeshig-Tobias's poems are clearly informed by mythic elements and characters derived from the oral traditions, while writing by authors such as the Cree poet Louise Halfe, Anishinabe writer Richard Wagamese, and Thomas King again is infused by the structural, rhythmic, syntactic, and phonetic qualities that characterize oral narrative. By "breathing new life into the stories" (McLeod 1998, 64), contemporary Native writers and storytellers ensure cultural memory, keeping the oral tradition alive for the generations to come. In view of the immense changes Canada's Aboriginal people have had to face since the arrival of Europeans, both the Aboriginal oral tradition and its written complement are forms of cultural affirmation, linking past to future for the Aboriginal people of Turtle Island.

# 2: The Whites Arrive: White Writing before Canada, 1000–1600

*Iain M. Higgins (University of Victoria)*

L IKE MOST MODERN NATION STATES, Canada was invented slowly, and like many nation states beyond Europe, it was invented by white colonizers who came from overseas. Indeed, the standard history of the name "Canada" itself retraces the nation's slow historical emergence as a product of European expansion and colonization. Originally a Huron-Iroquois word meaning "village" or "settlement," *kanata* entered the Euro-American record through Jacques Cartier's accounts of his explorations in the 1530s and 1540s, and referred to a region in the Laurentians (see ch. 4, Laflèche). Contemporary European mapmakers quickly borrowed the name from Cartier, using it still more vaguely to designate an area around the St. Lawrence River. The word's territorial extension continued across the seventeenth and eighteenth centuries as French and English expansion into First Nations territories increased, but a formal definition was not given until the late eighteenth century. Only after 1791, when the Constitutional (or Canada) Act was proclaimed, did the name Canada begin to receive official definition in constitutional documents, but even then it continued to expand its geographical reach until 1949, when Newfoundland and Labrador joined the federation.

It follows from this short history of Canada's name that there was no such thing as "Canada" in the period from 1000 to 1600 — except perhaps in the sixteenth century — and therefore no Canadian literature either. Accordingly, this discussion has to focus on the written record of successive European movements into the territory that would eventually be called Canada. For the sake of simplicity, though — unless there is an obvious reason to use another name — this pre- or proto-Canadian territory will be referred to here as Canada or North America, even if the literature concerned with it cannot yet accurately be called Canadian or North American.

Legend has it that enterprising Irish or "Alban" travelers were the first Whites to cross the Atlantic Ocean to North America in the sixth century. A few such intrepid travelers had, after all, reached Iceland even before the Norsemen, or Vikings, began colonizing it late in the ninth century, and as a result some people have wanted to imagine that the Irish made journeys still further west. The evidence for the Alban claim to priority in reaching Canada is, however, highly indirect and hardly convincing. It consists of the account of a saint's life, *The Voyage of St. Brendan*, which was set down in Irish sometime in the eighth century and reworked into Latin about two centuries later, and a reenactment in the 1970s by an indefatigable retracer of famous travels, Tim Severin (1940–). Severin's tale makes for entertaining reading and establishes that an Irish transatlantic voyage was possible but, ultimately, St. Brendan's journey remains a legend. Even more improbable is the journey of another supposed Celtic traveler to North America, that of Madoc, a Welsh noble, who, according to some accounts from the late sixteenth century, reached the continent near the end of the twelfth century.

Such firm evidence as we do have of early transatlantic travels reveals that the first-known Whites to come to North America were the Norse, who had begun expanding westwards from their Scandinavian homelands in the late eighth century. Progressing from raiding to settlement, and taking advantage of the then relatively ice-free conditions in the North Atlantic Ocean, the Norse pursued their course of expansion island by island, by both chance and design. They advanced all the way to Greenland, which received its deliberately propagandistic name from Eirik the Red in the late tenth century. The Norse continued their journeys still further into territories that they named flat stone land (*Helluland*), wood land (*Markland*), and even wine country (*Vinland*). Historians and geographers have long debated the exact location of these Norse-named territories, but the current scholarly consensus is that they designate Baffin Island, Labrador, and Newfoundland, respectively. The most contentious of these designations is that of Vinland, which some scholars have placed as far south as present-day New England, since modern Newfoundland lies north of grape-growing territory. Whatever the exact location of Vinland, though, the discovery in 1960 of the remains of a genuine Viking site (previous evidence had been either spurious or decidedly uncertain) at L'Anse aux Meadows in northern Newfoundland has confirmed that Norse travelers did in fact come to Canada.

For various reasons, the most pressing of them probably being economic, the Vikings did not stay long at L'Anse aux Meadows, but the evidence of their presence there has proved that the first works of European literature with an indirect claim to being Canadian are not pure fiction. Those works, the texts in which we first find the names Helluland, Markland, and Vinland, are the Old Norse narratives known today as *The Greenlanders' Saga* (*Grælendinga saga*) and *Eirik the Red's Saga* (*Eiriks saga rauða*). By their account, the first known European to see Canada was Bjarni Herjolfsson, and the first known explorer-settler was Leif Eirikson. Scholars believe that these two prose texts were composed in about the early and the mid-thirteenth century, respectively, although the manuscripts in which they survive were copied somewhat later. Neither of them is as fine a literary work as the better-known Icelandic sagas, such as those of Njall or Gisli, but they are important in that they reveal attitudes and experiences that would become commonplace in European writing about these unknown territories. For instance, European explorers assume the right to name the places that they have just encountered for the first time. "This land," says Leif Eirikson in *The Greenlanders' Saga*, "shall be given a name in accordance with its nature, and be called Markland, Wood Land" (Jones 1986, 192). In addition, the tales also feature accounts of things that are not local but were borrowed from other sources (usually earlier travel writings) and that serve to entertain the reader or to authenticate the account. Thus near the end of *Eirik the Red's Saga* we meet a dangerous "uniped" akin to the one-footed race that medieval people might have known from the tradition of the Marvels of the East. More significantly, the accounts of contact between the explorers and indigenous peoples (called Skraelings by the Norse) also present evidence of complex and typically wary interactions. Here, as elsewhere, these interactions usually involved a mix of trading, raiding (including "people raiding," when local people were taken back as slaves, samples, or souvenirs), and inadvertent comedy. Unexpected encounters often led to skirmishes, and these could be related realistically — as in the *Greenlanders'* laconic account of the battle that led to Thorvald Asvaldson's death from a stray arrow — or farcically, as in *Eirik's* account of a different battle that resulted in the Norsemen fleeing while a pregnant woman (Freydis) scared the Skraelings away by slapping a sword against her naked breasts.

These sagas seem to have been all but unknown outside the Norse world until the late sixteenth century. After L'Anse aux Meadows fell into disuse early in the eleventh century, Canada did not figure in the European imagination again until the later fifteenth century, by which time the Norse were abandoning their Greenland settlements as well. It is possible that after the twelfth century there were contacts between the Norse and the Inuit, who may have been moving into Greenland at that time, but no written record of them survives. European sources preserve vague evidence that Danish, German, and Portuguese voyagers may have been exploring in the North Atlantic during the late fifteenth century and early sixteenth century, but it is impossible even to link them firmly to Greenland, let alone to Canada. Slivers of archival evidence suggest that fishermen from Bristol in England may have known of the existence of what is now Newfoundland by the 1480s, but if so, this knowledge seems to have remained oral.

When Canada once again reliably entered the world of European letters, it did so in both Latin and English — the language of the nation that would help colonize it, although John Cabot, who undertook voyages to Newfoundland in 1497 and 1498, was not an Englishman but an Italian. A contemporary of Columbus, who in the 1490s was making his more famous expeditions to the "Indies," neither Cabot nor his two transatlantic journeys are especially well documented. Cabot was probably born Giovanni Caboto in 1449 or 1450, possibly near Naples or in Genoa, and seems to have died at sea off Newfoundland in 1498, leaving no written record of his explorations. Such sparse records as do exist come to us from other sources, including his son Sebastian (ca. 1476–ca. 1557), who made his own voyages of exploration in 1508–1509 and claimed partial credit for his father's discoveries. Sebastian's account, a Latin text taken from a map, was given wide circulation in Latin and English in Richard Hakluyt's (ca. 1552–1616) massive anthology of exploration history and colonial propaganda, *The Principall Navigations, Voiages and Discoveries of the English Nation* (first edition in one volume, 1589; second edition in three volumes, 1598–1600). Hakluyt's anthology has in very small parts some claim to being a work of proto-English-Canadian literature. The Cabot record in Hakluyt resembles the earlier Norse texts and other later European texts in its manner of bestowing names, noticing the ways of the indigenous peoples, and inventorying local features in a pleasant but unliterary prose. It also anticipates one of the most prominent and persistent features of Canadian writing well into the twentieth century, namely an unceasing focus on the land, the first peoples, and what would come to be called natural resources:

> In the yere of our Lord 1497 John Cabot a Venetian, and his sonne Sebastian (with an English fleet set out from Bristoll) discovered that land which no man before that time had attempted, on the 24 of June, about five of the clocke early in the morning. This land he called Prima vista, that is to say, First seene, because as I suppose it was that part whereof they had the first sight from sea. That Island which lieth out before the land, he called the Island of S. John upon this occasion, as I thinke, because it was discovered upon the day of John the Baptist. The inhabitants of this Island use to weare beasts skinnes, and have them in as great estimation as we have our finest garments. In their warres they use bowes, arrowes, pikes, darts, woodden clubs, and slings. The soile is barren in some places, & yeeldeth litle fruit, but it is full of white beares, and stagges farre greater then ours. It yeeldeth plenty of fish, and those very great, as seales, and those which commonly we call salmons: there are soles also above a yard in length: but especially there is great abundance of that kinde of fish which the Savages call baccalaos. In the same Island also there breed hauks, but they are so blacke that they are very like to ravens, as also their partridges, and egles, which are in like sort blacke. (Blacker 1965, 19–20)

If Hakluyt's translation of a single Latin paragraph on a map represents the first foretaste of an English-Canadian literature, Jacques Cartier's (1491–1557) *Relations*, which provide much more extensive accounts of his three voyages of exploration (1534, 1535–1536, and 1541–1542), represent the earliest anticipation of a French-Canadian literature (see ch. 4, Laflèche). After Cabot he was the first known White to make the transatlantic journey to what would become Canadian territory. Cartier was a sailor from Saint-Malo in Brittany who was commanded by the French king, François I, to search for both gold and a route to Asia. The third relation is a brief third-person summary of Cartier's explorations, but the previous two are first-person narratives that read like expanded versions of Sebastian Cabot's paragraph. All three texts have the same basic features as the Old Norse sagas and the Cabot record mentioned above (the factual inventories, for instance), but they give more information, whether geographical or ethnographical. In addition, they are attractive as (sometimes almost breathless) narratives that reveal glimpses of Cartier's own workaday consciousness, as in the following excerpt from the second relation:

> The next day, the second of the said month of September, we again came out of the said [Saguenay] river to make our way towards Canada and found the tide to be strong-flowing and dangerous, because southwards of the said river there are two isles around which, at more than three leagues, there are only two and three channels strewn with rocks as big as tuns and pipes [that is, as barrels and casks], and the tides were deceptive between the isles such that we thought we had lost our galleon there but for the help of our barques. (Cartier 1986, 135; my translation)

Lucky this time, Cartier was apparently not so fortunate on his third voyage, when the gold he discovered turned out to be fool's gold (iron pyrites) and the diamonds to be quartz. He received no further commissions as an explorer.

Martin Frobisher (1539–1594) — along with Humphrey Gilbert and John Davis the last of the sixteenth-century Whites to be associated with some written record of Canada — would have sympathized with Cartier's plight. On his three voyages (1576, 1577, and 1578) to find the Northwest Passage, Frobisher shipped plenty of worthless ore back to England as gold. He himself left no public record of his explorations, but three others (Christopher Hall, Dionise Settle, and Thomas Ellis) did, and these documents soon found their way into Hakluyt's *Voyages*. As one might expect, the three accounts contain the same features as the earlier records and they much resemble Cartier's in being unadorned narrative retellings of the journeys. Perhaps even more clearly, they fitfully articulate the designs that the White explorers had on the indigenous populations they encountered. Master Dionise Settle in his account of the 1577 voyage relates that the explorers prayed "that by our Christian studie and endevour, those barbarous people trained up in Paganisme, and infidelitie, might be reduced to the knowledge of true religion, and to the hope of salvation in Christ our Redeemer" (Blacker, 187). John Davis (ca. 1550–1605) made three northern voyages a decade later (1585, 1586, and 1587), coasting Greenland (which he brought back into European consciousness), Baffin Island, and Labrador, but devoted more energy to documentation than economic exploitation. One prominent feature of the records of these voyages, and a common one in European exploration narratives in general, are complaints about the thievishness of the local peoples. For example, Davis comments in the account of his second voyage: "our mariners complained heavily against the people, and said that my lenity and friendly using of them gave them stomacke to mischiefe: for they have stollen an anker from us, they have cut our cable very dangerously, [and] they have cut our boats from our sterne" (Davis 1880, 22–23).

Between Frobisher and Davis came Humphrey Gilbert (1537–1583), an early propagandist for exploration to find the Northwest Passage, whose fatal voyage of colonization in 1583 took him into Cabot's rather than Frobisher's and Davis's territory. Gilbert wrote much, but his own account of the Newfoundland voyage occupies only a short letter in which he describes the land as abundant in game and fish. Similar sentiments can be found in the longer Latin letter written in 1583 to Hakluyt by Stephen Parmenius (?–1583), a Hungarian scholar and poet, who accompanied Gilbert and died in a shipwreck in 1583. "But what shall I say, my good Hakluyt, when I see nothing but a very wildernesse? of fishe here is incredible abundance. . . . the whole lande is full of hilles and woodes" (Quinn [Hakluyt translation, 1589], 175). Parmenius also wrote a long Latin poem, *De Navigatione* (On Voyaging), which was published in London in 1582 and celebrated Gilbert's upcoming colonial expedition. The first overtly literary work (besides the Old Norse sagas) that is associated with Canada-to-be, the poem is too rhetorical for modern tastes and remains a curiosity less likely to attract readers than the plain-spun narrative and letters of exploration and early colonization.

Of all the works mentioned here, it is probably Cartier's *Relations* that have the best claim to be considered part of the prehistory of Canadian writing. Whether or not they count as more (pre-)Canadian, though, than the other early texts from the sagas to Parmenius's letter, they nevertheless have much in common with them, in their literary features as well as their cultural attitudes. Regardless of which national tradition(s) they belong to, such works are valuable not only in their own right, but also for the ways in which they anticipate many of the attitudes and assumptions that would manifest themselves in the work of European and European-Canadian writers to come. By 1600, then, the Whites had been coming to Canada for a long time, and although the records they left increased in length and detail, they continued to display many of the features and concerns that had already characterized the earliest travelers' transatlantic journeys to what later came to be called Canada. The reading of these earliest records thus reveals the continuities as well as the discontinuities in the cultural attitudes of the White writers of the Canada that took shape as a result of their exploration, expansion, and settlement.

# II. The Literature of
# New France, 1604–1760

# 3: Historical Background

*Guy Laflèche (Université de Montréal)*

NEW FRANCE IS A TERRITORY that once spread from Newfoundland to the Gulf of Mexico. As a French colony it included at least three main regions: Acadia, Canada, and Louisiana (not counting Brazil and Florida). In the context of Canadian history, the term refers to a period corresponding to that of the Ancien Régime in France, dating conventionally from 1534 (the first voyage of Jacques Cartier) to 1763 (the Treaty of Paris, which sanctioned the military conquest by Britain in 1760). New France was in fact the result of six major historical developments: first, the voyages of discovery, beginning officially in 1524 with Verrazzano, followed by Cartier's first voyage; second, the establishment of trading monopolies, starting with De Monts in 1604 (followed by the founding of Quebec City in 1608) and the establishment of the state enterprise Compagnie de la Nouvelle-France in 1627 (succeeded by the Communauté des Habitants in 1645); third, the Sovereign Council in 1663, when France imposed peace on the Indians and the territory of the colony expanded considerably; fourth, the onset of the Indian wars in 1684, further complicated by war with the British colonies; fifth, the "thirty-years peace" (1713–1744), which for the span of one generation allowed social and economic growth in the colony; and sixth, the resumption of war, which ended with the British conquest of 1760. Yet New France was much more than a territory, a period of history, or a colonial society. It was American France, a "France d'Amérique."

# 4: Literature on New France

*Guy Laflèche (Université de Montréal)*

T HE WRITINGS ON NEW FRANCE constitute a great marginal literature
spanning three centuries. The term "literature" has to be understood in
a broader sense here, since literary texts, or works possessing an aesthetic
value, were rare exceptions in this period. Such texts as did exist seldom concerned themselves with the French colony. Their subject was rather North
America and the Native Americans — in other words, the anthropology,
human geography, or, as it was called at the time, the natural history of the
New World. After the discoveries, explorations, and voyages came the long
and difficult missionary endeavors, conducted mostly by the Jesuits. As a
result, the literature on New France, throughout the seventeenth century,
drew a portrait of the Native American and of North America's tribes and
confederations on a two-dimensional cultural graph, with the one axis running from friends and allies (including the Mi'kmaq, Montagnais,
Algonquin, and Huron peoples) to enemies (the Iroquois Confederation,
the Abenaki), that is, from savages to barbarians, and the other axis running
from Christians to infidels. Native Americans were the main characters in
these writings, not the explorers or missionaries — and still less the governors, administrators, and military leaders of the colony. For New France —
unlike the Europeanization of the Dutch, British, Spanish, and Portuguese
colonies — was indeed an attempt to make America and the Native
Americans French, which also produced the opposite result, namely the
Americanization of the French in America. While attempts to found New
France in Brazil and later in Florida proved ephemeral, Canada, along with
Acadia and Louisiana, endured against all odds until 1760 — and even
beyond, as French America survived the military conquest by the British.
Thus the literature of New France remains the richest, oldest, and most
extensive in the history of the European expansion to North America.

In 1545 Jacques Cartier's (1491–1557) *Bref recit* ("A Short and Brief
Narration") which related his second voyage to America, conducted ten
years before (1535–1536), appeared in Paris. It is not known why Jehan
Poullet, Cartier's secretary, published this text, having in all probability
also written the accounts of the explorer's other two voyages to New
France in 1534 and 1541–1542. Neither is it known why Poullet published the account at this time, but from a literary point of view it makes

perfect sense: Similar to the earlier account of Verrazzano's voyage of 1524 (written in Latin but not published until an Italian edition appeared in Venice in 1565) and later ones by Captain Roberval and the pilot Jean Alphonse, the main importance of the three accounts of Cartier's voyages lay primarily in their political consequences and only secondarily in the value of the scientific or geographical information they contained. They were originally written as exploration reports for the French king François I. After the strategic information had outlived its usefulness, the accounts only resurfaced as insertions in scientific works. As a work of literature, the *Bref recit*, the tale of Cartier's second voyage — which took him from the Strait of Belle Isle all the way to Hochelaga (the site of present-day Montreal), followed by a hard winter at Stadacona (the site of present-day Quebec City) — is an extraordinary adventure story with a popular appeal, precisely because it was a true account of the discovery and exploration of a new continent and its peoples.

Hence, the *Bref recit* is primarily the logbook of a voyage of exploration, like Las Casas's report of Christopher Columbus's voyage in 1492. But when Cartier was on his second voyage to America, relations with the Indians had grown deeper and more personal — to the extent that the *Bref recit* is also a work of ethnographic reporting. The account introduces a captain commanding a flotilla of three ships and their officers, as well as two Iroquois interpreters, that is, two young captives who had just spent a year with him in France, and a great village chief. Last but not least, it features an entire village, Stadacona, which Cartier named "Canada," an Iroquois word meaning "village." The adventure tale begins as a sea story and turns into a tragedy, tragicomedy, and heroic epos. Cartier succeeds in reaching Montreal, despite opposition on the part of his native hosts, but he remains trapped by the ice in Quebec and at the mercy of the Iroquois villagers, who save his crew and his expedition by revealing to him a cure for scurvy. The narrative comprises three chapters on different themes: the St. Lawrence River, the Kingdom of Saguenay, and the country of the St. Lawrence Iroquois. Cartier's Iroquois are portrayed as having absolutely no shame whatsoever, going almost naked even in the dead of winter. Women enjoy total sexual freedom before marriage, while men may take several wives and divorce them at will. In France in 1545, Cartier's descriptions could not be regarded as anything but outrageously exotic.

Although the French exploration of America gave the world the masterpiece of Cartier's *Bref recit*, it was the simple narrations of individual travelers, rather than the grand explorations accounts, that proved most striking. The writings of cosmographer André Thevet (1516–1592), for instance, appear drab and bookish beside the vivid and moving eyewitness narrative of the Protestant Jean de Léry (1536–1613) in his *Histoire d'un voyage faict en la terre du Brésil*, published in 1578. The same applies to Samuel de Champlain's (1570–1635) accounts of his explorations, which took his readers from Acadia to the Great Lakes in five books published between 1604 and 1632 (the final volume includes the four previous books). A man of science, a geographer and explorer, but also a negotiator and diplomat among Indians, as well as a shipowner and politician among merchants and royalty, Champlain published works of colonialist propaganda, memoirs that offer a comprehensive survey of America and its Native peoples. From a literary point of view, these treatises are inferior, however, to the dramatic personal narratives of Pierre Biard (1567–1622) among the Mi'kmaq in 1611, Gabriel Sagard (1614–1636) among the Hurons in 1632 (see below), Paul Lejeune (1591–1664) among the Montagnais in 1634, and Jean de Brébeuf (1593–1649) again among the Hurons in 1636.

After a year in Quebec City, Paul Lejeune, the new superior of the Jesuits, decided to become a missionary among the Montagnais. During the winter of 1633–1634 he traveled with the Mestigoït family on their hunting circuit, accompanied by the shaman Carigonan. Even without the "sorcerer" (as Lejeune called him), the religious and missionary objective would certainly have proven improbable, since the conversion of the Montagnais to Christianity could not simply be brought about by magic. The winter hunt quickly turned into a Baroque adventure romance, for neither the prayers of the missionary nor the rituals of the shaman helped the hunters feed the group. To avoid being accused of leaving him to die, the Natives had to carry the gravely ill missionary back to Quebec City early in the spring. In fall, however, the missionary took his revenge, writing a vivid and spirited report about his winter experience in the Relation of 1634. He describes the Montagnais in minute detail — their food, hunting and fishing practices, clothing and ornaments, their good qualities and defects, their language and beliefs. The following passage, for instance, is a description of the drum of the Montagnais, which Lejeune saw in the hands of the shaman. The doctor as charlatan has always been a stock figure of comedy; here, he is trying to cure himself with a choreography worthy of the circus:

> Ils se seruent de ces chants, de ce tambour, & de ces bruits, ou tintamarres en leurs maladies, ie le declaray assez amplement l'an passé. . . . Par fois cest homme entroit comme en furie, chantant, criant, hurlant, faisant bruire son tambour de toutes ses forces: cependant les autres hurloient comme luy, & faisoient vn tintamarre horrible auec leurs bastons, frappans sur ce qui estoit deuant eux: ils faisoient danser des ieunes enfans, puis des filles, puis des femmes; il baissoit la teste, souffloit sur son tambour: puis vers le feu, il siffloit comme vn serpent, il ramenoit son tambour soubs son menton, l'agitant & le tournoyant: il en frappoit la terre de toutes ses forces . . .: il s'agitoit, il se tournoit de part & d'autre, faisoit quelques tours à l'entour du feu, sortoit hors la cabane, tousiours hurlant & bruyant: il se mettoit en mille postures; & tout cela pour se guerir.
> (Lejeune, 186, 188)

Lejeune's narrative is not only interesting for its ethnological information, but has a quite evident human or personal impact as well. For instance, it becomes clear enough that the shaman ritual is utterly the opposite of the learned mumblings heard around European sickbeds. Yet, from Lejeune's perspective, this shaman is the same baleful sorcerer who has refused the help of the very God who might easily deliver them all from sickness and famine. This incessant conflict between the shamans and the missionaries even came to blows on occasion, especially at the sickbeds of the dying, where the shaman was present for healing and the priest for baptism.

Certainly, the narrative, stylistic, and aesthetic form of Lejeune's 1634 Relation — with its interplay of comic situations, humor, and sarcasm — is exceptional. Its content, on the other hand, is quite representative of the literature of New France, since writers were describing the meeting of the French and the Natives — and generally in that order, as the writers were French, and the depictions of the Natives, however clear and vivid, must be read at second remove. Another example can be found in Pierre Biard's highly humorous description of the "grave-pit ritual" (a symbolical killing of a shaman lying in the grave, who thereby takes the sickness upon himself) from 1611. The exception to the general denigration of Native rituals and ceremonies was Gabriel Sagard, a Récollet missionary. In his *Grand Voyage du pays des Hurons* from 1632 Sagard also provides a description of the Aboriginals' "dances, songs and other ridiculous ceremonies." But his rendering of the Hurons' dances is quite different from that of the Jesuits. Sagard's main inspiration for this chapter is the 1606 account of the Mi'kmaq in New France by Marc Lescarbot, who in turn drew on Jean de Léry's account of Natives in Brazil in 1578. Despite his own peremptory judgments, Sagard comments very favorably on the Natives, whom he sincerely admired. The Récollet missionaries were Franciscans, and the spirit of Francis of Assisi can be found throughout their writings about New France, for example in Christian Leclercq's (1641–ca. 1708) *Nouvelle Relation de la Gaspésie* (1691) or in Louis Hennepin's (1626–1705) *Description de la Louisiane* (1683).

In stark contrast to Sagard, however, stands the account of another Récollet father, Valentin Leroux (1642–1708). Leroux's religious thinking on North American missions departed so far from Franciscan ideas as to espouse the fiercely anti-Jesuit stance of the Jansenist theologian and theorist Antoine Arnauld. Leroux expounded this theology in a major controversial work entitled *Premier Établissement de la foi dans la Nouvelle-France ou Histoire des colonies françaises* (1691); he attributed its authorship to his colleague Christian Leclercq. The work was a deliberate rewriting of the history set out by the Jesuits in their Relations. Leroux, whose thesis was as accurate as it was virulent, had little trouble showing that the Jesuit writings on New France were mere lies and propaganda. For him, the Jesuits were imposters and the Récollets were truly the first missionaries in the colony, arriving in Quebec in 1615, ten years before the Jesuits — who then blocked the Récollet fathers from returning to the colony. The Jesuits were exposed as liars, pretending to convert Indians in droves, even though there was not a single Native American church in the colony. Leroux branded them as cheats and hypocrites, who not only chivvied the dying into conversion and baptized dying babies unbeknownst to their parents, but also taught a form of Christianity that combined absurd devotions, rank prudery, and idiotic rituals.

The Jesuits had indeed established the colony of New France in 1632 with their own interests in mind — first and foremost, the evangelization of the Indians — so that throughout the entire seventeenth century the colony was virtually a theocracy. It was the Jesuits who, as their missions grew, expanded the French presence in America from Acadia and the St. Lawrence to the Great Lakes and down the Mississippi to the Gulf of Mexico. Consequently, they also produced the substantial bulk of the literature of New France, most notably the annual reports on missions in the colony from 1632 to 1672, the *Relations des Jésuites de la Nouvelle-France*. To these must be added the letters and spiritual writings, biographies and autobiographies, as well as numerous pious works, which the Jesuits sent back for the edification of their correspondents in France and Rome. A great deal of the material in the Jesuit Relations is rather monotonous, especially the interminable lists of edifying deeds performed by the good Christian savages. But every time the devil enters the stage or the threat of a war or Indian raid arises (as it frequently did), the Relations become heroic narratives of the missionaries' epic struggle against the forces of evil.

The high point of this missionary epic is the martyrdom of Goupil, Jogues, and Lalande in the Iroquois territory, followed by the deaths of Daniel, Gabriel Lalemant, Brébeuf, Garnier, and Chabanel in Huronia. These stories were retold and rewritten over three centuries, and the retellings became pieces of mythical hagiography in themselves, starting with the masterpieces of Jérôme Lalemant's (1593–1673) Relation of 1647 and Paul Ragueneau's (1608–1680) Relations of 1649 and 1650. Thus arose the first of the great myths of French Canada, the episode of the "Blessed Canadian Martyrs," crafted from the horrific accounts of the torture inflicted by the Natives on the Jesuit martyrs. In these tales, the Iroquois play the role of the Roman emperors and the Jesuits that of the early Christians. In fact, the Jesuits organized the entire Catholic literature of New France around this biblical typological analogy, with the Iroquois enemy as the reincarnation of the Egyptian armies attacking the children of Israel in the desert.

Also part of the Relations are the remarkable travelogues of Biard, Lejeune, and Brébeuf mentioned above. Even in their conventionally pious passages, the Jesuit writings are notable for their documentary value regarding the ethnology of the New World. The conversion of each Native

American was portrayed as a victorious combat against the shaman, who represented Satan. The missionaries often accepted a few minor compromises, for example, transforming the magical into Christian rituals. The Natives themselves had to make major compromises: marrying one wife only, forgoing divorce, and renouncing any aid from the shamans. "Comme je me mocquais d'eux," writes Paul Lejeune in his Relation of 1634, "et que je leur disais que les castors ne savaient pas ce que l'on faisait de leurs os, ils me répondirent: tu ne sais pas prendre les castors et tu en veux parler" (6, 210). The converse point of view, reported by Barthelmy Vimont (1594–1667) in the Relation of 1643, is equally dramatic: "C'est chose estrange, disaient-ils, que depuis que la priere est entree dans nos cabanes, nos anciennes coustumes ne nous servent plus de rien, & ce pendant nous mourrons tous à cause que nous les quittons" (24, 208). The Relations attracted a large readership in the seventeenth century and still today because they are easily accessible to the masses. In fact, while French intellectuals like Voltaire or Arnauld profoundly despised them, the numerous editions and reprints by Cramoisy, the Jesuits' official publisher in Paris, are proof that the Relations were bestsellers in their own time.

In addition, not only are the Jesuit writings in New France among the most numerous concerning French America, but the Jesuits inspired other writings in the same vein. The widow Marie Martin-Guyart de l'Incarnation (1599–1672), for instance, who founded a convent of Ursuline nuns in Quebec City in 1639, summarized, rewrote, or developed passages of their Relations in her own correspondence, which took the form of edifying letters. Although she wrote especially to her son Claude, this spiritual correspondence was not private but was intended for a form of publication that was quite common in the seventeenth century — the circular letter. This text format, which also includes some major relations or spiritual autobiographies, was often a form of leisure reading, even though Martin-Guyart expressed thoroughly Jesuit concerns in her thinking. In 1677 Claude Martin (1619–1696) wrote an edifying biography of his mother based on his correspondence with her, thereby partaking in another major development in the religious literature of New France. This development had produced, for instance, the extravagant biography of Catherine Longpré de Saint-Augustin, published in 1671 by Paul Ragueneau. Generally, such biographies more often took the form of "Lives," that is, short posthumous eulogies intended to be read aloud in monastic refectories. Using this kind of material, the nursing sisters of Quebec City wrote the annals of their community, recounting various incidents that occurred between 1636 and 1716. Marie Morin (1649–1730), a nurse in Montreal, attempted the same, but her manuscript remained a shapeless and incomplete rough draft.

The history of New France, then, was essentially written by the Jesuits. The establishment of the clerical, religious, and missionary history of the colony — which became its official history — was accomplished in three stages by three great Jesuit historical works: first, in Italian by Giuseppe Bressany (1652), then in Latin by François Ducreux (1664), and finally in French by François-Xavier de Charlevoix (1744). Charlevoix especially sought to set forth a factual history of the French colony on a monumental scale. These three Jesuit historians touched up or entirely rewrote the historical works of Marc Lescarbot, Gabriel Sagard, and especially Valentin Leroux — none of them sympathetic towards the Jesuit cause (see above). Charlevoix (1682–1761) succeeded in imposing the orthodox, missionary, and apostolic vision on the French colony (see below), particularly as his work was adopted and further developed by yet another great Jesuit historian, Camille de Rochemonteix, between 1895 and 1906. The result is that even the contemporary vision of New France is still that of the Jesuits, although the Franciscan-Jansenist history of Valentin Leroux provides a much more accurate and truthful account.

The most beautiful work of history about the colony, however, is the result of a historical collaboration. *L'Histoire du Montréal*, written by the Sulpician François Dollier de Casson (1636–1701) in 1672, was in fact dictated by Jeanne Mance (1606–1673), who, together with Maisonneuve, had founded Montreal in 1642. The book was composed at the end of her life as her spiritual testament — anonymously, for she insisted that Dollier de Casson present himself as the sole author. The twin authorship becomes apparent in the dual character of the work, though. On the one hand, readers sense a living presence in the eyewitness accounts of the elderly foundress and her view of Montreal as a fortified Holy City — although the town by that time had become a market for country folk and traders, who had long since lost any of the founders' illusions of creating the Ville-Marie. On the other hand, there is the vividly oral style of the Sulpician writer, who had arrived in Montreal only two years earlier and yet managed to write a living history of the heroic adventurers who fought for the settlement. For instance, it renders the speech of the Iroquois after the battle at the Long Sault against Dollard des Ormeaux and his sixteen brave companions:

> Si dix-sept Français nous ont traités de la sorte, étant dans un si chétif endroit, comment serons-nous traités lorsqu'il faudra attaquer une bonne maison où plusieurs de telles gens seront ramassés: il ne faut pas être assez fous pour y aller [attaquer Montréal], ce serait pour nous faire tous périr, retirons nous. (Dollier de Casson and Mance, 216–17)

Dollier de Casson's actual manuscript of *L'Histoire du Montréal* has never been published, and when it was rediscovered in 1845, it was put to use in rewriting history — a new, heroic version of the classical history of New France already developed by the Jesuits. At the time of the Révolution tranquille in the 1960s, the secular myth of Dollard des Ormeaux replaced the religious myth of the Blessed Canadian Martyrs, thanks in large part to the merits of Dollier de Casson's text, which is comparable in literary quality to the narratives of Jérôme Lalemant and Paul Ragueneau.

The most important of the authors who wrote about New France, the Baron de Lahontan (1666–1716), was undeniably a charlatan, an anticlerical, and a pamphleteer. And yet, he was the only real *writer* of all. Of course, Marc Lescarbot had published his *Muses de la Nouvelle-France* as an appendix to his 1609 *Histoire des navigations* (see ch. 5, Laflèche). Likewise, in the *Relation du voyage du Port Royal de l'Acadie*, published in 1708 by Marin Dières de Diéreville, the author's prose narrative alternates with passages in verse, while the novelistic fabrications of Mathieu Sagean (ca. 1700) and especially Claude Lebeau (1738) foreshadow the romantic exoticism of subsequent French tales of travel in America. Most remarkable among the latter, perhaps, is Chateaubriand's highly romanticized travelogue *Voyage en Amérique* of 1827, much of which comes straight out of Charlevoix's *Histoire*, by which it was largely inspired. Nevertheless, these romanticized travel accounts, which harbinger the literary exoticism of the Enlightenment, ultimately break free of the literature of New France to become new adventure tales, romances, and novels in the hands of French authors.

Louis Armand de Lom d'Arce, Baron de Lahontan, by contrast, is at the heart of the literature of New France, even though he single-handedly inspired the entire exoticist strategy French Enlightenment writings employed to criticize French society and institutions. Lahontan wrote his entire oeuvre in a single burst in three volumes and in three different genres. He had arrived in the colony in 1683, at the age of sixteen, and had left ten years later with a wealth of experience from which he crafted an exceptional work of literature. The first volume of his work (1703) gives an account of the French colony and America in the form of a series of letters. The second volume reports on the mores and manners of the Native Americans. It features a portrait of a true Noble Savage, who features two character traits that are entirely original in comparison to the rest of the literature of New France: First, Lahontan's savage has not to be converted, for he is yet a far better man than the Christian newcomers. Second, he has not to be Frenchified or Europeanized, for he is incomparably more civilized than the French colonists. Thus Lahontan introduced a critique of Western thought by contrasting it with the beliefs, customs, laws, and morality of the Native Americans. Comedy and humor dominate in the third volume, which went through dozens of editions. Entitled *Dialogues avec un sauvage*, it relates conversations of Lahontan with the Huron Adario on religion, laws, happiness, medicine, and love and marriage. The tone is saucy, irreverent, polemical, anticlerical, and antiroyalist, and few passages can in fact be taken seriously:

> Nos femmes, dit Adario, sont capricieuses, comme les vôtres, ce qui fait que le plus chétif sauvage peut trouver une femme. Car, comme tout paraît à découvert, nos filles choisissent quelquefois suivant leur inclination, sans avoir égard à certaines proportions: les unes aiment un homme bien fait, quoiqu'il ait je ne sais quoi de petit en lui; d'autres aiment un mal bâti pourvu qu'elles y trouvent je ne sais quoi de grand; et d'autres préfèrent un homme d'esprit et vigoureux, quoiqu'il ne soit ni bien fait ni bien pourvu de ce que je n'ai pas voulu nommer. Voilà, mon frère, tout ce que je puis te répondre sur le crime de la nudité. (Lahontan, 156)

Despite their striking differences, Lahontan's satire is no less American than the Jesuits' writings, even though his Adario and the latter's way of thinking have little in common with real Native Americans. The "truth" of Lahontan's writing instead arises from a stance of rebellion and systematic challenge: From Old France to New France, a New World was being discovered — the world of the Other, in which the French learned to negotiate with the Indians in an effort to preserve the best of both worlds and so make America their own. In this context, Lahontan's writings are a critique of France and Europe. It was easy enough for Lejeune to ridicule Carigonan's drum and the Natives' rituals; but the French also had to acknowledge what keen psychologists and effective healers the shamans were. And so criticism fired back, as in the dialogue on medicine, which mocks European science. Indeed, Lahontan can be said to have perfected this strategy of triggering genuine self-criticism via a reasoned critique of French manners and institutions through the lens of exotic cultures. A great deal of French Enlightenment thought has in fact its origins in New France, such as the articles on America and the Native Americans in Diderot and d'Alembert's *Encyclopédie* (from 1750 onward) and the major works in the new genre of the literature of reasoned critique through depictions from "exotic" points of view, for instance, Montesquieu's *Lettres Persanes* (1721) and Voltaire's *Le Huron ou l'Ingénu* (1767).

At the same time, the number of Jesuit writings continued to rise all through the eighteenth century. The Relations from New France changed in form and context, appearing in the *Lettres édifiantes et curieuses*, where letters from America were featured alongside letters from the Middle East, the Indies, and China. Also from New France came Joseph-François Lafitau's (1681–1746) treatise on *Les Moeurs des sauvages américains comparées aux moeurs des premiers temps* (1724). Popular for both its style and its illustrations, this book was the complete opposite of a serious scientific work. The author's naïveté has him comparing everything in Iroquois society to the Romans, Greeks, Egyptians, Sumerians, and Hebrews, in an attempt to prove that the Native Americans, the descendants of Noah, still preserve in their magical rituals Jehovah's first Christian revelation to Adam and Eve.

François-Xavier Charlevoix, together with his remarkable compendium of the history of New France (see above), published the historical *Journal d'un voyage dans l'Amérique septentrionale* in 1744. He borrowed the epistolary narrative formula from Lahontan's first volume, but his material was a compendium on America and its Native peoples, based almost entirely on the Jesuit Relations. The fact that all (or nearly all) parts of the *Journal* were derived at second hand did not prevent it from becoming a favorite among readers. François-René de Chateaubriand made it his source of inspiration for the *Voyage en Amérique* and the corresponding chapters about America of *Mémoires d'outre-tombe* (1848).

The literature of New France came to an end after the conquest of the French colony in 1760. There is, however, a relatively unknown book, the *Recherches philosophiques sur les Américains* (1768) by Cornelius de Paw, which had been republished no fewer than four times by 1774. This apparently learned work was in fact a series of polemical dissertations repeating banalities about America in the late eighteenth century from the viewpoint of the French colony.

In the mid-nineteenth century, Quebec rediscovered the literature of New France. Cartier's voyages were published in 1843, and the Jesuit Relations were republished in 1858. Over the next hundred years, historians pieced together the corpus of French texts on America, until in the 1960s, the first chapter of the history of Québécois literature was eventually published. In 1978 the first volume of Gilles Marcotte's *Anthologie de la littérature québécoise* appeared, written by Léopold LeBlanc and entitled "Literature of New France, 1534–1760," exactly the same title as the first chapter of the recent *Histoire de la littérature québécoise* (edited by Michel Biron, François Dumont, and Élisabeth Nardout-Lafarge, 2007). These chapters did not deal with actual writings *from* New France but with works *about* New France, however.

It is true enough that French writings *about* North America are not in any real sense the sources of Quebec's national literature. Nevertheless, the most important and significant of these works occupy a firm place in the culture of Quebec, being better known in Quebec than in France. Among them are some important masterpieces by French writers from the three greatest centuries of French literature: Léry's *Relation du Brésil* from the Age of Discovery, Lejeune's Relation of 1634 from the period of French classicism, and Lahontan's *Dialogues* from the dawn of the Enlightenment era. It might even be said that the literature of New France, with its intimate and precise knowledge of America and its Native peoples, marks the first achievement in the history of anthropology in Northeastern America, preceding the great works of Charles de Brosses, Auguste Comte, Émile Durkheim, Lucien Lévy-Bruhl, Claude Lévi-Strauss, and Rémy Savard. In short, although France lost its American empire, it preserved a rich heritage in its literature on New France.

# 5: Colonial Literature in New France

*Guy Laflèche (Université de Montréal)*

DESPITE THE VAST BODY OF LITERATURE about New France produced by French writers, it must be noted that before 1760 there was no literary scene in New France that could have rivaled that of France — neither in quality nor by extent. The French colony, conquered by military force in 1760 and ceded to Great Britain in the Treaty of Paris in 1763, was a colony in the strict sense — that is, a society still far from capable of taking charge of its own destiny. On the other hand, if Quebec today is a nation with a culture of its own, it is because by 1760 New France had already developed a French culture distinct from that of France, a culture that managed to resist the powerful temptations to assimilate with the dominant culture of Britain and English Canada. Yet in 1760 New France did not have a literature of its own, and this fact describes the situation for both the works from France that it incorporated and the literary works it produced — or can be assumed to have produced from today's perspective (the majority of texts were not preserved, since they were largely written for special occasions and were not accorded any greater importance).

The matter of a colonial literature in New France arises somewhat more plausibly with the establishment of the first trading settlements in Acadia in the early seventeenth century. Among the French documents of the Port-Royal colony (Biard, Massé, Champlain, Poutrincourt, and others) is one major work, the *Histoire des navigations* (1609) by Marc Lescarbot (ca. 1570–1642). Lescarbot was a young Parisian lawyer who sailed to Port-Royal in 1606, following his client Poutrincourt, who assisted in the ventures of Du Gua de Monts in Acadia. The *Histoire des navigations* gives an account of the French explorers in America and also contains the first historical description of the Mi'kmaq peoples. It featured as an appendix a collection of poems entitled *Les Muses de la Nouvelle-France*, mainly written for the amusement of the poet's fellow travelers and which would later appear as a separate publication. The collection contains a eulogy to De Monts and Poutrincourt, with the usual commonplaces on colonization and Christianization, as well as criticism of the Catholic clergy. Some verses, however, appear fresh and original, almost as if improvised; they are also quite autobiographical, as the poet evokes his profession, the architecture and life of the city, and the landscapes, forests, and countryside of France.

Bernard Émont (2004) has most aptly described the poetry of Lescarbot as "bardic." Émont discovered that the poet describes himself in his *Histoire de la Nouvelle-France* with the hope that French King Henry IV would continue to send to America "bardes chrétiens portant la fleur de lys au coeur." Lescarbot proposes and describes what he himself has in fact achieved, that is, a Gallic, or more specifically, Celtic poetry distinguished by its musicality, its Gallic themes, and its spirit of (especially religious) commitment. Lescarbot might be far from the aesthetic achievements of Ronsard and the Pléiade poets or the poetics of Malherbe, which dominated the poetry of France at that time, but even so, his poetry is entirely suited to its circumstances and certainly fit to herald the establishment of New France. Lescarbot identifies with those whose duty it is to serve the public: the entrepreneurs, sailors and merchants, the architects of colonization, and the missionaries — as well as the Souriquois (Mi'kmaq).

*Les Muses de la Nouvelle-France* singles out memorable events, such as the arrival at Port-Royal or the ship's return to France with Pont Gravé and a new crew. The first piece is entitled *Adieu aux François retournans de la Nouvelle-France en la France gaulloise*, dated 25 August 1606. *Les Muses* is comprised of a series of eulogies and sketches, which were written to accompany the various feast days and banquets, including humorous and at the same time grandiloquent odes and sonnets. The collection ends chronologically with the *Adieu à la Nouvelle-France*, dated 30 July 1607. More importantly, *Les Muses* includes two major works of colonial literature. The first one is "Le théâtre de Neptune," the first play ever performed in French in North America. The other one is an epic poem entitled "La deffaite des Sauvages Armouchiquois." In almost five hundred alexandrine lines, it recounts the treachery of the Abenaki people, who — believing that the French no longer supported the Souriquois (Mi'kmaq) — had murdered the young Panoniac in order to steal the goods he had come to trade. Seeking revenge, the Sagamos (Grand Chief) Membertou had reunited the forces of the allied nations and obtained support from the French in trade goods and in arms; under the pretext of coming also to trade, he and his people avenged Panoniac's honor. The story is very well told, full of ruses and reversals, and displays a fine rhetoric, style, syntax, and versification (akin to what would become the Baroque style in poetry half a century later). But the work's most notable quality is its literary "disinterestedness": Here is a composition written for the sheer pleasure of writing, endowed with the primary quality of all true literary works — pure aesthetic pleasure. It is also striking for its "North American" or "Native" content. Not only are all the main characters Native, but the narrator is also taking sides with some of them and vilifies others, never assuming the accustomed role of the aloof European. The poem abounds with minute observations of Native life, such as the importance of trade and the interplay of trading alliances, or the Native's customs of war:

> A cette charge ici quelques uns sont blessés
> Parmi les Souriquois; mais plus de terrassés
> Sont de l'autre côté: car de ceux-ci les fleches
> A pointes d'os, ne font de si mortelles breches
> Comme de ceux qui sont plus voisins des François
> Qui des pointes d'acier ont au bout de leurs bois. (Lescarbot, 210)

In short, Lescarbot had the sensitivity and open-mindedness to become North American in slightly more than a year. He also had real talent as a writer, producing the first North American literary work in the French language.

"Le théâtre de Neptune en la Nouvelle-France," on the other hand, is a perfect example of a work produced for a special occasion, and in that sense it is the most representative piece of *Les Muses de la Nouvelle-France*. Poutrincourt had left Lescarbot in charge of the colony, while he himself went off for the summer to explore the coastal routes taken by De Monts and Verrazzano. For Poutrincourt's return on 14 November 1606, Lescarbot had prepared a nautical spectacle in which Neptune welcomes the Sagamos or Grand Chief, who makes ready to create a new France under the aegis of the enterprising Sieur de Monts and King Henry IV. Poutrincourt's barque approached the fort of Port-Royal, suitably decorated for the occasion, and Neptune advanced towards him on a raft drawn by four tritons. There were then five speeches, followed by Poutrincourt's response (which has not been preserved). Next, four Indians offered gifts to the commander of the fort. The structure of this second part, despite its humorous touches, was inspired by the Natives' Grand Councils. Grandiloquence gives way to lyricism, but then slides into the burlesque, and the whole performance ends in a Rabelaisian spirit, with the entire company being invited to a Gallic feast. Critics have spilled so much ink debating the literary worth of *Les Muses de la Nouvelle-France* and its "Théâtre de Neptune" that some have forgotten the most important point: The entire colonial literature of New France was there from the start and would not be surpassed. As modestly talented as Lescarbot perhaps was, no other poet ever came from France and became North American, and so New France had to produce its own writers and poets. This is the true measure of the worth of the colonial literature of New France.

Like Lescarbot, Marin Dières de Diéreville (1653–1738) also spent a year in Acadia, though a century later. He authored a prolific body of poetry, and half of his account of his voyage to New France is written in verse. Unlike Lescarbot, however, not one of his poetical writings was North American or addressed to North American society in any way. His remarkable *Relation du voyage du Port Royal de l'Acadie* (1708), which appeared as a French text about America, shows by contrast the real originality and true value of Lescarbot's poetical works of 1609, which deservedly have earned a permanent place in French-Canadian colonial literature.

Between 1606 and 1607 the population of Port-Royal numbered only about fifty people (all male). In Acadia, such small societies continued to spring up over decades and even centuries. Champlain founded the Quebec City trading post in 1608, and it was here in the St. Lawrence River valley — first between Quebec City and Trois-Rivières and then as far as Montreal — that French society in North America, that is, New France, grew up. In 1627 the trading monopolies were replaced by a state company, the Compagnie des Cent Associés or the Compagnie de la Nouvelle-France. But the company's fleet was shipwrecked almost immediately — a stunning commercial setback. The French colony was even conquered for England in 1629 by the Kirke brothers. In 1632 the French had to start over again from scratch. Only then did the colony begin to grow with the "habitants" (colonists who owned their own land) on an economic basis, far from political authority. In 1645 the trading company Communauté des Habitants was established, and Trois-Rivières became the colony's metropolis. The next dramatic blow came with a powerful earthquake in 1663. Not long after, two large regiments of soldiers arrived and imposed the Peace of 1667 on the Indians, a prelude to many such enforcements. Most important of all, however, was the establishment of the Conseil souverain in 1663, the first genuine political authority, which made the colony a socioeconomic institution drawing its power directly from the Kingdom of France. The Conseil had to commit all its energy toward managing the formidable territorial expansion to the banks of the Mississippi and soon to the Gulf of Mexico. At the same time, the wars with the Indians transformed themselves into wars between colonies (these wars were the North American counterparts of the War of the League of Augsburg and the War of Spanish Succession). During the "thirty-years peace" from 1713 to 1744, a tiny population of less than 20,000 souls increased to more than 50,000. Obviously, compared to the English colonies on the Atlantic Seaboard (which by that time had well over a million inhabitants), the three French colonies — Acadia, Canada, and Louisiana — simply lacked weight.

Not surprisingly, among these 50,000 men, women, and children, there was not a single novelist; in fact, most people were illiterate. At the other end of the spectrum were a very small number of educated men: political leaders, officials, higher-ranking members of the clergy, and a few members of the liberal professions (surveyors, notaries, lawyers, and doctors). This elite consisted of devout Catholics, controlled by a theocratic power until 1663 at least and then ruled by a succession of bishops of Quebec and Jesuits. Under these circumstances, the time was not ripe for New France to develop a literature of its own. Education, when it existed at all, was confined to the most elementary levels, unless an especially bright pupil was destined for priesthood or one of the liberal professions. Private libraries (no public libraries existed) were so rare that there were probably not more than 25,000 books in the entire colony — most of them missals, books of hours, or other religious works. Nor was there a single printing house in the colony, where the printing trade was forbidden. Even the decrees of the political authorities and the bishops' own mandates were copied by hand and promulgated by being read aloud in public.

Theater in New France was a sort of periodic or random political event, as some governors of the colony undertook to stage one or two plays at their own expense. As early as 1640, both Governor Montmagny and the Jesuits were working to organize two theatricals in honor of the dauphin who would become Louis XIV. In 1646 Montmagny presented a performance in Quebec City, a dramatic work about which nothing is known, except that the Jesuit superior excused himself from attending out of respect for the church that he represented. Then came Governor Jean de Lauzon, who, for all his personal piety, brought with him the art of the French capital, with the result that two plays by Corneille were put on stage in Quebec City: *Le Cid*, on 16 April 1651, and *Héraclius*, on 4 December 1651. Finally, Governor Frontenac had Corneille's *Nicodème* and Racine's *Mithridate* performed in the winter of 1693–1694. The next winter, the governor undertook to have Molière's *Le Tartuffe* put on stage. Yet the bishop of Quebec and his preachers, whose sermons on decency and public morality figure among the great works of the colony, would not allow themselves to be ridiculed by this impious project. A few memorable ecclesiastical texts of the Canadian "Affaire Tartuffe" have survived, including the famous *Mandement sur les discours impies* (1651) and the *Mandement au sujet des comédies* (1651). Bishop Saint-Vallier won his case, though he had to pay the considerable sum of one hundred pistols to cover Frontenac's costs for withdrawing the play from production. In the end, "comedies, balls, dances, masquerades, and other dangerous spectacles" (Mandements, 1, 412) were prohibited and the actors excommunicated. In 1749 the intendant Bigot presided over grand balls at the risk of seeing his guests excommunicated.

Just as the church banned public theatricals, it was also to suspend the private theater performances held in the "collèges." These were formal welcome receptions, the first of which was Lescarbot's "Le théâtre de Neptune en la Nouvelle-France." In the same manner, though on a much more modest scale, the Jesuits wrote and prepared a formal welcome for Governor Louis d'Ailleboust on 20 August 1648 and for Jean de Lauzon on 18 October 1651. The Jesuits' reception for Governor Pierre de Voyer d'Argenson on 28 July 1658 is the most famous, simply because it is the only written text from an official protocol organized by the Jesuit teachers for the political authorities that has been preserved. The reception saw some protective spirits presiding at the presentations of the various groups: first the French, then the Hurons and Algonquins, followed at the end by all the other Native allies against the Iroquois, each of whose representatives presented their compliments in a welcoming speech. The last of these welcome receptions (of which any evidence has survived) took place on 25 January 1727 in honor of Bishop Saint-Vallier; both the text and its author's name, Père de La Chasse, have been preserved in the archives of the archdiocese. Hence, although theatricals existed, at the time of the military conquest there was no viable form of theater, no theatrical troupe, and no original theatrical work in New France.

As for poetry, the colony boasted, from its origins to its end, countless works in rhyme. The intendant Jean Talon, for example, exchanged a few private rhymes with the nursing sisters of the Hôtel-Dieu. Two other, more serious efforts aimed to portray the French colony from a poetic point of view. One of these poems, written by René-Louis Chartier de Lotbinière (1612–1680), is a somewhat burlesque jewel. The author had arrived in the colony at the age of ten and became a pupil of the Jesuits at the collège in Quebec. He took part in the Carignan regiment's expedition into the Iroquois territory in January 1666 and later became a highly esteemed official in the colony. On his return from the expedition, Lotbinière wrote the fine satirical poem "Sur le Voyage de monsieur de Courcelles gouverneur et lieutenant général pour le roy en la Nouvelle-France en l'année 1666, vers burlesques":

> La victoire auroit bien parlé
> De la démarche et défilé
> Que vous avez faict grand Courcelles
> Sur des chevaux faicts de fisselles.
> Mais en voyant vostre harnois
> Et vostre pain plus secq que noix
> Elle n'auroit peu nous descrire
> Sans nous faire pasmer de rire. (Lotbinière, 53)

After some five hundred octosyllabic lines, the poem concludes with ten alexandrines. The last lines read:

> En sérieux je diray que . . .
> La victoire vous doict ce qu'elle a de plus rare
> Puisque vos actions en domptant ce Barbare
> Ont eu pour fondement au sortir de ce lieu
> Le service du prince et la gloire de Dieu. (Lotbinière, 62–63)

In other words, in the dignified alexandrines, the governor had good intentions, but in the plain-speaking octosyllables, he mistook his enemy, never meeting the "barbarian" Iroquois in battle, but facing instead the barbarous winter conditions in Canada.

Just as the literature of France would rewrite the art of Greece and Rome, French-Canadian colonial literature had to rework everything in its turn. Writers thus did not need to start from scratch when they could take, for instance, Nicolas Boileau's *L'art poétique* (1674) as their model. Boileau governed the Republic of Letters in France and New France alike. He inspired the second great poem — next to Lotbinière's — of New France, which is highly remarkable both in terms of its literary quality and its social criticism: *Les Troubles de l'Église du Canada en 1728* (1733) by the young seminarian Étienne Marchand (1707–1774). An epic in five hundred alexandrine lines, it was a more successful example of classical style than Lotbinière's five hundred octosyllables. What is more, Marchand resisted the urge of the burlesque, creating a mock epic instead, which gave a tragic treatment to one of the most bizarre episodes in the history of New France. The story begins at the time of the death of Saint-Vallier and the question of his succession:

> Je chante les excès de ce zèle profane
> Qui dans les coeurs dévots enfanta la chicane
> Et qui dans une Église exerçant sa fureur
> A semé depuis peu le désordre et l'erreur.
> Sous ce masque un chanoine abusant d'un vain titre
> Fier de sa dignité, méprisant le chapitre,
> Pour soutenir les droits de l'archidiaconat
> Enterre de son chef un illustre prélat.
> C'est en vain qu'à l'envi partout on se prépare
> A lui rendre un honneur dont il fut trop avare.
> Lotbinière assisté d'un juge et d'un bourreau
> Le fait par des laquais traîner dans le tombeau.
> Muse, raconte-moi quelle jalouse envie
> De ces hommes de Dieu peut corrompre la vie
> Et comment en public, préchant l'humilité,
> Ils conservent dans l'âme autant de vanité. (Marchand, 132)

Readers will recognize the craftsmanship of Boileau's celebrated poem *Le Lutrin*, written in 1673, from which Marchand borrows the heroic-comic poetic form, a few rhymes, some turns of phrase, and a great deal of vocabulary. Marchand intented to rewrite *Le Lutrin*, a poem on the quarrel of 1667 between the precentor and the treasurer of the Sainte-Chapelle in Paris. However, he also aimed at an additional subject. Marchand's source, hence, is not the main issue, for his poem is not an imitation but a parody twice removed: While Boileau was parodying the great tragic poets (Racine in particular), Marchand pastiches Boileau on a subject of much greater satiric power, namely the question who was to manage the bishopric of Quebec until the appointment of a new bishop? The Quebec chapter promptly elected Boulard, a Quebec parish priest, as vicar-general of the diocese, with the support of the Governor Charles de Beauharnois; yet the Conseil Supérieur, controlled by the intendant Dupuis, appointed the archdeacon Chartier de Lotbinière to the position. Lotbinière lost no time asserting his authority in a truly spectacular, if underhanded, manner: He had the dead bishop's remains buried at night, in the greatest secrecy, before the grandiose funeral that was due to take place the next day. On 3 January 1728 a riot broke out in Quebec City. Marchand satirized the sordid political affair by presenting it as a small, insignificant incident, like that of the lectern in Boileau's poem. From an aesthetic point of view, Marchand's 482-line poem in two cantos is highly successful. The first pair of rhymes, "profane"/"chicane," suggests the everyday, the specialized, and the etymological meaning of both words. "Profane" comes from "profanation," which opposes the holy and sacred zeal expected of the representatives of church and state. "Chicane," at the time the poem was written, already had its weakened modern sense of a dispute or quarrel, but the word also denotes its precise legal sense, the abuse of judicial procedure. The poem's social, satiric, and moral scope is substantial, all the more so since the characters are indicated by their real names. Most of all, however, its aesthetic character is swept along by the mastery of the narration, for example, at the end of the first canto, when the narrator implores his muse to hold her tongue and not tell the crime that is central to the episode.

Marchand's poem marks the summit of the poetry and the colonial literature of New France, but it stands entirely isolated. It was composed in 1733, right in the middle of the "thirty-years peace" — a period that bears its name well in a colony always at war and which would soon resume combat in the War of Austrian Succession (King George's War) and the War of Conquest. By then, the embryonic colonial literature of the time would never see the light of day. For although a few notable pieces emerged in the period between the two major epics — Lescarbot's on the victory of the Souriquois in 1607 and Marchand's on the burial of Saint-Vallier in 1733 — the colonial literature of New France lacked further aesthetic achievements. There were private writings without literary pretensions, such as soldiers' journals and private correspondence. While these texts certainly count as colonial writings, they were never more than what their authors tried to make of them, in other words, documents: from the journal of Pierre de Troyes in 1686 or Louis-Henry de Baugny in 1687, to the journals at the time of the Conquest, including those of Montcalm or Lévis from 1756 to 1759, or the diaries about the siege of Quebec City by the nursing sister Legardeur de Repentigny and two anonymous soldiers.

From the considerable archive of private correspondence, three documents of general interest stand out. First, the letters of Marie-Andrée

Regnard Duplessis de Sainte-Hélène (who also wrote the annals of the Hôtel-Dieu) to Madame Hecquet de La Cloche at Abbeville in France (1720–1758); secondly, the letters by Sister Marie-Madelaine Hachard, a nun in New Orleans, to her father, published in Rouen in 1728; and above all, the nine volumes that Élisabeth Bégon wrote from Montreal to her son-in-law in Louisiana (1748–1753).

Born in Montreal, Élisabeth Bégon (1696–1755), the widow of Claude-Michel Bégon, crisscrossed New France with her husband, living in turns in the colony's three major towns, Montreal, Trois-Rivières, and Quebec City. She wrote to her son-in-law, Michel de Villebois, himself a widower, who had recently departed from the colony, leaving his daughter in her care. Élisabeth Bégon was a woman of experience, observing the details of colonial life, its everyday aspects as well as its political life, with a critical eye. It seems clear that she idolized her son-in-law Michel, to whom she writes with increasing intimacy and tenderness. In 1749 she left New France for La Rochelle, where she refashioned herself as a Native Canadian, an Iroquois woman. In her letters to her son-in-law in Louisiana she begins to quarrel with him. Their correspondence ends tragically, as the lonely, exiled woman learns of her correspondent's death in 1752, when her last letter is returned. The final paragraph of this letter bears witness to her sadness over their estrangement, when she mentions his health and asks for forgiveness, not knowing her correspondent would never read it:

> Adieu, mon très cher fils. Je vous demanderai toujours avec instance de ménager votre santé qui m'est infiniment chère, malgré tout le chagrin que vous m'avez donné. Aimez-moi et vos enfants autant que nous vous aimons, ce n'est pas peu dire, et ne grognez plus: il me semble qu'on peut se dire ce que l'on pense sans en venir aux duretés. Adieu, je t'embrasse mille et mille fois et serai, toute ma vie, ta tendre et trop bonne mère.
>
> (Bégon, 314)

Here, the colonial literature of New France symbolically comes to an end, if it can indeed be considered a literature. In a strict sense, the conclusion writes itself when the facts are set forth: Although there can be no doubt that there existed a culture which was the colony's own, distinct from the culture of France, this culture had no time to develop a literature of its own. Only a few major works can be numbered from a literary life that remained embryonic.

# III. The Literature of
# British Canada, 1763–1867

# 6: Historical Overview

*Dorothee Scholl (University of Kiel)*

POLITICALLY, BRITISH COLONIALISM IN CANADA began with the acquisition of Quebec (Treaty of Paris, 1763), yet the colonial coordinates had been set long before, in the Northwestern and Western territories as well as on the Atlantic coast. From the late eighteenth century onwards, the Hudson's Bay Company (founded in 1670) had developed a powerful influence in Canada's West. It had won a partially bloody and competitive battle with the North West Company in Montreal by the year 1821, when the latter was forced to merge with the Hudson's Bay Company. The Hudson's Bay Company exerted its near-monopoly over an area that extended from Hudson Bay to the Pacific coast until the company sold its territory in 1870 to the Dominion of Canada, which had been dismissed from its colonial status three years prior. As the fur trade had prevented the establishment of major agricultural settlements in the West, the Atlantic coast had become the first place for settlements. With the Peace of Utrecht (1713) the colony of Acadia, which had been predominantly inhabited by French settlers, was placed under British rule. In 1749, mainly for strategic reasons, the military Fort Halifax was founded in Nova Scotia (New Scotland), the English name for Acadia. The subsequent deportation of 7,000 Acadians in 1755 was an "ethnic cleansing" that later inspired authors including Henry Wadsworth Longfellow (1807–1882; *Evangeline*, 1847) and Antonine Maillet (1929–; *Pélagie-la-Charrette*, 1979).

Two major influences in Canada's colonial history were the survival of French culture and the birth of the United States. In 1758, during the French and Indian War between England and France, General Louis-Joseph de Montcalm's army successfully besieged the British troops in Fort Carillon on the shore of Lake Champlain and marked the occasion by raising the French-Canadian flag, which has ever since been called "le Carillon" (as opposed to the current flag of Quebec, the "Fleurdelisé") and which has become Quebec's national symbol. However, the French triumph was short-lived. Montcalm was beaten on 13 September 1759 in the battle on the Abraham plains on the doorstep of Quebec City. The war ended with the signature of the Traité de Paris in 1763, which determined that the French-Canadian territory was to be officially assigned to England. The American historian Francis Parkmann (1823–1893) noted the arrogance of the English position: "A happier calamity never befell a people than the conquest of Canada by British arms" (*The Old Regime in Canada*, 1874).

By contrast — especially after 1789 — the loss of Nouvelle-France left a deep wound in French Canada's collective consciousness, a wound that has erupted repeatedly and has not only been a major influence on the development of French-Canadian literature, but has perhaps even functioned as its very condition. The former colonizers became the colonized; the province of Quebec, until then referred to as "Nouvelle-France," fell under the rule of the Union Jack. After its political leaders had fled, the francophone society was weakened. Under the ensuing British rule the landed gentry, together with the Catholic clergy, lawyers, and doctors, formed the new elite. They decided to remain loyal subjects to the British crown, especially in the face of efforts by the American colonies to convince the francophones to side with them against England. After the Quebec Act (1774), the British government distanced itself from its original goal of assimilating the French Canadians. This laid the groundwork for the inner Canadian dualism, which is still virulent today. Not only did the province regain its old borders, but the restrictions put on the use of their French language, on the practice of the Catholic religion, and on the use of the French civil justice system were removed.

From 1783 onwards, North America has been dominated by two co-existent political philosophies: that of the United States, which considers itself a unique political experiment, and that of Canada, which represents a European window on the North American continent. British North America became a retreat for monarchistic-conservative thinking, underlined by the approximately 70,000 loyal fugitives from the United States (the so-called United Empire Loyalists), who maintained a strong political, sociological, and cultural influence in Canada. This act of emigration shifted the demographic weight towards the anglophone population. As a result, two new colonies were founded: New Brunswick, through the separation from New Scotland in 1784 and, at the instigation of the immigrants from the United States, Upper Canada (later called Ontario), through the separation from Quebec (then called Lower Canada) in the Constitutional Act of 1791. In contrast to the French "Canadiens," English Canada defined itself predominantly as non-American. English-Canadian national consciousness began more successfully to establish itself after the War of 1812 between the United States and Great Britain, in which Canadian militia, with the help of the British troops, gained a firm stronghold. Soon after, war heroes such as Laura Secord, who in 1813 made a difficult thirty-two-kilometer march to warn of an upcoming American attack, or General Isaac Brock and Shawnee chief Tecumseh, who had both died in their battle for the crown, appeared as part of the colonial inventory of folk culture. This war was the last military confrontation between Canada and the United States, both of whom, thanks to mutual border agreements (1818, 1846), like to point out that they have the longest undefended border on earth.

During colonial days, conjuring up the ghost of an American threat was a political tool often used by conservative elitists to play off the American myth of independence against the belief that the monarchy had been decreed by God. The so-called Révolte des Patriotes (1837–1838), which adopted republican slogans in Upper and Lower Canada, was by and large not a popular movement and was put down within two weeks. In his investigative report (1839) Lord Durham (1792–1840), sent from London, interpreted the rebellion not as a result of a desire for more democratic rights but as an ethnic war: "I expected to find a contest between a government and a people: I found two nations warring in the bosom of a single state. I found a struggle not of principles but of races." The merging of Upper and Lower Canada in the Act of Union in 1840 was aimed at anglicizing the French Canadians, whose belief in authority and tradition was supposed to be broken down. Yet the fact that English became the official language of the legislative branch as well as Durham's less-than-flattering description of French Canada only helped strengthen French-Canadian nationalism.

British North America had traditionally been a place of immigration. Starting in the 1820s, the end of the Napoleonic wars, the population growth in the British isles, the industrial revolution, and the great Irish famine in the 1840s together resulted in mass immigration into Canada, with the population swelling from 600,000 to 3.5 million people by the founding of the Dominion in 1867. By midcentury, the population of Upper Canada was larger than that of Lower Canada, as there had been no comparable immigration from France. In 1867, Canada gained independence from her colonial status via the (still effective) British North America Act, which established a British-style government in the Dominion. The main reason for the creation of this largely independent state was the fear that the United States might try to annex the still unsettled Canadian West — in fact, U.S. annexation efforts had dramatically increased during the American Civil War. Consequently, by 1870, the Dominion had increased its own efforts to encourage settlements in the prairies of the Canadian West, for example, through the Dominion Lands Act (1872) and the construction of the first transcontinental railway, the Canadian Pacific Railway (1881–1885).

# 7: English-Canadian Colonial Literature

*Gwendolyn Davies (University of New Brunswick)*

## Exploration Narratives and Settler Accounts from Central and Western Canada

IN HIS "CONCLUSION" TO THE *Literary History of Canada* (1965), Northrop Frye graphically imagines early travelers from Europe edging into Canada like tiny Jonahs "entering an inconceivably large whale," only to be swallowed by "an alien continent." The surrounding frontier, adds Frye, was vast and "unthinking," inevitably shaping the imaginations of those who encountered it. As such, the wilderness awaited mapping, a process that began along an east-west axis in the early days of Canada's social and economic development, but also included longitudinal pulls to the south. The body of Canadian literature that has emerged from this intersection of exploration, settlement, and development, notes Frye, not only "records what the Canadian imagination has reacted to" but also "tells us things about our environment that nothing else will tell us" (in Klinck 1965, 822–31).

As early as the seventeenth century, trader-explorers such as Henry Kelsey (ca. 1667–1724), working for the Hudson's Bay Company (HBC; founded 1670), began to develop scientific observations, daily logs, maps, and journals that would bring definition to Frye's "frontier" or "environment" even as they expanded the fur trade. As the first European to see the Canadian prairies and to witness an Indian buffalo hunt, Kelsey was unique in writing a preface in a poetic style to his 1693 journal, describing his journey down the Hayes River, his naming of places ("this neck of land I deerings point did call"), and his identification of flora and fauna ("Which hither part is very thick of wood / Affords small nutts with little cherryes very good"; *Canadian Poetry from the Beginnings*, 22–24). Company policy discouraged publication of explorers' records because of their perceived corporate sensitivity, so Kelsey's poetic prologue and prose journal were typical in not being published until much later (1929). Nonetheless, by the late eighteenth and early nineteenth centuries, a number of influential journals in this tradition had found their way into print, often reworked from the original by both the authors and their British sponsors or publishers.

Of these, *A Journey from Prince of Wales' Fort in Hudson's Bay to the Northern Ocean* (1795) by Samuel Hearne (1745–1792) has endured not only for its geographical and ethnographic detail but also for its often-anthologized description of the massacre of the Inuit by the Chipewyans at Bloody Fall near the mouth of the Coppermine River. Aged only twenty-six at the time of the expedition, Hearne remained haunted by the screams and agonies of a teenaged Esquimaux girl who, in her death throes, had wrapped herself around his legs as she twined "round their spears like an eel" (*Canadian Exploration Literature*, 125). Such graphic detail elevates Hearne's writing above the more matter-of-fact accounts of many early fur traders and explorers, revealing a distinctive narrative voice that is sensitive to cultural difference, the limited rights of eighteenth-century Native women, and his own vulnerability.

Far more expansive in its overview was Alexander MacKenzie's (1764–1820) *Voyages from Montreal through the Continent of North America to the Frozen and Pacific Oceans in 1789 and 1793* (1801). Traveling under the commercial aegis of the North West Company, formed in Montreal in 1783–1784 as a competitor to the HBC (before the two amalgamated in 1821), MacKenzie in 1789 discovered the MacKenzie River flowing from Great Slave Lake to the Arctic and in 1793 crossed the Rocky Mountains to become the first White man to reach the Pacific overland. MacKenzie lacked Hearne's sense of story, but his three-part narrative, informed by the intensity of his personality, provides readers with a sense of the significance of his geographical discoveries to the development of the fur trade. Although he and his men might cover only three miles a day, it would typically be a day in which they ascended a mountain, cut trees as they went, and pulled a heavy canoe behind them along with their supplies. The texture of Mackenzie's narrative is rich, whether he is describing the way in which a Native guide has mapped out directions for him on birch bark or his hesitant response to a dish of salmon roe, sorrel, and gooseberries. For all these reasons, and also because of the effective narrative editing by British writer William Combe, the *Voyages* were well received in Britain, the United States, Germany, and France, with a three-volume set being included in Napoleon's library on St. Helena (Klinck 1965, 28).

Accounts of other explorer-adventurers in the North and the West, including those of Alexander Henry (1739–1824), Peter Pond (1740–1807), Mathew Cocking (1743–1799), Simon Fraser (1776–1862), and Captain John Franklin (1786–1847), continued to be published throughout the nineteenth and twentieth centuries. Each — such as Franklin's *Narrative of a Journey to the Shores of the Polar Sea* (1823), in which eleven of twenty men died — relays its own tensions and sets of discoveries. However, the *Narrative of His Explorations in Western North America: 1784–1812* by surveyor and traveler David Thompson (1770–1857), published in 1916 and 1962 by the Champlain Society, survives as one of the richest in human and natural observation. With a penchant for character studies and vignettes, Thompson also brought a sense of irony to his text. Having worked first for the HBC and later for the North West Company after being educated at the Grey Coat School in Westminster (London), Thompson devoted twenty-seven years to mapping the West. By recording Aboriginal cultures, learning Native languages, and studying flora and fauna, he acquired the rich knowledge that imbues his narrative. Whether describing the securing of water while under siege, the importance of his scientific instruments for measuring the sun, moon, and stars, or the economic impact of the beaver on the well-being of an Indian community, Thompson's narrative voice is authoritative, descriptive, and humane. Unable to complete revisions to his journals before his death because of impending blindness, he nonetheless created an authoritative map of the West now lodged in the Archives of Ontario. He remains, in the view of many, the most significant land geographer, exploration writer, and scientific explorer of the early West in Canada (Warkentin 1993, 194).

The early explorers of the West and the North, including those searching for a Northwest Passage, helped to open up and map what Frye called the "alien continent." Nonetheless, the majority of them also represented the voice of corporate men who had journeyed and written in the service of mercantile expansion. Thus, in spite of the significant individuality that distinguishes the tone and content of each journal narrative, most of the trader-explorers initially wrote for the benefit of their employers and tended to be one-book authors (*History of the Book in Canada 2004*, 33–43). As such, they differed dramatically from literarily inclined emigrant settlers such as Susanna Moodie (1803–1885) and Catharine Parr Traill (1802–1899), two sisters who had left Great Britain with expectations that were surprised by their encounters with the wilderness.

Raised in the genteel environment of Reydon Hall near Southwold in Suffolk, Moodie and Traill immigrated to Upper Canada in the 1830s with their half-pay military husbands and eventually lived a mile apart on wilderness land in Douro Township near present-day Lakefield, Ontario. Whereas the challenge for the explorer-traders in the West had been to comprehensively explain geographical, ethnographic, and economic discoveries to their employers and readers, for the sisters the difficulty was to find within their genteel English experience the vocabulary that would capture their encounter with the wilderness and still preserve a sense of who they were. Thus Susanna Moodie, alighting on Grosse Isle in the St. Lawrence in her 1852 *Roughing It in The Bush*, sought "privets" and "filagree" among the vegetation; yet much of what she found she could only classify as "elegant unknowns" (Moodie 1852, 21). Similarly, her sister Catharine Parr Traill in Letter 10 of the autobiographical *The Backwoods of Canada* (1836) wrote home about the absence of ghosts, fairies, woodnymphs, druids, and hama-dryads in the forest around her, adding that

Canada was a "matter-of-fact" country. However, as the fictional letters that comprise *The Backwoods of Canada* progress, Traill is increasingly engaged by her new experiences. She discovers new words such as "stoup" (a North American verandah); in Letter 14 she is fascinated by the seasonal changes affecting various botanical species, and in Letter 18 she acknowledges that, although she and her husband have experienced many disappointments, she can foresee a future one hundred years hence when prosperity and comfort will replace the rude dwellings and wild forest that are now the lot of the emigrant.

Subsequent books by Traill, such as the children's novel *Canadian Crusoes* (1852), the practical-advice book *The Female Emigrant's Guide* (1854), and the botanical handbook *Studies in Plant Life in Canada* (1885), all translated her new world experience into a form of educational literature for others. This shows in particular in *The Female Emigrant's Guide*, which combines recipes, household hints, and comments on women's work with observations on female piety, affiliations with "home," and the new emigrant's proximity to nature. Traill missed her English home and, like her sister, reiterated for readers the sacrifices of emigration. However, she also unflinchingly upheld the importance of wifely loyalty and vigilant motherhood in starting anew in the bush, and looked for positive solutions.

In doing so, Catharine Parr Traill was never as self-dramatizing in her writing as her sister, who, adopting the stance of a beleaguered Victorian heroine and faithful wife struggling in the bush, employed caricature, story within story, mimicry, dialect, and pathos to make *Roughing It in the Bush: or, Life in Canada* (1852) a successful autobiographical book in both London and New York. Appealing to the popular interest in literary depictions of Yankee acuity and vernacular language (as did the contemporary Canadian writer Thomas Chandler Haliburton), Moodie revealed both her dependence on, and her repugnance for, Yankee characters among her backwoods neighbors. But as the skillful *animatrice* of her own emigrant drama, she also often deflected attention from herself by using the stories of others, such as the Englishman Tom Wilson, to illustrate the impact of the bush on the unprepared. And, in a sketch such as "Brian, the Still-Hunter," she effectively employed both her own voice and a tale within a tale to combine elements such as an eccentric woodsman, a lone dog called "Chance," a gory suicide attempt, and a night spent alone surrounded by wolves into an archetypal backwoods story designed to appeal to an audience seeking both pathos and sensation.

Moodie's memoir *Life in the Clearings* and her novel *Flora Lyndsey; or, Passages in an Eventful Life*, both published in London in 1853, built upon the themes of female emigration, but it was *Roughing It in the Bush* that unforgettably concluded with Moodie's claim that she would judge her sketches a success if they had deterred one other genteel family from immuring itself in the "prison-house" of the Canadian bush. Although Moodie's 1871 introduction to the first Canadian edition of *Roughing It in the Bush* tried to soften her 1852 conclusion by arguing a change of heart towards Canada, there remained enough ambiguity in Moodie's overall oeuvre to inspire Margaret Atwood's poetry sequence *The Journals of Susanna Moodie* (1971), in which she imaginatively recreated Moodie's sense of erasure by the wilderness as she looked into a mirror: "Hands grown stiff the fingers / brittle as twigs / eyes bewildered after / seven years, and almost / blind / buds, which can see / only the wind" (*Journals*, 25). Such a loss of human definition also informs Atwood's short story "Death by Landscape" in *Wilderness Tips* (1991) where iconographic Group of Seven paintings echo the same sense of uneasiness found in Moodie's settler sketches and reinforce Frye's polemical query in *The Literary History of Canada*, "Where is here?" (in Klinck 1965, 826).

## Manners and Mores: Early Literature and Culture in the Canadian East

In contrast to both the explorers' accounts of the West and the North and the early settler literature of central British North America were the narratives of navigators and traders from sixteenth-, seventeenth-, and eighteenth-century Europe who initially mapped and mythologized what is now the Atlantic coast of Canada (see ch. 2, Higgins). Accounts in Hakluyt's *Principal Navigations* (1598–1600) and *Purchas His Pilgrimes* (1625) focus primarily on the exploratory nature of the voyages and the perceived potential of the new-found land, although at least one ballad from 1584 survives, describing the stormy death of Sir Humphrey Gilbert and his gallants "fresh and green" while en route from "New-found-land" to England (Klinck 1965, 8–9). Set in the context of burgeoning seventeenth- and eighteenth-century British and American transatlantic trade, much early writing of what is now the Canadian East coast struck a note of both individual and mercantile opportunity, and mapped out in poetry, memoir, and ballad the perceived freedoms to which East-Coast colonists could aspire. Examples of early Atlantic provinces literature are Sir Richard Whitbourne's (1579–1628) prose *Discourse and Discovery of Newfoundland* (1620), where, in addition to climactic and living conditions, he fancifully describes a swiftly moving object swimming into St. John's harbor as a possible mermaid ("Marmaide or no"); Robert Hayman's (1575–1629) poetic *Quodlibets, Lately Come Over from New Britaniola, Old Newfoundland* (1628), where he celebrates the settlement of Harbour-Grace for being "Exempt from taxings, ill newes, lawing, feare" (*Canadian Poetry from the Beginnings*, 19–21); and Donncach Ruah MacConmara's (ca. 1716–1810)

1740s tavern poem, where he cleverly interweaves Irish Gaelic and English for dramatic political effect.

However, the founding of Halifax, Nova Scotia, in 1749 as a city planned from London inspired colonial immigration and literary initiatives, including the introduction of garrison theatricals, a printing press (1752), and a newspaper (*Halifax Gazette*, 1752). The anonymous "Nova Scotia: A New Ballad," published in *The Gentleman's Magazine* of London in 1750, invoked the familiar tune of "King John and the Abbot of Canterbury" to urge readers (as had Hayman's 1628 *Quodlibets*) to emigrate to a land where "No landlords are there the poor tenants to teaze, / No lawyers to bully, nor stewards to seize: / But each honest fellow's a landlord, and dares / To spend on himself the whole fruit of his cares" (*Canadian Poetry from the Beginnings*, 29). What is embedded in this simple tavern song is an appeal to the common man's desire for opportunity and human dignity, options reinforced by the publication of a "Plan of the Harbour of Chebucto and Town of Halifax" in the same magazine issue that shows a well-laid-out coastal city contiguous to the British navy, a benign forest, and an exotic, nonthreatening porcupine. Map and ballad thus become part of a process of defining a narrative voice in Atlantic Canadian literature very different from that of the eighteenth-century western explorers or the mid-nineteenth century settlers of Upper Canada such as Moodie and Traill.

Although the founding of Halifax in 1749, the defeat of the French in Quebec City in 1759, and the immigration of approximately 9,000 New England Planters (readers of the Bible and Bunyan) into what is now Nova Scotia and New Brunswick in 1760 provided a context for literary growth, it was the migration of up to 45,000 Loyalist exiles to British North America at the end of the American Revolution that stimulated the infrastructure on which pre-Confederation English-Canadian literature would grow. Representing all social strata, the Loyalists brought with them not only their experience of the social institutions they had left behind in the United States, but also the strong respect for literacy that was indispensable for the creation of a reading culture. To them can be credited the establishment of schools, universities, agricultural and reading societies, printing offices, booksellers, newspapers, and literary journals at a time when frontier conditions in British North America would not otherwise have seen such an expansion of a range of cultural institutions. Approximately 15,000 Loyalists settled in what was then Upper and Lower Canada, with the majority going to areas such as Newark (Niagara-on-the-Lake) and Kingston in Upper Canada, and to Quebec, Montreal, and the Gaspé peninsula in Lower Canada. However, the largest and most influential group in terms of cultural impact settled in what are now the Maritime provinces of Canada, including a significant number of graduates of American universities such as Harvard and Princeton and among them recognized poets such as Jonathan Odell, Jacob Bailey, Roger Viets, Joseph Stansbury, and Deborah How Cottnam. Although economics, geography, politics, and personal differences among the Loyalists prevented the establishment of a school of writing in the late eighteenth century in British North America, their cultural example nonetheless encouraged literary descendants such as Joseph Howe (1804–1873), Thomas Chandler Haliburton, Bliss Carman (1861–1929), and Charles G. D. Roberts (1860–1943) in the nineteenth century. In 1825 the poet Griselda Tonge (1803–1825) paid literary tribute to her Loyalist great-grandmother, the poet Deborah How Cottnam (1728–1806), in "To My Dear Grandmother on Her 80th Birthday," and both *The Acadian Magazine* in 1826 and *The British North American Magazine* in 1831 publicly acknowledged the Loyalist *Nova-Scotia Magazine* (1789–1792) as a standard and an exemplar. Periodicals such as *The Nova-Scotia Magazine* and *The Quebec Magazine/Le Magasin de Québec* (1792–1794; founded by a Scot, Samuel Neilson) were important in augmenting the role of newspapers in the late eighteenth century and in providing publishing venues for regional essayists, creative writers, and reviews of the latest books and periodicals from Great Britain.

Significantly, the Loyalists turned to poetry, travel accounts, play prologues, and personal reminiscences as a way of articulating their world vision, often circulating their writings by letter and through readings at private and semipublic events. Nonetheless, the increasing availability of printing establishments in communities stretching from Halifax to Quebec City to Newark (Niagara-on-the-Lake) in the late eighteenth century meant that in 1788 a writer such as the Reverend Roger Viets (1738–1811) of Digby, Nova Scotia, could publish in Halifax the first long poem in pamphlet form in Canada. His *Annapolis-Royal* was not only a topographical poem modeling the streets, buildings, and gardens around which the Loyalists could rebuild their community structure, but also a metaphorical poem embedding in lines of choral antiphony the spiritual center ("loud Hosannas") informing the displaced Loyalists' moral vision.

Even more significant than the note of domestic nation-building struck by such works was the tone of satire and irony introduced into Canadian literature by Loyalist poets, a number of whom (Bailey, Stansbury, Odell) had waspishly denounced the Sons of Liberty throughout the American Revolution. Once in exile in British North America, poet/clergyman/naturalist Jacob Bailey (1731–1808) turned from satirizing American republicanism to hudibrastically exposing New Light religion in Nova Scotia, an extension, in his view, of the chaos of the American Revolution. And Jonathan Odell (1737–1818), one of America's finest poets during the Revolution, eschewed the domestic verse and essay writing that had characterized his residence in Fredericton, New Brunswick, in the late 1700s to bitingly denounce the War of 1812 as a political extension of the American Revolution. Writers such as these set standards of satirical edginess in the post-Revolutionary period that were to endure and reverberate throughout nineteenth-century Maritime provinces literature. Developed around evolving settlements such as Windsor, Halifax, and Shelburne in Nova Scotia; Saint John, Fredericton, and St. Andrews in New Brunswick; and Charlottetown in Prince Edward Island, satirists bearing pseudonyms such as "A Little Bird," "Patty Pry," or "Censor" often turned to the columns of regional newspapers to expose the manners and morals of their time. Whether it was the delicious gossip of Halifax scandal in the satirical long poem "The Inquisition" (1805) by Sir Alexander Croke (1758–1842) or the moral irony of self-delusion in *The Mephibosheth Stepsure Letters* (1821–1823) by Thomas McCulloch (1776–1843), East-Coast Canadian literature in the pre-Confederation period was preoccupied with human fallibility and its consequences. "I was neither a great man nor a great man's son," Stepsure was to declare in Letter 10 of his newspaper satires in *The Acadian Recorder*: "I was lame Meph, whose highest ambition was to be a plain decent farmer" (*Mephibosheth Stepsure*, 106).

Yet by the time that he had signed "Gent." after his name in Letter 16, readers had already recognized the ironic discrepancy between illusion and reality. Moreover, sketches such as McCulloch's proved not only the efficiency of the newspaper as a means of disseminating literature to the masses, but also the effectiveness of the medium in focusing satire. McCulloch's success in exposing the follies and foibles of his neighbors in "our town" in anonymous, tightly written columns drew much response from regional readers, who, according to one correspondent, "looked with great anxiety for the arrival of the 'Recorder,' and on its receipt used to assemble in the shop of Mr. _____ to hear 'Stepsure' read, and pick out the characters, and comment on their foibles, quite sure that they and the writer were among ourselves. Great was often the anger expressed, and threats uttered against the author if they could discover him" (*Mephibosheth Stepsure*, xxxv).

McCulloch's satirical venue and style were not lost on his more famous literary contemporary, Thomas Chandler Haliburton (1796–1865), whose irreverent Yankee clock peddler, Sam Slick, first appeared in newspaper sketches in *The Nova Scotian* between 1835 and 1836 and then in book form as *The Clockmaker: Or the Sayings and Doings of Samuel Slick of Slickville* (1836). *The Clockmaker* was republished in Britain in 1837, reprinted and celebrated in the United States in 1837 as an illustration of "Yankee humor," translated into several languages including German, French, and Swedish, and even sold on the goldfields of Ballarat in Australia in the 1850s. "Sam Slick" became English-Canadian literature's first international success story. Although Haliburton's reworking of the Sam Slick figure in subsequent years became predictable, his original picaresque sketches reverberated with the vibrancy, rascality, and vivid aphorisms of his antihero. Sam's literary Yankee dialect and picturesque speech made expressions such as "raining cats and dogs," "as quick as a wink," "stick-in-the-mud," "it's no use to cry over spilt milk," and "upper crust" universally popular. And although Haliburton subliminally sympathized with the agriculture-based values that informed McCulloch's more subtle Stepsure sketches, he was nonetheless pragmatic enough to employ his entrepreneurial fast-talking Sam Slick as an agent of change, pushing Nova Scotia in particular, and British North America in general, into the industrial age. Although Sam may be a sentimentalist over memories of Slickville, Onion County, Connecticut, he invariably proves an insistent opportunist, an entrepreneur who sees not the sublimity of Niagara Falls but its potential for growth:

> "I guess it is a site," says I, "and it would be a grand spec to git up a joint stock company for factory purposes, for sich another place for mills ain't to be found atween the poles. Oh dear!" said I, "only think of the cardin' mills, fullin' mills, cotton mills, grain mills, sawmills, plaster mills, and gracious knows what sort o'mills might be put up there and never fail for water; any fall you like and any power you want, and yet them goneys the British let all run to waste. It's a dreadful pity, ain't it?" (Haliburton, *The Clockmaker Two* 1995, 377)

McCulloch's Mephibosheth Stepsure had warned against such speculative profits and the lure of fast money, valorizing a mixed farming economy and rural community values over the urbanization and mechanization of society. However, Haliburton's outrageous persona with his "go-ahead" message had more success in captivating the public's imagination than did McCulloch's self-righteous narrator. Sam Slick enjoyed popularity well into the twentieth century, in spite of the readers' increasing discomfort with Sam's blatant racism and sexism. Nonetheless, both writers highlight the importance of satire and irony in nineteenth-century Canadian literature, a thread that continued to emerge in subsequent years in novels such as James De Mille's *A Strange Manuscript Found in a Copper Cylinder* (written in the 1860s, published 1888), poems such as Archibald Lampman's "The City of the End of Things" (1894), and narrative sequences such as Stephen Leacock's *Sunshine Sketches of a Little Town* (1912) and *Arcadian Adventures with the Idle Rich* (1914).

However, by Stephen Leacock's (1869–1944) time, the nature of the satire had changed. Instead of the forward-looking correctives of McCulloch and Haliburton, premised as they were on an outcome of progressive change, there emerged in Leacock's writing a sense of loss in the face of urbanization and technological growth. Beneath the ironic humor and larger-than-life eccentrics of *Sunshine Sketches* lie dark insights into the irretrievable loss of an idealized rural past. As *Sunshine Sketches* draws to a close with "L'Envoi: The Train to Mariposa," its narrator bluntly destroys the illusion that the modern city dweller can recapture the small-town values of youth: "No, don't bother to look at the reflection of your face in the window-pane shadowed by the night outside. Nobody could tell you now after all these years. Your face has changed in these long years of money-getting in the city" (Leacock 1996, 145). McCulloch's "our town" of the 1820s and Leacock's Mariposa of 1912, Leacock's text implies, are separated by more than the passage of time.

# Fiction

While regionally written satirical sketches on manners and mores continued to engage readers well into the twentieth century, particularly in newspaper and journal format, a taste for the imported fiction of writers such as Sir Walter Scott, Washington Irving, John Galt, Catharine Maria Sedgwick, Charles Dickens, and Bulwer Lytton becomes apparent from the advertisements of booksellers and local stores. Writing from her forest home near Lake Washdemoak, Emily Beavan (1818–1897) in *Life in the Backwoods of New Brunswick* (1845) noted how eagerly settlers awaited the sound of the postman's horn as he passed through the fledgling community, delivering letters and papers. Without funds for book-buying, she explained, forest dwellers relied heavily on newspaper serializations of fiction to augment the settler's library of Bible, almanac, and sacred song book.

But not all popular novelists were from outside British North America. As early as the 1780s, the Loyalist Mather Byles's daughters of Halifax were delightedly writing to their aunts in Boston that they were reading the epistolary novel *The History of Emily Montague* (1769), written by Frances Brooke (1723–1789) after having spent several years in postconquest Quebec in the 1760s. Usually described as the first Canadian novel, *The History of Emily Montague* explores the courtship of three sets of lovers in Quebec in the years 1766 to 1767. Of the correspondents, Arabella Fermor and Ed Rivers are the most lively, and it is through them that Brooke advanced feminist arguments about women's marriage choices that resonated with contemporary readers. Employing the conventions of the sublime in describing sites such as Montmorency Falls, and making dramatic use of winter, the novel also achieves its effects by developing clever foil figures and by varying the length and tone of the letters written to England and within Quebec. It also popularized Quebec as an interesting historical subject and setting for fiction, thereby encouraging subsequent Canadian novelists such as Julia Beckwith Hart and Rosanna Leprohon to use postconquest Quebec as their settings.

However, Hart's (1796–1867) *St. Ursula's Convent, or The Nun of Canada* (1824), the first novel written in Canada by a native-born

Canadian, is very different in tone from Brooke's series of sophisticated social and moral observations. More in the tradition of a melodramatic romance for teenage readers, *St. Ursula's Convent* moves at a fast pace, creating an almost bewildering plot that includes imprisonments, an exchange of babies, an evil priest, and multiple marriages. Published by subscription throughout British North America, it never enjoyed the reputation of Rosanna Leprohon's (1829–1879) *Antoinette de Mirecourt or Secret Marrying and Secret Sorrowing* (1864), a postconquest Montreal romance of clandestine marriage that illuminated the cultural divide between the occupying British military and resident upper-middle-class French-Canadian families. Born in Montreal, educated in English, and married to a French-Canadian doctor, Leprohon brought to her novel a personal understanding of the complexities of anglophone and francophone cultures living side by side in Quebec. Thus *Antoinette de Mirecourt* is not only a historical novel about a young French Canadian's disastrous mismatch with a careless British military rake, but also a fictional parallel to wider political and social tensions. Translated into French, *Antoinette de Mirecourt* and other works by Leprohon enjoyed considerable popularity among French Canadians in Quebec as well as in English circles across Canada.

The audience's taste for historical fiction by writers such as Leprohon — and post-Confederation Canada's yearning for a sense of a Canadian past — led to an ongoing interest among nineteenth-century writers in setting their fiction in urban or rural Quebec. William Kirby's (1817–1906) *The Golden Dog* (1877) and Gilbert Parker's (1862–1932) *The Seats of the Mighty* (1896), novels that were enormously popular well into the twentieth century, were typical of the way in which stories of New France continued to fascinate readers long after the colonial period. Less prominent as a context in nineteenth-century Canadian historical novels was the clash of cultures that occurred when Europeans moved into traditional Aboriginal territory. However, at least two significant novels of the period between 1830 and 1850 used this confrontation as the backdrop to their historical plots. *Argimou: A Legend of the Micmac*, published in the Saint John periodical *The Amaranth* in 1842 and in book form in Halifax in 1847, was atypical of its time in urging that readers recognize the degree to which European settlements in traditional Aboriginal areas were destroying Aboriginal culture. Written by Douglas Smyth Huyghue (1816–1891) under the pseudonym "Eugene," the novel, set in Acadia in 1755, was not only a cry of conscience about what was happening to First Nations societies, but was also one of the first Canadian novels to describe the deportation of the Acadians.

Far more action-oriented than Huyghue's work was John Richardson's *Wacousta* (1832), which is set against the background of the 1763 Pontiac uprising extending from Lake Michigan to the southern Mississippi. Often described as Canada's first major gothic novel, it is a tale of personal betrayal, sexual titillation, and Aboriginal identity appropriation. Its author, Major John Richardson (1796–1852), lived a life as dramatic as anything he wrote. Of both Loyalist and First Nations ancestry, he fought as a volunteer in the War of 1812, was a teenage prisoner of war in Kentucky, served in the West Indies and Spain, lived precariously in London and Paris for twenty years, and returned to Upper Canada following the Rebellions of 1837–1838 in Upper and Lower Canada. Although his writing included poetry, journalism, and fiction, *Wacousta* remains his most remarkable literary work. Bringing all the principal characters together at the sieges of Fort Detroit and Fort Michilimackinac, Richardson draws on sentimental, sensational, and gothic novel conventions to develop a tale of disguise, coincidence, psychological fear (represented by the unknown in the forest), threatening sexuality, and the grotesque. Although Richardson in his 1851 preface to the modified New York reprint of *Wacousta* reminds readers of his indebtedness to American frontier-fiction writer James Fenimore Cooper, his own novel — replete with the image of a hound on a bridge at midnight lapping up spilt human brains and blood — always resonates first and foremost with gothic and sensationalist associations. Moreover, while obviously sympathetic to Aboriginal history (as evidenced in his 1828 epic poem *Tecumseh*), Richardson tends to sublimate his First Nations characters in *Wacousta* to the wider service of his tale of revenge.

# Poetry

Popular as fiction remained throughout the nineteenth century, poetry was by far the predominant literary genre to be written and read in pre-Confederation Canada. Valorized by the educated elite and religious conservatives alike, it was most frequently distributed in newspapers, periodicals, pamphlets, and in book form. As Carole Gerson has noted, the small English-speaking population of Lower Canada (Quebec) in the late eighteenth century (15,000 anglophones as compared to 140,000 francophones) meant that an English culture of letters was slow in developing there. However, as early as 1775–1776 the *Quebec Gazette/La Gazette de Québec* had launched a "Poet's Corner," and poets such as Thomas Cary, George Longmore, and Adam Kidd were typical in turning to local outlets in Quebec City and Montreal to distribute their work. In Upper Canada (Ontario), which had been divided from Quebec in 1791, printing establishments, newspapers, periodicals, and reading societies also evolved slowly, tending to emerge first in Loyalist-influenced communities such as Newark (Niagara-on-the-Lake) and Kingston, and in the provincial capital, York (Fleming, Gallichan, and Lamonde 2004, 393–96). When the Rebellions of 1837–1838 erupted in Upper Canada, they galvanized colonial emigrants such as Susanna Moodie to express in newspaper and periodical verse the depth of their political affiliation. "I must own that my British spirit was fairly aroused," Moodie notes, "and, as I could not aid in subduing the enemies of my beloved country with my arm, I did what little I could to serve the good cause with my pen" (Moodie, 278). While her husband was away fighting, Moodie boiled maple syrup, organized the repair of a sugar kettle, planted potatoes and corn, nurtured her children with dedicated purpose, and wrote verses and articles by the light of improvised rag candles. Rousing patriotic poems such as "An Address to the Freemen of Canada" and "The Oath of the Canadian Volunteers" represented her contribution to the defeat of Yankee republican principles ("'God and Victoria!' be your cry"), but the isolating side effects of the rebellions also sufficiently influenced Moodie to decide to leave the bush forever. On the distaff side of the rebellions, Anonymous's poem "The Fight at Montgomery's," published in William Lyon Mackenzie's New York-based *Mackenzie's Gazette* in August 1838, mourns the loss of freedom represented by the rebellions' failure and ends with the confirmation of exile, furtive hiding, and imprisonment for those who had supported the rebellions in Upper Canada.

Many of the poems published in British North America before and after the Rebellions of 1837–1838 — such as Thomas Cary's *Abram's Plains* (1789), Adam Hood Burwell's "Talbot Road" (1818), Oliver Goldsmith Jr.'s *The Rising Village* (1825), and Alexander McLachlan's *The Emigrant and Other Poems* (1861) — emphasized the importance of opening up the wilderness, developing individual farms, encouraging trade, and establishing roads, towns, churches, and schools as part of the process of building a new country. In Thomas Cary's (1751–1823) *Abram's Plains*, written in heroic couplets and drawing upon the conventions of topographical poetry, the narrator stands on the Quebec site of the 1759 Battle of the Plains of Abraham, surveying the perspective around him while at the same time seeing in his mind's eye the vast expanse of the St. Lawrence River system from the Great Lakes to the Atlantic (Bentley 1992, 40–42, 130–35, 173–76). As Cary travels over the "scenes of nature" identified as his focus in the preface, his mind's eye alights on significant landmarks such as Niagara Falls, a subject that he treats in the language of the sublime and one that was to become the focus of much English-Canadian landscape poetry in the nineteenth century. However, Cary's virtual journey also evokes memories of First Nations conflicts, of fur trade prosperity for Montreal, and of the 1759 battle that had taken place literally beneath his feet. General Wolfe's death during the battle becomes the symbolic structural center of the poem, with all things going back to it and all things radiating from it. In what is essentially a tribute to British rule in Lower Canada, as his mind's eye moves further down river and then back to his Quebec City location, Cary emphasizes the passing might of others

(Aboriginals, French, Americans), the enduring virtue of England, and the good fortune of French Canadians to now live under the imperial reign of King George. Just as Roger Viets's topographical poem *Annapolis-Royal* (1788) had celebrated English moral and social values as the foundation of an emerging Loyalist society in the aftermath of the American Revolution, so Cary's 1789 *Abram's Plains*, unified by the St. Lawrence River, sees a militarily and morally superior Britain as the unquestioned foundation of prosperity in central British North America.

Because of the sweep of history, the vastness of the land, and the arduous process of settlement that many eighteenth- and nineteenth-century Canadian poets were trying to capture, the long poem became a favored genre in nineteenth-century Canadian literature. One of the most widely read examples was *The Rising Village* by Oliver Goldsmith Jr. (1794–1861), published in London in 1825 and reissued in British North America in 1834. Inspired by his great-uncle's (Oliver Goldsmith Sr.) more famous Irish poem *The Deserted Village* (1770), Goldsmith Jr. divided *The Rising Village* into a three-part narrative structure: first, the physical, moral, and civil growth of the new community; next, the moral tale of Flora and Albert; and last, the promising prosperity of the newly settled rural area. In employing both the heroic couplet and the conventions of the picturesque to give form and manageability to the progressive sweep of his vision, Goldsmith, like Cary, nonetheless brought an unequivocal moral tone to his poem. While his description of the contents of the rural store and its capacity for mercantile success are vivid and engaging, his dismal picture of the quality of education in the emerging society holds little promise for cultural development.

Not all poets were preoccupied with the process of immigration and nation building, however, and pre-Confederation Canadian literature therefore reflects a variety of forms and subjects ranging from John Richardson's epic poem *Tecumseh* (1828), in honor of the great warrior chief beside whom he fought in the War of 1812, to Charles Sangster's descriptive voyage *The St. Lawrence and the Saguenay* (1856), intersecting divinity, love, nature, and artistic inspiration, to William Kirby's epic *The U.E.: A Tale of Upper Canada* (1859), an invention of history in the service of patriotism. While occasionally poets such as Adam Kidd (1802–1831) recognized in their poetry the destructive impact of Canadian "progress" on the culture of Aboriginal peoples (*The Huron Chief*, 1830), the works of nineteenth-century Aboriginal poets such as George Copway (Kah-ge-ga-gah-bowh; 1818–1869) and Pauline Johnson (Tekahionwake; 1861–1913) more prominently address issues of appropriation and loss ("O! tell me, ye 'Palefaces,' tell, / Where have my proud ancestors gone?"; Copway, *Canadian Poetry from the Beginnings*, 84–85). By straddling the divide between her Mohawk and non-Aboriginal heritage, Johnson became one of the most visible Canadian women poets of her generation. A consummate presenter of her work on stage, she would recite her "non-Aboriginal" poems in evening dress and then reemerge in buckskin to deliver moving poems of ancestral loss such as "The Corn Husker" (see ch. 9, Ware).

## Literary Dissemination

Although Pauline Johnson's first volume of poems, *The White Wampum*, was published in London in 1895, she was typical of many writers in the pre-Confederation period, especially women poets, in initially having published in ephemeral outlets such as newspapers and periodicals. As early as the 1750s, writers had submitted their works to British North American newspapers under pseudonyms. Archival documentation reveals that in the late eighteenth century, private correspondence, readings at social gatherings, and even school-writing exercises were ways in which local writers (especially female poets such as Deborah How Cottnam) disseminated their work. By the nineteenth century, however, publication in periodicals and newspapers had become a well-established practice. Moreover, the literary successes of writers such as Thomas McCulloch, Thomas Chandler Haliburton, Rosanna Leprohon, and Susanna Moodie, who followed successful periodical publications with books, set a positive model.

Writers such as Susanna Moodie and her sister Catharine Parr Traill, who at the time of their emigration had already established reputations in Great Britain, were fortunate in having family and publishing links in the old country to assist them in disseminating their work. However, even they found that restrictive British copyright laws and physical distance worked to their disadvantage. Thus Susanna Moodie was typical in seeking out literary periodicals such as Montreal's *Literary Garland* (1838–1851) or American newspapers such as the New York *Albion* as outlets for publication and sources of remuneration. Even as late as the 1890s, a Canadian writer such as Agnes Machar (1837–1927) of Kingston, Ontario, was lamenting the publication and readership limitations of Canada, noting, as she did in a letter to Douglas Sladen of Richmond-on-Thames in England, that it did not pay to publish books in Canada and that Canadian authors therefore had to try the United States or Britain.

Of the two, the United States was more accessible. The efficacy of what Machar was proposing had already been demonstrated by the success of midcentury novelists such as James De Mille and May Agnes Fleming, who had turned to New York publishers for distribution and financial recognition. Born in Saint John, New Brunswick (as was Fleming), De Mille (1833–1880) became an international favorite during the 1860s and 1870s while teaching History and Rhetoric at Dalhousie College in Halifax by day and writing for Harper Brothers of New York by night. Surviving correspondence indicates that De Mille would receive as much as

$2,000 from Harper's for a novel, with the firm first serializing the manuscript in *Harper's Magazine* and then publishing it in book form. De Mille died in 1880, the same year as his fellow Saint John novelist, May Agnes Fleming (1840–1880), who, having built a highly successful career publishing romances in Philadelphia, Boston, and New York periodicals throughout the 1860s, moved to New York in 1875. There she wrote exclusively for *The New York Weekly* and the *London Journal*, producing a book version with Carleton & Company once each serialization had run its course. Novels such as *Sybil Campbell: Or, The Queen of the Isle* (1863), *Guy Earlcourt's Wife* (1872), and *A Terrible Secret* (1874) brought her a vast readership, including translations in France. Her fifteen percent royalties with Carleton & Company made her one of the most financially successful writers of nineteenth-century Canada, and her publishers continued to publish under her name long after her death.

However, in writing for the American market, both Fleming and De Mille deliberately eschewed identifiable Canadian settings in order to appeal to a universal audience seeking romance, adventure, travel, and the exotic. Many Canadian writers faced this decision. Margaret Marshall Saunders (1861–1947), for instance, was the first Canadian writer to sell over a million copies of a novel. But she had to change the location of her award-winning bestseller *Beautiful Joe* (1894) from Nova Scotia to Maine in order to qualify for a prize from the American Humane Education Society and to have her novel published in Philadelphia. Thus, although by 1864 an emerging Canadian literary consciousness manifested itself in nationally produced publications such as Edward Hartley Dewart's anthology *Selections from Canadian Poets*, there remained a publishing-infrastructure that was disadvantageous to the emergence of a national literature. Confederation in 1867 became a symbolic as well as a functional turning point in that dilemma, gradually seeing, in the economics of centralization, the consolidation of publishing and editing in Montreal and Toronto. Nonetheless, Canadian writers of the post-Confederation period, like those of the colonial period, continued to find that population size, cumbersome copyright structures, and social conservatism all worked against keeping Canadian literary submissions at home. As in the colonial period, post-Confederation Canadian literature struggled to find a voice. That it was a conspicuously proud voice in its love of country was clear, but even among the much-touted post-Confederation poets, there was never any more unanimity for a "school" of writing than there had been among the Loyalist satirists of the colonial literary period. What did remain unchallenged was that, as Frye articulates in the "Conclusion" to *The Literary History of Canada*, Canadian literary and cultural history have always remained inextricably entwined.

# 8: French-Canadian Colonial Literature under the Union Jack

*Dorothee Scholl (University of Kiel)*

OVER THE COURSE OF THE EIGHTEENTH CENTURY the alienation between Canada and France continued to grow. In *Candide* (1759), Voltaire (1614–1778) ironically dubbed the French colony "quelques arpents de neige." On both sides of the Atlantic the French developed a sense of difference — geographically, culturally, linguistically, and psychosocially. The francophone Canadians began to consider themselves a "société distincte," particularly with regard to the anglophone population on the North American continent. After the French Revolution, this sense of difference matured into self-confidence. 1758 (French victory at Carillon), 1760 (surrender of Montreal), and 1763 (Traité de Paris) constituted important caesuras in French Canada's historical consciousness. The events connected with these dates would not cease to be reviewed and rewritten in French-Canadian literature, essays, and chansons, for example by François-Réal Angers ("Chant patriotique du Canada," 1838), Jacques Ferron (*Les grands soleils*, 1958), Félix Leclerc (*Un soir de février*, 1970), and Jean Bouthillette (*Le Canadien français et son double*, 1971).

## Journalism

The end of the eighteenth and the beginning of the nineteenth century saw the emergence of a decisively patriotic *littérature de combat*, which fought to defend the rights granted by the British parliament in the Constitutional Act of 1791. This "combat literature" — later to be strongly criticized by intellectuals like Michel Bibaud (1782–1857) — was published in newspapers and journals, initially most of them anglophone; however, there were also bilingual journals such as *The Quebec Gazette/La Gazette de Québec* (1764), a particularly valuable source on Canadian culture in the eighteenth century. Journals also provided a forum for the development and articulation of ideas for a new political formation and for utopian social designs. Inspired by Enlightenment thought, the founders of the *Gazette du commerce et littéraire de Montréal* (1778), Fleury Mesplet, Valentin Jautard, and Pierre du Calvet, used the freedom of the press to promote the utopia of a democratic and laicistic nation in which French and English Canadians would join the American striving for independence. The *Gazette* developed into a seminal voice for the mediation, dissemination, and discussion of the ideas of French Enlightenment.

Voltaire's influence on the press was omnipresent. The first French poem to appear in the *Gazette de Québec* was by Voltaire, an epistle in verse directed against the Catholic Church and ending with praise for Frederick II of Prussia. The French-Canadian clergy vehemently opposed the journals' "Voltairism"; not a few considered Voltaire the incarnation of the devil. Some journals printed heated disputes, but the freedom of the press was to be short-lived: With the ban on the *Gazette de Montréal* (1779) and the incarceration of its founders, the dream of an independent republic and of new social utopias was over, for the time being.

At the end of the eighteenth and during the first decades of the nineteenth century, literary production was initially confined to fragments in journals, which, particularly after 1830, thrived because of an improved infrastructure. Literature, often pointing toward a patriotic or nationalist background, was employed as a means to cope with the defeat by England and to construct a new "national" identity. Since the majority of the population could neither read nor write, at first only the educated upper class read the journals. Journalistic endeavors and the foundation of schools and libraries, however, advanced the literacy rate in the course of the nineteenth century. The gap between the people and its representatives decreased, although mistrust of political representatives was constantly rekindled. Authors who published their literary texts in journals were usually also active in politics or journalism. Journalism has even been described as the "cradle" (Michel Tétu) or the first "babble" (Gérard Tougas) of French-Canadian literature.

One of the first literary narrations, "Zelim," appeared under the pseudonym "Le Canadien curieux" in the *Gazette littéraire de Montréal* on 30 December 1778 and emulated the tradition of the "histoires orientales." This very short narration deals with the relationship between master and servant: A gardener working for a sultan finally realizes through divine inspiration that his subordinated position grants more advantages than the sultan's riches and power. The text triggered a long and fervent polemical debate in several journals. The anonymous author was accused of plagiarism; in the end, however, the text — like many others, including Jacques Ferron's (1921–1985) *Contes du pays incertain* (1962) — can be read as an allegory of the situation of the French Canadians. The short prose published in the journals often displayed a seemingly spontaneous style and dedicated itself to regional and sentimental topics; for instance, the stories by André-Romuald Cherrier (1821–1863) and his sister Odile (1818–?) or those by Joseph Doutre (1825–1886), whose narrations appear very modern. At times there were several versions of one and the same popular story. A case in point is a now-lost story — initially published in the English journal *The Truth Teller* in New York — of which the anonymous first French version from 1827 is attributed to Michel Bibaud. It evolves around the character of a converted Iroquois who refuses to return to her parents and dies a Christian martyr at the stake. The legend of the Iroquois inspired a whole range of stories, which, more or less influenced by James Fenimore Cooper's Leatherstocking novels, related the lives and mores of the indigenous population.

Authors who came to Canada because they served in the army also published in Canadian journals, for example, Joseph Mermet (1775–1820), who established contacts with francophone Canadians in Kingston. Mermet published various poems, among them epic as well as culinary pieces in the tradition of Rabelais's or Saint-Armant's "style gaulois." In short epigrammatic poems, the anti-Bonapartist Mermet shows his wit: "Ci-gît Napoléon premier / Dieu veuille qu'il soit le dernier." In "Tableau de la cataracte de Niagara" (1815) Mermet draws on the aesthetics of the sublime and expresses man's terror in the face of overpowering natural forces; in "Le Sicilien au Canada" he, like many before and after, moans about the Canadian winter. His heroic epos "La Victoire de Châteauguay," published in 1813 in *Le Spectateur canadien* (founded in 1813), celebrated the victory of Canada over the United States on 26 October 1813, after four hours of combat in which French Canada's loyalty toward the British Crown had allowed the English to recruit French Canadians to fight against the Americans. Apart from Mermet's famous poem, episodes from the War of 1812 (1812–1814) later also inspired historical novels (such as Joseph Doutre's *Les fiancés de 1812*, 1844) and narrations (such as Henri-Émile Chevalier's "La Batelière du Saint-Laurent," 1854).

## Literature between Cultural and National Identity Formation

Journalism played a seminal role in the constitution and propagation of a French-Canadian "national" identity. The same holds true for poems and prose texts published in journals and magazines, political speeches, sermons, and historiography. All these different text formats fostered the emergence of a literary field that aimed at the formation of a national identity by coming to terms with the past. 24 June 1834 — the day of John the Baptist — had been declared the official "national" holiday of French Canada (thus turning the "fête patronale" into a "fête nationale"); references to this particular holiday can be found in many literary texts even today. After the American War of Independence, the division into Upper and Lower Canada created new conflicts, and the national idea burgeoned

again: It was at this time that the ongoing topic of French Canada's disso-
ciation from English Canada fully emerged. Ideological pluralism, which
survived up to the middle of the nineteenth century, was gradually banned.
In the second half of the century, journals, too, began to reflect this
change in attitude towards the Enlightenment and the French Revolution:
Loyal to the Ancien Régime, French Canadians were shocked by the
Revolution and interpreted it as the result of French atheism and anarchy.

In the nineteenth century, about half a million francophones emigrated to the United States in search of a better life. At the same time,
thousands of new immigrants arrived from Ireland, Great Britain, and the
United States, immigrants who many French Canadians perceived as a
threat to their territory, language, and culture. Those intellectuals who did
not leave the country advocated a *littérature engagée* to counter emigration, to pave a common ground, and to preserve and propagate French
ways of life and traditions. To compensate for the lack of political independence, many texts promoted French Canada's cultural and religious
identity to the rank of national identity. From 1840, the authority of the
clergy had continued to grow, and it would largely influence journalism
and literature until the middle of the twentieth century. Catholicism also
created a sense of unity among different social classes, thus contributing
significantly to the constitution of a collective identity and the idea of
being a "nation différente." Yet a gap opened between folk and elite culture, with the latter unwilling to integrate the "Americanness" of the illiterate classes.

The precarious relation between English and French Canada developed more and more into an opposition on the grounds of wealth, education, ancestry, and moral values. Contemporaneous texts depicted this
opposition as a matter of racial difference. Furthermore, French-Canadian
society saw an inner division between those wanting to protect and preserve traditional values and those stressing the need to adjust to the
changed conditions and to enter a new era of capitalist "modernity."
Fighting the antifrancophone propaganda of the *Quebec Mercury* — which
on 27 October 1806 published the plea of a certain "Anglicanus" to
"unfrenchify" the province ("To *unfrenchify* it, as much as possible . . .
should be a primary object") — members of Parliament Bédard and
Blanchet founded *Le Canadien* in 1806, the first monolingual French-
Canadian journal and the voice of the eponymous party and the new elite.
From then on the antifrancophone *Mercury* and the nationalist *Canadien*
kept up a heated polemical debate. The following years saw the founding
of about thirty francophone journals, which provided the means to cultivate and preserve the French language, to appeal to a French-Canadian
identity, and to defy British assimilation politics. From this period stem the
first literary texts that strove to counter the cultural (and linguistic) mingling of French, American, English-Canadian, and British influences through

the revival of French Canada's old, "pure" traditions and customs. Journals such as *Le Courrier de Québec* devoted entire sections to the topic.

Étienne Parent (1802–1874), who had been in charge of the *Canadien* since 1831, used the journal to defend French institutions, the French language, the freedom of the press, and parliamentary democracy; he fought for the political rights of his compatriots and for the education of the working class. Parent's speeches at the Institut canadien de Montréal (which existed from 1844 until 1884) were fully in line with the institution's liberal outlook, and addressed various social, economic, pedagogical, political, and religious problems. Employing a religious rhetoric, Parent appealed to his compatriots' work ethos — usually spurned by the aristocratic mentality of a feudal society — and saw in the development of industrialization and modernization the only future for Quebec as a nation of free individuals. The members of the Institut canadien de Montréal (among them Jacques Viger, James Huston, Henri-Émile Chevalier, and Joseph Doutre) engaged with the existing institutions and tried to induce intellectual and social change. In 1858, the institute's library was denounced as heretical and anticlerical by the bishop of Montreal, Ignace Bourget.

At the beginning of the nineteenth century, nationalist-minded representatives of society joined the ranks of the so-called Patriots, who were active in the Parti canadien (since 1805) and the Parti patriote (since 1826), and who tried to push their aims in various journals. In 1834, the Patriotic Party published "92 Résolutions," which confronted the British government with radical accusations. The "Révolte des Patriotes" (1837–1838) under Louis-Joseph Papineau became a *lieu de mémoire* in French Canada's collective memory. Louis H. Fréchette (1839–1908) celebrated Papineau as a national hero in his eponymous historical drama from 1890.

After their defeat, the Patriots were deported to Australia. Their experience of exile became the subject of the famous song "Un Canadian errant" by Antoine Gérin-Lajoie (1824–1882), first published in the journal *Le Charivari canadien* under the title "Le Proscrit" in 1844, that is, in the same year the surviving patriots were pardoned and renaturalized. The song was later to be rewritten and varied by many other authors, and it stands as an important reference in French-Canadian literature to the present day.

> Un Canadien errant
> Banni de ses foyers,
> Parcourait en pleurant
> Des pays étrangers.

Following the reunion of Upper and Lower Canada in 1840, the francophones became a minority. Article 41 of the Act of Union (in effect until

1849) declared English to be the sole official language. Confederation (1867) made French Canadians even more of a minority: They now had to live among a protestant and British majority that dominated political life, and the officially bilingual state in fact became more and more anglophone.

## The Development of the Theater

The origins of French-Canadian theater remain disputed. Canadian author Antonine Maillet (1929–) named French poet and historiographer Marc Lescarbot (ca. 1576–1641) as its founder. To welcome the Sieur de Poutrincourt, who after a long absence returned to the colony on 14 November 1606, Lescarbot staged a "gaillardise" in the style of the nautical parades performed at Renaissance courts: "Le théâtre de Neptune en la Nouvelle-France" (see ch. 5, Laflèche). Since it ended with a call to get drunk, some critics vehemently refused to accept this "immoral" piece as the foundation of French-Canadian theater. They rejected Lescarbot also on the grounds of his not being a native and instead appointed Pierre Petitclair (1813–1860) the first genuine French-Canadian playwright. The latter's characters, however, were generally considered too imbecilic to offer ideal possibilities for identification: "Comment pourraient-ils nous toucher alors?" asked Jean-Claude Noël. After the cessation of all theater performances in the wake of the ban on Molière's *Tartuffe* (1694) by the bishop of Quebec, Saint-Vallier, the situation relaxed again under François Bigot (who would later become a character in novels and dramas himself). Salon pieces written for the amusement of the higher society were now put on stage, as we learn, for example, from the correspondence of Élisabeth Bégon (1696–1755). The so-called théâtre de société, which came into being in the 1730s, was performed at salons and also at military garrisons.

After the Défaite, French-Canadian theater of the secular sort was almost nonexistent. Apart from some vaudeville shows, theaters staged only French and English imports. Owing to difficult institutional conditions and severe censorship by the clergy, the situation for francophone theater remained a precarious one in the nineteenth century. A few ensembles vanished as quickly as they surfaced, and many pieces were either not performed at all or only in private or in schools, where they were controlled by the clergy. Like the novel, the theater was considered to be immoral. In addition, female parts had to be played by male actors (until 1880, when Sarah Bernhardt went on tour), because women were not allowed on stage. It needs to be acknowledged, though, that the same clergymen who condemned the uncontrolled and uncensored theater still promoted the study and performance of pieces from classicist French theater as an important aid in the school of life and as beneficial for their pupils' linguistic, intellectual, and cultural education. In monasteries and Jesuit schools, pupils studied and staged clerical dramas such as Pierre Brumoy's (1688–1742) *Jonathas et David ou Le triomphe de l'amitié* (1776), but their repertoire also included pieces by Corneille, Racine, Molière, Beaumarchais, and Hugo. Theaters outside of clerical institutions tried to reach society by holding up a mirror to it. Many pieces were actualized paraphrases of French dramas. While in France Romanticism had long since conquered the stage ("Bataille d'*Hernani*," 1830), French-Canadian theater and literature were still following the model of French classicism and only occasionally displayed affinities with Romanticism, for instance, in Hyacinthe Leblanc de Marconnay's (1794–1868) inventive comedy *Valentine, ou La Nina canadienne* (1836), which was set on the St. Lawrence River and featured a good-natured country yokel whose Quebec French met the romantic principle of "couleur locale."

Widely traveled and multitalented Louis-Joseph Quesnel (1746–1809) composed songs and musical pieces and published poems in the *Gazette de Montréal*. His vibrant comedy-operetta *Colas et Colinette ou Le Bailli dupé* (1808) emulated the style of Molière, Marivaux, and Beaumarchais. Young Colinette loves naive Colas, and Colas loves Colinette, but the old bailiff has his eye on her, too, and tries to enforce Colas's recruitment by the army to get rid of his rival. Eventually, the intriguer is unmasked, and Colas can marry Colinette. In his one-act comedy *Les Républicains français ou La soirée du cabaret* (1801–1802) Quesnel, who had been to Paris in 1789, tackled the French Revolution in a carnivalesque manner. The play is interspersed with absurd versions of patriotic and crude popular songs — 167 years before Michel Tremblay's (1942–) *Les belles-soeurs*. Quesnel employs grotesquerie and carnivalistic devices to warn his audience about the social and moral chaos ensuing from the Revolution. In his short one-act play *L'anglomanie ou Le dîner à l'anglaise* (1802) he condemns "English snobbery" and that of his compatriots, who let themselves be dazzled by rich English merchants and give up their traditional ways of life. In a clichéd yet amusing manner Quesnel shows the collision of two different nationalities. In the end, however, he calls for tolerance: "Un chacun vaut son prix; que l'Anglais soit Anglais. Et quant à nous, mon fils, soyons toujours Français."

Pierre Petitclair, too, drew his inspiration from contemporaneous ways of life. *Une partie de campagne* (published posthumously in 1865) deals with the problematic contrast between town and country. Protagonist William, having studied in town for a year, returns to his family and friends an arrogant man who imitates the manners of the British. *La donation* (1842) denounces the materialism of the rising bourgeoisie. The play is a culturally assimilated rewriting (pastiche) of Molière's *Tartuffe*, but in view of the "Affaire Tartuffe" (see ch. 5, Laflèche) Petitclair left out all religious dimensions. The French-Canadian Tartuffe (called Bellire) worms himself into the favor of Monsieur Delorval, a rich merchant in Quebec, in order to get a gift from him. Susette, Delorval's maid, finally unmasks the hypocrite. The farce *Griphon ou La vengeance d'un valet* (1837) draws on Shakespeare (*The Merry Wives of Windsor*) and Molière (*Les Fourberies de Scapin*). Petitclair's plays feature anglicisms and Canadianisms and partly attach differentiated linguistic styles to the individual characters. Of Petitclair's five plays, two have been lost: the drama *Le brigand* and the comedy of proverbs *Qui trop embrasse mal étreint.*

Antoine Gérin-Lajoie's *Le Jeune Latour*, a heroic drama in three acts and in alexandrine verse, is a tragedy in the tradition of Corneille. The play has no female parts at all. Applying the rules of his college, Gérin-Lajoie completely diverts from Corneille's thematic focus on love. The setting is Cap de Sable in Acadia, where young Roger Latour fights against the English. His father, loyal to England, tries to draw him on his side, but the hero remains faithful to France. With the retreat of the English the father becomes homeless. Since he cannot win over his son — as he had promised the English Queen — he cannot return to England but must endure the humiliating experience of having to ask his son for shelter. Whereas other authors saw the older generation as the advocates of French identity and accused the young francophones of current problems in society, it is here a father who lacks strength of character and power of resistance and who gets punished for it in the end. Gérin-Lajoie found the material for his historical tragedy in Michel Bibaud's *Histoire du Canada*. Bibaud presents an idealized portrait of the young Latour, a lone hero fighting the British and, in contrast to his father, immune to the lure of assimilation and collaboration.

## A French-Canadian Boileau: Michel Bibaud

Michel Bibaud was one of the leading literary figures of the nineteenth century. His poetry volume *Épîtres, satires, chansons, épigrammes et autres pièces en vers* (1830) was the first coherent collection of poems by a French-Canadian author. His historiographic oeuvre would not become as famous as that of François-Xavier Garneau (1809–1866) later on, but it became an important source of inspiration for many younger writers. Like Étienne Parent, Bibaud advocated a moderate position during the "Révolte des Patriotes" and he, too, was very active as a journalist. He founded the literary journal *L'Aurore* (1817–1819), was in charge of the *Spectateur canadien*, and brought into being several other journals: *L'Observateur* (1830), the *Magasin du Bas-Canada* (1832), *L'Encyclopédie canadienne* (1842–1843), as well as the monthly *La Bibliothèque canadienne* (1825–1830), where he published his *Histoire du Canada* in 1825 before it appeared in book form in 1837. In the first part (*Histoire du Canada sous la domination française*) Bibaud depicts the time prior to English conquest, including the more or less peaceful encounters with the indigenous population as well as with colonial America. Furthermore, he examines the political battles for independence. Bibaud appraises the political and clerical authorities according to subjective criteria and associates the "demise" of Nouvelle-France with the moral corruptness of the colonial rulers. A similar opinion can be found later in Joseph Marmette's (1844–1895) historical novel *L'intendant Bigot* (1862). The second and third part (*Histoire du Canada sous la domination anglaise*) — the latter published posthumously in 1878 — deal with Canada's history under English rule up until 1837 and praise the role of the French Canadians during the American invasion of 1775. Bibaud condemns the resolutions of the Patriots and their leader Papineau, whom he portrays as a madman, and diagnoses a moral and cultural decline resulting from misdirected separatist politics.

Bibaud's poetry followed the pattern and model of Nicolas Boileau (1636–1711), whose *L'art poétique* (1674) had been reissued by the Séminaire de Québec in 1829, at a time when the French Romanticists severely attacked Boileau and accused him of being too prosaic and lacking originality. Bibaud's poems were culturally assimilated rewritings of Boileau's poetic texts for a French-Canadian context, rewritings which would later provoke similar adverse reactions. Comparable to Boileau's influential poetics, which defined France's national identity on the maxims of reason, precision, lexical purity, and modesty, and hence strongly opposed Italianisms and provincialisms, Bibaud's satire "Contre la paresse" (1818) advocated a form of linguistic purism to cleanse Canadian French from "foreign" and "disruptive" elements like "tournures anglaises":

> La paresse nous fait mal parler notre langue
> Combien peu, débitant la plus courte harangue
> Savent garder et l'ordre, et le vrai sens des mots:
> Très souvent, au milieu d'une phrase française,
> Nous plaçons, sans façon, une tournure anglaise.
> Presentment, indictment, impeachment, foreman,
> Sheriff, writ, verdict, bill, roast-beef, warrant, watchman.

In the chronicles of his journal *L'Aurore* (1817–1819) Bibaud also practiced normative linguistic critique and education. In contrast to Quesnel, who sought to stimulate the intellect of his contemporaries through poetry, Bibaud believed the poet to be the leader and moral educator of his people, authorized to take — if necessary — vigorous action in the battle against "national" vices. With his satires on idleness, envy, meanness, and ignorance, Bibaud tried to mobilize the ethical attitudes of his readers. His classicism and his biting criticism, aimed at his contemporaries, were among the reasons why future literary historians would not acknowledge him as a poet or representative of French-Canadian literature.

# The Rapport Durham and Its Consequences

Sent from London to report on the revolt of the Patriots, Lord Durham (1792–1840) wrote in his report to Queen Victoria — published at full length in the London press in 1839 and in excerpts in *Le Canadien* — that the revolt was about the conflict between "two races," which could be solved if the "higher" race (the English) was allowed to rule the "lower" race (the French Canadians). Durham conceived of a civilizing mission by the English, namely to raise the generally inferior descendants of French ancestors to a nobler life, which he believed could only be achieved through radical assimilation politics: "They remain an old and stationary society, in a new and progressive world. . . . As to the national character which must be given to Lower Canada; it must be that of the British Empire." Durham's report became especially notorious for its statement that the French Canadians were a people without history or literature. Even shortly after its publication the Durham Report provoked outraged reactions, but at the same time had a catalyzing effect: Napoléon Aubin (1812–1890) announced a *Répertoire de la littérature canadienne ou Recueil choisi des divers écrits en vers ou en prose composés en Canada* and dedicated biting reports and satirical dialogues to Durham in his journal *Le Fantasque*. James Huston set out to compile an anthology of French-Canadian literature, and Garneau wrote a monumental history of Canada (as well as a poem "À Lord Durham"). The Durham Report triggered a recollection of French Canadian history and literature. It contributed to an unprecedented engagement with people's history, literature, and culture, and inspired contemporary authors to create a "national literature." Lord Durham's diagnosis does not cease to challenge French-Canadian authors even today: Jean-Claude Germain called the afterword to *A Canadian Play/Une plaie canadienne* (1979), which condemns Lord Durham, "Le Rapport du bonhomme."

However, Lord Durham was neither the only nor the first one to describe the cultural situation of French Canada as desolate. The first English-Canadian novel, Frances Brooke's (1724–1789) *The History of Emily Montague* (1769), for instance, argued that no genius could possibly spring from an icy climate, and certainly could not thrive in it. This climatic theory could also be found among French Canadians. At the beginning of the nineteenth century, Quesnel wrote a poem in verse to his friend and fellow poet Louis-Généreux Labadie (1765–1824; "Épître à M. Généreux Labadie," 1804), in which he complained about the lack of literary expertise in French Canada: "Pour nous, cher Labadie, dans ce pays ingrat / Où l'esprit est plus froid encore que le climat, / Nos talents sont perdus pour le siècle où nous sommes. . . ." Bibaud, whose *Histoire du Canada* charged Nouvelle-France with a "lack of events and history," made his compatriots' passivity and their craving for pleasure responsible for French Canada's want of great deeds, its lack of education, and its ignorance (only later would one see the cultural value of singing, making music, telling stories, and playing games — popular pastimes during long winter months). Many texts from this period formulate an awareness of belonging to a minority literature; the comparison with French literature particularly fostered an inferiority complex. The shortcomings of French-Canadian literature were constantly under discussion. Although this assessment needs to be revised and many texts still await a fresh reading, the fact remains that in both the authors' self-awareness and in their critics' opinion, French-Canadian literature occupied a comparatively low status. In 1867, the year of Confederation, Octave Crémazie (1827–1879) commented on the problem:

> Ce qui manque au Canada, c'est d'avoir une langue à lui. Si nous parlions iroquois ou huron, notre littérature vivrait. Malheureusement nous parlons et écrivons d'une assez piteuse façon, il est vrai, la langue de Bossuet et de Racine. Nous avons beau dire et beau faire, nous ne serons toujours, au point de vue littéraire, qu'une simple colonie.

Such self-degradations constitute obsessive motifs in French-Canadian literature, pervading historiographical as well as literary texts and chansons (for instance, Michèle Lalonde's [1937–] manifesto "Speak White" from 1970: "nous sommes un people inculte et bègue . . . nous sommes un people peu brillant . . . notre parlure n'est pas très propre"). Travelers to Canada gained a similar perspective: When French historian Alexis de Tocqueville came to Canada in 1831, he thought that time had stopped there. He expressed his surprise about the "backwardness" of the "Canadien français": in his view, a "mummified Frenchman from the last century." Other travelers, too, testified to this cultural time lag. Visiting Quebec in 1944, French surrealist André Breton ascribed the situation to the influence of the church and a lack of intercultural contacts. In every case the topic of cultural inferiority relies on argumentative strategies that judge cultural phenomena on the grounds of (historically variable) normative standards. French-Canadian literary criticism was still very much under the sway of French classicism at this time and judged French-Canadian literary production according to classicist aesthetic criteria — which accounts for the negative self-assessment of many French-Canadian authors in the eighteenth and nineteenth century. In addition, institutional matters concerning the production and reception of books (lack of publishing houses, censorship on religious grounds) played a role. Only with Romanticism did the negative picture change for the better.

# The Discovery of Romanticism as the Foundation for a New Literary Awareness and Self-Perception

Through individual travelers and the press Quebec slowly opened itself to Romantic ideas in the course of the nineteenth century and broke away from the spell of French classicism — much later than France itself. A new understanding between the former colony and the former motherland was found: In *Le Canadien* Étienne Parent published excerpts from Chateaubriand, Lamartine, and others, giving his compatriots an impression of French Romanticism. In addition, the religious dimension of French Romanticism, its critical stance towards Enlightenment philosophy, and Chateaubriand's visit to Canada all paved the way for a new rapprochement of the francophones on each side of the Atlantic. Leaving behind classicism's normative poetics, the transgressions of French Romanticism encouraged French-Canadian authors to do the same and to develop an awareness of the possibility of their own national literature.

The Romanticists' new perception of nature also inspired a fresh perspective on the unique beauty of the Canadian landscape. Visiting England and France in 1831, Garneau published his travel account *Voyage en Angleterre et en France dans les années 1831, 1832, et 1833* (1854–1855) as well as his poem "Le Canadien en France" in the *Journal de Québec*. Compared to the "picturesque" Canadian landscapes, France seemed monotonous to him. The discovery of Romanticism had triggered a change in mentality and a new self-confidence in French Canada. One glorified the culture of the farmers and défricheurs, and literary texts proudly celebrated the adventurous spirit of the pioneers and trappers ("coureurs de bois") — exotic figures to the French eye — as a distinctive characteristic of French-Canadian culture. With the Romanticists' affinity for the exotic also came the discovery of Native customs as a source of inspiration. Last but not least, the Romantic idea of originality prompted the recollection of one's origins and a more positive evaluation of the distinctive features of French-Canadian culture. With the help of poetry, people started to symbolically appropriate the land in a literary and emotional manner. Even the classicist Bibaud realized the potential of nature poetry to generate a genuine national literature and saw in the Canadian landscape a source of inspiration for future poets.

An author to mediate between French and French-Canadian Romanticism was the French socialist Henri-Émile Chevalier (1828–1879). An exile to Canada since 1848, he and others were not considered genuine French-Canadian authors by some literary critics. Most of his novels and stories first appeared as feuilletons in Canadian journals, later in book form in Paris. In his historical novella "La Batelière du Saint-Laurent" (first published in *La Patrie* in 1854 under the title "L'Héroïne de Châteauguay") Chevalier dealt with the War of 1812 and suggested that the English owed their power in North America to the French Canadians. Chevalier dwelled on the savageness and cruelty of the Natives, who massacre the heroine's parents. Like Balzac in his *Comédie humaine*, Chevalier's theory and practice of the novel drew on metaphors from the theater. He collected his stories and novels as "Drames de l'Amérique du Nord"; the individual episodes were called "Scènes de la vie canadienne." His novels and novellas abound with sudden turning points, incredible coincidences, and melodramatic adventures. The depiction of the Natives, the landscape, the exotic, and the picturesque take in much room. Chevalier caters to the expectations of a French audience and to the marketing of the exotic, thus frequently toying with clichés. In *Les derniers Iroquois* he deals with Papineau and the revolt of the Patriots of 1837–1838. The popular novel *L'île de Sable* (1854; also known as *Trente-neuf hommes pour une femme*) recalls an adventurous legend from the sixteenth century — passed on by, among others, Marguerite de Navarre — according to which a stern Roberval, on his mission to colonize the New World, marooned his relative Marguerite de La Rocque and her lover on an island.

The first genuine French-Canadian novel also situates itself on the boundary between history and legend, the author's description of his text as a historical novel being but a typical device to claim authenticity. Philippe Aubert de Gaspé the younger (1814–1841) was a journalist at *Le Canadien* and *Mercury* as well as at *L'Abeille* in New Orleans. With Aimé-Nicolas Aubin he founded the journal *Le Télégraphe* and wrote for Aubin's *Fantasque*. His novel *L'influence d'un livre* appeared in 1837, twenty-six years before his father's novel *Les anciens Canadiens* (see ch. 10, Kirsch). The text unites elements from crime and adventure novels, fantastic folk legends, and from the black romanticism of the *roman gothique*. Initially de Gaspé only published the third chapter in *Le Télégraphe*. Journalists attacked him vehemently, finding his text too modern: In their view, the author had better followed the example of Boileau, not Hugo. On the grounds of French normative poetics from classicism, the novel was dismissed for its lack of *vraisemblance*. Aubert de Gaspé responded to this critique with a preface that referred to the Romanticists' reform of the classical canon. Employing a rhetoric of modesty and *captatio benevolentiae*, he tries to legitimize a "new aesthetics":

> Le siècle des unités est passé; la France a proclamé Shakespeare le premier tragique de l'univers et commence à voir qu'il est ridicule de faire parler un valet dans le même style qu'un prince. . . . J'offre à mon pays le premier roman de moeurs canadien, et en le présentant à mes compatriotes je réclame leur indulgence à ce titre. Les moeurs pures de nos campagnes sont une vaste mine à exploiter. . . . Le Canada, pays vierge, encore dans son enfance, n'offre aucun de ces grands caractères marqués, qui ont

fourni un champ si vaste au génie des romanciers de la vieille Europe. Il a donc fallu me contenter de peindre des hommes tels qu'ils se rencontrent dans la vie usuelle.

The characters in the novel were far from ordinary, however. The intricate plot focuses on Charles Amand, who wants to make gold with the help of magical spells from a book. To achieve his goal he tries to get the hand of a hanged man ("la Main-de-Gloire"), but his cabbalistic magical methods show no result. Embedded in the core story are further reports with legend-like elements such as the story of Rodrigue Bras de Fer, who fears neither God nor the devil, and the story of Rose Latulipe, who dances with the devil. Similar gothic tales can be found in *Les anciens Canadiens* by the elder Aubert de Gaspé (1786–1871); the Abbé Henri-Raymond Casgrain (1831–1904) even argued that it was in fact the father who wrote the episode on Rose Latulipe.

The structure of *L'influence d'un livre* is picaresque. Next to the assessment of society from within, there is also the outsider's perspective, provided by a character named Saint-Céran, who may be considered the author's voice. Saint-Céran loves Amand's daughter and observes society, also its privileged members, with a highly critical eye. His critique of society — its superstition, ideological isolation, exclusion of the "Other," patriarchal ways, education of its daughters by their mothers, and its striving for material wealth — balances the idealized representations of French Canadians in later novels. The text also includes references to Enlightenment philosophy; the preface ends with a quotation from Voltaire. As in his father's novel, the individual chapters often begin with an introductory quotation, and the chapters themselves feature quotations from authors of world literature but also from folk songs.

The novel can be symbolically linked to its period. An enlightened mentality, embodied by Saint-Céran, struggles with a world of magic and superstition, which — as the author suggests in the last chapter — will survive as long as loneliness and isolation dominate people's lives. Aubert de Gaspé the younger thus indirectly criticizes the idealized and idyllic self-stylization in many of his contemporaries' works and later particularly in the *roman du terroir*. This critique was probably one of the reasons why *L'influence d'un livre* was not published in its entirety until 1953.

## Satirical and Patriotic Prose: Napoléon Aubin

A friend of Aubert de Gaspé, Aimé-Nicolas Aubin was a universal talent of immense productivity and originality. His admiration for Napoléon Bonaparte had inspired the epithet "Napoléon." Being of Swiss nationality, he is usually excluded from French-Canadian literary histories. Aubin came to Canada in 1835, where he started a very active cultural life. He ran a salon, wrote poetry, composed, and set poems to music (for example, the "Chant patriotique du Canada" by François-Réal Angers, 1838). He founded a theater group, kept a printing business, drew, engraved, wrote dialogues and narrations, and was busy as a scholar. Aubin taught chemistry at the École de Médecine de Québec and invented a lighting appliance, the "appareil à gaz Aubin." He also contributed to several journals, for example, *La Minerve* and *L'Ami du peuple*, and edited Garneau's *Histoire du Canada*. He described himself as an "observateur étranger," "flâneur," "fantasque," "Démocrite," "Héraclite," and "père Bonsens" (in 1865, he founded the journal *Les Veillées du Père Bonsens*).

In 1837, Aubin brought into being the satirical journal *Le Fantasque*, which (like *Le Charivari* in France) featured numerous caricatures and ironically if not sarcastically confronted the authorities following the motto: "Je n'obéis ni ne commande à personne, je vais où je veux, je fais ce qui me plaît, je vis comme je peux et je meurs quand il faut." In the tradition of Democritus, Aubin went by the principle "Rions de tout, c'est mon principe," particularly with regard to politics. He opposed his contemporaries' obsession with (national) identity by propagating a "negative" or "trickster identity," which envisions an unstable and fickle individual escaping every fixed opinion. His self-representation as a court jester certainly made him less vulnerable to censorship, but it was also an expression of his helplessness in view of the ideological conflicts of his time. His means were akin to those of the satirists at *Charivari* and of grotesqueries, namely deformations of names, comparisons with animals (one journalist Cauchon becomes a "cochon," governor Poulett Thomson a "poulet"), and stereotyping ("Jack Canuck" for English Canadians, "Jean-Baptiste" for French Canadians, "Uncle Sam" for Americans, "John Bull" for the English). Aubin's *Fantasque* may be understood as a counterprogram to "combat journalism" (see below), because its author either refrained from any specific position at all, or else claimed freedom of speech as well as the instability of positions in the context of the "fantasque." Nothing and nobody, least of all Lord Durham, escaped his humorous, ironical, and bitingly cynical derision. Aubin's cynicism, his creativity, and his literary qualities make the *Fantasque* a unique literary and historio-cultural document. In *Le Fantasque* and in *La Minerve* Aubin published various poems, songs, and romantic narrations. "La lucarne d'un vieux garcon" is about the voyeurism of an old bachelor, who observes bizarre incidents from his skylight window and has to realize that appearances are deceptive. In the melancholy love story "Une chanson — un songe — un baiser" two lovers embark on a canoe tour to the Northwest; when the girl drowns, the song "À la claire fontaine" becomes a tragic parable for the man. In 1839, *Le Fantasque* also published Aubin's utopia *Mon voyage à la lune*, a piece of social criticism in the style of Cyrano de

Bergerac. At a time when many French Canadians did not think well of their former motherland, Aubin adopted a cosmopolitan stance and appealed to the bonding ethos of "égalité, liberté, fraternité."

In the course of the nineteenth century more humorous and satirical papers turned up: *La Citadelle* (1858), *L'Observateur* (1858), and *La Scie* (1863). With their epigrammatic style and their potpourri of anecdotes, observations, stories, poems, and amusements they not only formed part of France's tradition of satirical papers in the nineteenth century but also of that of the French *Almanachs* of the eighteenth century.

## The Call for a National Literature

After the traumatic experience of the "Révolte des Patriotes" and the Durham Report, the French-Canadian intellectuals attempted to reconstruct a national identity from the past. From about the middle of the nineteenth century their new self-understanding — inspired by Romanticism — manifested itself in texts that praised nature and the rural community and glorified conservative values and national unity. The aim of these texts was to create a national literature and construct a socially, religiously, and linguistically homogeneous collective identity. An imagological analysis reveals that the stereotypical images of the "Other" in these texts were shaped by resentment and xenophobia. The French-Canadian character was depicted as virtuous, pure, and pious (in contrast to the materialistic, atheist, and libertine "Other"). The so-called *mythe du terroir* arose, that is, the mythologizing of the soil as the site of French-Canadian national identity. Patrice Lacombe's (1807–1863) *La terre paternelle* (1846) and Pierre-Joseph-Olivier Chauveau's (1820–1890) *Charles Guérin* (1853) were the first representative examples of this ideology, which lent itself particularly to the novel. The basic structure in the *roman du terroir* was usually a conflict between father and son; often, the biblical story of the prodigal son served as a semiotic code: A father wants to pass on his land to his son, but the latter leaves "la terre paternelle" to seek an adventurous life in the city, where he finds only misery and death; if he survives, he repents and returns to his father's soil and forgiveness. Lacombe's novel is considered the genre's prototype: The author polemically breaks with the adventurous fantasy and black romance of the *roman gothique*. He also critically relativizes the oral stories transmitted by adventurers and travelers, which had held a powerful sway over the audience's imagination. Lacombe's novel is set in a rustic environment and argues for conservative values, moral edification, and the heroism of French Canada's struggle for survival. Yet in some regards the text is different from later novels. Young Charles, son of a farmer, yearns to go North after meeting other travelers and discovers within himself the soul of a "coureur de bois." To bind his elder son to the land, the father signs it over to him, but the son cannot handle it. His materialism destroys any bond there is, so that in the end the land has been cheated, betrayed, and sold by everyone. All of a sudden the younger brother returns a rich man and becomes a hero, because he is able to buy back the land. The years in the wilderness have served as a kind of "initiation rite" (Lemire 1980) to brace his masculinity.

Encouraged by European Romanticism and its interest in oral narratives, French Canadians also discovered the culturally constitutive and formative role of orality and other nonliterary cultural forms: Old folk legends, stories, anecdotes, and songs were now systematically collected and written down, and in that way gained an enhanced status as well as access to the people's collective memory. After 1845, numerous literary and philosophical institutions were founded: L'Oeuvre des bons livres, the Société des Amis ou Cercle littéraire et philosophique, the Société canadienne d'Études littéraires et scientifiques, the Lycée canadien, the Club des anciens, and the Institut canadien de Montréal, which would become a center of liberal thought. James Huston (1820–1854), a member of the Institut canadien, with the help of his friends collected poems, theater pieces, and literary prose in journals from the eighteenth and nineteenth century in order to make his compatriots familiar with a "national" literature. The result was an anthology in four volumes entitled *Le répertoire national* (1848–1850). The first page featured the folk song "À la claire fontaine." Huston had announced in his program to have found "les meilleures productions des littérateurs canadiens." Excluded from the anthology, though, were politically and religiously engaged texts, which made up a very significant part of this literature; more harmless and often even banal productions dominated the collection instead. Huston's canonization thus fostered the commonly held opinion that the beginnings of French-Canadian literature were pretty meager and negligible. Huston drew on the Romantic myth of the Cultural Ages in describing his own culture as emerging from its childhood: "La littérature canadienne s'affranchit lentement . . . de toutes ses langues de l'enfance. Elle laisse la voie de l'imitation pour s'individualiser, se nationaliser."

A new attempt to create a national literature — in a different manner and with different criteria — was undertaken by a group of literary men who met in the bookstore of poet Octave Crémazie in Quebec and called themselves the Club des anciens. In many regards the group is comparable to the French Romanticist circle (Cénacle) and in fact was in touch with it through the French Romanticist Charles Nodier. The Club des anciens was founded in 1858, exactly one hundred years after the victory at Carillon. The group's name was programmatic: They aimed at bolstering up the self-esteem that had been wounded with the capitulation of 1760 and at rescuing the culture of "old times." More importantly, they sought to establish the preconditions for a new understanding of culture and literature.

They collected and published old stories and legends, thus preserving them in the people's collective memory. "J'ai campé sur les bords de nos lacs et de nos rivières," wrote Joseph-Charles Taché (1820–1894) in his preface to *Forestiers et voyageurs* (1863); "j'ai vécu avec les hommes de la côte et de la forêt, avec les sauvages; j'ai recueilli plusieurs de leurs récits, et je les écris pour tâcher de faire qu'on puisse les lire, quand on ne pourra plus les entendre raconter." The meetings at the Bibliothèque Crémazie generated the École patriotique de Québec (see ch. 10, Kirsch) and the literary journal *Soirées canadiennes* (1860), founded by Casgrain, which — like *Le Foyer canadien* (1863) — addressed an interested readership at home; from March 1862 *Soirées canadiennes* also published excerpts from *Les anciens Canadiens* by Aubert de Gaspé the elder.

After English- and French-Canadian historiographers had painted a predominantly negative picture of French-Canadian culture in the first half of the nineteenth century (see, for example, William Smith, Robert Christie, Jacques Labrie, Michel Bibaud, Jean-François Perrault, or Isodore Lebrun), the situation changed fundamentally with Garneau's *Histoire du Canada* (in three volumes 1845, 1846, and 1848). The book's national inspiration, which makes it a foremost reference point in the process of French-Canadian self-perception, was influenced by the author's travels in Europe, particularly his confrontation with the Romantic vision of the Polish and Irish struggle for liberation. His monumental historiographical work was an apology for French-Canadian culture and its traditions. Following French historians such as Augustin Thierry in their conception of history, Garneau finds his land's past and present shaped by the political oppression and socioeconomical marginalization of a militarily defeated people, which tries to survive by preserving its cultural heritage — particularly its Catholic denomination and French language. The individual family in the village community constitutes the core of this resistance. In this manner the old pioneers' legendary heroism of constant sacrifice can be connected to a present that builds on the loyalty to one's home and a new feeling of "national pride" instead of inferiority complexes. "Il y a quelque chose de touchant et de noble à la fois à défendre la nationalité de ses pères, cet héritage sacré," wrote Garneau in his preface.

Just as Chateaubriand's *Génie du christianisme* (1802) developed into the "bible of Romanticism," the *Histoire* — not least thanks to its literary rank — came to inspire numerous writers, so that Garneau was even hailed as the "père de la littérature québécoise" (Gilles Marcotte). Garneau also tried to overcome the inferiority complex of French Canada in regard to feudal France in the seventeenth century by making a virtue out of necessity:

L'on se tromperait fort gravement si l'on ne voyait dans le planteur qui abattit les forêts qui couvraient autrefois les rives du Saint-Laurent, qu'un simple bûcheron travaillant pour satisfaire un besoin momentané. Son oeuvre, si humble en apparence, devait avoir des résultats beaucoup plus vastes et beaucoup plus durables que les victoires les plus brillantes qui portaient alors si haut la renommée de Louis XIV.

Garneau's *Histoire* invested the simple and modest farmer with a new dignity. Where Quesnel, Bibaud, Crémazie, and others had lamented the French-Canadian passivity, lethargy, and mindlessness, Garneau saw genius, energy, and the necessary power of resistance to survive in a hostile environment. Drawing on typical race discourses of his time, Garneau declared the opposition to assimilation a heroic endeavor; he even suggested that the descendants of the Gaul were a chosen people, whose ethnic and ideological unity and struggle for survival constituted a victory in itself. This argumentation was intended to compensate for the defeat of 1760.

In a similar manner Crémazie's poetry transformed the idea of colonization by applying it to the cultivation of the land through the French-Canadian population. He introduced historiography's messianic ideology and the *mythe du terroir* of the novel into the genre of poetry. In 1858, he celebrated the centennial of Montcalm's victory with the solemn hymn "Le drapeau de Carillon." The passionate patriotism of this poem made Crémazie a likely candidate for being Quebec's first national poet. Another hundred years later, Charles Wugk Sabatier set Crémazie's text to music, further perpetuating its appeal to the people's collective memory of Carillon and their mourning for the loss of Nouvelle-France. Crémazie also contributed the introductory poem to Aubert de Gaspé the elder's novel *Les anciens Canadiens*, which is often falsely attributed to de Gaspé himself, and which evokes the situation before 1760. Like his friends from the Club des anciens, Crémazie wanted to preserve the Ancien Régime in his compatriots' collective memory and to protect French Canada's cultural heritage — also in view of postrevolutionary France. He published his poems in several journals (like *L'Ami de la Religion et de la Patrie*); they were collected only posthumously in *Oeuvres complètes* (1882). His texts contained dramatic appeals to the reader, for example, the famous "Colonisation," which first appeared in 1853 under the title "Premier jour de l'an 1853" in the *Journal de Québec*:

> Devant vous se déroule un monde magnifique
> Qui veut de vos efforts l'aide patriotique.
> Votre langue et vos lois, votre religion,
> L'avenir tout entier de la race française
> Voulant se conserver sur une terre anglaise,
> Tout est dans ce seul mot: COLONISATION.

Through his poems Crémazie tried to shake his compatriots out of their "lethargy" and "apathy" and inflame their resistance against English hegemony. He conjured up heroic ideals of their French ancestors ("Chant du vieux soldat canadien," 1855) and compared the wave of anglophone immigrants to a threatening flood. Those French Canadians who had emigrated to California in the hope of a better life, Crémazie asked to stay and resist the lure of gold. He called the emigrants "déserteurs" and argued for spirituality, morality, and higher ideals instead of materiality, and for love of one's native land instead of Wanderlust. Crémazie and others employed this utopian contrast between spirituality and materiality in the service of a messianic ideology and national typology that identified the French Canadians with spirituality, intellect, and a pure soul, and denounced the English Canadians as materialist and consumerist. A sense of mission developed, which would further grow after 1860. Crémazie — who was to die in exile himself — conveyed in his poems a kind of psychopathology of the exiled human being: His lack of roots caused emotional disturbance, his escape into the materialist mentality of the Other destroyed his soul. In contrast, Crémazie found those who did not emigrate to possess a pure, beautiful, and harmonic soul; the land was no longer associated with its adverse inhospitability but praised for its motherly hospitality as well as for its beauty:

> Salut, ô ma belle patrie!
> Salut, ô bords du Saint-Laurent!
> Terre que l'étranger envie,
> Et qu'il regrette en la quittant.

A similar tone to Crémazie's poems (some of them were later set to music) also distinguishes the famous chanson "O Canada! mon pays! mes amours!" by Sir Georges-Étienne Cartier (1814–1873), which appeared in *La Minerve* on 29 July 1835:

> . . . L'étranger voit avec un œil d'envie
> Du Saint-Laurent le majestueux cours;
> À son aspect, le Canadien s'écrie:
> O Canada! mon pays! mes amours!

Shortly before his flight in 1862, Crémazie published a poem that exceeds the frame of patriotic inspiration and promotes him to the rank of precursor to anticonformist poetry in the twentieth century: "La promenade des trois morts," a fragment of some one hundred verses. Though obviously influenced by French Romanticist Théophile Gautier and his theme of the macabre, the poem can be considered innovative insofar as it positions itself at the weak spot in the French-Canadian system of norms where the reverence for heroic deeds gets challenged by the belief in the triviality of earthly death: "La promenade" does not conjure up Quebec's "great" dead but deals with simple, rural people in the face of death, also a prominent topic in the oral tradition. Crémazie stages the *danse macabre* without referring to either a rewarding or punishing hereafter. This prompted some contemporary critics to accuse him of violating Christian morals and embracing Protestant ideals. Although Crémazie wrote to the Abbé Casgrain that he had already composed the second and third part in his mind, the text would ultimately remain uncompleted.

Adolphe-Basile Routhier's (1839–1920) "O Canada" — which Calixa Lavallée (1842–1891) set to music on the occasion of French Canada's national holiday on 24 June 1880 — reaches back to the emphatically patriotic tradition of the nineteenth century and constitutes its high point:

> O Canada! Terre de nos aïeux,
> Ton front est ceint de fleurons glorieux!
> Car ton bras sait porter l'épée,
> Il sait porter la croix!
> Ton histoire est une épopée
> Des plus brillants exploits,
> Et ta valeur, de foi trempée,
> Protègera nos foyers et nos droits.

In the twentieth century the hymn became the official national anthem for all Canadians, with the numerous English versions obviously modifying the text. Routhier's "Chant national" brings the diverse elements of French-Canadian nationalism to a synthesis: the myth of origin and the glorification of a great past, the reference to military and religious identity, and concomitantly the stylization of French Canada as victim and martyr, the intimate relation to nature (allusions to the St. Lawrence River), the reference to French ancestry and to national character, the concept of the national genius, the battle for rights and freedom, messianism, and the prophetic role of Saint John the Baptist as a symbol of French Canada's mission to bring the world spiritual renewal.

Apart from patriotically engaged hymns there were also simple folk songs about nature, love, and a life in solitude; for example, the famous anonymous "À la claire fontaine":

> À la claire fontaine
> M'en allant promener
> J'ai trouvé l'eau si belle
> Que je m'y suis baigné
> Il y a longtemps que je t'aime
> Jamais je ne t'oublierai.

"À la claire fontaine" became a prominent motif in French-Canadian literature. Some regarded the simple love song as the unofficial national anthem and related it to French Canada's fate: "Jamais je ne t'oublierai" was connected to the "national" motto "Je me souviens," thus divesting the song of its subjective love theme in favor of the nation's collective memory. Moreover, the song also prompted a debate about whether it was an authentic expression of French-Canadian identity or a cultural import from France.

More than 10,000 mostly anonymous songs have been preserved: ballads, dance songs, lullabies, love songs, wedding songs, laments, pastoral lyrics, shanties, songs by raftsmen and lumberjacks, isolated refrains one sang at work, spiritual songs, and more. These texts can partly be traced to medieval songs of courtly love and the tradition of troubadours and jugglers; they are partly original French-Canadian productions or rewritings of old French songs. Ernest Gagnon edited a collection of more than one hundred folk songs (*Chansons populaires du Canada*, 1865–1867), but it was only at the beginning of the twentieth century — when Marius Barbeau presented a new collection of thousands of songs — that one fully acknowledged songs to be among the most vital sources of the French-Canadian literary tradition.

Because of its ideological engagement, French-Canadian literature from the period between 1763 and 1867 was often not considered "literary" (in the sense of Roland Barthes and other representatives of the *nouvelle critique*). In recent times this assessment has been corrected; however, many texts still await a thorough analysis, and many that were forgotten or withheld need to be rediscovered. In the wake of secularization numerous texts by clergymen have since been banished from the collective memory as well.

# IV. From the Dominion to the Territorial Completion of the Nation, 1867–1918

# 9: English-Canadian Literature, 1867–1918: The Making of a Nation

*Tracy Ware (Queen's University)*

THE PERIOD FROM CONFEDERATION to the First World War saw the slow emergence of a strong national economy and a vibrant national literature. The nation started with four provinces under the British North America Act of 1 July 1867: Ontario, Quebec, New Brunswick, and Nova Scotia. They were followed by Manitoba in 1870 (after the previous year's Red River Insurrection), British Columbia in 1871, Prince Edward Island in 1873, and Alberta and Saskatchewan in 1905. The next year, the Latin phrase that became the national motto, "A mari usque ad mare" ("from sea to sea") was inscribed on the head of the mace of the Saskatchewan Legislative Assembly. It was the era of John A. Macdonald, prime minister from 1867 to 1873 and again from 1878 to 1891, and Wilfrid Laurier, prime minister from 1896 to 1911. While very different in character, both combined a deep respect for British political traditions with a pragmatic Canadian nationalism. As Donald Creighton writes in *Dominion of the North* (1944), Macdonald followed "three interrelated national policies of western settlement, transcontinental railways, and protective tariffs." The railway was completed in 1885, the same year in which Louis Riel was executed in Manitoba for his role in the Northwest Rebellion (1885) — clearly, nationality was never without its discontents, especially in Quebec, where sympathy for Riel led to a movement away from Macdonald's Conservative Party. The tariff was a response to an American one as well as an expression of Macdonald's own economic nationalism and the growing manufacturing interests of central Canada. Laurier attacked the tariff when the Liberals favored reciprocal trade with the United States in 1891, but as prime minister he adopted Macdonald's nationalism, and he had the good fortune to govern during the years of prosperity that accompanied the growth of the West and the increased immigration during the first decade of the twentieth century. It was, after all, Laurier who said in 1904 that "the nineteenth century was the century of the United States. I think that it is Canada that shall fill the twentieth century." Accordingly, he did not agree with those who hoped to see Canada play an increased role in the British Empire through Imperial Federation, such as Stephen Leacock, who claimed in 1907: "I that write these lines am an Imperialist because I will not be a Colonial." As Creighton argues, both Laurier and Macdonald regarded imperial federation and continental union as threats to Canadian nationality. Laurier decided to build a Canadian navy rather than contribute to the British one, but when he returned to the idea of reciprocal trade with the United States, he lost the 1911 election to Robert Borden, who preferred Canadianism over Continentalism. As Leader of the Opposition, Laurier spoke against the introduction of conscription in 1917, and while the valor of the Canadian troops in the First World War remains important in the national memory, the "conscription crisis" revealed the countervailing tendencies that persist in Quebec nationalism. As Jonathan Kertzer (1998) has argued, such events make it impossible to narrate Canadian history as the unfolding of a confident master narrative. Even the national anthem "O Canada," while based on a song composed by Calixa Lavallée in 1880, did not become official until an English version was adopted by Parliament in 1980.

One reason that Canadian writers faced fewer obstacles than Canadian politicians is that they always had the option of publishing abroad. One of the first to do so was James De Mille (1833–1880), a Professor of Classics at Acadia from 1861 to 1865 and at Dalhousie from 1865 until his death. Perhaps because of his debts from running a bookstore in Saint John, he wrote historical romances, mysteries, parodies, and a textbook, *Elements of Rhetoric* (1878). *The Dodge Club* (1869) is a parody of travel writing that mocks both American tourists in Italy and the Italians who try to exploit them. *The Lady of the Ice* (1870) shows De Mille's facility and his comic potential, as, for instance, in the farcical episode in which a duel ends without violence because the participants are deterred by the harsh Quebec climate. His most important novel, *A Strange Manuscript Found in a Copper Cylinder*, was published posthumously in New York in 1888. In an elaborately framed narrative, four travelers find a manuscript that purports to describe the Antarctic adventures of one Adam More, whose very name evokes the utopian tradition initiated by Thomas More's *Utopia* (1516). The manuscript tells of More's encounter with the Kosekin, who carry selflessness to the extent of preferring poverty over wealth and death over life. Bewildered at this inversion of his own values, More longs for "some one among this singular people who was selfish, who feared death, who loved life, who loved riches, and had something in common with me." The authenticity of the manuscript is debated by the four travelers, two of whom accept it as authoritative, and one regarding it as a satirical hoax. Whatever the individual reading of this ambiguous novel, it serves as a useful reminder that early Canadian authors were not necessarily concerned with early Canada.

Three writers who, in contrast to De Mille, took the national route demonstrate the difficulties that this involved. William Kirby (1817–1906) was a poet, editor, and historian whose most important work, *The Golden*

*Dog* (1877), can be considered the best of the many Canadian historical romances written from "the long shadow of Sir Walter Scott" (Gerson 1989). What made the novel so successful — in addition to a story of intrigue, love, and murder — was the research that Kirby devoted to New France; *The Golden Dog* was a success both in its original version and in Léon-Pamphile Lemay's French translation of 1884. Because his first publisher failed to register the Canadian copyright, however, Kirby earned nothing from either of these editions. According to George Parker (1985), his total earnings — for a novel that has never been out of print since — were about one hundred dollars from an 1897 edition that he misleadingly claimed to be authorized. The lack of international copyright agreements between Canada, Britain, and the United States remained a problem until the 1890s — too late for Kirby, who never wrote another novel. Isabella Valancy Crawford (1850–1887) faced even greater difficulties. A single woman trying to make a living by writing stories and poems for Canadian and American newspapers and journals in the 1870s and 1880s, Crawford published one collection at her own expense in 1884 (*Old Spookses' Pass, Malcolm's Katie, and Other Poems*), but she sold only fifty of the thousand copies printed. She wrote on both topical ("Canada to England") and traditional themes ("The Hidden Room"), and her extensive use of both classical and Native mythology in such poems as "Malcolm's Katie" and "The Dark Stag" led James Reaney to call her a mythopoeic poet. One of her most successful publications was *Winona; or, the Foster-Sisters*, a prize-winning novel when serialized in 1873. Crawford died before finishing her most ambitious work, posthumously published as *Hugh and Ion* in 1977. Confronting similar difficulties, Susan Frances Harrison (1859–1935) published some of her work at her own expense throughout her long career as a writer and professional musician. She published two novels, *The Forest of Bourg-Marie* (1898) and *Ringfield* (1914), several collections of poetry, notably *Pine, Rose and Fleur de lis* (1891), and an influential anthology, *The Canadian Birthday Book* (1887). Her short stories would probably have made a bigger impact if *Crowded Out! and Other Sketches* (1886) had not been privately published in Ottawa. Most of these stories reveal Harrison's fascination with Quebec. The title story, however, depicts the unhappy fate of a Canadian artist in London, and the last story, "The Gilded Hammock," is a fine satire of the wealthy in New York, anticipating Leacock's *Arcadian Adventures with the Idle Rich*: "Even a worm will turn, and public opinion is very often a little vermicular, let us say," says the narrator, as the heroine learns how to manipulate her own image with the help of her clergyman cousin.

A good summary of the Canadian writer's plight comes from Goldwin Smith (1823–1910). Smith had taught history at Oxford before leaving for Cornell University, where he taught from 1868 to 1871. He then moved to Toronto, where he established such periodicals as *The Bystander* (1880–1890) and *The Week* (1883–1896). At first sympathetic with the nationalists of the Canada First group (Colonel George Taylor Denison III, Henry Morgan, Charles Mair, William Foster, and Robert Grant Haliburton), Smith could not share their interest in Imperial Federation. He soon became convinced that Canada's future involved union with the United States, as he argued in *Canada and the Canadian Question* (1891). By 1894 he held that "without any disparagement of our native genius, we must answer that no such thing as a literature Canadian in the local sense exists or is likely ever to exist." The population of Canada was so much smaller than that of the United States, the diversity of the regions so great, and the lack of interest in Canadian writers so apparent that Smith saw only one solution: "The breasts of some of our Canadian birds of song throb with patriotism, but on opening an American magazine you will find them, at least as soon as they are feathered, warbling on a foreign bough." Mistaking blending for confusion, Smith could hardly have been more wrong, for by this time the Confederation Poets had achieved an international reputation for the unmistakeably Canadian works that they published in Canadian, American, and British journals and that largely avoided the simplistic nationalism favored by Canada First.

If these poets constitute a group it is mainly because of the leadership of Charles G. D. Roberts (1860–1943). His first volume, *Orion, and Other Poems* (1880), "connected the poetry of Canada with all that is excellent in English poetry the world over," according to Duncan Campbell Scott. Archibald Lampman went further, in his memorable tribute from one Canadian writer to another:

> Like most of the young fellows about me [at the University of Toronto] I had been under the depressing conviction that we were situated hope-lessly on the outskirts of civilization, where no art and literature could be, and that it was useless to expect that anything great could be done by any of our companions, still more useless to expect that we could do it our-selves. I sat up all night reading and re-reading *Orion* in a state of the wildest excitement and when I went to bed I could not sleep. It seemed to me a wonderful thing that such work could be done by a Canadian, by a young man, one of ourselves. It was like a voice from some new par-adise of art calling us to be up and doing.

A clear sign that these poets had escaped a colonial attitude shows in the criticism that Lampman feels free to make of his elder peer, especially of his patriotic and love poems. Against such shortcomings Roberts's achieve-ments remain: first, "The Tantramar Revisited," which sets its speaker's impossible desire for a place beyond the "Hands of chance and change" against the ever-changing tides of Roberts's beloved Tantramar; second, such classical poems as "Actaeon," which Lampman thought would "stand comparison favourably with Tennyson's 'OEnone' "; and third, the thirty-seven sonnets about rural life in New Brunswick that form the title sequence of *Songs of the Common Day* (1893). The key to these sonnets, which had sometimes appeared first in American journals, is not that they are uniquely Canadian, but that they are distinctively regional. "The Herring Weir," for instance, is a modified Petrarchan sonnet that features seven colors in succession in the octave, while the sestet describes the weir in the language of the common day:

> The herring weir emerges, quick with spoil.
> Slowly the tide forsakes it. Then draws near,
> Descending from the farm-house on the height,
> A cart, with gaping tubs. The oxen toil
> Sombrely o'er the level to the weir,
> And drag a long black trail across the light.

With this frame drawn in the mud, the poem finds a way to adapt the sonnet to a landscape of constant change. Most of Roberts's best poetry was written in the last two decades of the nineteenth century, when, as D. M. R. Bentley demonstrates in *The Confederation Group of Canadian Poets, 1880–1897* (2004), he worked tirelessly to advance the cause of Canadian literature. To survive as a writer, after he quit his job at King's College in 1895, Roberts had to subordinate poetry to prose: Between 1896 and 1904, he wrote a history of Canada, five historical romances, a romance set in the contemporary Tantramar (*The Heart That Knows*, 1900), and a fable about humanity's relation to nature (*The Heart of the Ancient Wood*, 1900). He compiled several collections of the animal stories that he, along with Ernest Thompson Seton (1860–1946), started writing in the 1890s, and these proved to be so popular and at the same time controversial that Roberts was even called to the White House to discuss the matter with President Theodore Roosevelt. Through the efforts of Roberts more than any other writer, Goldwin Smith's attack on Canadian literature became blunted. Because he was interested in both classical and indigenous mythology, wrote a sequence of *New York Nocturnes* (1898) as well as a sequence of New Brunswick sonnets, and translated the French of Quebec writers Phillippe-Joseph Aubert de Gaspé (1786–1871) and Louis Honoré Fréchette (1839–1908), Roberts is a fine example of the "blending" described by Sara Jeannette Duncan in *The Imperialist* (1904): "It was a sorry tale of disintegration with a cheerful sequel of rebuilding, leading to a little unavoidable confusion as the edifice went up. Any process of blending implies confusion to begin with; we are here at the making of a nation."

The first writer to profit from Roberts's influence was his cousin Bliss Carman (1861–1929). In his first collection, *Low Tide on Grand Pré: A Book of Lyrics* (1893), the title poem, which gives an erotic charge to the return poem, is probably his best:

Was it a year or lives ago
We took the grasses in our hands,
And caught the summer flying low
Over the waving meadow lands,
And held it there between our hands?

Carman lived most of his adult life in the United States, where he worked as an editor for such journals as *The Independent, The Chap-Book*, and *The Atlantic Monthly*. He achieved an international popularity, especially with the *Songs from Vagabondia* books (1894–1901) that he wrote with Richard Hovey (1864–1900). His other collections include *Behind the Arras: A Book of the Unseen* (1895), *Ballads of Lost Haven: A Book of the Sea* (1897), *By the Aurelian Wall and Other Elegies* (1898), and *Sappho: One Hundred Lyrics* (1903). Carman's career was marred increasingly by his prolixity and mystical pretensions, but his influence pervaded the poetry of England and North America at the end of the nineteenth and the beginning of the twentieth century, when Ezra Pound called him "about the only living American poet who would not improve by drowning."

Modern poets and critics often followed E. K. Brown in preferring the Ottawa poets, Lampman and Scott, to their more flamboyant peers. Archibald Lampman (1861–1899) published his first and most important volume, *Among the Millet*, in 1888, and he remained steadily productive until his early death. As a socialist ("The Land of Pallas") and a skeptic ("To an Ultra Protestant"), he did not share Roberts's support for Imperial Federation or Carman's interest in mysticism. He was probably the best stylist among the Confederation poets, especially in such nature poems as "Among the Timothy" or "Heat," in the haunting "City of the End of Things," and in sonnets such as "Winter Uplands," where he creates a remarkable winter pastoral:

The stars that singly, then in flocks appear,
Like jets of silver from the violet dome,
So wonderful, so many and so near,
And then the golden moon to light me home –
The crunching snowshoes and the stinging air,
And silence, frost and beauty everywhere.

Duncan Campbell Scott (1862–1947) worked for the Department of Indian Affairs and was Deputy Superintendent-General from 1913 to 1932. He started to write after meeting Lampman, and his first collection, *The Magic House and Other Poems* (1893), contains poems dedicated to each of the other Confederation poets, as well as "In the Country Churchyard," an elegy for his father. *Labor and the Angel* (1898) and *New*

*World Lyrics and Ballads* (1905) feature the first of his poems on the First Nations, which have received much critical attention, often adverse in recent years. "Indian Place Names," for instance, assumes that "the race has waned and left but tales of ghosts." For some critics, all of Scott's work on the First Nations is consistent with the policies of assimilation that he followed as an administrator, while others find more sensitivity in "A Scene at Lake Manitou" and other later poems. His most frequently anthologized story, "Labrie's Wife" (first published in *The Witching of Elspie* in 1923), offers the strongest resistance to the official attitudes that today strike us as offensive: The protagonist Archibald Muir's racism and sexism make him fear the laughter that he associates with Natives and women, while the mistaken identity in the title confirms his unreliability; in the end the laugh is on him, and Muir has to recognize the greater humanity of his young assistant. Scott also wrote a short-story cycle, *In the Village of Viger* (1896), which examines the impact of change on a small Quebec town. Seven of the stories had previously appeared in *Scribner's*, and the book was published in Boston.

Pauline Johnson (1861–1913) must have been influenced by Roberts, who gave her a manuscript copy of *Songs of the Common Day*. She called the Tantramar "the spot that every lover of Canadian literature longs to see" and held that "for another to sing of Tantramar would be almost plagiarism; its very name is so wedded with Roberts, that to sever them would be an arrant literary divorce." Although she wrote of both nature ("Low Tide at St. Andrews") and nationalism ("The Good Old N.P.," her tribute to Macdonald's "National Policy"), she is best known for the poems and stories in which she powerfully claims her identity as a woman born on the Six Nations Reserve of a Mohawk father and an English mother. Johnson performed many of her own poems as "the Mohawk Princess" in sensationally popular readings that started in 1892. She would appear first in a buckskin dress with a bear-claw necklace, her father's hunting knife, and, after 1895, a Huron scalp, and then return in the second half in a formal gown. Her performances were a great success with a growing audience in Canada, the United States, and England, but her hectic schedule eventually took its toll on her health. Her first volume, *The White Wampum* (1895), appeared under the names "E. Pauline Johnson" and "Tekahionwake" and includes such poems as "Ojistoh," "The Song My Paddle Sings," and "A Cry from an Indian Wife." In the last poem, set during the first Riel rebellion, the speaker urges her lover to

> Go forth, and win the glories of the war.
> Go forth, nor bend to greed of white men's hands;
> By right of birth we Indians own these lands,
> Though starved, crushed, plundered, lies our nation low . . .
> Perhaps the white man's god has willed it so.

This defiance was part of Johnson's appeal, though the sense of a "crushed" nation echoes the idea of racial extinction that rightly concerns critics when it appears in Scott and other writers. In "The Corn Husker" (1896) the members of an unidentified tribe are compared to "dead husks," though Johnson is careful to state that they are oppressed by "might's injustice" and not by some inevitable force. In any case, Johnson valued Canadian unity over racial purity: "White Race and Red are one if they are but Canadian born," she wrote in the preface to her second book, *Canadian Born* (1903). She could be sharply critical of depictions of the First Nations, as in her essay "A Strong Race Opinion: On the Indian Girl in Modern Fiction" (1892). The very word "Indian," she complained, "signifies about as much as the term 'European,' but I cannot recall ever having read a story where the heroine was described as 'a European.'" She called for an end of the "'doglike,' 'fawnlike,' 'deer-footed,' 'fire-eyed,' 'crouching,' 'submissive' book heroine." In "A Red Girl's Reasoning" (1893) a marriage ends when the title character throws away her wedding ring and tells her intolerant husband: "that thing is as empty to me as the Indian rites to you." In her last years, she wrote stories that appeared first in periodicals and then as *Legends of Vancouver* (1911), *The Moccasin Maker* (1913), and *The Shagganappi* (1913).

Other notable poets of the period include William Wilfred Campbell (1860–1918), who collaborated with Lampman and Scott on *At the Mermaid Inn*, a weekly column on the arts that ran in the Toronto *Globe* from February 1892 to July 1893. Campbell is best remembered for his poems set in the area around Lake Huron and Georgian Bay, though he also wrote novels, histories, and closet dramas. His *Collected Poems* (1905) so impressed American steel magnate Andrew Carnegie that he ordered a special edition for his libraries. Three other poets long associated with the Confederation group are Frederick George Scott, Francis Sherman, and Theodore Goodridge Roberts. Frederick George Scott (1861–1944) wrote one novel (*Elton Hazelwood*, 1891), several books of poetry, and *The Great War as I Saw It* (1922), a memoir of his experience as chaplain to the Canadian troops in the First World War. Francis Sherman (1871–1926) wrote pre-Raphaelite verse, including a fine elegy for William Morris ("In Memorabilia Mortis," 1896). Theodore Goodridge Roberts (1877–1953), Charles's brother, wrote such romances as *The Harbour Master* (1913) as well as poetry. Among the period's female writers were Agnes Ethelwyn Wetherald and Sophia Almon Hensley. Agnes Ethelwyn Wetherald (1857–1940), working in both Canada and the United States, was well known for her poetry and prose; Jennifer Chambers has studied the "poetic dialogue" between Wetherald and Helena Coleman (1860–1953), the author of *Songs and Sonnets* (1906) and *Marching Men: War Verses* (1917). Sophia Almon Hensley (1866–1946) knew and admired Charles G. D. Roberts when he taught at

King's College; her interest in women's causes after she moved to New York City appears in verse in *The Heart of a Woman* (1906) and in prose in *Love and the Woman of Tomorrow* (1913). Two very different talents emerged towards the end of this period: Marjorie Pickthall and Robert Service. Marjorie Pickthall (1883–1922) shows her keen understanding of myth and legend in *The Drift of Pinions* (1913), *The Lamp of Poor Souls and Other Poems* (1916), and in the posthumously published *The Woodcarver's Wife and Other Poems* (1922). Robert Service (1874–1958) produced rollicking ballads of life in the North that have remained popular since they started to appear in, for instance, *Songs of a Sourdough* (1907).

Financial exigencies were always more pressing for novelists than for poets, who would not expect to live off their earnings. 1893 — the year in which the Confederation poets saw the publication of some of their most important books — proved to be a crucial historical marker. Before then, the New Brunswick-born May Agnes Fleming (1840–1880) earned as much as ten thousand dollars a year for her popular novels that appeared first as installments and then as books in America. Her success makes her a trailblazer of sorts: Fleming was often the sole Canadian writer in the "cheap libraries" that Canadian publishers began to produce in the 1880s. In the following decade, however, several Canadian publishers included Canadian writers. For these publishers, the key to financial success came when they imported plates for new paper-covered Canadian editions of books that had been published elsewhere. According to George Parker, "this trend began in 1892, and by 1893 new fiction in paper covers took Canada by storm." In 1896 Gilbert Parker's *The Seats of the Mighty* was a great success in its Canadian copyright edition, and in 1899 Robert Barr's *The Adventure of Jennie Baxter* sold three thousand copies in Canada. Gilbert Parker (1862–1932) was an Anglican deacon who moved to Australia in 1885 and to England in 1889. His first success came with *Pierre and His People* (1892), a collection of stories about the Canadian Northwest — which he had never seen. He wrote several romances about Quebec past and present, among which *The Seats of the Mighty* (1896), about the Battle of Quebec, is the best known. With his collected works appearing in a lavish "Imperial Edition" of twenty-three volumes in 1912, he became a member of Parliament in 1900, a knight in 1902, a baron in 1915, and a member of the Privy Council in 1916. Robert Barr (1850–1912) declared in 1899 that the average Canadian "loves whiskey better than books," but the sales of his own book that year told a different tale. After working as a teacher and principal, he got a job as a reporter for the *Detroit Free Press* in 1876, then moved to England in 1881, where he knew such writers as Stephen Crane and Arthur Conan Doyle. He wrote twenty novels, among them *In the Midst of Alarms* (1894) and *The Measure of the Rule* (1907), and many short stories, including detective stories, historical romances, and satires.

One writer who achieved great international success without leaving Canada was Ralph Connor, in George Parker's words "the miracle that the Canadian book trade had been unconsciously waiting for." Ralph Connor was the pseudonym of Charles Gordon (1860–1937), who explained later that "my sole purpose was to awaken my church in Eastern Canada to the splendour of the mighty religious adventure being attempted by the missionary pioneers in the Canada beyond the Great Lakes by writing a brief sketch of the things which as clerk of the biggest presbytery in the world I had come to know by personal experience." His first sketches appeared in book form as *Black Rock: A Tale of the Selkirks* (1898), in which a missionary states: "The Church must be in with the railroad . . . If society crystallizes without her influence the country is lost, and British Columbia will be another trapdoor to the bottomless pit." The novel focuses more on the drama of salvation than on work in the mines and lumber camps, but its homiletic manner found readers who liked it precisely because it was not conventional. *Black Rock* was followed by *The Sky Pilot: A Tale of the Foothills* (1899), *The Man from Glengarry* (1901), and many other novels. Gordon/Connor claimed that these first three titles sold five million copies, and many of his novels have remained in print within Canada and elsewhere. *The Man from Glengarry* remains of interest to students of Canadian literature, for it combines with its moral concerns an affectionate account of the area (Glengarry county near Ottawa), where Gordon grew up. As the preface states, while the old way of life is gone, "in the Canada beyond the Lakes, where men are making empire, the sons of these Glengarry men are found." The hero eventually winds up in British Columbia, from where he travels to Ottawa to urge Prime Minister Macdonald to build the railway.

An even greater success began in 1908 when Lucy Maud Montgomery (1874–1942) published *Anne of Green Gables*. In Anne Shirley, the red-haired orphan who seeks "scope for imagination" and decides that "one can't stay sad very long in such an interesting world," Montgomery created the single most famous character in Canadian literature. The unforgettable first novel, soon translated into other languages, was followed by seven sequels, several films, and, in recent years, stage versions, a long-running television series, and a small tourist industry. As a local joke has it, the home of Anne of Green Gables that draws crowds of pilgrims is "the place where someone who never lived, never lived." Montgomery was involved in legal battles over the publication and film rights to the character, securing the former and losing the latter, and her executors have continued the fight. Next to the Anne of Green Gables series, she published poems and as many as forty-three stories a year (her astonishing output for 1906), and selections from her journal have been edited in five volumes by Mary Rubio and Elizabeth Waterston. Many Canadian writers grew up under the spell of Anne, though some (including Alice Munro) were more taken with

Emily, the heroine of *Emily of New Moon* (1923), *Emily Climbs* (1925), and *Emily's Quest* (1927).

Less famous than Montgomery, Sara Jeannette Duncan (1861–1922) is invaluable for the literary historian. In her early writing for American and Canadian newspapers in the 1880s, she wrote about, among other subjects, Canadian culture and women's issues, often with subtle irony. In her columns in *The Week*, she wisely argued that "it is not necessary . . . to suppose that because people are reading foreign books they are not also reading home productions," and she cogently defended literary realism against the conventional taste for romance: "The novel of to-day is a reflection of our present social state. The women who enter into its composition are but intelligent agents in this reflection and show themselves as they are, not as a false ideal would have them." She turned some of the articles based on her travels into her first book, *A Social Departure: How Orthodocia and I Went Round the World by Ourselves* (1890), which Archibald MacMechan later called "the wittiest book of travels ever written by a Canadian." It was followed by such novels as *The Simple Adventures of a Memsahib* (1893), *A Daughter of Today* (1894), and *Cousin Cinderella; or, A Canadian Girl in London* (1908). Much of her later work is set in India, where she moved after marrying in 1890. She was thus far from her native Brantford when she depicted it, lovingly and ironically, in the fictional town of Elgin in *The Imperialist* (1904), which she dedicated to her father. As the novel opens, the population of Elgin is quite cheerful about its blending of cultures, celebrating Queen Victoria's birthday with a game of lacrosse (a French name for a Native game) and speaking with something of an American accent. Lorne Murchison, the protagonist, wants a stronger national identity and turns to Imperial Federation. When he joins a deputation to England to seek "improved communications within the Empire," he cannot understand the accents that he encounters, and he himself is mistaken for an American. In a devastatingly ironic detail, when Lorne returns to Elgin to discuss his trip and his plan for protected trade between England and Canada, the narrator notes that his family has American furniture and reads an American paper along with their local one. At the end of the novel, Lorne's defeat as a politician is followed by his failure as a suitor and the probable failure of the idea of Imperial Federation, and he has to be called back from Florida to resume his legal career. Duncan's irony conceals her own attitude to Imperial Federation, but she must have been both sympathetic toward the ideal and shrewdly pragmatic about the outcome (see ch. 13, Dvorak).

Several other writers of fiction marked the period. Agnes Maule Machar (1837–1927) expressed her passionate Christian feminism in poetry, essays, and fiction; her best novel, *Roland Graeme: Knight. A Novel of Our Time* (1892), is one of the few examples from this period to examine the problems of industry and labor. Margaret Marshall Saunders

(1861–1947) became famous for *Beautiful Joe: An Autobiography* (1893), an animal story that became an international bestseller. Edward William Thomson (1849–1924) was a journalist and editor in Toronto, Montreal, Boston, and Ottawa, and a friend of Lampman and Wetherald. He collected his short fiction in *Old Man Savarin and Other Stories* in 1895, which he revised as *Old Man Savarin Stories: Tales of Canada and Canadians* in 1917. The title story, featuring a regional dialect, and "Miss Minnely's Management," which examines the difficulties of working for the fictitious New England journal "The Family Blessing," both continue to be anthologized. Francis William Grey (1860–1939) wrote plays, poems, essays, and one novel, *The Curé of St. Phillipe: A Story of French-Canadian Politics* (1899), which does for Quebec what Sara Jeannette Duncan did for Ontario. After attending the University of Toronto, Norman Duncan (1871–1916) moved to New York to work as a reporter. In 1900 he published *The Soul of the Street: Correlated Stories*, a sequence about New York's Syrian community. That same year he arranged with *McClure's Magazine* to write about outport life in Newfoundland, and several books followed, including another sequence, *The Way of the Sea* (1903). Patrick O'Flaherty calls "The Fruits of Toil," the concluding story, "arguably the finest piece of fiction ever written about oldtime Newfoundland." Nellie McClung (1873–1951) published a story about twelve-year-old Pearlie Watson in 1905, which was expanded into *Sowing Seeds in Danny* (1908), selling over one hundred thousand copies. It was followed by *The Second Chance* (1910) and *Purple Springs* (1921) to form a trilogy tracing Pearlie's growth into an activist for temperance and suffrage. McClung, who was elected to the Alberta legislature in 1921, wrote more novels, an autobiography, and *In Times like These* (1915), a landmark feminist work. Robert Stead (1880–1959) began to write his prairie novels during this period, including *The Homesteaders* (1916) and *The Cow Puncher* (1918), both of which were popular successes. Edith Eaton (Sui Sin Far; 1865–1914), the daughter of an English father and a Chinese mother, was born in England, raised in Montreal, and eventually moved to the United States. "After all I have no nationality and am not anxious to claim any. Individuality is more than nationality," she maintained, and wrote both fiction (*Mrs. Spring Fragrance*, 1912) and essays about the Asian-American community. Martin Allerdale Grainger (1874–1941), who was born in England and educated at Cambridge before moving to British Columbia, wrote only one novel, *Woodsmen of the West* (1908). His attitude towards life in the western logging camps contrasts sharply with Ralph Connor's, as when he argues that "on the whole, the good-fellowship atmosphere of a loggers' saloon seems to supply some of the same sentimental food as the music, books, and stage plays and other emotional influences with which the educated man nourishes (and too often satisfies) his sentimental nature." The book focuses on the character of Carter, whom the narrator both fears and admires, "for among the clinkers and the base alloys that make up much of Carter's soul there is a piece of purest metal, of true human greatness, an inspiration and a happiness to see."

To conclude the period under discussion, Stephen Leacock (1869–1944) brings together several of the patterns traced above. His first books were *Elements of Political Science* (1906), an influential textbook, and *Baldwin, Lafontaine, Hincks: Responsible Government* (1909), followed by *Literary Lapses* (1910) and *Nonsense Novels* (1911). The latter contain the comic sketches and parodies that he continued to write for a widely expanding audience over the next three decades. "Hannah of the Highlands; or The Laird of Loch Aucherlocherty," for instance, mocks the Scottish historical romance tradition by depicting two families who "differed on every possible point. They wore different tartans, sat under different ministers, drank different brands of whisky, and upheld different doctrines in regard to eternal punishment." His most famous book, *Sunshine Sketches of a Little Town* (1912), is both a regional idyll and a searching examination of the nostalgic attitudes that made the genre so popular (see ch. 7, Davies). The satire includes the narrator and almost everyone else in the small town of Mariposa, where "everybody . . . is either a Liberal or a Conservative or else is both," and a politician's reference to wending his "way towards that goal from which no traveller returns" is taken as a plan to move to the United States. In the conclusion, "L'Envoi: The Train to Mariposa," the narrative switches to the second person, so that the reader becomes one of those "sitting here again in the leather chairs of the Mausoleum Club, talking of the little Town in the Sunshine that once we knew." That club returns in *Arcadian Adventures with the Idle Rich* (1914), a caustic satire of advanced capitalism. In the opening chapter, the English aristocracy confronts the new power of American capital when Lucullus Fyshe entertains the Duke of Dulham:

> And the Duke . . . decided that just as soon as Mr. Fyshe should give him a second glass of wine, that second glass should cost Mr. Fyshe a hundred thousand pounds sterling.
>
> And oddly enough, at about the same moment, Mr. Fyshe was calculating that provided he could make the Duke drink a second glass of the Mausoleum champagne, that glass would cost the Duke about five million dollars.

In such passages, Leacock's Toryism is subordinated to the understanding of economics that he gained when he studied under Thorstein Veblen at the University of Chicago: The aristocrat and the plutocrat differ only in the scale of their avarice. *Arcadian Adventures* is a satire of what Veblen called "conspicuous consumption" and "the conduct of universities by business men." Thus, Dr. Boomer, the university president, boasts that a series of lectures on the Four Gospels was founded by Mr. Underbugg "on the sole stipulation that any reference . . . to the four gospels should be coupled with his name." The book ends with the triumph of plutocracy, as "Bands of Dr. Boomer's students armed with baseball bats surrounded the polls to guarantee fair play. Any man wishing to cast an unclean vote was driven from the booth; all those attempting to introduce any element of brute force or rowdyism into the election were cracked over the head." Other writers would depict the city more sympathetically, but no one had a shrewder sense of the contradictions of capitalism than this Canadian Tory.

Many of the writers discussed here continued to write long after the end of the First World War, especially Roberts, D. C. Scott, Service, Montgomery, McClung, Stead, and Leacock. Their enduring popularity in Canada became a source of animosity among the younger generation, especially in the field of poetry. F. R. Scott's (1899–1985) "The Canadian Authors Meet" (1927), for instance, mocks a literary milieu in which "Carman, Lampman, Roberts, Campbell, Scott / Are measured for their faith and philanthropics, / Their zeal for God and King, their earnest thought." It did not matter then to Scott or to his friend and fellow poet and critic A. J. M. Smith (1902–1980) that such values had little to do with the best work of the Confederation poets — Lampman was a skeptic and a socialist, while Carman's popularity was initially an American, and not a Canadian, phenomenon. But there are at least three ironies here: First, although the Canadian modernists often singled out Carman for abuse, he was read appreciatively by such modernists as Ezra Pound and Wallace Stevens; second, Scott and Smith mocked the very idea of nature poetry in their youthful polemics, but it is their own nature poetry (such as Smith's "The Lonely Land," 1926) that has been most influential; and third, although the modernists opposed distinctively Canadian to "universal" themes, the Confederation poets frequently appeared in the leading international journals, while Smith became "world-famous across Canada / for urging cosmopolitan standards," in Frank Davey's cruel phrase (from *The Louis Riel Organ and Piano Company*, 1985). A modernist reaction was probably inevitable, but in Canada that meant a wholesale rejection of the past, and not just of the immediately preceding generation. Later, Smith came to recognize that the older poets "had not read Hulme or Eliot or Dylan Thomas, but we must not condemn them entirely for having read Wordsworth, Shelley, Keats, or Matthew Arnold — as most of them, and I think fruitfully, had" ("Eclectic Detachment: Aspects of Identity in Canadian Poetry," 1961). By applying this kind of flexibility and tolerance to all previous eras, recent Canadian literary history has avoided what E. K. Brown calls "the provincialism of time."

# 10: French-Canadian Literature from National Solidarity to the École littéraire de Montréal

*Fritz Peter Kirsch (University of Vienna)*

## Historical and Cultural Developments

AFTER THE REBELLION OF 1837–1838 was crushed, the signs of a tendency towards defense and retreat in French-Canadian society increased. After 1791, following the division into a western Upper Canada and an (initially) almost exclusively francophone Lower Canada ("Bas Canada") in the East, the "Canadiens" — the term was not changed to "Canadiens français" until after the middle of the nineteenth century — had attempted a strategy of cooperation and rivalry with their anglophone partner, trying first to exhaust all possibilities within the parliamentary system. The failure of the liberal-patriotic rebellion and the political signals and measures coming from London in the wake of this defeat led to a conflict between resigned willingness to conform on the one hand and a need for "national" affirmation on the other, a conflict that would leave its mark on the cultural life of the francophone population for a long time to come. To be sure, the politics of assimilation — initiated by Lord Durham's report (1839) — failed and were replaced by the federal government's recognition of the francophones ("accommodation"). Nevertheless, the British North America Act of 1867 continued to feed ethnically motivated fears as well as economically motivated feelings of frustration in the face of the "Anglais"-dominated economy.

The constitution of the Dominion of Canada and the inclusion and/or annexation of new territories in the West and East were accomplished without the participation of the French Canadians, who had been reduced to the status of provincials, and in part directly against their wishes. Once a space without borders for the expansion by "voyageurs," North America from then on opened itself to the French Canadians primarily when they set out for the cities of English Canada or New England as economic emigrants. The feeling of helplessness and isolation would deepen with each event that demonstrated the unbalanced power distribution within Canada, including the suppression of the Métis movement in

Manitoba and Saskatchewan and the execution of Louis Riel in 1885. At the end of the century, the francophones of Quebec showed their outrage at the closing of French-Catholic schools in the other Canadian provinces, but to no effect. They protested in vain against Canada's participation in England's wars (both the Boer War of 1899 and the First World War sparked dissent in Quebec). Because resistance on political or military grounds had proved ineffective, the forces that finally gained the upper hand in French-Canadian society were those that fought for an assimilation with the British ruling system and simultaneously for a conscious closing of ranks between the clergy and the citizenry. The tensions within Quebec society allowed a system of norms and values to arise in Quebec City and Montreal that was primarily focused on resistance to external influences and the protection of French culture. This defensive stance would be palpable in the course of literary history in the nineteenth century and even in a substantial part of the twentieth century.

French-Canadian literature in the second half of the nineteenth century evinced a drive for definition and assertion of its own identity, which, in intensity and determination, far surpassed the patriotism characterizing the centuries following the Conquête of 1759–1763. At first glance, this need for affirmative self-interpretation seems to manifest itself above all in the nurturing of nostalgic memories of the old days of Nouvelle-France and in the desire for an intensification of the cultural ties with the former motherland. In fact, however, the authors involved in such endeavors were most interested in founding a French-Canadian national literature, which despite important influences from France did not run parallel to French literature. The anglophone literature of Canada only slowly managed to release itself from British models because of continuing colonial ties. The francophones' feeling of isolation, in contrast, accelerated the new orientation of Quebec's literature. The Catholic Church played a seminal role in this process: Through its loyalty to the London government, it succeeded in removing a large number of restrictions initiated by Protestants in positions of power, and under the energetic leadership of the reforming bishop Ignace Bourget, it greatly increased its political influence. Under the influence of the specifically inner-Canadian cultural conflict, large portions of the francophone population were more willing to work together with the clergy than had been the case at the beginning of the century. This explains the continually decreasing influence of the Institut canadien de Montréal, founded in 1844, which the liberal forces of Quebec had originally rallied around (see ch. 8, Scholl). Slowly, literature — as an institution and as the scope of verbal art — relinquished part of its unwieldiness and placed itself in the service of a system of ideological guidelines and social models that alone claimed to secure the survival of the national community in a perceived hostile environment. Canada, as part of the British Empire and at the same time part of a continent dominated by anglophones, was perceived by many francophones as an overpowering opponent.

Whenever the conservative French-Canadian value system was challenged from outside, however, its inherent contradictions surfaced. When the upswing in the American economy after the Civil War reached a peak and spread to Canada in the 1880s, the socially and economically marginalized French Canadians were increasingly challenged by capitalist modernization. While the political and socioeconomic imbalance between the linguistic communities prevented francophones from participating equally in the continental upturn in industry and trade, the elite of clergy and citizens attempted to compensate for the collective experience of marginality by strengthening traditionalist positions. At the heart of these positions were Catholicism, memories of Nouvelle-France, and loyalty to the land which was cleared and cultivated by the first French settlers (see the so-called agriculturist ideology, "terroirisme," or *mythe du terroir*). Additionally, the French language remained sacrosanct in its normative variant, although the difference between spoken Canadian French and the standard of Paris kept growing. A similar rift marks the literature of this period, which voluntarily placed itself in the service of ruling norms and values, yet was also forced to accept that the ideal of homeland loyalty was threatened by a cruel reality that could not be fought but at best could be depicted in literature as unjust, by contrasting it to moral ideals. From the viewpoint of the twenty-first-century reader, it is this contradiction that lends interest to an aesthetically rather modest literary production.

Even if it seems legitimate to place the beginnings of French-Canadian literature back in the missionary reports and occasional writing of Nouvelle-France (see ch. 5, Laflèche), it is still worth noting that not until the middle of the nineteenth century can the development of an independent literary life be identified. As late as the 1830s, book production in French-speaking Canada was barely developed and was restricted to only a dozen titles, half of which were political tracts, schoolbooks, or other nonfiction. Books imported from France were rare and expensive because they could only be ordered via London and the English trade houses. Public libraries in Quebec — in contrast to anglophone Canada — were few and far between, and limited primarily to parish libraries whose collections were strictly censored according to church dictates. A quarter century later, however, the number of books published in Quebec had tripled (thanks to the successful expansion of a subscription system) and the portion of works of fiction and poetry had greatly increased. The expansion of the school system ("collèges classiques") produced a larger number of potential readers with a fairly homogeneous education (that is, molded by the church, which also controlled the educational system). At a time in which illiteracy was still widespread in rural areas, this new generation of readers — primarily self-employed amid few francophone professionals (journalists, doctors, pharmacists, notaries, and politicians) — strengthened the ranks of the reading public. The middle of the nineteenth century also saw the founding of reading circles as well as literary associations in Quebec cities. The members of this literary field recruited each other from the clergy and educated citizenry, that is, from those groups that had been significantly involved in the definition and development of a national identity. The canon of values developed by this elite was rigidly adhered to, not only in magazines and newspapers, but also in the selection of books in libraries and bookstores. What harmonized with the socially consecrated strategies for (cultural) survival ("survivance") was accepted, while subjective or experimental poetry, the novel, and drama fell prey to the censors. For several decades, most French-Canadian authors voluntarily placed themselves in the service of the national cause. Not until the end of the nineteenth century did a growing discontent manifest itself in the face of a cultural-political situation that some artists considered a hostile environment to literature.

## "National" Romanticism

From the middle of the nineteenth century, French-Canadian authors, shaped by the traumatic experiences of the failed Rebellions and the union regime, subjected history to a reinterpretation that viewed the period of Nouvelle-France as a heroic age of explorers, soldiers, and missionaries, and the Conquête of 1759 as a national catastrophe. French-Canadian writers enthusiastically imitated the representatives of French Romanticism in the motherland, whose epic-lyric works demonstrated the path to a national community through the centuries. Particularly popular were texts that combined a historical development with a spiritual release, whether reflecting a Catholic concept as in the case of Alphonse de Lamartine's *Jocelyn* (1836), or opening theosophical perspectives like Victor Hugo's *La légende des siècles* (1859). In 1855 it became clear to what extent the recollection of the French inheritance reflected a social need, when for the first time since 1760 a ship from France anchored in Quebec, causing great commotion and giving strong new impulses to national self-confidence. This loyalty to the former mother country only stretched so far, however, as an integration of admired models from overseas did not come into conflict with the ideological guidelines of French Canada. Thus neither the cult of the individual of French Romanticism nor the spiritual inheritance of the Enlightenment and the French Revolution was adopted. The indexation of literature that "corrupts customs" by the Office des Bons Livres (founded in 1844) limited the number of imported books from Paris. Over the course of the nineteenth century, the model function of French literature would be reduced to authors defending the monarchy and the church, for example in works by Louis Bonald, Joseph de Maistre, and Louis

Veuillot. In Quebec, it was above all the old ultramontane France that was venerated.

Some critics have called François-Xavier Garneau's (1809–1866) *Histoire du Canada depuis sa découverte jusqu'à nos jours* (1845–1848) the most significant work of French-Canadian literature of the nineteenth century. In part because of its compelling style, Garneau's historical work had a strong and lasting effect on later generations (see ch. 8, Scholl). Its liberal views, however, were rejected by later historians such as Jean-Baptiste Antoine Ferland and Étienne-Michel Faillon and replaced by a position that further emphasized the religious mission of the French Canadians. From the viewpoint of these authors, the colonization of the New World by France was a work of God, intended to allow the golden age of the original church to rise again. Thus Adolphe-Basile Routhier (1839–1920) stated in the "chant national" of 1880 that heaven showed Canadians the path in the New World. This pious interpretation of national history was by no means irreconcilable with a weakening distinction between the two "founding peoples," which was still very strong in Garneau, but seemed less opportune over the course of the consolidation of the clerical-bourgeois value system in a period when the francophone elite strove for an accommodation of sorts with the English-Canadian leadership.

Around 1860, members of the educated elite met regularly in Quebec City for discussions of literature, art, and culture. Academics such as François-Xavier Garneau, ministers such as Pierre-Joseph-Olivier Chauveau, members of Parliament such as Antoine Gérin-Lajoie (1824–1882), and members of the clergy such as the Abbé Casgrain (1831–1904) belonged to its circle. They met in churches, newspaper editorial offices, parliamentary offices, or in the bookshop of the writer Octave Crémazie (1827–1879). Their discussions revolved around the renewal of French-Canadian literature through works that would reflect their patriotic-traditionalist principles. This exchange of ideas, however, led neither to the institutionalization of the group nor to a shared manifesto. For this reason, some French-Canadian literary historians have reservations about using Camille Roy's term "École patriotique de Québec" for such a loose affiliation. Still, the members of the group were united by the joint striving for a native, patriotic literature: The production of the past decades — adventure novels, folklore-fantasy, and occasional poetry — was regarded as a wild growth that needed to be tamed.

The civilizing claim of the French Canadians was fundamentally different from the Promethean inspiration of French Romanticism, which at least since Hugo's "Préface" to the drama *Cromwell* (1827) had taken the entire material and spiritual universe as the playground of literature in order to give the ideal figure of the "poète mage" the opportunity to develop the highest force of language. Neither did the Tellurism of the American Walt Whitman have any equivalent in francophone Canada of the nineteenth century. The literary theory that Casgrain conceived along with the other patriots of the "Quebec School" avoided such tones and instead emphasized the survivalist character of French-Canadian culture. In keeping with Casgrain's concept, which could well be characterized by the term Messianism, it was the mission of the literarily active "Canadiens français" to encounter opponents (who in the past had included the Iroquois and now the English Canadians and Americans) with the same maximum amount of discipline as their admired founding figures. They believed that Canadian literature should be serious and shaped by loyalty to the great past, to the Catholic faith, and to the French language. It should not react to humiliation and rejection of the "chosen" people with hateful polemics, but with a dignity that would force the rest of the world to show respect. The path that French-Canadian literature would travel in theory and practice was delineated: For Casgrain's intellectual heir Camille Roy — literary historian, "homme de lettres," university instructor, and churchman, who had a lasting influence on French-Canadian literary criticism from the beginning of the twentieth century — the literary production of French Canada had in the nineteenth century already constituted itself as an independent literature "in the service of the nation."

The first publication by Casgrain bore the title *Légendes canadiennes* (1861). This collection of prose narratives was intended, according to its editor, to save the orally transmitted legends from impending oblivion — "today more than ever" — and to support the national self-confidence of the French Canadians, much as the medieval heroic lays (*Chansons de geste*) had done for the French. Collections of this kind were then published several times by different authors. They did not draw sharp lines between legends, fairy tales, and ghost stories from the oral culture of the farming population (*contes*) and anecdotes from French-Canadian history. Through an idealistic depiction of great deeds by soldiers or missionaries, patriotic awareness was to be strengthened in broader sections of society. The civilizing power of Christianity in the beginnings of Nouvelle-France was celebrated, as was the resigned fight for the survival of a people that had not been adequately supported by their motherland France.

Without question, the nineteenth-century authors of francophone Canada, with their rich offerings of folk songs and stories, helped preserve their oral culture in writing. The folklore traditions provided an important basis for the envisioned nationalization of French-Canadian literature by the "École patriotique de Québec." During 1865–1867, Ernest Gagnon's important collection of folk songs *Chansons populaires du Canada* appeared. At the beginning of the twentieth century, Édouard-Zotique Massicotte was able to appraise a quantitatively rich production in the field of narrative writing in his anthology *Conteurs canadiens-français du XIXe siècle* (1902). The lively interest in oral traditions encouraged the cultivation of the French language and at the same time inspired literary production; a striking example of this is the work of Adjutor Rivard (1868–1945), who came to prominence in 1902 as a cofounder of the Société du parler français and made a name for himself as the author of vivid sketches from village life (*Chez nous*, 1914; *Chez nos gens*, 1918). Amid efforts towards a "national" literature, collectors and retellers drew on French-Canadian oral tradition and did not hesitate to use this material liberally, even more loosely than the European fairy-tale researchers of the nineteenth century. For example, in the narrative works of Joseph-Charles Taché (1820–1894; *Trois légendes de mon pays*, 1861; *Forestiers et voyageurs: Études de moeurs*, 1863), much of the sensuality and "wildness" of the stories of woodsmen and Indians was sacrificed in the Christianization of the tales.

The literary production of jurist, journalist, and politician Louis Honoré Fréchette (1839–1908) led the patriotic inspiration founded by Garneau and the "École patriotique de Québec" to its climax. His 1880 volume of poetry *Les fleurs boréales, Les oiseaux de neige: Poésies canadiennes* was recognized by the Académie Française with the Prix Montyon. In the same year, the writer was awarded numerous honors in Paris, and Victor Hugo received him personally. His most famous work, *La légende d'un peuple* (1887), a collection of short prose texts (almost exclusively written in alexandrines), was modeled after Hugo's *La légende des siècles*, the second and third series of which had appeared in 1877 and 1883. In fact, Fréchette had only adopted the national inspiration of Hugo's model, while consistently avoiding the latter's staging of the lyrical I between prophetic impetus and immersion. Fréchette also took different paths to the French Romantics insofar as his epic was not dedicated to the history of humankind, but to the wanderings of the French Canadians through time, as requested by the nationally minded historians of the nineteenth century. Fréchette divided the texts of his collection into three "époques," the first evoking the age of explorers and settlers, the following two covering the battles against the English and the development up to the present under the régime britannique. The panorama is framed by a prologue and an epilogue that span the whole breadth from the discovery of America by Columbus to the civilizing mission of present-day France. The French Canadians are depicted as the children of an admirable mother country, of which they have proven themselves worthy through heroism and self-sacrifice and for which they could serve as a source of inspiration. In his texts Fréchette viewed America as an immense space — from the mouth of the St. Lawrence to the Mississippi — and animated it literarily with his visions of history.

Fréchette distinguished himself also as a dramatist with the relatively successful plays *Félix Poutré* (first performed in 1862, published in 1871), *Papineau*, and *Le retour de l'exilé* (both 1880). All these texts deal with the failed Rebellions of the Patriots of 1837–1838. In the first of the two plays Fréchette deviated from the principles of French-Canadian traditionalism, insofar as his protagonist Félix Poutré, as a prisoner of the English, attempts to avoid the impending gallows by feigning madness, rather than heroically accepting death. The limits of Fréchette's patriotism are also visible in poems like "Le drapeau anglais" (1890), where he developed the myth of a Canadian duality, with the constitution of 1867 being seen as a pact between two unified founding nations striving for a shared ideal.

Along with epic poetry, French-Canadian poetry in the nineteenth century was defined by so-called mood poetry, which evokes the transient moment, and by poems featuring anecdotes of an idyllic or dramatic nature. William Chapman (1850–1917), despite his fame as a French-Canadian patriot, would have liked to claim his place as the "Bard of America" in the competition with the Parisian Parnassus poets, the Provençal Frédéric Mistral, or at least with his older compatriot and contemporary Fréchette. Yet, lacking great visions, he created poetic anecdotes and inspiring episodes from history and the present (in collections like *Les feuilles d'érable*, 1890, and *Les rayons du nord*, 1909), which are characterized by clever use of rhetoric rather than by linguistic power. The horizon of inspiration on which the poets of this period were moving was very limited. Every poet who dealt with historical topics felt obliged to take a solemn stance. Nonetheless, nostalgia could also strike more cheerful chords, as long as the principles of Catholic bourgeois morality were respected. This is the case, for instance, in a poem by Nérée Beauchemin (1850–1931) on a resolute ancestor, who long ago emigrated to the New World from Saint-Malo: "Par un temps de demoiselle sur la frêle caravelle" ("Ma lointaine aïeule," *Patrie intime*, 1928). With regard to present times, the poet could devote himself to the simple facts of rural life, the advent of spring, or write in discreet melancholy about the transitory quality of youth. In the texts from Pamphile Le May's (1837–1918) collection *Les gouttelettes* (1904), for instance, the little details of everyday life are continuously drenched in the light of emotions. Religious sentiment was manifested in general not as a struggle in the soul, but as humility and devotion. This could produce delightful linguistic miniatures of bittersweet melancholy, such as those by Alfred Garneau (1836–1904), the son of the great historian. Alfred Garneau's son Hector collected his father's *Poésies* and published them in 1905, partly as a foundation for his own work, which would radically renew French-Canadian poetry between the world wars and at the same time emphasize the groundbreaking function of the homeland poets of the nineteenth century.

## The French-Canadian Novel: Entertainment Value and Adherence to Norms

Throughout the entire nineteenth century, the encounters between French immigrants and Native peoples provided an important source of inspiration for the French-Canadian novel. The French Romantic François-René de

Chateaubriand proved himself an important groundbreaker for later "Indian novels" with his stories surrounding the Natchez people (see, for instance, *Atala ou Les amours de deux sauvages dans le desert*, 1801). Of particularly lasting influence, however, were the Leatherstocking books by the American novelist James Fenimore Cooper, whose depiction of exciting chases and battles was frequently connected by French-Canadian authors with the conflicts of the soul illuminated by Chateaubriand. According to a familiar plot scheme in texts of this kind, a noble Indian girl comes into contact with Whites, converts to Christianity, and finds herself in a conflict between her family who wants her back and the French youth who loves her, a conflict that is usually fatal. Often these portrayals served to glorify the heroic "coureur de bois," who strengthened the "national" self-confidence as a founding figure of Nouvelle-France. Yet the trapper, as mentioned above, was subject to a process of adaptation to Christian morality in the second half of the nineteenth century.

The transition from the distant age of heroes and adventurers to the compromises of the present is particularly well illustrated by *Une de perdue, deux de trouvées* by Georges Boucher de Boucherville (1814–1894). The novel first appeared in the feature pages of a newspaper, beginning in 1849; it was then published in installments up until the first years of the twentieth century by a total of seven French-Canadian papers (publication in book form 1874). The author followed a very old tradition — reaching from the Hellenistic love story to the *Mémoires et aventures d'un homme de qualité* by the Abbé Prévost — by arranging the travels of the brave Captain Pierre de Saint-Luc, whom fate leads from Louisiana to Canada and finally to Central Europe, in the form of a colorful series of adventures. Scurrilous intriguers and cruel pirates attempt to rob the hero of his inheritance, but at the end he is able to defend his rights, and he finds his beloved Clarisse. The Rebellions of 1837–1838 is also touched on, though the intentions of the rebels and their leader Louis-Joseph Papineau are significantly weakened, not least with respect to the author's (who turns up by name in the course of the novel) efforts to free himself from the suspicion of bearing all too much sympathy for the liberal cause. The transition to the supremacy of a value system that not only implies an adaptation to the current situation but also the nostalgic admission of one's own cultural identity is thus clearly demonstrated.

The rod by which the historical novels of the period after 1860 are measured is without a doubt Philippe Aubert de Gaspé's (1786–1871) *Les anciens Canadiens* (1863), which was written when its author was already over seventy. The paradigmatic quality of this text is based primarily on the successful combination of European and autochthonous themes. Aubert de Gaspé is so closely indebted to Sir Walter Scott's novels that he even took the name of his protagonist, Archibald de Locheill, from Scott's *Waverley* (1814). The confrontation near the end of the Seven Years War between the "Anglais" and the "Français," both of whom seek to gain the upper hand on military and on moral grounds, mirrors Scott's antagonism between Anglo-Saxons and Normans, English and Scots. With respect to the complex relationships between the figures involved in the military conflict, Scott provided many impulses as well. At the same time, Aubert de Gaspé drew on the repertoire of French-Canadian oral culture, which he enriched with experiences from his own life. Written in a seemingly spontaneous and at times very amusing style, the novel is a rich source — literarily, cultural-historically, sociologically, and anthropologically — of orally transmitted narratives, fairy tales, witch stories, legends, anecdotes, songs, customs, prayers, national celebrations, and detail about the gastronomy and costumes of the "old Canadians." The author distanced himself from the tenets of French classicist aesthetics: "Cet ouvrage sera tout canadien par le style. . . . Que les puristes, les littérateurs émérites, choqués de ces défauts, l'appellent roman, mémoire, chronique, salmigondis, pot-pourri: peu importe!" This blend of anecdotes, reflections, and memories related in a conversational tone would become even more apparent in Aubert de Gaspé's *Mémoires* (1866). What at first seems to be a chatty style reveals itself upon closer inspection to be the clever strategy of a great narrator.

Aubert de Gaspé used Garneau's historiographical work as the source for his novel. In both works the return to the past forms the starting point for the construction of identity and pursues the goal of confronting people with their own past and thus strengthening the feeling of community. The title *Les anciens Canadiens* refers to the time before 1760 when French Canadians still lived within the system of seigneurs. The novel is characterized by a paternalistic ethos, in which each individual is satisfied with his designated place in society and the relationships between different races and classes function on the basis of mutual respect. The author criticizes France for having deserted the French Canadians at the siege of Quebec in 1760, leaving the victory to the English. "Le roi de France ne payait à ses alliés sauvages que cinquante francs la chevelure d'un Anglais; le monarque anglais, plus riche, ou plus généreux, en donnait cent pour une chevelure française!" Towards the English conquerors, on the other hand, the author is more conciliatory. The hero of his novel, the rich, aristocratic Catholic Jules d'Haberville, is a friend of the Scot Archibald Cameron de Locheill, "orphelin sur une terre étrangère," whose deceased mother was a Catholic Frenchwoman, however, and who was raised with Jules among the Jesuits. The friendship turns cloudy when war breaks out between England and France and both are forced to fight on different sides. After France's defeat, Archibald is rich and Jules is poor. Archibald loves Jules's sister Blanche, who, like many women of the time, has to choose between marrying a poor French-Canadian noble or a rich Englishman. Blanche refuses Archibald and with this heroic refusal — like the heroine in Louis Hémon's later *Maria Chapdelaine* — places collective values and the code of honor above the interests of the individual.

The novel *Jacques et Marie: Souvenirs d'un peuple dispersé* (1866) by the Acadian Napoléon Bourassa (1827–1916) is also based on a wealth of oral traditions that the author collected from his surroundings. The story of an engaged couple, separated for several years by the catastrophe of the Grand Dérangement — the expulsion of the Acadians by the English military — does not, however, lead to a contest of magnanimity between opponents, which is characteristic of Aubert de Gaspé's work. Instead, the English rival of the honest Acadian Jacques is a true scoundrel who drives Marie into a cruel dilemma of conscience, in which, however, she is able (like Longfellow's Evangeline in the eponymous verse epic of 1847) to prove herself a true heroine and the living symbol of a suppressed people. Yet the author's efforts to portray the protagonists with psychological accuracy and to exactly reconstruct the historical events through a series of poignant episodes keep the myth from excessively dominating the novel.

The historical novels that were to appear in the following decades reflected a shifting interest away from "realistic" components. In the context of a "national" value system that was increasing in importance in this period, the historical roles of religion and of the church were continually being enhanced. At the same time, romance writers attempted to diffuse the conflict with the English Canadians. In some cases this led to a polemic distancing from "enlightened" France, which was not only accused of scandalously neglecting its Canadian outpost and abandoning it at the hour of its greatest need, but occasionally also appeared in the dubious light of criminal and ruinous mismanaging of the colonial finances. The figure of the last governor of Nouvelle-France, François Bigot, was a particular target for novelists such as Joseph Marmette (1844–1895), who in *L'intendant Bigot* (1872) causally links the doings of his greedy protagonist to the defeat of the heroic "Canadiens."

With its liberal position and enmity towards England, the Patriots' movement of 1837–1838 was not popular among the writers of historical novels in the late nineteenth century. For some (such as Ernest Choquette, *Les Ribaud, idylle de 1837*, 1898), the rebels were demagogues who had tried to damage the good relationship between francophones and anglophones. Others demonstrated a cautious understanding but refrained from expressing their political opinion openly. The comrades-in-arms of Papineau found their enthusiastic defenders primarily in France, where Jules Verne, for example, took up their cause (*Famille sans nom*, 1889). Paradoxically, traditional norms and values did not strengthen the willingness of writers to fit themselves in with Canada as ruled from London. In 1895, the journalist Jules Tardivel (1851–1905) published his novel of ideas *Pour la patrie: Roman du XXe siècle*, in which he argued for the independence of francophone Canadians. The goal of French-Canadian history for this author was to erect an independent theocracy on the banks of the St. Lawrence.

The hegemony of traditionalism in Quebec society also encouraged a politics of settlement through clearing still-untouched areas in the north of the province. Inseparable from the name of the priest Antoine Labelle, who had been promoting the colonization of areas north of Montreal since the end of the 1860s, acquisition of land was intended to specifically counteract the emigration from rural areas of French Canada to the industrial centers of the United States. Contemporary literature supported efforts of this kind in various ways: through the transfiguration of country life in the *poésie du terroir* (which manifested itself throughout the whole period as a diffusely present tendency), through traditionally oriented essays, but above all in the realm of the novel in the form of the *roman du terroir*.

The fiction of the influential politician Antoine Gérin-Lajoie differs especially in its practical aspect from the pioneer work of the Quebec farm novel, Patrice Lacombe's (1807–1863) *La terre paternelle* (1846). Gérin-Lajoie's diptych *Jean Rivard, le défricheur* (1862) and *Jean Rivard, économiste* (1864) do not read so much as a moralizing warning against the corrupt influences of the city on those who allow themselves to be seduced into giving up the home turf, but rather more as progress-oriented handbooks for material success. To escape the unemployment that threatens francophone youth in the city, the protagonist Jean Rivard plans to develop a plot of land in the wilderness. The wealth he laboriously acquires is not restricted to the securing of his own existence in the sense of becoming self-sufficient, but extends with time to the entire region. His pioneer success provides for the development of new roads, the profitable combination of agriculture and manufacture, and even the development of educational institutions and a press — so that nothing prevents his ascent to becoming mayor and member of Parliament. This text, drawing both on the physiocratic legacy of the French Enlightenment and on principles of Anglo-American economic liberalism, lends the dominant traditionalist worldview of the time an optimistic aspect, working with solid, practical arguments, which would continue to have a significant effect on politics and on the cultural life of the province Quebec for a long time. At the beginning of the twentieth century, the novels of, for instance, Damase Potvin (1879–1964; *Restons chez nous*, 1908; *L'appel de la terre*, 1918) read like propaganda in the service of agriculturalism. Ernest Choquette (1862–1941) in *Claude Paysan* (1899) attempted to intensify the portrayal of emotional movements and conflicts in the farm novel, which were for the most part ignored by Gérin-Lajoie.

Félicité Angers (1845–1924) published several historical novels under the pseudonym Laure Conan. They expressed the pioneers' chivalric spirit and willingness for self-sacrifice in the battle against Native Americans and the English, as in *À l'oeuvre et à l'épreuve* (1891), *L'oublié* (1900), and *La sève immortelle* (1925). In her most famous text, *Angéline de Montbrun*, however (published 1881–1881 as a serial novel in the *Revue canadienne*, 1884 in book form), the pioneers' heroism, which was so typical for the French-Canadian literature of the late nineteenth century, moves into the background and is replaced by a messianic attachment to the homeland. The main character Angéline de Montbrun's beloved father, who has run a small farm since his wife's death, commits himself, despite his noble birth, body and soul to agriculture, because in his eyes only the bucolic virtues can secure the continuity of the French legacy in the New World. Largely because of the passages structured as an epistolary novel, the reader is reminded of Jean-Jacques Rousseau's *La Nouvelle Héloïse* (1761), where people striving for perfection seek to establish an ideal society within the framework of a farm. But the most powerful source of inspiration for the novel is Garneau's historical work, which father and daughter attentively read and discuss. When father Montbrun is killed in a hunting accident, Angéline is thrust into deepest despair. Neither the love for her fiancé Maurice nor any other hope of earthly happiness can relieve her pain, whose deepest roots touch the condition of the entire French-Canadian people. For the heroine, the only hope of an existential balance can be found in work, charity, and the church's support. Several commentators of the nineteenth century have emphasized the autobiographical nature of this novel: The heroine's worship of her father is said to reflect an unhappy romance of the author herself. On the other hand, critics have pointed to an incestuous component in the relationship between father and daughter. From today's perspective, such interpretations demonstrate the difficulty the older French-Canadian criticism must have had with a text of this psychological depth, which went beyond the scope of pious patriotism without questioning its ideals.

# Traditionalism and "Americanness" at the Turn of the Century

In 1901, two thirds of Quebec's population lived in the country; in 1911, it was still fifty-five percent. The industrial development on the North American continent encouraged French-Canadian migration to the cities. With its attractive location at the confluence of railroad lines and waterways, Montreal rose to become the economic center of Canada during the second half of the nineteenth century. The anglophone middle class of Montreal profited in particular from this situation, supported by a number of cultural institutions: McGill University, the outstanding library at the Fraser Institute, the Montreal Museum of Fine Arts, and several good theaters. The francophones were in the majority, thanks to the migration of very large families from rural areas since 1865, so that Montreal became the second largest "French" city after Paris. This was, however, in sharp contrast to the sociocultural weakness of the French-speaking population compared to the anglophones: French Canadians had fewer financial means available to them, and their room for creativity was limited by church control. Still, the situation for obtaining books printed in French in Montreal had slowly improved.

Beginning in the 1880s, the traditional agricultural-messianic models were further challenged by progressing industrialization and urbanization. The dynamic economic metropolis Montreal was at the same time the Canadian city where the lower classes suffered the worst living conditions. The province of Quebec developed into the region with the highest percentage of city dwellers; unemployment, hunger, and need were daily issues for the urban proletariat. The francophone population still bore the mentality of the village, with their willingness to conform to the principles of traditionalism. But critical voices also began to be raised, which argued for the renunciation of bucolic ideals and for the consistent assimilation of French-Canadian society to the economic life of the country as inspired by U.S. American models. The critical analysis of the economic situation, which had already been put forward by the journalist Étienne Parent in the first half of the century, reached a new peak with Édouard Montpetit and Errol Bouchette, who answered Curé Labelle's "Emparons-nous du sol" with "Emparons-nous de l'industrie." Both fought for the modernization of the economy by French Canadians themselves and thus against the development of the land by external investors, as tolerated by traditionalist forces. Other important representatives of political journalism like Henri Bourassa and Olivar Asselin (who together founded the newspaper *Le Devoir* in 1910) also subjected the system of French-Canadian norms and values to a differentiated analysis, paving the way for future criticism of this system.

In literature, criticism was at first only tentative and contradictory. One of its most important voices was that of the École littéraire de Montréal, founded in 1895. The origins of this group probably lie in the Bohemian milieu of young students — Jean Charbonneau (1875–1960) and Louvigny Testard de Montigny (1876–1955) are usually mentioned as initiators of the École — who revolted against the ruling orientation of society and culture and gathered a circle of nonconformist writers. Their goals were manifold: A certain state of neglect of the French language in the context of urban diglossia fed the desire for a newly founded literary society that would occupy itself with the elevation of the linguistic-cultural level. Additionally, there was a growing discontent among the educated with respect to the dominant traditionalist norm and value system that hampered the forces of renewal in French-Canadian literature and caused the differences with other countries, above all with the motherland France, to continually increase. With the École littéraire de Montréal there was for the first time an organization that partially dissociated itself from the traditional interest of defending the Catholic faith and the integrity of the ethnic group: Of the nineteen registered members in the years from 1895 to 1900, not one belonged to the clergy or to the leading circles of the French-Canadian bourgeoisie; several saw writing not as a hobby or pastime but as a serious occupation, if not a calling. They initially met in the private apartments of the president or secretary; beginning in 1898 the public was also admitted to the sessions that then took place in the history-charged Château de Ramezay (built in 1705, and once the residence of the French governor). In 1900 the first collected volume of the group appeared, *Les soirées du Château de Ramezay*, with a patriotic introduction by Charles Gill (1871–1918). The book consists predominantly of lyric texts produced within the École. Attempting to free themselves from the traditionalism of their predecessors, the authors sought their models among the French writers of the symbolist-decadent era, particularly Baudelaire and Verlaine. The contemporary French preference for the Far East, especially for Japan, China, and the South Seas, produced echoes in francophone Canada as well. However, the legacy of French Romanticism and Parnassus poetry was still highly influential for several members of the École littéraire de Montréal. After all, traditionalists such as Nerée Beauchemin and Pamphile Le May were still very active at the beginning of the twentieth century and published some of their most representative works at the same time as the École littéraire de Montréal. In this context it is understandable that the boldness of a Mallarmé or Rimbaud found little resonance even among those francophone writers who declared themselves open to innovation.

The first period in the history of the École was shaped by an extraordinary talent, Émile Nelligan (1879–1941). Nelligan was introduced to the Montreal circle by Arthur de Bussières in 1897 and dominated the lyric production of the group from this point on — until the outbreak of a mental illness that would end the career of the young poet in 1899. While the other poets who belonged to the group from 1895 through the 1930s, or who were associated with it (numbering, approximately, seventy), lacked neither diligence nor ambition, very few were able to offer more than rhetorical skill and goodwill. The poet and painter Gill attempted in *Le cap éternité* (1919) to express his fascination for the St. Lawrence in a plethora of alexandrines. Albert Lozeau (1878–1924), kept bed-ridden by illness, devoted his lyrical work to isolation and the slow stream of time that carries the waiting person along (*L'âme solitaire*, 1907). Arthur de Bussières (1877–1913), like his French model José-Maria de Hérédia, dreamt of picturesque far-off countries and conjured up the temples and landscapes of an imaginary Japan (*Les Bengalis*, 1931). Names like Gonzalve Desaulniers (1863–1934) and Lucien Rainier (1877–1956) are associated with the odd pleasant poem, without having introduced new styles into the literary landscape. In the second phase of the École, the increasing tension between the aestheticism of its founders and rival attempts to emphasize more strongly French-Canadian poetry's connection to the landscape (without following the well-trodden paths of traditionalism) led to a temporary division of the group (1907–1913). Poets more closely tied to the homeland such as Albert Ferland (1872–1943) gathered around the magazine *Le Terroir*, whose ten fascicles were published in book form in 1910. "Exotics" like Paul Morin, René Chopin, and Marcel Dugas, who in turn founded a short-lived magazine (*Le Nigog*, 1918), formed an opposing group. The publication of the École's second anthology, *Les soirées de l'École littéraire de Montréal* in 1925, signaled the peaceful coexistence of the various tendencies. In this third and last phase, Jean-Aubert Loranger (1896–1942) towered above the general mediocrity.

The complete absence of national-traditionalist inspiration in Nelligan, who since a groundbreaking essay by his executor and editor Louis Dantin (1902) has been considered the most talented French-Canadian author of the nineteenth century, is partially explained by the circumstance of his mixed heritage: His father, of Irish background, was anglophone, his mother francophone. To be sure, Nelligan's deep uneasiness with the cultural scene dominated by traditionalism is characterized by a sense of contradiction that can also be found in other turn-of-the-century authors. Yet the radicality of his claim to a life in the service of art earns him a special position. Equally familiar with the literatures of England and France, he chose to orient himself towards French (or francophone) models. For topics, he rarely referred to Canada's history or present; instead, his lyrical oeuvre was molded by those tendencies that also shaped nineteenth-century French literature: Romanticism, Parnassism, symbolism, and decadence. He shared the search for the perfect form with contemporary French writers, as well as the oscillation between longing for fulfillment and the frustrated withdrawal from society, between the dream of tropical paradises and death fantasies. But the religious fervor that is typical of Nelligan's image of women and that is expressed in extreme feelings of guilt is as much a reference to the Quebec context as is the negatively colored nature sentiment that operates in "Soir d'hiver" in the vision of an overpowerful winter:

> Ah! comme la neige a neigé!
> Ma vitre est un jardin de givre.
> Ah! comme la neige a neigé!
> Qu'est-ce que le spasme de vivre
> À la douleur que j'ai, que j'ai!
>
> Tous les étangs gisent gelés,
> Mon âme est noire! Où vis-je? où vais-je?
> Tous ses espoirs gisent gelés:

Je suis la nouvelle Norvège
D'où les blonds ciels s'en sont allés.

Pleurez, oiseaux de février,
Au sinistre frisson des choses,
Pleurez, oiseaux de février,
Pleurez mes pleurs, pleurez mes roses,
Aux branches du genévrier.

Nelligan's image of the poet was neither inspired by the titanism of the leading writers of French Romanticism nor by Rimbaud's alchemy of the word that caused the poet to search for the absolute, but rather by a yearning for purity and moral perfection in harmony with the traditional stock of Quebec norms and values. Nelligan's tragic life — spending forty-one years between his psychic collapse and his death in a mental institution — gave rise to his mythical portrayal as a heroic rebel in conflict with a conservative society. In truth, he rather put his finger on the existential condition of the society that would form the starting point of the cultural criticism of the twentieth century.

The contradiction that French-Canadian authors were living with at the beginning of the twentieth century became particularly evident in the lyrical work of Jean-Aubert Loranger, who can be seen as the most important representative of the last generation of the École littéraire de Montréal. Loranger's poems can both be taken as an implicit commentary on Nelligan's work and as a foreshadowing of future deconstructions of the traditionalist system of norms — for example, by Hector de Saint-Denys Garneau (1912–1943). The collection *Les atmosphères* (1920) outlines the area of conflict between writers who strive for an expansion of the repertoire of forms and themes and those who remain connected to countryside and village. Loranger demonstrated the two sides of the same coin: On the one hand, there was no escaping loyalty to inherited values, while on the other, the fragility of these values was becoming apparent, thus spurring the dream of a freer form of art. Loranger summarized this conflict in the image of the ferryman who enables others to go on their journey while he himself — although constantly in motion — remains in the same place. In the author's texts, which vary between poetry and prose, traditional forms and Haikai techniques from the Far East, traveling proves itself as illusory as being rooted in one's own soil.

# The (Anti-)Homeland Novel Between Tradition and Renewal

Like other cultural norms with a claim to absolute validity, the French-Canadian "survivance" ideology profited from scandals and heretical deviations, often because these had a revitalizing effect and slowed processes of stagnation within the dominant order. Equally, the symptoms of an increasing tension between loyalty to the inherited and the desire for renewal were multiplying around the end of the nineteenth century. Arthur Buies (1840–1901; son of the Scot William Buie, having added another consonant to his name to make it look more French) is particularly noteworthy in this context. Among the journalists of Quebec, Buies, who fought by the side of Garibaldi in Italy, held the critical spirit of the liberals aloft and was unsparing in his anticlerical jabs in his brilliant essays and reports on the country and people of Quebec (for example, "Chroniques, humeurs, caprices," 1873). This left-wing journalism demonstrated that the liberal legacy of the Institut canadien had survived all attacks and was capable of vital development.

In the realm of the novel, *Jeanne la fileuse* (1878) by Honoré de Beaugrand (1848–1906), a plea for French-Canadian emigrants to the United States (who the author felt did not deserve to be stamped as traitors or deceived fools), received little recognition. In 1904, Rodolphe Girard's (1879–1956) novel *Marie Calumet* appeared, a nonconformist text that undermined the foundations of the French-Canadian norm system by means of a carnivalesque treatment of the village theme and a crude satire of the priest and his cook. Just a few years later Albert Laberge (1871–1960) in *La Scouine* sketched the picture of a run-down village world colored by human coldness, ignorance, and greed, which seems much crueler than the one portrayed by the French naturalist Émile Zola in *La Terre* (1887), lacking as it does the latter's mythical portrayal of nature.

Louis Hémon's (1880–1913) novel *Maria Chapdelaine* (1914) fills a unique position in French-Canadian literature, not least because of its success as an international bestseller. For several generations this book was seen as the symbol of Quebec conservatism. Then the attempt was made to rehabilitate Hémon by referring to his social inspiration. In fact, this complex author can best be understood by considering his intercultural orientation: Hémon was born in France and came from a bourgeois family in Brittanny, which he fled as a youthful nonconformist to London. There he struggled by as a sports reporter and writer of stories about ordinary people. The texts written in this period were rediscovered after the success of *Maria Chapdelaine* and enjoy a growing critical interest today. It is a hard, depressing, big-city world that is described here, full of social injustice and unattainable longings. Hémon turned his back on this milieu and went to Canada, leaving a wife and child in dire straits. Before again following his Wanderlust at the age of thirty-three and falling victim to an accident, he discovered human warmth and security in a francophone farming village on the Lac Saint-Jean, and with the zeal of a neophyte adopted the cause of those loyal to the homeland Quebec.

In *Maria Chapdelaine* Quebec's traditionalist system of norms, as cemented in François-Xavier Garneau's history, is combined with the cult of rootedness in the home, as the Breton Hémon could have found it in the work of Provençal bard Frédéric Mistral. Like Mistral's Mirèio in the eponymous work, Maria is also a simple country girl who is inspired by inner voices to heroic self-sacrifice, in the same Joan of Arc model.

> Alors une troisième voix plus grande que les autres s'éleva dans le silence: la voix du pays de Québec, qui était à moitié un chant de femme et à moitié un sermon de prêtre. . . . Elle disait: "Nous sommes venus il y a trois cents ans, et nous sommes restés . . . Autour de nous des étrangers sont venus, qu'il nous plaît appeler des barbares; ils ont pris presque tout le pouvoir; ils ont acquis presque tout l'argent; mais au pays de Québec rien n'a changé. Rien ne changera, parce que nous sommes un témoignage. De nous-même et de nos destinées, nous n'avons compris clairement que ce devoir-là: persister . . . nous maintenir . . ."

By deciding to remain true to farming life despite all temptations, Maria proves herself a match for relentless nature, as well as for the temptations of the American cities. Seen against Hémon's own life and work, the novel points at a score to be settled with both the France of the triumphant bourgeoisie at the time of the Third Republic and with the England of the Victorian Age, which he saw as dominated by capitalist brutality. Hémon's polemic stance paradoxically provides the Quebec value system with a literary formulation that can be received as an unqualified idealization of tradition. If, however, the novels and novellas written in England are considered, the double misunderstanding at the source of the *Maria Chapdelaine* myth becomes clear: Those who only see the arch-conservative prophet of French-Canadian messianism in Hémon have failed to notice that this nomadic social critic wanted to set up a monument to the Quebec village where he found shelter for a while. He himself misunderstood the intercultural situation of his hosts in that he compared them with the resistance of French regions towards the centralism of Paris, rather than having a critical look at the scope of the opposition between traditionalism and "Americanness" in French-Canadian culture.

# Beginnings of a New Theater

In a climate of moral rigor among the French-Canadian public and in the face of effective censorship on the part of the church, francophone theater of the nineteenth and early twentieth centuries in cities like Montreal or Quebec barely expanded beyond tentative beginnings. Nonetheless, there was a strong interest on the side of the population in theater; this was demonstrated by the success of the flourishing English-language theater in

Montreal, which also drew a francophone audience, as well as by the enthusiasm with which French troupes were received on tours. The high point of this series of guest performances were the tours of the French theater star Sarah Bernhardt (1844–1923) with pieces like *Hernani* by Victor Hugo and *La Dame aux Camélias* by Alexandre Dumas (the younger). They provided the strongest impulses for a gradual professionalization of the French-Canadian theater industry that started with the founding of permanent structures at the end of the 1880s (Compagnie franco-canadienne in 1887, Les Soirées de famille in 1898, Le Théâtre des variétés in 1898). One of the main problems with theater in Quebec was the absence of a French-Canadian repertoire of top-quality plays. The authors of the nineteenth century, constantly at pains to avoid excommunication by the moral authorities, had little more to offer than patriotic festival plays, pious melodramas, or trite comedies of mistaken identity. Not until after the turn of the century would this change: One of the founders of the École littéraire de Montréal, Louvigny Testard de Montigny, came to attention with a comedy about gossip as the social game of French-Canadian bourgeois society. The use of polyphony as a structural principle and the vernacular language in this play with the programmatic title *Boule de neige* foreshadow one of the most important pieces of Quebec literature of the twentieth century, *Les belles-soeurs* (1968) by Michel Tremblay (1942–).

# V. The Modern Period, 1918–1967

# 11: Politics and Literature between Nationalism and Internationalism

*Julia Breitbach (University of Constance)*

IN 1926 THE POET A. J. M. SMITH (1902–1980) found Canada immersed in "an age of change, and . . . a change that is taking place with a rapidity unknown in any other epoch. . . . Ideas are changing and therefore manners and morals are changing. It is not surprising, then, to find that the arts, which are an intensification of life and thought, are likewise in a state of flux" ("Contemporary Poetry"). At this point in its history, Smith argued, the forces of modernization had already transformed the country so thoroughly as to infuse it with a new zeitgeist, engendering both a specifically modern mindset (unheard-of ideas, manners, and morals) and an equally iconoclastic artistic scene. While Smith's assessment — with the verve and rhetoric of a modernist innovator — eclipses the many premodern continuities in Canadian society, culture, and artistic practice at the time, it is certainly right in diagnosing "a nation in ferment" (Pacey 1976, 119). In fact, it was the collective experience of change — induced by closely intertwined political, economic, social, and cultural developments — which gave fresh momentum to the idea of a Canadian nation in the first place. Building on the milestone of Confederation, the first half of the twentieth century saw a refueled debate on the merits and drawbacks of national autonomy, with agendas of political and cultural nationalism forming a sometimes harmonious, sometimes conflictual alliance. Given Canada's particularly entangled position as a simultaneously bicultural, colonial, and North American country, these discussions mainly evolved within the triangle of nationalist, internationalist, and continentalist orientations and ambitions. The constant negotiations of Canada's political and cultural profile at home and abroad paved the way for the country's ultimate coming-of-age in the second half of the twentieth century. It is understood here that the forging of a nation as the result of historical events, social developments, and political decisions cannot be separated from the successful pursuit of a *cultural* national identity (see Corse 1997). Nor can this cultural emancipation — as it was, for instance, spurred on by the advocates of Canadian modernism in the first decades of the twentieth century — be conceived without taking into account the sociohistorical and political context.

The desire to assess, sharpen, and defend Canada's national interests on the political stage became unprecedentedly urgent with the country's engagement in the First World War, when the experience of military commitment and allied victory triggered a revision of Canada's international standing and, particularly, her relation to the British Empire. The wave of national sentiment and pride at having won the war seemed to suggest what the liberal prime minister Wilfrid Laurier had already expressed in 1904 with pronounced self-confidence: "The nineteenth century was the century of the United States. I think we can claim that it is Canada that shall fill the twentieth century." Such promotion, as the comparison with the American success story implied, could hardly be achieved if Canada did not wrest more rights of political self-determination and -representation from the mother country. Canada had entered the war automatically under British command, but in light of the substantial war effort and the sacrifice of about 65,000 Canadian lives (out of a population of eight million people) the Canadian government increasingly demanded a greater say in British warfare for the Dominions, which resulted in the creation of the Imperial War Cabinet in 1917. At the end of the war — owing to the persistence of prime minister Robert Borden — Canada (along with Australia, New Zealand, and South Africa) signed the 1919 peace treaty of Versailles in her own right, if still indented under the British signature. Simultaneously, the Dominions became founding members of the League of Nations, obtaining separate representation. Delivered rather abruptly to the realm and responsibility of international politics through the Great War, Canada's policy in the League of Nations reflected the country's special double interests, as a branch of the global British Empire on the one hand, and as part of the North American continent on the other hand. The latter position doubtlessly had its share in Canada's refusal to accept the collective security clause in Article Ten of the Covenant of the League of Nations, which obliged all members to engage in the military defense of any other member against external aggression. Isolationist tendencies in foreign affairs, to be continued in the 1930s, drew the country closer to the United States (which had not joined the League of Nations), as did the steadily growing economic ties, especially extensive U.S. investment in Canada. In 1927 this special continentalist relationship became symbolically cemented with the establishment of Canada's first diplomatic mission abroad in Washington, DC (raised to the status of embassy in 1943). With regard to Great Britain, on the other hand, Canada did not seek independence but equality, which was granted and officially formalized in, respectively, the Balfour Declaration (1926) and the Statute of Westminster (1931):

> [Dominions are] autonomous communities within the British Empire, equal in status, in no way subordinate one to another in any respect of their domestic or external affairs, though united by a common allegiance

to the Crown, and freely associated as members of the British Commonwealth of Nations.

A landmark on the way towards national sovereignty, the Balfour Declaration steered Canada's gradual emancipation over the next decades, manifesting itself, for example, in the formal establishment of Canadian citizenship in 1946 and being eventually completed with the Canada Act of 1982, when Great Britain abandoned its right to make laws affecting Canada, including the Constitution.

Providing a fitting example for the aforementioned close ties between political and cultural nationalism, E. D. Blodgett (2003) has commented that the new "sense of maturity" acquired during the First World War prompted, among other signs of cultural emancipation, the urge to create a national narrative of Canada's literary past — not least to nourish in turn a sense of national unity among Canadians. Hence, the first English-Canadian literary histories appeared during and after the war, striving to define and describe English-Canadian literature, locate its origins, and relate or else contrast it with British and American literatures: Thomas Guthrie Marquis's chapter on "English Canadian Literature" in *Canada and Its Provinces: A History of the Canadian People and Their Institutions* (1914), Ray Palmer Baker's *History of English-Canadian Literature to the Confederation: Its Relation to the Literature of Great Britain and the United States* (1920), Archibald MacMechan's *Headwaters of Canadian Literature* (1924), Lionel Stevenson's *Appraisals of Canadian Literature* (1926), Lorne Pierce's *An Outline of Canadian Literature (French and English)* (1927), J. D. Logan and Donald G. French's *Highways of Canadian Literature: A Synoptic Introduction to the Literary History of Canada (English) from 1760–1924* (1928), and V. B. Rhodenizer's *Handbook of Canadian Literature* (1930). Glenn Willmott (2002) has observed in these pioneering texts the recurring trope of the "nation-as-youth" gradually coming of age, as, for instance, in MacMechan: "The young nation has a soul, which is striving to be articulate" (14); or in Rhodenizer: "Canada is a young country . . . characterized by simplicity, sincerity, eagerness, romanticism, idealism, optimism, courage, and the spirit of adventure, and all of these qualities are found in Canadian litera-ture. The attitude of youth toward convention is often inconsistent, and this is true also of the spirit of Canadian literature" (263–64).

Successful in the war and foreign politics, Canada did not fare as well on the home front, where relations between Ottawa and Quebec — still strained from late nineteenth century conflicts such as the Manitoba Schools Question and the execution of Métis leader Louis Riel — were opened into an even wider rift with the so-called Conscription Crisis of 1917. Quebec vehemently opposed — in the end to no avail — Prime Min-ister Borden's decision to legislate compulsory military service because of a shortage of enlisted men. (When in 1942, then Prime Minister Mackenzie King would also take back his promise not to impose conscription and conducted a plebiscite on the question, Quebec, not surprisingly, again voted against the general draft.) Apart from the wedge of discontent dividing English and French Canada, the country also saw the call to arms of a mutinous working class, who, demanding its share in the economic revival induced by the war, fought for better working conditions in a wave of strikes across the country. Tensions culminated in the 1919 Winnipeg General Strike of 30,000 workers, which the federal government, driven by the specter of Bolshevism, brought to a violent end after six weeks. However, it survived in the nation's collective memory as a significant social touchstone and symbol of class conflict. Another challenge to Canada's domestic politics came with the rising numbers of immigrants (a record of 400,000 in 1912), especially those from non-English- or non-French-speaking countries. Since the beginning of the century the rapid growth of agriculture and the wheat boom in the western provinces (leading to the foundation of two new provinces, Alberta and Saskatchewan, in 1905) had been fueled by the influx of British and American immigrants, who constituted the vast majority of newcomers from 1900 to 1920 (about seventy-five percent of about 3.4 million altogether). In contrast, immigrants with a different ethnic background — regulated through quota systems and the introduction of an English literacy test — often came to populate the industrial centers of Canada's expanding cities, changing the ethnic and cultural composition of an increasingly urbanized and industrialized society. Another marginalized group on the rise, Canada's female population seized the day and successfully pushed its case for women's suffrage onto the federal level with the 1917 Wartime Elections Act, which gave voting rights to women in military service and those related to serving men. The federal franchise was expanded in the following year to include all Canadian women, with the exception of Quebec, where women were enfranchised only in 1940.

From a period of warfare and domestic upheaval, the country entered the doldrums of the Great Depression in the wake of the 1929 U.S. stock market crash and was severely hit by the global effects of economic collapse. Unemployment and inflation soared, and a lingering drought in the prairie provinces forced thousands of farmers to abandon their lands. The government introduced relief measures, partly modeled on Franklin D. Roosevelt's New Deal. More radical initiatives arose with the growing political awareness of farmers and workers, resulting in the formation of two new political parties, both emerging from the province of Alberta. The Cooperative Commonwealth Federation, founded in 1932 and forerunner to the New Democratic Party (1961), was a coalition of farmers, labor representatives, and intellectuals from the League for Social Reconstruction (including F. R. Scott), which advocated government ownership of primary industries and a social welfare system; the Social Credit Party, founded in 1935 by William Aberhart, envisaged the distribution of dividends (social credit) to augment the population's purchasing power. As the decade drew to a close, the country recovered from the hardships of the Depression and with the onset of the Second World War it saw another economic upsurge. Canada had entered the war, this time independently, a few days after Great Britain on 10 September 1939, mobilizing more than a million men and women and mourning 42,000 lost lives during the six years of combat. Again, the war experience accelerated political and social transformations at home, such as the introduction of unemployment insurance (1940) and the increased access of women to the labor force. It also brought the country even closer to the United States, as Prime Minister Mackenzie King and American President Roosevelt agreed on a Permanent Joint Board of Defense in 1940, and Canada came to occupy a mediating role between Great Britain and the United States before the latter entered the war in 1941. Though arguably not as epochal as the First World War in forging Canada's national identity — and also generating less tumult and tension on the home front — the Second World War still further advanced Canadians' pride and self-confidence, providing a springboard for the explosion of creative energies and cultural ambitions in the ensuing decades.

This cultural boom — lending the epithet "Canadian Renaissance" to the 1960s and 1970s — was to a large extent stimulated by an unparalleled level of institutional support in the 1950s. Significant steps to promote the arts on a national scale had already been undertaken in the 1930s, with, for instance, the establishment of the Dominion Drama Festival in Stratford (1932), the Canadian Broadcasting Corporation (CBC, 1936), and the National Film Board (1939). An even more decisive landmark in Canada's cultural history, however, was the famous Massey Report of 1951, named for the Commission's chairman Vincent Massey (1887–1967), who would go on to be Canada's first native-born governor general from 1952 to 1959. Based on a 1949 Royal Commission on National Development in the Arts, Letters and Sciences, the Report issued recommendations as to the government's investment in Canada's cultural traditions and future development, arguing

> that it is desirable that the Canadian people should know as much as possible about their country, its history and traditions; and about their national life and common achievements; that it is in the national interest to give encouragement to institutions which express national feeling, promote common understanding and add to the variety and richness of Canadian life, rural as well as urban. (Massey Report, Part 1, ch. 1)

In order to foster Canada's national profile in and through the arts — especially in the face of "the American invasion by film, radio and periodical" (ibid., ch. 2) and the brain drain of talents headed south of the border — the Canada Council and the National Library were founded in 1957, and substantial financial support was granted to cultural institutions and projects throughout the country.

Of course, such concerted intervention on the part of the federal government could not have been sparked if numerous individual efforts on smaller scales had not already prepared a vital cultural scene in the preceding decades. In contrast to official cultural politics, these endeavors arose, according to Willmott, in a "volatile ferment of ad hoc, local, and amateur means and media," often interlocking, out of necessity, the contents and forms of innovative art with the existing infrastructure of mass culture and thus providing less a radical break with than a "turning inside out" of traditional genres and markets (6–8). Yet despite the strong influence of mass culture and nineteenth-century traditions — manifesting themselves, for example, in the above-mentioned imperialism of American pop culture, the popularity of Canadian magazines such as *Maclean's* (1911) and *Chatelaine* (1928), and the public's continued delight in historical romances and regional idylls — Canada experienced both an increasing institutionalization and professionalization of artistic practice and the emergence of an avant-garde movement, which strove to enhance the quality and international standing of Canadian arts and letters. The avant-garde ushered in a period of modernism, which has been — if not altogether denied (Robert Kroetsch) — the subject of an ongoing debate, ranging from traditional, rather negative assessments as "belated" or "marginal" to more recent affirmative evaluations as an "alternative" or "medial" "counterpoint" to international modernism (see Irvine 2005).

In the context of Canadian writing the new professionalism emerged most visibly in the founding of the Canadian Authors Association in 1921, called into being in response to unfavorable copyright legislation. The CAA soon became a mouthpiece for the material interests of Canadian writers, successfully lobbying for fairer working conditions and financial benefits, such as special income tax privileges. It also developed into a central organ for promoting Canadian writing — which turned out to be a mixed blessing after all. A major achievement was indubitably the CAA's initiation of the Governor General's Award in 1936, Canada's most prestigious national literary prize, which today is annually distributed in fourteen categories for works in both English and French. The CAA itself had assumed the role as judge until the establishment of an independent board in 1944, and in 1959 handed over the administration to the Canada Council. On the other hand, the CAA's literary preferences and politics, as advertised in the pages of *The Canadian Bookman* (1919) and later *Canadian Author & Bookman* (1943), earned the association the reputation of traditionalism, conservatism, and parochialism, clinging to the outdated, colonial poetics of Victorian sensibilities that made Canadian productions automatically second-best to their British models. Even worse, many modernist writers and critics held that the CAA encouraged mediocrity, endorsing unremarkable writers on the sole grounds of their Canadian nationality rather than their literary merits:

> Whatever sympathy one may feel for the aims of the Canadian Authors' Association and however eagerly one may hope for the creation of a worthy national literature, it is impossible to view the excesses of "Canadian Book Week" in a favorable light. . . . the commercial boosting of mediocre Canadian books not only reduces the Authors' Association to the level of an advertising agency but does considerable harm to good literature. After all, it is not so much Canadian books that we should like to see the public buy, as *good* Canadian books; and as there are not very many of these latter yet, we should be very well content with a public that would buy merely good books, regardless whether their writers are English, American, German or Japanese. (*The McGill Fortnightly Review* 1.2 [1925])

Such boosting of the national cause at all costs offended the proponents of modernist innovation, who often responded with scorn and polemics to the CAA's activities, as, for instance, F. R. Scott (1899–1985) in his poem "The Canadian Authors Meet" (1927/rev. 1935; see ch. 12, York):

> O Canada, O Canada, O can
> A day go by without new authors springing
> To paint the native maple, and to plan
> More ways to set the selfsame welkin ringing?

Canadian modernists were themselves divided over the question if and how to advance the case of an explicitly *national* literature. In order to shed the stigma of epigonality and colonial mentality, should Canadian writers adhere to an international orientation, attempting to draw level with the established national literatures of British and European provenance? Or should they embrace the continentalist model, creating Canada's own "homemade world" (Hugh Kenner) of native modernism in the vein of American writers William Carlos Williams or Sherwood Anderson and the like? Or was there even the chance for an "isolationist" alternative, that is, a Canadian literature based on unique, incomparable characteristics — as exemplified perhaps in the realm of painting by the Group of Seven (1920–1933), which combined the traditional subject of landscape painting with original, postimpressionist forms? Last but not least, was Canada's national literature maybe in fact a regional and thus highly diversified one, "discovering in a western grain field, a Quebec *maison*, or in a Montreal nightclub, a spirit and a consciousness distinctly Canadian" (Leo Kennedy 1929)?

The exchange of such conflicting views was nowhere more prominently pursued than in the emerging scene of little magazines. Despite its
taxing position in-between the market dominance of popular presses and
the conservative tastes of the educated elite, the little magazine turned out
to be — in the words of poet, editor, and publisher Louis Dudek
(1918–2001) — "the most important single factor behind the rise and
continued progress of modernism in Canadian poetry" (Dudek and
Gnarowski 1970, 203). In contrast with established academic periodicals
like *Queen's Quarterly* (1893) or the *University of Toronto Quarterly*
(1931) — which has devoted an annual issue "Letters in Canada" to
Canadian publications in the arts and humanities since 1936 — the typical
little magazine was usually a rather volatile, short-lived phenomenon,
more fervent in its debates and more avant-gardist in its poetics. Among
the most influential publications of the 1920s were *The Canadian
Forum* (1920–), as well as the iconoclastic *McGill Fortnightly Review*
(1925–1927; founded by Smith and Scott) and the *Canadian Mercury*
(1928–1929; founded by Scott and Kennedy), all of which basically
espoused international modernism and cosmopolitan aesthetics. In the
1930s leftist agendas came to the fore in, for instance, *Masses* (1932–1934)
and *New Frontier* (1936–1937). The vital role of the little magazine as a
platform for progressive literary debates found its epitome in the legendary
quarrel between the publications *Preview* and *First Statement* (both
1942–1945), represented by the respective editors Patrick Anderson and
John Sutherland. The left-wing *Preview* continued the cosmopolitan,
international outlook of the *McGill Fortnightly Review* and the poets of the
McGill Movement/Montreal Group — A. J. M. Smith, F. R. Scott, Leo
Kennedy, and A. M. Klein — and envisioned the poet as affecting social
change, "a humanist leader of the modern movement" (Anderson in
*Preview* 21 [1944]). *First Statement*, subtitled "A Magazine for Young
Canadian Writers," on the other hand, promoted a "native strain" (Dudek
1976) in writing and the continental orientation toward American modernism, accusing *Preview* of its alleged "colonial pull toward British literature." Sutherland and his poets — such as Louis Dudek, Irving Layton,
and Kay Smith — cultivated the image of a rough-hewn, anti-intellectual
kind of poetry in tune with North American realities and ways of speech.
Nevertheless, both publications would eventually merge, under the editorship of Sutherland, in *Northern Review* (1945–1956), which featured
not only poetry but also fiction and criticism. The erstwhile battle of editors still reverberated, however, in Smith's and Sutherland's proclamation
of alternative canons in their rival anthologies *The Book of Canadian
Poetry: A Critical and Historical Anthology* (1943) and *Other Canadians:
An Anthology of the New Poetry in Canada 1940-1946* (1947). In 1936
Smith had already waged another war, this time against Canada's persistent
adherence to traditional, conservative poetry: His preface to the anthology

*New Provinces*, edited by Scott and featuring the Montreal Group plus E. J. Pratt and R. Finch, had been rejected on the grounds of being too aggressive, but would be included in the anthology's 1976 reissue (see ch. 12, York).

What A. J. M. Smith et al. had done for English-Canadian poetry, Raymond Knister (1899–1932) did for the English-Canadian short story. Himself a writer of short stories, as well as a poet, editor, and literary and cultural critic, Knister mainly distinguished himself through his untiring educational and promotional efforts on behalf of English-Canadian literature in general and short-story writing in particular. In his critical essays he was the first to give an encompassing assessment of the English-Canadian short story, putting it in a predominantly North American context. Of utmost importance for the genre proved his "benchmark anthology" (New 1990, 44) *Canadian Short Stories* (1928), commissioned and published by Macmillan, which featured representative writers from both the nineteenth and twentieth century, for instance, Duncan Campbell Scott and Morley Callaghan. In addition, the anthology took stock of the genre as a whole, providing a "List of Canadian Short Stories in Books and Magazines" (280 texts by 112 writers) and a list of "Books of Short Stories by Canadian Authors" (ninety-one volumes by forty-seven writers). With regard to his own work, Knister exemplifies the difficult professional stand of the Canadian writer of his time, who usually faced a strenuous negotiation of bread-and-butter-jobs and artistic vocation. He also serves as a case in point for the Canadian modernist's peculiar oscillation between high-end avant-garde magazines (*The Midland*, Iowa City; *Poetry*, Chicago; *This Quarter*, Paris) and the payroll of popular presses (*Toronto Star Weekly*, *Maclean's*, *Chatelaine*), thus indeed turning the latter "inside out" through modernist innovation (see Willmott above). Further, Knister's simultaneous appearance in international avant-garde publications (alongside Ezra Pound, James Joyce, and Ernest Hemingway) and in Canada's emerging little magazines (*The Canadian Forum*, for instance) reflects the aforementioned heated debate on Canada's national versus international literary orientation. Knister's criticism contributed to the discussion in a differentiated manner (see, for example, "The Canadian Short Story," 1923; "Introduction: The Canadian Short Story," 1928; "Canadian Literature: A General Impression," 1975; "Canadian Literati," 1975). He acknowledged the far better infrastructure of the American publishing industry and professional situation of American writers; but he also ardently warned against surrendering to a commercialized or Americanized mass culture that demands and produces only formulaic, easily marketable texts. Similarly, he firmly believed in Canadian literature as an up-and-coming *national* literature — the "expression of an indigenous mode of life and thought" ("Canadian Literature") — and relentlessly strove to promote the qualities of Canadian writing among his own incredulous country (wo)men. Yet, he also strongly advocated the exposure of Canadian literature to international standards, contexts, and traditions and argued particularly for a pronounced North American orientation.

Knister's introduction to *Canadian Short Stories* had put the genre at the forefront of Canada's literary emancipation as an increasingly self-confident player on an international stage: "In nothing have we more clearly passed an epoch than in the short story, here in Canada. Literature as a whole is changing, new fields are being broken, new crops are being raised in them, and the changes apparent in other countries show counterparts in our development." Significantly, the short story would indeed soon rise to unprecedented prominence and excellence, eventually becoming a leading genre during the Canadian Renaissance. Here and elsewhere, the cultural energies of the first half of the twentieth century — poised as they were between national, continental, and international commitment and ambition — had laid the groundwork for a still more far-reaching national awakening of Canadian literature and (cultural) politics in the decades to come.

# 12: English-Canadian Poetry, 1920–1960

*Lorraine York (McMaster University)*

S PEAKING OF THE PERIOD from 1920 to 1960, Margaret Atwood stated in her introduction to the *New Oxford Book of Canadian Verse* (1982) that "this, for me, is the age that only the usual Canadian cautiousness and dislike of hyperbole prevents me from calling golden." The years between 1920 and 1960 were indeed a period of prodigious activity and contention in English-Canadian poetry, and the contentiousness was as productive a force as was the energetic publishing of poems, collections, manifestos, and little magazines. These were also, of course, years that were overshadowed by two world wars; and those global events were felt most powerfully in the poetic activity of the period: in a wave of postwar modernist poetic practice in the 1920s, in a slowing of poetic production in the 1930s, when the Depression and then another looming war delayed the appearance of a number of poetic voices, and in a reinforcement of a sense of political urgency in the works that did appear during this time.

## Modernism Revisited

Until recently, this period in the history of Canadian poetry had followed a strongly defined, well-established narrative. This familiar story has now been both challenged and refined. Typically, the narrative of poetic activity in Canada between the years of 1920 and 1960 had been a tale of triumphant modernism: of a sweep of postwar cosmopolitanism that left earlier poetics in the dustbin of literary history, followed by a quiet, otherwise-preoccupied period of the 1930s, and culminating in a dramatic conflict between competing poetic forces of aestheticism and political consciousness during the 1940s and 1950s. To a degree, this narrative has a good deal of truth to it. But it can only benefit from and be deepened in complexity and interest by a concern for the exceptions and shades of gray that were usually ignored. The narrative of modern English-Canadian poetry has been overwhelmingly a conservative one. This view persists to this day, and even literary histories of the period that seek to disrupt this well-worn narrative still tend to neglect other relations of power — gender, race, sexualities — that animate it. Recent reinvestigations of the nature of Canadian modernism, invigorated by a 2003 conference "The Canadian

Modernists Meet" at the University of Ottawa, make exactly this point, and have spearheaded an attempt to reread Canadian modernism, in poetry and other genres, by paying close attention to the historical exclusions that the earlier narrative has enabled.

One sign of the increasing industrialization of writing in Canada was the formation of professional societies, such as the Canadian Authors Association (CAA), founded in 1921. As part of the canonical narrative of Canadian modern poetry mentioned above, the CAA often figures as a symbol of mediocrity and mindless national boosterism, most explicitly and infamously in F. R. Scott's (1899–1985) much-quoted poem "The Canadian Authors Meet":

> Expansive puppets percolate self-unction
> Beneath a portrait of the Prince of Wales.
> Miss Crotchet's muse has somehow failed to function,
> Yet she's a poetess . . .

The stuttering alliteration of the opening line neatly skewers poetic mediocrity, while the imperial portrait underneath which these poetasters ply their trade glances at the colonialism of their poetic ventures. Also folded into this critique of cut-rate colonial derivativeness is a sexist broadside against the feminization of poetry that feminist critics of Canadian modernism have not been slow to notice.

One of the new insights afforded by more recent investigations into modernist poetry in Canada is a reminder of how marginal an enterprise it was in the 1920s. If one subscribes to the received narrative of modernist iconoclasm, then the movement appears to have been triumphant from the outset: a sudden, revolutionary overturning of Victorian and Romantic aesthetic and poetic practice. But as scholars such as Brian Trehearne, in his study *Aestheticism and the Canadian Modernists* (1989), have shown, the stirrings of modernist poetry in Canada took place amid a great deal of conflict and continued adherence to earlier poetic practices. Aestheticism is Trehearne's choice of one such earlier influence, and he convincingly traces its workings in poets such as A. J. M. Smith and F. R. Scott. Of other poets of the period who have been reckoned "minor," such as Neil Tracy, Frank Oliver Call, Frederick Philip Grove, Louis Mackay, Leo Kennedy, and Robert Finch, Trehearne asks why, if modernist poetry held such sway, these poets chose to keep writing in fairly traditional verse forms? Such questioning is salutary, for it allows us to see the coming of modernism to Canadian poetry in all its complexity: The new aesthetics and forms did not simply sweep away all that had come before, but came into contact and conversation with previous poetic movements.

Quoted above as an instance of modernist iconoclasm, Scott's "The Canadian Authors Meet" had first been published in the *McGill*

*Fortnightly Review* in 1927, founded by Scott as a student, together with A. J. M. Smith and Leon Edel. Here, the poem had ended in a somber tone:

> Far in a corner sits (though none would know it)
> The very picture of disconsolation,
> A rather lewd and most ungodly poet
> Writing these verses, for his soul's salvation.

In a later version, which appeared in the influential modernist anthology *New Provinces* (1935), the final stanza was excised, and the poem closed on its dominantly satirical tone:

> O Canada, O Canada, O can
> A day go by without new authors springing
> To paint the native maple, and to plan
> More ways to set the selfsame welkin ringing?

Clearly, this particular excision makes for a more effective satirical impact of the poem as a whole, and can easily be explained on that basis. But scholars have found other implications in Scott's revision. Trehearne, for instance, sees in the excised stanza evidence of Scott's involvement in Decadent poetics: For who, he asks, but a decadent poet was so keenly aware of his or her sinfulness ("ungodly poet") and yet yearned so passionately for "his soul's salvation"? Dean Irvine suggests a literary historical reading, arguing that, in 1927, modernism was still a marginal presence on the Canadian poetic scene; well might Scott's poet find himself scribbling disconsolately, far away in his corner. By the time *New Provinces* appeared — self-described as the first anthology of modernist Canadian poetry — literary modernism could so clearly be seen to have carried the day that the original ending of Scott's poem no longer seemed appropriate. Both readings reveal much about the way in which modernism in Canadian poetry is now being understood and revised. It is considered a decidedly more complicated movement than formerly assumed, and critics and literary historians now hesitate to see it as the product of a groundswell of revolutionary poetics. Instead, modernism in Canadian poetry is being read as a fascinating amalgamation of Victorian, Romantic, decadent, aestheticist, *and* modernist practice. Moreover, it was a mixed, contested poetic import, and its success served as an occasion to rewrite its history, effectively obscuring its complicated, hybrid, and tenuous beginnings.

# A. J. M. Smith and E. J. Pratt

One poet who is both credited with embodying a new modernist aesthetic and whose work has been productively reread for this sort of complexity is A. J. M. Smith (1902–1980). Many of his best-known poems have been reprinted and taught over the years for precisely their exemplary modernism. For instance, a poem like "The Lonely Land" (originally entitled "Group of Seven" after the consciously nationalist school of painters that included A. Y. Jackson and Lawren Harris) joined a modernist aesthetic with a nationalist flavor that, together, ensured its status as an emblematically modern Canadian poem for years to come:

> Cedar and jagged fir
> uplift sharp barbs
> against the gray
> and cloud-piled sky;
> and in the bay
> blown spume and windrift
> and thin, bitter spray
> snap
> at the whirling sky;
> and the pine trees
> lean one way.

Still, reading Smith as influenced by the cosmopolitan modernism of T. S. Eliot, Ezra Pound, and H. D. alone downplays the manifold creative influences at work in his poetry, and more recent scholars have discerned the influence of aestheticism and surrealism in his writing.

Smith joined to his poetic practice a long career as a critic and anthologist, penning manifestos for the new movement even when he settled in the United States to teach at Michigan State University (academic, like other jobs, were scarce in Canada during the Great Depression). In a now famous passage from a rejected preface to the anthology *New Provinces*, he lambasts the poetry that appeared in earlier anthologies:

> The Canadian poet, if this kind of thing truly represents his feelings and his thoughts, is a half-baked, hyper-sensitive, poorly adjusted, and frequently neurotic individual that no one in his senses would trust to drive a car or light a furnace. He is the victim of his feelings and fancies, or of what he fancies his feelings ought to be, and his emotional aberrations are all out of proportion to the experience that brings them into being. He has a soft heart and a soft soul; and a soft head.

The preface was rejected not only by the publisher, Macmillan, but also by Smith's coeditor and fellow contributor E. J. Pratt (1882–1964), because of its wholesale dismissal of all previous Canadian poetry. Pratt threatened to withdraw from the project, and Macmillan threatened not to publish the volume at all. As Smith later reflected, the preface was indeed brash and arrogant, but he felt that its harsh tone would have been beneficial to the project of an evolving Canadian poetry.

This controversy demonstrates Canadian poetic modernism's contestatory nature. Clearly, there were manifold modernisms at work here. Consider, for that matter, the poetry of Pratt himself, who is sometimes hailed as Canada's first modernist poet. His volume *Newfoundland Verse*, which appeared in 1923, represents, according to some critics, the first modernist verse published in Canada. In a short lyric like "The Shark," for instance, he moves from a traditional-sounding iambic meter to a sparer free verse and reveals a fascination with the meeting points of industrialization and nature that would characterize his entire oeuvre:

> He seemed to know the harbour,
> So leisurely he swam;
> His fin
> Like a piece of sheet-iron,
> Three-cornered,
> And with knife-edge,
> Stirred not a bubble
> As it moved
> With its base-line on the water.

But Pratt also wrote long epic, mythic poems full of archaic and scientific terminology about the Titanic, Brébeuf, and the construction of the Canadian Pacific Railway. Hailed by Northrop Frye as Canada's epic bard, Pratt produced, in these long poems, formidable narratives of the grand struggles of history. Densely packed with the technical languages of science, mythological reference, and archaisms, they produced an impression of historical opera. A particularly striking case in point is the description of the Laurentian Shield in "Towards the Last Spike":

> On the North Shore a reptile lay asleep –
> A hybrid that the myths might have conceived,
> But not delivered, as progenitor
> Of crawling, gliding things upon the earth.

Lines like these are not easily reconciled with the conventional notions of modernist poetry as iconoclastic revolution. As has often been remarked, although Pratt is associated with the advent of modernism in Canadian poetry, he belonged to no school, and clearly he was not willing to burn all bridges with preceding poetics.

# Female Voices

Though recent scholarship has been eager to refine the history of modern poetry in English Canada, one aspect has remained largely untouched: its gendered exclusions. In many ways, this is a by-product of the way in which male participants in these movements narrated their literary history. The most infamous example is that of Louis Dudek and Michael Gnarowski's volume *The Making of Modern Poetry in Canada* (1967): A valuable casebook of primary documents regarding poetic practice from the 1920s to the 1950s, it nevertheless tells the story of that "making" as an almost exclusively male endeavor; P. K. Page (1916–), who emerged in the 1940s, is the only female poet to merit mention in their volume — in a mere three sentences. More recent readings of the period, such as Trehearne's *Aestheticism and the Canadian Modernists*, retain the masculinist air. In his 1999 study *The Montreal Forties* Trehearne makes good on this neglect to some extent, devoting a substantial chapter to Page. In his introduction he diminishes the role of feminist criticism for the study of Page's work, however: "Criticism of her poetry through the unifocal lens of gender has ironically concealed her central place among male poets" (5). This seems a too easy and troubling dismissal: Leaving aside for the moment the assumption that gender approaches are "unifocal," there is also the questionable assertion that feminist attention to female poets somehow lifts them out of their contemporary milieu. It seems as though this decontextualizing effect has been more often the work of masculinist literary historians rather than of feminist revisionists.

Indeed, as Wanda Campbell and others have pointed out, women came to the fore with important collections of poetry during this period. Dorothy Livesay (1909–1996), for instance, published her first collection of poems, *Green Pitcher*, in 1928 and would go on to have a long and remarkable career well into the 1980s. A critical commonplace has been to associate Livesay's early poetry with the modernist avant-garde movement of imagism (Ezra Pound, H. D., etc.), as well as with the stylistics of American Romanticist Emily Dickinson, and to marginalize it as derivative, as a mere apprenticeship to her own distinctive contribution to Canadian poetry. Those influences are certainly felt there, but there is also a stylistic flexibility that is suggestive of some of her formally freer later poems:

> I cannot shut out the light —
> nor its sharp clarity.
> The many blinds we draw,
> you and I,
> the many fires we light
> can never quite obliterate

> the irony of stars
> the deliberate moon
> the last, unsolved finality of night.

In a collection that otherwise invites comparisons with Pound, H. D., or Dickinson, these lines display a skillful mixture of poetic practices past and present, rather than a monochromatic palette of styles. An undergraduate at the University of Toronto when her first collection was published, Livesay already shows Canadian modern poetry being written in the variegated way that recent scholars of the field suggest that it was.

Other representatives of the decade, though less critically recognized than Livesay, were the poets Louise Bowman (1882–1944) and Katherine Hale (1878–1956), whose works have recently been reappraised by Wanda Campbell. Publishing in the early 1920s, both figure as early Canadian practitioners of free verse. Lines by Bowman, for instance, bear a remarkably flexible style, self-consciously mirroring her dual commitment to poetic tradition and innovation that she explicitly ponders in "Darkness":

> It seems to be a foregone conclusion;
> That if I worship the new gods
> Sincerely, in the sunshine —
> I must not pray in the moonlight,
> By the shrines of the old gods
> Where the cherry blossoms still shine.
> But sometimes in the darkness
> I mistake the shrines.

Literary histories of modern Canadian verse tell about early experiments with free verse by Frank Oliver Call (1878–1956) — who divided his 1920 collection *Acanthus and Wild Grape* into formally metered poetry (symbolized by the classical "acanthus") and free-verse poems (suggested by the untamed "wild grape") — but they have not, until very recently, included accounts of such experiments by Bowman. And though one is likely to find A. J. M. Smith's "The Lonely Land" in almost any anthology, Katherine Hale will be missing:

> It looms up larger than I dreamed;
> Roadways of rock
> And canyons full of light;
> Niched balconies for pines bent all one way;
> Small birds in flight,
> Dashing against the dark
> Of that vast rocky flank

Over the next two decades, more female poets came to national prominence, and they were by no means as absent from the trendsetting 1920s
as standard literary histories of the period suggest.

# The 1930s and 1940s

The 1930s and 1940s were tumultuous times, and Canadian poets increasingly felt called upon to respond to them in their writings. The period
began with Canada plunged into the Depression and, from there, into the
Second World War. The most direct, material implication of these shatter-
ing world events for Canadian poetry of the time was the delay in book
publication of several of the period's most promising poets until after the
war. The Depression had a devastating effect on the publishing industry in
Canada, and one must also take into account the wartime paper shortage.
Also, poets were organizing as never before, and not just in the name of
improving working conditions for writers, as the CAA continued to do.
Dorothy Livesay, along with thirty-four other writers and intellectuals,
founded the Progressive Arts Club in 1932, the same year that *Signpost*
appeared. It collected poems from the late 1920s, but in the 1930s and
1940s Livesay would turn to a more explicitly political poetry. The
Progressive Arts Club, for its part, sponsored writings and performances
that raised awareness of social conditions, including the presentation of
agitprop drama. F. R. Scott, along with historian Frank Underhill, formed
the League for Social Reconstruction in the same year, a group dedicated
to working for social equity. Such groups mirror the formation on the larger
political scene of new parties and organizations such as the Cooperative
Commonwealth Federation (CCF) in 1932, the democratic socialist forerunner of today's New Democratic Party, and the founding of the Social
Credit party in Alberta in 1935, a party founded on monetary policy that
would seek to make workers shareholders and distribute a form of credit to
them for their labor. A fascinating memoir of this period and of the role of
art therein is Livesay's *Right Hand, Left Hand* (1977), which details her
association with the Communist Party of Canada, the links between her
social activities and her writing, and her growing awareness that class politics in Canada was, at this point, far from reckoning with gender politics: In
theory, she writes, women were comrades in the struggle; in practice, they
were still chained to the kitchen — a rueful insight that women would
rediscover in the civil rights and anti-Vietnam movements of the 1960s.

Livesay's writing of the 1930s and 1940s is neatly summed up in her
well-known poem "Day and Night." Echoing — and inverting — the title
of Cole Porter's song of carefree lovers clad in evening wear, Livesay's pul-
sating rhythms recreate, instead of a luxurious ballroom, the clanging of
factory machines:

> One step forward
> Two steps back
> Shove the lever,
> Push it back

The rhythms also owe a great deal to the agitprop performances sponsored by groups like the Progressive Arts Club; not surprisingly, given Livesay's political stance at the time, the poem ends with a ringing call to revolution:

> The wheel must limp
> Till it hangs still
> And crumpled men
> Pour down the hill.
>
> Day and night
> Night and day
> Till life is turned
> The other way!

What is somewhat surprising is that, in spite of Livesay's explicit connections with the Communist party, and the menacing reference to the "crumpled men" whose sacrifice is seen as necessary to class revolt, Livesay won the Governor General's Award for poetry for her 1944 collection *Day and Night*. Though the awards were still under the governance of the CAA, this marked the first year that an independent jury undertook the judging of the awards.

## Ethnic Communities

During the 1930s and 1940s, and particularly during the war, relations among ethnic communities as well as classes were tested, and once again the poetry of the time shows evidence of the tension. Anti-Semitism was not only present but unabashedly visible; it was not uncommon in the 1930s to see signs forbidding Jews at resorts, clubs, or beaches in Manitoba, British Columbia, Nova Scotia, and Quebec. In June of 1939, the government of Liberal William Lyon Mackenzie King refused to let the "St. Louis," a boat filled with 907 Jewish refugees from Europe, land on Canadian soil. This instance is the most appalling example of the anti-Semitic immigration policy in place for some years. Between 1933, the year of Hitler's accession to power, and 1939, the outbreak of the Second World War, Canada only accepted four thousand Jewish immigrants, the lowest number among Western countries. Domestically, 21,000 Japanese Canadians were interned or sent to work or detention camps in 1942; often families were split up and their property seized by the government.

Livesay's documentary poem "Call My People Home," which treated the forced evacuation of Japanese Canadians, was aired on CBC Radio after the war in 1949. For some years, Livesay had been drawn to the documentary form, inspired by experiments by John Grierson at the National Film Board and by American poet Archibald MacLeish's radio documentaries on American themes. Increasingly, she came to see the documentary form as having a special resonance for Canadian poetry. In an influential article, "The Documentary Poem: A Canadian Genre" (1969), she emphasized the importance of irony as a by-product of the mixture of document and subjective interpretation that is fundamental to the genre. In this, she influenced generations of poets after her who were drawn, for a wide range of reasons, to the documentary mode: Robert Kroetsch, Daphne Marlatt, and Michael Ondaatje, to name but a few.

Another poet of the time who was inspired by the question of relations among Canadian ethnic communities was A. M. Klein (1909–1972), arguably the most brilliantly original poet of his generation. Like Livesay and Scott he was committed to political activism; a lawyer and poet, he also was vigorously involved in the Canadian Zionist movement in the 1940s, serving as editor of prominent publications for the cause, and running, in 1948, as a CCF candidate in Montreal. Poems from his first two collections, *Hath Not a Jew* (1940) and *Poems* (1944), frequently delve into his own cultural background. As a learned student of Talmud and fluent in both Hebrew and Yiddish, Klein explored through his poetry ethical questions about tradition, justice, and the besetting problem of evil. Other poems, like "Psalm XXXVI: A Psalm Touching Genealogy" from *Poems*, are moving testimonials to community, specifically the responsibility of the individual to the group:

> Not sole was I born, but entire genesis:
> For to the fathers that begat me, this
> Body is residence. Corpuscular,
> They dwell in my veins, they eavesdrop at my ear,
> They circle, as with Torahs, round my skull,
> In exit and in entrance all day pull
> The latches of my heart, descend, and rise —
> And there look generations through my eyes.

Such a lyric is not only religious, but profoundly political, when read in the context of Klein's poetic career and his political milieu. Scholars like Zailig Pollock have argued that, for all of his attachment to his culture, Klein still felt torn between it and the freedom that literary modernism seemed to offer. A confident break from the past of the sort that Smith and Scott were at least overtly proposing in the 1920s, however, would not come without troubling consequences in Klein's view. At the same time, Pollock has maintained that Klein's attachment to his heritage made the rootlessness often associated with modernism deeply unattractive to him.

In his 1948 collection *The Rocking Chair and Other Poems* Klein turned his attention to the question of relations among various ethnic communities. Writing out of Quebec's rich mixture of ethnicities, Klein sought to find and meditate on parallels between his Jewish heritage and that of the Québécois, whom he saw as a comparable nation of people who persisted through time. For all that, however, Klein's depiction of Quebec has raised political hackles, for he wrote nostalgic poems about "this static folk," as he calls them in "The Rocking Chair." Similarly, his well-intentioned lyric "Indian Reservation: Caughnawaga," though explicitly condemnatory of the economic conditions found on the reserve, tends to draw upon the myth of the dying race that has been so forcefully critiqued by indigenous scholars.

## Postwar Developments

In the same collection of poems, and acting as its ringing moment of closure, is Klein's best-known poem, "Portrait of the Poet as Landscape." An original foray into the condition of the poet as shunned minority, this poem both mourns contemporary disregard for poetry and glories in the love of language that creates and, ironically, revivifies the poet:

> For to praise
> the world — he, solitary man — is breath
> to him. Until it has been praised, that part
> has not been. Item by exciting item —
> air to his lungs, and pressured blood to his heart —
> they are pulsated, and breathed, until they map,
> not the world's, but his own body's chart!

The poem closes with a synthesis of mourning and celebration for this "solitary man" who "lives alone, and in his secret shines, / like phosphorus. At the bottom of the sea." The poetic gift shines richly, but undetected by many. The text describes the inhospitable climate for poetry in Canada in the 1940s — before the 1950s saw a turn to the fostering of national culture, as embodied in the establishment of the Canada Council and its program of grants in 1957, and the gradual enlargement of publishing venues after the war.

For female poets, this gradual opening up of postwar publishing was a boon. A commanding voice to emerge in those years was that of P. K. Page, who began publishing in periodicals in the early 1940s, then in a collection with four other poets in 1944, and finally in her first solo collection, *As Ten, As Twenty*, in 1946. Her poetry is philosophically rich, technically demanding, and deeply concerned with vision and spiritual search. Some of her poetry from the 1940s reflects social concerns; one of her best-known poems, "The Stenographers," explores the realm of mechanization, thematically similar to Livesay but in a language that is much more highly worked:

> In the felt of the morning the calico-minded,
> sufficiently starched, insert papers, hit keys,
> efficient and sure as their adding machines;
> yet they weep in the vault, they are taut as net curtains
> stretched upon frames. In their eyes I have seen
> the pin men of madness in marathon trim
> race round the track of the stadium pupil.

The opening of this last stanza shows technical dexterity, with the consonance, alliteration, and meter neatly recalling the mechanical rhythms of typing. But it is the closing, terrifyingly condensed image that captures the quality of most of Page's poetry. Thus, attempts to pigeonhole Page's work as aestheticist or as political may simply be asking the wrong questions of that oeuvre. Recently, Shelley Hulan has suggested that Page's poetry confounds other attempts at categorization, in this case the assumption that Canadian modernist poets were wary of emotion: In Page's poems intellection and emotion are not conceivable as opposed dualities; even in the early lyric "The Stenographers" the justice of such an observation seems clear.

What the case of Page and of another female poet of the 1940s, Anne Marriott (1913–1997), makes clear is that although women took advantage of the increase of publication opportunities after the war, they did so working under particular, gendered restraints. As Marilyn Rose observes of Marriott, who rose to prominence in 1939 with the publication of the long poem *The Wind Our Enemy*, powerful male mentors played a significant role in her career. In the case of Marriott, it was Dorothy Livesay's father, the respected journalist J. F. B. Livesay, who recommended the poems to the editor Lorne Pierce at Ryerson Press in Toronto. Later cited by Livesay as one of Marriott's representative documentary poems, *The Wind Our Enemy* is an entrancing sequence that positions the wind itself as protagonist. Marriott won the Governor General's Award with her next volume, *Calling Adventurers!* (1941), which also featured documentary narrative. But as the 1940s wore on, Marriott wanted, like most poets, to experiment with other forms and modes, and so she moved away from the long documentary poem to shorter lyrics. These proved less attractive to some of her mentors and publishers, and there followed a long poetic silence between the end of that decade and the 1970s. Rose also argues that the vagaries of Marriott's life, that is, the moves necessitated by her husband's work, had the effect of removing her from the sustaining circle of other modern women poets like Livesay, Page, Miriam Waddington, and Kay Smith.

However, female poets like Livesay and Page persisted into the 1950s and beyond, and they were joined by other poets who took modern poetry in Canada in new directions. Earle Birney (1904–1995) was a perfect example of a modern poet whose practice was nourished equally by the old and the new. He is best known for his 1942 work "David," a poetic narrative of a young man who must face the ethical decision of offering death to his friend who is horribly injured during a mountain-climbing expedition. During war, a time notoriously rife with such dilemmas, the poem resonated with readers (a fact that would distress Birney in later years, for he faced continuing speculation over whether the poem was based on his own experience). Birney also has a special place in Canadian poetic history as a supporter of innovative writing; in revising his poems in the 1960s, he followed contemporary practice and replaced conventional punctuation with spaces. He was also at the forefront of experiments with concrete and sound poetry, and defended the work of other, new poets, who were working in such media.

Raymond Souster (1921–) shared with Birney this fostering of newer poetic voices and techniques. In the 1950s, along with Dudek and Irving Layton, he helped to bring the work of American Black Mountain writers (Charles Olson and Robert Creeley) to the attention of the Canadian poetic community, and later, in 1966, he edited the anthology *New Wave Canada*, which was an important early outlet for experimental and younger poets, such as Daphne Marlatt, Victor Coleman, bpNichol, and Michael Ondaatje. Souster's own poetic practice was not experimental so much as it was dedicated to the expression of poetic images in colloquial diction; in many ways, his writing harks back to imagist poets like William Carlos Williams or the Canadian W. W. E. Ross (1894–1966). Politically, this affiliation was born of a desire on Souster's part to offer social commentary in a way that is accessible to all; to quote from a poem he wrote in 1969 ("Get the Poem Outdoors"):

> Get the poem outdoors under any pretext,
> reach through the open window if you have to,
> 　kidnap it right off the poet's desk

Irving Layton (1912–2006), who had been publishing poems in the 1940s, only came to the attention of a Canadian audience in the 1950s, mainly as a result of being promoted by influential American poets. Robert

Creeley praised his poetry, and William Carlos Williams wrote an admiring preface to his first selected volume, *The Improved Binoculars* (1956). Layton's ebullient, Lawrentian poetry influenced a generation of poets to come, who would also find inspiration in the works of contemporary American poets, particularly the Black Mountain poets Creeley and Olson. This Layton joined to an energy and philosophy reminiscent of Nietzsche, to create a poetry that was forceful and emotive. As he writes in his tribute "The Birth of Tragedy":

> And me happiest when I compose poems
>> Love, power, the huzza of battle
>> are something, are much;
> yet a poem includes them like a pool
>> water and reflection
> In me, nature's divided things —
>> Tree, mould on tree —
>> have their fruition;
> I am their core. Let them swap,
> bandy, like a flame swerve
> I am their mouth; as a mouth I serve.

As the 1950s wore on, poets like Layton and Louis Dudek (1918–2001), who saw themselves alienated from the earlier aesthetics espoused by Smith and Scott in the 1920s, were joined by poets who took a very different path in that they turned to the study of myth as a signifying system. In contrast to Layton's passionate verve, they coolly presented a poetry of witty mythic allusion. The seminal influence here was the scholarship of Northrop Frye, who in his 1947 study of William Blake, *Fearful Symmetry*, embarked on his structuralist study of myth. In his *Anatomy of Criticism* (1957) Frye refined and further classified his systematic thinking about myth and genre (see ch. 22, Rosenthal). What poets in the 1950s learned from Frye — some of them directly, as students — was the possibility of myth as a structuring system. The two poets who rose to prominence in this regard were James Reaney and Jay Macpherson. Reaney (1926–) wrote poems that fused Frye's mythic structures with the documentary urge that had long been a strain in Canadian poetry; in poems set in his hometown of Stratford, Ontario, he saw the customs of the small town through the lens of larger mythical dimensions.

Jay Macpherson (1931–), whose most celebrated collection is *The Boatman* (1957), displayed a distinctive capacity to write of mythological tales and figures using a witty, flippant, epigrammatic style; a good example is the opening of "Euronyme II":

> Come all old maids that are squeamish
> And afraid to make mistakes,
> Don't clutter your lives up with boyfriends:
> The nicest girls marry snakes.

Not surprisingly, she counts as a major influence on one of the most celebrated poets to emerge from Canada in the very next decade: Margaret Atwood, whose lyrics "Helen of Troy Does Countertop Dancing" and "Circe/Mud" clearly owe a great deal to Macpherson.

## Conclusion

Whatever the narrative that one describes in writing about English-Canadian poetry during the eventful years between 1920 and 1960, one thing is certain: The observation about Canadian modernism that irks most scholars in the field — novelist and poet Robert Kroetsch's claim that "Canadian literature evolved directly from Victorian into Postmodern" — can only sound viable if one imagines a clichéd cosmopolitan modernism. That particular version of modernism was glimpsed but briefly in the manifestos of Smith and Scott, and even then, recent scholars have convincingly shown that it does not tell the entire story of modern poetry in Canada or even the story of the poetic oeuvres of these individual poets. What was being written between 1920 and 1960 was no missing link on the evolutionary march to postmodern playfulness — it was a richly varied, complexly articulated poetry that continues to be unearthed.

# 13: The English-Canadian Novel and the Displacement of the Romance

*Marta Dvorak (Université Paris 3–Sorbonne Nouvelle)*

ACCORDING TO NORTHROP FRYE, English-Canadian literature is marked by a five-century-long oscillation between the romantic tendency, on the one hand, moving in the direction of myth and metaphor and their formulaic units, and the realistic tradition, on the other hand, moving in the opposite direction, displacing or adjusting such improbable formulas so as to produce verisimilitude (Frye 1976, 36–37). English-Canadian cultural production can thus be situated at opposite extremes. In the period between 1918 and 1967, a large part is grounded in the themes and motifs of the folktale, in the structures of the mythopoeic or marvelous, and in the implausible, erotic, and often violent world of romance. Simultaneously, a large part of cultural production, derivative of a society fascinated by history as well as by social observation, has long been anchored in documentary or expository material for which English-Canadian film, poetry, life writing, and historical and historiographical fiction are well known.

Among the best-known writers resorting to mythical and romantic formulas, and claiming entitlement to the freedom to "lie" — that is, to make full use of the imaginative faculty — is the American Nathaniel Hawthorne. In the introductory chapter to *The Scarlet Letter: A Romance* (1850), entitled "The Custom-house," Hawthorne provided the framework for an artistic manifesto on the prerogatives of the "romance writer" to create a "neutral territory, somewhere between the real world and fairyland, where the Actual and the Imaginary may meet, and each imbue itself with the nature of the other" (66). The themes and motifs of the folktale, of fantasy, and the supernatural have always belonged to the stylized formulas of prose romance. Writers of the burgeoning genre of the novel, as Northrop Frye has remarked, essentially displaced the structural features of romance with which readers were familiar and grounded them in ordinary experience. The highly coded patterns and predictable, often flat characters of contemporary Canadian popular literature — be it the thriller, the Western, the (neo)gothic, or science fiction and fantasy, which Frye in *The Bush Garden* terms "formula-writing" (234) — belong to the domain of romance. At the risk of oversimplifying, several distinctions can be made: Realism keeps the action horizontal, generating an illusion of logic and causality, while the more sensational romance makes use of the affect for purposes of persuasion, and moves from one discontinuous episode to another. The romance writer tends to choose a subject remote in time, while the realist deals with contemporary experience, but the divergent frameworks function in each case to promote or critique certain social values.

## Forms of Romance

Frances Brooke's (1724–1789) *The History of Emily Montague* (1769), the earliest novel to emanate from the North American continent, is replete with the coincidences, melodramatic disclosures, mistaken identities, and *dei ex machinae* of the popular romance. Yet underlying the work one can discern the undercurrents of triangular geopolitical relations (England; the newly acquired colony of what is today Quebec; and the older and more restless Thirteen Colonies; but also the English gentry; the newly displaced, expatriate colonials; and the established French seigneurial class). The focus on love and marriage is actually an indirect but didactic reflection on social order, and an interrogation of political, social, religious, and philosophical issues, which oscillate between the transgressive dynamics of satire and the conservative dynamics of sentimentalism. Moreover, Brooke's romance is exemplary of an identifiable epistemological dimension of the genre, which exposes the problematic relations between truth and perception or subjectivity, and which stages through techniques such as multiple points of view a certain indeterminacy and instability — all concerns that modernism and postmodernism subsequently engage with, as they will with the discontinuity and fragmentation of the romance.

Brooke's romance, but also the nineteenth-century historical romances of John Richardson (*Wacousta; or, The Prophecy: A Tale of the Canadas*, 1832), Rosanna Leprohon (*Antoinette de Mirecourt or Secret Marrying and Secret Sorrowing: A Canadian Tale*, 1864), William Kirby (*The Golden Dog: A Romance of Old Quebec*, 1877), or Gilbert Parker (*The Seats of the Mighty*, 1896), to name but a few examples, have influenced early to mid-twentieth-century literary production in Canada, from Mazo de la Roche and Ralph Connor to Emily Carr and Thomas Raddall. They have also ushered in the twenty-first century, for instance, with Guy Vanderhaeghe's *The Englishman's Boy* (1996) and Margaret Atwood's formula writing, dipping into the codes of the gothic, fantasy, detective novel, and near-future fiction (*The Handmaid's Tale*, 1985; *Alias Grace*, 1996; *The Blind Assassin*, 2000; and *Oryx and Crake*, 2003). These authors' works all teem with actions that do not obey a narrative function, but nonetheless serve expository, dramatic, and didactic functions. The recurrent parties, dinners, picnics, games, and other celebrations described at length in these texts conform to the representative or symbolic acts of social cohesion best described as ritual, which Frye terms "the epiphany of the myth, the manifestation or showing forth of it in action" (Frye 1976, 55). Ritualized actions such as the feast were traditional motifs or objects of description in medieval literature and serve to encode an ideology or clash of ideologies and the ascendancy of a social class — such as the French and English elites surrounding the British conquest of New France. These ideologies of another time and/or place are presented through the cultural filter of the author, whose discourse conditions the readers' responses to the attitudes and values specifically promoted or undermined. Near-future fiction such as that of Margaret Atwood or Hugh MacLennan (*Voices in Time*, 1980) participates most clearly in the reform-oriented dynamics of satire, as the cataclysm that triggers the future dystopia is invariably the result of the mindset and practices of the society to which the readers belong and with which they can, sometimes uncomfortably, identify.

Clearly an influence on Ontario writer Mazo de la Roche's (1879–1961) *Jalna* saga (*Jalna*, 1927, and its fifteen sequels culminating in *Morning at Jalna*, 1960), which represents imperial English Canada from a Loyalist perspective, the United Empire Loyalist William Kirby (1817–1906) explicitly praises in the concluding chapter of *The Golden Dog* the "noblesse and people of New France . . . [who] gave their allegiance loyally and unreservedly to England, upon their final abandonment by the Court of France" (314). Kirby points out that when the Thirteen Colonies revolted, the French Canadians remained loyal to their new crown in spite of the appeals to join the Americans sent out by Washington, the Congress, and, ironically, by the French military officers and admirals La Fayette and D'Estaing. His lengthy descriptions of rituals throughout thus generally contrast the wholesome pleasures of the respectable families settled in New France with the debaucheries of the depraved representatives of the Ancien Régime of Louis XV and the Marquise de Pompadour. These passages — which constituted half of the original edition of 678 pages — were unfortunately cut in the abridged New Canadian Library edition (1969), whose truncated 320-page version is the only one available to contemporary readers.

Readers are allowed an inkling of Kirby's mastery of the rhetorical tradition of the descriptive pause in the chapter presenting Bigot, the corrupt Royal Intendant of New France. Obeying the conventions of the portrait, which requires a movement from exterior to interior qualities, the author sets up a horizon of expectation by first describing a drunken feast in Bigot's château. Carved representations of "Bacchus enthroned on a turn of wine, presenting flowing cups to a dance of fauns and satyrs," are surrounded by "real" silver cups which are brimming over or which "lay overturned amid pools of wine that ran down upon the velvet carpet," in turn surrounded by "overturned" chairs and revelers "in the garb of gentlemen, but all in disorder and soiled with wine," their countenances "inflamed, their eyes red and fiery, their tongues loose and loquacious" (*The Golden Dog*, 35). A figure purportedly incarnating the stability of absolute royal and even divine power is thus placed under the sign of irrationality, disorder, excess, ex-stasy, and dissolution, in the double sense of looseness through dissipation but also through disintegration and destruction, suggesting the disruption of the social structure — the social contract becoming as unbound as the alliteratively loose, loquacious tongues. The tearing up of the social fabric is consolidated through the vestimentary motif of Bigot's followers dressed "in the garb of gentlemen," which furthermore suggests a trope central to the work, that of illusion/delusion/usurpation.

Kirby's romance, published in the late nineteenth century, presents a plot unfolding a century earlier. So does Emily Carr's (1871–1945) *The Book of Small* (1942), a retrospective mixture of anecdote, sketch, portrait, autobiography, and essay exemplifying the loose episodic structure of the romance, which projects its voice back over half a century to a geopolitical and temporal space of mutation. The child narrator-protagonist participates in the transformation of Victoria from colonial outpost to administrative capital. She is born into a community striving "to be more English than the English themselves" (76) in the year British Columbia joined Confederation, in which all notions of propriety were imported from England along with the furniture, oven, and dishes. The romance thus presents the processes of acculturation as well as individual and national identity construction at work. The collision of imperial *doxa* with a New World axiological positioning is conveyed through the rituals of Navy balls, church services, family Bible readings, Sunday dinners, and public holidays, but also through the descriptions of the spaces representing diverse stages of cultural identification, from the prim English garden, symbolizing an affiliation with Great Britain and the ascendancy of English values, to the new field of wild Canadian lilies and the cow yard, sites of indigenization. While Small's oldest sister in her starched frocks prefers to play in the tidy garden, Small — the first child of the family to be born on New World soil — enjoys the freedom of the muddy cow yard, singing to the cow not in the "trained" voice Small's mother suggests would be more proper, but with unconstrained exuberance, "boiling over like the jam kettle" (31). Notions such as mimicry and authenticity (see Bhabha 2001) are addressed both metonymically and metaphorically, as in the scene in which Small's mother and a lady friend nostalgic for England sing all their "old" songs, including "God Save the Queen" and "Rule Britannia." Contrasting these songs spilling over from another time and place with the little girl's original cow-yard songs, the narrator makes a complex form of analogy: "Small's songs were new, fresh grass snatched as the cow snatched pasture grass. The ladies' songs were rechews — cudded fodder" (33). The proportional metaphor posits a multilateral system of interconnections in which the mothers' resuscitated old songs are to Small's original improvisations what imported, cudded fodder is to pasture grass. What is implied is that creation rooted in new territory is to take ascendancy over mimeticism and replication (see Dvorak 2007).

Carr's romance is a gentle one, which partakes only obliquely in "the cyclical movement of descent into a night world and a return to the idyllic world" which Frye has identified in the genre (1976, 54). It does present the vertical perspective Frye has theorized, namely an idyllic world and a demonic world respectively above and below the ordinary world of experience. Alongside passages of epiphanic contemplation evoking an Arcadian stability, harmony, and light, one finds eruptions of violence, darkness, and disquiet. These occur when a world of vice the child narrator cannot grasp, such as that of saloons or of chain gangs, is evoked. The descent into the realm of disorder and suffering, analogous to the disrupted inner landscape of the unconscious, of dream or madness, can occur in quite ordinary places, such as the butcher's shop, redolent of suffering, murder, and cannibalism, in which creatures are rushed "from life to meat" and the piglets are "pink and naked as bathing babies" (120–21); or at sites of play such as the regattas, when torture and cruelty provide amusement.

This is a far cry from the demonic world of Kirby's *The Golden Dog*, complete with Gothic staples (a corrupt royal court, a castle, a deserted watchtower, a secret passage, a midnight rendezvous, a ghost, a seduced and betrayed maiden, and a beautiful, scheming, cold-hearted siren) and the entire panoply of murder and eroticism found in Jacobean revenge tragedies with their artful variants on poison and stabbing. It is a far cry, too, from the demonic world of Richardson's (1796–1852) *Wacousta*, a sensationalist account of the Indian uprisings against British forts in the 1760s. The text's emphasis on savagery, blood, and horror targeted the readers' appetite for exoticist discourse and their taste for the monstrous, which would usher in Romanticism, but also the strong neogothic current of the twentieth-century artistic scene, from the cinema (David Cronenberg) to the novel (from Timothy Findley's *The Last of the Crazy People*, 1967, to Barbara Gowdy's *Mister Sandman*, 1995) or the suspense novel and thriller (Arthur Hailey's bestsellers such as *Hotel*, 1965, and *Airport*, 1968, come to mind). *Wacousta* was notably adapted for the stage in 1978 by playwright James Reaney. The Hurons of New France are revisited by Brian Moore (1921–1999) in *Black Robe* (1985), the somber tale of a Jesuit missionary that blends eroticism and martyrdom. While Moore had obtained the Governor General's Award for *The Luck of Ginger Coffey* in 1960, he had previously honed his skills at romance formats by writing thrillers under pseudonyms in the 1950s, skills particularly discernable in *The Black Robe*. And Thomas Raddall's (1903–1994) *His Majesty's Yankees*, published in 1942 but set in the period of the American

Revolution and its colliding political and social systems, also contains the structural features and motifs of imprisonment and escape, love and scheming, and land and sea battles, including an attack on a fort. Interestingly, as with Kirby, the extravagant features are mixed with real events, and the intrusion of utterances in the present tense posits absolute, universal truths, imbuing historicity with veracity. Rooted in the Maritimes — the region with the oldest and arguably strongest literary tradition, counting among its twentieth-century novelists Ernest Buckler, Frank Parker Day, Charles Bruce, Hugh MacLennan, Alden Nowlan, and Lucy Maud Montgomery, Raddall authored other historical romances including *Roger Sudden* (1944), *Pride's Fancy* (1946), *The Warden of the North* (1949), and *The Nymph and the Lamp* (1950). He is equally well known for his collections of short stories, and his writing, never stilted, is at its finest when deploying the symbolic overtones of the title story of *The Wedding Gift* (1947), originally published in *Story Magazine* in 1935.

Western writer Ralph Connor (pseudonym of Charles William Gordon, 1860–1937) was a minister and a missionary as well as the author of international bestsellers focusing on the frontier, among the earliest *Black Rock: A Tale of the Selkirks* (1898), *The Sky Pilot: A Tale of the Foothills* (1899), *The Man from Glengarry: A Tale of the Ottawa* (1901), and *The Prospector: A Tale of the Crow's Nest Pass* (1904). His was popular formula fiction featuring melodramatic adventures and binary structures, heroic or villainous stock characters of the Western involved in predictable situations in which the clash of good and evil is happily resolved for the good of the community. Celebrating rituals such as the logging-bee, which promoted the pioneer values of industriousness and solidarity, his works are suffused with Christian principles and the aesthetics of sentimentalism, which readers expecting literature to teach as well as to entertain found immensely satisfying. The works published in the 1920s and 1930s first focused on contemporary economic issues such as the 1919 Winnipeg General Strike or the stock market crash, and subsequently projected readers back to the American War of Independence and the War of 1812, offering discursive investigations of the historico-political issues that have shaped Canadian identity. Alberta writer Howard O'Hagan's (1902–1982) *Tay John* (1939), the story of a mixed-blood Indian compared to the Messiah, blends referential historical fact with myth and magic. Some of O'Hagan's later pieces, written for adventure magazines on figures such as Grey Owl and Albert Johnson (the Mad Trapper of Rat River), were collected in *Wilderness Men* (1958) and influenced writers such as Rudy Wiebe, Jack Hodgins, and Michael Ondaatje.

It was for didactic purposes that prairie suffragette and social activist Nellie McClung (1873–1951) wrote popular romances. Her trilogy *Sowing Seeds in Danny* (1908), *The Second Chance* (1910), and *Purple Springs* (1921), which denounced institutional misogyny and the harmful effects of alcohol on the family and community, essentially promoted Christian virtues and the values of wholesome rural life. Also celebrating pioneer life and virtues were Grace Campbell's (1895–1963) wartime best-sellers *Thorn-Apple Tree* (1942) and *The Higher Hill* (1944), set in early nineteenth-century Ontario. While Canadian artists influenced by William Morris and *art nouveau* often became involved in book design by provid-ing illustrations, Campbell's *Thorn-Apple Tree* was an exceptional work in that Group of Seven member Franklin Carmichael not only provided the woodcuts but also directed the typography and completed the book design. Manitoba writer Robert Stead's (1880–1959) popular romances of pioneering (*The Homesteaders*, 1916, and *Neighbours*, 1922) borrow the traditional motifs of the Western, but a preoccupation with social issues brought the writer to produce arguably realist fiction, which is often com-pared to that of Grove and Martha Ostenso and investigates the brutish dynamics of rural life, as for instance in *The Smoking Flax* (1925) and *Grain* (1926).

# Realism

At one end of the spectrum, then, there are writers of romance engaging with the paradigms of folktale in order to fashion New World configura-tions of epic adventure. Mikhail Bakhtin has observed that the epic is based "on the immanent unit of folkloric time" (Bakhtin 1996, 218), the repre-sentation of an absolute, completive past totally separated from the time and evaluative plane that the speaker shares with his/her audience. He judiciously remarks that "to portray an event on the same time-and-value plane as oneself and one's contemporaries (and an event that is therefore based on personal experience and thought) is to undertake a radical revo-lution, and to step out of the world of epic into the world of the novel" (Bakhtin 1996, 14). These considerations lead in turn to questions of high and low, of the idealized and the familiar, of the completed and the ongo-ing, and to the category of literary realism. The term, an elastic one, can indeed be taken loosely to signify — in opposition with the fabulously cos-mic or extravagantly heroic dimension of epic and romance — plausible action, characters modeled on ordinary society's common ways of life, and a logical or even historically verifiable narrative development organized into coherent, unified segments leading to a form of closure. These are intended to give the illusion of copying nature, or of reflecting, as would a mirror, an alleged truth — or at least the reality that the narrator or receiver perceives as authentic and seeks to emphasize or consolidate.

Sara Jeannette Duncan's (1861–1922) novel *The Imperialist* (1904) was among the first to examine the contemporary political and economic tensions surrounding the triangular trade relations between England, the

United States, and Canada from the knowledgeable position of a freelance correspondent, editorial writer, and columnist for major international newspapers. An expatriate, Duncan presents in meticulous detail the strategies of the imperialists striving to establish a special trade agreement with England, whose free-trade policy granted Canada no preferential treatment as a loyal dominion without access to the economies of scale of its American neighbor. Duncan's idealistic young imperialist, Lorne Murchison, urges his fellow citizens to resist American influence: "American enterprise, American capital, is taking rapid possession of our mines and our water-power, our oil areas and our timber limits" (*The Imperialist*, 266), words that strike a chord in readers who have experienced the 1980s debates surrounding the North American Free Trade Agreement. But the author's casual mention of a neighbor's "pretty feet in their American shoes" (144) astutely draws attention to the Canadian community's already voracious appetite for American goods. Duncan systematically mocks Canadian provincialism, the tastes of a raw society valuing size and ostentation. The omniscient narrative voice reminds the reader that the "value of carriage and clothes are relative," pointing out that, although elegant by Canadian standards, "in Fifth Avenue Lorne would have looked countrified, in Piccadilly colonial."

Duncan's ironic devices, such as the adroit combination of exaggeration and understatement which debunk the small-town parochialism exemplified by the fictional small town of Elgin, anticipate those that Stephen Leacock deployed in *Sunshine Sketches of a Little Town* (1912) to mock Mariposa. One finds the identical use of a fallible narrator whose triumphant enumeration trivializes what it sets out to celebrate: "[Main Street's] appearance and demeanor would never have suggested that it was now the chief artery of a thriving manufacturing town, with a collegiate institute, eleven churches, two newspapers, and an asylum for the deaf and dumb, to say nothing of a fire department unsurpassed for organization and achievement in the Province of Ontario" (*The Imperialist*, 24–25). Yet the distanced perspective of displacement also allows Duncan to construct a caustic satire of the English sociopolitical system and its institutions. Her mouthpiece Lorne points out the already dwindling economic prospects of an overpopulated England which cannot feed its own people or keep capital "drawing away to conditions it can find profit in — steel works in Canada, woolen factories in Australia, jute mills in India" (*The Imperialist*, 138). Also held up to ridicule is the gap between the global and the local, the political and economic issues at stake on an international scale, and the apolitical concerns of the English community focused on the small: "Pick up a paper, at the moment when things are being done . . . against them — when their shipping is being captured, and their industries destroyed, and their goods undersold beneath their very noses — and the thing they want to know is — 'Why Are the Swallows Late?'" (149).

In spite of its digressive, episodic mode and its playfully intrusive narrative voice, Duncan's style has been classified in the category of realism. The verifiable accuracy of the social, historical, and geographical details that the writer provides with a certain pretension to objectivity does give the illusion of representing an identifiable world, the idea at the heart of the realist aesthetic. Other twentieth-century writers in Canada have insisted on a more extreme interpretation of realism that has affinities with the naturalist movement in its suspicion of idealism and beauty and its interest in the squalid. One can playfully simplify the distinction by saying that realism strives to represent life with all its blemishes, while naturalism focuses almost exclusively on the blemishes. Frederick Philip Grove (1879–1948) and, decades later, David Adams Richards (1950–), who from his first novel *The Coming of Winter* (1974) starkly depicted the underclass of New Brunswick, can be considered the leading exponents of naturalism in Canada.

Born Felix Paul Friedrich Greve in Prussia and raised in Hamburg, Grove was an expatriate who began his writing career in Germany and is also known to German readers for his translations of French authors such as Flaubert, Balzac, and Gide. After living in France and then in the United States, he finally settled in Manitoba and set out to represent the life of the pioneer immigrants arriving in unsettled territory and struggling with a hostile environment. His first novel in English, *Settlers of the Marsh* (1925), is considered to be one of the first works of prairie realism. The novel was censured for being indecent, and Grove's later novels such as *Our Daily Bread* (1928), *The Yoke of Life* (1930), and *Fruits of the Earth* (1933), albeit containing strong pastoral overtones, also set out to depict human failings and appetites as well as societal deficiencies. As can be seen in his essay "Realism in Literature," Grove saw no contradiction in positing — along with the idealists — that his perception and representation of the world were not subjective, but corresponded to an absolute, universal truth. In spite of a certain clumsiness with respect to characterization and focalization, as well as stilted language and a reliance on cliché, Grove went on to win both critical and popular acclaim. The decision of the major Canadian publisher McClelland & Stewart to reprint his work in its popular paperback series of Canadian classics further consolidated his rank in the canon.

Among the first Canadian novelists to focus on representing the extensive migration to the West, particularly the Scandinavian immigrant experience, was Laura Goodman Salverson (1918–1960), born in Winnipeg of Icelandic immigrant parents. Her novels *The Viking Heart* (1923), *When Sparrows Fall* (1925), and *The Dark Weaver* (1937) blend a documentary meticulousness with a bleak metaphysical vision which contrasts interestingly with her romantic adaptations of Norse sagas in *Lord of the Silver Dragon: A Romance of Leif the Lucky* (1927). It was not until the late

1950s that another realist novel by a Central European immigrant, John Marlyn (1912–2005), depicted the experiences of a community of other than Anglo-Saxon and Germanic origin, which had dominated publishing and distribution up until the end of the Second World War. Although Canada has long been among the most urbanized societies of the world, a large part of Canadian fiction until the postcentennial era was set in the small town or rural area, with their accompanying symbolic resonances. An exception is *Under the Ribs of Death* (1957) by John Marlyn, who was born in Hungary and grew up in Winnipeg. Set in an urban center rather than in farming communities, the novel deals with a young Hungarian's struggle against poverty and discrimination in the underprivileged North End of Winnipeg. The voice is that of the traditional third-person omniscient narrator, the time frame is linear with conventional chronological markers, and the narrative structure is based on cause and effect, moving from prohibition to transgression, and from act to reward or punishment. There is an undeniable overreliance on cliché, and the protagonists themselves are clearly stock characters. Sandor's father embodies the historical transitions from feudal society to modern and from agrarian to industrial. Moreover, he is the epitome of both the self-made man of the American Dream and the cultivated (self-taught) working man from Central Europe, for whom learning is sacred and who sits around in a barber shop discussing Bertrand Russell and the nature of reality.

The Canadian prairies have continued to produce strong storytelling in the second half of the twentieth century and beyond, with writers such as Rudy Wiebe, Margaret Laurence, and Robert Kroetsch. Critics from Laurie Ricou (1973) to Claire Omhovère (2007) have argued that this was where the landscape most shaped creative expression. Among other earlier leading figures of the prairie novel were two writers very different in scope and approach: Sinclair Ross and W. O. Mitchell, both reputed short-story writers as well (see ch. 14, Nischik). Ross (1908–1996) is better known for his first novel *As for Me and My House* (1941) than for the subsequent *The Well* (1958). Unlike Grove's melodramatic writing, with its heavy use of rhetorical questions and exclamations, Ross's novel, set — like his short stories published in the 1930s — in the Dust Bowl of Saskatchewan during the drought and Depression, is a more minimalist representation of gray misery and despair. The focus on the domestic sphere (whose intimacy is skillfully relayed in diary form) against the backdrop of an economic system as implacable as pitiless nature, is quiet and understated and thus all the more moving. Ross's style later evolved to take the shape of modernist fragments of interior monologue in *Sawbones Memorial* (1974). Also published in the 1940s and set in rural Alberta was *Who Has Seen the Wind* (1947) by W. O. Mitchell (1914–1998). A novelist, essayist, fiction editor, and author of popular radio and television scripts as well as short stories, Mitchell possesses a savory regional language celebrating the land and its community in a pastoral yet exhilarating fashion. He has often been likened to Mark Twain, and his 1981 novel *How I Spent My Summer Holidays* compared to *Huckleberry Finn*. Mitchell's effortless use (like that of Jack Hodgins decades later) of the oral idiom and its power of invention — which he termed the "magic lies" of folklore — as well as his control of structure and rhythm and his recourse to incongruity place him in line with the best comic writers. The idealism and sentimentality of Mitchell's work — a sentimentality also present, albeit in a different manner, in Ross's works — corresponded to the tastes of the early period, but then went out of fashion. Recently, there has been a renewal of interest, along with a rediscovery of writers from other regions such as Ernest Buckler, whose similar love of the land and focus on family and community also came to be viewed as old-fashioned, only to be valued later. Yet in spite of Mitchell's elegiac pastoral mode and Emersonian idealism, he, too, is firmly anchored in realism, visible in his mimetic representation, his logical, ordered unfurling of plot development, and his attention to authentic depiction of regional speech and behavior. The literary realism of Victorian writers was still the most powerful current in Canadian writing at a time when the transcontinental movement of modernism was already at its height in Europe and the United States, and the Canadian predilection for historical fiction was just as strong in the second half of the twentieth century. This applies to novels written in an identifiably realist vein (for instance, the social realism of Jane Rule's homoerotic *Desert of the Heart*, 1964), but also to those suffused with romantic, but also modernist or postmodern dynamics, such as those of Morley Callaghan, Margaret Laurence, Robert Kroetsch, Rudy Wiebe, and Leonard Cohen.

# Hybridization

Students of narrative, fascinated by genre theory and typological classification, argue that genres provide sets of expectations that serve both as a writerly code and as a readerly guide, and generate a particular relation between text and world (Culler 1994, 136). Nonetheless, with respect to the empirical identity, purity, contamination, or hybridization of literary genres, theoreticians diverge widely. The epistemological crisis of the modern age has led to the destabilization of genre distinctions, with boundaries often blurred. Writers such as Hugh MacLennan (1907–1990) and Frank Parker Day (1881–1950) have been labeled both realistic — that is, rich in factual detail — and romantic, which shows the limitations of such categories. In 2005, almost eighty years after its initial publication in 1928, Day's *Rockbound* won the CBC's popular "Canada Reads" contest. Its appeal may lie in its epic, romantic qualities, discernable in the opening description of the young protagonist David through the sublime style and analogy with the semidivine hero of the Greek legend of Jason and the Golden Fleece:

> Though he looked it not, he was a man of destiny — in small things, it is true, yet in relation to the universe all things upon this earth are small — and this voyage in his yellow dory, a voyage of destiny, less spectacular than Jason's but requiring none the less courage and resolution. For Jason had with him forty heroes and had but to meet a dragon, while David was alone and had to meet Uriah. (*Rockbound*, 3)

Such high style and epic analogies jar at first reading with the sociological orientation and the dialect derived from Low German spoken by the fishing communities on the islands of Mahone Bay: "I owns one tent' o' dis island t'rough my grandfader old Edward Jung, same as you owns your shares" (*Rockbound*, 5). Yet Day's dialect is actually a stylized way of speaking English and carries a dramatic function. Considered to be a representative of antimodernist naturalism, Day is also a perfect illustration of the paradox underlying such a movement: on the one hand, a rejection of industrialized societies, deemed inauthentic; on the other, an interest in primeval or primitive settings (in the sense of early or original), which converges uncomfortably with the taste for exotic settings inherent to the romance. Charles Bruce (1906–1971), primarily a poet, is equally well known for his novel on rustic Nova Scotian life, *The Channel Shore* (1951). Its frequent recourse to the scene or dialogue creates an effect of immediacy and authenticity, and conforms to the didactic tradition of the Socratic dialogue, a trademark feature of realists such as Charles Dickens or George Eliot, who were concerned with the moral improvement of their readership. Bruce's *The Township of Time* (1959), a saga subtitled *A Chronicle*, unfolding from 1786 to 1950 and comprised of connected stories, significantly appends a full genealogy of its characters. These nonetheless stand for social types, representatives of various stages of transplantation from Old World to New. One can cite the series of antithetical parallelisms describing Mrs. Mervyn, who is encountered in a two-room hut but wears gloves and a satin dress and is made to embody — through the shift to the plural pronoun — all the dysfunctional immigrants who are unable to adapt, "unable now to let the symbols go. To face the fact that here, now, they must start again, that two generations lay ahead before the rags and homespun would again be satin, the log walls white clapboard, the parlor panelled oak" (*Township*, 6).

Hugh MacLennan's didactic, committed novels are among the first in Canada to concern themselves primarily with national, social, and political issues. A strong nationalist, MacLennan can thereby be counted among the intellectuals such as Marshall McLuhan, Northrop Frye, and Harold Innis, who all elaborated theories on national culture. His warnings against an economic, technological, and cultural takeover on the part of the United States were made against the backdrop of the Massey Commission's similarly alarming conclusions (in 1951), which incited the Canadian government to promote national cultural production. MacLennan's *Barometer Rising* (1941) projected readers back to the notorious 1917 Halifax Explosion, when the explosion of a munitions ship in the harbor, of a force unequalled in human history until the atom bomb, leveled the city and caused a tidal wave and conflagration. The metaphorical, even apocalyptic, overtones of the narrative invite a political reflection on, more specifically, Canada's role in the war, and, more generally, on the nature and consequences of postcolonial relations. *The Precipice* (1948) subsequently investigated U.S.-Canadian relations, while *Each Man's Son* (1951) recorded life in the mines of Cape Breton Island through the psychological filter of father-son rivalry. *Two Solitudes* (1945) addressed the tension of English-French relations in Quebec (as would the subsequent *Return of the Sphinx*, 1967), a tension that has troubled the country up to the present day. The novel provided Canadian writers with a staple theme and contributed a label to a cultural phenomenon. Yet, while MacLennan grounded his writing in the mimetic realist mode, meticulously researching data so as to faithfully depict a referential reality, a strong symbolic, even allegorical, dimension underlies the surface level of event and characterization. Thus the larger canvas suggested by the local microcosm in *Barometer Rising* arguably anticipates the shift to near-future fiction with his last novel, *Voices in Time* (1980), which surprised his readership. Moreover, one can detect a predilection for certain modernist practices, such as the interest in psychology, the play with epic and recourse to biblical and mythological rhythms and allusions, and, more specifically, the structural Homeric parallels exploited by James Joyce.

Toronto writer Morley Callaghan (1903–1990), a contemporary of MacLennan, Ross, and Mitchell, has also been classified among the realists, and associated with American naturalist writers such as Theodore Dreiser, Sinclair Lewis, and Sherwood Anderson — especially for his first novel, *Strange Fugitive* (1928), but also for the books published in the 1930s, *It's Never Over* (1930), *A Broken Journey* (1932), and the highly successful *Such Is My Beloved* (1934), *They Shall Inherit the Earth* (1935), and *More Joy in Heaven* (1937). He briefly belonged to the expatriate circle of modernists in Paris, but Callaghan's writing does not adhere to the iconoclastic inventions of James Joyce or Gertrude Stein, and tends to conform to realist literary conventions concerning chronology, causality, voice, and closure. The influences of Ernest Hemingway and Scott Fitzgerald are discernable, however, for his writing does subscribe to the early modernist aesthetic advocating simple spoken English, repetition, and an interest in psychological activities rather than in events. A prolific short-story writer as well as a novelist, Callaghan continued to publish highly acclaimed books for over half a century. *The Loved and the Lost* (1951), which like the generically hybrid *The Many Coloured Coat* (1960) is set in Montreal, was awarded the Governor General's Award.

Norman Levine (1923–2005) is as well known in Europe and North America for his poetry and short stories (many broadcast by the BBC and CBC) as for his autobiographical fiction *The Angled Road* (1952) — a war novel whose romanticism has been contrasted with Norman Mailer's brutally naturalistic *The Naked and the Dead* (1948) — and *From a Seaside Town* (1970). Like Mordecai Richler, Levine depicts poor (often Jewish) urban neighborhoods, and the modernist influence is discernable with respect to time, subjectivity, fragmentation, and the contrapuntal play of past and present, memory and experience, mind and world. Also hybrid are the earliest novels published by Robertson Davies (1913–1995), Canada's most important playwright in the 1940s and 1950s, who subsequently established an international reputation as a major novelist, essayist, and skillful ironist in the 1970s. The early Salterton trilogy (set in a thinly disguised Kingston), *Tempest-Tost* (1951), *Leaven of Malice* (1954) — which won The Leacock Memorial Medal for Humour — and *A Mixture of Frailties* (1958), dips into both the extravagant mode of romance and the realistic mode of social critique, with precise social observation made to serve a gentle Horatian satire of small-town Ontario. *A Mixture of Frailties* deploys a modernist practice that anticipates the postmodern as well as postcolonial predilection for writing back to master narratives. Like Malcolm Lowry (*Under the Volcano*, 1947), who overtly used intertexts as writerly building blocks in the manner of the painterly collage, Davies used the ancient romance by Apuleius as both recognizable material embodying a cultural continuum and the stuff of creative transformation (involving turning *The Golden Ass* into an opera).

At the opposite pole on the axis of irony, there is Mordecai Richler (1931–2001), internationally recognized as a superbly caustic satirist. His texts excel in representing a recognizable world, depicting events such as the 1929 stock exchange crash and the Spanish Civil War (*The Acrobats*, 1954). Some critics detect the influences of Hemingway, Dos Passos, and Scott Fitzgerald, and the existential stances of Sartre and Camus in the early texts written during or soon after his brief stay in Paris among other expatriate writers such as James Baldwin and Mavis Gallant, or during his subsequent eighteen-year-long stay in England. Richler stands as a reminder that Canadian writers in the 1950s — even the most well-known ones such as Callaghan or MacLennan — could not make a living from their fiction alone, or needed to go abroad in order to establish careers for themselves, especially before the government's commitment to subsidize the arts nationwide materialized in the creation of the Canada Council for the Arts in 1957. In his first article, published in the Canadian magazine *Maclean's* in 1958 and entitled "How I Became an Unknown with My First Novel," Richler related with mordant irony the two years he had spent in Canada working for the CBC while revising the manuscript of his first novel for his London publisher. Realizing that the four hundred copies of his new novel which his Canadian distributor had consented to order for the domestic market would generate a total of $32 in royalties, he decided to leave for London. Many of his works, such as *The Apprenticeship of Duddy Kravitz* (1959), which was adapted for the screen by Ted Kotcheff in 1974, represent with remarkable authenticity of voice and rhetorical control as well as infectious humor the experience of growing up in a working-class Jewish neighborhood in Montreal, that is, on the margins of both the powerful Anglo-Saxon Protestant community which still controlled the affairs of the province, and the francophone Catholic community which was to take up the reins after the Quiet Revolution and which founded the Parti Québécois in the 1960s. In *Son of a Smaller Hero* (1955) and subsequently in *St. Urbain's Horseman* (1971), he interrogated notions of commitment and responsibility. The novels explore the place of Jews in a modern, secular society with an irreverence that drew the wrath of the Jewish community, anticipating the francophone Quebec community's outraged reactions in the 1990s to satirical essays targeting a certain tribal, xenophobic mindset. Richler delighted in debunking the myths of his time. In *A Choice of Enemies* (1957) he challenged the *doxa* of martyrdom, which the American film directors who had fled McCarthyism were constructing for themselves in London, treating them not as idealistic victims but as "poseurs." *The Incomparable Atuk* (1963, entitled *Stick Your Neck Out* in the American edition) and *Cocksure* (1968) — an extravagant fable about an aging Hollywood film director cannibalizing his associates to keep his body functioning — denounced through caricature both the powerful American entertainment industry and a newly fashionable Canadian nationalism. Richler's later novels would go on to use postmodern techniques, such as multiple labyrinthine narrative lines, and continued to draw on a vast cultural scope analogous to that of his erudite contemporary Robertson Davies (see ch. 23, Kuester).

Among the Canadian writers frequently seen as operating within the conventions of realism was Margaret Laurence (1926–1987), one of the most important writers to emerge from the cultural space of the prairies and one of the major figures of the literary revival of the 1960s and 1970s. Her first novel, *This Side Jordan* (1960), was set in Ghana, where she had lived for several years. It was soon followed by *The Stone Angel* (1964), the first of the Manawaka cycle, comprising four novels and a collection of linked stories (*A Bird in the House*, 1970), which had been published separately in magazines throughout the 1960s. Having been influenced by Ross and Mitchell, the Manawaka cycle in turn nourished a whole generation of writers. Set in the fictional small town of Manawaka, which embodied an era and a mindset shaped by geography as much as by history, it depicts the repressive Puritan spirit of the Scots-Presbyterian founders who forged a community in the face of hostile conditions. *The Stone Angel* presents communities split along fault lines generated by race and ethnicity, but also sets out to examine the cohesive force of language which contains society and moulds an aggregate of individuals into a community. Laurence attempts to capture the workings of consciousness and the acquisition of language, subverting the codes of realism by articulating shifts from inner voice to outer dialogue, memory, dream, and fantasy through inner films, changes of typeface, and visual layout. She configures various genres such as the Künstlerroman, and deconstructs the details of dailiness with unreliable narrators, shifting points of view, and an increasingly destabilizing manipulation of time and duration, notably recurrent ellipses and flashbacks and flashforwards — techniques favored by the modernists and subsequently adopted by postmodern writers.

# Modernism

Robert Kroetsch (1927–), a critic as well as a poet and novelist, notoriously asserted that Canadian writing moved directly from Victorianism to postmodernism. The preceding discussion has aimed to show that, on the contrary, the modernist movement, which arrived later in Canada and which evolved almost imperceptibly into the postmodern current, did influence novelists working in the realist mode, resulting in hybridized practices. Adding to the formal diversity, one can moreover identify certain Canadian writers who wholly adhere to facets of modernist aesthetic practices, such as discontinuity and fragmentation, or metafictional preoccupations, for modernism is undeniably changeable in form. Sheila Watson immediately springs to mind, as do Mavis Gallant, A. M. Klein, Elizabeth Smart (*By Grand Central Station I Sat Down and Wept*, 1945), Ernest Buckler, and Leonard Cohen.

Mavis Gallant (1922–), born in an anglophone enclave of Montreal, emigrated in order to earn her living as a writer, and has lived in France since the 1950s. Recognized internationally as one of the best short-story writers in the English language and a superb ironist (see ch. 24, Nischik), her writing is marked by formal modernist experimentation such as stretching or condensing conventional forms. She developed the longer short story favored by Katherine Mansfield and Thomas Mann, for instance with the novella *Pegnitz Junction* (1963), in which the opening rhetorical accumulation blends the referential external world of post-Second World War Germany with the awareness of mental landscapes. It obliges the reader to switch between the different logics and points of view contained in the adjuncts: "She was a bony slow-moving girl from a small bombed baroque German city, where all that was worthwhile keeping had been rebuilt and which now looked as pink and golden as a pretty child and as new as morning" (*Pegnitz Junction*, 3). With *Green Water, Green Sky* (1959), she had previously chosen to condense the novel to the utmost, further hybridizing it through its episodic structure which resembles the story cycles she and Alice Munro were the first to revive in the twentieth century. Gallant's texts are self-reflexive, nonlinear, multilayered, polygeneric, open-ended constructions based on clusters of images, fragmented points in time, memory, and perception. They alternate between the extreme stasis of descriptive pause and the ultimate speed of ellipsis, and reverberate on multiple paradigmatic levels. Such modernist features move her imperceptibly into the postmodern current, and her second novel, *A Fairly Good Time* (1970), destabilizes with recurrent flashbacks and flashforwards and dips into life writing's devices of staging the self, such as the journal and the letter, alongside the shifts from external observation to interior monologue.

Gallant's interest in formal effects, her fascination with the mechanisms of language and the writing process itself, is analogous with that of British Columbian writer Sheila Watson (1909–1998), author of *The Double Hook* (1959), often acclaimed as the first truly modernist Canadian novel and compared to T. S. Eliot's *The Waste Land*. Watson's writing, intensely preoccupied with language as visual sign and aural music, is dislocated — rather like Gertrude Stein's — through recurrent recourse to nominal sentences, noncompletive present participles, repetition, echo, ellipses, and a spatialized form centered on stanza-like chapters and blanks: "James walking away. The old lady falling. There under the jaw of the roof. In the vault of the bed loft. Into the shadow of death. Pushed by James's will. By James's hand. By James's words: This is my day. You'll not fish today" (*The Double Hook*, 11). Also discernable is a Faulknerian privileging of image over discourse, of the poetic over the narrative, the symbolic over the informational, and inner vision over external reality:

> Still the old lady fished. If the reeds had dried up and the banks folded and crumbled down she would have fished still. If God had come into the valley, come holding out the long finger of salvation, moaning in the darkness, thundering down the gap at the lake head, skimming across the water, drying up the blue signature like blotting-paper, asking where, asking why, defying an answer, she would have thrown her line against the rebuke; she would have caught a piece of mud and looked it over; she would have drawn a line with the barb when the fire of righteousness baked the bottom. (*The Double Hook*, 11–12)

The biblical and mythological rhythms and allusions, recourse to foreign words, or lexical dislocations and word play that characterize Watson's writing are equally to be found in *The Second Scroll* (1951), the only novel written by poet A. M. Klein (1909–1972). Brought to Canada from the Ukraine as a child by orthodox Jewish parents, Klein grew up in the already cosmopolitan environment of Montreal, and his work stimulated other writers such as Matt Cohen, Mordecai Richler, and Leonard Cohen to write about the experiences of the Jewish community. Written after a trip to the newly created state of Israel, *The Second Scroll* traces the Jewish people's wanderings throughout Europe, North Africa, and Canada in search of a new homeland. It is rooted in a vision of international flux, the two geographically opposite but ontologically similar poles being the two lands of welcome: Israel and Canada, both kaleidoscopes of origins, languages, and customs. Reminiscent of the structural Homeric parallels of Joyce (on whose *Ulysses* Klein wrote an ambitious commentary), the text fuses Oriental and Western cultures, resorts systematically to polyphonic prose, neologisms, foreign words, and intricate literary and religious intertextuality, based mainly on the Pentateuch. In a similar vein, Adele Wiseman (1928–1992), born in Winnipeg and also the child of Jewish Ukrainian emigrants, constructs her first novel, *The Sacrifice* (1956), in a dialogic manner around a biblical intertext. The narrative of Abraham and Isaac provides an allegorical backdrop to a modern tale of displacement and exile, in which the arrival of the Jewish immigrants in the prairies between the two world wars also resonates on a symbolic, universal plane that spills beyond the boundaries of the referential framework.

The poet, songwriter, and performer Leonard Cohen (1934–) was also born in Montreal into a Jewish family, with roots in Russian Lithuania. Cohen studied at McGill University, where Hugh MacLennan taught Canadian literature, but then went on to Columbia University in New York, where he mixed with members of the Beat Generation such as Allen Ginsberg and Jack Kerouac. Idolized from the 1960s for his escapist themes and magical, mystical, even surrealistic lyrics blending highbrow and mass culture, Cohen grounded his appeal in traditional rhyming prosody and decorative imagery which was heavily mythological, drawing on Hassidic but also Greek sources, Cohen having lived for years on the island of Hydra. His first novel *The Favorite Game* (1963) is a portrait of the artist as a young Jew in Montreal. His second novel *Beautiful Losers* (1966) was the most controversial work of fiction to be published in Canada in the latter half of the twentieth century. Many found it shocking and offensive, while others hailed it as *the* major modernist work since James Joyce. Cohen frequently employs the Joycean technique of stream of consciousness and onomatopoeic seriation: "yug yug sniffle truffle deep bulb bud button sweet soup pea spit rub hood rubber know girl come head bup bup one bloom pug pig yum" (*Beautiful Losers*, 68). With its Rabelaisian low style, imprecations, and obscenity as well as abundant recourse to hyperbole and bathos, Cohen's novel transgresses codes of decorum and creates a Canadian brand of the grotesque. He plays with what the dominant culture sees as tragic or macabre, and dips into colonial hagiography irreverently. Describing Jesuit missionaries proselytizing in New France, the narrator depicts one priest sucking the toes of the saintly Iroquois virgin Kateri Tekakwitha, ostensibly to warm them; yet the increasing onomatopoeic gusto ("Gobblegobblegobblewoggle. Slurp") and bathos produced by anachronism — "his tongue going like a wind-shield wiper" — suggest otherwise. Inscribed in a long tradition of contestatory writing, the ensuing comic effects are similar to those produced by major satirical writers throughout the ages advocating inversions of values (such as Jonathan Swift, Alfred Jarry, and Jean Genet). At the core of the carnivalesque laughter is a bedrock of social criticism intended to challenge established doctrines and conventions with respect to religious institutions, political movements, or simply American corporate and popular culture. The criticism, foregrounding an axiological gap between Madison Avenue and the Canadian community, oscillates between frontal attack, designed to generate moral indignation, and playful parody, designed to produce detached amusement.

Among the key literary figures of modernist production paving the way for the postmodern is Ernest Buckler (1908–1984), a writer-farmer from Nova Scotia who emerged from a bookless rural society but went on to study philosophy at Dalhousie University and the University of Toronto alongside writers and cultural theorists such as Hugh MacLennan, Marshall McLuhan, Northrop Frye, and Harold Innis. Yet, as would West Coast writer Ethel Wilson (1888–1980; *Swamp Angel*, 1954; *Love and Salt Water*, 1956; see ch. 14, Nischik), Buckler distanced himself from the movement yoking art to nationalistic purposes that was gathering momentum in the early 1950s. He had produced countless short stories, radio plays, and essays in the 1940s, and his elegiac first novel, *The Mountain and the Valley* (1952), was published the same year as Hemingway's *The Old Man and the Sea* and Steinbeck's *East of Eden*. Buckler's aesthetic practices call up the aesthetic philosophy developed by Joyce's mouthpiece, Stephen Dedalus, in *A Portrait of the Artist as a Young Man*, and his rhetorically fecund writing also evokes the highly figurative, metaphorical language of Faulkner. Buckler was preoccupied with the manner in which reality manifests itself to our senses, and with the nature of being itself. Joycean epiphanies and Emersonian fusions of consciousness and the universe pepper his texts: "It was a kind of instant Zen, come by with no effort at all. Perhaps in the most humdrum hour it would strike you right out of the blue, and for the length of one dazzling pulsebeat lift you higher than a June of kites into that sky of skies where the glass between inside and outside melts completely away" (*The Mountain and the Valley*). At the same time, like many other modernists such as Joyce, who had triggered an international resurgence of interest in Aristotelean, neoplatonic, and Renaissance studies, Buckler was interested in the relationship between language and the world, and was particularly fascinated by the metalinguistic faculty.

Buckler's novels (his second novel, *The Cruelest Month*, was published in 1963) and his fictional memoir *Ox Bells and Fireflies* (1968) — a hybrid text blending autobiographical writing with contemplative prose poems, essays, anecdotes, portraits, and sketches — disrupt in different ways the readers' expectations of linearity and story. Yet, as with W. O. Mitchell, the audience cherished his celebration of domesticity, of the humble elements that make up the everyday lives of ordinary people, in an incantatory, incremental style that explores the relationship between words and things. Readers are also attracted to his strong ethical vision that questions the place of the individual within society and explores the social ties that bind the community together. Buckler's texts are a crossroads between the old and the new, grounded in idealist and romantic currents of thought, yet connecting Canadian literature to international modernist concerns and anticipating postmodern issues and practices ranging from a strong ethical and social consciousness involving epistemological preoccupations and a privileging of the ex-centric to an aesthetic grounded in literary and linguistic theory.

While Northrop Frye has shown that the novel has developed transnationally by displacing the structural features of the romance, this chapter has argued that displacement is the quintessential feature of Canadian writing, endowing it with an identifiable specificity. The heuristic but often binary displacements on chronological, thematic, and stylistic planes postulated by Bakhtin and later Frye are rendered highly complex by Canadian writings. The multiple generic and narratological displacements as well as aesthetic hybridizations underlying Canadian fiction from the eighteenth century to the modern period have generated in distinctive albeit diverse manners a certain indeterminacy and instability which can be seen as leading almost ineluctably to postmodernism. It is not surprising, then, that Cambridge University in 1993 hosted an international conference on the theme "Canada: The First Postmodern Nation?"

# 14: The Modernist English-Canadian Short Story

*Reingard M. Nischik (University of Constance)*

IN ITS MAIN LINE OF DEVELOPMENT, the English-Canadian short story is a relatively recent literary phenomenon, spanning a little more than a hundred years to the present. It began to coalesce as a national genre in the 1890s, with writers such as Isabella Valancy Crawford, Susan Frances Harrison, Ernest Thompson Seton, and Charles G. D. Roberts. Yet it was only with the advent of the modernist short story in the 1920s that the English-Canadian short story fully emerged as a distinct literary genre, and with the works of Morley Callaghan and others joined the realm of world literature.

The modernist development of the English-Canadian short story is closely connected to the life and works of Raymond Knister (1899–1932). Knister was important in the genre's early stages as well as in the development of Canadian literary modernism in general. His importance in regard to the Canadian short story rests on his contributions to the poetics of the Canadian brand of the genre, on his early attempts — as editor of Canada's first anthology of English-Canadian short stories — to create a canon of the genre, and on his own short-story production.

In "Democracy and the Short Story" (written in 1920, first published in 1975), Knister emphasizes the unrivaled excellence of the contemporary American short story and relates its significance to the large number of short stories published in the United States and their distribution in widely circulating popular magazines. At the same time he denounces the "Americanization" of the genre, against which he would like the Canadian short story to take a stand ("The Canadian Short Story," 1923). Knister understands "Americanization" to mean the commercialization of short-story writing, fostered by the success of correspondence schools with their stereotypical plot and formula stories that leave no room for innovation. Instead, Knister promotes — as did T. S. Eliot in his seminal essay "Tradition and the Individual Talent" (1919) — individuality and originality as well as a pronounced consciousness of technique and form in order to achieve technical versatility and variation, often in an indirect, concealed manner ("The great art is that which is concealed"). Though not using the term explicitly, he advocates a "new form" (391), the modernist short story. For Knister (whose equally noteworthy lyrical oeuvre is, significantly, indebted to the imagist movement), short fiction is linked to precise observation, narrative economy, stylistic succinctness, as well as concise, "objectifying" images to indirectly convey feelings and emotions (see Eliot's "objective correlative"). Knister's sparsely plotted stories open up a new, realist dimension, as opposed to the schematically structured plot story. "If his [the new writer's] eye be true and his emotions universal and directed, he will be one of the artists for which Canada has awaited to heighten the consciousness of portions of her life. And it may be that a time will come at which he can find a publisher awaiting him in his own country" ("The Canadian Short Story").

Knister's influential role in the development of Canadian literature in general and the Canadian short story in particular manifests itself in his editorship of *Canadian Short Stories* (published in 1928 by Macmillan, Toronto), the first anthology of English-Canadian short stories and Knister's first book — a pioneering work published after twelve years of extensive reading, "exactly what Canadian literature needed," according to E. J. Pratt (1928). Knister himself wrote about a hundred short stories, fifty of which are available in print today. Among his best-known stories are his farm stories (for example, "The First Day of Spring," "Mist-Green Oats," "The Strawstack," "The Loading"), set in southwestern Ontario and mainly focusing on male protagonists and their experiences of initiation (such as first love), disillusion, guilt and innocence, tensions between family members — in particular between father and son — and death. The vague, hardly realistic hopes and tentative attempts of the protagonists to overcome their sense of confinement on the farm often pivot on their imaginative identification with and spiritualization of nature in all its mythic beauty — in stark contrast to the numbing chores of a monotonous farm life. In his farm stories, Knister introduces the reader to his characters' inner worlds with distinctively modernist narrative techniques such as subjective narrative focalization, allusion, ellipsis, epiphany, and indirect, symbolistic rendering of information. His "state-of-mind stories" (for instance "Elaine," "The Fate of Mrs. Lucier") reduce the external plot even more, ultimately condensing it to the function of merely intimating an awareness of their female protagonists' consciousnesses.

A third group of stories draws on Knister's brief work experience in the United States: his "Chicago stories" or "crime stories" (for instance "Hackman's Night," "Innocent Man"). Knister's stories paved the way for the modernist short story in Canada. They deal with a wide range of themes and employ a variety of narrative styles, demonstrating a general competence in narrative strategies. Once in a while, however, the author's narrative techniques and his use of language betray some of his texts as "beginner's stories," which would have profited from revision at a more mature artistic stage (which, dying at thirty-three, he did not live to see).

"Elaine," for example (Knister's fifth story), overuses modernist strategies such as ambiguity, allusion, ellipsis, and the portrayal of consciousness to the point of excessive obscurity, as does "The Loading." Stylistic inconsistencies such as unclear pronoun referents, clumsy sentence rhythms, inadequate vocabulary, and awkward expressions occasionally disturb the quality of Knister's innovative stories.

Frederick Philip Grove (1879–1948), a friend of Knister's and twenty years his senior, had his first short stories published in 1926. Grove is primarily known as the first significant prairie novelist in Canada to write in a realist or naturalist manner, his semiautobiographical novels, with their deliberate mingling of fact and fiction, anticipating later postmodernist strategies. Ever since 1972, when Douglas O. Spettigue exposed Grove's spectacular autobiographical lie (unmasking Grove as the German writer and translator Felix Paul Greve, who had faked suicide in Germany and established a new identity as Grove in Canada), the interest in Grove's fascinating persona has tended to eclipse the study of his work. But the 1970s also saw the belated rediscovery of Grove as an author of short stories. Like Knister, Grove managed to publish some pieces during his lifetime (mainly in the *Winnipeg Tribune Magazine* in 1926 and 1927), but did not live to see a collection of his stories. *Tales from the Margin: The Selected Stories of Frederick Philip Grove* was not published until 1971, introducing an astonished readership of Grove insiders to a multifaceted short-story oeuvre that is at least on a par with the author's novels. Until then, knowledge of Grove's short stories had been by and large confined to the frequently anthologized story "Snow" (1932; published in an earlier version under the title "Lost" in 1926), which, in a naturalist manner, reflects key elements of Grove's novelistic oeuvre: the setting in an inhospitable prairie landscape, here in the depths of winter; the overpowering, inevitable influence of the natural or social environment on taciturn characters whose fate appears to have been determined in advance; the detailed, realistic portrayal of setting (particularly the natural surroundings), characters, and plot; the depiction of hardship and privation in the lives of the pioneers, who do not so much act as react — even to the point of downright fatalism at the end of the story. The symbolically coded *in medias res* beginning of "Snow" reveals how vividly Grove's writing used the Canadian prairie as a formative setting for the modernist Canadian short story — a pioneering achievement indeed, which would soon inspire writers such as Sinclair Ross and later W. O. Mitchell, Margaret Laurence, and Rudy Wiebe.

Although Grove's classification as a prairie writer builds on a central aspect of his work, a full appraisal of his short-story oeuvre finds a greater variety than is usually acknowledged. His settings, for example, embrace a diversity of Canadian landscapes and cities, as well as the coastal region of northern France in the important story "The Boat," and even the indeterminate, allegorical "far-away-country" in the anagrammatically titled story

"In Search of Acirema" (that is, "America"). Grove's protagonists, despite appearing and feeling insignificant in the face of a seemingly omnipotent nature, are far from one-dimensional or repetitive. Stories such as "Saturday Night at the Crossroads" present an array of succinctly drafted individuals, like the penny-pinching Jewish merchant Kalad and his "hag" of a wife as well as friendly farmer Sunny Sam. Grove also commands a broad range of narrative tones, which exceeds what would be expected to accompany the unmitigated tragedy he is usually associated with in his best-known story "Snow"; he employs irony (for example, in "The Sale"), life-affirming optimism (see the ending of "Lazybones"), and even humor (in "The Extra Man").

Grove is a writer whose literary work remains as hard to pin down as his biography, and critics have labeled Grove's style an example of realism (psychological, social, or regional), naturalism, symbolism, and even existentialism. A correlation with "modernism" is missing in this context — and rightly so. Grove clearly stands in between tradition and modernity. As the first important English-Canadian writer of realist or naturalist stories, publishing about thirty years after Duncan Campbell Scott's and Sara Jeannette Duncan's short-story collections, Grove wrote in the vein of American authors of the last decades of the nineteenth century, such as Bret Harte, Mark Twain, Ambrose Bierce, Stephen Crane, and Jack London. Notwithstanding the importance of Grove's efforts to establish the postromantic, realist short story in Canada, his narrative style in the late 1920s obviously lagged behind the avant-garde modernist writings of his Canadian contemporaries such as Raymond Knister and Morley Callaghan.

With Morley Callaghan (1903–1990), the Canadian short story in the late 1920s caught up with world literature, particularly with the American short story. Callaghan's productive period ranges over almost seven decades, until his death in 1990. His first short story, "A Girl with Ambition," appeared in the Paris journal *This Quarter* in 1926, and his main phase of short-story writing stretches from the late 1920s to the early 1950s. Although Callaghan, like Knister and Grove, initially suffered from the still underdeveloped literary infrastructure in Canada at the time, he had already been successful in his younger years, especially in the United States and in Europe. Callaghan was "Canada's first great internationalist" (Boire 1992), and he soon saw his short prose published in collected form. His first short-story collection, *A Native Argosy*, appeared in 1929, published by Scribner's in New York and Macmillan in Toronto. Not counting his novellas, Callaghan wrote more than a hundred short stories. They were often first published in *The New Yorker* or *Scribner's Magazine*, and later appeared in four collections: *A Native Argosy*, comprising the early work; *Now That April's Here and Other Stories* (1936), featuring the stories of the 1930s, arguably his prime creative phase; the (most representative) collection *Morley Callaghan's Stories* (1959), combining a selection from the earlier collections with twelve new stories; and finally *The Lost and Found Stories of Morley Callaghan* (1985), presenting stories that had hitherto not been collected.

Callaghan charted the big city for the Canadian short story: Most of his stories are set in his hometown Toronto, but some — particularly in the later collections — are also set in New York or Montreal. At the same time, his stories also feature small-town or rural settings, especially in southern Ontario. In his first collection in particular — still heavily influenced by the naturalist tradition — Callaghan shows a preference for characters at the margins of society, isolated outsiders in constant struggle with themselves and with their social environment, whom the author, although displaying an implicitly moralistic tone, nonetheless depicts in their individuality and dignity. In his later stories, too, Callaghan portrays lower-middle-class characters, dealing with their problems in private relationships and questions of social acceptance. The moral-didactic tendency towards the "human condition" (Callaghan) of his early texts explains their similarity to the genre of the parable, their interlocking of realist and symbolist narrative levels; exaggerating his case, Milton Wilson in 1962 spoke of "Callaghan's uneasy mixture of parable and case-history, of hagiology and sociology."

Callaghan's contribution to the further development of the modernist style of writing in the short story is irrefutable. Like Knister, he de-emphasizes plot in favor of fragmentary reflections on his characters' inner worlds rather than extraordinary external events, and points out the significant in the everyday. Further trademarks of his narrative style are the ironic narrative voice, the ambiguity of plot and language, and, above all, the laconic diction, which has time and again evoked associations with Ernest Hemingway. Callaghan summarizes his modernist credo in the following way: "Tell the truth cleanly. . . . Strip the language, and make the style, the method, all the psychological ramifications, the ambiance of the relationships, all the one thing" (*That Summer in Paris*, 1963), which suggests modernist techniques such as "objective correlative," epiphany, and imagism. Callaghan's vocabulary and syntax, particularly in his early work, create a deceptively simple and direct, deliberately repetitive, unadorned style. The combination of narrative techniques that objectify and document while engaging the reader was inspired to a large extent by Callaghan's side job as a journalist for the *Toronto Daily Star* (where he also met Hemingway). Hemingway and Fitzgerald, in particular, recommended young Callaghan to editors and publishers in Paris and New York and thereby helped him to achieve an early and abiding international success. Beginning in 1928 and for the ensuing fourteen years, Callaghan's short stories were included in the annual volumes *Best (American) Short Stories*. As Callaghan remarked: "I was the only guy I knew of in America somehow selling my noncommercial stories in the great commercial market and staying alive." Indeed, the prolific Callaghan not only brought the Canadian short story international standing and praise, he was also the first to prove the genre profitable in the literary market.

Sinclair Ross (1908–1996), on the other hand, who was only uncovered as an outstanding author in the 1970s, could not make a living from his writing and supported himself as a bank clerk. Compared to Callaghan, Ross produced a fairly small oeuvre, which owes its considerable reputation mostly to his early work, his first novel *As for Me and My House* (published 1941 in New York) and his short stories first published in the 1930s and 1940s. Ross was the first modern Canadian short-story writer whose stories were primarily published in Canadian magazines, mostly in the Canadian scholarly journal *Queen's Quarterly*. Against the cultural background of the 1930s in Canada, the Canadian literary magazines' acceptance of Ross's, that is, a Canadian writer's, works at the time may be due to his less experimental style compared with Knister's and Callaghan's, a style that, with regard to form and narrative technique, is rather more conventional. His preferred setting, in the early stories in particular, of the Canadian prairie during the Depression era may also have contributed to his early acceptance in Canada. Form, setting, and theme link Ross to his predecessor Grove. The first collection of his short stories, *The Lamp at Noon*, consists almost exclusively of pieces from this geographical and historical context, thereby introducing Ross as the first native-born prairie writer, who uses the Saskatchewan prairie not only as a documentary setting but as a region of the mind, opening up to the reader the psychological world of the characters. Following the example of the immigrant Grove, Ross turned against the earlier romance-like if not sentimental representation of the prairie (for instance, in the works of bestselling author Ralph Connor, 1860–1937), and in the process firmly established the Canadian realist prairie short story.

Among the idiosyncracies of narrative representation in Ross's prairie stories are the close connections between humans and their natural environment, with the prairie farmer repeatedly pitted against an extreme climate, struggling for physical and mental survival in the face of what seems to be overpowering and indifferently cruel nature; the isolation and alienation of the individual in that environment; the spatial and psychological isolation between husband and wife; and the imminence of death. In a modernist fashion, Ross's narrative economy transforms external incidents and images into symbolic, indirect expressions of the characters' inner states (for instance, the "lamp at noon" burning in defiance of the surrounding darkness of the sandstorm). In Ross's classic stories, the desolate conditions in the prairie region in the 1930s, when economic depression and years of drought went hand in hand, are often expressed by emotional and communicative deficits in hopeless relationships between man and woman. Both sexes display conventionally gendered behavior, outdated from today's point of view: the emotionally repressive, outward-oriented male, who gains his self-esteem from the successful managing of his daily work, in particular the subjugation of nature, versus the lonely housewife confined to the domestic sphere, who feels neglected emotionally as well as sexually and strives in vain to alter her frustrating existence. The continual disappointment of hopes and dreams in these depressing stories frequently occurs in the context of parent-child relations, when parents, especially mothers, struggle to help their children to overcome the local and mental restrictions they themselves must submit to. Ross repeatedly writes from a child's point of view and thereby also produced some "initiation stories" (for example, "Cornet at Night," "The Outlaw," "The Runaway," "A Day with Pegasus," "Circus in Town," "One's a Heifer," and "The Flowers That Killed Him"). As Laurence Ricou commented on Ross's "puritan" prairie fiction, "An empty, unproductive and oppressive existence in an empty, unproductive and oppressive landscape makes an intense fictional impact." The manner in which Ross — despite his predominant portrayal of extreme deprivation and human limitations — nevertheless finds meaning in existence and human dignity in his characters raises the significance of his stories of the 1930s and 1940s far above their temporal and regional frame. That his short stories cannot be reduced to this immediate context is shown particularly by his later pieces, such as "Spike" and "The Flowers That Killed Him," which explore "the criminal mentality and the motivation for the crime" (Ross). His short prose also features urban settings (though only in "Saturday Night"), deals with the lives of soldiers (for example, "Jug and Bottle"), and even displays a comical streak (for instance, "No Other Way," "Saturday Night," "The Race," and "The Outlaw").

Ethel Wilson (1888–1980), whose short stories first appeared between 1937 and 1987 (about one-third of them posthumously), took the short story all the way to the Far West of Canada: More than half of Wilson's nearly thirty published stories (the best of which were collected in *Mrs. Golightly and Other Stories* in 1961) are at least partially set in Vancouver, with others set in the rural interior regions of British Columbia, Canada's westernmost province. Even stories with locations outside British Columbia frequently feature Vancouverites as protagonists, for instance, "Haply the Soul of My Grandmother" and "We Have to Sit Opposite." Although Wilson more than any other writer established Vancouver, her place of residence for many years (1898–1980), on the literary map, she is not a "city writer" like her contemporaries Morley Callaghan and Hugh Garner. For even in the stories set in Canada's westernmost metropolis, Wilson underlines the contrast between Vancouver's urban identity on the one hand and the more natural, rural aspects of both the city itself and the wider region on the other. She thereby often divests the picturesquely situated city of all typically metropolitan characteristics (thus preserving the image of Vancouver as a frontier town, a vestige of an earlier phase in the city's history, which Wilson herself experienced after emigrating to Vancouver from England in 1898 at the age of ten). Wilson frequently portrays Vancouver as a liminal space, a space of transition and even escape, but also as the awaited sanctuary from disappointing if not dangerous human relationships (symbolized by the repeatedly described "flying birds"), for example in "The Window" and "Till Death Us Do Part." Echoes of an arcadian contextualization of the big city are continually undercut by the depiction of threats arising from urban and adjoining areas, ranging from juvenile delinquency (in "Fog") to murderous intentions and homicide (in "The Window" and "Hurry, Hurry"). In the final analysis, however, pastoral yearnings are not satisfied by natural settings either. The brief story "On Nimpish Lake," for example, presents flora and fauna, and especially birds, as admirable protagonists, while the three fishermen hold hardly more than walk-on parts; the American tourist in particular appears downright out of place in the natural idyll ("'I'm just crazy about this lake. I'm just crazy about Nature anyway. I thought I'd like to stay here a week but I think I'd get kinder [sic] restless.'"). And yet, the symbolically fashioned end of the story — which can be said to cite the romantic heightened awareness of man towards nature — concludes this example of Wilson's "nature writing," despite its epiphanic pathos, on an antipastoral, melancholy note: "He [the lame man] felt a queer exaltation, a sudden flash that was deepest envy of the wild geese, strongly flying and crying together on their known way, a most secret pain." Even an encroachment of horror upon the beauties of nature can be found in stories like "Hurry, Hurry" or "The Birds." Human existence in both the city and in natural settings in Wilson's stories turns out to be precarious, if not dangerous ground for the protagonists, who are often depicted as lonely and alienated. Not without reason does the epigraph to *Mrs. Golightly* by Edwin Muir state: "life '. . . is a difficult country, and our home.'"

With regard to theme, characters, and narrative technique, Wilson's stories are very diverse. Among the best known are "Mrs. Golightly and the First Convention" and "We Have to Sit Opposite" (both 1945), which are set, respectively, in the United States and in Europe — two texts interspersed with irony and comedy, yet conveying a grim level of meaning. The latter story, for example, stages the intercultural confrontation between two cultured Canadian ladies and a lower-class German family in a train compartment en route to Munich in the 1930s, not only parading common national stereotypes of both countries, but also dealing in retrospect with the then-impending international threat of Nazi Germany. As these stories demonstrate, the polishing of preferably simple words and sentences to a highly concise and elegant style has become the author's trademark.

As Ethel Wilson's contemporary, the poet Dorothy Livesay wrote in a review: "What F. P. Grove struggled for and did not attain, what Knister grasped at, and what Ethel Wilson found and perfected, was the need for a wholly original way of handling language."

A paradox only at first sight, Wilson has even been likened by some critics to her contemporaries Virginia Woolf and Katherine Mansfield, but she has received relatively little critical attention. The reason why this talented writer ultimately did not achieve a standing in world literature comparable to that of Woolf's or Mansfield's partly stems from the precarious literary constellations in Canada at the time. It is also a result of Wilson's very slow artistic development, in particular the relatively short creative phase in which she actually published (she had her first short story printed at the age of forty-nine, her first novel when she was fifty-nine, and she stopped writing after her husband's death in 1966), and moreover reflects her conscious and modest contentment with being a wife in the first place and a writer only secondarily (if she identified with this role at all). Her slim oeuvre still made her English Canada's most important female modernist writer (Eric Nicol hailed her "First Lady of Letters in Canada"), who would later inspire even more eminent writers such as Margaret Laurence (1926–1987) and Alice Munro (1931–): "I *was enormously* excited by her work because the style was such an enormous pleasure in itself. . . . It was important to me that a Canadian writer was using so elegant a style . . ., that a point of view so complex and ironic was possible in Canadian literature" (Munro 1983).

With the prolific Hugh Garner (1913–1979), who published short stories from 1938 through a creative period of four decades, the Canadian short story became a popular genre in a wider sense. Garner wrote a hundred stories, which were often first published in Canadian popular magazines such as *Chatelaine, Canadian Home Journal,* and *National Home Monthly* and were reprinted in five collections during the author's lifetime: *The Yellow Sweater,* 1952; *Hugh Garner's Best Stories,* 1963; *Men and Women,* 1966; *Violation of the Virgins,* 1971; and *The Legs of the Lame,* 1976. Especially until the early 1960s, Garner professed his interest in reaching a large audience (in 1951 alone, he sold seventeen stories to Canadian magazines). Garner's artistic credo could be said to pander to the reader: "I believe, along with W. Somerset Maugham, that the first duty of a writer of fiction is to entertain" (Garner 1952). This approach, together with Garner's undeniably great narrative talent, probably made him the most widely read short-story author in Canada in the 1950s. For the same reason, though, literary critics have often remained skeptical, mistrusting Garner's popular success and the style that he cultivated to achieve it (for instance, his stock repertoire of drastic plot elements). His frequent anti-intellectual statements and his candidness — for example, in his autobiography *One Damn Thing after Another* (1973), in which he discussed his often hasty creative process under the pressure of deadlines — did not help him with the critics either. Consequently, and also as a result of some clichéd or formulaic, too "well-made" qualities of some of his most popular stories, Garner is still a disputed and barely studied author among literary scholars. One may well agree with Paul Stuewe's classification of Garner as a "lowbrow," "middlebrow," and "highbrow" writer all in one (Stuewe 1985, 112). Garner is particularly known today for his short-story oeuvre, not least thanks to the frequent anthologization of some of his classic stories (including "One-Two-Three Little Indians," "The Yellow Sweater," and "The Legs of the Lame"). In such pieces, particularly from his early phase, Garner proves his narrative expertise in the tradition of Ernest Hemingway and displays a sure command of the genre's form.

Like Callaghan, Garner is basically a city writer, with a strongly developed sense of place. Most of his stories are set, more or less discernibly, in Toronto (see also his paramount novel on Toronto's *Cabbagetown*, 1950), but sometimes also in Montreal or elsewhere in Quebec. Garner adheres to a social-realist agenda. What sets him apart from the American realists he takes as examples (such as Theodore Dreiser), however, is the moralistic, even sentimental dimension of some of his stories. In his settings and themes, Garner is a genuinely Canadian writer; in his preface to *The Yellow Sweater* he remarks: "These are Canadian stories; the people in them are all Canadian; the locale is Canada . . ., and they were written in Toronto and . . . Quebec" (Garner 1952). Characteristic aspects of Garner's writing can be traced, for example, in his most frequently anthologized story, "One-Two-Three Little Indians" (1950). The story relates the tragic impact of racism on an indigenous family, thereby illustrating the grim situation of Native Canadians trapped between their economic dependence on tourism on the one hand and miserable living conditions on the other.

Joyce Marshall (1913–2005) has received even less critical attention than Garner, and unjustly so. Well-known Canadian novelist and short-story writer Timothy Findley (1930–2002), for one, considered Marshall one of Canada's best short-story writers. She published her first story in 1936, and many of her more than thirty stories were first read on CBC Radio. Her three collections *A Private Place* (1975), *Any Time at All and Other Stories* (1993), and *Blood and Bone/En chair et en os* (bilingual edition, 1995) document her most creative phase, from 1952 through 1995, and explore in various ways the effects of modernity on human consciousness in an often urban setting (Toronto, Montreal). Faced with a world that seems alien and inscrutable to them, Marshall's characters struggle for a sense of identity by projecting their own aspirations and speculations onto their surroundings, thus repeatedly substituting ersatz images for authentic contact with their environment. In a process of extensive self-reflection, Marshall's almost exclusively female protagonists (who are of all ages) oscillate between feelings of alienation and the insignificance of existence and the search for insight. In none of Marshall's texts is the unbridgeable gap between human beings as symbolically highlighted as in "The Old Woman" (1952), her most frequently anthologized story. The secluded setting in northern Quebec and the isolation of the English protagonist Molly, who after three years of separation has joined her Canadian husband Toddy there, mirror the characters' inner worlds and the impossible love between them: Years of loneliness in the Canadian wilderness have left Toddy utterly transfixed by the lure of nature and hence incapable of human interaction. The electrical power station where he is employed and which he personifies as "The Old Woman" becomes a substitute for his wife — the end of the story sees him succumbing to complete isolation, to madness, with his wife left to cope with this gruesome situation. Timothy Findley describes the story as "the story of a woman's emancipation and a man's enslavement" (1993).

Among Marshall's modernist stylistic techniques are *in medias res* beginnings, allusions, and experimental narrative forms. A good example is "The Heights" (1993) from *Any Time at All*. Featuring young Martha, who spends her childhood as an anglophone in French Quebec, the story establishes an internal discourse on Martha's different stages of development right at the beginning of the story by introducing a second narrative consciousness, a "ghost" from the past, to comment in retrospect: "All through this story . . . you'll have to imagine the occasional presence of another person, watching, weighing, adding things up. . . . The strange thing is that I don't remember her . . . though she must often have been in the same place at the same time, since she saw many of the same things. Or so she says." Marshall's stories probe the mental worlds of characters in twentieth-century Canada who find themselves in an acute phase of uncertainty but do not completely lose track of their aim to better understand themselves and their environment. In the course of her career Marshall's narrative style increasingly developed postmodernist traits, as structural and thematic aspects of her third collection *Blood and Bone/En chair et en os* clearly show. The story "Kat," for example — consisting predominantly of a conversation — denies the reader a spatial reference system any more specific than a "room" in the "city," emphasizing the universality of the story's thoughts and implications, which seem to speak and stand for themselves. According to Marshall, this self-reflexivity may hint at the constructedness of literary texts ("Stories don't always end"), but at the same time also at their enduring connection to reality ("Some things are never fully understood").

Sheila Watson (1909–1998) definitively marks the transition from modernist to postmodernist paradigms in English-Canadian literature and in the Canadian short story, and her significance for Canadian literature is larger than her slim oeuvre would suggest (two novels, only five short stories, some essays in literary criticism). Her literary work stems almost exclusively from the 1950s, although some texts were published much later, for instance, the story "And the Four Animals" (1980). Watson's long literary silence, which extended from around 1958 to her death in 1998, that is, for about forty years after her most creative decade, remains an enigma in Canadian literary history. Under the title *Five Stories*, Watson's short stories were not collected until 1984, after they had previously appeared as *Four Stories* in 1979 (before the publication of "And the Four Animals").

Watson was particularly interested in narrative aesthetics and its renewal through a turn away from the realist, regional paradigms that had dominated Canadian fiction until then. She expands the suggestive ambiguity of modernist texts towards a hermetic and abstract system of multiple meanings, producing texts of intricate intertextuality and complex intransparency, which are aimed primarily at an educated audience. Her allegorical compositions often draw on ancient mythology (four of her five short stories refer to Oedipus; she also mentions, for instance, Antigone, Ismene, Atlas, and Daedalus), but also on more recent European mythology and literature, for example, the Bible, Shakespeare, James Joyce, Gertrude Stein, Freud, and Jung. These extremely dense, impersonal allegories feature fragmentary plots, in which splinters of meaning from the realm of mythology and literature are superimposed in a collage-like fashion on aspects of Canada in the twentieth century, thus creating an abstract, seemingly unreal level of meaning. Watson's texts use stripped-down plot and imagery, symbols, allusions, and associations to construct an open, complex framework of meaning, which — in a self-referential and postmodernist manner — engenders literature on literature and emphasizes the text's level of discourse (rather than its plot). Watson's elaborate language links her fiction to prose poetry, for instance, in "And the Four Animals," the earliest text in *Five Stories*, and the shortest, at only three pages. Shirley Neuman argues convincingly for an interpretation of this story as "one of the most concise histories of mankind's journey from Creation to Apocalypse ever told" (Neuman 1982, 48). Watson's most frequently anthologized story, "Antigone" (1959), still presents a roughly comprehensible plot, namely the story of Antigone's cousin, in love with Antigone rather than with her sister Ismene. Antigone, outspoken and individualistic, revolts against her father's system of order and discipline by burying a bird on the premises of the mental asylum (Watson grew up in such a place, as the director's daughter). As Shirley Neuman summarizes the story:

> The Provincial Mental Hospital of Watson's childhood and its inmates are transformed and undercut by their allegorical conflation with characters from Greek tragedy. Watson's Antigone is no princess burying a dead brother in the six feet of soil due to him, . . . Creon no longer rules Thebes but a land where Atlas eats dirt, Helen walks naked and all is but

> a demented inversion of Greek myths and Greek tragedies. . . . This
> modern parable provides no moral resolution of its dualities. (Neuman
> 1982, 48)

Stephen Scobie has argued that Watson's fundamental combination of
conflicting elements might in itself be considered either modernist, a form
of duality, or postmodernist, a form of duplicity — a position that once
again emphasizes Watson's watershed function (pointed out by George
Bowering) in contemporary Canadian fiction. As a female writer, Watson's
position on the threshold between different literary paradigms confirms
Barbara Godard's thesis (1984) that women's social eccentricity predis-
poses them to the role of innovators in literary history: "Women have long
been pioneers in new subjects, new forms, new modes of discourse." The
development from Wilson to Marshall to Watson, as it has been traced
here, thus anticipates the explosion of female creativity in Canadian writing of the 1960s, also in the genre of the short story.

# 15: Early English-Canadian Theater and Drama, 1918–1967

*Jerry Wasserman (University of British Columbia)*

AFTER FOUR YEARS OF CARNAGE Canada emerged from the Great War in 1918 bloodied but victorious, with a strengthened sense of national confidence and pride. The nation shared a feeling that it had come of age, its soldiers having proved themselves equal to any other combatants in their courage, ability, and self-sacrifice across the western front, at Vimy Ridge, and in the fields of Flanders. Canadian attitudes towards Great Britain changed significantly. Though English Canadians still considered theirs a British nation, they could no longer be content to be treated like colonial children by the mother country whose men they had fought alongside on the road to victory. The Canadian government began to insist on equality of political representation, sending its own delegation to the postwar negotiations at Versailles. Within a decade it would appoint Vincent Massey its first ambassador to Washington, and the British embassy no longer presumed to speak on behalf of Canadian interests in the United States.

The end of the war also brought about changed relations and attitudes towards the United States. Long-held prejudices against the presumed arrogance of Americans were reinforced by the self-congratulatory attitudes of their politicians and press, who boasted that American intervention had won the war. Canadians bitterly pointed out that the United States had joined the fighting three years after Canadians entered the war and that, relative to population, Canada had suffered ten times more casualties. Nevertheless, the United States and Canada had fought together as allies, and the United States emerged from the war rich and powerful, while Britain was exhausted and nearly broke. Increasingly, Canadians realized that their future lay with their North American neighbor. In fact, 1921 proved to be the last year in which the value of Canadian trade with the United Kingdom exceeded that between Canada and the United States. Canadians no longer feared the threat of American political annexation as they had throughout the nineteenth century. And yet, fear of American economic and cultural domination would become a Canadian obsession in the 1920s and beyond.

Postwar Canadian nationalism and the accompanying ambivalence towards the two great English-speaking powers that had shaped so much of

Canada's destiny provided a springboard for Canadian theatrical development over the next decade. Professional theater in prewar Canada had been dominated by commercial American theatrical syndicates operating out of New York, and to a lesser extent by British touring companies. In the face of imported commercial theater, organizations like Toronto's Arts and Letters Club (established 1908) had attempted to create a Canadian equivalent of the European art theater, an initiative temporarily put on hold during the war. But even the war years had seen some cultural momentum. The amateur Little Theatre movement began taking root with the establishment of the Ottawa Drama League (1913), the University of British Columbia Players' Club (1915), the University of Toronto Players' Club (1913), and the University College Alumnae Dramatic Club (1917). Within a few years of the war's end came a virtual explosion of community-based arts organizations. The West alone saw a short-lived attempt by Carroll Aikins (1888–1967) to create an artistic Mecca in rural Naramata, BC, with the Home Theatre (1920–1922), the founding of the Vancouver Little Theatre and the Community Players of Winnipeg (1921), and little theaters in New Westminster and Saskatoon (1922) and in Calgary (1924). Calgary Little Theatre's opening double-bill of short plays by J. M. Barrie and Susan Glaspell was typical of these companies' repertoires, drawing primarily on contemporary English, American, and Irish work. But they also encouraged the production of original Canadian scripts. One of the most prolific Canadian playwrights of the 1920s, Isabel Ecclestone Mackay (1875–1928), had her Glaspell-esque play *The Second Lie* premiered by the University of British Columbia Players' Club in 1920 and subsequently remounted as part of Hart House Theatre's first all-Canadian bill in 1921.

Hart House was the jewel in the modest crown of Canadian postwar theatrical development. Built in 1919 on the University of Toronto campus by Vincent Massey (1887–1967), an Arts and Letters Club member and heir to a family fortune, the five-hundred-seat theater with the best technical equipment in the country became the center of amateur production in Toronto for the next two decades. American-born Roy Mitchell (1884–1944), its first artistic director (1919–1921), was a force in New York City's burgeoning Little Theater movement and had even greater influence in Toronto. Mitchell's aversion to commercial values, embodied in his book *Creative Theatre* (1929), helped shape Hart House's programming, dominated by Euripides, Shakespeare, and George Bernard Shaw in his years there, along with the all-Canadian evening which would become a staple of Hart House seasons. Mitchell's successors updated the Hart House repertoire, adding work by such modernists as Henrik Ibsen, William Butler Yeats, and Eugene O'Neill. The 1922 season included a production of Carroll Aikins's melodrama *The God of Gods*, set amid a confused version of First Nations culture on the Canadian West Coast. In 1927 Aikins became Hart House Theatre's first Canadian-born artistic director.

Many of the Group of Seven painters belonged to the Arts and Letters Club, and some of them — Lawren Harris, A. Y. Jackson, J. E. H. MacDonald — lent their talents to Hart House productions as designers and scenic artists. In the manifesto accompanying their first major exhibition in Toronto in 1920, the Group of Seven advocated a distinctive indigenous style and subject matter for Canadian painting. Similar nationalist notions might have carried over into Hart House theatricals, but they found ambiguous form in the plays of Merrill Denison (1893–1975). Trained as an architect, Denison came to Hart House as its first art director but soon became its major dramatist. Of the eight original Canadian scripts Vincent Massey published in the first of his two volumes of *Canadian Plays from Hart House Theatre* (1926), three were by Denison. Among them, Denison's *Brothers in Arms*, written in 1921 for the theater's first all-Canadian bill, was the most produced Canadian play of its time, with over five hundred performances by the end of the decade.

In one-act Hart House comedies like *Brothers in Arms*, *The Weather Breeder*, and *The Prize Winner*, and in his full-length tragedy *Marsh Hay* (unproduced until 1996 at the Shaw Festival), Denison created vivid stage-realist portraits of backwoods Ontarians speaking a rural Canadian vernacular. His first and last plays for Hart House, *Brothers in Arms* and the full-length *Contract* (1929), also satirized Toronto's urban elite and the Canadian business establishment. Unlike the ruggedly beautiful northern landscapes of the Group of Seven's paintings, Denison's theatrical Canada was *The Unheroic North*, the title he gave to the 1923 publication of four of his stage plays. By the end of the decade, hoping to make a living as a playwright and frustrated by the apparent impossibility of doing so in Canada, Denison emigrated to the United States, bidding farewell with an essay, "Nationalism and the Drama" (1929), in which he despaired at the possibility of there ever being a Canadian theatrical culture or homegrown drama that would not be merely a branch-plant of American theater.

Postwar nationalism and the Canadian aesthetics of the Group of Seven finally found their theatrical champion in Denison's associate Herman Voaden (1903–1991), who worked mostly outside Hart House, producing plays in the Toronto high school where he came to teach in 1928. Having studied contemporary dance, German expressionist theater, and the plays of Eugene O'Neill, about whom he wrote his MA thesis, Voaden developed a multimedia, antirealist theatrical aesthetic that he called "symphonic expressionism." Music, lighting, choral speech, and choreographed movement were more important than character and plot. As in many Group of Seven paintings, the Canadian landscape itself was a dominant, almost mystical element in Voaden plays with titles like *Rocks* and *Earth Song* (both 1932), *Hill-Land* (1934), and *Murder Pattern* (1936).

Voaden also encouraged the writing and production of new Canadian plays by others, especially those who shared his aesthetics. In 1930 he edited a collection called *Six Canadian Plays*, chosen, as he explained in the preface, from among forty-nine entries to a playwriting contest he conducted (with Merrill Denison as one of the judges): "An exterior northern setting was required, and it was suggested that contestants follow in mood or subject matter the paintings of artists whose work they considered Canadian in character. The result is that the plays are infused with the vigorous, outdoor spirit of Canada" (viii). Cultivating the Canadian spirit in homegrown cultural productions was, for Voaden, like generations of anglophile Canadian nationalists before him, one way of resisting the dangers of creeping Americanism. In an essay typical of his proselytizing spirit, he wrote, "Second-rate road shows and third-rate movies are vehicles for an unwelcome American influence," an influence which he feared would "in time override our national and British character . . . turning our energies into material channels" at the expense of "our spiritual integrity." Voaden's cultural nationalism led him to advocate a national drama league, a network of amateur and educational theater organizations across the country that might effect "a Canadian Renaissance in art and literature" ("A National Drama League," in Rubin 1996, 78).

By the early 1930s Canada's string of little theaters would reach from Victoria, BC, to the Maritimes, representing every major city and many of the nation's smaller communities. The national drama league that emerged as the Dominion Drama Festival aimed to connect these institutions with one another in order to improve and develop the quality of the work they produced. But it was also one of a number of defensive maneuvers aimed at holding back the rising tide of American cultural products threatening to overflow the border and snuff out what little indigenous progress was slowly being made on the Canadian cultural front. Canadian editorialists in the 1920s echoed Voaden in constantly warning of the threat to Canadian values (not to mention Canadian commercial interests) posed by the American newspapers and magazines Canadians preferred to their own, and by the powerful new entertainment media of moving pictures and radio dominated by American studios and networks. Radio and movies, along with the deep economic depression that began in 1929, did away with much of what remained of the second-rate road shows Voaden scorned, the touring companies from the United States that had largely monopolized Canadian professional theater. With those "alien" influences (as they were characteristically called) gone, Canadians might be able to fill the gap by developing their own cultural infrastructure, but only if the new cultural invaders could be held at bay.

While various quota systems, levies, and other discouragements were proposed — nearly all without success — to help Canadian companies compete with American print media and movies, concrete progress was made regarding radio and live theater. With the rapid popularization of radio in the mid-1920s, American networks quickly developed a slick commercial product so that nearly all the most popular radio shows among Canadians were American. In response, prominent Canadians (among them the omnipresent, influential Vincent Massey) lobbied the federal government to create a noncommercial Canadian national radio network to compete with U.S. programming. The Canadian National Railway's network of stations, which used to broadcast radio entertainment to the travelers on its trains, already provided something of a model. In 1930 Merrill Denison wrote a series of radio plays about Canadian history called *The Romance of Canada* for the CNR network, directed by the acclaimed British director Tyrone Guthrie, who would help found the Stratford Festival a quarter of a century later. Two years later, prime minister R. B. Bennett announced the formation of CRBC, the Canadian Radio Broadcasting Corporation, intended as an "agency by which national consciousness may be fostered and sustained and national unity still further strengthened" (quoted in Nash 1994, 88). In 1936 CRBC became the CBC, a key institution in the future development of Canadian drama.

Voaden's dream of a national drama league came to fruition around the same time, again with the help of Vincent Massey, who became the first Chairman of the Dominion Drama Festival, created in 1932 under the patronage of Canada's new Governor General, Lord Bessborough. It was Bessborough who coined the organization's unofficial slogan: "The spirit of a nation, if it is to find full expression, must include a National Drama" (Lee 1973, 116). Steered by a British peer and by Canadians like Voaden and Massey, who were unabashedly suspicious of creeping Americanism, the Festival aimed at building the kinds of cultural defenses that Massey, in his famous *Report* (1951) twenty years later, would argue that Canada lacked in its relations with its powerful southern neighbor.

Officially, the Festival intended to provide opportunities for Canadian amateur theater practitioners — strung out as they were in isolation across the nation's huge geographical expanse — to cross-fertilize, see each other's work, and improve their own through competition and feedback from professional adjudicators like British director Rupert Harvey, who judged the first DDF Finals in 1933. Little theater companies from eight provinces had competed and triumphed in local and regional festivals, then made their way to Ottawa for this gala event, which saw trophies presented for the best productions in both English and French. The following year, to encourage the writing and production of new Canadian plays, a trophy with a one-hundred-dollar cash prize was established for the best original Canadian play in the competition. The fact that this award was sponsored by and carried the name of a British director, Sir Barry Jackson, was only one of many ironies associated with the DDF. Another was that the adjudicators at the Toronto regional festival ruled Voaden's own plays ineligible, arguing that their multidisciplinary modernism made it impossible to judge them according to the DDF's conventional evaluation system.

Despite chronic complaints about its aesthetic conservatism and excessive concern for social rather than artistic values, the Dominion Drama Festival lasted until 1970 and certainly helped to encourage the growth of amateur theater in Canada. It served as a training ground for many of the artists who would professionalize Canadian theater after the Second World War, providing opportunities for actors, directors, designers, and playwrights to learn their trades in a functioning theatrical environment, albeit one that could not pay them for their work.

Among those benefiting from the stimulation provided by the DDF were three talented women from Alberta. Producer/director Elizabeth Sterling Haynes (1897–1957) and playwrights Elsie Park Gowan (1905–1999) and Gwen Pharis Ringwood (1910–1984) were active in the Edmonton Little Theatre, the University of Alberta, and the Banff School of Fine Arts. The latter, destined to become a key training institution for Canadian theater artists, was established in 1933 with Haynes as its first instructor. Gowan, one of the most frequently staged prairie playwrights of the 1930s and 1940s, was among the first to be produced professionally when her play *The Last Caveman* was toured by Sidney Risk's Everyman Theatre across Western Canada in 1946. Ringwood, who went off to the University of North Carolina to study folk drama in the late 1930s, emerged as a strong voice of Western regionalism with a series of folk tragedies about the prairies and, later, British Columbia. Her stark prairie-gothic melodrama *Still Stands the House* (1939) remained the most frequently anthologized Canadian play for decades.

Another important manifestation of the Little Theatre movement in the 1930s was a body of plays and performances with an overtly political agenda that came to be known as the Workers' Theatre. As the Depression deepened, left-wing Progressive Arts Clubs established themselves in most of Canada's major cities and adopted the notion that art could be a weapon in their political struggles. A short-lived but spectacular example of the genre was the lively, powerful agitprop play *Eight Men Speak*, written by four members of Toronto's Progressive Arts Club in protest against capitalism, repressive legislation, and the imprisonment of Communist union leader Tim Buck in the Kingston Penitentiary. It got only one performance, to a large Toronto audience in 1933, before being shut down by the police department's Red Squad. But within a few years even the conservative Dominion Drama Festival opened itself to this kind of work: A production of American playwright Clifford Odets's pro-union play *Waiting for Lefty*, mounted in support of a longshoreman's strike in Vancouver, made its way to the 1936 DDF Finals, as did Toronto's Theatre of Action with its production of Irwin Shaw's antiwar play *Bury the Dead* in 1937. Even outside the Workers' Theatre movement theatrical protest became commonplace and respectable. Adjudicator Harley Granville-Barker awarded London (Ontario) Little Theatre the trophy for best production at the 1936 final for the first Canadian play to be so honored by the DDF, W. Eric Harris's *Twenty-Five Cents* (1936), a harshly naturalistic drama about the disintegration of a family under the pressures of urban poverty.

Best production and best Canadian play awards for 1938 went to *The House in the Quiet Glen* (1937), a play set in Northern Ireland, written by a recent Irish immigrant to Toronto, John Coulter (1888–1980). Inspired by the example of Dublin's Abbey Theatre, as many Canadian cultural nationalists had been since its establishment in 1904, Coulter argued in his 1938 essay "The Canadian Theatre and the Irish Exemplar" that what the Abbey's plays had done for Ireland — reflecting back to audiences "Irish mugs in Irish mirrors" — Canadian playwrights and theaters could do for Canada by choosing subject matter from their immediate environment and history (Coulter in Rubin, 121). Taking his own advice, Coulter would soon turn his playwriting attentions to Canadian history and become an important figure not only in Dominion Drama Festivals to come but also for CBC Radio and television drama and the emerging professional stage.

Coulter was one of many Canadian playwrights who found increasing opportunity for their work on CBC Radio. Original plays had been broadcast on Canadian radio since the 1920s, but what came to be called the golden age of Canadian radio drama began with the appointment of Andrew Allan (1907–1974) as National Supervisor for the CBC in 1943. Allan had been producing innovative radio plays from Vancouver during the 1930s with a repertory company of writers and actors, many of whom he brought with him to Toronto. Allan established two key drama series, *Stage* in 1944 and *CBC Wednesday Night* in 1947. Both ran weekly for many years, broadcasting live from the studio hundreds of original scripts and adaptations which Allan commissioned from Canadian writers. He also employed a regular group of actors, musicians, and directors. Everyone was paid for their labor, a rarity in a Canadian cultural field that was still overwhelmingly amateur. Many of the actors — John Drainie, Don Harron, Jane Mallett, Frances Hyland — would soon become mainstays of the new professional theater. The same held true for playwrights like Lister Sinclair (1921–2006) and W. O. Mitchell (1914–1998), who also established significant bodies of dramatic work for radio.

The outbreak of the Second World War put the Dominion Drama Festival on hiatus and saw many theater artists who were working on the amateur stage or in professional radio join the armed forces. Troop entertainments such as The Army Show were broadcast by CBC and provided valuable training for performers like the soon-to-be-famous comedy team of Johnny Wayne (1918–1990) and Frank Shuster (1916–2002). Andrew Allan's *Stage* productions continued airing throughout the war, many of them taking on taboo themes like racism, abortion, and religious intolerance. By 1945 *Stage* was lauded by international radio organizations and even *The New York Times* as North America's highest quality dramatic series. Like the First World War, the Second World War provided enormous momentum for Canadian cultural endeavors. Once again Canada emerged victorious, its economy booming, its national pride reinforced by its sacrifices and successes on the wartime world's stage. With demobilization and the resumption of peacetime normalcy, many people sought to professionalize Canadian theater. In Toronto, Vancouver, Ottawa, and Montreal, they were soon successful.

The prime mover on the Toronto scene was actress, teacher, and director Dora Mavor Moore (1888–1979). She had been the first Canadian to attend London's Royal Academy of Dramatic Arts and on her return became a mainstay of Hart House and other amateur theaters in Toronto. In 1937 Moore established the Village Players, a company that operated out of high school auditoriums in the winter and out of a barn in the yard of her Toronto home in summers. When the war ended she decided to turn professional, and when a basement auditorium in the Royal Ontario Museum became available for performances, she announced the formation of the New Play Society, a professional company whose members would be paid fifteen dollars per production. Their first show, J. M. Synge's *Playboy of the Western World* (1907), was staged in 1946. Though it was by no means the first homegrown professional stage production, in many ways it signaled the real beginning of professional theater in Canada.

The New Play Society not only blazed the trail of professionalism, but set a standard for new Canadian companies in its insistence on creating a body of Canadian work for performance. Over the next few years the company produced plays by well-known writers Lister Sinclair and Harry Boyle (1915–2005), the novelist Morley Callaghan (1903–1990), and Dora's son Mavor Moore (1919–2006), who created the company's most popular production, the legendary satirical revue *Spring Thaw* (1948), which made gentle fun of Canadian institutions, public figures, weather, and Canada's most prominent city: "We All Hate Toronto" was one of the show's most popular songs. By the time of its final incarnation in 1985, *Spring Thaw* was the world's longest-running annual topical revue. For the 1949–1950 season, six of the ten NPS productions were new Canadian plays — including John Coulter's sweeping epic *Riel* (1950), with Mavor Moore in the role of the Manitoba Métis who organized a rebellion against the Canadian government in the 1880s, was executed, condemned as a traitor by English-Protestant Canada, and memorialized as a martyr by French-Catholic Quebec. Modeling Riel on so many ambiguously heroic Irish rebels and martyrs, Coulter's play not only initiated new interest among writers and historians in Riel himself, but also created a paradigm for Canadian historical drama that would be followed well into the 1970s.

In Vancouver, director Sydney Risk established his Everyman Theatre company in 1946 and kept it alive until 1953. Ottawa's Canadian

Repertory Theatre opened in 1948 and lasted until 1956, featuring in its casts many of Canada's future stars, including Christopher Plummer, William Hutt, Amelia Hall, and William Shatner. In Montreal, the professionalization of French-language theater rode on the brilliant success of Gratien Gélinas (1909–1999), a radio personality whose persona of a working-class street kid named Fridolin became so popular that Gélinas built a series of annual stage revues around him called *Les Fridolinades* (see ch. 20, Scholl). In 1948 he wrote a sentimental family melodrama based on a grown-up version of Fridolin and played the part himself. The play, *Tit-Coq* (1948), was a phenomenon. Identifiably French-Canadian characters spoke colloquial Quebec French, and audiences were thrilled to see, as Coulter had predicted, (French-)Canadian mugs in (French-)Canadian mirrors. The production ran for over two hundred performances in Montreal, went briefly to Broadway, then reopened in Toronto in 1951 for a long, successful run in English translation. Gélinas became the most famous theater artist in Canada. Clearly, indigenous drama had struck a chord.

Meanwhile, the cold war quickly replaced the postwar peace. With the growing threat of nuclear conflict between the United States and the Soviet Union, the outbreak of the Korean War, and the military and economic weakness of Britain after the war in Europe, Canada was increasingly drawn into the American orbit. The United States and Canada became partners in NATO and NORAD (the North American Air Defense Agreement), fought together in Korea, and shared in the "Red Scare." Between 1948 and 1953 Canada's military expenditures grew from seven percent of its budget to forty-three percent. But from a cultural perspective, ironically, the real threat seemed closer to home. While Canada had established its credentials as a major international player economically and militarily, it still lagged far behind culturally, artistically, and educationally. Why had Canada produced so few creative artists of note? Why were its cultural institutions, including its theater, so poorly developed? In 1949, to answer these questions, prime minister Louis St. Laurent asked Vincent Massey to chair a Royal Commission on National Development in the Arts, Letters and Sciences. After two years of investigations and hearings, the 1951 Massey Report, as it came to be known, concluded that "the forces of geography" had conspired to put a nation of fourteen million (Canada's population at the time) alongside a country ten times as populous and many more times as culturally aggressive. Strung out in a narrow band across five thousand miles of border, Canadians had "not even the advantages of what soldiers call defense in depth" against the "American invasion by film, radio and periodical," and the newest entertainment medium, television (*Report*, 13, 18). Given the tenor of the times, military metaphors seemed most appropriate. In the end, the Massey Commission concluded that defense expenditures were important, but "it would be paradoxical to defend something which we are unwilling to strengthen and enrich, and which we even allow to decline. . . . Our military defences must be made secure; but our cultural defences equally demand national attention . . ." (274–75).

Psychologically, the *Report* produced significant consciousness raising among Canadians. Concretely, it recommended the establishment of the Canada Council for the Arts, Letters, Humanities and Social Sciences. That recommendation, implemented in 1959, changed the face of Canadian arts and culture generally, and Canadian theater specifically, more than any other single development in the nation's history. Modeled along the lines of the British Arts Council, the Canada Council provided federal funding for Canadian artists and arts institutions, allotted by peer-review juries at arm's length from the government itself. In principle it formally acknowledged the significance of art and culture to the life of the nation. In practice the Council provided both foundational and ongoing funding for individuals and institutions — playwrights, other theater artists, and theater companies. It meant that Canadian professional theaters that accepted Council funding — in fact the great majority since 1959 — would be nonprofit organizations. And once the money began flowing in significant amounts, it produced a cultural explosion, a Canadian cultural revolution. Within a decade of its implementation, a fully-fledged Canadian professional theater culture and infrastructure would come into being.

Even while the Canada Council was still being conceptualized, other significant developments were taking place. In Toronto, which would continue to lead the way for theater in English Canada, more new professional companies followed in the path of the New Play Society. A group of actors led by John Drainie (1916–1966) and Lorne Greene (1915–1987) founded Jupiter Theatre in 1951. The two of them starred the following year in Jupiter's production of *The Moneymakers* by Ted Allan (1916–1995), an autobiographically based play about a Canadian screenwriter in Hollywood who gets caught up in and ultimately denounces American cultural imperialism, materialism, blacklisting, and Red-bashing. *The Moneymakers* would also be the first stage play adapted for broadcast on CBC television, which went on air in the fall of 1952 and would become nearly as important as radio in affording dramatists the opportunity to earn a living in the 1950s and 1960s. Crest Theatre, founded in 1954 by brothers Donald (1928–1998) and Murray Davis (1924–1997), became known for its very high level of acting talent and was Toronto's most important company until it shut down in 1966. Some Canadian plays were incorporated into its mostly international repertoire. The Crest introduced to English-speaking audiences the hard-hitting *Zone* (1953), a play about urban ennui by Marcel Dubé (1930–), Quebec's most important playwright, along with Gélinas, in the 1950s. It also produced *A Jig for the Gypsy* (1954) and *Hunting Stuart* (1955) by English Canada's most prominent playwright of the postwar decade, Robertson Davies (1913–1995).

Robertson Davies, who would turn from playwriting to become Canada's most significant novelist of the 1960s, had established himself as a major figure in the amateur theater of the late 1940s with plays like *Overlaid* (1947), *Fortune, My Foe* (1949), and *At My Heart's Core* (1950), which took aim at the Philistine sensibilities of a Canada he sought to transform. As a journalist, too, writing under the pseudonym Samuel Marchbanks, Davies consistently criticized the hostile physical and spiritual conditions under which Canadian artists were forced to labor. He submitted a lengthy brief to the Massey Commission in the form of a dramatic dialogue about the state of Canadian theater and its dire need of federal funding, to help move it from an amateur activity to serious professional status and to upgrade the facilities in which it took place. Having worked as an actor in 1930s London for Tyrone Guthrie, Davies enthusiastically agreed to help Dora Mavor Moore convince Guthrie to come to Canada and head a bold new venture that a businessman named Tom Patterson had dreamt up for the economically depressed town of Stratford in southwestern Ontario. Davies and Moore, and of course Massey, would all join the board of the Stratford Shakespearean Festival that opened in 1953 with Guthrie as its first artistic director.

The word most often used to describe the Stratford Festival's inauguration was "triumphant." Staging Shakespeare in small-town Ontario under a tent (for the first few summers before a permanent structure was built in 1957), Guthrie managed to give the Festival a legitimate international profile. Under Guthrie's supervision the thrust stage was designed by Tanya Moiseiwitsch to emulate the original Globe Theatre's configuration, and the design turned out to be hugely influential. Guthrie's policy of hiring a few British and American stars (Alec Guinness and Irene Worth in the first season) and fleshing out the rest of the company with Canadian actors (many of whom went on to significant fame) provided box-office attractiveness for the company and important experience for the actors. Stratford's opening was reported and reviewed around the world, giving Canadian theater instant credibility, and a spin-off company was formed — The Canadian Players — to tour Shakespeare and the classics across Canada during the winters. Yet Stratford would prove to be a site of remarkable contention within Canadian theatrical circles. In its first few decades, many argued that Stratford was a neocolonialist venture, Canada's marquee theater devoted to Britain's marquee playwright, run until the 1970s by British artistic directors. As soon as Canada Council money came on stream, Stratford became Canada's most heavily funded company. And yet it hardly produced or encouraged Canadian playwrights. Today, with four stages, a virtually year-round schedule, and annual revenues exceeding ten million dollars, a more fully Canadianized Stratford

Festival — albeit one still primarily dedicated to Shakespeare — remains an important element in the Canadian theatrical landscape which, in the 1950s, it dominated.

Even with the higher international profile afforded Canadian theater by Stratford, Canadian dramatists were generally unable to make any impact outside the country during this era. Patricia Joudry (1921–2000) was one exception. In the 1940s and early 1950s she became a mainstay of CBC Radio drama and spent time in New York as a highly paid writer for an American radio sitcom. Turning to the stage with domestic dramas like *Teach Me How to Cry* (1955) and *Semi-Detached* (1960), she succeeded where few Canadians ever had, getting productions on Broadway and London's West End. But ironically, Joudry never really found an audience in Canada.

The growing professionalization of Canadian theater was most significantly marked by the establishment of the Manitoba Theatre Centre (MTC) in Winnipeg in 1958 as a result of the merger of two amateur companies. Led by directors Tom Hendry (1929–) and John Hirsch (1930–1989), who would remain major players in the burgeoning Canadian theater scene of the 1960s and 1970s, MTC was the first in what would become by the end of the 1960s a nationwide network of "regional" theaters anchoring a newly formed Canadian professional theater structure. The rationale for the regional theater system reflected the long-held desire among Canadian cultural leaders for a "national" theater, some of the findings and recommendations of the Massey Commission, as well as the logic and experience of the Dominion Drama Festival. Given Canada's vast geography, a single national theater company or building seemed impractical, a notion with which the Massey Report concurred. The DDF had shown the success of organizing Canadian amateur theater around regional models. MTC offered itself to the province of Manitoba as a regional theater center, which would provide main-stage productions in the city plus a children's theater company, a touring arm to bring professional plays to outlying communities, and a theater school. This regional model for a decentralized, de facto national theater was embraced and supported by the new Canada Council, which offered funding for such organizations in other provinces. By the end of the 1960s, Vancouver, Halifax, Edmonton, Regina, Montreal, Calgary, Fredericton, and Toronto would all house major companies, each providing a professional center for theater in their respective province or region.

The Massey Report had also remarked on the need for advanced theater training facilities in Canada and had recommended the establishment of a National Theatre School. The school of that name was founded in Montreal in 1960, with separate English and French components. It would be a key element in the feeder system that was developing alongside the infrastructure of the new professional companies. Along with the Banff

School of Fine Arts, the National Theatre School and a network of university drama programs across the country (the University of Saskatchewan was first in 1945, with many soon to follow) would produce a huge wave of young artists as the baby boomers began graduating in the mid-1960s.

Along with the regionals some other major festival theaters were founded in the early 1960s, modeled loosely on Stratford. The Shaw Festival, established in Niagara-on-the-Lake, Ontario, in 1962, had Andrew Allan as its first artistic director. It soon became, and remains, Canada's second most highly subsidized theater and another ironic symbol, some would argue, of Canada's lingering colonialism. A different sign of the times was the founding of Prince Edward Island's Charlottetown Festival in 1964 as part of that province's centennial celebrations. Like Stratford and Shaw, Charlottetown was as much about tourism as it was about theatrical art. Nevertheless, the decision of its founder, Mavor Moore, to commission an all-Canadian program for what would turn out to be the first season of a permanent festival, was profoundly significant. One of the shows he cowrote was a musical adaptation of a hometown favorite, Lucy Maud Montgomery's (1874–1942) young adult novel of Prince Edward Island, *Anne of Green Gables*. First staged in 1965, *Anne* would go on to become a perennial hit, produced every year of the Festival, and a template for the Festival's mandate — to produce only original Canadian work, including musicals. This was an extraordinary commitment at a time when Canadian professional theater still barely existed, yet it was a definite sign of the times.

Prince Edward Island was not the only jurisdiction celebrating its centennial in the 1960s. Canada's own one hundredth birthday was imminent. The major event to mark the occasion was to be the 1967 world exposition in Montreal. But the nationalism and national self-examination sparked by the coming centennial reached into other areas, too. In 1964 Liberal prime minister Lester Pearson asked Parliament to adopt a new Canadian flag — the Maple Leaf — to replace the Red Ensign, a version of the British Union Jack that seemed one of the last vestiges of Canada's colonial origins. A fierce debate ensued, with Conservative John Diefenbaker leading the vehement opposition. The debate and the eventual adoption of the new flag with its indigenous national symbol were prologue to the intense national consciousness that would mark the years around the 1967 centennial. Just at the moment when Canadian theater was achieving its apotheosis, this strong nationalist impulse — part patriotism, part national self-critique — would irrevocably help shape its ultimate manifestation. There were other powerful forces at work, too, in remarkable synchronicity: The Quiet Revolution in Quebec, set loose by the death of long-time ultraconservative Premier Maurice Duplessis in 1959, was fully underway. The increasingly unpopular Vietnam War, racial violence, and the assassinations of John F. Kennedy, Robert Kennedy, and

Martin Luther King Jr. in the United States alienated many Canadians, especially the young, in the mid- to late-1960s, and consequently intensified Canadian national feeling. This inevitably spilled over into the developing theatrical culture. More than ever, Canadians wanted their own cultural institutions, in which they could tell their own stories. The youth revolution of the 1960s gave added impetus to these developments. Experimentalism and antiauthoritarianism, the creeds of the Counter Culture, were anathema to the old and traditional ways. A professional Canadian theater was new, and anything seemed possible.

The Dominion Drama Festival, which would fold in 1970, was already an anachronism in the newly professionalized Canadian theater scene. But for centennial year the Festival required for the first time that all plays entered into competition in both French and English (there were sixty-two of them) come from Canadian playwrights. More importantly, the federal government made special funding available to cultural institutions specifically for centennial projects, and some major theaters used it to commission new Canadian plays. This was a watershed moment: All across the country Canadian theater artists were performing plays about Canada by professional Canadian playwrights. The Charlottetown Festival produced an English translation of Gratien Gélinas's *Yesterday the Children Were Dancing* (1967), a play about a liberal Quebec politician and his radical separatist son. At the Manitoba Theatre Centre in Winnipeg the audience saw *Lulu Street* (1967) by local journalist Ann Henry (1914–), a story of the 1919 Winnipeg General Strike. John Coulter wrote yet another version of the Riel saga, *The Trial of Louis Riel* (1967), performed in Regina where Riel had been tried for treason and condemned to hang in 1885. Even Stratford got into the act, producing *Colours in the Dark* (1967) by local playwright James Reaney (1926–2008), a surreal personal/cosmic multimedia history in the poetic style that Reaney had begun establishing in 1960 with *The Killdeer* (a play Mavor Moore considered the best yet written in Canada to that date) and which he would bring to maturity in the 1970s in his trilogy *The Donnellys*, felt by some critics to be the best Canadian plays of that decade.

Two other signature plays premiered in 1967. *Fortune and Men's Eyes* by Toronto playwright and director John Herbert (1926–2001) had been workshopped at Stratford and read by various artistic directors, but no one in Canada wanted to produce this play about homosexuality and violence in a Canadian prison. It premiered in New York, off-Broadway, in 1967, ran for a year, and soon became the first Canadian play to attain extensive international success. Like Herbert, George Ryga (1932–1987) refused to draw pretty dramatic pictures of the Canada he saw around him. Raised in a poor Ukrainian family in northern Alberta, Ryga had strong political sympathies for the poor, the marginal, and the oppressed. After studying theater at Banff, he moved to the interior of British Columbia and in 1962 wrote a controversial half-hour drama for CBC television called *Indian*, dramatizing the pain and despair of a Native man in the face of systemic Canadian racism. In 1967 British Columbia's regional theater, the Vancouver Playhouse, commissioned Ryga to write a centennial play. The result was *The Ecstasy of Rita Joe*, the lyrical tragedy of two young Native people who emigrate from their rural reserve to Vancouver in search of a better life, only to find cultural alienation, racial discrimination, dead-end jobs, and ultimately violent deaths.

*Rita Joe* was a revelation. Powerful and poetic, it utilized sophisticated epic and expressionist theatrical techniques to tell a contentious, unflattering story of Canadian injustice in the midst of the centennial's national self-congratulations. And yet it was a critical and popular success. No longer could artistic directors credibly claim that no Canadian plays were worth producing, that audiences would not come to see them, especially if they treated difficult subjects, or that new plays were box-office poison (though artistic directors of large Canadian theaters would in fact continue to use these arguments for some years to come as their rationalization for refusing to produce new Canadian work). Despite the rear-guard actions against Canadian plays carried on by many of the regionals for some time still (actions that would in part result in the "alternate" theaters of the 1970s, which would come to supersede the regionals in importance), 1967 marked the point of no return. Canadian theater was a *fait accompli* and Canadian scripts would become increasingly important to it as the culture entered its next phase.

# 16: French Canada from the First World War to 1967: Historical Overview

*Ursula Mathis-Moser (University of Innsbruck)*

## From the First World War to the Stock Market Crash

ON THE POLITICAL LEVEL, the end of the First World War brought no significant changes for Quebec: The province was governed by the Liberals (1897–1936), and it had not been forgotten that this party had spoken up for Louis Riel in 1885 and had supported pan-Canadian francophone nationalism under Honoré Mercier (prime minister 1887–1891). On the national level, the Liberals had found in Wilfred Laurier a prime minister (1896–1911) who was capable of compromise and was a skillful advocate for a federalist Canada. In addition, he knew how to mobilize the European immigrants and how to affect a rapprochement between his party and the French-Canadian bishops. The economic growth, which had carried over into the next century, further contributed to the positive image of the Liberals. In contrast, the conservative government in Ottawa, which had been in office since 1911, was criticized for entering the war (1914) as well as for the draft (1917), both of which actions Quebec had vehemently opposed. Thus the Liberals were in the voters' good graces in the provincial elections. The party question was overlaid with a second problem, namely that of the relationship and the representation of the two founding nations in the government. While the French-Canadian nationalists — among them Henri Bourassa — had, prior to the war, demanded a bicultural state that would accord both peoples equal rights throughout the nation, the majority of the anglophones only tolerated the French Canadians in Parliament and in Quebec. This resulted in the French Canadians' disappointed withdrawal from the national scene and a refocusing of their national-political efforts on the province of Quebec.

In economic terms, too, the First World War had — after temporary upheavals — at first only intensified already existing tendencies: Liberal politics focused on the province's natural resources, encouraged investment from outside, and discovered hydro-electric power. With the second industrial revolution, non-iron metals became more important and the demands on the forestry sector increased with the growing need for paper and wood. The fact that both were predominantly exported to the United States was, however, problematic, as it strengthened the (economic) ties to the anglophone world. At the same time, agricultural production dropped, making up only thirty-seven percent of Quebec's total production right after the First World War. And despite the growth in manufacturing industry (thirty-eight percent), the massive exodus of the rural population to the United States and the Canadian West, which had begun at the end of the nineteenth century, still continued apace. In contrast, the big cities — above all Montreal — exerted an ever-growing appeal: In 1921, the urban population outnumbered the rural population for the first time in the province of Quebec, and after a temporary stop in expansion caused by the war, Montreal passed the million mark by 1930. Despite weaknesses in the city infrastructure, the 1920s generally ushered in better living conditions, as they did for Montreal's francophone population. A francophone middle class developed, and the labor unions initially joined the Fédération américaine du Travail. However, the fact that the interests of women, who had been entering the job market in droves, were not being satisfactorily represented called for other measures. The first pioneering initiatives were set in motion by the anglophone feminists of Montreal, but there were also francophones — for example, Marie Gérin-Lajoie and Idola Saint-Jean — to be found fighting in their ranks. At first they had little success: Female suffrage, which became a federal law in 1919 and came into effect in the provinces between 1916 and 1922, did not prevail in Quebec until 1940.

This situation is easier to understand when an additional factor is considered: Above and beyond the power games of the parties and of the federal versus the provincial governments, the Catholic Church maintained a great influence in Quebec in the 1920s. Not only did it control the education system, social services, and family structures, but it profoundly influenced public ideology. Changes in public life were met with skepticism and defensive strategies; secularist France and the rapidly transforming city were its bogeymen. Thus the church tried, on the one hand, to make its presence felt in the daily life of the urban workers by supporting the founding of Catholic unions in 1921 and by "protecting" the workers from socialist and communist appeals. On the other hand, they still placed their hopes in rural Quebec, for which they had decreed "la revanche des berceaux" since the time of the British conquest, certainly since 1840. Given the economic liberalism and the flourishing economic situation, Louis Hémon's (1880–1913) well-known sentence from *Maria Chapdelaine* (1914) "au pays de Québec rien ne doit mourir et rien ne doit changer" cynically summed up the position of the church. At the same time, the clergy, who had been fortified through the arrival of French religious orders after 1905, gained not only in power but also in prestige, expressed in such external symbols as massive church edifices, public ceremonies, and pilgrimages.

Through their monopoly of the education system and their influential contacts to capital resources alone, the church ultimately dominated the press.

# The Depression

The 1920s ended disastrously: The effects of the 1929 New York stock market crash, which caused a worldwide financial crisis, arrived in the province two years later and led to a massive crisis. The economy collapsed and was only slowly able to recuperate. Montreal, as the center of international trade, was hit especially hard, with the unemployment rate rising to thirty percent. Poverty and uncertainty spread. The economic difficulties intensified the social, mental, and linguistic tensions between the founding nations, ultimately unleashing a wave of intolerance toward the Jewish population as well as allowing socialist and communist ideas to gain ground. The decline of exports and the fact that Quebec laborers were no longer needed in the United States had drastic consequences for those living in rural areas. The church was confronted with difficulties, too. The welfare system had grown out of all manageable proportion; as a diversionary measure a new ruralization program was implemented, which aimed at the northern parts of Quebec, but it ultimately failed. At the same time, the traditionalist values of the *mythe du terroir*, which were fraught with aspects of the typical Catholic-nationalist discourse as it had been practiced by Lionel Groulx (1878–1967) even before 1930, experienced a revival.

The historian Groulx, whose name is associated with newspapers such as *L'Action française* and *L'Action nationale*, and with novels such as *L'appel de la race* (1922), sculpted a vision of an independent, francophone, Catholic province, in which the church would train an intellectual oligarchy conscious of its historical mission to lead the people. He countered individualization with the unifying principles of religion and nation; the individual was to be swallowed up in the mystique of the collective. His slogan "maîtres chez nous," which would reappear during the Quiet Revolution, was aimed not only at the revitalization of agriculture but also against the crowding out of francophones from the capital market, which Victor Barbeau (1896–1994), among others, had already tried to counteract through cooperatives. A whole generation of young nationalists learned from Groulx. Their sympathies were more in line with the European corporative state model of the 1930s than with British-American liberalism. Finally, with the emergence of a Christian-based social program in the École sociale populaire (Joseph-Papin Archambault), liberalism was also called into question from within the church. A first election success for the conservative Maurice Duplessis (1936) and the Union nationale party, which was established as an antiliberal coalition, can be seen as an expression of the general dissatisfaction with the liberal apparatus. However, the Liberals managed to reassert themselves with Adélard Godbout's late attempts at reform (1939–1944).

# The Second World War, Duplessis, and the Révolution tranquille

Despite a negative referendum, Ottawa had decreed mobilization and military deployment in Europe in 1944, but with Quebec's new economic boom brought about by war production, the protests were less fierce than they had been during the First World War. For the first time, the federal government also showed itself willing to take on social responsibility in the sense of Keynesianism and the New Deal (unemployment insurance, family assistance payments). For the time being, unemployment seemed to be under control and again the labor market experienced an inflow of female workers. Montreal became a center for important industries in aeronautics and technology.

Nevertheless, both the 1940s and the 1950s presented a contradictory picture. On the one hand, the positive development continued, albeit intermittently, until 1957, observable in such phenomena as population growth, urbanization, and immigration (especially from southern Europe), the rise of the middle class, the improvement in the level of education, and the spread of mass media. On the other hand, this development again entailed the exploitation of native resources, and once more there were certain sectors (above all agriculture) and certain parts of the population that were not able to participate in the general boom. Quebec had definitely stopped being an agriculturally dominated province. Urbanization, industrialization, and the increasingly nonconfessional unionism of the labor force threatened the clerical benefice, and church membership sharply decreased. The official ideology, however, was proclaimed by Conservative Maurice Duplessis, who finally came to power in 1944 and pursued an authoritarian, antiunion, nationalistic government policy until 1959. He focused on rural Quebec, religion, traditional family structures, and law and order, and put his energy into improving the economic situation in the rural areas (Crédit agricole, electricity); at the same time, he boycotted every union activity and persecuted any political, intellectual, or artistic activity that aimed at modernization (Loi du cadenas). Adherence to the principle of small-property ownership did not deter him from trying afresh to bring American capital into the country. He pursued a policy of autonomy towards Ottawa, and while respecting the constitution, reacted fiercely to attempts at centralization and "Canadization" (introduction of provincial taxes, 1954). Thus in a bizarre way "la grande noirceur" ("the great darkness") linked paternalistic traditionalism with a belief in progress and free enterprise.

Nevertheless, opponents of the tenacious power of the church and the provincial government, most of them from intellectual circles, began to take action in the "darkness." During the Vichy Regime, Quebec had already become an adoptive country for French writers and thinkers; they brought an unorthodox Catholicism into the country, which found its expression in magazines such as *La Nouvelle Relève* (1941) and *Cité libre* (1950). *Cité libre*, which counted the later prime minister Pierre E. Trudeau among its circle, took a stand against the excesses of clericalism, nationalism, and capitalism; under the influence of personalism, emphasizing the person as the fundamental category for explaining reality, they argued for a liberal rationalism, for education, and political liberalism. Also as a result of the war, the publishing business experienced an enormous boom through the publication of French classics and formerly listed in the censorship index. For the first time voices for the liberalization of the education system began to be heard. In 1949, the archbishop of Montreal, Joseph Charbonneau, showed solidarity with the striking asbestos workers; soon radio and television began to transmit opinions that did not toe the official line, and introduced the audience to American pop culture. The manifesto *Refus global* (1948) finally proclaimed a clear "No" to the "great darkness," which abruptly came to an end in 1959 with the death of Duplessis.

With the slogan "In the nick of time" Jean Lesage and his "équipe de tonnerre" scored a sensational election victory for the Liberals in 1960. Generally, 1960 is considered the beginning of the so-called Révolution tranquille or Quiet Revolution (the term was coined by *The Globe and Mail*), which in less than ten years rapidly ushered Quebec into the modern world. Sometimes the years 1957 and 1965 are also mentioned as milestones: 1957 as the year in which it was finally acknowledged that the wartime market had been saturated, the domestic industries were outdated, the francophone employees financially discriminated against, and that for the first time there was again a stagnation in the economy; 1965 as the year in which Quebec nationalism revealed a new uncompromising profile. All in all and from a purely French-Canadian perspective, however, the year 1960 is of greater importance than 1967, which is often mentioned in English-Canadian history books: In 1960 Lesage opened the way for a lasting modernization and "Frenchification" of the province. Supported by those powers that had been marginalized under Duplessis — the intellectuals, the unions, the officials, and the media — he managed to create a strong governmental apparatus, put social measures into effect, and rejuvenated the health and education systems. In 1964, the Ministère de l'Éducation was founded, the annual expenditures for education and health increased by twenty-one percent, and unemployment decreased from 9.2 to 4.7 percent. A new self-confidence made itself felt, which was not only the result of the better job and educational opportunities, but also of the large collective projects such as the federalization of hydro-electric power (1962), the dam project Manic 5, and the construction of the Metro in Montreal. Quebec soon presented itself as an independent political entity (1961 Maison du Québec in Paris), while internally the Catholic Church experienced an unprecedented loss of power. The province was secularized in an incredibly short time, and society opened up. However, several goals, such as political independence and the reduction of government debts, had not been achieved.

# 17: French-Canadian Poetry up to the 1960s

*Ursula Mathis-Moser (University of Innsbruck)*

## Diversity of Voices

IN THE DOGGED STRUGGLE between progressive and conservative forces that, in varying intensity, took place in every genre in French-Canadian literature during the time between the end of the First World War and the 1960s, poetry proved to be the driving force of innovation. It managed to overcome the ideology and aesthetic perceptions of the past and, until the beginning of the 1960s, became French Canada's dominant genre. In the interplay of regionalism and exoticism, of nationalistic "homeland" discourse and an emerging national consciousness, of classical mimetic and surrealistically inspired poetry, of verse, vers libre, and the complete liberation from formal constrictions, almost everything was experimented with. It is difficult, however, to establish exact temporal borderlines, as many tendencies occurred simultaneously and oscillated between progressive and regressive. Individual poets of high renown unjustifiably overshadowed so-called minor poets, so that some of them were only discovered in the 1970s.

## Regionalism versus Exoticism

In the years after the First World War the old debate between regionalists (*terroiristes, Américanistes*) and exoticists (*Parisianistes*) continued. While the former emphasized the self-sufficiency of Canadian literature, the latter saw themselves both in a francophone and in an international context. The manner in which the regionalists patriotically turned to the landscape and the local customs as well as to the North American wilderness stood in direct contrast to the poetics of the exoticists, for whom art was sufficient unto itself. They advocated individual artistic freedom and formal experimentation. Although Canadian subjects were not explicitly excluded, the most significant creative impulses came from the experience of exile, a sense of alienation, and a distance from the uneducated masses. The most important representative of the regionalists was undoubtedly

Alfred DesRochers (1901–1978), while the central figure among the exoticists was Jean-Aubert Loranger (1896–1942), who was succeeded by Hector de Saint-Denys Garneau (1912–1943) and Alain Grandbois (1900–1975). While the École littéraire de Montréal absorbed more and more regionalist elements, the exoticists provided the cultural environment for the emergence of the magazines Le Nigog (1918) and La Relève (1934). In addition, female and socially critical voices were raised for the first time.

Just as Blanche Lamontagne-Beauregard (1889–1958) had done with the Gaspésie region at the beginning of the twentieth century, DesRochers immortalized the area around Mont d'Orford with his poetry; he also eulogized the North and the entire American continent, to which he felt deeply attached. In À l'ombre de l'Orford (1929) the poet already goes beyond regionalism in that he reconciles a strikingly realistic description of the local manners and customs, the landscape, and the adventurous life of the lumberjacks with the formal principles of the Parnasse. DesRochers was not only a master of the sonnet, but also a skillful juggler of the "mots rares" so esteemed by the exoticists, which he, of course, took from the language of the people. Thus, with the help of Canadianisms, archaisms, anglicisms, and technical vocabulary, he created an authentic Canadian poetry, inspired also by the folk song. In terms of content, DesRochers's lyrical discourse was shaped by patriotism and traditionalism. Although his realism found no regionalist echo in the narrow sense of the word, Jean Narrache (Émile Coderre; 1893–1970), one of the first Quebec monologists, and Clément Marchand (1912–) at least indirectly drew on his work in that they focused on the image of the city — albeit in a less dynamic way than Robert Choquette (1905–1991) in his Metropolitan Museum (1931). Narrache's Quand j'parl'tout seul (1932), which was written during the Depression, depicts the living conditions of the workers in East Montreal and imitates the language of the people. The lyrical I, however, displays xenophobic, anti-Semitic tendencies and is ultimately resigned. It is unable to go beyond the mere representation of reality in the sense of a critical analysis of social conditions. Marchand's Les soirs rouges (1947), depicting the monstrous city, equally leads the reader astray: Here again there is no condemnation of the unequal distribution of wealth; in fact, Marchand's poetry never went beyond socially romantic images, neither in its form nor in its content. All in all both Marchand and Narrache lagged behind the critical anglophone voices of the 1930s.

Jean-Aubert Loranger came, chronologically speaking, before DesRochers, however aesthetically speaking he was a predecessor of Saint-Denys Garneau; Loranger's Atmosphères (1920) and Poèmes (1922) prove him to have been a torn mediator between the modern and the traditional, who — notwithstanding his work on the Nigog — also wrote regionalist narratives. His volumes of poetry are hybrid constructions that can be placed somewhere between the narrative, the prose poem, and the haiku. He dispensed with rhyme but not with punctuation, even though he was the first to publicly take a stand against it, and he combined the freedom of composition with a reevaluation of poetry's inherent rhythm. Thematically he focused on loneliness and *errance*, but above all on being torn between an annihilating departure and the renunciation of one's own transcendence. This is wonderfully illustrated in "Je regarde dehors par la fenêtre": The windowpane is an interface between the dominant outer world and an artificially exaggerated interiority, which affords a temporary equilibrium. The poem suggests, however, that it will not be possible to permanently remain in this "entre-deux."

Impulses in the direction of modernism came from a group of female writers who have often been overlooked. Parallel to the increasing number of female journalists, the first breakthrough for poetry written by women came in the years between 1925 and 1935 with writers such as Jovette-Alice Bernier, Simone Routier, Medjé Vézina, Éva Sénécal, and Hélène Charbonneau. They broke with the Jansenist-puritanical ideas of their environment, pleaded for the right to individuality and emotion, and claimed desire to be the central source of love and female existence as such. Formally, despite their leanings towards romanticism and Parnasse, they showed signs of extending classical prosody through free verse. Like Loranger, they paved the way for the innovations of the following generation.

## New Horizons: The Poet Generation of the "Big Four"

In this period of interplay between progress, stagnation, and regression, the decade from 1934 to 1944 was a phase of intense innovation, and was mainly carried by the generation of the "Big Four": Hector de Saint-Denys Garneau, Alain Grandbois, Rina Lasnier, and Anne Hébert. To speak of a "generation" may neglect its members' individual characteristics, or else conceal that the "Big Four" — except for Saint-Denys Garneau — were active far beyond the 1940s; it also diverts attention from other important innovators such as Loranger, Vézina, Routier, and François Hertel. Yet there are striking parallels between the "Big Four" that are impossible to ignore. The high value they placed on form went hand in hand with the search for a language that was not worn out and that could express the existential and metaphysical experience of the individual poet and his or her spiritual quest. All four were strangers in a society indifferent to artists, a society that negated body and intellect, cultivated the myth of national unity, and forced literary critics to be the guardians of tradition. Equally, they opposed empty rhetoric and the constraints of classical rules and regulations. They were familiar with French symbolism, postsymbolism, to some degree with *Renouveau catholique*, with the intellectual environment of *La Relève* and *Esprit*, and with thinkers such as Emmanuel Mounier and Jacques Maritain. Their texts have often been compared to a "voix" or "voie du dedans": Frequent themes were the experience of inner exile, entrapment, intellectual suffocation, silence, and solitude, and the alienated and seeking individual, manifesting themselves in screams or violent visions.

Hector de Saint-Denys Garneau is primarily known as a poet with a strong musical sensibility and a deep love for photography; but he was also a painter who evoked the beloved landscape of his home — the area of Sainte-Catherine-de-Fossambault and Charlevoix — in (mainly) untitled pictures, on which he wrote extensive comments (posthumously published in the *Journal*). With his idiosyncratic use of color, his restless brushstrokes, and his renunciation of spatial perspective, he made a major contribution to Quebec painting of the 1930s, which he also discussed in countless articles. Saint-Denys Garneau was also one of those precocious poets like Émile Nelligan (1879–1941) or Arthur Rimbaud, whose art was born from a crisis. Highly talented, raised in a family with strict Jansenist ideals, and fostered by the Jesuits, he later saw himself as having been cheated out of his early promise. A sense of guilt and excessive self-expectations made it impossible for him to accept his own ambivalence. After initially working for *La Relève* and then suffering from a heart ailment, he fell into a deep crisis in 1935, which stimulated his creativity but also intensified his loneliness. Hurt by the criticism of his *Regards et jeux dans l'espace* (1937), which would soon be ranked among world literature, he withdrew it from the market and died in total isolation at the age of thirty-one.

*Regards et jeux dans l'espace* is a text of ambivalences. It can be regarded as an artistic transposition of an individual's experience of suffering and psychic development, but at the same time it serves as a metaphor for the collective condition of Quebec and its intellectual elite. Its twenty-eight poems lead the reader in seven sections from a playful innocent orientation in space to an inevitable confrontation with failure and death. This dualism, which provides a frame for the beginning and the end of the volume, is intensified by the organization of the poems in opposing pairs, often creating an effect of ironic refraction. Contrast ultimately determines the inner texture: Like Baudelaire the poet aspires to the ideal; like Baudelaire he speaks of "Spleen." Still, the first sections appear to express something positive. Although the introductory "C'est là sans appui" depicts the poet's unease, he could attain his balance if he were only allowed to tame the wild stream. The poet is also symbolized in the child who claims the right to both the freedom and the seriousness of play, that is, the playful reconstruction of the world and the word. However, play, dance, vision, and even the grandiose evocation of the color, movement, and voice of the shimmering leaves of the Canadian woods are not enough to maintain the precarious equilibrium: "The center is not in the middle." The I and the world split, and the search for beauty and harmony comes to an end with the recognition that salvation is impossible — which the ailing poet captures in a macabre way in the words "Je suis une cage d'oiseau." In the final, impressively unadorned poem the poet gives the reader at least an ambivalent ending, with the lyrical I ambiguously walking "à côté d'une joie."

Various elements of modernism can be observed in Saint-Denys Garneau's writing: These are the basic lack of an answer, the ironic distance and, at the same time, introspective stance of the lyrical I, the belief in poetry as an intellectual field of inquiry, and the emphasis on poetry's self-referentiality. Above all, Saint-Denys Garneau's modernism manifests itself in his language: The poems are precisely composed and carefully polished, so that all elements relate to each other in the sense of a "jeu d'équilibre." The poet employs a simple vocabulary, organizing it in varying repetitions. He mostly refrains from using punctuation and employs an elliptical syntax to produce ambivalent meanings. In terms of meter, he chooses free verse, which he places in typographical space and shapes through capital lettering and the use of enjambment. Finally, his poetry is conveyed by the rhythm of the spoken word. In his posthumous volume of collected poems, *Solitudes* (1949) — all of which were written before 1938 — the tone remains serious despite occasional positive reminiscences and the use of biblical cadences. The poet reminds us of the affinity between the human individual and Jesus Christ and constitutes the female as the mediator between the self and transcendence.

Although there are many differences between the poetry of Saint-Denys Garneau and Alain Grandbois, they share common ground: They both explore the depths of existential questions, use a predominantly somber tone, and practice radical formal innovation. Nevertheless, the succeeding generation, which wrote in a Quebec that was passing through a period of transition, could identify more with Grandbois than with Garneau, for the latter's poetry expressed a helplessness that could not but end in silence. With the triptych *Îles de la nuit* (1944), *Rivages de l'homme* (1948), and *L'étoile pourpre* (1957) Grandbois — who also produced a narrative oeuvre — demonstrated his poetic development. In contrast to Garneau he was a cosmopolitan, who traveled for over twenty years in the orient and occident and published in China as well as in France. He is known, last but not least, for his treatment of love, the female, and eroticism, and as a poet who, in a grammatical alternation between past and present tense, was able to "narrate" and comment on contemporary women and men influenced by the war experience.

In *Îles de la nuit*, into which he integrated his *Poèmes d'Hankéou* (1934) and several of Alfred Pellan's pictures, Grandbois wonders about human existence. The opening poem describes the basic experience of *angoisse*, which is countered by an unquenchable desire for lucidity. It is exactly this lucidity, however, that is denied to the lyrical I because the islands of the night know nothing but emptiness, exile, loneliness, and transience. Instead of clarity the lyrical I discovers a happiness that is already "buried" and an absoluteness that is unattainable. Shortly thereafter, in *Rivages*, contingency, earth, and the present moment become central themes, establishing an antithesis to the cosmos and to transcendence. *L'étoile pourpre* seems like an endless evocation of earthly desire, as the couple in "Noces" dives through the ocean during the act of love, with the purple star, a symbol of poetry, as their guide. Microcosm and macrocosm are in harmony, extending the moment in time. This correspondence is evoked through "waves" of words rising and falling like religious hymns, which evoke Saint-John Perse and Paul Claudel, and which will be smoothed out and shortened in Grandbois's later collections. Grandbois chooses free verse, strings anaphors together in litany-like ensembles, and plays with assonance, alliteration, and interjection. He also eliminates punctuation but emphasizes the syntactical unity of the verse through his renouncement of enjambment and the use of capital letters. The single word is rich in symbolic meaning, implying a wide array of multiconnotative imagery, and exerting a hermetic effect that places it somewhere between postsymbolism and a surrealistic style. In contrast to André Breton's *écriture automatique*, however, the poet consciously and artistically interferes with the "dictates" of the unconscious.

Rina Lasnier (1915–1997) also invites her readers into her own world. Up to 1995 she had published more than twenty volumes of poetry (*Images et proses*, 1941; *Escales*, 1950; *Présence de l'absence*, 1956; *Mémoire sans jours*, 1960). She found inspiration in the familiar environment of Quebec and the tradition of Christian spirituality, which she sought to renew from within. Alienation, mysticism, and love are her major themes: Alienation occurs when the individual allows herself or himself to be distracted from the constraints of the human condition and to be seduced into indifference. However, it can also arise in a land such as Quebec, which Lasnier sees as weak, reviled, and riven in its religious and national self-image. With this assessment she contributed significantly to the recognition of her generation, which was often reproached for its unpolitical "inward journey." Lasnier opposes alienation with the mystic quest for the "infini," the unity of body and mind, of the natural and the supernatural. The mystical poem can never be a substitute for prayer, though, because the creative-formative element dominates. The aim of her poetry is not to enter a spiritual space empty of human life, but rather to bring the human drama into this space; for this reason her Christ figures display modern, revolutionary traits. She depicts love — the eternal driving force of poetry — as the unity of sensuality, Eros, and *charité*, in that moment when the gaze transforms into touch.

Lasnier's extensive work evolves around recurring features: She starts with ordinary, everyday perceptions, recording their most subtle nuances, in order to ultimately direct the reader's attention to the invisible, the non-material, the metaphysical. In some of her poems the latter is represented by God, Christ, Mary, or figures from the Old Testament (*Le chant de la montée*, 1947), while other poems do not need this type of reference or leave it open as a possibility; still other poems lead from the concreteness of nature to the invisible universe of the poet ("Beauté"). Lasnier also plays with form: Verse, free verse, and poetic prose, long and short forms alternate with each other, revealing the poet to be a master of the "small image." She likes to prefix her lyrical texts with comments and links diverging discourses. The frequently elliptical syntax makes her texts seem hermetical, yet she succeeds in expressing the unsayable with vital emotion — which explains why her poetry was partly considered too daring and sensual in the 1940s.

Another female poet who also put her stamp on the generation of the "Big Four" was Anne Hébert (1916–2000), mainly known as a novelist and daughter of a renowned literary critic as well as cousin of Saint-Denys Garneau. Her *Les songes en équilibre* (1942), *Le tombeau des rois* (1953), and *Mystère de la parole* (1960) were trend-setting works of poetry. The triptych, which was followed by further collections in 1992 and 1997, was celebrated as an awakening from a time of isolation into the "age of words," as a criticism of Duplessis's ideology, and as a statement that drew its force from interdiscursive strategies. Hébert called into question conventional vocabulary and conformist clichés — such as the role of women — and she also vehemently challenged religious concepts by way of recontextualization and remotivation. In *Tombeau* only the glass-like clarity of the first poem "Éveil au seuil d'une fontaine" is reminiscent of the fragile "dreams in balance" ("songes en équilibre") that Hébert uses to evoke the innocent world of childhood through symbols recalling Saint-Denys Garneau — the gaze, the game, the dance, air, and light. The "inner tears" of introspection and loneliness follow immediately, and even the humble, embroidering, open female hands are not able to dispel them. As "Petit désespoir" finally verbalizes it: "Mon coeur est rompu / L'instant ne le porte plus." Thereupon the lyrical I produces images that are powerful despite their simplicity: It plunges into the night and silence of the oceanic depths, and the complaint of a dead bird echoes the injured and alienated inner voice of the lyrical I. Paradise is destroyed, the realms of childhood are enshrouded in sadness. The lyrical I is overcome with helplessness, then destructive anger ("Inventaire"). In a macabre fashion, it dissects its own heart and polishes its bones ("Inventaire," "La chambre fermée," "La fille maigre"), scoffs at the conventional world in which everything seems to be in order — "Les morts dessous / Les vivants dessus" ("En guise de fête"), and invents countless images of entrapment. These images speak of an inner suffocation, of the "little dead girl" on the doorstep and of the oppressive external world ("Une petite morte"), which traps every sign of vitality in enclosed spaces, coffins, and walls. Still, even "sous la pierre" the heart stubbornly continues to beat ("Retourne sur tes pas"); the murderer of the lyrical I had forgotten to cover up the beauty of the world and to close its desirous eyes. Thus in the ghostly "Tombeau des rois," a ray of light appears, despite death and blindness, in the darkness.

*Mystère de la parole* is introduced by a text in which Hébert dismisses ideological commitment and the aiming at edification for her poetry, and instead demands the radical internal coherence of the work of art and its exact correspondence to the poet's inner experience. The text already points towards a new era: Quebec is apostrophized as a land that has to be discovered, named, and possessed. In so doing, Hébert speaks of "la solitude rompue comme du pain par la poésie": The written word is the place that conquers silence and despair. Without becoming political, a new lyrical I comes to the fore and asks that one's love for the world be expressed through words that speak for everyone ("Mystère de la parole"); it is to God that man wishes to offer the fragrant homemade bread ("Naissance du pain"), and the lyrical I self-confidently accepts its own ambivalence ("Je suis la terre et l'eau"). After the destructive past has been banned, Hébert finds in Eve of Genesis an unorthodox model, new life, and a new universal language. Thus the way for the next generation is paved, and this is also true with regard to Hébert's style: Like Garneau, she sought to reduce language to the essential, abandoned classical verse, and made rhythm and sonority the driving force in her poetry. At the same time, however, the bareness and conciseness of *Tombeau* did not exclude the softness of biblical cadence in *Mystère*. Her imagery and symbols are drawn from the same semantic fields as those of her contemporaries, especially Saint-Denys Garneau, but they do not primarily serve the purpose of painful inner scrutiny. Instead, once freed from familiar associations ("La fille maigre"), they are employed to question tradition and the past. Hébert even borrows from surrealism, which also set the tone for the imagery of her poems of the 1990s. "Interiority" was thus the stepping stone for confronting the changing world.

# Time of Refusal

Challenging traditional values can also take on the form of an eruption that abruptly makes room for all that has been dammed up. In 1948, two manifestos appeared within six months: *Prisme d'yeux* (in the circle around Pellan) and Émile Borduas's (1905–1960) *Refus global*, which was signed by a group of fifteen artists. The central concern of both publications was the cultural and ideological reform of the province. Influenced by surrealism, which Borduas and the automatists had become acquainted with through Pellan, they stood for the revolutionary ethical principle of the unity of art and life. They saw the spontaneous act, devoid of intentionality, as the impulse for a liberation and change that could not even be stopped by social reality. The archenemies — politics, religion, and nationalism — were to be met with antagonism; the externally controlled, fearful individual should realize his or her individual possibilities by following his or her "desire" in "luminous anarchy": "Nous poursuivons dans la joie notre sauvage besoin de libération." The nine texts of the illustrated manifesto *Refus global* caused a scandal. It is true that its rhetoric of binary opposition, which Borduas set in contrast to monolithic rational thought, still lacked the typical traits of *écriture automatique*; Borduas to some extent even employed familiar ideologemes, although in a new form. The self-image of the province, however, was shaken to its foundations, and his postulation of the unity of life and art cost Borduas his job at the École du meuble. Whether as a transformation or as a radical break, *Refus global* stands as one of the most significant catalysts of Quebec modernism. It inspired texts that sought to express the spirit of renewal in a language of uncompromising radicalism, even though most of them would only be acknowledged in the 1970s in a second wave of surrealistically inspired poetry. Irrespective of this, they heralded a new order: Poetry became the place of the imagination, where anger at the traditionalists was given vent to, where their discourse was deconstructed, and where the liberated self was already playing with the idea of a new "we." Individually, of course, each poet went his own way: If *Les sables du rêve* (1946) by Thérèse Renaud (1927–2005) was considered the first "automatic text," then Claude Gauvreau (1925–1971) went even beyond surrealism with his poetry of "automatisme surrationnel," which penetrated to the depths of the unconscious through the vehemence of emotion rather than passive "receptivity." Roland Giguère (1929–2003) was near to classical surrealism, and Gilles Hénault (1920–1996), who frequented diverse literary groups (among others, La Relève), combined surrealistic visions with social protest and a North American consciousness. Paul-Marie Lapointe (1929–) discovered — initially without any contact with the automatists — a specific North American surrealism which displayed affinities with jazz, but was inspired by "ancient cultures."

A student of Borduas and coresponsible for the publishing house Mithra-Mythe, Claude Gauvreau — whose "objets dramatiques" appeared in part in *Refus global* — made a major contribution towards modernization with *Étal mixte* (1950–1951), *Brochuges* (1957), and other collections. In his works, the ethical principle of the unity of life and art gradually transformed into an aesthetic principle, and Gauvreau ultimately fell into a tragic reclusiveness. He was, however, not solely an innovator but, extremely well read, he inscribed Tristan Tzara, Antonin Artaud, Henri Michaux, François Rabelais, Paul Verlaine, and Hector de Saint-Denys Garneau into his texts. The unmasking of the obstructers of "le rêve total" occurs with a scream, in a tirade aimed at the clergy and the bourgeois in "Ode à l'ennemi":

Mourez
cochons de crosseurs de fréchets de cochons d'huiles de cochons de caïmans de ronfleurs de calices de cochons de rhubarbes de ciboires d'hosties de bordels de putains de saints-sacrements d'hosties de bordels de putains de folles herbes de tabernacles de calices de putains de cochons

In his "langage exploréen" the poet makes full use of every imaginable liberty — from bold metaphors, lexical polyphony, syllabic conglomeration, and echolalie, to sound combinations of the comic strip. Beyond this, he was also well known as a performing artist and dramatist, who gave a voice to the misunderstood artist in such unusual and linguistically powerful pieces as *Les oranges sont vertes* (1972).

In contrast, Roland Giguère, who was a typographer, painter, poet, and founder of the avant-garde publishing company Erta, stood in direct contact with the French surrealists. Giguère, who had also signed the manifesto *Prisme d'yeux*, knew André Breton personally and had cooperated with surrealistic groups during long sojourns in France. Like Gauvreau, he, too, was not recognized until the 1960s, when he published *L'âge de la parole* (1965), *La main au feu* (1973), and *Forêt vierge folle* (1979), in which Giguère illustrated his development as a poet and painter. Although he loved the "darkness" of the text, he did not go as far as Gauvreau in experimenting with language. His material was the image, the metaphor, which blends into the sonorous flow of the words and often undergoes a symbiosis with the visual form. The word should "nommer, appeler, exorciser, ouvrir," and powerfully initiate a new start.

Gilles Hénault's lyrical oeuvre, the complete collection of which was published in 1972, is thematically similar, but politically more sharply focused. Self-educated, a committed unionist, art critic, cofounder of *Cahiers à la file indienne*, and later the head of the Musée d'art contemporain in Montreal, Hénault first published in magazines, then with Erta (*Totems*, 1953), and finally with L'Hexagone (*Sémaphore*, 1962). The surrealistic influence can be seen above all in his early work, that is, in the flow of images and in the irony, but there is no *écriture automatique* in any strict sense. In terms of content, Hénault pursued the vision of an autonomous individual who returns to his origins, respects the indigenous people, and liberates himself from immobility, capitalistic compulsions, and obedience to the Catholic Church.

Finally, Paul-Marie Lapointe, who was influenced by Rimbaud and Paul Éluard, also situates himself at the crossroads in his brilliant first work, *Le vierge incendié*, which was published in 1948 by Mithra-Mythe. His second work, *Arbres*, which is reminiscent of André Breton's litanies, did not appear until 1960; further volumes followed up to *écRiturEs* (1980), in which Lapointe plays with the freedom of words, letters, and sounds, in part spatially, with an absolute *gratuité*. The form of *Le vierge incendié* is also very striking: Prose poems and texts in free verse are combined into rectangular pictures, which are that are given shape through the empty spaces between the words. Within these pictures, associations flow between surreal nominal groups. The constant movement of "signifiant" instead of a fixed meaning gave Lapointe the reputation of a deconstructive poet. Within his word clusters, he speaks of aggression and violence, of eroticism, rage, and revolt, but in some of the poems also of the possibility of transforming man and the world. Similar to Gauvreau in many ways, Lapointe has become, like the former, one of the most important reference points in Quebec poetry in the 1970s.

## Poetry and the Collective

The magazine *Cité libre*, which united Catholic activists, unionists, and leftist intellectuals in the early 1950s, was one of those organs that, in the spirit of Mounier and *Esprit*, cultivated innovative thought and made a significant contribution to the liberation from dogmatism and nonage. The founding of the publishing house L'Hexagone (1953) by Gaston Miron (1928–1996), Olivier Marchand (1928–), and others proved to be even more important because it gave poetry a social "location" and the poet a new status. Aside from the modern classics, L'Hexagone primarily gathered new voices such as Jean-Guy Pilon, Jean-Paul Filion, Claude Fournier, Fernand Ouellette, Luc Perrier, Françoise Bujold, Yves Préfontaine, and Michel van Schendel. These authors shared a desire for the revaluation of the community and a belief in collective destiny — a national consciousness that, however, distanced itself from any ideas of rightist nationalism. They began to assume social responsibility and to trust the power of words; in the process, linguistic experimentation gave way to a new clarity of language. The dictum "name-change-act" was reminiscent of Sartre's "literature of commitment," although in this case it was actually poetry which was the agency of revolt. Ultimately, a personal brand of editorial politics came into being that, in the following years, brought forth a flood of publishing companies that in their own way bore witness to the dynamic quality of Quebec poetry. Yet until the 1960s, the poets were slowly feeling their way towards self-definition. In his "Notes sur le non-poème et le poème" (1965) Miron states that the prerequisite is an admittance of one's own colonization, the latter being the root of the painful experience of collective inferiority, ontological depression, and political as well as historical nonexistence. The francophone population had been delegated to the junk room of history, their language deformed beyond recognition, their name refracted through the view of the Other:

"Mon nom est *Pea Soup*. . . . Mon nom est *Frog*. Mon nom est *dam Canuck*. Mon nom est *speak white*." In contrast to earlier times, however, the recognition of weakness and collective unease did not lead to a withdrawal but to a new beginning. In this process, literature had a fundamental task: It reflected the existential situation of the French Canadians, verbalized exile and alienation, and at the same time strove to overcome the inner conflict and contribute to the formation of a national culture. The goal of this "poésie du pays" was a new land, a new language, and a new human being; its themes included the description of the status quo, of historical forces and daily life, nature, verbal powerlessness, but also of the victory over *angoisse*, the rediscovery of the body, speech, and the self — even if this entailed howling and pain.

Miron's path was that of the great national poet and fighter. Himself a publisher and as of the 1960s a member of diverse political groups, he did not agree until 1970 to have a complete edition of his major work *L'homme rapaillé* published. *L'homme rapaillé* speaks of a lyrical I that is gradually reconstituting itself, whose mirror is shattered, whose hope has ebbed, and whose face has been destroyed. With unmistakable clarity, the lyrical I criticizes the course of history that has turned it into "le sous-homme, la grimace souffrante du cro-magnon / l'homme du cheap way, l'homme du cheap work / le damned Canuk." "Dépoétisé dans ma langue et mon appartenance / déphasé et décentré dans ma coïncidence," the lyrical I lands in Montreal. From the very beginning, however, an accompanying voice can be perceived that becomes even stronger in "La marche à l'amour," but also in "La Batèche": The clenched fist, the wind, love, poetry, and finally the land — "mon Québec ma terre amère ma terre amande" — will wrest the lyrical I out of its agony. Finally in "L'octobre" it fiercely declares its vision of the future — "Nous te ferons, Terre de Québec," for a committed future — "l'avenir dégagé, l'avenir engagé" — is standing at the door. Miron's poetry lives from the power of its language. The man of "tortured" words, who defends the community as an "anthropoet" in the "place publique," suffers from the distorted grimace of the mother tongue. In contrast to many of his contemporaries, he saw the lexical impoverishment of the *joual* as a problem that could be averted through an authentic native language that distanced itself from both regionalism and an aseptic internationalism. Miron's poetry impresses the reader with its rhythmic power, its hetero-metrical verse lines and anaphors, but also with its litany-like segments. The lyrical I constantly summons a you, be it in the form of the beloved one or the beloved "pays." The accumulation of imperatives, vocatives, and interjections is an expression of the never-ending plea to the Other, the social component of the text. Independent of this, the dynamic quality of the texts originates in their hybrid nature: The juxtaposition of prose and poetry, of colloquial language and its poetization, of orality and the written form, of transparently inserted anglicisms and curses, as well as of the private and the public, all correspond to the poet's refusal to accept a "version définitive." Poetry is a process; it is the path to self-discovery on which Miron tries to reconcile "le concret, le quotidien, un langage repossédé et en même temps l'universel."

What L'Hexagone began in the 1950s was carried forth in the 1960s with the publication of over four hundred volumes of poetry, a boom in poetry unheard of, which reached its peak in 1965, before the novel came to the fore. In addition to those poets already mentioned, two poets stand out: Alongside Miron, Jean-Guy Pilon (1930–), the long-standing director of *Liberté*, is considered to be one of the most important representatives of the new literary scene. In *Recours au pays* (1961) he illustrates in a masterly way, through recourse to typical metaphors of cold and snow, the journey from homelessness to the fullness of "belonging" — the land, which had been an absence, should now be born: "tu es pays à enfanter." In a similar fashion Gatien Lapointe (1931–1983), the founder of Écrits des Forges, sings about a new beginning and a reappropriation of one's own land. In his well-known *Ode au Saint-Laurent* (1963), which is written in simple language, he not only establishes manifold relationships to his native land, but also captures its specific American quality. Not long thereafter, however, a radicalization of the political climate and the poets' convictions took place. In 1963, the first bombs exploded, and the magazine *Parti pris* (1963–1968) proclaimed independence, "laïcité," and socialism as its credo. Within the circle of *Parti pris*, Jacques Brault (1933–), Paul Chamberland (1939–), and Gérald Godin (1938–1994) set the tone with texts that were once more full of anger and rage, but also expressed the determination of an entire generation of poets.

Jacques Brault, who wrote fascinating critical studies of Grandbois, Saint-Denys Garneau, Miron, and others, became famous above all for *Suite fraternelle* (1963). The inconspicuous death of his brother in the Second World War becomes a symbol for the non-existence of an inconspicuous people — "bourré d'ouate et de silence" — which cannot liberate itself from its own ambivalence. In sweeping verse, punctuated by impressive passages of short verse, Brault prepares for the change: "Debout face aux chacals de l'histoire face aux pygmées de la peur," the Quebec people will eventually overcome the shameful past and witness fresh green sprouting from his brother's grave.

Paul Chamberland's poetry from the early 1960s, *Terre Québec* (1964) and *L'afficheur hurle* (1965), is even more forceful than Brault's before Chamberland, like Brault, went in completely new directions. He addresses the theme of the "pays" only in the first part of *Terre Québec*, while in the second and third parts we hear the voice of love as well as mystical tones. In *L'afficheur hurle*, however, the poet becomes more biting: Powerful cascades of words without punctuation force out the long, injured howl of him who has been humiliated, of him who has no more language and is slowly dying "à petit feu," "poliment / dans l'abjection."

Finally, in *Les cantouques* (1967) Gérald Godin deliberately employs a "langue verte, populaire et quelquefois française," which in its use of phonetic deformation and word contamination can be understood as a picture of helplessness and incapacitation, of destruction and psychic misery. He also vehemently condemns the status quo; in his texts the strident, almost cynical outcry against colonialization and alienation replaces the condition of wordless agony. Together with his fellow combatants, Godin built up a "poésie d'urgence," whose roots could be followed back at least as far as the group of poets of L'Hexagone, and which combined a commitment to reality, provocation, orality, and verbal power. Thus Quebec poetry had become identical with the national cause: In it, according to Claude Beausoleil, all poetic elements merged into a "discours engagé sur la voie d'un projet social et politique, ayant comme objectif l'indépendance du Québec."

# 18: The French-Canadian Novel between Tradition and Modernism

*Doris G. Eibl (University of Innsbruck)*

## The Rise and Demise of the Farm Novel

As IN THE PRECEDING DECADES, the development of the French-Canadian novel after 1918 was closely connected to the nationalism of Quebec's Catholic intelligentsia: In 1866 Abbé Henri-Raymond Casgrain demanded that the novel should advocate the French language and Catholicism, as well as concentrate on regional themes, country life, and the memory of Nouvelle-France. Camille Roy's speech "La nationalisation de la littérature canadienne," held in 1904 in the Société du parler français, built upon Casgrain's theses and led the way for virtually all novels produced until 1930. In order to adequately perform its function as a Canadian "épopée chevaleresque" and as a "gardienne toujours fidèle des intérêts supérieurs de la race et de la nationalité," French-Canadian literature should above all be inspired by an authentic Christian faith, as well as comply with the creed: "Faisons ici une littérature qui soit à nous et pour nous."

Roy's demands were echoed by the nationalistic writings of historian Lionel Groulx (1878–1967), who in *La naissance d'une race* (1919) advocated the purity of the French-Canadian race and even spoke of a "race supérieure." Groulx established a concept of Nouvelle-France as a "terre d'élection," not unlike the American concept of the "city upon a hill." Similar to Roy, Groulx saw the regionalist-agriculturalist literature as the only authentic expression of the French-Canadian national character. Strictly speaking, his novel of ideas *L'appel de la race* (1922), which was published under the pseudonym Alonié de Lestres, does not belong to the genre of the farm novel, but it does postulate the inescapable victory of the "instinct de la race" over the feelings of the individual — an attitude that readers had been well acquainted with ever since Louis Hémon's *Maria Chapdelaine* (1914), perhaps the most famous farm novel. Groulx's text describes the return of the French-Canadian lawyer Jules de Lantagnac to his roots, having established himself in the anglophone milieu of Ottawa, and his fight against the ban of French classes in Ontario.

Farm novels are texts that focus on the life of French-Canadian farmers. Among the approximately seventy farm novels published between 1920 and 1960, one has to distinguish between original and serious portrayals of French-Canadian country life — such as Claude-Henri Grignon's *Un homme et son péché* (1933), Ringuet's *Trente arpents* (1938), or Germaine Guèvremont's *Le survenant* (1945) — and predominantly propaganda-fueled and simplified *romans à these* like Damase Potvin's *L'appel de la terre* (1919), Harry Bernard's *La terre vivante* (1925), or Louise-Philippe Côté's *La terre ancestrale* (1933). While the first group features detailed depictions of the rural milieu, the second group restricts itself to preaching Catholicism and traditional French-Canadian lifestyles, which are only possible within the borders of the countryside, far away from the sinful city. Whoever leaves the "terre paternelle" and moves to the city (or the United States) will only experience disappointments. The happiness of sons and daughters depends on their returning home and renouncing the material temptations of Protestant capitalism.

The farm novel reached its qualitative peak in the 1930s with the works of, for instance, Léo-Paul Desrosiers, Félix-Antoine Savard, and Ringuet (alias Philippe Panneton). It maintained its readership and supporters during this period of political and social tumult and despite the increasing urbanization of Quebec (by 1929 around sixty percent of Quebec's population lived in urban areas) and the growing interest in both urban and psychological novels. The continuing appeal of the rural genre was ultimately connected with the disastrous consequences of the stock market crash of 1929, from which Quebec only recovered with the economic boom during the Second World War. During the 1930s, the nationalist camp strengthened its position both among intellectuals and politicians. As urban unemployment steadily increased, it favored the return to subsistence farming and the settlement ("colonization") of the northern regions, promoted by government programs.

However, the most significant farm novels of the 1930s show that the embellished picture of country life as conveyed by the agriculturalist discourse did not correspond in any way to reality. It was not their moral weakness, their neglect of tradition, or their materialism that drove the sons and daughters of farmers into the cities or the industrial areas of the United States. Rather, it was the "terre" itself, which, though praised in farm novels, inflicted a life full of deprivation on her children. Léo-Paul Desrosier's (1896–1967) novel *Nord-Sud* (1931) reveals several reasons for mass emigration into the cities, such as the difficult climatic conditions and the impossibility of cost-efficient farming on the newly settled land. These reasons were later also used to explain the inescapable failure of the last major colonizing efforts of the 1930s. In contrast to earlier farm novels, the figure of the renegade son is not depicted negatively in *Nord-Sud*. In fact, he features the characteristics of the adventurer in the tradition of the trapper ("coureur de bois") without being categorically condemned for his nomadic lifestyle. However, as Desrosiers's other works show — such as the fur-trading novel *Les engagés du Grand Portage* (1938) or the historical farm novel *Les opiniâtres* (1941), both nationalistically inspired — the author is by no means trying to question the colonization efforts or to enhance the image of the trapper. *Les engagés du Grand Portage* most critically depicts the daily life of the fur trapper, the intrigues of the profiteers of the fur trade, the harshness and the deprivations of the life of the "voyageur" in the forests of the North, as well as the confrontations with Natives. The penniless hero of the novel, Louison Turenne, hires himself out as a "voyageur" to English fur-trading companies, but dreams of settling down. Following the traditional dichotomy between the upright, honest country people and the unfair and ambitious urban population, and between the exploitative English and the exploited French Canadians, Desrosiers's novel juxtaposes the French Canadian Turenne, who remains true to himself, and the morally perverted city dweller Nicolas Montour, whose naive ambitions are unscrupulously exploited by his anglophone bosses.

Félix-Antoine Savard's (1896–1982) farm novel *Menaud, maître-draveur* (1937), which has become a French-Canadian literary classic, also deals with the ideological and economic confrontation between French Canadians and the English. Savard dispenses with the norms of the farm novel insofar as the protagonist Menaud is not a sedentary farmer but a raftsman, who represents the solitary, independent, and liberated adventurer in the tradition of the trappers and who fights against the financial dominance of the English and the selling off of the country. Thus Savard's novel pays tribute to both of the great traditions of French Canada, that of conquest and that of a sedentary lifestyle. The author's appreciation for the adventurer must be seen in connection with his commitment to the colonization efforts in the years of economic crisis: In *L'abatis* (1969) the priest Savard describes the colonization projects as a "croisade du retour à la terre." A vision of a crusade of some sorts also pervades *Menaud, maître-draveur*, in which a voice resonates that had already induced Maria Chapdelaine to follow the tradition of her people: Menaud's daughter Marie reads to her father from the last chapter of Hémon's novel *Maria Chapdelaine*; in addition, the early death of the mother as well as the emotional confusion of the daughter are reminiscent of Hémon's seminal novel. The daughter has to decide between Délié, who collaborates with the English, and Alexis Tremblay, called Lucon, who has a spiritual bond with Menaud. Menaud works for the English at the beginning of the novel, then plans a failed rebellion against them, and finally falls into insanity. It is in this state of mental derangement that he exclaims with surprising clarity: "Des étrangers sont venus! Des étrangers sont venus!" — a quote from *Maria Chapdelaine*, which paraphrases the precarious situation of the French Canadians. By avoiding any idealization of the French-Canadian situation at the end of the novel and by depicting Menaud's individual fate as that of French Canada, Savard's text can be understood as an epic warning to the reader.

*Menaud, maître-draveur* might appear idealistic and patriotic in comparison to Ringuet's *Trente arpents* (1938). Ringuet (1895–1960) — an atheistic doctor and later the Canadian ambassador to Portugal — originally published his first novel with Flammarion in Paris. It is commonly accepted as the last farm novel in Quebec's literary history and ranks as a masterpiece of the genre. At the same time, it is considered to be Ringuet's best work, his later novels (*Fausse monnaie*, 1947; *Le poids du jour*, 1949) being inferior in quality. Readers and critics alike have been captivated by the realistic depiction of the peasant family Moisan and the land in *Trente arpents*, by the rise and fall of the protagonist Euchariste Moisan, and by the portrayal of the changes in rural society between 1887 and 1932. The historic contextualization of Euchariste's story, the meticulous rendering of his milieu, and the authentic use of rural parlance from the beginning of the twentieth century (as well as the "franglais" used by Euchariste's cousin, who emigrated to the United States) suggest that the novel should be read in the tradition of naturalist aesthetics. Time and again Ringuet subtly shows how the characters' fates are determined by the anthropomorphized "terre." The author thus manages to draw a picture of rural life that overcomes its regional context and is universally valid. In addition, using Euchariste as an example, Ringuet depicts the problematic situation of the peasants who have to decide between traditional agricultural practices and new technologies. Euchariste's exile, in which he scrapes together a living working as a night watchman in New England, is tragically irrevocable. It stands for the uprooting of the peasantry and metaphorically for the disintegration of the conservative-idealistic ideology. The author's withdrawal from the didactic-ideological program of the farm novel and the naturalist aesthetics of *Trente arpents* put the novel in the tradition of a few literary works that, starting at the beginning of the twentieth century, undermined the prescribed literary model, for example, Rodolphe Girard's *Marie Calumet* (1904), Albert Laberge's *La Scouine* (1918), and Claude-Henri Grignon's *Un homme et son péché* (1933). These authors turned away from the ideological embellishing of country life and depicted the rural lifestyle realistically, without omitting its negative aspects.

Claude-Henri Grignon's (1894–1976) main work has achieved considerable popularity in Quebec, especially after its adaptation for radio, television, and the stage. The innovative character of *Un homme et son péché* is based on the realistic depiction of the protagonist Séraphin Poudrier, whose pathological avarice and sadistic behavior cause the early death of his wife Donalda, twenty years his junior. The character study of the ruthless money lender and scrooge — whose relationship with his "terre" is marked by an unusually pronounced indifference (for him only financial gain counts) —

can also be interpreted as a metaphor for a purely materialistic society: When Séraphin's farm burns down, his charred body is found clasping a piece of gold in one hand and some oats in the other. Thus, despite its realistic style, the novel remains bound to agriculturalist, traditional ideals, which were still valid for the farm novel of the 1940s and 1950s.

As did her cousin's *Un homme et son péché*, Germaine Guèvremont's (1893–1968) *Le survenant* (1945) also counts among the most successful Quebec novels, which can again be explained by its frequent adaptation by the media: In 1947 CBC Radio broadcast a program based on the novel, and the years between 1954 and 1960 saw a television version of *Le survenant* and *Marie-Didace* (1947), the latter being the second part of a planned trilogy about the Beauchemin family. In *Le survenant* the characteristic conflict between the peasant and the trapper is considered in a fresh light. Instead of the traditional description of the peasant's relationship with his "terre," the text focuses on the portrayal of interpersonal relationships. The farmer Didace Beauchemin is amicably attached to a stranger called Survenant, while Didace's son Amable and his wife Phonsine see him as a threat, similar to the majority of the other villagers, who greet him with suspicious curiosity. However, for the patriarch Beauchemin, Survenant embodies the perfect son, and his neighbor Angélina Demarais sees in him her long-awaited life partner. Yet Survenant, who outdoes Amable in vitality and love of life, does not mutate into a better farmer. When he disappears just as suddenly as he had entered the life of the Beauchemins, the villagers find their prejudices confirmed, while Didace and Angélina hope for his return. With the subtle creation of the trickster figure Survenant, who ingeniously manages to avoid any strict typecasting, Guèvremont succeeded in giving a differentiated analysis of French Canada's developing collective consciousness, which opened itself to the dynamic power of influences from outside.

The literary production of the 1940s and 1950s partially contests the assumption that the publication of *Trente arpents* marks the end of the farm novel. The distanced narrative authority launched by Ringuet as well as his naturalistic milieu description were indeed not imitated in the farm novels of the following two decades — both characteristics were rather taken up by the urban novel. Nevertheless, there were several authors who strove for a less formulaic treatment of the genre. Novels such as Léo-Paul Desrosiers's *Sources* (1942), Pierre de Grandpré's *Marie-Louise des champs* (1948), and Aimé Carmel's bestseller *Sur la route d'Oka* (1952) centered on the return of the purified protagonist to the country. Albertine Hallé's *La vallée des blés d'or* (1948) dealt with the colonization of northern Ontario, and Jules Gobeil's *Le publicain* (1958) told the story of the tragic life of Henri Millar, whose ambitious and bigoted parents force him into the priesthood. In addition to nationalist novels such as Rex Desmarchais's *La Chesnaie* (1942), which tackled the topic of Quebec's possible independence and whose racist undertone culminated in anti-Semitic declarations and a glorification of

Salazar's dictatorship, other novels such as Bertrand Vac's *Louise Genest* (1950), Harry Bernard's *Les jours sont longs* (1950), and René Ouvrard's *Débâcle sur la Romaine* (1953) described the fascination with the forests and the North, yet were still clearly committed to traditional dichotomies. Only in the 1960s, in André Major's *Le cabochon* (1964), Laurent Girouard's *La ville inhumaine* (1964), or Jacques Godbout's *Le couteau sur la table* (1965), can there be found an innovative continuation of the form of writing that Ringuet demonstrated in *Trente arpents*.

The mythic attractiveness of the woods and the northern countryside, as well as encounters with Inuit culture, were elaborately described for the first time in Yves Thériault's (1915–1983) *Agaguk* (1958). After numerous journeys, Thériault, who occupied a leading position at the Department of Indian Affairs between 1965 and 1967, devoted himself nearly exclusively to writing and produced a total of sixty-five publications, among them several novels for adolescents. Oscillating between folklorization and ethnographic sensitivity, *Agaguk* describes the Inuits' confrontation with the elements, with life and death, and with their worst enemy, the White man, whose destructive influence had already been a topic in Desrosiers's *Les engagés du Grand Portage*. However, Desrosiers's protagonist was a francophone voyageur, whereas at the end of the 1950s Thériault focused on the autochthonous perspective, which was particularly convincing in the first-person narration *Ashini* (1960). Thériault's novels *Aaron* (1954), *Agaguk*, and *Ashini* put the social outcast — be it a Jewish immigrant, an Inuit, or a Native North American — into the spotlight.

# The Urban Novel*

The history of the urban novel in Quebec begins with feuilleton novels, which were initially still committed to French models, though set in Montreal or Quebec City. *Les mystères de Montréal* (1879–1881) by Hector Berthelot (1842–1895) as well as the novel of the same title (1893) by Auguste Fortier (1870–1932) marked the beginning of this highly entertaining genre. Not only did these novels adapt the patterns of the French examples to French-Canadian conditions, but they also contributed to the development of the later urban novel. Some of the main characteristics of the latter were inherited from the farm novel, though. Montreal already plays a prominent role in the prototype of the farm novel, Patrice Lacombe's (1807–1863) *La terre paternelle* (1846). The topic of the city can also be found in several other farm novels such as *Jean Rivard, le défricheur* (1862) and *Jean Rivard, économiste* (1864) by Antoine Gérin-Lajoie, in Hémon's

*The section "The Urban Novel" was written by Rolf Lohse (University of Göttingen).

*Maria Chapdelaine*, and in Ringuet's *Trente arpents*, where urban space is depicted in a clearly negative way as a place of temptation and corruption, and thus appears as the counterpart to the country, where salvation and prosperity prevail. This negative evaluation of the city was also characteristic of the first urban novels. At the end of the nineteenth century, short stories, such as "L'encan" (1875) by Napoléon Legendre, were exclusively located in an urban setting, but it was not until the first decades of the twentieth century that truly urban novels, such as *Mirage* (1913) by Alfred Mousseau and the exceptional realistic novel *Le débutant* (1914) by Arsène Bessette, were written and published.

The central topic of Ubald Paquins's (1894–1962) novel *Jules Faubert* (1923) is the relationship between city and country, which also points to the antagonism between the anglophone upper classes and the wider francophone population. The thriving Montreal paper dealer Jules Faubert manages to accumulate a large fortune, thus proving that French Canadians are just as capable of financial success as anglophone merchants. However, at the height of his prosperity, his business disintegrates. The novel's plot is closely interwoven with the city of Montreal, where Faubert runs his business and leads a life that is focused on social status and material wealth. The city, with its means of transportation and communication, sharply contrasts with the country, which provides the paper producer with his key resource, yet also serves as a place of recreation. It is in the country that he seeks refuge from the turmoil of his feverish city existence. The novel thus describes the double role of the country from the perspective of the urban *homo economicus*.

The idealization of nature is one of the most typical elements of the French-Canadian urban novel, and already in Arsène Bessette's (1873–1921) *Le débutant* the city-dwelling protagonists yearn for a life closer to nature, hoping to rediscover their true selves in the countryside. Claude Robillard's (1911–1968) novel *Dilettante* (1931) is set in the milieu of well-to-do Montreal adolescents, who pursue the temptations of the American lifestyle but also live in an atmosphere of mutual manipulation and sexual concupiscence. Modern existence finds its expression in the fast pace of the city, in the quick sequence of parties where the protagonists meet, and also in the frenzy of speed that they experience while driving their cars. The fact that the novel is set in Montreal is so obvious that it is not even explicitly mentioned. The actions of the characters, their purpose in life, the locations where they meet, the ways they spend their time together, the things they talk about, and their means of transportation are all closely linked to the urban space. The country only appears as the destination of car excursions; the youngsters' attitude towards the country residents is characterized by ignorance and condescension. The characters love and respect each other, but they also have strong inhibitions to break the resigned silence and speak about difficult situations. Consequently, the picture of the city is an ambivalent one: On the one hand, the urban space tolerates the coexistence of different life concepts and ensures a high degree of freedom, but on the other hand, life remains subject to special restrictions, which are the result of the opportunistic pursuit of individual goals.

Jean-Charles Harvey's (1891–1967) novel *Les demi-civilisés* (1934) also ties in with this analysis of urban society. It describes the formative years of the first-person narrator and protagonist, Max Hubert. He measures the dishonest citizens of Quebec, the "demi-civilisés," against the moral integrity of the country dwellers, who live in a world of honesty, persistence, loyalty, and the willingness to be self-sacrificial. Openly anticlerical statements as well as Harvey's attempt at a synthesis of traditional values and social liberty awakened the suspicion of the clerical board of censors, who explicitly and officially condemned the author. Harvey was forced to resign from his position as chief editor of the newspaper *Le Soleil*. This censorship helped the novel achieve lasting success; during the Révolution tranquille it gained the reputation of a "martyr text."

The topic of social ascent as well as the question of moral values came to occupy the center of the urban novel. *Les Velder* (1941) by Robert Choquette (1905–1991) was published at the same time that the radio feuilleton "La Pension Velder" was broadcast (between 1938 and 1942). It tells the love story of Élise Velder, the daughter of a Belgian emigrant who runs a guesthouse in Montreal, and Marcel Latour, a young ambitious lawyer. After having overcome several obstacles, which are mainly connected with the social differences between Élise and Marcel and the personal rivalries of the mothers Joséphine Velder and Mona Latour, the couple marries, which propels the social rise of the Velder family.

Roger Lemelin's (1919–1992) first novel, *Au pied de la pente douce* (1944), moves the focus from Montreal's middle class to Quebec City's working class, describing the latter's (ultimately doomed) aspiration to a better life. Lemelin portrays the life of adolescents from Quebec's neglected quarter Saint-Sauveur during the prewar period in a picturesque, partially caricatured way, with a special focus on forms of religious life. At the center of the novel is the rivalry between aspiring young Denis Boucher and Jean Colin, who both have affections for Lise Lévesque. In the course of the plot, however, Jean becomes fatally ill and dies, while Denis loses his job and begins writing with increasing success. Nevertheless, Denis does not succeed in detaching himself from his milieu and, like his peers, is trapped in a stagnating society. The fact that he finally cannot realize his dreams of a better life has often been linked by critics to the state of French-Canadian society in the prewar era. The novel denounces the paralysis of society, its inability to find new goals and to free itself from narrow-minded self-referentiality and xenophobia. Lemelin's second novel, *Les Plouffe* (1948), can be read as a sequel to *Au pied de la pente douce*: It is also set in the city of Quebec, and some of the characters from the first novel reappear. The novel, whose episodic plot was subsequently expanded for a perennial television series, is set immediately before the Second World War. The story is told from the perspective of different members of the Plouffe family, who describe the colorful life in the Saint-Sauveur quarter. This includes sports, political and religious events, as well as diverse conflicts between the various characters. The central storyline circles around the mother who is trying to keep the family together, while its male members strive for independence.

Gabrielle Roy's (1909–1983) *Bonheur d'occasion* (1945) is considered the seminal urban novel and substantially raised public awareness of this genre. Under the title *The Tin Flute* it also became a bestseller in English Canada and the United States. In vivid naturalistic pictures the novel describes the life of the unemployment-stricken working class of the Montreal quarter Saint-Henri, where people live in dreadful apartments wedged between rail tracks and industrial plants. The plot takes place between February and May 1940. The young waitress Florentine Lacasse falls in love with the ambitious blue-collar worker Jean Lévesque, who intends to become an engineer and settle in the wealthy quarter of Westmount. At his side Florentine hopes to make her dream of emotional as well as material security come true. When she gets pregnant, however, Jean leaves her. She is forced to marry Emmanuel, whom she does not love and who later joins the army to fight in the war. They move to an apartment in Ville LaSalle, which, compared to Saint-Henri, is an improvement, yet still not what Florentine had originally envisioned. The descriptions of the miserable life of the Lacasse family, providing a backdrop for Florentine's story, reflect the deteriorating situation of the working class. The unstable father, Azarius, is unable to provide for his family. The mother, Rose-Anna, who has followed her husband to Montreal, refuses any state subsidies because of her peasant pride. Finally, it is the war that creates the jobs that the despairing unemployed seize in great numbers.

*Bonheur d'occasion* has often been imitated, for example, by Roger Viau in his *Au milieu, la montagne* (1951). Here, as in *Bonheur d'occasion*, the economic crisis forces the men into unemployment. Early on in her life the young Jacqueline Malo discovers that she has to take care of herself. When she meets Gilbert Sergent, who comes from the wealthy bourgeoisie and falls in love with her, she seizes the opportunity. However, the class barriers between bourgeoisie and working class make their love impossible. Viau's novel clearly shows that the assumption of a homogenous French-Canadian society, united in solidarity, is but an illusion.

## The Psychological Novel

The genre of the psychological novel had already been initiated in the late nineteenth century with Laure Conan's (1845–1924) *Angéline de*

*Montbrun* (1884), but was not revived until the 1930s. In 1931 Éva Sénécal's (1905–1988) *Dans les ombres* and Jovette Bernier's (1900–1981) *La chair décevante* were published in Albert Lévesque's series "Romans de la jeune génération." By concentrating on psychological novels, Lévesque strove to give Quebec prose a new direction. The lyrical undertone in Sénécal's first novel corresponds with the romantic worldview of the protagonist Camille L'Heureux, who, during the absence of her husband, falls in love with an American but resumes her marital duties after her spouse returns. As is the case in Bernier's novel, the landscape in *Dans les ombres* mirrors the inner life of the protagonist. However, Bernier also uses surprisingly innovative language to describe the inner conflict of her heroine, Didi Lantagne, language that in its telegraphic and syncopated tautness plausibly conveys the emotional impressions of the first-person narrator.

*L'initiatrice* (1932) by Rex Desmarchais (1908–1974) was also published by Lévesque's publishing house. By having the two protagonists, the first-person narrator and the mysterious Violaine Haldé, get acquainted while reading Lamartine's *Méditations poétiques*, the author alludes to the reception of French Romanticism in Quebec. In the stylized natural landscape that surrounds the "Castel," where Violaine and her mother live in seclusion, the twenty-year-old son of the village doctor introduces the young woman to Romantic poetry. While she opens herself to the poetry, the first-person narrator falls in love with her but has to come to terms with the fact that Violaine does not seem to share his affections. Only after her death does Violaine's mother reveal her daughter's illegitimate descent as the reason. While Sénécal and Bernier almost completely neglect the historical context in their novels and concentrate on the psyche of their middle-class protagonists, the autobiographically inspired novel *L'initiatrice* is scattered with allusions to the constantly growing Moloch Montreal and the increasing Americanization of Quebec's economy. The "Castel," for example, shrouded in mystery for the protagonist, is transformed into a factory by the Oklahoma Match Co., the romantic memories of his meetings with Violaine overshadowed by the industrial décor.

In the prologue to Desmarchais' *L'initiatrice* the author mentions those premises that motivated the movement of intellectual renewal at the beginning of the 1930s. In addition to a series of newly founded journals (*Opinions*, 1929; *La Relève*, 1934; *Vivre*, 1934; *Les Idées*, 1935), the psychological novel can be regarded as the movement's main instrument. For the young generation of writers and journalists the enemy was no longer the English. Instead, their criticism focused on all-embracing American materialism, which mainly manifested itself in the platitudes of mass culture. The journal *La Relève*, founded by Robert Charbonneau and Paul Beaulieu, became the young intelligentsia's mouthpiece against the systematic appropriation of cultural life by the church. Diagnosing a spiritual crisis, the followers of *La Relève* turned against the shallowness of a culture that only served the stylization of the past, at the expense of the present. Renamed *La Nouvelle Relève* in 1941, the journal emphasized the priority of the individual over material necessities and collective demands, thus advocating the principles of liberal Christian humanism. Consequently, Robert Charbonneau's (1911–1967) novels focus on the evaluation of the protagonists' inner lives. In several articles, which were collected in 1944 in *Connaissance du personnage*, the author expressed his concerns. The protagonists in *Ils posséderont la terre* (1941) are tormented by existential insecurities, resulting from the struggle between evil and good, love and hate, sin and virtue, and from the search for a Christianity-inspired ideal. While Charbonneau's first novel, *Ils posséderont la terre*, responded to these existential insecurities with an increase of metaphysical moralizing, Julien Pollender, the protagonist in *Fontile* (1945), counters it with social and political commitment.

Absence of meaning, absurdity, lack of passion, cultural alienation, and a desperate, mostly spiritual search for the meaning of life are the characteristics of the majority of the psychological novels of the 1940s and 1950s, despite all their differences. In his first novel *Le beau risqué* (1939) François Hertel (1905–1985) depicts the spiritual search and development of the adolescent Pierre Martel. However, in his later trilogy consisting of *Mondes chimériques* (1940), *Anatole Laplante, curieux homme* (1944), and *Le journal d'Anatole Laplante* (1947) he addresses the problems of writing and reflects on the psychological dimension of the writing process. In doing so the author dissolves the borders between dream and reality with almost surrealistic ease. Hertel distances himself from Quebec's literary tradition by ironically having his protagonist state: "J'étais devenu flasque et vide comme un roman québécois." And his judgment of Quebec's readership is by no means less severe when he claims: "N'oubliez pas que vous écrivez pour des lecteurs qui n'ont rien lu." In his philosophical-theological essay *Pour un ordre personnaliste* (1942) Hertel had already criticized this tradition indirectly, along with nationalism, which determined all aspects of social life at the time.

The rebellion against the suppression of the individual through social dogmas was often portrayed in violent, hate-filled mother-son relationships. Françoise Loranger's *Mathieu* (1948) and Jean Filiatrault's *Chaînes* (1955) can be considered exemplary for the devaluation of maternal authority. From the nineteenth century onwards, and particularly in the farm novel, the mother stood for all the values from which the younger generation wished to distance itself. Loranger's (1913–1995) *Mathieu* depicts the bleak picture of Mathieu Normand, whose desolate psychic state is expressed in his cynical interaction with others. Through his diary — a means of introspection frequently applied in psychological novels — the reader gains insights into the cruel relationship between Mathieu and his mother, which he can only escape by leaving the city. In nature and through sports Mathieu not only strengthens his physical condition, he also gains new insights about himself.

The first part of Jean Filiatrault's (1919–1982) *Chaînes* is linked to *Mathieu*: In both novels the mother figure, who has been abandoned by her husband, has an emotionally problematic relationship with her son. In Loranger's novel the mother's destructive scorn for her son can be explained by the fact that for her he has become the epitome of his father. In Filiatrault's novel, by contrast, the mother projects her conjugal love onto her son Serge, which has equally destructive consequences. In addition to the problematic absence of the father and the omnipresence of the mother, Filiatrault also focuses on incest, a topic which, although there are no actual occurrences of it, is subliminally present throughout the novel. Although independent from each other as to content, the two parts of the novel are strongly linked by the recurring image of the cat: The first part ("La Chaîne de feu") ends with the mother killing a cat, and in the second part ("La Chaîne de sang") the protagonist Bastien Patry confesses to having killed his cat and his mother, whereupon he commits suicide. The novel deals with an individual's struggle in a symbolic constellation recalling the situation of Quebec, where the active father figure has been excluded in favor of the triad of Terre-Mère-Église.

Whereas in Filiatrault's novel the existential hopelessness reaches a pronounced psychoanalytical dimension, in Robert Élie's (1915–1973) *La fin des songes* (1950) the psychological analysis and the typical elements of the urban novel overlap. Marcel Laroque's inability to communicate keeps him at a painful distance from his environment and turns him not only into a passive observer of his own foreignness, but also into a sarcastic critic of his social surroundings, which he condemns in his diary. It is in this diary that Marcel encapsulates his metaphysical emptiness in one sentence: "Cherche Dieu dans ta vie et un immense vide répond à l'appel de ce mot." Marcel leads a mediocre existence in a poor quarter of Montreal and, lonely and bitter, he finally commits suicide. His alter ego Bernard Guérin, who is financially better off, attempts to find a way out through political commitment, which, however, results in his leading an inauthentic bourgeois life. The author, who was committed to the spirit of *La Nouvelle Relève*, draws an awkward picture of a disillusioned generation that, by illustrating its social consequences, clearly rejects the ideological and cultural idealization of the past.

In her novels *Alexandre Chenevert* (1954) and *La montagne secrète* (1961) Gabrielle Roy also deals with fundamental existential problems. Alexandre Chenevert, a fifty-two-year-old bank teller, is haunted by guilt about his dead mother and proves to be unable to have a normal relationship with his clients, his few friends, and his daughter. The third-person narration repeatedly switches to the protagonist's interior monologue, which, at the moment of his death, blames God for the cruelty of his woes.

In *La montagne secrète* Roy describes the life and suffering of the artist Pierre Cadorai. He lives in solitude in northern Canada and is possessed by the idea of painting a particular mountain. A trip to Paris allows him to become acquainted with great works of art, but confines him to a miserable life that ultimately leads to his premature death. In Roy's late work autofictional and autobiographic texts play a central role; in *La petite poule d'eau* (1950) the author deals with her experiences as a young teacher in a remote area in Manitoba. In three parts she tells the story of the Tousignant family's aspirations to found a school, the actual running of the school, and the helpfulness of Father Joseph-Marie. In several volumes of short stories and novellas — *Rue Deschambault* (1955), *La route d'Altamont* (1966), *Cet été qui chantait* (1972), and *Ces enfants de ma vie* (1977) — Roy, relying on autobiographical fiction, writes about key events in her childhood and adolescence. Her actual autobiography (in two volumes, *La détresse et l'enchantement*, 1984, and *Le temps qui m'a manqué*, 1997) was published after her death in 1983.

As Roy had done in *Alexandre Chenevert* and Élie in *La fin des songes*, André Langevin (1927–) in his novel *Poussière sur la ville* (1953) also links the topic of city life with existential experiences: The loneliness, isolation, and desperation of the protagonist is reflected in the picture of the dreary and dust-covered mining town Macklin. Shortly after moving to Macklin, the young doctor Alain Dubois and his wife Madeleine grow apart. While Madeleine turns her attention to the womanizer Richard Hétu, Alain turns to alcohol to quench his jealousy and frustration. His desperation reaches its climax when Alain discovers that Madeleine has killed her lover Hétu and thereupon committed suicide. The hostility of the inhabitants of Macklin persuades Alain to leave, but three months later he returns with a new determination to stay. *Poussière sur la ville* is the second novel in a trilogy completed by *Évadé de la nuit* (1951) and *Le temps des hommes* (1956). Loneliness and the inability to rationally and emotionally cope with existential challenges, conflicts, and failures are the central themes of all three works.

The strong influence of existentialism on the psychological novel of the late 1940s and 1950s can, above all, be ascribed to the cultural and sociopolitical vacuum in which a whole generation of authors felt trapped. As an important part of publishing during the Second World War was shifted from France to Quebec, the French literary scene, even if only for a short time, gained some influence in the "belle province." Other important factors for the further development of the novel were war experiences and the historical, cultural, and mental effects of the war. Both Roy and Lemelin made the Second World War a central theme of their works and dealt with it from a local perspective. In *55 heures de guerre* (1943) by Francharme, alias Pierre Tisseyre (1909–1995), the war itself becomes the setting, as in Jean-Jules Richard's (1911–1975) *Neuf jours de haine* (1948), in which the soldiers are not portrayed as heroes but merely as human cannon fodder. The novels of the 1950s massively criticized the social system, asking for new parameters of identity, and finally leading to the discourse of decolonization in the 1960s. The latter's first indicators are noticeable at the end of the decade in the strongly socio-critical novels of Jean-Jules Richard (*Le feu dans l'amiante*, 1956), Pierre Gélinas (*Les vivants, les morts et les autres*, 1959), and are especially well elaborated in Gérard Bessette's *La bagarre* (1958).

The protagonist of *La bagarre*, Jules Lebeuf, is a student of literature who finances his studies by doing cleaning work for municipal transport services. He aspires to becoming an author and represents, in contrast to the sickly middle-class Augustin Sillery, the active Québécois. However, Jules does not succeed as a writer because he lacks his own voice and language, a shortcoming he tries to compensate for by committing himself to the trade union. The use of *joual*, the language of the Montreal working class, in the dialogues already foreshadows the 1960s and forms a stark contrast to the artificially precious language of the bourgeois Sillery. Gérard Bessette (1920–2005), a professor of literature, owed his breakthrough to the novel *Le libraire*, which was published in Paris in 1960. This novel, as critics in the early 1960s emphasized, simultaneously honors the French *nouveau roman* and the existentialist novel. References to Jean-Paul Sartre's *La nausée* (1938) or Albert Camus's *L'étranger* (1942) are especially striking in Bessette's depiction of the protagonist Hervé Jodoin. Like Antoine Roquentin (*La nausée*) and Meursault (*L'étranger*), Jodain, who works in a bookstore in the lifeless town of Saint-Joachim, lives in an existential vacuum, which becomes accessible to the reader through the diary-like narration. Indifference and the excessive consumption of alcohol characterize the protagonist's life. In Jodain's self-depiction the subtle criticism of the incapacitating clerical influence on intellectual life plays a central role. Whereas Bessette's *Les pédagogues* (1961) as well as *La bagarre* and *Le libraire* remain bound to traditional narrative schemes, the author found a new form of articulation in *L'incubation* (1965) by breaking up the syntactic and structural coherence of the narrative frame through numerous insertions in brackets as well as the minimal use of punctuation. As later in *Le cycle* (1971) and *Les anthropoïdes* (1977), Bessette already applies the stream of consciousness technique in *L'incubation*, which serves his psychoanalytical interests. Bessette's commitment to psychoanalysis also marks his later and strongly autobiographical novels, which focus on the academic milieu and the work of the literary critic (*Le semestre*, 1979; *Les dires d'Omer Marin*, 1985).

## Colonial Counterdiscourse and Aesthetic Fractions

The history of Quebec in the 1960s was marked by political, economic, and cultural change as a consequence of drastic reforms at all levels of social life.

The shift from a defensive to an active nationalism often resulted in an aggressive nationalistic policy in commerce, education, and culture as well as in the radicalization of the independence movement. This shift also artic- ulated itself as a central ideological concern in the novels of the Révolution tranquille, whose authors, on the wave of the francophone colonial counter- discourse, joined the sociopolitical commitment of Albert Memmi (*Portrait du colonisé*, preceded by *Portrait du colonisateur*, 1957), Frantz Fanon (*Peau noire masques blancs*, 1952; *Les damnés de la terre*, 1961), and Jaques Berque (*Dépossession du monde*, 1964). In addition to novels that continued the psychological trend of the 1950s under new formal premises, especially those works whose authors were connected to the journal *Parti pris* can be considered representative of the spirit of the Révolution tranquille and the push for political and cultural emancipation.

"Laïcisme, socialisme, indépendance" was the slogan of the journal *Parti pris*, a slogan that was created in October 1963 by André Brochu, Paul Chamberland, Pierre Maheu, André Major, and Jean-Marc Piotte. This journal, along with *Liberté* (1959), became the most important instrument of the new generation. The so-called *partipristes* distanced themselves from the traditional myths of French-Canadian society and turned to the depiction of the incapacitated Canadien français, who from then on was referred to as the Québécois. The latter's social estrangement was revealed in his degenerated language, the *joual*, which was often interpreted as the expression of his situation as "colonisé" and of his cultural dispossession. Simultaneously, the publishing house Les Éditions du Parti pris released titles such as Laurent Girouard's *La ville inhumaine* (1964), André Major's *Le cabochon* (1964), and Jacques Renaud's *Le cassé* (1964), as well as Pierre Vallières's renowned essay *Nègres blancs d'Amérique* (1968). In addition to the colonial counterdiscourse, which the three novels more or less successfully apply through critical realism, they all share the same setting, namely the city of Montreal. It is a place of alienation and social exploita- tion, which in *Le cabochon* stands in stark contrast to the mythic North. At the center of Major's (1942–) developmental novel (Entwicklungsroman) is Antoine, called Cabochon (a roundly cut gemstone) by his mother. He breaks out of his milieu, fights for himself, and after a long trip to the North finds his way back to his roots. The protagonist's search for identity is situated between the traditional opposite poles of the individual versus collective, nomadic versus sedentary lifestyles, and the self versus the Other. It is also a search for an individual calling, which for Antoine means that he wants to write for the collective benefit. As he follows his vocation, he is confronted with the difficult question of how to capture the banality of his milieu in an authentic literary language. The novel once again takes up the theme of the nomadic lifestyle, which also plays a central role in Jean-Jules Richard's *Journal d'un hobo* (1965). The individual freedom of Richard's protagonist, however, shows a new, more relaxed way of dealing with constraints of all types, and goes beyond the strict ideological discourse of the *partipristes*. Furthermore, in *Le cabochon* Major contemplates the question of whether, and in which form, writing constitutes a central step in the process of individual and collective emancipation and thus raises a topic that, although looking back on a long tradition in French-Canadian literature, had not been treated in such detail in an individual work before. In the 1960s the topic of writing and literature, as well as language in general, was dealt with in numerous novels such as Laurent Girouard's *La ville inhumaine* and Jacques Godbout's *Salut Galarneau!* (1967). In Girouard's (1939–) *La ville inhumaine* writing also plays a central role, insofar as the second part of the text focuses on the creation of a novel entitled "La ville." The title is a reference to the city in which the Québécois fail, which is exemplified by the suicide of the author-protagonist Etienne Drolet. Jacques Renaud's (1943–) *Le cassé* deals with a similar problem, namely the lack of language as a consequence of cultural and social incapacitation. Although both Major's Antoine and Girouard's Etienne Drolet are confronted with the problems of their alienated milieu, their ability to reflect on linguistic and social alienation in the writing process still provides them with a certain sense of self-determination. In contrast, Renaud's inarticulate protagonist Tit-Jean is at the mercy of his hopeless situation, because he is unable to give tangible reasons for his desperation and to locate the enemy. He consequently turns his aggressions against his own milieu and thus against himself: "Il n'a jamais connu ni stabilité, ni sécurité materielle. . . . Son élément, c'est la bagarre, une ville hostile, la violence." Towards the end of the novel it becomes clear that Renaud's Montreal does not offer any room for the francophones. The omnipresent violence has to be understood as an expression of revolt, resulting from the feeling of an all-encompassing confinement.

> . . . c'est une île torturée, assommée, hideuse dans sa poliomyélite.
> Montréal étendu dans ses meurtrissures sous la lune.
> Montréal tanné.
> Montréal monnayé.
> Montréal en maudit.
> Gagne de chiens!
> Qui ça?
> Tout le monde!
> Fesser! Frapper! L'air sent la violence à plein nez. Le gaz carbonique et
> le mensonge.

The informal language used in Girouard's, Major's, and Renaud's novels contributes to the cathartic effect of their critical realism. The use of *joual* may be evidence of the linguistic impoverishment of the French-Canadian working class: Jean-Paul Desbiens writes in *Les insolences du Frère Untel*

(1960) that "parler joual, c'est précisément dire joual au lieu de cheval. C'est parler comme on peut supposer que les chevaux parleraient s'ils n'avaient pas déjà opté pour le silence et le sourire de Fernandel." The use of *joual* in literary texts, however, can be seen as a way of raising awareness of the colonial suppression of the Québécois. In the *Parti pris* journal in 1965, Gérald Godin defends his use of *joual*: "Nous refusons de servir à maquiller par notre beau langage le langage pourri de notre peuple." In contrast, Hubert Aquin time and again referred to the dead end into which *joual* led Quebec literature, considering its compulsory use as a restriction of authorial freedom. When after the October Crisis in 1970 the colonially accentuated discussion of the situation of Quebec slowly died down, *joual* had nevertheless secured a fixed position as a literary option, losing its explicit political connotation in the following decades.

Quebec novels influenced by colonial counterdiscourse distinguished themselves less through formal innovation than through their determined protest against the status quo of Quebec society, a protest that had been articulated since the early 1960s in numerous, formally more traditional novels. Authors criticized the inherited moral concepts and revolted against the tyranny of the traditional family, against bigotry and social hierarchies, as well as all authorities that supported a value system alienating humans from themselves. The psychological novel of the 1960s revalued the status of the individual, as opposed to society. The break with the past often saw the individual fall into hopeless despair and loneliness. The early novels of Gilles Archambault ( *Une suprême indiscrétion*, 1963; *La vie à trois*, 1964) illustrate this, as do Claude Jasmin's *La corde au cou* (1960) and *Délivrez-nous du mal* (1966), Réal Benoit's *Quelqu'un pour m'écouter* (1964), Adrien Thério's *Le mors aux flancs* (1965), Gilbert Choquette's *L'apprentissage* (1966), and Jacques Hébert's *Les écoeurants* (1966). These authors almost obsessively focus on all the topics that had previously been excluded, particularly on the body and on sexuality. Roger Fournier's (1929–) novels ( *Inutile et adorable*, 1963; *À nous deux!*, 1965) have in fact a pronounced pornographic dimension. Jacques Benoit (1941–) has his protagonists, Jos and Myrtie in *Jos Carbone* (1967), surrender to each other in the mythic atmosphere of the woods, revealing a sensuality that differs greatly from the cold, mostly violent depictions of bodily attraction in other novels of the 1960s.

The break with the values of the past, the escape from traditional relationships, and the engagement with traumatic childhood experiences, self-discovery, the body, and sexuality also characterized the emerging field of women's literature, which slowly established itself in the course of the 1960s. In addition to very traditionally constructed novels as, for example, Claire France's (1927–1976) *Autour de toi Tristan* (1962), there were also exceptional publications such as Claire Martin's (1914–) memoirs *Dans un gant de fer*, which were published in two volumes ( *La joue gauche*, 1965;

*La joue droite*, 1966) and were honored with the Governor General's Award. After *Doux-amer* (1960), a depiction of women's difficult situation in relationships, the author in her memoirs unsparingly evaluates her childhood, depicting the devastating effects of growing up in a society characterized by oppression, stupidity, and a deep aversion towards culture. These topics are also dealt with in Andrée Maillet's (1921–1995) *Les remparts de Québec* (1965). In Maillet's novel the protagonist transgresses — "Hier dans la nuit du vingt-six au vingt-sept juillet, je me suis promenée toute nue dans les Plaines d'Abraham" — and thus uncovers the mask of the traditional discourse regarding the French-Canadian nation: "Nue et les mains vides, effrayée par l'inconnu, je ressemble à ma nation." Diane Giguère (1937–), the granddaughter of Jean-Charles Harvey, takes up the topic of problematic relationships between mothers and daughters in *Le temps des jeux* (1961), a topic that had already been addressed by Marie-Claire Blais in *La belle bête* (1959). While in Giguère's second novel, *L'eau profonde* (1965), the symbolic search for her father forces the young protagonist into a torturous and demeaning relationship with an older married man, *Le temps des jeux* sees the daughter taking revenge on her mother, who neglects and abandons her and deprives her of any chance to find her place in society.

Literature by female writers of the 1960s also approached the subject of homosexuality for the first time. Louise Maheux-Forcier (1929–) discusses female homosexuality in her trilogy (*Amadou*, 1963; *L'île joyeuse*, 1964; *Une forêt pour Zoé*, 1969), which reflects upon the female body and its desires. Hélène Ouvrard's (1938–1999) scandalous novel *La fleur de peau* (1965) traces the problematical self-discovery of Anne, who falls in love with the homosexual Stéphane. Dealing with the difficult analysis of the alienated body and ill-treatment during childhood, and distancing themselves from the moral values of the postwar period, authors such as Monique Bosco (1927–2007; *Un amour maladroit*, 1961) and Yvette Naubert (1918–1982; *La dormeuse éveillée*, 1965) also turn to the issue of the Shoah. Whereas Bosco's protagonist, Esther, who emigrated to Montreal, manages to overcome her traumatic experiences through psychoanalysis, Naubert's main character, the German Jew Hans, takes refuge in suicide as the only way of forgetting the murder of his parents by the Nazis. Naubert's second novel, *L'été de la cigale* (1968), is set in the United States and depicts the story of Tom Gordon Henderson, who against his family's will marries Lorraine Hope, a Black woman. Against this backdrop the novel deals with the history of slavery and the unsolved problem of racism in the United States.

The years 1965 and 1966 were of particular importance for the further development of the Quebec novel. Works such as Jacques Godbout's *Le couteau sur la table* (1965), Hubert Aquin's *Prochain épisode* (1965), and Réjean Ducharme's *L'avalée des avalés* (1966) definitely tied in with the European and American avant-garde. In 1962 the writer, journalist, and filmmaker Godbout (1933–) published *L'aquarium*, which is set in Ethiopia, where the author had worked as a French teacher in the mid-1950s. The novel's formal design and narrative point of view is reminiscent of the French *nouveau roman*. However, it is the unconventional structure of *Le couteau sur la table*, its fragmented montage, the seemingly random oscillation between past and present in the eighty-five story fragments, the insertion of explanatory or commenting footnotes or remarks in brackets, which interrupt the flow of the text. The systematic change from French to English in numerous dialogues, as well as the frequent use of English expressions, sometimes even whole sentences, marks an aesthetic break, a break that mirrors the numerous breaks in the life of the first-person narrator, and, in a broader sense, those with traditional values in the 1960s. In the following years and decades Godbout masterfully shifted back and forth between formal innovation and distanced irony, which made him a favorite with the reading public. In novels such as *Salut Galarneau!* (1967), *D'amour P.Q.* (1972), *L'isle au dragon* (1976), *Les têtes à Papineau* (1981), *Une histoire américaine* (1986), *Le temps des Galarneau* (1993), or *Opération Rimbaud* (1999), he remained faithful to his credo (formulated in *Le Réformiste*, 1975): "Écrire . . ., c'est faire un choix, c'est refuser de se laisser porter par les idées reçues, c'est être conscient de la précarité des échanges, c'est assumer l'angoisse de la mort, c'est rejeter la famille et l'héritage."

The novels of Marie-Claire Blais (1939–) are dominated by outsiders who are in pursuit of the absolute and break with society. Criminals, thieves, pyromaniacs, homosexuals, prisoners, and those weary of life are portrayed against the backdrop of the inhospitable Quebec winter landscape and its icy coldness, the darkness of the woods, and the dubious worlds of bars, prisons, and mental institutions. In her early works Blais, who was awarded the French prix Médicis for *Une saison dans la vie d'Emmanuel* (1965), combined fantastic and naturalistic elements and turned the societal pariah into a romantic, yet infathomable hero. In *Une saison dans la vie d'Emmanuel* the central elements of the farm novel and its system of values undergo a subtle deconstruction. The author achieves this by reversing the empty pledges of the *roman de la terre* into their despicable opposites: The farmer becomes a violent alcoholic who rapes his wife and beats his children, the benevolent village priest becomes a parasite, the religiously exalted daughter turns into a prostitute, the friar into a pederast. The literally dirty world of the adults contrasts with the world of dreams and imagination, where the young brothers Jean Le Maigre and Le Septième seek refuge. Faced with an inhuman existence, writing becomes a magical place of survival for Jean Le Maigre. Writing also plays a central role in the trilogy *Manuscrits de Pauline Archange* (1968), *Vivre! Vivre!* (1969), and *Les apparences* (1970). Even though Blais approaches the issue of homosexual tendencies quite often in her work (for example in *Le loup*, 1972), it was only in her later novels such as *Les nuits de l'Underground* (1978) or *L'ange de la solitude* (1989) that she seems to explicitly deal with her own homosexuality. In *Les nuits de l'Underground* this is achieved by a lyrical and almost mystical staging of lesbian passion. In *L'ange de la solitude* Blais deals with homosexuality through the story of young lesbians who share an apartment and try to overcome the death of one of their roommates. The fact that the author, after three decades of literary productivity, is still fascinated by outsiders can be seen, in an impressive and stylistically convincing manner, in *Soifs* (1995), which consists of a single, 315-page-long sentence recalling the breathless abysms of Western society at the end of the twentieth century.

Hubert Aquin's (1929–1977) literary work made him the epitome of the *écrivain maudit* of the 1960s, particularly after his suicide in March 1977. Aquin and his novels have to be analyzed from a different perspective from works of critical realism, because in the dispute between content and form, he clearly preferred formal experiments. Aquin is considered the most radical of the modern authors of his generation, and is sometimes even referred to as postmodern. Nevertheless, his work remained in touch with the experiences of his time, down to even the smallest details of its baroque complexity. The depiction of the writing process reflects the broken self-image of the French-Canadian people who, as the author explains in "L'art de la défaite" (1965), are not able to speak about themselves as winners, but see themselves caught up forever in the founding myth of the defeat on the Plains of Abraham (1759), part of a latent conflict in Aquin's works between historical and individual determinism on the one hand and dedication as a process through which one acquires self-determination on the other. From the late 1950s onwards Aquin worked as a producer and director for the Office national du film and Radio Canada, and in 1961 he joined the RIN (Rassemblement pour l'Indépendance Nationale). In 1964 he was arrested for illegal possession of firearms and as a result spent several months in prison and subsequently in a mental hospital. His first novel *Prochain épisode* (1965) — the immediate result of his stay in the psychiatric ward — blurs the boundaries between reality and fiction. The narrator, a political prisoner in a psychiatric clinic, attempts to write a spy novel whose protagonist, an FLQ fighter, is to execute the history professor H. de Heutz in Switzerland, but returns to Montreal without having accomplished his mission. In Montreal he is arrested and interned in a mental institution. In addition to the obvious parallels with the author's own biography, it becomes apparent at the end of the novel that the supposedly fictitious story could also be the prehistory to the narrator's own detention in the clinic. In *Trou de mémoire* (1968) Aquin creates a similar subtle suspense between fiction and autobiography by blurring the boundaries between different narrative levels. As later in *L'antiphonaire* (1969) and

*Neige noire* (1974), he confronts the reader with a world of violence and powerlessness and thus subtly maneuvers the reader into an unbearable disorientation, similar to that of the colonized.

Since the publication of his first novel *L'avalée des avalés* (1966), honored with the Governor General's Award, the speculations about Réjean Ducharme (1941–) have continued. In 1967 in *La Presse* the author explained his refusal to present himself to the media and his readers with the right of the published text to be seen independent of its author. This refusal to conform to the conventions and demands of the literary market partially corresponds to the denial of Ducharme's young protagonists to adapt to an adult world. With surprising consistency they continue their search for the absolute, in whichever form, and refuse to integrate themselves into an arbitrary and often absurd adult world, which in *Le nez qui voque* (1967) is ruled by sexual drives. The identity of the characters is based on their determination not to surrender to the inevitable division between ideal and reality (as seen from the perspective of the adults). In Ducharme's novels the revolt against the pragmatics of the symbolic order reveals itself most impressively in the author's linguistic portrayal of his characters. Ducharme is an ingenious creator of word games and neologisms, which are reminiscent of improvised language games but in fact aim at the reacquisition of language, its absurd, comical, and uncanny features. These were already prominent in *L'avalée des avalés*:

> Je hais tellement l'adulte, le renie avec tant de colère, que j'ai dû jeter les fondements d'une nouvelle langue. Je lui criais: "Agnelet laid" Je lui criais: "Vassiveau" La faiblesse de ces injures me confondait. Frappée de génie, devenue ectoplasme, je criai, mordant dans chaque syllabe: "Spétermatorinx étanglobe" Une nouvelle langue était née: le bérénicien.

Simultaneously a playground and a combat zone, language is a momentary place of freedom, yet this freedom is illusory. Although Bérénice Einberg in *L'avalée des avalés* is able to create her own language — the "bérénicien" — out of her hate for the adult world, she cannot stop reality's invasion into the absoluteness of her amour fou for her brother, similar to Ducharme's other protagonists, Mille Milles and Chateaugué (*Le nez qui voque*), Iode Ssouvie and Asie Azothe (*L'océantume*, 1968), André and Nicole (*L'hiver de force*, 1973), and Fériée and Vincent (*Les enfantômes*, 1976). After the success of the films *Les bons débarras* (1980) and *Les beaux souvenirs* (1981), directed by Francis Mankiewicz, for which Ducharme had written the screenplays, and his play *Ha ha!* . . . (1982), it was only in the 1990s that further novels followed (*Dévadé*, 1990; *Va savoir*, 1994; *Gros mots*, 1999). These novels continued the dissonant linguistic virtuosity of the early texts. It would be presumptuous, even wrong, however, to reduce Ducharme's novels to political metaphors, even if many of the archetypal features of the "holy" martyr (a recurrent theme in Quebec literature) can be found, particularly in Johnny, the protagonist in *Gros mots*.

The impressive and quick development of the Quebec novel during the years of the Révolution tranquille not only illustrates the extent and effectiveness of the control of cultural life by the church and state before 1960, but also the mechanisms of self-censorship that particularly the novelists in the 1950s subjected themselves to. Just as in the first decades of the twentieth century, the novels published during the Révolution tranquille mirrored the explosiveness of the question of Quebec national identity. This no longer, however, took place in the form of a defensive self-depiction which paid homage to an anachronistic provincialism. Novelists rather projected the answer to the identity question into the future and linked it increasingly with the call for an independent Quebec. The vision of independence proved to be an ideal projection screen for the latent desire for authenticity and absoluteness, whose phantasmagorical dimension became especially clear in Ducharme's figures. From the mid-1970s onwards, the specific consciousness of a lack of identity or the latent insecurity with respect to identity was articulated independently from colonization. From then on problems of identity, which the literature of the 1960s still understood as a consequence of colonization by English Canadians, was conceived of as a general component of modern human existence.

# 19: The French-Canadian Short Story

*Doris G. Eibl (University of Innsbruck)*

THROUGHOUT THE NINETEENTH CENTURY and at least until the 1940s, the development of the French-Canadian short story, both thematically and formally, paralleled that of the novel. The generic boundaries of the novel and the different forms of short prose cannot always be clearly determined, and scholars and the authors themselves are often vague in their distinction between *nouvelle, conte, histoire, récit, légende, chronique,* and *mémoire*. Thus, Patrice Lacombe's *La terre paternelle* (1846) has been categorized both as a novel and as a *nouvelle*, Albert Laberge's *La Scouine* (1918) has occasionally been regarded as a short-story collection, and Jacques Ferron's novels as "grands contes."

In the first decades of the twentieth century, authors such as Adjutor Rivard, Lionel Groulx, Frère Marie-Victorin, Damase Potvin, Clément Marchand, and Blanche Lamontagne-Beauregard produced short prose that was ideologically indebted to agriculturalism and focused on French-Canadian country life being threatened by rural exodus, technology, and Americanization. In these works, the francophone population represents both the values inherited from France and those of Catholicism. Literary adaptations of historical events and picturesque depictions of country life — all claiming to be anthropologically authentic — resulted in an idealizing realism. The authors of the 1920s such as Frère Marie-Victorin (1885–1944) particularly emphasized the "vieilles choses, vieilles gens," which were folkloristically overdrawn and enjoyed great popularity. Only a few writers managed to break away from the agriculturalist and moralizing discourse dominating the majority of short stories, most of them published in periodicals. Similar to Stephen Leacock's (1869–1944) *Sunshine Sketches of a Little Town* (see ch. 7, Davies), the humor in Jean-Aubert Loranger's (1896–1942) *À la recherche du régionalisme* (1925) stems from an ironic distance to the rural milieu — which also applies to his numerous later short stories circling around the figure of Joë Folcu. Albert Laberge's (1871–1960) short-story collection *Visage de la vie et de la mort* (1936) features social sketches inspired by naturalist aesthetics, juxtaposing fanatic and ignorant rural "habitants" with an exploited urban population unable to cope with its striving for social advancement. By depicting the general hopelessness of the figures, leading to alcoholism and ugly vulgarity, the author severely criticizes French-Canadian self-perception. In addition, he clearly rejects the existing social hierarchies, which were supported rather than undermined by agriculturalist and retrogressive nationalism.

Léo-Paul Desrosiers's (1896–1967) first short-story volume, *Âmes et paysages* (1922), deals almost exclusively with historical and regional topics in a psychologically plausible way. *Le livre de mystères* (1936) focuses completely on the inner life of his protagonists, their passions, and their secret conflicts. Hence Desrosiers, along with Jean-Charles Harvey (1891–1967), can be considered the pioneer of the psychological short story of the 1940s and 1950s. While Desrosiers's psychological analyses reflect a spiritual quest and enrich the tradition of regionalist literature through a differentiated depiction of his characters, Harvey's collections of texts (*L'homme qui va*, 1929; *Sébastien Pierre*, 1935) decidedly reject nationalist-Catholic ideals and reveal the pessimistic worldview of the author. Harvey emphasizes the abyss of the *conditio humana* and the enslavement of people through war, famine, ignorance, and injustice.

Since the beginning of the twentieth century the short story had belonged to the preferred genre of women writers, who, as for instance Gaëtane de Montreuil (1867–1951) in *Coeur de rose et fleur de sang* (1924), dealt with historical topics from the time of Nouvelle-France, childhood memories, and local events, or commited themselves to regionalism, as did Blanche Lamontagne-Beauregard (1889–1958) in *Récits et légendes* (1922), *Légendes gaspésiennes* (1927), and *Au fond des bois* (1931). Most female authors were particularly interested in social problems, which distinguished them clearly from their male colleagues. Without betraying their patriotic convictions or striking any type of social criticism, they preferred to deal with poverty and oppression, underprivileged children and orphans consigned to their fate, forced marriages, and unhappy relationships. Their depictions of exemplary individual cases were often extremely emotional and dramatic and, through the invocation of pitiful pictures, tended to be moralizing. Love always played a central role, be it in the works of Anne-Marie Gleason (1875–1943; she published under the pseudonym Madeleine and is considered one of the first important female Quebec journalists) in *Le long chemin* (1913) and *Le meilleur de soi* (1924), or in those of Marie-Rose Turcot (1887–1977; *L'homme du jour* 1920; *Stéphane Dugré*, 1932) and Marie-Antoinette Grégoire-Coupal (1905–1984; *Le sanglot sous les rires*, 1932). Not surprisingly, the authors abstained from discussing sexuality in their texts, and love was defined as the virtuous devotion of the woman to her duties as a wife and mother, in correspondence with the general negation of sexual desire in French-Canadian literature of the early twentieth century.

At the end of the 1930s, when regionalism was replaced by a vehemently critical depiction of rural reality, a pronounced social criticism and exoticism emerged in short-story writing. The cliché of the rural idyll was deconstructed among others by Yves Thériault and Jean-Jules Richard, whose short stories also display formally innovative aspects. In *Contes pour un homme seul* (1944) Thériault (1915–1983) places his figures in mostly remote areas where, surrounded by unpredictable and troubling natural occurrences such as storms or snow, they succumb to their animalistic instincts. In the story "Simon-la-main-gourde" the protagonist of the same name ties a farmer's son to a plow and slits his veins in order to obtain a better harvest from the soil through this blood sacrifice. The superstition and misplaced moral values of the rural population lead to mindless violence against others or self, for example, in "Lorgneau-le-Grand," in which a woman is hanged for accidentally causing the death of her child, or in "La Jeanette," in which a father kills himself and his dishonorably impregnated daughter. Thériault's chiseled characters, the dramatic tension in human relationships, and the depiction of nature as a threat contrast with the conventional and palliating picture of traditional regionalist short stories, a contrast which is further stressed by the author's partially raw and archaic language and his use of ellipses.

Only three of the thirteen short stories that Jean-Jules Richard (1911–1975) collected in *Ville rouge* (1949) are set in a rural milieu, but they are by no means less violent than Thériault's stories: Two of the three stories end with a murder. The violence that the impoverished or cynical city population sees itself exposed to in Richard's social scenarios matches the moral and physical cruelty of the rural population. Frequent sequences of short sentences create suspense and give an impression of restlessness. Behind this restlessness lies an undefined and sometimes nearly hysterical quest, which drives the protagonists from one place, one desire, and one disappointment to the next, relentlessly striving to communicate with their fellow beings. On their journey through life, which has no actual destination, the urban characters especially become mouthpieces of the author's criticism of Quebec society — a society trapped in self-referentiality and thus the victim of self-inflicted powerlessness.

Predominantly known as a poet, Alain Grandbois (1900–1975), who lived in France from 1925 to 1938 and returned to Quebec after the Second World War broke out, published *Avant le chaos* (1945), an autofictional and for the time unusually modern volume of short stories. In the conventional Quebec literature of the 1940s and 1950s, Grandbois's work stood out: In the tradition of Marcel Proust, his short stories recall "parcelles de temps perdu," which Grandbois sought to reanimate in literature, as pointed out in the foreword of the collection. He chose exotic settings such as Djibouti, Constantinople, Hanoi, Shanghai, and Macao, but also Paris and the Côte d'Azur, which he knew from his own travels. The author, who is recognizable to the reader particularly in the first-person narrator, tried in each narration afresh to define his own identity as *auctor*. On the one hand, the collection stages the figure of the wealthy, good-looking, well-educated American dandy who amuses himself in Europe and the rest of the world and who recalls the stereotypical image of the 1920s American expatriate. On the other hand, the volume is a true homage to literature itself and refers to the author's intensive examination of the problems of writing. Besides the first-person narrator, most of the other protagonists are also somehow involved in literature. Ultimately, their intensive traveling can be understood as a quest for their true selves, which they strive to find by discovering the real as well as the literary world.

With respect to their innovative and cosmopolitan aspects, Grandbois's short stories did not trigger an immediate response from other writers. The publication of Anne Hébert's (1916–2000) *Le torrent* (1950), in contrast, touched upon the spirit of the day. Of the five stories of the collection, written between 1938 and 1947, "Le torrent" belongs to the best-known short stories of Quebec literature. The opening lines have been quoted many times: "J'étais un enfant dépossédé du monde. Par le décret d'une volonté antérieure à la mienne, je devais renoncer à toute possession en cette vie." For the readers and critics of the 1950s and especially those of the 1960s — in 1963 a second edition was published, including two new short stories — Hébert's work was emblematic of the situation of Quebec society, its incapacitation and alienation. The title story itself is an allegory of the spiritual and cultural plight of Canada's francophone population. In the 1980s and 1990s this interpretation was broadened by taking into account the story's mythological dimension. Nevertheless, the deliberate isolation in which the character Claudine trains her son François to complete submission and abdication is a clear reference to the ideological and literary discourse that has been omnipresent in Quebec ever since the mid-nineteenth century. The key events of the story — the son's refusal to conform to his mother's expectations for him to become a priest, the violence of the mother which causes the son's deafness, and finally the son's murder of his mother — create, in their concentrated depiction from the perspective of the first-person narrator François, an atmosphere of unbearable suspense, which accompanies every glance, gesture, and word, and simultaneously attests to François's enormous existential emptiness. Even after his mother's death François remains her prisoner: "J'ai porté trop longtemps mes chaînes. Elles ont eu le loisir de pousser des racines intérieures. Elles m'ont défait par le dedans. Je ne serai jamais un homme libre." He can only liberate himself from captivity by committing suicide.

In comparison to Hébert's *Le torrent*, Gabrielle Roy's (1909–1983) short-story volume *Rue Deschambault* (1955) proved to be almost traditional. Similar to Adrien Thério (1925–2003) in *Contes des belles saisons* (1958), Roy in her eighteen short stories deals with childhood memories. Numerous parallels can be found between the life of the author and that of the protagonist and narrator Christine. The narrator describes the key moments of her development from a small child to a young woman against the backdrop of the francophone milieu of Saint-Boniface, Manitoba, and hence allows glimpses into the life of a francophone enclave that had only rarely been depicted in French-Canadian literature. Adrienne Choquette's (1915–1973) *La nuit ne dort pas* (1954) and Claire Martin's (1914–) *Avec ou sans amour* (1958) sharply contrast with the nostalgic, yet differentiated tone of Roy's short prose. It was particularly Claire Martin's ironic and sometimes even sarcastic analyses of lonely existences that foreshadowed the favorite literary topics of the Révolution tranquille.

The 1960s saw the publication of countless short stories, featuring a wide variety of aesthetic approaches and ranging from the socio-critical realism "médinnequébec" of André Major (1942–; *La chair de poule*, 1965) and Marcel Godin (1932–; *La cruauté des faibles*, 1961) to the magical realism — peppered with surrealistic elements — of Claude Mathieu (1930–1985; *La mort exquise*, 1965) to the truly macabre fantastic aesthetics of Michel Tremblay (1942–; *Contes pour buveurs attardés*, 1968), reminiscent of H. P. Lovecraft. The most outstanding figure of the 1960s, however, was Jacques Ferron (1921–1985), general practitioner, author, and cofounder of the Parti Rhinocéros, which appeared repeatedly as a "guerrilla idéologique" during the election campaigns from 1963 onwards and which ridiculed Canadian politics with ironical and satirical comments. Ferron participated in all the essential political and social debates of his time, and during the October Crisis of 1970 he even acted as mediator between the government and the kidnappers of Labour minister Pierre Laporte. The generic classification of Ferron's writings is difficult. Besides *Contes du pays incertain* (1952) and *Contes anglais et autres* (1964), which were collected in *Contes* together with four new stories in 1968, Ferron, starting in the early 1960s, also published novels which are often labeled "grands contes." Marcel Rioux, sociologist and author of the essay *Jacques Ferron malgré lui* (1978), maintains that Ferron's complete works belong to the genre of the conte, even if individual stories were published as novels. In fact, all the author's prose texts are to a certain extent "contes savants," and the story *Papa Boss* (1966) may even be called a "conte philosophique." At the center of Ferron's texts one repeatedly finds the problematic yet indispensable relationship between the individual and the collective, for example, in the very complex and sensitively humorous "grand conte" *Cotnoir* (1962). The author was also concerned with the question of individual and collective memory; Ferron refused to rely on official historiography, which he denied any credibility, in *Historiettes* (1969): "Qu'on sache que je m'occupe d'histoire parce que la sottise des historiens me fâche, . . . ces jocrisses qui . . . ont été des faussaires et ont tout fait pour mettre le passé au temps mort — et pourtant l'histoire vit comme un roman." As can be seen in, for instance, *Le ciel de Québec* (1969) or *Les confitures de coings* (1972), Ferron focused on memories which are "alive," in the sense of a positive, open, and creative confrontation of both the individual and the collective with the past. Thus it is not surprising that Ferron frequently reworked and expanded his own already published texts, quoted himself without restraint, incorporated published texts in new ones or, as in *Le ciel de Québec*, produced an intertextual scenario with numerous literary, mythological, biblical, and historical references, which the author arbitrarily distorted.

The parallels in the development of the Quebec novel and short prose, which are especially prominent on the content level, can be explained by the fact that the majority of the short stories that entered the literary canon had been written by novelists. The oral aspect that formally characterizes many short stories testifies to the vitality of the oral tradition, especially before the Révolution tranquille, a tradition whose importance for Quebec's identity and collective memory also formed a topic in numerous novels. Narratives, particularly in the rural genre, frequently described the evening gatherings (the so-called "veillées") of village inhabitants who exchange news and tell stories. It was only in the late 1970s that the Quebec short story began to disengage itself from its linguistic and formal commitment to the oral tradition. The radicality of this break opened the path to striking literary innovations.

# 20: French-Canadian Drama from the 1930s to the Révolution tranquille

*Dorothee Scholl (University of Kiel)*

## Institutional Framework

THE LATE DEVELOPMENT OF FRENCH-CANADIAN THEATER is above all a result of its institutional framework: For a long time, secular drama was decried as amoral and was therefore prohibited. The clergy, in particular, who made a decisive contribution to the history of drama by encouraging the performance of plays in the collèges for the purpose of classical education, rhetorical training, and the moral edification of pupils, rejected the performance of "profane" texts. Beginning with the 1930s, however, the influence of European theater led to a modernization in the repertoire and the performance practice of clerical theater. Many clergymen also composed their own plays, for example, Antonin Lamarche (1899–1967) and his brother Gustave (1895–1987), who achieved great success with *Jonathas* (1931) and the open-air theater piece *La défaite de l'enfer* (1938), and who also wrote numerous mystery plays, clerical plays, and dramatic fragments. Émile Legault (1906–1983) — who has since been acknowledged as the founder of modern French-Canadian drama — wrote clerical plays, too, and welcomed avant-gardist tendencies, for instance, in matters of stage decor. He broke away from the limitation to a religious repertoire and performed not only Christian but also secular classical and modern plays, for example, by Molière, Jean Anouilh, T. S. Eliot, Carlo Goldoni, Luigi Pirandello, and Jean Cocteau, as well as by Jacques Copeau, whose aesthetics had a strong influence on him. In 1937 Legault founded the amateur group Les Compagnons de Saint-Laurent at the Collège Saint-Laurent in Montreal, which later became a professional institution and produced the theater magazine *Les Cahiers des Compagnons*. The chansonnier Félix Leclerc (1914–1988) was part of the Compagnons ensemble, beginning in 1942 as a temporary actor and later becoming an author. In 1948 his play *Le p'tit bonheur* was performed, which consists of a series of short, partly realistic, partly fantastic scenes of Canadian life, and praises the "small blessedness" of everyday life in the spirit of the eponymous chanson. In fact, many of Leclerc's chansons are, according to his daughter,

"small plays." Through their tours, the Compagnons reached national vis-
ibility, and through their performance art as well as their innovative interpretations of classical and modern plays, they contributed to the general
dramatic effusion of the 1940s. Further groups and institutions with an
international repertoire resulted from Legault's ensemble, such as the
Centre dramatique des Compagnons, the Compagnie du Masque, the
École Nationale de Théâtre, and the Théâtre du Nouveau Monde.

The number of tours abroad continuously increased, and the exchange
with performers from Europe was also on the rise. As new theaters and
new companies gradually emerged, the repertoire continued to expand,
national and international theater festivals were brought into being, and
acting schools were founded. Authors often combined several functions
successively or simultaneously in the course of their careers (chansonnier,
actor, dramatist, artistic director, director, choreographer, stage and cos-
tume designer, professor at a training center) — a phenomenon that can
be encountered to this day and can be traced back both in a positive and
in a negative sense to the institutional infrastructure. Beginning in the
1950s, radio and television provided the possibility of professional employment for writers and actors, making a significant contribution to the development and propagation of scenic art in series such as "Les Nouveautés
dramatiques" (1950–1962), to which (among others) Yves Thériault,
Hubert Aquin, and Claude Gauvreau contributed. Some authors wrote
their plays specifically for the new media. New genres appeared, such as the
"téléthéâtre" or the "radioroman," and many plays were henceforth mul-
timedia-oriented, employing structural techniques such as unmediated
change of scene or film-inspired flashbacks.

# Theater as a (Distorting) Mirror to the Popular Mind

As a reaction to the decidedly international orientation of theater as of the
1930s, various authors attempted to present French-Canadian themes and
problems to a wider audience. Through their "realistic" drama, these
authors wished to encourage French Canadians to become aware of their
collective identity. The plays contain various topoi of French-Canadian
identity construction: The relation between Canada and Quebec, for
instance, was described as a personified parent-child relationship, whereby
Quebec is impersonated by the abandoned child (topos of the orphan or
bastard) who rebels against his parents (topos of the "fils révolté") or succumbs to them (topos of the victim). Theater thus became the scene for a
symbolic representation of the Québécois identity, but it also offered an
opportunity to question the status quo and present alternative lifestyles. In

this sense it contributed to the emergence of an ideological pluralism and, ultimately, also to the mentality change that the Révolution tranquille brought about. The collective mentality structures and character features nourished by the colonial and clerical background, such as self-disdain, submission to authority, servility, and fear of change, were made a theme of on the stage. The reference to Quebec is not always stringent in the individual plays, but it suggests itself in many cases. In the following, such potential interpretations will be pointed out, with the caveat that the identity-related interpretation is, in some cases, only possible in hindsight. Many of these plays can exist as autonomous works, or must be rediscovered as such; furthermore, there are authors such as as Paul Toupin (1918–1993), whose plays (*Brutus*, 1951; *Chacun son amour*, 1957; *Le mensonge*, 1960) and drama theory (*L'écrivain et son théâtre*, 1964) refused to make concessions to public taste and intentionally backed away from specifically Canadian themes.

The actor and Shakespeare performer, translator, and author Gratien Gélinas (1909–1999) is widely considered to be the first authentic dramatist of Quebec, since he dealt with French-Canadian themes and created in his plays figures that achieved a strong identificatory effect through their ability to articulate the consciousness of the common man in their colloquial language and likable simplicity. Gélinas also belongs to the founding figures of multimedia stage plays: For a series of radio, theater, and television sketches he created a comical, clown-like character called Fridolin who, for the duration of a decade, gave voice to the attributes of the common people with a caricaturing, satirical intent and in an entertaining fashion. As a symbolic figure of the French Canadian, Fridolin marks an important stage in the representation of identity. He is a kind of picaro, an adventurous rogue, who scrutinizes society with a critical gaze and common sense. Fridolin "suffers from suffering," and his characteristic expletive "souffrance de souffrance!" became a leitmotif of the so-called *Fridolinades*, which enchanted audiences between 1938 and 1947.

With his first drama *Tit-Coq* (1950), which originated in the Fridolinade *Le conscrit* and was later adapted for the screen, Gélinas created, as he himself called it, a "théâtre national et populaire." The three-act play structured in "tableaux" tackles in a novelistic, almost filmic fashion the topic of the bastard child who grows up in an orphanage and is confronted with the problem of having to fight as a soldier for England in the Second World War; the political background is the second "crise de la conscription" (1942; see ch. 16, Mathis-Moser). During Christmas celebrations with the family of a friend, Tit-Coq falls in love with the latter's sister who, although smitten in turn, is forced by her family into marrying another man while Tit-Coq does his military service in England. Just like Bousille in *Bousille et les justes* (1959), Tit-Coq becomes the projection screen of the simple and honest everyman who fails to realize his dreams and to change the conditions of his existence. In his two-act play *Hier, les enfants dansaient* (1967) Gélinas also took up a current political problem: the conflict between a fed-eralist-minded politician and his son, who is part of a separatist association. The play reflects Gélinas's own confrontation with this politically charged topic, one set against the background of the Révolution tranquille and the increasingly forceful clarion calls of separatists for national independence. While Gélinas's plays preserved their connection to the urban working class still rooted in its rural background, Marcel Dubé (1930–) sympathized with the younger generation of this class and became the mouthpiece of their new needs, wishes, and requirements prompted by industrialization and the expansion of the American way of life.

Dubé wrote over three hundred works for radio, television, and the stage, and his dramatic oeuvre had a decisive impact on Quebec's theater scene for three decades. Dubé was influenced by Anouilh, whose *Antigone* (1944) he adapted for the French-Canadian stage, and whose young hero-ine of resistance deeply impressed him. His plays are — in keeping with his own statements — partly autobiographical and revolve around the themes of childhood, youth, coming-of-age, and their implicit demands and re-sponsibilities. They try to pull at the heartstrings of the viewer and provoke pity through the tragedy and failure of the depicted destinies. The young protagonists in Dubé's theater aim to break out of their dependency on the grown-ups' world. Along with friends, Dubé founded the company "La jeune scène" in 1950, for which he wrote his first texts, *Le bal triste* (1951) and *De l'autre côté du mur* (1952). In the latter play, which was also adapted for television, the image of the wall expresses the confinement in the prison of a retrograde society and points at the same time to "the other side," the utopia of an ideal society, in which the individual has the chance of self-realization.

Dubé's drama *Zone* (first performed in 1953) was celebrated in the press as a national triumph. A backyard hero with the ironic nickname Tarzan smuggles American cigarettes into Canada to earn a little money and save himself and his adulatory cronies from the grim prospects of a dis-mal existence. But happiness is not possible in this social "zone." Tense dialogues evoke the dreary atmosphere of the working-class environment and the hopelessness of a naive and defiant youth in conflict with the law and its guardians. Tarzan's attempt at escaping from the drab monotony of everyday life fails as lamentably as his escape from prison, and he dies a martyr for a generation bereft of all future prospects. In *Florence* (1958) Dubé grapples with the issue of emancipation from a female perspective. Florence is the female counterpart to Tarzan in *Zone*. Similarly to Louis Hémon's (1880–1913) Maria Chapdelaine, she stands in conflict with tra-ditional values and the desire to evade them. But in contrast to Hémon's heroine, Florence wants to break out of her life, her "house of boredom," and refuses marriage with its implicit responsibilities and transformations:

"Je veux pas devenir une machine à faire des enfants, je veux pas devenir une machine à faire du ménage, une machine à engraisser et à vieillir. . . . Je veux pas d'homme qui va se laisser bafouer toute sa vie, qui fera jamais de progrès, sous prétexte qu'il est honnête . . . ça vaut pas la peine d'être honnête si c'est tout ce qu'on en tire." Florence bears witness to a paradigm shift in the evaluation of valid moral principles and delivers a demythologizing portrayal of the French-Canadian woman. What is more, the oppressed woman who becomes aware of her strength and refuses to comply with tradition can be regarded as a symbolic representation of Quebec in the throes of the Révolution tranquille.

Joseph, the hero of Dubé's *Un simple soldat* (1958), is also a collective symbolic figure. After his return from the Second World War, Joseph does not know what to do with himself, joins the war in Korea, and dies there not as a national hero but as "a simple soldier." The play ends with young Fleurette's quip: "Quand on est mort, on n'a pas besoin de médaille." Joseph is depicted as a drifter and a failure whose every job fails to please or succeed. He enmeshes himself more and more tragically in his hopeless situation and finally succumbs to his own weakness of will. His persistence in passivity and isolation reflects the mentality of French Canadians under the conservative government of Maurice Duplessis (1944–1959). Dubé works with a filmic change of scene and interrupts the very lively and intense dialogues with melancholy song inserts and poetic scenes. In later plays, such as the melodramatic thriller *Octobre* (1964) and the social critique *Les beaux dimanches* (1968), the author sketches characters who have sacrificed their youthful dreams to material interests and pleasures, and whose childlike candor has flipped into hypocrisy. Dubé's plays can thus be perceived as an indirect confrontation with French existentialism, and his failed heroes as reversals of the Sartrean heroic ideal.

Françoise Loranger (1913–1995) was also extremely active on the Quebec cultural scene, and her plays similarly express generational conflict and its implicit clash of values, as well as the wish for emancipation. In contrast to Dubé, however, Loranger attempted to present possibilities of existential liberation. In the middle-class family drama *Encore cinq minutes* (1967) Gertrude, a woman of the working class, refuses to allow her son's girlfriend, who is working on a dissertation on the exploitation of the poor, to move into her house. The space that Gertrude inhabits becomes a symbol of Lebensraum, while the generational conflict escalates into a class struggle. In the end, Gertrude breaks the vicious circle of her self-imposed alienation and dares to free herself from the people she used to cling to and who are now clinging to her. She manages to be herself and to acknowledge the others in their alterity. The "téléthéâtre" *Un cri qui vient de loin* (1967) also deals with the self-recovery that comes with inner liberation. The play consists to a large extent of stage directions and in several respects anticipates the contemporary "théâtre d'images." The protagonist's

dreams, fears, and memories are rendered through mythological and religious allusions (the motifs of Hercules and Christophorus), abrupt shifts
in lighting, and fluid transitions and flashbacks to the protagonist's childhood. These devices lend the play the surreal character of a dream and contribute to its uncanny power as much as do the poetic use of clichés
(images of the bride, of the North) and the psychological intensity in the
characters' performance and dialogues. At the core of *Un cri qui vient de
loin* is the inner liberation of a nameless protagonist ("Lui") who, as a
child, had witnessed his mother's passionate affair with another man and
whose repressed cry breaks out twenty years after the fact. He finds himself in a situation similar to his father's back then: His wife meets her lover
while he travels to the "Grand Nord" as a trapper. The theme of the passive woman in the grip of boredom at home and of the active man exploring the woods, an ever-present theme in French-Canadian literature, is
revisited here from the female perspective and reevaluated: The woman's
unfaithfulness is interpreted as a consequence of the man's inability to settle down. Yet the play ends on a conciliatory note with the protagonist's
nonverbally mediated renouncement of his adventurous journeys to the
North and his hope of winning his wife back.

With the ambiguous psychological drama *Double jeu*, directed by André
Brassard in 1969, and the "comédie patriotique" *Le Chemin du Roy* (1969),
Loranger entered a new creative phase (see ch. 33, Scholl). She intensified
her use of audio-visual effects in order to act upon the audience's subcon-
scious, and allowed more room for improvisation under the influence of the
Living Theatre. The text, which also contains musical inserts, is no longer
considered as something irrevocably set in stone, but as an organic object
that can undergo transformations ("work in progress"). The actors mingle
with the audience and thus incorporate the spectators into the play.
"Flirting" with the audience has been extremely popular with many French-
Canadian dramatists and directors up to this day.

## Theater under the Sign of the Avant-Garde

Jacques Languirand (1931–) approached in his plays the theater of the
absurd or the "théâtre de l'insolite" in the tradition of Eugène Ionesco. He
diverged, however, from this, and from avant-garde theater in general, by
placing himself, like Dubé, in the tradition of Anouilh. Yet similarities with
the theater of the absurd — both in theme, formal and aesthetic means, and
Languirand's dramatic theory — cannot be overlooked: farce, clown comedy, alienation into the grotesque, multilayered structures and the resulting
ambiguity, doublings, archetypal patterns, symbolical significance of
objects, puns, illogism, the inability to communicate and the isolation of
the figures, deformed language and mutilated characters (deafness), the

parody of traditional practices, the oscillation between tragedy and comedy, banality and pathos. As Ionesco did in France, Languirand distanced himself from the "théâtre populaire" by rejecting the concept of mimesis in the sense of a realistic representation of psychological and social facts, and also by denying linguistic concessions. In the three-act play *Les insolites* (1955), which was, according to Languirand's own indications, the fruit of his experiments with the surrealistic *écriture automatique*, four men are located in a bar. By chance (in the surrealistic sense of "hasard objectif"), the woman they all talk about happens to be the same person, namely Brigitte, who has betrayed her husband Jules with the other three men. The play has overtones of Beckett and Pirandello and stages the motif of meaningless and aimless waiting, as well as the duality between the individual and social roles, between happiness and misfortune. This basic pattern is modified seven years later in *Violons de l'automne*. Two elderly men, both named Eugène, compete for the same woman, who during her engagement with one of them has had an affair with the other. In the end, the "aristocratic" Eugène murders his troublesome double. The motif of the double or the divided self, which appears in various guises in French-Canadian and other literatures, dominates Languirand's entire dramatic work as well as his novel *Tout compte fait, ou L'Eugène* (1963), which in many respects can be said to offer a key to understanding Languirand's drama. In typically authorial passages, Languirand voices his conviction that man carries in himself a double, an "homme des ténèbres," who is repressed under normal circumstances and who only surfaces in the imagination — or in literary fiction.

Languirand's *Les grands départs* (1958), which lends itself to interesting comparisons with Loranger's *Une maison . . . un jour* (published in 1965), premiered on television and reflects the general atmosphere of lethargy and apathy during the period of the "grande noirceur" under Duplessis. The disconnected figures soliloquize on and on without acknowledging each other's presence. Similarly to Chekhov's and Beckett's characters, they await a change in their stagnant situation, expecting a "great awakening," seated on furniture amid a scene of removal. Each attempted escape is doomed to fail, because deep down they fear freedom and change. Hector, the protagonist of the play, is a writer manqué. He was conceived and received as an embodiment of the French Canadian. He gives great orations and devises majestic plans that are never realized. His wife Margot prefers to make herself at home in the comfort of the household and resists any transformation. The doldrums are deepened by the grandfather, who, as a result of an argument with Hector, is left paralyzed and motionless, and is treated by the others like a piece of furniture. The grandfather's paralysis symbolizes a hesitation to act, just as Hector's inability to write expresses a spiritual lameness. The play ends with a *coup de théâtre*: At the end of the third and last act, the grandfather rises from the chaos of removal and idle talk and leaves with his luggage, loudly slamming the door behind him.

The public's reaction to Languirand's drama was comparable to the European response to the theater of the absurd: He was accused of abstraction, formalism, opaqueness, deception, vulgarity, bluffing, and hermetic elitism. Languirand's deforming alienation of reality offended an audience who wished to see theater as a mirror of the individual and collective self and its environment. With *Klondyke* (1970), Languirand turned towards the multimedia collective theater and discovered "Americanness" as an essential component of the French-Canadian identity. The play is a spectacular adventure piece that evokes the Yukon gold rush in 1896 and as "théâtre total" attempts to create an operatic synthesis of the arts, combining text, music, ballet, choreography, and photographic and filmic means, as well as stage design.

Claude Gauvreau (1925–1971) also failed to fulfill the audience's expectations at the outset of his career. Gauvreau is considered the *enfant terrible* among the dramatists of his time. He was expelled from the Jesuit College because he painted obscene pictures and propounded heretical views. Likewise, his provocative texts sparked scandals and polemics. Gauvreau joined the "automatist" movement and contributed to the surrealist manifesto *Refus global* (see ch. 17, Mathis-Moser). He staged his first play, *Bien-être* (1947), together with his partner, the actress Muriel Guilbault; the play created a stir because of its avant-gardist modernism. After Guilbault's suicide in 1952, Gauvreau spent some time in psychiatric institutions and also took his own life in 1971. The death of his partner and the ensuing trauma constituted the obsession of many of his plays. During his stay at the Saint-Hilaire clinic he composed his first long play, *L'asile de la pureté* (1953), which was not performed until 1988. In the play, a poet wants to subject himself to a purifying diet in order to maintain an immaculate memory of his dead beloved through ascetic practices. *La charge de l'original épormyable* (1977; written in 1956) with its tragic hero Mycroft Mixeudeim, *La reprise* (1977; written in 1958–1967), and *Les oranges sont vertes* (1977; written in 1958–1970) also revolve around the obsessive motif of the authentic individual and artist, who is left behind after the death of his lover and muse and then tries to come to terms with this loss in an unsympathetic and hypocritical environment. Gauvreau also wrote texts for the radio, among others *Automatisme pour la radio* (1961) and *L'imagination règne* (1963–1967), and composed poetry for the stage, which he recited himself in ceremonial scenic readings. After his death many of his poetic and narrative texts continued to be performed on stage, for example, in the 1988 "Spectacle Gauvreau" under the direction of François Barbeau, who staged a series of texts from *Poèmes de détention* (1986–1970), *Beauté baroque* (1952), and *Étal mixte et autres poèmes* (1948–1970).

Gauvreau's literary and psychological record is to some extent comparable to that of Antonin Artaud, whom Gauvreau met personally and who opened up new avenues for him. *Les oranges sont vertes* especially is reminiscent of the French theorist of the "théâtre de la cruauté" (*Le théâtre et son double*, 1938) and of his stage plays, but also harks back to the avant-garde drama of Alfred Jarry and Guillaume Apollinaire. The performance of *Les oranges sont vertes* on 13 January 1972 introduced a wider audience to the hitherto little-known Gauvreau and triggered a heated debate. Only after the publication of his *Oeuvres créatrices complètes* (1977) was Gauvreau canonized as a serious author on the French-Canadian literary scene. His poetic language is unusual and radical in an etymological and metaphorical sense: Gauvreau tried to return to the origins — of language, of imagination, and of theater itself. He referred to his own language as "exploréenne," exploring and sounding the depths of language and orchestrating words, word fragments, and sounds down to babblings and silence. His search for the absolute always remained true to the motto "Créer le pur!" (*Beauté baroque*).

Like Gauvreau, Sauvageau (1946–1970; actually Yves Hébert) also experimented with words and sounds and played with linguistic and phonetic ambiguousness; moreover, his drama also stands under the influence of Artaud and his concept of the "théâtre total." After dedicating himself first to the representation of family conflicts in an expressive way (*Les mûres de Pierre*; *Papa, je ne veux pas rentrer chez moi, maman m'attend*, both 1977), he switched to the operatic music spectacle with *Wouf wouf* (1970), which requires a more extravagant use of theatrical machinery as well as more performers. At the play's center is a young poet called Daniel, a modern version of the *poète maudit*. Daniel feels exposed to the pressure of consumer society and its overflow of contradictory signs, which *Wouf wouf* describes by invoking varied elements from the fields of literature, advertising, sports, leisure, religion, and the Americanized everyday life of Quebec society (with its references to bingo games and fast food). Daniel wishes to live according to his own principles of pleasure and, ultimately, descends to an animal level, which also results in a "degeneration" of his language. The neo-Baroque spectacle includes interludes, acrobatic insertions, dances, choruses, street scenes with demonstrations and funereal processions, sports reports, and ritualistic scenes, as well as literary parodies (of Racine's *Phèdre* from 1677, for instance) and to a certain extent anticipates contemporary theater. In the 1970 play *Mononstres et manattentes (Ohé! toi qui louches, fais-moi peur)* Sauvageau also picked up themes and techniques of the European avant-garde, for example, from Jarry's *Ubu roi* (1896) and Ionesco's *Jacques ou La soumission* (1954), where the hidden demonic streak in man breaks out. Yet Sauvageau's drama also introduced elements from the repertoire of American fantasy, thrillers, and horror films (Dracula, Frankenstein), although his treatment of all these features remains playful and parodic. Laurent Mailhot (2001) characterized Sauvageau's drama as the "drama of America's white Indians," under the sign of disempowerment, dysfunction, and ridicule, which opposed the status quo to the wild and the primitive, as well as to the blasphemous.

# Epic and Lyrical Aspects of Drama, Dramatic Aspects of the Epic and the Lyrical

Whereas some playwrights distanced themselves from the literary text, there were, on the other hand, authors whose main body of work consisted primarily of short stories or novels, but who also produced interesting texts in the field of drama, such as Jacques Ferron, Anne Hébert, and Yves Thériault. What their dramatic works share is an introspective tendency and an unmasking and demythologizing function: In contrast to those authors who, in whatever fashion, always stage or improvise a "popular spirit," they channel the consequences and the problems of the situation specific to Quebec before and during the Révolution tranquille (seclusion, prevention of all contact with the outside world, communication problems, generational conflict, emancipatory ideals) through the mirroring in individual consciousness. In matters of linguistic composition and scenic design these authors also exceed the one-dimensionality of an insider's language and symbolism. They use drama to orchestrate the conflict of various perspectives and to achieve detachment and reflection through this interplay of visions.

Anne Hébert's (1916–2000) well-known novel *Kamouraska* (1970) lent itself to a stage adaptation (2003) not least thanks to its "dramatic" structure. With her plays, which in turn display epic proportions, Hébert tackled the psychosocial and religious issues of her epic and poetic work. The detective play *La mercière assassinée* (1967; first performed in 1958) tells the story of a female serial killer who is herself murdered. The action takes place in the French countryside, where the French-Canadian journalist and amateur detective Jean Rivières sets out to investigate the secrets behind the psychological drama of the French murderess. Jean is a kind of "ingénu" in the tradition of Voltaire, a man who observes the society of the "ancienne France" and its preconceptions with an impartial eye and relativizes its values through his point of view. Hébert plays with the clichés of national autostereotypes and heterostereotypes:

LA MARQUISE: Parlez-moi, monsieur, parlez-moi la langue du Canada, je vous en prie . . .

JEAN: Kamouraska, Kénogami, Chicoutimi, Caughnaeaga, Chibougamau, Richebouc, Yamaska, placotter, magasiner, t'avais ben enbelle, O.K. All right, on est paré, t'es ben smatte . . .

LA MARQUISE: Mon Dieu! Qu'est-ce qu'il a dit? C'est terrifiant!

LE JUGE: Je n'en ai pas la moindre idée. Ce garçon est sauvage et n'a aucune éducation!

LA MARQUISE: Ça sent le Nouveau Monde à plein nez! Aucune éducation!

The clash between different mentalities also supplies the basic conflict in the parable *Le temps sauvage* (1966). In contrast to historical time, "wild time" is static and ritualistic, a vicious circle without change or progress. This novelistic four-act play, whose plot extends over six months, describes a family that lives in the mountains, completely cut off from civilization, whose members get on each other's nerves in the tight domestic atmosphere. When Agnès, the mother of the family, takes her late sister's daughter into her home, the crisis comes to a head. The rancorous woman, let down by life, religion, and love, unconsciously takes out her hatred of her sister, who pinched the lover of her youth, on the urbane and cosmopolitan niece and on her own children. In the demonic and barbaric wilderness, she wishes to gather them around her in keeping with her own visions of salvation. The psychological drama can at the same time be read as a gloss on the situation of Quebec: The mother who cloisters herself away from progress must admit in the end that progress — the emancipation of her children and their passage from wilderness into civilization — cannot be hindered. The revolt of the younger generation points to the upheavals and advances of the Révolution tranquille.

Yves Thériault (1915–1983), another writer who is known primarily as a novelist, turned even more radically towards the archaic and the primitive as a means of expressing the specific features of French-Canadian culture. Thériault, who worked for some time as a government representative for issues concerning the Natives, supplied engaged and critical comments on the civilization and "knowledge" of the White population from the perspective of the indigenous peoples. Thériault composed countless radio plays and stories for Radio-Canada. He defined the radio play as "littérature pour l'oreille" and mediated the uncivilized, wild, and telluric through an archaic, stylized language that approximated oral speech. The "radio-théâtre" *Le samaritain* (1958) is structured in brief sequences. Clément, who becomes a Good Samaritan, lives with his wife Christine outside of and isolated from the village community. He could be classed in the literary category known as "défricheur," since he ventures into the wilderness to find sources of water for the rural community. The eeriness of nature, evoked through a lyrically archaic language, is contrasted, as with Hébert, with the safety and protection of the home. Moreover, the figure of the father in Thériault's *Le marcheur* (1968) can be considered a male foil to the mother in Hébert's *Le temps sauvage*. In a naturalistic fashion, the play shows the suffocating atmosphere of the rural, patriarchal milieu, which is put under a social and psychological microscope. The *mythe du terroir* is deconstructed by the pitiless exposure of the cruelty of the rural world. The basely motivated characters prove their wretchedness and worthlessness, just as Hébert's protagonists do, in relation to the sublimity of nature and their inherited culture. Extralinguistic signs take up symbolic significance and contribute to the tension and intensity of the play: Victor, the father, whose steps on the upper floor of the house never cease to tyrannize the family, is at death's door. He dictates instructions and rules to his wife and children, who are to be severely punished if they fail to comply. The tyranny of the upper floors points to a patriarchal image of God, marked primarily by the fear of authority. At the play's premiere, Thériault was forced to give in to censorship and rewrite the ending of the text: The members of the family, who suffered under the father's oppression their entire lives, finally forgive him. Thériault also opposed any interpretation of his play as a regional allegory: "J'ai fait une oeuvre d'imagination, sans prétendre qu'elle collait à une réalité, à notre réalité."

Jacques Ferron's (1921–1985) drama, in its literary quality, also matches the author's narrative and essayistic output. Ferron himself saw his dramatic work as preliminary exercises for his prose, but the mere fact that he repeatedly revised his plays — there are different versions of several of them — suggests that his artistic aspirations were in fact higher than he acknowledged. Ferron masters French-Canadian traditions of orality as well as the classical French repertoire, and he plays with these traditions with unmistakable originality and aplomb in his own works, which revolve around universal issues such as love, religion, and the homeland. He elaborated on his own conception of theater in *L'impromptu des deux chiens* (1972), which continues the metadramatic tradition of the "impromptu" and of the "canine conversation" as a form of cynical dialogue (Greek *kynikós*, canine). A snappy altercation is involved, one between Ferron in the role of the author and Albert Millaire as the director. Millaire favors collective achievement and scenic art, whereas Ferron privileges the individual author's work and the linguistic work of art:

> FERRON: Le spectaculaire l'emporte sur la littérature, il la balaie à grands coups de bruits et de lumières: on peut faire passer n'importe quel texte, et même se passer de texte, les acteurs improvisant leurs cris en français comme en anglais, n'importe comment. Que devient l'auteur dramatique dans tout cela? Il s'en va, il n'est plus rien.

In the end the two yapping dramatic artists reconcile after realizing that neither can exist without the other.

Ferron's plays often contain metadramatic insertions and humorous allusions to literary texts as well as to past and present concerns of French-Canadian identity. In Ferron's sketchy texts, the banal is inflated to fantastic proportions, while the fantastic and the supernatural are revealed as self-evident and mundane. In the brief sketch *La mort de monsieur Borduas* (1968; written in 1949), for instance, the group of automatists around Paul-Émile Borduas and Gauvreau appear as *dramatis personae*, and the presumably dead Borduas, whom everyone imagines to have reached the "paradis surréaliste," appears in the flesh on the stage. In many of Ferron's texts, the motif of madness also plays an important part. In *Tante Élise ou Le prix de l'amour* (1956) the cranky old spinster Élise gathers information from a hotelier on the procedures of her niece's wedding night, after having the bed and various pieces of clothing removed from the hotel room in the hope that the unbridled passion of the newlyweds would require no external accessories. In *Le Don Juan Chrétien* (1968; first version 1957) Ferron provides a burlesque deconstruction of the Don Juan myth. The commander's libidinal energy is, in this case, misguided: Instead of aiming at his wife, it is directed at his horse, Arthur, and under the spell of this illusion he tries to "humanize" the animal. However, he undergoes a much stronger transformation from a crazed lover of horses towards becoming a gentle husband. On the dramatic level, appearances are broken through a distortion of illusion that places the myth itself under reconsideration: "DON JUAN: Je ne suis qu'un mythe, un mythe dont la présence dans l'histoire servira à comprendre la condition des femmes jusqu'à cette génération." The imaginative confrontation with myth, fairytale, and legend provides Ferron with an opportunity to reflect and analyze the present in light of the past. Modern myths are questioned with critical irony and made accessible to the reader's own reflection. Next to mythical, fantastic, and burlesque themes, Ferron's drama also turned to historical topics. In *Les grands soleils* (first version 1958; last version 1968) he dealt with the Patriots' Rebellions of 1837–1838 and with the controversial national hero Jean-Olivier Chénier, "homme incertain," and made a theme of the kind of forgetfulness of history that borders on complete amnesia.

The invocation of history or of individual historical personalities was a common phenomenon in drama during and after the Révolution tranquille. Theater was connected with the aspiration for national independence and aimed to educate "national" consciousness, but it could also — as in feminist drama — seek to revise or reinterpret traditional historiography in order to reform collective consciousness. Within French-Canadian culture, theater had an immense political and ideological significance in mirroring the relationship between the audience and reality. It expressed, and at the same time challenged, the public sphere, presented pluralistic ways of life, and offered a platform to disseminate ideas and ideologies, to bestow on these a body and a voice through the actors' presence on the stage, to revive the past, and renew or counteract collective traumas.

# VI. Literature from 1967 to the Present

# 21: Sociopolitical and Cultural Developments from 1967 to the Present

*Sherrill Grace (University of British Columbia)*

IN 1967, CANADA CELEBRATED ITS CENTENARY, the hundredth anniversary of Confederation, but there are many other defining years and events which have come to be seen as foundational or transformative for the country's history. The First World War marked Canada's entry onto the world stage as a nation separate from Great Britain (while still part of the British Commonwealth); the Second World War consolidated Canada's national stature and independence and paved the way for a number of significant cultural and social developments during the cold war years that would have their major impact after 1967. Vincent Massey, the country's first Canadian-born Governor General (1953–1959), submitted his Report of the Royal Commission on National Development in the Arts, Letters, and Sciences in 1951 and, as a result of Massey's recommendations, the Canada Council for the Arts was created and began funding artists, publishers, and scholarship in 1957. In 1977, the SSHRC (Social Sciences and Humanities Research Council), an offshoot of the Canada Council, was established. Without these two strategic organizations the cultural and scholarly landscape of Canada as we know it today would be a different one. The Stratford Festival (founded in 1953) opened in its permanent building in 1957 and has gradually come to be recognized as one of Canada's top national theaters. Jack McClelland began his important New Canadian Library series (which facilitated the teaching of Canadian Literature in schools and universities) that same year. In short, the political vision and financial support for cultural endeavors that would pave the way for the surge of national pride we now associate with the centennial year and the two decades that followed have their roots in the 1950s and early 1960s. That was also the period when the National Theatre School of Canada opened in Montreal (1960), the Shaw Festival in Niagara-on-the-Lake was founded (1962), and several major regional theaters emerged (such as the Neptune Theatre in Halifax, Nova Scotia, and the Playhouse in Vancouver, British Columbia, both in 1963, and the Citadel Theatre in Edmonton, Alberta, in 1965). George Grant

(1918–1988) published his now famous treatise *Lament for a Nation* in 1965, but the cultural life of Canada was nonetheless poised to blossom as it had never done before.

1967 saw not only the country's centennial, but also a series of major cultural events: George Ryga's (1932–1987) classic play *The Ecstasy of Rita Joe* premiered at the Vancouver Playhouse; *Louis Riel*, the first major full-scale Canadian opera, with libretto by Mavor Moore and music by Harry Somers, was staged at Toronto's O'Keefe Centre; at the Théâtre du Nouveau Monde in Montreal, Michel Tremblay (1942–) launched his extraordinary career with *Les belles-soeurs*; CBC Radio, which had commissioned Glenn Gould to create a centennial composition, broadcast Gould's contrapuntal masterpiece *The Idea of North*; and in New York, John Herbert's (1926–2001) controversial prison play *Fortune and Men's Eyes* opened to acclaim (no Canadian theater was prepared to risk a production). In addition, "Expo '67" — the Canadian Universal and International Exhibition "Man and His World/Terre des Hommes" — brought millions of international tourists and Canadians from across the country to Montreal to enjoy the spectacle. The nation-building process that could be said to have begun in 1867 and had been confirmed in blood during the First World War found its cultural and artistic apogee in the centennial year.

In the last three years of the 1960s, national pride was further enhanced by the opening of the National Arts Centre in Ottawa (1969), by the founding of many small presses such as Talonbooks (1967), a leading publisher of Canadian drama, and the House of Anansi (1967), established by young writers like Margaret Atwood (1939–) and Dennis Lee (1939–), as well as several important small presses in Quebec inspired by the nationalist Quiet Revolution, as, for instance, Leméac and VLB-Éditeur. At the same time several theaters and theater companies were being founded (such as Theatre New Brunswick, Theatre Calgary, Montreal's English-language Centaur Theatre, and Toronto's Theatre Passe-Muraille), and the Canadian Music Centre, which today has branches across the country, opened in 1969. By 1970, Canada (including Quebec) was poised for a decade of nationalist fervor and cultural activity that, in retrospect, signaled the beginning of the most exciting, innovative, and confident decade in Canada's cultural history.

On the sociopolitical scene, matters were much less optimistic during the late 1960s and the 1970s, despite the election of the flamboyant Pierre Elliott Trudeau as Liberal prime minister in 1968. International problems such as the Cuban Missile Crisis, the assassination of American President John F. Kennedy, the continuing horror of the Vietnam War, and the assassination of American civil rights champion Martin Luther King Jr., all had serious impacts on Canada and intensified Canadians' (from politicians like Trudeau to many intellectuals and artists) resistance to America's influence on Canadian life. At home, Canadians faced one of the worst periods of civil unrest in the country's history, climaxing when an extremist wing of the Quebec separatist movement, the FLQ (Front de Libération du Québec), kidnapped and murdered Quebec cabinet minister Pierre Laporte in October 1970. In response to this act of terrorism, Trudeau invoked the War Measures Act and, for the first and only time in Canadian history, civil liberties were suspended during peacetime. The reverberations of the October Crisis in Quebec, and of the federal government's reaction, have continued for many years and fueled the rise of Quebec's popular separatist party, the PQ (Parti Québécois), which was founded in 1968 and soon won provincial elections under the charismatic leadership of René Lévesque. Since then, the PQ has held two referenda on the question of Quebec separation, but to date the province has chosen to remain within the federation. Trudeau, who had moved so quickly to implement the War Measures Act, was also quick to curtail federal support for the arts, the national media, and for publishing; instead, he championed official bilingualism, multiculturalism (the Multiculturalism Act became law in 1988), and the repatriation of the Canadian Constitution from Westminster in London, England, with its Charter of Rights and Freedoms (1982).

For many Canadians, Trudeau is still considered as the architect of a contemporary, post-1970 Canada, a nation that celebrates its separate identity from Great Britain, France, and the United States: Its respect for cultural and linguistic diversity, human rights, and international peace-keeping (a legacy of previous prime minister Lester B. Pearson) constitutes its unique role in world affairs and characterizes the Canadian voice in such important international bodies as the United Nations and the G8 (the international organization of the Group of Eight democratic states). Not until the 1990s would this proud image begin to be tarnished by military scandals involving Canadian armed forces (in Somalia and Rwanda), political and security failures regarding the 1985 Air India disaster, the mishandling of the Maher Arar case, and, above all, by the treatment of First Nations peoples in their land claims settlements, by the slow response of church and state to the disclosure of evils perpetrated through the Residential School system, and by the Quebec provincial police response to Kahnawake Elders during the Oka Crisis of 1990. Most recently, Canada's failure to meet its obligations under the 1997 Kyoto Protocol, which it ratified in February 2005, has created tensions at home, embarrassment abroad, and a crisis for the Canadian Arctic. By 1999, when the map of Canada changed for the first time since 1949 (the year that Newfoundland joined Confederation) with the creation of Nunavut out of the former Northwest Territories, the country seemed well on the way to closer military and economic ties with the United States, first through the Free Trade Agreement (FTA) of 1988 and then through the North

American Free Trade Agreement (NAFTA) of 1992. These pressures to merge with the powerful neighbor to the south, along with the Canadian government's more recent response to the American "war on terror" in the wake of the 2001 World Trade Center attacks and the escalation of military intervention in Afghanistan, have led some intellectuals (such as Ian Angus, Frank Davey, and Robert Wright) to argue that Canada is now postnational or even that its sovereignty is merely virtual, a computerized image of a national identity about which younger generations know little and care less. According to this scenario, George Grant's "lament" was a few decades too early but nevertheless prescient.

In terms of artistic production the forty years from 1967 to 2007 were anything but bleak. In fact, the number, variety, and quality of Canadian writers, visual artists, musicians, and filmmakers are surprising for a nation of only thirty-three million inhabitants. The teaching of Canadian literature in universities, a rare phenomenon in the late 1960s, is now *de rigueur.* No serious English department can fail to offer a wide range of undergraduate and graduate courses in the field, and at least three generations of professors specializing in Canadian literature are currently teaching and conducting research in Canada's universities, while the flourishing of Quebec literature since 1967 is such that the subject is often taught separately from its English- or French-language partner as Québécois literature. Moreover, Canadian Studies programs, established in the 1970s, continue to flourish at home and abroad and offer interdisciplinary approaches to Canadian literature, history, and the arts. None of this would have been possible without the institutional developments of the 1950s and 1960s which, in turn, provided the fertile ground necessary for the support of literature and its sister arts.

One sign of this confident cultural position can be located in the celebration and secondary study of several of Canada's key thinkers — from Harold Innis (1894–1952), Northrop Frye (1912–1991), and Marshall McLuhan (1911–1980) to Charles Taylor (1931–) — who, along with leading historians, have traced the contours of a national identity that is constantly evolving. Another sign of this productivity, and one of the most striking, is the rise to preeminence of the historical novel, which has become so important that almost all of Canada's major writers have experimented with the genre: Margaret Atwood, George Bowering, George Elliott Clarke, Jack Hodgins, Robert Kroetsch, Michael Ondaatje, Jane Urquhart, Guy Vanderhaeghe, and Rudy Wiebe are only a few examples of the most senior and prolific writers to have taken Canadian history as their domain. The events they have chosen to explore typically concern the cultural encounter between indigenous peoples and settlers or explorers in the Canadian West and North, the meaning of Canadian participation in both world wars and the consequences of that participation on the home front, as well as the examination and/or celebration of mythic figures from the past such as John Franklin, Jerry Potts, George Vancouver, Walter Allward, Louis Riel, and Grace Marks. Poets and playwrights have also been very productive over the past forty years, in part because there are small presses to publish poetry and an audience who likes to read it, and in part because a multitude of small theaters (as distinct from the larger, regional ones) focus on work-shopping and producing new Canadian plays. It is in rich soil like this, cultivated over several decades and supported by national institutions, that major authors like Margaret Atwood, Alice Munro, Michel Tremblay, Sharon Pollock, Tomson Highway, Robert Kroetsch, Michael Ondaatje, and Rudy Wiebe earned their national as well as international reputations.

Further strong indicators that Canadian culture has thrived since 1967 can be found in the many excellent anthologies of Canadian literature published since the early 1970s, in the longevity of top-ranking journals such as *Canadian Literature*, which will celebrate its fiftieth anniversary in 2009, or *Voix et images*, the Quebec journal founded in 1967, as well as in the sharp increase in the writing of biography. Biography in Canada takes many forms, and its importance as a genre that enhances and expands our understanding of the country and its historical figures is crucial. In addition to major multi-volume dictionaries of biography, encyclopedias, and the *Who's Who of Canada* (begun as an annual publication in 1980), Canada is witnessing a proliferation of literary, artistic, and more traditional biographies of public figures, such as sports stars and politicians, as well as the increased publication of memoirs and autobiographies. Many recent biographies of artists such as Margaret Atwood, George Ryga (1932–1987), Sharon Pollock (1936–), Gwendolyn MacEwen (1941–1987), Sheila Watson (1909–1998), Joyce Wieland (1931–1998), Tom Thomson (1877–1917), Emily Carr (1871–1945), Frank Scott (1899–1985), Mordecai Richler (1931–2001), Gabrielle Roy (1909–1983), and Émile Nelligan (1879–1941) have won major prizes and national recognition. Moreover, playwrights like Marie Clements (1962–), Lorena Gale (1958–), Linda Griffiths (1956–), Tomson Highway (1951–), Robert Lepage (1957–), R. H. Thomson (1947–), Michel Tremblay, and Guillermo Verdecchia (1962–) have developed their own treatment of both individual and group biography and autobiography in plays that explore identity through personal and national histories.

Canadian filmmaking has always faced considerable hurdles, struggling to survive in the shadow of Hollywood. Documentaries about Canadian history or the Arctic, about various national regions and communities, and about Canadians at war — many of them directed and produced by the NFB (National Film Board) — have maintained the highest standards since the mid-1950s and won numerous awards, but feature films must compete in a North American market saturated by Hollywood movies. Nevertheless, a number of important, award-winning filmmakers have emerged since the 1980s — Denys Arcand, David Cronenberg, Atom

Egoyan, Guy Madden, and Anne Wheeler, to name just a few of the more senior examples. In 2001 Inuk filmmaker Zacharias Kunuk gained international acclaim at Cannes for his spectacular Inuit film *Atanarjuat (The Fast Runner)*, and Sarah Polley's (1979–) successful *Away from Her* (2006), based on a story by Alice Munro, signaled the debut of an important new director who develops Canadian material with universal themes. The recent production history for Canadian culture on CBC national radio and television, however, gives less cause for optimism. Without doubt, the best years of CBC support for the arts (theater, classical and popular music, and fiction readings) were the 1960s and 1970s; beginning in the 1980s, federal regulations concerning the promotion of Canadian content have been reduced by the CRTC (the Canadian Radio and Television Corporation, founded in 1968) to such a degree that media images of the country and its people are becoming rare. Globalization and free-market competition are usually cited as the reasons for this shift in cultural programming, and its practical consequence is the Americanization of the Canadian *habitus* (especially, but not exclusively, in English Canada). Given the central importance of communications to the history of Canada (whether the early fur trade routes, the continental railways, or the radio and now the Internet), this trend toward Americanization is troublesome.

Nevertheless, other forces counter this general trend. In Canada it is once again the cultural institutions that champion the country's development by preserving the full range of its history and identity and by celebrating and exhibiting its material culture and works of art. In 1988 the stunning new National Gallery of Canada/Museé des beaux-arts du Canada, designed by Moshe Safdie, opened in Ottawa, and in 1989 the Canadian Museum of Civilization/Musée canadien des civilizations, designed by Douglas J. Cardinal, opened just across the Ottawa River in Gatineau, Quebec. In 2005 the Canadian War Museum/Le Museé canadien de la guerre opened in Ottawa with magnificent displays of war art by some of the country's leading painters, as well as more traditional artifacts of war. Canadian artists have also turned their attention to events outside Canada: Some of the most exciting writing in the country is being been done by novelists and playwrights who choose to look beyond national borders, for instance, to examine the war in Iraq, Canadian involvement in antiterrorism activities, and the renewed threats to democracy at home associated with racial profiling and prejudice. Where artists and intellectuals in the late 1960s and 1970s worked to "Canadianize" the public, today an understanding of Canada is inextricably bound up with several decades of immigration, of ethnic and linguistic diversity extending far beyond the old parameters of First Nations-French-English concerns, and with major global issues. To be Canadian in the early twenty-first century is to see this circumpolar nation within a wide context of global responsibility and international debate.

# 22: English-Canadian Literary Theory and Literary Criticism

*Caroline Rosenthal (University of Constance)*

## "Where is Here?": Literary Nationalism in the 1960s and 1970s

WHILE AT THE BEGINNING of the twentieth century literary theory and criticism had been busy tackling the question of whether there was a genuinely Canadian literature at all, a new cultural self-awareness arose in the late 1950s. As internationally Canada was poised between the traditional model of Great Britain and the overwhelming cultural, economic, and political influence of the United States, cultural unity and self-confidence in its own literary and cultural achievements developed slowly. Unlike the United States, Canada lacked founding myths and master narratives that could be applied to the nation as a whole because of the intranational dualism of English Canada and Quebec. Anglophone literary theory in the 1960s has to be understood as a reaction to both Quebec's Quiet Revolution, which triggered social reforms and sparked nationalism in Quebec, as well as to the publication of the Massey Report (1951), which displayed anti-American tendencies and conjured up a new Canadian nationalism, especially in English Canada. The Massey Report — named after its chairman Vincent Massey (1887–1967) — was the work of an independent committee that advised the Canadian government in the improvement of the arts, letters, and sciences. It maintained that from the time of the Second World War Canada's national identity had neither been threatened by economical nor political forces but instead by the predominance of a commercialized U.S. American mass culture. This cultural critique caused a stir in Canada and in 1957 gave rise to the foundation of the Canada Council. This institution continues to commit itself to the promotion of the arts and has, since 1959, been awarding Canada's most prestigious literary prize, the Governor General's Award (established in 1936). Both in English Canada and Quebec, the cultural climate of the 1960s was shaped by the search for a national identity that was believed to be particularly evident in a genuinely Canadian literature. Literary theory thus blossomed into a sociopolitical force, as it reflected and fostered a national consciousness. New literary journals emerged — for instance, the quarterly *Canadian Literature* (founded in 1959) — and numerous small publishing houses were established that devoted themselves exclusively to Canadian literature and often originated upon authors' initiatives (see ch. 11, Breitbach). Canadian literature was introduced to a wider audience, for instance, through the series New Canadian Library, launched by McClelland & Stewart in 1958. Under the editorship of Malcolm Ross (1911–2002) it reprinted Canadian classics and made them accessible to a large public in inexpensive paperback editions. Against this background, literary criticism in the 1960s and early 1970s sought to define Canadian literature as a *national* literature. It identified recurrent symbols, motifs, and themes in Canadian texts that were believed to not only reflect a certain literary tradition but to reveal a national character as well.

The writings of Northrop Frye (1912–1991) came to be of paramount importance for this national endeavor. While Frye's international reputation derives primarily from his work on English Romanticism, Shakespeare (Governor General's Award for nonfiction in 1986 for *Northrop Frye on Shakespeare*), and T. S. Eliot, he published extensively on Canadian topics as well. The search for recurrent myths and symbols characterizes Frye's oeuvre in general, from his early books such as *Fearful Symmetry* (1947) — a study of William Blake — to the encyclopedic *Anatomy of Criticism* (1957) — a taxonomy of the structural principles of literature that seeks to promote literary criticism to the rank of an exact science — to his more recent work on the influence of the Bible and biblical typology on Western literature in *The Great Code* (1982) and *Words with Power* (1990). Frye claimed that a culture's collective unconscious manifests itself in recurrent plot patterns, images, and motifs, which make the particular text a mirror of fundamental human experiences and at the same time anchor it in a larger context of tradition. Frye heavily drew on C. G. Jung's work on archetypes, and like Jung he was criticized for the assumption that myths and their archetypical makeup hold a universal claim. While Marxist and feminist theoretical approaches dismissed this universality because it creates the illusion of coherence by completely ignoring differences of race, class, and gender, deconstructivist critics complained about Frye's logocentrism, that is, the fixing of linguistic meaning by the agency of some extralinguistic, transcendental presence. On the other hand, Frye has been described as a precursor to (post)structuralism. Paul Ricoeur, Julia Kristeva, and Hayden White, for example, have underlined their strong indebtedness to Frye's oeuvre, one that thoroughly mapped the cultural conditions and structures of narrative.

One basic tenet of Frye's writing is the assumption that mythical symbols and images in a language constitute the epistemological framework for all our mental processes. According to Frye, literature is an imaginary second order next to nature. While this "order of words" (Frye 1957, 17) continuously changes and expands by integrating new texts, it is nevertheless stable because it relies on common myths. Frye understood myth as a structural principle that manifests itself in the metaphors, images, and symbols of a text, thus revealing its underlying meaning. The task of literary criticism is to unearth, in a scientific, systematic manner, those myths and symbols that tell about fundamental human experiences. Frye described literature as "conscious mythology" (Frye 1971, 232) that provides a society with the structural principles of storytelling and offers an imaginary perspective on the real world. Literature thus plays a fundamental part in shaping cultural and national identities.

Frye studied philosophy and English at Victoria College from 1929 and from 1933 onwards was registered for theology at Emmanuel College, University of Toronto. Although he was eventually ordained as a priest by the United Church of Canada in 1936, as a student minister he soon turned exclusively towards literary studies. After obtaining his master's degree in English Studies at Oxford, he came back to Canada to teach at Victoria College, where he stayed for the next fifty years despite numerous offers from international universities. Frye contributed to the foundation of a Canadian literary tradition in various roles: as a university professor and administrator, as the editor of *Canadian Forum*, and as a literary and cultural critic. After 1950 he wrote annual surveys of Canadian poetry for the *University of Toronto Quarterly* in which he not only analyzed lyrical texts but established general criteria for the description of Canadian literature. These chronicles make up the core of the essay collection *The Bush Garden: Essays on the Canadian Imagination* (1971), which gathers Frye's main writings on Canadian literature. Other essays on Canadian literature and culture can be found in *The Educated Imagination* (1963), *The Modern Century* (1967), and *Divisions on a Ground* (1982). Frye's most influential essay in the context of Canadian literary studies is his "Conclusion" to Carl F. Klinck's (1908–1990) *Literary History of Canada* (1965; reprinted in *The Bush Garden*, 1971).

In this essay, Frye coined the term "garrison mentality" in relation to Canada's early colonial position. The term describes the bearing of the first settlers, who sought to defend their culture against a hostile natural environment by forming guarded communities. For Frye, "garrison" denoted "a closely knit and beleaguered society [whose] moral and social values are unquestionable" (Frye 1971, 226). He was able, on the one hand, to trace a successive emancipation of Canadian literature and culture from this "garrison mentality" and, on the other, to point out an imaginative continuum in Canadian literature. Frye identified the experience of utmost emptiness in an unfathomably vast land as central to the Canadian imagination. Since Canada — in comparison to the United States — has almost no Atlantic seaboard, the arriving traveler has the feeling of being "swallowed" by a giant whale: "To enter the United States is a matter of crossing an ocean; to enter Canada is a matter of being silently swallowed by an alien continent" (217). Such an experience of isolation and alienation had many consequences for the formation of cultural identity in Canada. Frye even argued that Canadian identity does not constitute itself around the question "Who am I?" but around the question "Where is here?" (Frye 1971, 220). The latter query, which explores the correlation between space and subjectivity and the role of the imagination in this context, has become a leitmotif of Canadian literary and cultural theory. The reflection on "here," however, has increasingly shifted from approaches that took landscape as a given, to theoretical stances that stress the construction of space and landscape through cultural practices and discourses. Frye had conceptualized the Canadian landscape as an "unseizable virginity," as he claimed that no other nation had so thoroughly integrated the unknown, unnamed, and unrealized in its collective consciousness. In contrast to the United States, where the frontier had progressed ever more westward and people could either stay in the populated areas along the East coast or else settle in the West, in early Canada psychological and geographical frontiers were omnipresent, making it almost impossible to bridge the vastness of a sparsely populated land: "In the Canadas [referring to upper and Lower Canada before Confederation in 1867], the frontier was all around one, a part and a condition of one's whole imaginative being" (220). Precisely this experience engendered a "garrison mentality," which Frye credits with having fostered positive developments in Canadian culture as well. Since the settlers in their "closely knit" communities had need to solve conflicts with the help of arguments, they came to trust in an "arguing intellect"; Frye considered the latter to constitute the basis for philosophical positions in the nineteenth century that defined conscience and intellect as the maxims of any cultivated society.

Frye's "Conclusion" also engages with the pastoral myth in Canadian literature. Despite the representation of a seemingly hostile landscape, Canadian literature also shows man's yearning for a harmonious relation to nature. While literature had first been dominated by nostalgic or sentimental manifestations of this pastoral myth (which stressed the indifference of nature towards man), a later literary phase had generated a more idyllic kind of pastoral definition. Nature was still feared for its mystery and power of deception, but was now also seen as representing an order and spiritual unity that man had violated. If at the incipient stage of Canadian society man had stood alone against nature, later periods saw a triangular process between nature, society, and the individual, in which the latter became an ally of nature in opposition to society. Frye found the pastoral myth in Canadian literature to span a range from an idealized yearning to become one with nature to the longing for death inspired by the experience of nature's dark and terrrible elements. He described the pastoral movement in Canadian literature as "a quest for the peaceable kingdom" (Frye 1971, 249).

Frye's seminal influence on Canadian literary theory and criticism as well as his outstanding role in the formation of a national literature also shows in the work of his disciples. With his metaphor of the "garrison mentality," Frye had not just described Canadian literature but had in fact created a new myth. Successive critics built on this myth, as well as on his method to use the analysis of myths and mythologies to establish a national canon of literature, while at the same time locating Canadian literature within the larger context of world literature. Inspired by Frye, these critics isolated recurrent symbols and themes in Canadian texts that would not only tell about the individual author's literary imagination but would reveal a national character and a particular literary tradition. Important studies in this respect are D. G. Jones's *Butterfly on Rock: A Study of Themes and Images in Canadian Literature* (1970), Margaret Atwood's *Survival: A Thematic Guide to Canadian Literature* (1972), John Moss's *Patterns of Isolation* (1974), and in a wider sense also W. H. New's *Articulating West* (1972) as well as Laurence Ricou's *Vertical Man/ Horizontal World* (1973). Jones examined individual works by Canadian authors for biblical themes and images that would allow the inference of a "common cultural predicament," since they imaginatively secure collective dreams and fears. His study aimed at establishing a line of tradition in Canadian literature and at the same time strove to create a feeling of belonging to a common culture. Moss, too, applied Frye's methods in *Patterns of Isolation* by looking at different manifestations of exile in Canadian literature. Among the important texts of early Canadian literary and cultural theory is *Contexts of Canadian Criticism*, edited by Eli Mandel (1922–1992) in 1971. The collection continued in the vein of thematic criticism — so called later because its adherents looked for themes and symbols that would testify to a national character — but its mode of self-critical reflection already anticipated a paradigm shift. An interdisciplinary anthology of texts by Frye and other prominent voices (among them George Grant, Marshall McLuhan, Henry Kreisel, Harold A. Innis, and Dorothy Livesay), *Contexts* wanted its readers to grasp and experience the literary tradition of Canada as an "invisible country." The alleged artistic barrenness of the land had to be fertilized through the kind of "authentic identity" that unfolds as a "conceptual space" between literary works. The most prominent example of thematic criticism inspired by Frye was Margaret Atwood's *Survival*.

Although Margaret Atwood's (1939–) international renown rests primarily on her extensive fictional oeuvre, she has played a vital role in Canadian literary and cultural politics as a journalist, editor, university lecturer, and political activist, as well as a literary critic. Compared to her prolific output as a writer of fiction, her critical work is less voluminous, but it has nevertheless helped to define Canadian literature as a national literature and has introduced it to an international audience. Apart from numerous interviews, reviews, and newspaper articles, Atwood's major critical works are *Survival* (1972), *Second Words* (1982), *Strange Things* (1995), *Negotiating with the Dead* (2002), and *Moving Targets* (2004). Atwood herself has always put the creative act of writing above the analysis and critique of literature; in an interview with Geoff Hancock she quipped: "As a theorist, I'm a good amateur plumber" (1987). Her critical work is inspired more by her own reading and writing experience than by theoretical discourses, and it illuminates her own fiction as much as Canadian culture. George Woodcock (1912–1995) has appropriately described her literary and cultural essays as "practical-mediational criticism — as distinct from the academic-theoretical kind" (1981, 236).

No other text of Canadian literary criticism was so popular at its time or triggered so many fervent and controversial reactions among contemporary readers and critics as did Atwood's *Survival: A Thematic Guide to Canadian Literature*. If Earle Birney (1904–1995) in his frequently cited poem "Can. Lit." (1962; revised in 1966) had still poignantly concluded that Canada lacked literary models and key texts ("it's only by our lack of ghosts we're haunted"), the scene changed for good with the advent of *Survival* — for irrespective of its acceptance or dismissal, it became a milestone of Canadian cultural criticism. It was modeled on Frye's work, appearing at a time of budding nationalism when CanLit (the institutionalized national canon of Canadian literature) as a distinct corpus of texts did not yet exist. In her preface to *Survival*, Atwood reminisces how at school she would draw the Union Jack, read English authors, and sing "Rule Britannia," but outside the classroom would devour Canadian literature. Although initially she did not recognize the latter as a national literature, she noticed that the depicted experiences and imaginative worlds coincided much more with her own reality than the British texts read at school. Atwood wrote *Survival* from her own experience as a reader of Canadian literature, calling it an "easy-to-use-guide to CanLit" for students and teachers making their first contact with Canadian literature. The book neither wanted to analyze individual Canadian authors nor provide a survey of Canadian literature, but rather aimed at discovering recurrent "patterns of theme, image, and attitude," which characterize Canadian literature as a national literature. Literature thus not only became the mirror of a "habit of mind" but a map to guide the reader through a distinctive culture, through Canada as a mental space.

*Survival* drew on Frye's already mentioned thesis that Canadians, rather than asking "*Who* am I?," were preoccupied with the question of "*Where* am I?" in the sense of "Where is here?" While the question "Who am I?" applied to countries where "here" had been sufficiently delineated, in a Canadian context "here" denoted a cultural no-man's-land, always inferior to "there," that is, to the cultural identity of England or the United States. Literature in particular could help to define this precarious "here" as the place of collective perception and identity. Atwood argued in *Survival* that every nation and culture constitutes itself around a central symbol, be it a word, an idea, or an image. For the United States, for example, it is the frontier, which permeates its literature in countless imaginative variations. Building on Frye's metaphor of the garrison mentality, Atwood declared "survival" to be the predominant theme of Canadian literature, with the term implying both a physical and a spiritual or cultural dimension. While "survival" makes up the central theme, one leitmotif of Canadian literature is the representation of victims. This "victimization" applies to individual works as well as to Canadian literature as a whole, since Canada's postcolonial position characterizes it as a "victim society." *Survival* distinguishes between four "victim positions": to deny that one is a victim; to realize that one is a victim but to explain this as an act of fate or the will of some higher power; to acknowledge that one is a victim but to refuse to accept this role as inevitable; to be a "creative non-victim." While in the moment of literary production writers are by definition in the fourth position, their texts can still describe the other three positions, as frequently happens in Atwood's own works.

*Survival* became a national bestseller and was met with general acclaim because many readers for the first time found their experiences described as genuinely Canadian. From the camp of literary theory, however, it was often severely criticized for its sweeping generalizations and for reading literature as the reflection of a national consciousness. Although *Survival* was never planned to be a thorough theoretical study but more as a literary polemic intended to spark an interest in Canadian themes, the text was often read prescriptively and thus misunderstood as a fatalistic appraisal of Canadian identity. In an essay from 1973, in which Atwood countered the accusations, she said: "*Survival* was fun to attack. In fact, it still is; most self-respecting professors of CanLit begin their courses, I'm told, with a short ritual sneer at it" (reprinted in *Second Words* 1982, 105). Here Atwood particularly responded to the harsh critique of Robin Mathews and took the opportunity to clarify her concerns in *Survival*. Against the widespread misunderstanding that her book was a negative assessment of Canadian culture because it saw survival as a main theme in Canadian literature, Atwood stressed that to her the will to survive is the opposite of desperation and resignation. While her critics demanded positive models in Canadian literature, Atwood found it vital to stress the victimization of postcolonial Canadian society as a necessary precondition for its literary development. She claimed the strength of Canadian literature lay precisely in its ability to neither glorify nor demonize the ambivalences and dualities that resulted from the relation to nature and from the colonial position, but to preserve this conflict through language and imagination.

After *Survival* Atwood has continued to analyze themes, myths, and motifs in Canadian literature in various frameworks, which mirror many currents of Canadian literary criticism, from its postcolonial and nationalist beginnings to postmodern paradigms. Published in 1982, *Second Words* is a collection of reviews, small journalistic pieces, and critical essays covering the time between 1960 and 1982. The texts reflect topics that are central to Atwood's oeuvre in general, such as the role of the female artist, national differences and conflicts between the United States and Canada, and characteristic features of Canadian identity, as well as questions of human rights. *Second Words* has a strong political agenda and can be read as a comment on Canadian cultural politics over three decades. *Strange Things: The Malevolent North in Canadian Literature* (1995) returns to the analysis of myths transformed into literature. These myths are, however, no longer read as immediate representations of human experience, but as mediated products of cultural preconceptions. The book consists of four talks that Atwood gave at Oxford University in 1991 in a lecture series on Canadian literature. All of them explore the ongoing fascination with the wilderness — particularly the North — in Canadian literature. Atwood examines the mystical quality and gothic imagery inspired by the North, as well as the narrative rendering of historical events, for example, the failure of the Franklin expedition, and of mythical figures like the Wendigo. The last essay in the collection looks at how female authors have rewritten traditional Northern imagery, which had often contrasted a passive female nature with that of an active male explorer. *Negotiating with the Dead: A Writer on Writing* (2002) also derived from a lecture series, given at Cambridge University in 2000. It deals with the moral and social responsibility of the author, especially the female author, and looks at the motivations of and influences on writers. The eponymous main thesis of the book is that all writing stems from the fear of and fascination with death, and that the author — like Orpheus — has to retrieve his or her story from the realm of the dead. *Moving Targets* (2004; published in Great Britain with a slightly altered text selection and introduction as *Curious Pursuits* in 2005), like *Second Words*, gathers shorter literary texts — reviews, addresses at award presentations, introductions to anthologies, tributes to Canadian authors — which demonstrate Atwood's far-reaching literary and cultural engagement since 1982. The book is subdivided into three different periods that are all briefly introduced to provide the texts with the political and historical background of their time as well as to locate them within the context of Atwood's own fictional work.

## "Surviving the Paraphrase": Postnational Tendencies

What was later to be labeled as "thematic criticism" — that is, the writings of Frye, Jones, Moss, Atwood, and others — created the basis for a national canon of literature by presenting shared characteristics in the work of Canadian authors, thus establishing a new sensibility for CanLit. In the mid-1970s a canon of Canadian literature was further consolidated and institutionalized in curricula and through magazines; in 1959, for instance, the quarterly *Canadian Literature*, with George Woodcock as its first editor, was founded. Thematic criticism was, however, also severely criticized for its conceptualization of both culture and nation as well as for its literary objectives and methods. Its opponents criticized that, for the sake of propagating a national and cultural unity, the internal differences that characterize Canada were disregarded. They felt uneasy about the fact that ethnic and regional differences — with their inherent tensions of urban versus rural, center versus periphery — were ignored, and instead called for a literary criticism that would generalize less and pay more tribute to diversity. Subsequent approaches no longer saw the task of criticism in analyzing texts for common national characteristics but instead returned to the study of individual authors and their works. In the 1980s, Canadian literature was discussed beyond the context of thematic criticism both in Canada and abroad. A case in point is, for instance, the Canadian-German-European cooperation *Gaining Ground: European Critics on Canadian Literature*, coedited by Robert Kroetsch and Reingard M. Nischik in 1985, which gathers literary theory and criticism on Canadian literature from as many as seven countries.

Dissociating itself from thematic criticism, Canadian literary theory in the 1980s and 1990s was stimulated by poststructuralist, postmodern, phenomenological, and feminist methods and theories that were applied to a Canadian cultural context. Under the influence of such approaches, critics questioned the universality of national myths and furthermore perceived reality as the effect of particular representational strategies. Concepts like landscape, geography, or region were no longer considered as givens but were seen as shaped by the onlooker's consciousness and created through social practices and discourses. However, even if the predominantly nationalistically oriented period in Canadian literary theory had run its course by the mid-1970s, critics continued to determine the specific characteristics of Canadian literature and literary theory. This dynamics generated what Robert Lecker called a "conflicted narrative" (Lecker 1995), that is, a literary theory driven by the duality of wanting to affirm and at the same time negate "Canadianness," to be both national and postnational, to think of Canada as both construct and reality. Canadian literary theory and criticism to this day continues to stress that Canada's "other" position — in between Great Britain and the United States and informed by the dualism of English Canada and Quebec — accounts for a characteristically ambivalent self-understanding, which also manifests itself in literature. In this manner, Canadian literary theory since the 1980s has examined textual strategies that work to confirm and at the same time challenge cultural paradigms, for example, instances of irony, parody, and self-reflection in texts.

One of the precursors to a literary theory that sought to examine Canadian literature for its specific qualities without adhering to a thematic and nationalist agenda was writer and critic Frank Davey (1940–). In his talk "Surviving the Paraphrase" (reprinted in his eponymous book from 1983) — which Davey gave at the inauguration of the Association of Canadian and Quebec Literatures at York University in 1974 — he severely attacked the objectives of what he then termed "thematic criticism." He bemoaned thematic criticism's neglect of a text's intrinsic qualities (such as language or narrative structure) for the sake of identifying only those themes that were thought to reveal something about Canadianness. In this manner, thematic criticism propagated a false cultural unity and lost sight of the individual text's meaning. In contrast to structuralism, it did not isolate formal patterns but structures on the content level, which were supposed to speak about culture, not the text itself. Concomitant preconceptions of nation and landscape proved to be far more problematic, since they took for granted what is in fact only created through subjective perception and its description. Davey equated thematic criticism with bad sociology and even literary determinism because it reduced literary texts to previously selected themes. Furthermore, its method was dubious since it ignored cultural contexts and their dynamics and instead reduced literary texts to paraphrases of a static culture: "The movement here is towards the paraphrase — paraphrase of the culture and paraphrase of the literature. The critic extracts for his deliberations the paraphrasable content and throws away the form" (1983, 3). As an alternative to approaches that value the cultural content more than the text itself, Davey proposed methods that again analyze the form and meaning of texts, albeit without neglecting their cultural contexts (such as phenomenological approaches).

Davey, too, wanted to work out the specific characteristics of Canadian literature, but via a detailed analysis of individual authors rather than by looking for recurrent cultural themes. He has contributed to this aim in various monographs and also in two handbooks, such as *Our Nature — Our Voices: A Guidebook to Canadian Literature* (1973) and *From There to Here* (1974), which provide short critical introductions to Canadian authors across the centuries. Like Atwood, Davey combines the roles of writer and critic. He is cofounder of the influential group of poets *Tish*, and he is among the founders and editors of the journal *Open Letter*, which publishes experimental texts and innovative literary theory. Next to many volumes of poetry, Davey published several monographs on Canadian authors, for instance, Earle Birney (1971), Louis Dudek (1981), and Atwood (1984). In *Reading Canadian Reading* (1981) he subjected his own writing to a critical revision. Davey's belief that Canadian literary theory has to emancipate itself from the task of unearthing national characteristics becomes particularly evident in his book *Post-National Arguments* (1993), in which he examines Canadian identity and literature after 1967 in the wake of globalization and the Free Trade Agreement. The study analyzes sixteen contemporary novels that still evoke a Canadian context but substitute national discourses through discourses on community, neighborhood, and intimacy.

## "Incredulity Towards Metanarratives": Postmodern and Postcolonial Theories

Under the influence of postmodern and postcolonial theories, discourses concerning nation and space gained a new quality in the 1980s and 1990s. The threat to national unity from separatist movements in Quebec, along with the rise of globalization and the Free Trade Agreement between Canada, the United States, and Mexico, lent a renewed urgency to questions of location and subjectivity. In contrast to earlier times, however, the question of "where is here" was now seen in the larger framework of postcolonial and postmodern politics and theory. The crisis of "here" was no longer regarded as resulting from Canadian history, geography, or a specifically Canadian mentality, but from a narrative crisis in general. The inevitable gap between the linguistic and narrative patterns available in a culture and the unprecedented experience of an unknown land made it impossible to describe the experience of the subject in a new environment. Many themes and concerns of Canadian literary theory changed their focus under the influence of postcolonial, feminist, and postmodern theories. According to postcolonial theories, one basic problem of White settler colonies like Canada, New Zealand, or Australia was that the "imported" English language lacked the means to adequately describe the land and the new experiences. Since language is not a neutral medium but is always imbued with cultural inscriptions and values, it failed in capturing the New World. This discrepancy between experiential reality and the available representational means created a feeling of inauthenticity among the settlers. In addition, the binary terminology of the Old World could not but degrade the New World — in comparison to the motherland — as uncultured and uncivilized. The settlers felt forced to keep up their "British" identity in order to define themselves against the land's "Otherness," whether that meant the indigenous population or the wilderness, but at the same time they saw a need to distinguish themselves from the Old World. Postcolonial theories found this ambivalence to create a "double vision," that is, an inherently dual kind of self-perception. In order to define themselves as colonizers, settlers had to affirm the extant symbolic orders of language and culture while simultaneously having to challenge these orders from within in order to create new narrative and linguistic patterns that would capture their experiences and environment in more accurate ways. Former settler colonies thus increasingly cultivated a gesture of "writing back" that sought to disclose thematic and structural differences in the language, culture, and literary traditions of the colony and its motherland. In the case of Canadian literature, the epithet "postcolonial" entails certain problems, though, particularly in view of the relation between colonizer and colonized. Donna Bennett (1945–), Thomas King (1943–), and others have stressed the difficulty in clearly delineating a postcolonial period in Canadian literary history, as well as the open question as to who actually bears a colonizing influence on English-Canadian literature, Great Britain or the neoimperialist United States. Above all, the postcolonial argument becomes highly ambivalent in the face of Canada's internal colonization, that is, the predominance of White mainstream culture over indigenous cultures.

Postmodern and postcolonial theories share the assumption that reality lies within, not outside the act of representation, and that representation is the result of certain power structures and interests. Thus texts can never represent reality in an "authentic" manner, but can only depict it from a particular perspective. For English-Canadian literature the gesture of "writing back" meant to overwrite old narratives, previous representations of Canadian reality. Authors rewrote Canadian stories, and history by transforming early-settler and exploration accounts into parodistic and ironic fictions. Literary theory was primarily interested in studying the preconditions of narrative, demonstrating the ideological makeup, cultural perspective, and cultural predicaments of storytelling. The authority of historiography came under attack because its narrative quality, which inevitably introduces a subjective component, was stressed. History was now perceived as one story among many other possible stories, and alternate histories were written, particularly from the perspective of indigenous and immigrant authors as well as feminist writers. Yet not only its postcolonial position sharpened Canada's awareness that history and stories are always (re)constructed from certain perspectives and tied to certain cultural contexts. Concepts of nation and history were also perceived as fragile narrative constructs in view of the differences between the "two solitudes," Quebec and English Canada, and the polyphony of the "Other Solitudes" (Hutcheon 1990), that is, the great ethnic diversity within both groups (which was still enhanced by the Multiculturalism Act of 1988). In literary theory this did not, however, result in a further interrogation of a specifically Canadian identity, but in fundamentally questioning traditional conceptions of identity, nation, and narration. Under the influence of poststructuralist, postmodern, and feminist theories, these concepts were no longer considered as given but perceived as shaped by their cultural context. Issues of representation, language, and narrative became more and more vital to the discussion of literature. The thematic focus on *what* is represented gave way to the central question of *how* and *by whom*. Whereas Canada's postcolonial situation, its presumed emptiness, and its lack of a national mythology had been initially dismissed as clear disadvantages — for they were thought to prevent human subjects from positioning themselves in the land, the literary tradition, or the nation — more recent approaches drew precisely on these characteristics to find Canada predestined for poststructuralist and postmodern theories. What had previously been dismissed as a lack now became Canada's most prominent asset.

Robert Kroetsch (1927–) had already argued in the 1970s that Canadian literature had skipped modernism by moving from Victorianism straight to postmodernism (Kroetsch 1974). Although in its provocative overstatement the argument is untenable, many critics share its basic assumption that Canadian literature is predestined for postmodern paradigms as they evoke and renegotiate concerns that have been at the heart of Canadian culture from the start. While Frye in his "Conclusion" in 1965 had maintained that Canada (in contrast to the United States) still awaited its period "of a certain magnitude," which every nation needs to ingrain its imagination and develop a tradition, many critics saw Canadian cultural history enter this stage with the advent of postmodernism. Marshall McLuhan once called Canada a "borderline case" (McLuhan 1977) because this huge, bilingual land neither possessed a geographical nor an ethnic center; and until today, Canadian literary theory continues to be keenly interested in borders, boundaries, and spaces-in-between.

Linda Hutcheon (1947–) considers "shape-shifting," the crossing of generic boundaries, to be the literary equivalent of McLuhan's thesis and finds the postmodern affinity of Canadian literature to be particularly evident in textual instances of polyphony, ambiguity, and the creation of difference through ironical ruptures. Hutcheon has had international renown since the 1980s, having published more than twenty books and anthologies on postmodernism and the function of irony and parody. Hutcheon employs and combines theoretical approaches and methods from New Historicism, postcolonial theory, deconstruction, reader-response theory, and feminist theories. Although she has at times been attacked for this eclecticism, it in fact realizes her theoretic claim to avoid unifying narratives. Self-referentiality and generic boundary-crossings are prominent methods in Canadian literary theory; they are also employed, for instance, in the feminist literary approaches of Barbara Godard (1941–) and Daphne Marlatt (1942–). Hutcheon regards postmodern theories as particularly productive for Canadian literature because their preference for parody and irony allows for the undercutting and destabilizing of fixed orders from within without dissolving them altogether. She describes postmodernism as a paradoxical phenomenon, "one that uses and abuses, installs and then subverts, the very concepts it challenges" (Hutcheon 1988a, 3); it thus perfectly matches the dualities and paradoxes in Canada's cultural history, which need to be dealt with through narrative. Hutcheon developed her thinking on postmodernism primarily in *A Poetics of Postmodernism* and in *The Canadian Postmodern: A Study of Contemporary English-Canadian Fiction* (both 1988), an analysis of the specific postmodern forms to be found in Canadian literature. Hutcheon sees postmodern Canadian novels as characterized by self-referential textual strategies that, through deliberate ruptures and contradictions, render the underlying conditions of their own narrative, a development that is, once again, fostered by the absence of a comprehensive national mythology. Other postmodern strategies such as the renegotiation of the hierarchy between center and periphery or the mingling of fact and fiction also have a bearing on Canada's cultural history. Hutcheon notes that irony and parody as agents of an ideological critique, which subverts the system from within, lend themselves not only to the concerns of Canadian literary studies but also to feminist studies. Critics like Donna Bennett (1986) and Coral Ann Howells (1991) have shown that female Canadian writers often combine their experiences of marginalization in both national and gendered contexts in order to describe victimization, alienation, and powerlessness in their novels.

Feminist theories, which drew on postcolonial and postmodern approaches, are a prime example for the creative adaptation of international currents to a specifically Canadian context. Volumes such as Smaro Kamboureli and Shirley Neuman's collection of essays *A Mazing Space: Writing Canadian Women Writing* (1986) and Godard's *Gynocritics* (1985) demonstrate the innovative and boundary-crossing character of Canada's feminist literary theory since the 1970s. Linguistic, cultural, and generic boundaries were challenged and supposedly mutually exclusive theoretical positions combined. This productive strength stemmed not least from the fact that feminist critics overcame the linguistic and cultural boundaries *within* Canada by integrating English and French theories. A case in point is the Tessera Collective, a group of English-Canadian writers and artists (among them Godard, Marlatt, Kathy Mezei, Gail Scott, and Louise Cotnoir), who made the innovative work of feminists from Quebec accessible for the English-Canadian literary scene and connected it with anglophone theories. Intercultural conferences as well as the founding of the feminist magazine *Tessera* contributed to this endeavor. The volume *Collaboration in the Feminine* (1994), edited by Godard, gathers a selection of texts from 1984 to 1992, that had first appeared in *Tessera*. Among the theoretical positions that the collective made fruitful for English Canada was, next to *écriture au féminin*, also fiction theory — two approaches that had been developed in Quebec predominantly by

Nicole Brossard (1943–). Fiction theory blurs the boundary between fiction and theory in order to show that theory, too, is subjected to narrative patterns and cultural preconceptions, and so possesses no greater authority than fictional texts. Fictional texts, in turn, can have an effect that is just as normative and ideological as theoretical positions. Fiction theory can be understood as a feminist practice of reading and writing aimed at dismantling ideological concepts in language and narrative. *Écriture au féminin* marks a specifically Canadian consideration and further development of *écriture féminine*, a feminist approach that advocates a style of writing outside the patriarchal symbolic order. While *écriture féminine* was criticized for its alleged essentialism, which supposedly equates being a woman with a feminine style of writing, *écriture au féminin* stresses the textual nature as well as the provisional and self-reflexive components in such an undertaking by translating "female writing" into "writing *in* the feminine."

Hutcheon looks at postmodern writing primarily as a "problematized return to history." While modernism had turned away from history, postmodernism shows a renewed interest in history, not, however, to authenticate fiction, as earlier periods had done, but on the contrary to question the authority of historiography. Hutcheon coins the term "historiographic metafiction" for texts that mingle fact and fiction to render the narrative quality of both literature and historiography. Just like storytelling, the writing of history has to rely on narrative patterns that are informed by certain cultural, ideological, and linguistic parameters and can thus never be objective or absolute. For defining "historiographic metafiction" as a subgenre of the postmodern novel, Hutcheon builds on the work of historian Hayden White. In the 1970s White had argued that "proper history" cannot be separated from its metahistorical, that is, interpretative level, and had made a distinction between "facts" and "events": While "events" actually happened, we only learn about them through narrative mediation, so that "facts" are always narrativized events; and narrative, because it is bound to a cultural context and relies on representational means, is never neutral. For White, subjective components enter the writing of history on various levels: on an aesthetic level as the historian has to select the events that he finds fact worthy and put them into a specific narrative form, and on an epistemological level because an analytical paradigm has to be chosen for interpreting facts. Furthermore, the ideological and historical context of the time plays a role just as important as the moral intentions of the individual author. History, White concludes, is always the history of the present, written and interpreted from a specific point of view in time. Hutcheon's term "historiographic metafiction" now denotes a genre, which, in a metafictional manner, reflects on the conditions of its own making and simultaneously questions the difference between literature and historiography. In contrast to the historical novel, historiographic metafiction usually refrains from the portrayal of heroes and rather turns to eccentric and marginalized figures. It does not use history to lend a higher authority to literature, but uses literature to underline the fictional quality of historiography.

In reference to Jean-François Lyotard's statement that postmodernism is characterized by an "incredulity towards metanarratives" (1984), Hutcheon observes that postmodern novels challenge the authority of universal myths by disrupting the reality effect/"effet de réel" (Roland Barthes, 1968) that is created through specific narrative structures. Meta- or master narratives are narratives — myths, historiographies, fictions — that are assigned a superior status in a given culture, thus enjoying a higher authoritative power than other texts and professing an outstanding claim to truth and objectivity. While earlier Canadian literary theory had lamented the absence of a national master narrative (something comparable to the American Dream, for instance), this lack now undergoes a positive reassessment. Kroetsch, for instance, locates Canada's greatest potential precisely in the absence of one authoritative narrative. He sees Canada defined by a fragmentary and paradoxical narrative, yet "this very falling-apart of our story is what holds our story together" (Kroetsch 1989, 21–22): "Disunity" becomes the Canadian strategy of unity. According to Kroetsch, Canada's genealogy is fundamentally postmodern, because it can neither pinpoint its national founding moment nor come up with heroes who would be suitable as protagonists of a master narrative.

Kroetsch has impacted on postmodern Canadian literature as a writer, critic, and literary theorist. One of the cofounders of *Boundary 2: A Journal of Postmodern Literature*, since the 1970s he has promoted a literary criticism that is thoroughly grounded in theory. His most influential essays were collected in *The Lovely Treachery of Words: Essays Selected and New* (1989). For him, a skepticism towards space and language, but also towards national identity, is characteristic of Canadian literature, which, in a postmodern fashion, asks how knowledge becomes possible in the first place and how it can be mediated. Like Hutcheon, Kroetsch examines and practices strategies of postmodern irony and parody in order to shed light on the connection between subject, space, and history while challenging the very conditions of these concepts.

William H. New (1938–) is another prominent contributor to this field. Since the 1970s he has participated in establishing Canadian literature and literary theory as a professor, but mainly as the editor of numerous handbooks, literary histories, and anthologies. While teaching at the University of British Columbia he edited the journal *Canadian Literature* for seventeen years and published more than forty books. His *Encyclopedia of Literature in Canada* (2002) shows the comprehensiveness of New's long engagement with Canadian literature and culture. In 2004 his merits were rewarded with the Governor General's International Award for Canadian Studies. As early as in *Articulating West* (1972), New has analyzed Canadian literature for its conceptions of space and the interaction of subject, landscape, and symbolic orders. The book, written in the tradition of Frye, assumed a duality between the (also linguistically) established "East," on the one hand, and the unarticulated, discursively uncharted "West" on the other, which was still awaiting a language and symbolic order of its own — an order that would, however, turn it into a "new East." In his later publications, which integrate poststructuralist and postmodern approaches, New continues to deal with the relation between space, subject, and language, for example, in *Land Sliding: Imagining Space, Presence, and Power in Canadian Writing* (1997) and *Borderlands: How We Talk about Canada* (1998). *Borderlands* examines how Canada's national identity constitutes itself on "borderline metaphors" that elucidate time-honored Canadian issues such as regionalism, separatism, and multiculturalism. All of New's texts analyze how the location of Canadian identity on borders and in spaces-in-between engenders ironic ruptures in literary texts, which name and disclaim things at the same time.

New's *Land Sliding* contributes to a field of theory that can be subsumed under the term New or Cultural Geography. New Geographers understand space not as something neutral or simply given but as the effect of complex discourses, symbolic orders, and social practices that are informed by issues of class, ethnicity, and gender. Just as postmodern theories had investigated "the making of history," New or Cultural Geographers want to analyze "the making of space." This inspired projects in literary studies that looked at correlations between the textual construction of identity and the cartographic construction of the Canadian landscape. The fictional and critical texts of Aritha van Herk (1954–) are especially important in this context. In "Mapping as Metaphor" (1982) she had already claimed that cartography is not an objective representation of spaces and places, but a subjective interpretative mode similar to fiction. Her text *Places Far from Ellesmere: A Geografictione* (1990) crosses every generic boundary. As the neologism in the subtitle already hints at, the text positions itself on the boundary between autobiography, fiction, literary theory, and cartography and interprets place discursively, that is, as a possible position for the subject, which s/he may assume in the act of reading. The book can also be seen as a feminist counterdiscourse to both the masculine generic tradition of the Western as well as to traditional narratives of the North that render the male hero as active explorer and the female landscape as his passive territory. Van Herk suggests to rewrite Northern narratives as well as their underlying cultural predicaments.

Since Canada has always defined itself as a Nordic nation, the North as discursive space and plane of projection is given much attention in more recent Canadian literary criticism. Sherrill Grace (1944–) further develops van Herk's approach of "gendering the North," but also examines in a more general sense how very persistently images of the North have shaped Canadian literature and culture. In *Canada and the Idea of North* (2002) she explores the prominent role that the North has played for Canadian literature, art, and popular culture, particularly as it relates to the formation of a national identity. She also considers how both the national idea and the conception of North as "home" have changed with the foundation of Nunavut, and how new, different portrayals of the North challenge old representations and narratives. Rudy Wiebe (1934–) was one of the first authors who tried to substitute an indigenous for a Eurocentric perspective in both fictional and critical texts. This paradigm shift already shows in the title of his novel *A Discovery of Strangers* (1994), which defines the White explorers of the Franklin expedition as "strangers" to the land and describes their "discovery" both through the indigenous Yellowknife and the landscape itself. In *Playing Dead: A Contemplation Concerning the Arctic* (1989), Wiebe reflects this paradigm shift in a theoretical context by disclosing the gaps and ruptures in narratives of White explorers. John Moss in *Enduring Dreams: An Exploration of Arctic Landscape* (1996) delineates the various restrictions underlying linguistic and narrative representations of the North. While van Herk has been criticized for reading the North as a blank space for feminist reinscriptions, thus ignoring the indigenous population, Wiebe has been reproached by some critics for his appropriation of an indigenous perspective. An alternative to such critical discourses is offered by approaches that seek to map the North via indigenous narratives themselves. A pioneering survey on the topic is Robin McGrath's study *Canadian Inuit Literature: The Development of a Tradition* (1996). Valerie Alia's *Un/Covering the North: News, Media, and Aboriginal People* (1999) chooses an intermedial approach to examine misrepresentations of the indigenous population and the North itself.

The question of "here," the focus on the relation between subject and place, still prevails in Canadian literary theory; however, the parameters for defining both identity and space have vastly changed. Canadian theory no longer strives to assure itself of a national identity and literature, but shows that concepts such as nation, space, and identity rely above all on power structures and representational strategies that define "here" from a multitude of different perspectives. Whereas Canadian literature, theory, and criticism in former times concentrated on representations of nature or the small town, which have permeated the literary tradition and have relegated the representation of cities to the margins, contemporary theory explicitly turns to the analysis of urban space (Edwards and Ivision 2005). The literature of immigrants, who contributed not only their cultural background but narrative paradigms to capture their experiences to the literary tradition, gained prominence. Non-English backgrounds have become more and more important for defining postcolonial English Canada so that the question of "where is here" has been increasingly replaced by "who is here," a question that solicits a myriad of different answers (Bennett 2002).

# 23: The English-Canadian Novel from Modernism to Postmodernism

*Martin Kuester (University of Marburg)*

IN THE LAST QUARTER OF THE TWENTIETH CENTURY English-Canadian literature has firmly established itself on the international stage — above all in the novel and short-story genre. The production and reception of a national Canadian literature gained significant impetus during the 1960s and 1970s. The process of maturity for Canadian literature was greatly influenced by the cultural atmosphere surrounding the centenary of the Canadian Confederation in 1967, but the process itself had begun much earlier, as is indicated by the active support for Canadian literature by the Canada Council for the Arts from the late 1950s onwards. However, it was only after the celebrations of 1967 that Canadian literature came to be regarded as an expression of national identity. As a result, there was soon talk of a Canadian Literary Renaissance, although in fact it was really more a matter of birth than of rebirth. Commenting on this phenomenon, Walter Pache noted in 1997: "When the centenary of Canadian Confederation came around in 1967, this event was celebrated with a World Exposition in Montreal and the introduction of a new flag: 'two red bands rampant and a red maple leaf rampant on white, looking like a trademark for margarine of the cheaper variety, or an owl-kill in snow,' as it is described in Atwood's novel *Cat's Eye* (1988). Growing national pride and an acerbically ironic internationalism appeared to be the two poles between which Canada's national consciousness alternated."

In the context of the literary renaissance of the 1960s and 1970s, much Canadian literary criticism has tended to view Canadian literature above all in relation to the definition of national self-awareness. Patriotic identification does not so much occur along formal and stylistic lines as along the lines of themes considered to be typically Canadian. Such a central theme is the definition of Canadian identity as distinct from the English mother country and, obviously today more than ever, from the economically and militarily dominant United States. A work that has come to be regarded as one of the 1970s manifestos on the theme of Canadian identity is *Survival* by Margaret Atwood, one of the few volumes of literary criticism which has also turned out to be a great success with a wider audience. In this book, first published in 1972, Atwood presents survival in a hostile environment — be it in a literal or metaphorical sense — as *the* central theme of Canadian literature (see ch. 22, Rosenthal). The related question of Canadian identity and its survival certainly remains one of the central themes of English-Canadian literature until the present. The focus of this search for identity and self-awareness has shifted distinctly, however, from a preoccupation with the two so-called founding nations England and France to other national and regional aspects of Canada. For example, the literature of the Native inhabitants of Canada, the First Nations, increasingly became the focus of discussion, so that an Aboriginal author like Thomas King could land a bestseller with his novel *Green Grass, Running Water* (1993). On the other hand, within the framework of Canadian multiculturalism, the works of immigrants from other parts of the world, for example, from Asia and the Caribbean, have also received more and more attention.

While this interest in Canadian themes and attitudes encourages engagement with and the production of Canadian literature, in the course of the 1980s and 1990s literary critics such as Linda Hutcheon and David Williams (who came to prominence as a novelist as well) also identified typically prominent Canadian genres such as the artist novel and the historical novel. In addition, Hutcheon postulated a typically Canadian literary attitude, namely irony. This irony may well be brought about by the Canadian situation of English-French bilingualism or by the original Canadian inferiority complex in relation to the mother countries or the United States.

The search for identity can be established particularly well as a theme in the historical novel, in which either writing about history itself becomes a topic or the author explicitly reflects upon the genesis of the work that he or she is writing. To describe this literary genre, which critics agree is particularly prominent in Canada, Hutcheon coined the term "historiographic metafiction," to which genre belong the majority of the works under discussion here. For example, novels by Rudy Wiebe, Margaret Atwood, Timothy Findley, Guy Vanderhaeghe, and Robert Kroetsch discuss the problems inherent in writing about history, specifically Canadian history. Historiographic metafiction addresses various themes and approaches ranging from feminism to fascism and postcolonialism. The other genre in which the Canadian novel retains great significance is the Bildungsroman and — more specifically — the Künstlerroman (artist novel). This subgenre can be observed in the writing of authors such as Margaret Laurence and Alice Munro, as well as in postmodern experimental novels (see Williams 1991).

## Established Authors: Robertson Davies and Mordecai Richler

Among the more established authors who have been part of the literary scene since the 1950s is Robertson Davies (1913–1995). Davies achieved acclaim not only as a novelist but also as a journalist, literary critic, and dramatist. For Davies, as for many of his compatriots, experiences gained in Europe — particularly in England, where he studied at Oxford and worked as an actor at the Old Vic Theatre in London — were of central importance; Davies presented a distinctly anglophile image in his later role as the Master of Massey College at the University of Toronto.

From the 1950s onwards, Davies's novels were mostly published as trilogies (the Salterton, Deptford, and Cornish trilogies). The settings span the Canadian small-town idyll, which is often suffocating for the protagonists, the metropolis Toronto and its university, and finally Europe, specifically England and Switzerland. The latter was especially interesting to Davies as the birthplace of C. G. Jung's archetypal theory in psychoanalysis. In the Deptford and Cornish trilogies, the amusing and ironical analysis of society and its foibles is complemented by an in-depth study of the characters' personal weaknesses. This growing psychological depth corresponds to a change from third-person to first-person narrative perspective. The novel *Fifth Business* (1970), the most successful part of the Deptford trilogy, is Davies's narrative masterwork. It retraces the life of a history teacher, Dunstan Ramsay, who strives to emancipate himself from traditional Presbyterian moral attitudes. The novel takes the form of a long letter, in which Ramsay recounts the far-reaching consequences of a snowball thrown in the distant past by his childhood friend and rival, Boy Staunton. This snowball, meant for Ramsay and hiding a stone at its core, hits a woman who is henceforth regarded as odd. For Ramsay, who escapes the suffocating life of small-town Canada by participating in the First World War, the battlefields of Flanders become a pivotal experience: He has the vision of a Madonna who is an exact likeness of the woman hit by the snowball, and consequently — and surprisingly for a Protestant — develops a great interest in hagiography. Later, in Switzerland, the home of Jungian psychoanalysis, a wise woman explains to him that his role in life is that of "fifth business," an important supporting role in opera. Ramsay's role in the novel indeed proves fatal for Boy Staunton, who apparently commits suicide after Ramsay confronts him with the very stone that had been hidden in the fateful snowball many years earlier.

Davies's satire about the foibles of a provincial and colonial society is superseded by his exposing previously unacknowledged character dimensions in his protagonists. The depiction of the crises in his figures' lives is based on his study of Jungian psychoanalysis. It draws on Davies's insight that it is indispensable for a balanced — and eventually individualized — character to acknowledge these formerly hidden dimensions, but also on the character's ability to recognize a deeper meaning of existence. This is the reason that in *The Manticore* (1972), the second volume of the Deptford trilogy, psychoanalytical dialogues are of central importance, while in the third volume, *World of Wonders* (1975), the world of magic is presented from the point of view of a magician. Jung's influence is still visible in the novels of the Cornish Trilogy. The first volume, *The Rebel Angels* (1981), belongs to the tradition of the satirical campus novel, whereas its sequels deal with the realm of the fine arts, the question of truth and deception (*What's Bred in the Bone*, 1985) and the realm of music (*The Lyre of Orpheus*, 1988). Davies here combines his interest in these spheres with his favorite bias towards a satirical description of society.

The discrepancy between puritanical Canadian reality and the human need for a holistic existence encompassing both body and soul is also at the center of Davies's final novel, *The Cunning Man* (1994). Like *Fifth Business*, this novel again deals with the solving of a crime, this time the death of a cleric, which is connected to the recollection of a fulfilled life. In line with the holistic principle, Davies conjures a view of the Canadian metropolis Toronto as a collection of "village" communities. Although Dunstan Ramsay makes a brief appearance as an inspiring history teacher with an interest in hagiography, this novel is in fact narrated by Jonathan Hullah, the "cunning man" of the title. Hullah is one of the many rather odd members of the Anglican congregation of St. Aidan's. At the end of his career as a strange but successful holistically oriented physician, he meditates on the various stages of his life: his youth spent in the North, where he learned about Aboriginal healing practices; his school and university days in Toronto; his activities as a field doctor, experimenting with alternative medicine during the Second World War, and as a police physician. Hullah's reminiscences, which teem with details of the Toronto of the 1930s to 1970s, are inspired by a young attractive journalist. In the course of the novel, this young woman becomes the widow of Hullah's murdered godson, and Hullah falls in love with her. Confronted with a mass of personal memories, Hullah decides to write an *Anatomy of Narration* from his own perspective, that of a well-read dilettante. His text corresponds to contemporary literary theories of deconstruction and follows the pattern of Robert Burton's seventeenth-century *Anatomy of Melancholy*. It thus becomes a prime example of the type of intertextuality so distinctive of Davies's work. The novel closes on a phrase that can also be read as a worthy conclusion to the life of a significant author: "This is the Great Theatre of Life. Admission is free but the taxation is mortal. You come when you can, and leave when you must. The show is continuous. Good-night."

Another novelist who established himself early on is Jewish-Canadian author Mordecai Richler (1931–2001). Since the 1950s he has been counted among the leading innovative Canadian authors, whether it be with the representation of the Jewish community of Montreal and Canada in novels such as *The Apprenticeship of Duddy Kravitz* (1959), *St. Urbain's Horseman* (1971), *Joshua Then and Now* (1980), and *Solomon Gursky Was Here* (1989), or later in his final work, *Barney's Version* (1997). Richler's focus is almost always on the Jewish-Canadian community, originally centered in the Montreal district around St. Urbain Street, but later including the entirety of the Jewish-Canadian diaspora. This focus is at times affectionate; often, however, as in the case of the character Barney Panofsky from his final novel, it is characterized by a bitingly ironic perspective.

In his realist narrative prose Richler draws upon his ethnic background within Canada, but he also makes use of his experiences in London's media industry and in the European cultural scene dominated by expatriates. In *The Incomparable Atuk* (1963) he describes the neopicaresque adventures of an Inuit poet in Toronto. In *Cocksure* (1968), one of his two novels that won a Governor General's Award, Richler chooses as his main character a naive Canadian who experiences the collapse of ethical values in a series of farcical situations set in London. *St. Urbain's Horseman* (1971), Richler's second Governor General's Award winner, combines realistic description with mythical symbolism in the portrayal of his main character, Jake Hersh. Hersh, whose biography often runs parallel to Richler's own, has to deal with his personal history as well as the collective past of the Jews during the Holocaust. In his dreams he evokes the strong figure of the avenging horseman alluded to in the novel's title. Although readers might have been put off by Richler's grotesque humor and complex narrative structure, this did not keep the book from becoming a popular success. *Joshua Then and Now* (1980) once again shows Richler's literary versatility in a story focusing on a Jewish-Canadian journalist with a Montreal background who is — among other things — an avid Nazi hunter but who also finds himself in a self-engineered, morally compromising situation.

Like most of Richler's works, the novel *Solomon Gursky Was Here* (1989) starts out in Montreal. It then expands beyond the city's urban Jewish community and traces the fictive family history of the Gurskys. Emerging from impoverished immigrant beginnings in the nineteenth century the Gurskys become members of the leading circles of industry and business and finally one of the most powerful producers of alcoholic beverages in North America. This development brings them in contact with historical personalities such as Al Capone and Joseph Kennedy, the patriarch of the Kennedy dynasty. In his earlier Montreal-based novels, Richler cultivated a largely conservative narrative style. Here, however, he departs from a realistic depiction and constructs a partly humorous, partly mythical story which features the whole world as its stage. The story encompasses historical events from John Franklin's expedition to the Arctic in the nineteenth century via the prohibition years in Canada to the hijacking of an Israeli airplane bound for Uganda in 1976. Like many other contemporary Canadian novels, *Solomon Gursky* also features the figure of a historian, Moses Berger, who attempts to reconstruct the life story of Solomon Gursky from unreliable and often manipulated historical records. Solomon has mysteriously disappeared, yet there are indications that he is not actually dead. The evidence rather suggests that he surfaces wherever in the world Jewish interests are at stake.

*Barney's Version* (1997) differs the most from the realist form of Richler's early novels. It relates the (fictitious) autobiography of Barney Panofsky, a film director who suffers from Alzheimer's disease. In a postmodern manner, the novel constantly focuses on the writing, rewriting, correcting, and revising of the very text that the readers have in front of them. Richler's insistence on bodily functions seems to combine superficial realism and acerbic satire so that one might view the novel as a postmodern counterpart of Jonathan Swift's satires. Not unlike Swift, Richler polemically attacks political issues of his time — in this case, for example, Quebec language regulations.

## Innovative Form and Content in the 1960s and 1970s: Postmodernism, the Role of Female Authors, and Regionalism

One of the most prominent literary innovators in the field of the Canadian novel is Leonard Cohen (1934–), who is also a successful poet and well-known singer. Like Mordecai Richler, Cohen hails from the Jewish community of Montreal. His *Beautiful Losers* (1966) became one of the first postmodern Canadian novels. It is an "experimental monument to the sixties" (Moss 1981, 46), condemned as blasphemous by some, praised as a cult novel by others. In the controversial book Cohen tests the boundaries of what is possible in the Canadian novel, which had hitherto been rather conservative. He makes use of a provocative combination of religion, anthropology, and sex, juxtaposing the story of an Aboriginal saint from the seventeenth century and a team of narrators fueled by sex and drugs. *Beautiful Losers* cannot but unsettle those readers who expect a coherent and complete depiction, because Cohen is at pains to emphasize narrative ambiguities, the " 'blanks' segmenting the text" (Heidenreich 1989, 95), and the blurring of boundaries.

Among the most striking features of contemporary Canadian literature is the number and significance of female authors who have left their mark on the Canadian novel in recent decades. The narrative experimentation of authors such as Margaret Atwood, Margaret Laurence, or Audrey Thomas may not be as radical in formal terms as that of their male colleagues Leonard Cohen, Robert Kroetsch, or George Bowering, but the message of their novels, shaking as it does the foundations of outdated patriarchal structures, is therefore all the stronger. Since the late 1960s Margaret Atwood (1939–) has without a doubt become the leading voice of Canadian literature: The news magazine *Maclean's* even dubbed her the

"Queen of CanLit." Her early novels are characterized above all by a feminist and patriotic Canadian stance. In later works she explores themes of social and ecological criticism. Atwood employs and develops innovative formal techniques, such as historiographic metafiction (see ch. 22, Rosenthal). Almost all of her novels, the only exception being the recent dystopian novel *Oryx and Crake* (2003), depict the various plots from the perspective of female characters, often in extreme situations.

Atwood's first novel, *The Edible Woman* (1969), still presents a rather passive image of a woman's role in society, using the metaphor of the woman made of dough, which the protagonist Marian McAlpine bakes for her boyfriend. In contrast, Atwood's later works include numerous examples of the Bildungsroman, in which women gain a more confident self-image. The novel *Surfacing* (1972) can be read as an illustration of the theses Atwood put forward in her introductory volume to Canadian literature, *Survival* (1972). The novel depicts the return of a young woman to those places in the wilderness of Quebec where she spent her youth. The search for her lost father eventually becomes a search for her own identity as a woman and as a Canadian, not least because she mistakenly identifies a group of tourists who are destroying nature as Americans instead of Canadians. The existential confusion of the protagonist is poignantly expressed at the beginning of the novel: "Now we're on my home ground, foreign territory."

In *Bodily Harm* (1981) Atwood combines criticism of society's misogyny with criticism of the political machinations of the United States as a quasi-colonial power in Latin America. Canada's relationship to the United States is a recurring central theme in her novels and poems, as it is in her political work, in which she, along with many other intellectuals, opposed the creation of a North American free trade zone. Her motivation stems from the fact that she fears the loss of an independent Canadian culture within a unified North American market. Canada's relationship to the United States is also an important theme in Atwood's historical novels. For example, *Alias Grace* (1996) problematizes women's role in society and in the penal system of the nineteenth century by relating the case of historical figure and alleged murderer Grace Marks, who finally moves to the United States. A similar theme can be found in the earlier dystopian novel *The Handmaid's Tale* (1985; film adaptation in 1990 by Volker Schlöndorff on the basis of a script by Harold Pinter), which is set in the near future in the area of the New England states, where an extremely misogynistic totalitarian system has been set up on the basis of a narrow fundamentalist interpretation of the Bible. Under this system, the female protagonist loses all her rights and becomes the handmaid of a leading politician. Her only task is to bear a child for her master, because his own wife, like most other women, has become barren in the wake of apocalyptic wars and the destruction of the environment. Although it is set in the future, the novel becomes an example of Canadian historiographic metafiction: The epilogue reveals that the plot has been reconstructed by historians in the twenty-third century and subjected to a one-sided interpretation. The theme of coming to terms with the past and the possibility of rewriting and misrepresenting bygone times is also central to the novels *The Robber Bride* (1993) and *The Blind Assassin* (2000). Atwood's dystopia *Oryx and Crake* (2003), on the other hand, deals with the dangers of an unquestioning belief in research and science, which plunges the world into chaos. Atwood's enormous success, not only with literary critics but also with her readership, can be explained not least by the fact that she tackles vital themes of contemporary society in her novels. These include the danger of religious fundamentalism, the risks of the American struggle for global hegemony, the role of women in the past, present, and future, and the threat of environmental destruction. For many, Atwood has come to be *the* public voice of Canada.

Canada has produced a significant number of distinguished female authors, many of whom originate from the central Canadian province of Ontario and, accordingly, set their works there. An example is Alice Munro (1931–), whose short-story collections are often, but not exclusively, set in southwestern Ontario. In contrast, Margaret Laurence (1926–1987), who represents the western Canadian province of Manitoba, chooses the fictitious small town of Manawaka as the focal point and the prairies as the central context for her most famous works. Like Mordecai Richler, Laurence spent long periods of time in London (as well as in Africa). With her confidently feminist, persuasively pacifist, and moral voice, her works are viewed as provocatively confrontational by many conservative readers. Laurence's oeuvre comprises a whole cycle of novels and short stories that often — as in *The Stone Angel* (1964) — present the developmental potential of female protagonists in a traditionally patriarchal prairie society. The semiautobiographical artist novel *The Diviners* (1974) represents the zenith of her work. In this novel, the writer Morag Gunn deals with her beginnings in Manawaka, her confrontation with the Scottish roots of her ancestors, and her emancipation and artistic development, as well as her experience of society's subliminal animosity, not only towards artists but also towards Canadian Aboriginals. This is illustrated through the fate of Morag's daughter Pique, whose father was a Métis (the Métis are descendants of Aboriginals and European fur traders in the prairie provinces Manitoba and Saskatchewan). The protagonists' confrontation with their European ancestry through a journey back to the European homeland — which in the end turns out not to live up to the myths that surround it — is a theme that also distinguishes the work of other contemporary Canadian novelists such as Jack Hodgins and Alistair MacLeod. In Laurence's artist novel, the protagonist Morag even comes to the conclusion that myths are more important than historical facts: "The myths are my reality."

Aritha van Herk (1954–) is an important successor to Laurence. Van Herk, too, conjures the feminist but also regional voice of the Canadian West. She comes from the prairie province of Alberta and describes the experiences of women emancipating themselves from their destiny in novels such as *Judith* (1978), the story of a pig breeder, or *The Tent Peg* (1981), the story of a young woman who disguises herself as a man and joins the all-male world of a team of geologists. Probably van Herk's most memorable female character is Arachne Manteia in *No Fixed Address: An Amorous Journey* (1987), who, not unlike Odysseus, crosses the sea of the prairie in her car and finally disappears in the open spaces of the Canadian North. Van Herk "explores" further formal literary and geographical regions in her "geografictione" *Places Far from Ellesmere* (1990), a semiautobiographical, experimentally feminist exploration of the Canadian West and North with intertextual references to Tolstoy's *Anna Karenina* (1878), who "should have escaped to Ellesmere." In the novel *Restlessness* (1998) the protagonist Dorcas flirts with death and with the man who is supposed to kill her in a hotel. This man delays the deed, in a reversal of Scheherazade's tactics, by spurring her on in the telling of more and more tales.

Daphne Marlatt (1942–) and Audrey Thomas (1935–) have been important feminist authors since the 1970s. Both have made British Columbia their home, although neither of them was born in Canada. While Marlatt first made her name as a poet, in *Ana Historic* (1988) she contributes to Canadian historiographic metafiction from a radically feminist-lesbian perspective by describing the attempt of a young woman to reconstruct the life of a Mrs. Richards (a pioneer in the city of Vancouver in the nineteenth century) based on sparse archival records in which women barely register. The novel takes the form of a stream of consciousness or interior monologue of the narrator Annie. It constructs the personality and background of another Annie (the later Mrs. Richards), who comes to Vancouver as a teacher, soon marries, and thus disappears from the archival records. In the poem that concludes the novel, the two Annies from the nineteenth and twentieth centuries eventually become one: "We give place, giving words, giving birth, to / each other — she and me. you."

In the feminist historical novel *Isobel Gunn* (1999) Audrey Thomas reworks material that has already been treated by the Scottish-Canadian poet Steven Scobie (1943–) in his epic poem *The Ballad of Isabel Gunn* (1987). It is the story of a young Scottish woman in the early nineteenth century who, in order to escape the poverty of her homeland, dresses up as a man and travels from the Orkney Islands to North America. Still disguised as a man, she finds work with the Hudson's Bay Company at Fort Albany on Vancouver Island and works as hard as her male colleagues. Her true gender is discovered only when she bears the child that is the product of a rape by the only person who knows her secret. She is sent back to

Scotland while her child remains in Canada. Working with sparse information from historical archives and with legends told on the Orkneys, Thomas reconstructs how it was possible for Isobel Gunn to remain undetected for so long in the almost exclusively male society of a fur-trading post, where the only other women were the wives of the Natives. As her narrator she chooses the teacher and cleric Magnus Inkster who, like Isobel, is an outsider in the fort. Thomas simultaneously demonstrates the important role that the Aboriginals, particularly the women, play in keeping life going, both for the fort and for Isobel.

Kristjana Gunnars (1948–), originally from Iceland, weaves her Icelandic heritage into her stories and poems. The line between poetry and prose, between fiction and nonfiction, between novel, autobiography, and literary criticism is often blurred in her books. Accordingly, her texts are full of intertextual references to world literature. Her first novel, *The Prowler* (1989), is unpaginated, contains 167 chapters mostly shorter than one page, and entertainingly describes important events in the life of the narrator, such as her spartan upbringing in Iceland or her schooldays in Denmark and the United States. A central aspect of the novel is the narrator's ongoing commentary on the act of writing itself — and particularly on the act of writing as a woman. The prowler of the title becomes a metaphor for the threat of crime, but also for the attitude of author and reader towards the text, which is explicitly addressed in the book. In *The Rose Garden: Reading Marcel Proust* (1996) Gunnars links reminiscences of a stay in Trier (Germany) with the depiction of a romantic relationship as well as with reflections on Marcel Proust and other authors and on feminist literary theory.

One of the most successful female Canadian authors was Carol Shields (1935–2003). In 1957 Shields, who was born in the United States, became a Canadian citizen by marriage. By the 1990s she had established herself as one of the most important literary representatives of Canada on the international stage. Her literary success is crowned by the novel *The Stone Diaries* (1993), a fictional autobiography which won the Canadian Governor General's Award as well as the American Pulitzer Prize (1995). In numerous novels, including *Small Ceremonies* (1976), *The Box Garden* (1977), *The Republic of Love* (1993), and *Larry's Party* (1997), Shields depicts the day-to-day lives of apparently unremarkable characters in a way that might look superficial or simplistic at first glance. Yet on the contrary, situations from everyday life become material for exciting and entertaining, but also innovatively structured and technically skillful narratives. The spectrum of her novels ranges from the heavily autobiographical, humorous study of life in an academic household — the narrator of *Small Ceremonies*, like Shields herself, writes a book about the early Canadian poet Susanna Moodie — to the scenes of a marriage depicted in two complementary novels (*Happenstance*, 1980, from the perspective of the husband,

and *A Fairly Conventional Woman*, 1982, from the perspective of his wife) to *Swann: A Mystery* (1987), a mixture of campus and crime novel. *Larry's Party* depicts the life of a landscape gardener and labyrinth constructor. Shields's last, very personal work *Unless* (2002), written during her battle against cancer, depicts the threat of external influences to a family idyll. The middle-class life of an author and translator is upset by the fact that her daughter decides, completely unexpectedly and initially inexplicably, to quit university, withdraw from society, and live on the streets of Toronto. It is only in the course of the novel that the real reason for the daughter's behavior becomes clear: She has witnessed a young Muslim woman's self-immolation in public. This event and other coincidences lead the protagonist to radically rethink her philosophy of life.

## Region as Challenge: Further Innovations from the West and East of Canada

Both the Canadian literary scene and Canadian politics have seen continuous rivalries between the center, Toronto, and the periphery. In this context, Margaret Laurence's works, for example, contribute not only to the Canadian tradition of the feminist Bildungsroman, but also to literary regionalism and to the establishment of the Canadian prairie as a literary setting. Similarly important as a representative of prairie literature, and perhaps even more essential as a representative of postmodern experimentation in the Canadian novel, is poet, literary theorist, and novelist Robert Kroetsch (1927–). Kroetsch has been described by Linda Hutcheon as "Mr. Canadian Postmodern" and is the most important proponent of postmodern literary theory and practice in Canada. Kroetsch grew up on a farm in the prairie province of Alberta. In his literary work, particularly in the Out West trilogy of novels and in his long poems, he represents the Canadian prairie in an innovative literary manner. In his poems about the newly settled land, he often uses "prosaic" texts, such as the catalogue of a seed merchant, as an intertextual model, answering to a lack of European and literary reference points. His novels, which are set in a fictional prairie landscape, often exaggerate and parody reality and also feature frequent intertextual references to such literary models as Homer's *Odyssey*. In *The Studhorse Man* (1969), for example, Kroetsch has the last horse inseminator, Hazard Lepage, travel with his stallion from farm to farm across the endlessly flat "sea" of the prairie, just as the mythical Odysseus sailed aimlessly around the Mediterranean Sea (see also van Herk's *No Fixed Address*). Above all, however, Kroetsch depicts the prairie region in three distinct historical phases of the twentieth century: in the 1930s, dominated by economic depression and drought (*The Words of My Roaring*, 1966), towards the end of the Second World War (*The Studhorse Man*), and in the

1970s (*Gone Indian*, 1973). In the process, his experiments with narrative perspective become all the more complex. This also holds true for his subsequent novels, for example, *Badlands* (1975), *What the Crow Said* (1978), *Alibi* (1985), and *The Puppeteer* (1992), in which he experiments with feminist, postmodern, and other narrative strategies. In *Badlands* the daughter of a paleontologist frees herself from the shadow that her dead father still casts over her life by using his not always entirely reliable field notes to reconstruct "on location" his search for dinosaur skeletons in the Alberta "Badlands," and in so doing uncovers his deception. In *What the Crow Said* a magic-realist plot unfolds on the border between the prairie provinces of Saskatchewan and Alberta. The laws of nature do not hold here, so that stunning incidents such as a young woman copulating with a swarm of bees or the existence of a talking crow seem quite normal. In the pair of novels *Alibi* and *The Puppeteer*, Kroetsch's characters are searching for their own identity. This is particularly true in the case of oddly named William William Dorfendorf, who purchases curiosities all over the world for the millionaire Jack Deemer. These novels pose a particular challenge to the reader, because the writing process often commands the center of attention, and the reader can never be certain to what extent the competing narrative authorities may be trusted.

Kroetsch takes a new narrative direction in *The Man from the Creeks* (1998), in which he tells the story of the Yukon gold rush at the end of the nineteenth century from the perspective of an eyewitness who was a child at the time and is now well over one hundred years old. In an intertextual manner, the narrative line results from the fact that the narrator's mother is the heroine of a well-known ballad by the Canadian poet Robert Service (1874–1958). (Service himself worked in the Yukon territory as a bank clerk at the time of the gold rush.) Kroetsch also finds an ideal narrative and reflective medium in his heavily autobiographical collection of essays, *A Likely Story: The Writing Life* (1995). In these personal essays he connects aspects of literary theory with humorous and very readable personal reminiscences and observations.

No less important than the experimental regional novels of Robert Kroetsch are the works of Rudy Wiebe (1934–). In his novels, which are generally set in the Canadian West or have a strong thematic link to it, Wiebe mainly focuses on the history of minorities in Canada. The reason for this may be found in Wiebe's being a member of the Mennonite community, a pacifist religious group originating from northern Germany and Frisia, many followers of which emigrated to Canada via the region of Danzig, Ukraine, and Russia. The Mennonites have maintained German as the language of religious services until today, and many of them still speak Low German in their everyday life. Initially, in novels such as *Peace Shall Destroy Many* (1962) and *The Blue Mountains of China* (1970), Wiebe analyzes his own personal relationship with the conservative, hierarchical structures of the Mennonites and recounts aspects of their history, for example, their flight from Ukraine and Russia to North and Latin America. He also depicts, however, the fate of Native Canadians: in *The Temptations of Big Bear* (1973), using the example of the Cree chief, or in *The Scorched-wood People* (1977), with the fate of Métis leader Louis Riel. *A Discovery of Strangers* (1994) explores, from the perspective of Native Canadians, the first polar expedition of the Englishman John Franklin. Franklin's failure and disappearance in the Arctic has become an important myth in Canada's collective memory and search for identity, exemplified, for example, in the work of Atwood and Richler.

Wiebe's historical novels are among the most impressive but also the most linguistically complex examples of the experimental historical novel in Canada. In the novel *Sweeter Than All the World* (2001), Wiebe returns to the history of the Mennonites and their journeys, presenting an epic overview. Wiebe's sensitive and stylistically experimental method of rendering the position of ethnic minorities has spawned criticism, however, not least from representatives of the First Nations, who have accused him of appropriating their voice. Nevertheless, in works such as *Stolen Life: The Journey of a Cree Woman* (1998) — which Wiebe wrote together with an Aboriginal woman, Yvonne Johnson, a descendant of the chief Big Bear — it becomes obvious that his intention is to echo and amplify the voice of the minority rather than distort or manipulate it.

The history of the Mennonites is also a central theme in Sandra Birdsell's (1942–) novel *The Russländer* (2001). In her earlier works, Birdsell's main concern had often been with the rural population of Métis and Mennonite background in the province of Manitoba. In *The Russländer* Birdsell describes in a striking manner the life and persecution of the Mennonites in the Soviet Union at the beginning of the twentieth century. She does this from the perspective of a woman who has escaped persecution in Russia and is now living in a retirement home in the Canadian city of Winnipeg, where she tells her story to a young man. Another writer who artistically draws upon her Mennonite background is Miriam Toews (1964–), who in *A Complicated Kindness*, winner of the 2004 Governor General's Award, impressively describes the dire fate of an adolescent girl in a conservative and very hierarchically structured rural community.

An author who represents the Canadian Pacific West is George Bowering (1935–). Bowering has also made a name for himself in poetry with his postmodern experimentation; in November 2002 he was appointed as the first Canadian Parliamentary Poet Laureate for a period of two years. In his novels he utilizes and parodies a wide range of genres, from the historical novel to the crime novel and the Western. Thus, his novel *Caprice* (1987) concludes not with a lone anglophone male hero riding westward into the sunset, but rather with a French-Canadian heroine riding eastward. Bowering's most important contribution to Canadian historiographic metafiction comes in the form of his postmodern "historical novels" such as *A Short Sad Book* (1977; see Gertrude Stein's *A Long Gay Book*, 1932) and, above all, the provocative *Burning Water* (1980). In the latter novel he retells the story of the European "discovery" of his home province, British Columbia, from the perspective of the Native inhabitants, who are not much interested in being "discovered." The novel is full of intertextual references and wordplay. In addition, Bowering suggests that the main representatives of the colonization of the North American Pacific Coast, captains Vancouver from Britain and Quadra from Spain, had a homosexual relationship. In the course of his experiments with narrative perspective, the narrator "George Bowering" also mentions that he (the narrator), the novelist, the seaman George Vancouver, and the then King of England (George III) all have the same first name, so that the latter can be ambiguously, ironically (and correctly) be referred to in the novel's prologue as "George the Third." Ironically enough, the narrator moves to Europe in order to have the necessary distance to write about the discovery of his "homeland." Alongside these playful treatments of Canadian history, Bowering authored a revisionist but certainly serious history of the province British Columbia (*Bowering's B.C.: A Swashbuckling History*, 1996).

Jack Hodgins (1938–) is an important novelist from the Pacific province of British Columbia, more specifically, Vancouver Island. After a first collection of short stories published in 1976 (*Spit Delaney's Island*), he came to be known for the 1977 novel *The Invention of the World*. Stylistically, this work is reminiscent of the magic realism of Latin American authors such as Gabriel García Márquez. It exhibits numerous historical, historiographic, and metafictional features. *The Invention of the World* tells the story of a "colony" founded by a charismatic Irishman on Vancouver Island on 6 January 1900, the Feast of the Epiphany. Meanwhile, this colony had to make way for a camping ground, though its former inhabitants, or rather victims, still live on the island and meet with other extremely idiosyncratic and colorfully depicted characters. In an exaggerated, carnivalistic representation, celebrations such as weddings and festivals take on mythical proportions and significance. In the work of the character Strabo Becker, a historian who wishes to reconstruct the history of the "Revelations Colony of Truth," the striving for a historiographic and documentary style becomes particularly evident. It is no exaggeration to say that Hodgins, who lives on Vancouver Island and until 2002 taught there at the University of Victoria, has put his home region and its colorful mixture of eccentric characters on the literary map of Canada. In later novels Hodgins focuses on other communities of the island. In *Broken Ground* (1998) he depicts the islanders' confrontation with the outside world, demonstrating to what extent the wartime experiences of the protagonist in France and their consequences can endanger the established lifestyle in the intimate surroundings on the Pacific Coast far away from the European battlefields.

The relationship between the United States and Canada in the course of the nineteenth and twentieth centuries — which is largely friendly in nature but still retains an imbalance of power — is also the focus of the skillfully constructed historical novel *The Englishman's Boy* (1996) by the Western Canadian writer Guy Vanderhaeghe (1951–). The novel centers on a massacre of Aboriginals carried out by American trappers on Canadian soil in the 1870s. One historical consequence of this "Cypress Hills Massacre" was the founding of the Royal Canadian Mounted Police, the Mounties, who subsequently ensured that, in comparison to the American Wild West, the settlement of the Canadian West proceeded much more peacefully. On the one hand, the plot unfolds from the perspective of the "Englishman's Boy," a young American who is drawn into the disputes with the Aboriginals. On the other hand, a second narrative perspective is introduced when in the 1920s a Canadian scriptwriter in Hollywood is supposed to interview an aging cowboy about the old Wild West. This cowboy, who also occasionally works as an actor, turns out to be the Englishman's Boy, who had participated in the massacre. However, his true and sobering version of the story falls victim to the nationalistic pathos of a megalomaniac American film producer and his belief in a heroic settlement of the West. The cowboy is so embittered by the misrepresentation of his story that he shoots the producer dead at the premiere of the film, while the scriptwriter abandons his Hollywood career and returns to Canada. The two perspectives on the massacre — the American perspective of "manifest destiny" and the alternative Canadian perspective — are in the end supplemented by the perspective of the real victims, the Aboriginals, whose traditional way of life is destroyed by the settlement of the West.

It is not only from Western Canada that important innovative impulses for the Canadian novel have emerged. In the Maritime provinces, novelist David Adams Richards (1950–) develops his own successful style of realism in the description of the working class of the Miramichi region in New Brunswick. The Newfoundland author Wayne Johnston (1958–) makes use of the genre of the historical novel in *The Colony of Unrequited Dreams* (1998) to create a fictional biography of Newfoundland premier Joe Smallwood, who, in 1948, led the province (which had until that time been a directly dependent colony of Great Britain) into Canadian confederation. This novel is one of the best examples of Canadian historiographic metafiction, making use of experimental artistic devices such as the invention of Smallwood's muse and opponent Fielding, whose version of events competes with and completes that of the first-person narrator, and the intertextual reference to a real historiographic text written in the colony during the late nineteenth century. In *The Navigator of New York* (2002) Johnston describes the race to the North Pole at the turn of the twentieth century. In his fictionalized, revisionist version of events, he invents a young Newfoundlander who joins the competition between Robert Peary and Frederick Cook. The young man accompanies Cook, who had been the apparent winner of the race, but who is later suspected of cheating. His young companion later discovers not only that he is the product of an extra-marital affair between his mother and Cook, but also that the ambitious Cook quite obviously did not shy back from manipulating his findings.

## The Canadian Novel on the Threshold of the Twenty-First Century: Internationalization and Diversity

In the period stretching from the 1970s to the turn of the century, Timothy Findley (1930–2002) is one of the most important voices in Canadian literature. After a career as an actor, Findley became one of the most celebrated Canadian dramatists and novelists. With his historical novel *The Wars* (1977), in which he develops a specifically Canadian paci-fist stance, he makes a pivotal contribution to literature about the First World War. In this novel, as in several others, Canada's participation in the First World War is viewed as a transformative experience and an initiation ritual leading to Canada's acceptance as an independent nation, but it is also seen as the moment at which Canada loses its innocence. The novel *Famous Last Words* (1981) is a political thriller about the period of fascism and the Second World War. The "source" of the novel are the writings that (fictitious) poet Hugh Selwyn Mauberley has left on the walls of a Tyrolean hotel. Mauberley in turn is of course the creation of the American poet and fascist sympathizer Ezra Pound (from his poem "Hugh Selwyn Mauberley," 1920). In the novel Findley illustrates how British and North American politicians, including members of the royal family, run the risk of succumbing to the enticements and intrigues of a worldwide Nazi con-spiracy. In other novels Findley describes or allegorizes Canada's relation-ship with the United States, for example, in his depiction of the Hollywood film industry in *The Butterfly Plague* (1969) or in his crime novel *The Telling of Lies* (1986), which attacks the conducting of medical experiments on Canadians under the auspices of the American secret ser-vice. In general, the threats and temptations to which people in the mod-ern world are exposed appear ever more starkly in Findley's novels. Intertextual references form a central stylistic element of his novels, for example, references to the Bible in his feminist version of the story of Noah's ark in *Not Wanted on the Voyage* (1984), to British First World War literature in *The Wars*, to Ezra Pound in *Famous Last Words*, and to C. G. Jung in his novel *Pilgrim* (2000). Through his use of intertextuality, Findley becomes an important practitioner of the intertextual parodic technique of "repetition with a difference," which Linda Hutcheon views as a pivot of Canadian historiographic metafiction.

Whereas in the 1970s and 1980s typical metaphors of Canadian literature, such as the question of survival, could still be deemed meaningful, at the threshold of the twenty-first century similar statements about Canadian literature and the Canadian novel can hardly be put forward any longer. Canadian literature today is multifaceted and, as its success outside of Canada demonstrates, has established itself as an international literature, with themes and authors who have come to Canada from all over the world. Because of the official policy of multiculturalism, Canada is obviously in a better position and more willing than other countries to adopt these streams and influences from outside. Thus the reader is presented with a broad spectrum of authors and styles of writing. On the one hand, there are authors such as the highly successful Native North American author Thomas King (1943–), who represents the First Nations in a highly amusing and intellectually stimulating mixture of intertextual quotations from world literature and parodic references to literary clichés about "Indians." Recently, he has even authored (under a pseudonym) "traditional" crime novels, with the difference that King's private detective is an Aboriginal (*Dreadful Water Shows Up*, 2002, published under the pseudonym Hartley GoodWeather). There is also, for example, Yann Martel (1963–), whose novel *Life of Pi* (2001) navigates the waters of magic realism in telling the story of an Indian boy who crosses the Pacific in a lifeboat with a tiger. Internationally successful authors such as Michael Ondaatje, Anne Michaels, and Rohinton Mistry offer a wide variety of styles and themes, and thus can scarcely be considered to be representatives of a clearly defined national literature of Canada, unless one is willing to agree on a very broad definition of what a Canadian novel is or can be today. In saying this, it should be noted that the term and the concept of a national literature is, especially in recent Canadian literary criticism, the subject of controversial debates. As far as the international success of Canadian novels is concerned, Alistair MacLeod's (1936–) winning of the 2001 International IMPAC Dublin Literary Award for *No Great Mischief* (1999) and the awarding of the British Booker Prize to Margaret Atwood for *The Blind Assassin* in 2000 and to Yann Martel for *Life of Pi* in 2002 speak for themselves.

The historical novel and the problematization of the act of writing about history remain of vital importance in Canadian writing. One of the most successful contemporary Canadian authors who draws on the traditions of the historical novel and the artist novel is Michael Ondaatje (1943–), who, born in Ceylon (today Sri Lanka), grew up in Great Britain, and now calls multicultural Toronto his home. His earlier works, such as

*The Collected Works of Billy the Kid* (1970) about the American Western hero or *Coming through Slaughter* (1976) about the jazz musician Buddy Bolden, approach their protagonists through the genres of historiography and documentary. *Running in the Family* (1982) then heads in the direction of the autobiographical artist novel, while the protagonists of *In the Skin of a Lion* (1987) become increasingly aware of their role in the development of a modern multicultural society. Historically based political novels, such as *The English Patient* (1992) about the end of the Second World War in Italy and *Anil's Ghost* (2000) about the civil war in Sri Lanka, go beyond the framework of Canadian politics to deal with questions of postcolonial emancipation. Ondaatje arguably found the inspiration for his English patient in the Hungarian Count Almásy, who had been an explorer in the Sahara in the 1930s as well as a spy in the desert war. His love affair with the wife of a fellow explorer is one of the narrative strands of the novel. In another strand, he lies seriously wounded in an Italian villa towards the end of the Second World War, incapable of remembering his own identity, guarded and cared for by a Canadian nurse and a soldier from India. A love relationship develops between Hana, the nurse, and Kip, the Indian. While the novel is very poetic in style and highly complex in form, its political position is not always easily identified, not least because strong human bonds develop between the four characters. The political message — with the exception of the strongly anticolonial position of the Indian who serves in the English army but in the end is appalled when he hears about the bombing of Hiroshima — tends to fade into the background in favor of human relationships and the fascinating inscrutability of the English patient.

Traditionally, Canadian literature has embedded conflicts such as the world wars in the context of Canada's coming-of-age as a nation. Many representatives of multicultural Canadian literature add to this the memory of those who were just able to escape the pogroms of Europe's fascist and totalitarian past. In *Fugitive Pieces* (1996) the Jewish author Anne Michaels (1958–) from Toronto relates in a very poetic — in the opinion of some critics, too poetic — style how seven-year-old Jakob Beer, the first-person narrator of the first half of the novel, is saved from the Nazis by the Greek scientist Athos (who has lost his own parents at the hands of the Nazis). Athos takes Jakob to a Greek island and hides him from the Germans. After the war the two find their way from Greece to Canada, where Athos becomes a professor and Jakob attends university and becomes a poet and translator. In the second part of the novel, a posthumous literary relationship develops between Jakob, who in the meantime has returned to Greece and died there, and the young university lecturer Ben from Toronto, who is searching for the poet's writings on a Greek island. Ben functions in this section as the first-person narrator and, at times, addresses Jakob directly, although the latter now only exists in his literary work. In addition, Jakob serves as a connection to the generation of Ben's parents: "You died not long after my father and I can't say which death made me reach again for your words." Ben's parents, too, suffered in Hitler's concentration camps and, throughout their lives, were haunted by their traumatic memories. Ben's search for Jakob's writings, which exhibit the handwriting but not the message of a scientist, is eventually successful. Throughout the search, Ben keeps a photo of his parents before him and he comes to the conclusion: "I see that I must give what I most need."

The perspective of emigrants from Eastern Europe, particularly from Ukraine, is represented by Janice Kulyk Keefer (1952–), who herself comes from a family with Ukrainian roots. With *The Green Library* (1996) she created a moving novel about a Canadian woman who is torn from her daily life as an English-Canadian middle-class woman when she discovers from a photo that has been sent to her anonymously that she is the daughter of a Ukrainian who had come to Canada as a "displaced person" and with whom her mother had an affair after the end of the Second World War. Through this discovery she is once more confronted with her youth and the past. She travels to Ukraine to resume contact with the love of her youth, Alex, the son of her family's former cleaning lady. In this way, the representative of the New World is confronted with European conflicts from the time of the Nazi regime and of Communist totalitarianism. Even if the love affairs of the protagonist's natural father with her mother and with the Ukrainian cleaning lady and her daughter do seem somewhat artificial, the author is nonetheless able to fascinate the reader with the depiction of European-Canadian family relationships after the fall of the Iron Curtain.

In the second half of the twentieth century, European emigrants only made up a minority of the new Canadians. Needless to say, this development is reflected in the literary scene through contributions from authors who have come to Canada from regions such as the Caribbean, Africa, or Asia. Many of them — like Rohinton Mistry (1952–), who immigrated from India and has become an internationally successful novelist with Booker Prize nominations and other important prizes for his novels — set their works in their countries of origin so that Canada often only appears in the sidelines, as a destination for a planned emigration, or as the starting point for a retrospective perspective on a plot line set in far-off places. Mistry's novels *Such a Long Journey* (1991), *A Fine Balance* (1995), and *Family Matters* (2002) are thus set in India, largely within the Parsi religious community in Mumbai. The novels highlight the difficulties of the religious minority in multicultural Indian society as well as generational problems. In *A Fine Balance* Mistry illustrates the problems of the Indian caste system, using, among other things, the chaotic situation under the emergency laws proclaimed by Indira Gandhi.

Given the multifaceted nature of the novels written in Canada today, and given the changes brought about by the policy of multiculturalism and the departure from overly obvious national characteristics, the designation "Canadian novel" has become particularly inclusive. It should also not be forgotten that a cyberage author such as Douglas Coupland (1961–), who has created and named *Generation X* (1991) and whose novels are set in an internationalized world, is also a Canadian. In the twenty-first century there are many authors who consider themselves Canadians with a certain patriotism, and — judging by his nonfictional publications such as *Souvenir of Canada* (2002) and *Souvenir of Canada 2* (2004) — even Coupland seems to go in this direction. But there are just as many who prefer to think of themselves as contributors to an international literature and depict the once traditional search for Canadian themes in a rather ironic way. Alongside the genres of the historical novel, historiographic metafiction, and artist novel, which have been presented here as central, there are other literary fields in which Canadian authors today interact with their colleagues the world over. The result is that today even less than in the past can literary influences be determined on the grounds of the national literature to which an author belongs. A Canadian author such as Yann Martel was born in Spain and writes about an Indian boy who crosses the Pacific to Mexico on a lifeboat; this author then wins the most important literary prize in Britain and hits international headlines because he is accused of borrowing too heavily from a Brazilian work, which he claims to have known only through a review by an American novelist. An author like Timothy Findley writes about the enmeshment of members of the British royal family and American magnates in an international fascist conspiracy and can therefore publish his work in England only after the death of the persons involved. An author like Margaret Atwood apparently sells as many copies of her books in Germany as she does in Canada (see Holzamer 2000, 18), even though — or perhaps because — most of her plots are set in Canada. The Canadian novel has, on the one hand, declared the whole world as its stage. At the same time, it has quite obviously come a long way from the situation in which Hugh MacLennan complained that Canadian settings would nip the interest of the American reading public in the bud. Even if in recent years great Canadian novelists such as Carol Shields and Timothy Findley have sadly passed away, there is certainly no shortage of innovative and highly readable successors.

# 24: The English-Canadian Short Story since 1967: Between (Post) Modernism and (Neo)Realism

*Reingard M. Nischik (University of Constance)*

## The Short Story after 1967

THE ENGLISH-CANADIAN SHORT STORY got off to a hesitant start in the twentieth century. To a considerable extent this was due to the lack of appreciation that Canadian literature had to face in its own country at the time and the limited publication facilities in Canada that resulted. Early short-story writers such as Knister, Grove, and Callaghan were thus forced to find their way into print mainly outside the country. The collected stories of all the major modernist writers, except for Callaghan and Garner, appeared decades after their conception, that is, in the 1960s, the period known as the Elizabethan Era of Canadian literature or the Canadian Renaissance.

The explosive development of Canadian literature in the 1960s, partly boosted by new supportive cultural policies, had a particular impact on the short story. Owing to the fact that short stories typically enjoy multiple publication — a first printing in a magazine, followed by publication in later collections by a single author and/or in anthologies — the genre relies particularly heavily on a flourishing print industry. Indeed, the Canadian Renaissance finally saw the growth of the kind of literary infrastructure that is necessary for a vital national literature. Publishing houses specializing in Canadian literature were founded, such as House of Anansi Press, Coach House Press, Talonbooks, and Oberon Press. Several literary magazines were inaugurated as well (*University of Windsor Review*, est. 1965, *Wascana Review*, est. 1966, *Malahat Review*, est. 1967, *Lakehead Review*, 1968–1977), providing an essential forum for short-story writing. These periodicals, which had low circulations and are often referred to as "little magazines," were kept above water by government subsidies, and still are to some degree: Even in the late 1990s, the Canada Council granted a total of $400,000 yearly to some thirty English-language literary magazines in Canada. Despite the odd voice of protest, such as John Metcalf's (see below), these cultural measures did much to promote a diverse, competitive literature, including short-story writing. Norman Levine (1923–2005), known primarily as an author of short stories (eight collections between 1961 and 2000), memorialized literary debuts and the importance of the little magazines in his story "We All Begin in a Little Magazine" (1972).

Another underwriter of Canadian short-story writing was the public Canadian Broadcasting Corporation (CBC) with its various radio programs featuring the reading of Canadian short stories, sometimes by the authors themselves. The internationally unique program *Anthology*, initiated and produced for more than twenty years by Robert Weaver, is of particular interest here, as it broadcast weekly readings of Canadian literature for over thirty years (1953–1985). While *The New Yorker* is considered to be the most prestigious American venue for short-story publication, Weaver's *Anthology* was for a long time its Canadian counterpart. Every year about forty stories by well-known and lesser-known Canadian writers were broadcast to an average audience of 55,000 listeners per week. Not only did Weaver recognize the affinities between radio and the short-story genre, he also edited important anthologies of Canadian short stories. With Oxford University Press he launched the *Canadian Short Stories* series in 1960, which comprised five volumes by 1991 and documents the evolution of the Canadian short story in one of its most important phases. Moreover, Weaver together with Margaret Atwood edited *The Oxford Book of Canadian Short Stories in English* in 1986 and *The New Oxford Book of Canadian Short Stories in English* in 1995, both of which have become standard works.

With the first volume of his series *Canadian Short Stories* in 1958, Weaver initiated a practice that other editors would later take up, namely the cautious inclusion of French-Canadian short stories in English translation. In his introduction Weaver writes:

> This book is . . . the first comprehensive anthology of Canadian stories to make any attempt to include fiction from both cultures. There have been good reasons for restricting Canadian anthologies to writing in one language, and there is no sense pretending that even today there is a consistent or vital connexion between the literatures of French and English Canada. But in the past few years some short stories from French Canada (and a good deal of poetry) have been published or broadcast in translation, and it seemed worth recognizing this important, if hesitant, meeting of the two cultures by reprinting three of those stories here. (Weaver 1960, x)

The French-Canadian stories (*contes*) in this case are by Ringuet, Anne Hébert, and Roger Lemelin; later collections feature, among others, Gabrielle Roy, Jacques Ferron, Gilles Vigneault, and Roch Carrier (see Nischik 1994). Regarding the contrast between English- and French-Canadian short-story writing, critical consensus long reigned that "[the] short story is not a major literary form [in French Canada]" (Owen and Wolfe 1978, 7). On the other hand, the less established French-Canadian *conte* is more open to narrative experimentation than the English-Canadian short story, which by and large leans more towards realism and modernism. Moreover, recent developments in French-Canadian short prose in the 1980s and 1990s led critics to speak of the 1980s as the "golden age of short prose" in Quebec, without denying that short prose in Quebec remains a "genre plutôt pour *happy few*" (Michel Lord; see ch. 30, Eibl).

The only writer to match Weaver's indefatigable support of the Canadian short story is John Metcalf (1938–). A productive and acknowledged writer of short stories, novellas, novels, and literary and cultural criticism, Metcalf has contributed significantly to the short-story genre not only through his creative work, but also by editing countless anthologies and book series (see Nischik 1987). In his somewhat controversial, sometimes aggressive critical style, Metcalf argues in favor of the traditional realist-modernist strain of the short story, whose representatives are included in his approximately forty anthologies, many of them meant for the classroom (for example, *Sixteen by Twelve: Short Stories by Canadian Writers*, 1970; *Making It New: Contemporary Canadian Stories*, 1982). In addition, he has figured in almost all of the strikingly numerous book series of Canadian short-story anthologies, for instance, *Best Canadian Short Stories* or *New Canadian Stories*. In *Best Canadian Stories* he repeatedly gave newcomers the chance to publish in an established forum, and thus greatly stimulated up-and-coming generations of writers.

While Weaver and Metcalf prefer the more conventional narrative forms of the Canadian short story, Geoff Hancock, editor of *Canadian Fiction Magazine* between 1975 and 1998, supported experimental, postmodernist short fiction in particular. In various articles and edited anthologies (for example, *Illusion One/Illusion Two: Fables, Fantasies and Metafiction*, 1983; *Moving Off the Map: From 'Story' to 'Fiction,'* 1986) he encouraged the rejection of the realist-modernist tradition in fiction. As he wrote in the introduction to *Illusion*, with an overstated sideswipe at prairie realist Sinclair Ross, "Gone at last are those boring fictional depictions of the prairie depression. . . . The illusionists are filling in those blank spaces on the literary map of Canada by uncovering the fantastic." He even states, "Canadian Literature begins again" (Hancock 1983, 9, 8). Hancock's partiality for postrealist narratives also explains his fondness for French-Canadian short fiction, which he tried to make accessible to an English-speaking audience in articles as well as book editions (for example, *Invisible Fictions*, 1987). However, despite such influential and zealous defenders as Hancock, the postrealist short story did not bloom to the extent in English Canada that it did in the United States (or, for that matter, in French-Canadian literature), not even during postmodernism's heyday in the 1960s and 1970s. Although partly experimental, deconstructive, and self-referential, the Canadian short story was less committed to these features in and of themselves than its American counterpart and more often combined them with the traditional Canadian interest in realist representation. Robert Kroetsch's well-known dictum that Canadian literature skipped the modernist phase and after nineteenth-century Victorianism reached directly into postmodernism is therefore questionable in the case of the short-story genre, too: To this day, the Canadian short story is marked by a clear predominance of modernist and neorealist narratives over outright antirealist, postmodernist styles.

In the past decades an impressive number of collections, book series, and anthologies of Canadian short stories have appeared at an unusual rate even by international standards, which testifies to the prominent position of the short story on the Canadian literary scene (and also to the continued state support of literature in Canada). The stories are collected and grouped according to various criteria: author, quality and representativeness, region, era, ethnicity, gender, etc. At the beginning of the 1980s German critic Helmut Bonheim had written that "the short story has been the most active ambassador of Canadian literature abroad" (Bonheim 1980-81), while Canadian critic David Arnason similarly stated that "the short story has always been a popular literary genre in Canada, and it is the form of Canadian writing that has traditionally had the largest appeal to international audiences" (Arnason 1983, 159). The Canadian editor of a short-story anthology at the turn of the millennium even described the contemporary Canadian short story as "the literary equivalent of a national display of fireworks" (Thomas 1999, vii). The high standing of the short story in Canada is also shown by its popularity with literary prize juries: Since 1978 about one third of the books awarded the most prestigious literary prize in Canada — the Governor General's Award — have been short-story collections, among others by Alice Munro (three times), Mavis Gallant, Guy Vanderhaeghe, and Diane Schoemperlen. The Canadian Giller Prize, in existence since 1994, has also been repeatedly awarded for short-story collections. Demanding stories by prominent Canadian authors such as Margaret Atwood, Alice Munro, Mavis Gallant, Alistair MacLeod, and W. D. Valgardson, to name just a few, were often first printed in Canadian magazines of large circulation, such as *Saturday Night*, or in American magazines such as *The New Yorker*, *The Atlantic Review*, or *The Saturday Evening Post*. What Knister had claimed in the 1920s with regard to the contemporary American short story — that strength in the numbers of short stories written and published help to raise the genre's general level of quality — proved true in Canada as well half a century later.

# The Montreal Story Tellers

The so-called Montreal Story Tellers contributed notably to the success of short fiction in Canada. This group of writers living in Montreal at the time was founded by Metcalf in 1970 and included Clark Blaise, Hugh Hood, Ray Smith, and Raymond Fraser. With the exception of the lesser-known Fraser (1941–), all members remained active in the short-story genre even after the group's dissolution in 1976. Their official title, the Montreal Story Teller Fiction Performance Group, points out their distinctiveness: Metcalf and company wanted to show that not only poetry, but also the short story lent itself to public reading, perhaps even more so. The readings, as the group members sometimes self-ironically recall in their memoirs (published in Struthers 1985), were intended as performance events and took place before audiences of up to 150 listeners, mostly at universities or colleges, but also in schools and bookstores, especially in the Montreal area.

Metcalf was not only the founder but the most important member of this relatively short-lived group. Over the years he developed into an even more active anthologist of Canadian short fiction than Weaver, but also into an acid-tongued, uncompromising critic of the Canadian literary scene. While nationalism and thematic criticism held sway over literary Canada, Metcalf raised his voice against subsidizing mediocre literature, irrespective of its themes, its focus on content related to Canada, or other aspects that he considered ancillary; for him the only acceptable yardstick of a still-budding national literature was literary excellence (see among others Metcalf's controversial works *Kicking against the Pricks*, 1982; *The Bumper Book*, 1986; *Freedom from Culture: Selected Essays 1982–1992*, 1994; as well as his memoirs, *An Aesthetic Underground*, 1996).

Besides his other merits, Metcalf is counted among Canada's best short-story writers and was dubbed "one of Canada's best-kept literary secrets" by the American *Harper's Bazaar*. He has published six short-story collections (among them *The Teeth of My Father*, 1975; *Selected Stories*, 1982; *Adult Entertainment*, 1986; *Standing Stones: The Best Stories of John Metcalf*, 2004). Some of his longer prose narratives are best described as novellas ("Polly Ongle," "Travelling Northward," "Private Parts: A Memoir," "Girl in Gingham," "The Lady Who Sold Furniture"), as is one of his most recent publications, *Forde Abroad: A Novella* (2003). Metcalf the critic once referred to his own narrative style as experimental. But in his literary work he relies on the modernist narrative tradition rather than on postmodernist innovation, which he once dismissed as a frequent excuse for poor, sloppy writing. A good example of Metcalf's style is "Gentle as Flowers Make the Stones" (1975). The story describes the struggles of poet and translator Jim Haine, above all in relation to his creative writing, and his attempts at gaining public recognition in a social context that proves hostile to art. Events such as Haine's poetry reading or the sex scene that follows with a woman from the audience are recounted from Haine's perspective, with Metcalf embracing Joycean stream of consciousness and simultaneity in his narrative technique. "Gentle as Flowers Make the

Stones" is a satirical turn on the exclusive demands that art makes on a writer's life — Haine reveals himself to be committed to his literary work only.

Considering Metcalf's critical take on Canadian culture and its politics, his particular interest in the satirical artist story comes as no surprise (see also "The Teeth of My Father," "The Years in Exile," or "The Strange Aberration of Mr. Ken Smythe" from 1973, the latter contrasting different cultures, with a German music group and its conductor Herr Kunst playing a central, parabolic role). A further subcategory of the short story that Metcalf masters in equal measure is the initiation story (see, for instance, "Early Morning Rabbits" or "Keys and Watercress").

Clark Blaise (1940–) has published six short-story collections to date, as well as three novels and five partly autobiographical nonfiction works. The thematic content of his story collections is hinted at in their titles: *A North American Education* (1973), *Resident Alien* (1986), and *Man and His World* (1993). Beginning in 2000, Porcupine's Quill Press (for which Metcalf is editorial advisor) began publishing a four-volume project, *The Selected Stories of Clark Blaise*, that combines selected, already published stories with some of Blaise's more recent ones, structuring the individual volumes according to the cultural geographies they cover: volume 1, *Southern Stories*, 2000; volume 2, *Pittsburgh Stories*, 2001; volume 3, *Montreal Stories*, 2003; volume 4, *World Body*, 2006. This project testifies to Blaise's cosmopolitanism and cultural mobility, which is traceable to his childhood. Born in 1940 in North Dakota (his first citizenship being American) to an English-Canadian mother and a French-Canadian father, he changed schools twenty-five times as a result of his parents' nomadic lifestyle, so that even as a child he was used to travel between Canada and the United States. Together with his Calcutta-born wife and fellow writer Bharati Mukherjee he settled in Montreal from 1966 to 1978, which left its mark on his early work in particular ("I've always thought of myself as a French Canadian, but . . . I was writing in English, not in French," Blaise in Wahl 1997, 51). In 1973 Blaise was granted Canadian citizenship; he regards himself as Canadian but today lives in the United States. Blaise's fiction has also been referred to as a sequential fictional "autobiography," centering on a socially estranged male protagonist whose identity is permanently under threat. This predicament may be considered the epitome of the "North American condition" concerning "rootlessness, homelessness, . . . dislocating contrasts to be found among juxtaposing groups within North American culture" (Davey 1976, 73).

The frequently anthologized short story "A Class of New Canadians" (1970; collected in *A North American Education*) is representative of Blaise's vast short-story oeuvre. Eighteen months before the story opens, protagonist Norman Dyer has left the United States upon receiving his PhD and has come to Montreal, which has made him feel like a "semi-permanent, semipolitical exile." He works as a lecturer in English literature at McGill University and teaches a colorful group of new immigrants from all over the world. His arrogant, self-absorbed attitude towards his students sums up the fragility of the idealized concept of multiculturalism known as the Canadian Mosaic (according to which Canadian society is made up of diverse ethnic groups with equal rights and opportunities). Dyer's positive image of Canada not only seems artificial, it also fails to win over the immigrants (some of whom regard Canada merely as a stepping stone to the United States), thus uncovering the frequently precarious identities of Blaise's protagonists. The story's final scene shows Dyer as an insecure and fearful "resident alien." Other exceptional short stories by Clark Blaise include "A North American Education," "Eyes," "Going to India," "Notes beyond a History," "I'm Dreaming of Rocket Richard," "How I Became a Jew," "North," and "Identity."

The thematic and stylistic heterogeneity of the Montreal Story Tellers also shows in the works of Hugh Hood and Ray Smith. Hood (1928–2000) prided himself above all on his novelistic work, especially his *roman-fleuve,* the novel series The New Age/Le nouveau siècle, published at regular intervals beginning in 1975 and planned to include twelve volumes, the last of which appeared on schedule in 2000, shortly before Hood's death. Hood's intention in this ambitious project was to delineate a fictional panorama of contemporary Canadian culture. Set against the vastness of his complete works, Hood's reception by critics and audiences alike seems moderate, and he is appreciated above all as a writer of short stories. His collected stories, published over forty years between 1962 (*Flying a Red Kite: Stories*) and 2003 (*After All!: The Collected Stories V*), comprise ten original book publications plus several volumes of reprinted stories, which makes Hood one of the most prolific Canadian short-story writers. Most of his stories are located in eastern metropolises (Toronto, Montreal); the bilingual Hood was indeed the only one of the Montreal Story Tellers who lived in this city throughout his writing life. His second collection *Around the Mountain: Scenes from Montreal Life,* deliberately published at the time of the EXPO World's Fair in Montreal in 1967, conveys an almost documentary attention to detail — Hood's style has in fact often been described as journalistic. A self-professed Catholic and a professor at the University of Montreal for over thirty years, Hood is regarded as one of Canada's most intellectual writers. In his apparently accessible and, in his own phrase, "super-realistic" and often allegorical writing style, he combines realistic elements with supernatural, transcendental aspects, uncovering philosophical and religious questions in the mundane patterns of daily life. Some representative examples of his highly polished stories include "Flying a Red Kite" and "Three Halves of a House" (from *Flying a Red Kite*), "Going Out as a Ghost" (from *Dark Glasses,* 1976), as well as "Getting to Williamstown" (from *The Fruit Man, The Meat Man & The Manager,*

1971). Despite some formal innovations (such as the comatose first-person narrator in "Getting to Williamstown," who supplies the central perspective and thereby lends the plot a dreamlike, surreal touch), Hood's narrative style remains largely traditional.

Ray Smith (1941–) is the most experimental of the Montreal Story Tellers. The fact that he published three short-story collections between 1969 and 1986, and two novels as late as the 1990s, is evidence of his initial predilections in matters of genre, although clear genre boundaries are difficult to establish with this postmodernist author. His best-known stories include "The Princess, the Boeing, and the Hot Pastrami Sandwich" (from his short-story cycle *Lord Nelson Tavern*, 1974) and "Cape Breton Is the Thought-Control Centre of Canada" from his eponymous first story collection (1969). "Cape Breton" belongs unmistakably to the 1960s, an age that also questioned conventions in literary terms. As the text self-referentially proclaims, we are dealing with "compiled fiction," a piecemeal, fragmentary collection of dialogues, reflections, aphorisms, and miniature stories, thirty-one fragments in all. Insofar as thematic threads are still discernible, these fragments deal with the precarious national identity of post-colonial Canada at the time of the Canadian Renaissance — especially in connection with the economic threat posed by the United States — with writing and art, and with relationships and love. The text also rejects any "sense of an ending," to use Frank Kermode's phrase, and closes instead with the following rather anti-American paragraph: "For Centennial Year, send President Johnson a gift: an American tourist's ear in a matchbox. Even better, don't bother with the postage."

## The Three Leading Authors of the English-Canadian Short Story: Alice Munro, Mavis Gallant, and Margaret Atwood

While the Montreal Story Tellers, who were so instrumental in the development of the short story as a genre, were all male, the three most highly regarded and at the same time best-known short-story writers in Canada today are female. The first of these is Alice Munro (1931–), the master of short fiction in Canada. This judgment derives also from the fact that Munro writes exclusively short stories, and thereby represents the very rare case of a writer committed to a single literary genre. Between 1968 and 2004, Munro published eleven collections of short stories as well as two volumes of selected stories, although *Lives of Girls and Women* (1971) and *Who Do You Think You Are?* (1979, published as *The Beggar Maid* in the United States and Great Britain) can be described as short-story cycles because of the unifying interconnectedness of the individual stories. Munro often addresses specifically female themes, such as restrictive gender roles in rural and small-town milieus (for example, "Boys and Girls" from *Dance of the Happy Shades*, 1968), complex and difficult mother-daughter relationships ("The Peace of Utrecht" from *Dance*), gender-related professional issues ("The Office" from *Dance* or "The Ottawa Valley" from *Something I've Been Meaning to Tell You*, 1974), emotional enslavement in love relations ("Dulse" from *The Moons of Jupiter*, 1982), and problems of aging in female characters ("The Moons of Jupiter" from *Moons* or "What Is Remembered" from *Hateship, Friendship, Courtship, Loveship, Marriage*, 2001). One of Munro's trademarks is her elaborate style, which not only fulfills high aesthetic demands but also attains an unusually complex expressiveness, for instance, through its idiosyncratic combining of seemingly paradoxical adjectives ("People's lives, in Jubilee and elsewhere, were dull, simple, amazing, and unfathomable — deep caves paved with kitchen linoleum," *Lives*, 249). Munro's stories also achieve her self-proclaimed purpose of reaching her readers' emotions.

Munro's writing has had a considerable impact on the literary world (in a listing in *Time Magazine* at the beginning of the twenty-first century, she was counted among the one hundred most influential personalities alive today, a rare honor for a writer of fiction). Her first short-story collection, *Dance of the Happy Shades*, was awarded the Governor General's Award for fiction in 1968 (and she has won this coveted prize twice again since then). Since the publication of *Lives of Girls and Women* her new books have regularly topped bestseller lists. The first appearance of many of her stories in *The New Yorker* testifies to the international dimension of her work. Munro is also the most frequently anthologized author of short stories in Canada. As with Atwood, Munro's skill is proven in a narrative and linguistic style that never lacks complexity or fails to challenge the reader, yet her stories are also popular with a large readership. Munro is something of a "writer's writer," who often interweaves poetological questions into her texts (for instance, in "Epilogue: The Photographer" from *Lives* or "Material" from *Something*), deftly switches between traditional and nonlinear, digressive narratives ("Dulse"; "White Dump" from *The Progress of Love*, 1986), celebrates multiple narrative perspectives ("Fits, from *Progress*, or "The Albanian Virgin" from *Open Secrets*, 1994) and Joycean epiphany, and subtly blends the mundane with the extraordinary ("Miles City, Montana" from *Progress*). Even the short-story form itself serves one of Munro's central arguments concerning the impenetrability and fragmentariness of the human condition and the episodic, fleeting nature of experience that never coagulates into a consecutive, cumulative sequence (for which the novel form would seem more appropriate): "And what happened, I asked myself, to Marion? . . . Such questions persist, in spite of novels" (*Lives*, 247).

Mavis Gallant (1922–), the second most anthologized short-story writer in Canada, grew up bilingual in Montreal, moved to Europe in 1950 at the age of twenty-seven and traveled extensively. Since 1960 she has been living and writing in Paris as the best-known expatriate author of Canadian origin writing in English. Unlike Munro, Gallant has tried her hand at other genres as well, having written two novels and various journalistic essays, but the short story is still closest to her, for poetological reasons similar to Munro's. With her emigration to France as well as her frequently European settings, characters, and themes, Gallant belonged for a long time to the ranks of Canada's lesser-known writers, at least with her early collections (*The Other Paris*, 1956; *My Heart Is Broken*, 1964), although she always thought of herself as a Canadian (Gallant once referred to this as "the national sense of self"). Her books were first published in the United States and England; the first to appear in Canada was *The End of the World and Other Stories* (1974). It was only with the publication of *From the Fifteenth District* (1979) that Canadian critics and scholars, somewhat belatedly, acknowledged Gallant to be one of the best short-story writers.

Having found brief employment as a journalist, her international literary career began in the early 1950s when she submitted one of her stories to *The New Yorker*. Her second submission, in 1951, made it into print. In 1964 *The New Yorker* negotiated a first-option contract with Gallant, which resulted in the hitherto longest cooperation between a writer and this distinguished magazine. Virtually all of Gallant's approximately one hundred stories have been first published there, a singular achievement, which was, however, a hindrance to Gallant's reception in Canada from the 1950s up to the 1970s.

Gallant's situation as an emigrant has had a lasting effect on her work from a thematic and narrative point of view. Time and again she writes about immigration and exile, outsiders, psychological rootlessness in place and time, socially estranged foreigners in Europe and North America, cultural conflicts and failed communication, multi- and transculturalism (often against the historical background of the Second World War and the postwar period), about political and social rifts reflected in individual destinies and mentalities. The setting of several of her short-story collections is predominantly or even exclusively Paris, her adopted home (see, for example, *Overhead in a Balloon: Stories of Paris*, 1985). *The Pegnitz Junction* (1973) deals with Germany and the Germans. *Home Truths: Selected Canadian Stories* (1981), the collection for which she received the Governor General's Award for fiction in Canada, provides Canadian readers with some critical views of their homeland and of themselves. The breadth and variety of her settings, characters, and themes make Gallant one of the most flexible, cosmopolitan authors in Canada. Her typically distanced, apparently uninvolved narrative voice has been attributed by scholars to her own personal situation as an immigrant and could partly be responsible for her modest readership compared to Munro's or Atwood's. Although her detached narrative voice may be a subject for debate ("There is something rather chilling in Gallant," Rooke 1986, 267), what particularly commands respect is her nuanced, polished style, often drenched in wry humor, understatement, or more or less subtle satire.

The thematic and technical breadth and complexity of her narrative art, which also comprises novellas (for example, "The Pegnitz Junction"), is reflected in some of the most frequently anthologized of her short stories, such as "The Ice Wagon Going Down the Street," "Acceptance of Their Ways," and "My Heart Is Broken" (from *My Heart Is Broken*), "The Moslem Wife," "The Latehomecomer," and "From the Fifteenth District" (from *From the Fifteenth District*), as well as in "In Youth Is Pleasure" (from *Home Truths*). Although herself nationally "dislocated, perhaps forever" — like her character Lottie Benz in "Virus X" from *Home Truths*, a young Canadian of German ancestry whose visit to Strasbourg in 1953 unsettles her formerly secure sense of home and belonging — Gallant with her eleven short-story collections published over forty years (including *The Selected Stories of Mavis Gallant*, 1996, which comprises fifty-two of her stories) remains an international flagship figure of the English-Canadian short story, honoring the multicultural, cosmopolitan inclination of contemporary Canadian letters.

Margaret Atwood (1939–) has placed less emphasis on the short-story genre than Munro and Gallant. Atwood, the acknowledged figurehead of Canadian literature — not only for the exceptional quality of her writing but also because of the volume and versatility of her output — has concentrated on novels and books of poetry. But she has written a considerable body of short stories, in which she is on the whole more experimental than either Munro or Gallant as far as genre conventions are concerned, extending and blending them, for instance, with those of poetry and the prose poem. Her collections *Dancing Girls* (1977), *Bluebeard's Egg* (1983), and *Wilderness Tips* (1991) contain stories that are in formal terms relatively conventional and are still anchored in the tradition of psychological realism. *Dancing Girls* gives a glimpse of the thematic resourcefulness of the author: "The Man from Mars" and "Dancing Girls" shed critical light on Canada's national dream of multiculturalism; "Giving Birth" creates a metapoetical parallel between the human act of conception and creative writing; "A Travel Piece," "Under Glass," and "Polarities" outline psychological problems and pathological developments, in the case of "Polarities" set against the background of an uneven power struggle between Canada and the United States. Other stories in the collection, such as "A Travel Piece," "The Resplendent Quetzal," "The Grave of the Famous Poet," "Hair Jewellery," and "Lives of the Poets," employ motifs of traveling in various contexts, while a central theme of the collection is relationship crises that result in identity conflicts, mostly on a personal but occasionally also on a national level.

Atwood places her stories in a specifically Canadian context, even more so than Munro, which is particularly obvious in stories from *Wilderness Tips* such as "Hairball," "Death by Landscape," "The Age of Lead," and "Wilderness Tips," as they take up Canadian settings (the "wilderness" but also the metropolis of Toronto), Canadian history (the Franklin expedition in search of the Northwest Passage), Canadian national challenges (ecological issues, the proximity to and difference from the United States, Canadian identity, multiculturalism), and Canadian myths (Sir John Franklin, the Canadian Mosaic). In addition, and to a greater extent than Gallant and even Munro, Atwood confronts the differences between the sexes and the difficulties of gender relations, not only in her formally more conventional stories (for example, "Uglypuss" and "Bluebeard's Egg" from *Bluebeard's Egg*), but especially in the experimental short texts in *Murder in the Dark: Shorter Fictions and Prose Poems* (1983), for instance "Worship," "Iconography," "Liking Men," and "Women's Novels."

Atwood's later short-prose collection *Good Bones* (1992) regards gender aspects from an even more critical perspective, with the remarkably well-read Atwood making intertextual use of classic works of world literature and also of popular culture texts. Her short dramatic monologue "Gertrude Talks Back" rewrites Shakespeare's *Hamlet*, the quasi-prose poem "Men at Sea" references Charles Baudelaire's poem "L'homme et la mer," while "The Little Red Hen Tells All" takes up an English children's story, and the delicious "Making a Man" alludes to certain types of texts in women's magazines, especially the recipe format. Atwood's short fiction also reveals her talent of lending a humorous if not comical twist to even the most serious matters, while preserving their intellectual complexity. As a storyteller, Atwood experiments in her short stories with narrative structure (exemplified by the alternating point of view in "The War in the Bathroom," the montage-like composition in "The Age of Lead," and the dense intertextuality in "Bluebeard's Egg"). Atwood the stylist (and poet) is revealed in the linguistic brilliance of many of her stories.

# Regionalism and the Short Story

In its initial stage of development in such a vast country, the modern Canadian short story was closely linked to regional themes and to rural and urban backgrounds. In contemporary Canadian literature an increasing cosmopolitanism is noticeable, which is often reflected in a much wider and more varied choice of setting (see, for example, Blaise's fictional geographies). But even in connection with the contemporary short story, one can still distinguish distinct regions spanning literary Canada from coast to coast. There are the large cities in the East (Toronto, Montreal, Ottawa), which serve as backdrops for stories, for instance, by the Montreal Story Tellers, Atwood, and Austin Clarke. Vancouver, the western metropolis, is often the chosen setting for writers like Audrey Thomas and Jane Rule. And there are the more rural regions, including the prairies, the Pacific coast, and the Atlantic provinces.

The prairie writers W. O. Mitchell, Margaret Laurence, Rudy Wiebe, and Guy Vanderhaeghe, though treading in the footsteps of their forerunners, the prairie realists Grove and Ross, adapt and renew this tradition in various ways. Mitchell (1914–1998) was one of the most successful screenwriters in Canada, also a playwright, yet is today mainly well-known for his novels, such as *Who Has Seen the Wind* (1947). Mitchell's short-story collections *Jake and the Kid* (1961) and *According to Jake and the Kid: A Collection of New Stories* (1989) became bestsellers in Canada — partly because the stories, which began to appear in 1942 in both Canadian and American magazines, were rewritten by Mitchell for a radio format (and aired over about 250 CBC programs between 1950 and 1956) — and were finally adapted for television. It was only after they had acquired this media publicity that the texts were released in book form as short-story cycles. Mitchell's writing invests the prairie story with a more cheerful, humorous streak. With their coarse humor, which draws from the oral tradition and that of tall tales, their emphasis on small-town local color, and their child protagonist and his relationship to a fatherly mentor, Mitchell's texts gave the prairie short story new impulses and twice won him the Stephen Leacock Award for Humour. Their sentimental, leveling, roughly moralizing aspects led Margaret Laurence to conclude in her review of *Jake and the Kid* in 1962 that these stories addressed "a younger audience" in particular.

Margaret Laurence (1926–1987) herself delivered one of the best Canadian short-story cycles with *A Bird in the House* (1970) as part of her exceptional Manawaka fiction series, which is set for the most part on the prairie. Written over eight years and, according to Laurence, "the only semi-autobiographical fiction I have ever written," *A Bird in the House* recounts the making of an artist in a cycle of eight stories. The writer-to-be Vanessa MacLeod grows up in the 1930s in Manawaka, a fictional small town on the prairie, modeled upon the author's own home town Neepawa in Manitoba. The events are related from the perspective of a grown-up, forty-year-old Vanessa, but the focus is nevertheless on the experiences of the growing child. Through her writing, among other things, Vanessa tries to break out of the constricting family and gender roles that are imposed upon her by a patriarchal small-town community. Her purpose is to escape the stifling life script based on family life that her mother had to resign herself to. The text delivers a realistic evocation of small-town life and social structures in the Canadian prairie, subtle character sketches, and a gradual thematic buildup in the manner of a Bildungsroman. Another essential feature is the accessible style and the balanced, consistent tension between the experiencing and the reminiscing Vanessa, the latter learning to reconsider, as a "professional observer," the judgments of her younger self.

Casting off chains of limitation is for Laurence a central theme, which her prairie works mostly address in connection with the empowerment of female characters. Her African stories, inspired by her years in Africa between 1950 and 1957, have been read as a thematic preparation for this, yet most of them were written later than her prairie stories. Collected in *The Tomorrow-Tamer* (1963), these stories — including "The Rain Child," "A Gourdful of Glory," "Godman's Master," and "The Tomorrow-Tamer" — are set against the African struggles for independence and revolve around the topic of freedom, its chances and challenges, from the political to the personal.

Rudy Wiebe (1934–) grew up in the prairie provinces Saskatchewan and Alberta, where he still lives. As a Mennonite he is a member of a religious minority; his parents had been persecuted on religious grounds and emigrated from the Soviet Union to Canada. Wiebe is mainly known as an author of novels in which he recounts the experiences of the Mennonites in the New World, but he also directs his attention towards other minorities such as the Indians, Inuit, and Métis, particularly in the Canadian West. Many of his works recreate landmarks and figures of Canadian history, yet his pronounced authorial voice takes sides with the minorities and reconsiders official historiography (see ch. 23, Kuester). From 1970 onwards Wiebe edited various short-story anthologies, and between 1974 and 1995 he published three collections of his own stories: *Where Is the Voice Coming From?* (1974), *The Angel of the Tar Sands and Other Stories* (1982), and *River of Stones: Fictions and Memories* (1995). The opening sentence of Wiebe's best-known and most complex story, "Where Is the Voice Coming From?," already points to one of his central themes, namely the difficulties of writing and rewriting history and the complexity of perspective and form in fictional representation, both aspects often being correlated. Although Wiebe's writing leaves behind the limitations of realistic storytelling from a narrative as well as thematic point of view (see, for example, "The Angel of the Tar Sands") and shares characteristics with a postmodernist style, Wiebe still believes in the meaningfulness of language and existence. He struggles for a better understanding of their complex nature in his highly experimental works, despite occasionally leaning a little too much towards the didactic and the moral. Stories such as "Where Is the Voice Coming From?" or "The Naming of Albert Johnson" (both based on historical facts) make it clear that Wiebe accords a larger truth value to fiction than to official historiography, not least because the former gives voice to indigenous, that is, marginal aspects in Canadian cultural history. Such epistemological problems trickle down into narrative form, especially in "Where Is the Voice Coming From?" In this metafictional story that exposes history and literature as artificial constructs, the narrator becomes ever more aware of this difficulty of story construction while trying to piece together the story of Almighty Voice, a young Cree Indian, who for his various crimes was tracked down and killed in the nineteenth century by the Canadian Mounted Police. The narrator realizes in the course of a disillusioning narrative process that the numerous but fragmentary historical "facts" are contradictory, and that a coherent picture of events, also taking into account the indigenous perspective, is thus quite impossible to achieve. Language itself also threatens to hinder rather than ensure access to truth. Almighty Voice's death cries remain incomprehensible to the storyteller, encoded as they are by intercultural difference — a "wordless cry" that nevertheless reaches beyond the narrative at hand, not least because of the homophony between "Cree" and the French "cri": "I say 'wordless cry' because that is the way it sounds to me. I would be more accurate if I had a reliable interpreter who would make a reliable interpretation. For I do not, of course, understand the Cree myself" (86–87).

Belonging to a younger generation of prairie writers, Guy Vanderhaeghe (1951–) is sometimes referred to next to Wiebe as a "man's writer" (for instance by Aritha van Herk), as he describes the Canadian prairie primarily from a male perspective. Vanderhaeghe received the Governor General's Award for fiction for his first book, *Man Descending: Selected Stories* (1982). Especially with this first collection, Vanderhaeghe developed the tradition of the Canadian prairie story. There followed *The Trouble with Heroes: And Other Stories* (1983) and *Things as They Are? Short Stories* (1992). These titles are programmatic in that Vanderhaeghe's male protagonists, mentally drained antiheroes, have become ill at ease with conventional male codes of behavior and face up to their weaknesses and their failure to come to terms with life (see especially "Man Descending" and "Cages"). Some of his stories deal with younger protagonists ("Reunion," "The Watcher," "Drummer").

One of the best-known male writers of the Canadian West coast is Jack Hodgins (1938–). Deeply rooted on Vancouver Island all his life, Hodgins has immortalized this western region of Canada in various novels, but also in his two short-story cycles, *Spit Delaney's Island* (1976) and *The Barclay Family Theatre* (1981). His works characteristically feature hopelessly entwined family relations (the latter volume portrays seven sisters and their extended families), eccentric characters, fantastic burlesque twists and turns, and a hyperbolic style. They convey a sense of place in connection with living on an island, the boundaries it creates and those it dissolves. Hodgins (1979–80) regards "the line between water and land as a kind of separation between one kind of reality and another." His stories also highlight the beauties of nature of the Canadian Pacific Northwest.

Alden Nowlan, who died at the age of fifty in 1983, and David Adams Richards (1950–) are known above all as poets and novelists of the Maritimes, but they also published short-story collections in the tradition of hard realism that delineate what Janice Kulyk Keefer has called an "anatomy of poverty" of the rural inhabitants of the Atlantic provinces (Nowlan, *Miracle at Indian River*, 1968, and *Will Ye Let the Mummers In?*, 1982; Richards, *Dancers at Night*, 1978). This also applies to the main representative of the short story of the Maritimes, Alistair MacLeod (1936–), who has also published an internationally successful and prize-winning novel, *No Great Mischief* (1999). His high reputation in Canada and beyond is mainly based on the sixteen stories that appeared in his two short-story collections, *The Lost Salt Gift of Blood* (1976) and *As Birds Bring Forth the Sun and Other Stories* (1986), as well as in his collected stories (*Island: The Collected Stories*, 2000). Even before his stories had been collected, some of his texts were selected for *Best American Stories*, which considers stories first published in American magazines during the year prior to selection ("The Boat," 1969, and "The Lost Salt Gift of Blood," 1975). Other excellent stories by MacLeod include "The Closing Down of Summer" (1976), "The Road to Rankin's Point" (1976), "As Birds Bring Forth the Sun" (1985), and "Vision" (1986). MacLeod's conventionally structured, highly polished stories describe in an elegiac, occasionally lyrical style his semi-autobiographical narrator's departures from and returns to Cape Breton (MacLeod himself splits his time between Windsor, Ontario and Cape Breton), the loss but also the maelstrom of local and family bonds. His first-person narratives render an almost palpable impression of the region, with their precise descriptions of ruggedly beautiful landscapes, the hardships of physical work, and the poor economic conditions in the Maritimes. His most frequently anthologized story is "The Boat," a vivid text that is representative of MacLeod's style and proves once again how so-called regional stories can still convey universal meanings.

## Female Writers between Compliance, Innovation, and Rebellion

The roughly equal representation of well-known female and male authors that characterizes Canadian literature also applies to the short story. Not only do the three leading writers of the Canadian short story happen to be female, but such a large number of female authors have written in the genre that this even gender distribution seems self-evident today. It is noteworthy, however, that this state of affairs has partly resulted in a gender-sensitive and gender-oriented writing style in Canadian short fiction and in Canadian literature in general.

Margaret Laurence is a pioneer of gender-conscious writing from a female perspective in Canada. Her works delineate the psychological, emotional, and intellectual development of female characters in a man's world, her short-story collection *A Bird in the House* (1970) being paradigmatic in this respect (Laurence in 1977: "I was dealing with a lot of the stuff Women's Lib is talking about right now. . . . My generation of women came to a lot of the same conclusions, but they did it in isolation: you weren't supposed to say those things out loud"). Marian Engel, Jane Rule, Audrey Thomas, and Carol Shields — all born within five to nine years after Laurence (who was born in 1926) — pursued these approaches in various forms. Despite the fact that Marian Engel (1933–1985) mainly thought of herself as a novelist (her best-known novel being *Bear*, 1976), she published two remarkable short-story collections, *Inside the Easter Egg* (1975) and *The Tattooed Woman* (1985). In these stories, most of whose protagonists are middle-aged women, Engel addresses typically "female" issues, such as the socialization of girls and women to define Self in relation to the Other, the consequences of aging, illness, and surgery for women, and the female body ("The Tattooed Woman," "The Confession Tree"). But Engel also finds ways of transcending such limitations through imagination and self-determined writing, whatever code might be chosen for it. A good example is the title story "The Tattooed Woman," first published in 1975. An unnamed forty-two-year-old woman, a housewife, hears her husband's confession about his affair with a twenty-one-year-old colleague. The shocked protagonist responds to this disclosure by carving signs, such as houses, trees, and stars, into her skin, and through this form of "writing" she fashions the body that has been "discarded" by her husband into a work of art. Ironically, this act makes her visible and confident again: "I am an artist, now, she thought, a true artist. My body is my canvas. . . . I am Somebody . . ., and at the same time beautiful and new." Towards the end of her life, Engel gradually shifted from a realistic writing style to a fantastic, surreal, postmodernist style, before her early death in 1985.

Jane Rule, born in the United States in 1931, settled in Vancouver in 1956 and in 1976 moved to Galiano Island, one of the Gulf Islands situated between the mainland and Vancouver Island. Early in her career she became a prominent mouthpiece of the gay and lesbian rights movement after the success of her debut novel *Desert of the Heart* (1964), which describes a homoerotic relationship between two women and was later made into a film (*Desert Hearts*, 1985). In her numerous novels and essays, Rule repeatedly addressed the topic of (mostly female) homoeroticism. Timothy Findley (1930–2002), who sometimes dealt with male homosexuality in his three collections of short stories and more often touched on the broader theme of gender in relation to masculinity, insisted that the significance of his work goes beyond his sexual orientation. The same applies to Rule (Rule: "The real problem is not homosexuality, but homophobia"). In an accessible, transparent, structurally conventional manner, her stories tackle unconventional gender issues in an undogmatic, open-minded, and compassionate way, although her earlier texts in particular do not ignore the difficulties of otherness. Examples of this are the collections *Theme for Diverse Instruments* (1975) and especially *Outlander: Short Stories and Essays* (1981), with its stories "Lillian" and "Outlander." A representative example of her even more relaxed later work is "Slogans" from *Inland Passage and Other Stories* (1985). In this story, three women take turns retelling their life stories to each other at their twenty-fifth anniversary class reunion. The long-time couple Nancy and Ann radiate supreme contentment, whereas Jessica, divorced and suffering from cancer, talks of nothing but broken marriages, her own and those of many former classmates. The title story "Inland Passage" is exemplary of the strong regional component of Rule's work, which makes use of the local color and picturesque landscapes of western Canada. Her better-known stories also include "The End of Summer," "Joy," "Brother and Sister," and "My Father's House," which deal with childhood and family issues as well as with the past and present lives — and love lives — of elderly female protagonists. Rule has retired from writing after a career of three decades (Rule in 1993: "I have written what I wanted").

Like Jane Rule, Audrey Thomas (1935–) and Carol Shields (1935–2003) were also born in the United States and later received Canadian citizenship (both in the 1970s). The work of the prolific Thomas, who once described herself as a "B.C. writer," has an especially strong regional component. After her move to Canada in 1958 she settled down in British Columbia, for the first eleven years in Vancouver, then, like Rule, on Galiano Island. Thomas has published as many short-story collections (seven) as novels and has contributed to the development of the Canadian short story over thirty years, both technically and thematically. Her first short-story collection *Ten Green Bottles*, published in 1967, three years ahead of Laurence's *A Bird in the House*, initiated the portrayal of uniquely female modes of experience in a radically new, authentic, and strongly autobiographical way in Canadian literature. For instance, her earliest story, "If One Green Bottle" (first published in *The Atlantic Monthly* in 1965), deals with miscarriage. Written using a consistent stream of consciousness technique, the story places Thomas among the formally flexible, experimental postmodernist writers of short fiction in Canada. Thomas foregrounds the level of discourse (for instance, by transcribing lexicon entries and using intertextual references) and self-referentially addresses the topic of writing itself, which she often describes as a liberating act, particularly for female characters. Her strong, playful interest in language sometimes informs her choice of titles, as in "Initram" ("Martini" spelled backwards). In "The Man with Clam Eyes" from *Goodbye Harold, Good Luck* (1986), the title is based on an unintentional misspelling ("clam" for "calm"), and the self-referential aspect of language and its conditioning of reality, which permeate the entire story, are also reflected in the plot. Like Laurence, Thomas spent some years in Africa, which functioned as a catalyst for her writing and left traces that went beyond her early work (see, for instance, "Xanadu," "Rapunzel," "Two in the Bush," and "Out in the Midday Sun"). Other stories focus on mother-daughter relationships and family bonds in general (see her collection *Real Mothers*, 1981), the critique of the relationship between the sexes, and the reappraisal of female gender roles (see her 1971 Vancouver story "Aquarius," in *Ladies & Escorts*). Thomas also confronts themes such as the liminal space between sanity and madness or, in more general terms, between dreams and reality.

Carol Shields, who died in 2003, had a remarkable writing career, begun in her forties after having raised five children. Particularly well-known are her prize-winning novels *Swann: A Mystery* (1987) and *The Stone Diaries* (1993). But it is particularly in her short-story collections *Various Miracles* (1985), *The Orange Fish* (1989), and *Dressing Up for the Carnival* (2000) that Shields proves herself to be not only a realist-modernist writer, but one also open to postmodernist experimentation, with the publication of her first short-story collection marking a turning point in her oeuvre. The focus on the female experience of a home environment, for which she was initially reproached by male critics, was gradually reevaluated and eventually celebrated as her trademark (this artistic creed of hers is spelled out particularly clearly in her late story "Soup du Jour"). Her writing may indeed record exceptional, even miraculous aspects of everyday life, but the author never looks away from the greater or lesser tragedies of human existence. Her characters belong to the upper middle class. As a result of her long career as a university lecturer and her marriage to a Canadian professor, she often deals with the academic world in an ironic or even parodic tone, for example, in "The Metaphor Is Dead — Pass It On" or "Mrs. Turner Cutting the Grass" (both from *Various Miracles*). The latter story sets the eventful life of a simple woman in the outskirts of Winnipeg against episodes from the life of an unappealing professor at a Massachusetts college. Shields's works often display a joyful, optimistic attitude. Examples of this are stories such as "Pardon" (which hyperrealistically and humorously transforms personal relations into gestures of apology), "Various Miracles," and "Absence." Placing great emphasis on family in her personal life, Shields's stories often deal with family issues, such as marriage, mother-daughter relationships, and love, as well as the experience of aging (for example, in "The Orange Fish," "Milk Bread Beer Ice," "Love so Fleeting, Love so Fine," "Flitting Behaviour," and "Chemistry"). The satirical take on academic life in stories like "Our Men and Women," "Ilk," and "A Scarf" proves nevertheless that Shields is capable of reaching outside her familiar field of domestic fiction and addressing larger social issues.

Among the generation of younger female writers, born in the 1940s and 1950s, are Sandra Birdsell, Isabel Huggan, Katherine Govier, and Diane Schoemperlen. Birdsell (1942–) has resided in Manitoba and Saskatchewan all her life, and the prairie environment and milieu of these provinces have had an impact on the settings and choice of characters in her works (various immigrant groups, but also Mennonites and Métis). Birdsell's first two short-story collections, *Night Travellers* (1982) and *Ladies of the House* (1984), were republished in one volume under the title *Agassiz Stories* in 1987. If slightly misleading, the subtitle of the American edition, *A Novel in Stories*, rightfully points to the cyclical nature of Birdsell's short fiction. Agassiz is the name of a fictional place in Manitoba, which serves as a setting for the saga of the Lafreniere clan (with a Métis father and a Mennonite mother) over three generations, with an emphasis on its female family members. The partly self-inflicted marginality and dependence of women as well as the situation of the working-class and ethnic minorities prompt Birdsell to describe larger structures of exclusion, isolation, repression, and discrimination; the possibility of change is regarded largely pessimistically in these texts, particularly in connection with the plight of women. Her better-known stories include "Flowers for Weddings and Funerals," "Keepsakes," "Judgment," and "Night Travellers" (all from the eponymous collections), as well as "The Man from Mars" (from her fourth collection, *The Two-Headed Calf*, 1997).

## Multicultural Diversity and the Short Story

The contemporary Canadian short story owes its diversity in part to its numerous multicultural voices. The many contributions to the genre from writers of different ethnic backgrounds can only be hinted at here.

The most important representatives of Native short fiction are Thomas King (1943–), with two short-story collections (see, for instance, his stories "Borders," "One Good Story, That One"), and Lee Maracle (1950–), with one collection (see her stories "Yin Chin," "Bertha"). The best-known and most prolific representative of Caribbean-Canadian literature is Barbados native Austin Clarke (1934–), who published seven collections of short stories between 1965 and 2003 (see, for instance, *Choosing His Coffin: The Best Stories of Austin Clarke*, 2003). Dionne Brand (1953–; *Sans Souci and Other Stories*, 1988, see especially "Sans Souci," "Photograph") and Neil Bissoondath (1955–; *Digging Up the Mountains*, 1986; *On the Eve of Uncertain Tomorrows*, 1990) are writers from Trinidad. The foremost proponent of the Asian-Canadian short story is Rohinton Mistry, born in Bombay in 1952, who mostly writes about his former home country India, for example, in his 1987 collection *Tales from Firozsha Baag* (see "Condolence Visit" and "Swimming Lessons").

In Canada, not only the so-called ethnic minority writers, but also writers with European backgrounds often deal with problems of migration and diaspora, the history and culture of their native countries, and intercultural themes of immigration and assimilation in multicultural Canada. A representative of Icelandic-Canadian literature is Kristjana Gunnars (1948–), who emigrated from Iceland in 1968 (*The Axe's Edge*, 1983, and *The Guest House and Other Stories*, 1992). Another writer with an Icelandic background, with three short-story collections to his credit, is Canadian-born W. D. Valgardson (1939–), whose work was shaped by his growing up in Icelandic enclaves in Canada (see his stories "Bloodflowers" and "A Matter of Balance"). Besides radio and television scripts, Valgardson published six short-story collections between *Bloodflowers: Ten Stories* (1973) and *The Divorced Kids Club: And Other Stories* (2002). The versatile Janice Kulyk Keefer (1953–), also active in the field of literary criticism as a professor at the University of Guelph, reveals a strong awareness of her Ukrainian cultural background in her work, which on a literary level reflects her theoretical concept of "transculturalism." Keefer has published three short-story collections (*The Paris-Napoli Express*, 1986; *Transfigurations*, 1987; and *Travelling Ladies*, 1990).

# The Contemporary English-Canadian Short Story and the Challenges of Modernism, Realism, Postmodernism, and Neorealism

Taking a panoramic view of the Canadian short story since the 1960s, several things stand out: first, the diversity and vitality of the genre, partly deriving from the fact that almost all major writers in the fascinating "postnational" literature that is Canadian literature have made contributions to the short story; second, the relative high number of short-story cycles in Canada, a tendency that brings this genre closer to the novel without relinquishing the unity of the individual short story — above-mentioned works by Munro, Gallant, Laurence, Hodgins, Hood, Birdsell, Clarke, Smith, Mitchell, and Mistry, as well as Mordecai Richler (*The Street*, 1969) testify to this phenomenon; and finally, the primacy of the modernist-realist tradition of storytelling in the English-Canadian short story.

Having established themselves as short-story writers, some authors — such as the aforementioned Smith, Thomas, Wiebe, and Engel, as well as some who have not been dealt with here, such as Leon Rooke, George Bowering, Matt Cohen, and Dave Godfrey — have turned away from or outgrown the genre conventions of the realist-modernist short story, redirecting the genre onto an antirealist, surreal, metafictional, postmodernist path (although all of them continued to produce stories in the realist-modernist vein — see Bowering's "Apples" or Matt Cohen's "Keeping Fit" — and never fully abandoned this writing style). The most prolific and most anthologized among these authors is Leon Rooke (1934–), who has published eleven short-story collections and three volumes of selected stories (most recently *Painting the Dog: The Best Stories of Leon Rooke*, 2001, including "The Woman Who Talked to Horses," "Wintering in Victoria," and "Art"). George Bowering (1935–), now retired literature professor at Simon Fraser University in Burnaby, British Columbia, and editor of postmodernist stories as well as of critical articles, has published four short-story collections. Best known is his programmatic "A Short Story," a metafictional text that emphasizes the artificiality of writing by giving the individual subsections generic, self-referential titles such as "Setting," "Characters," and "Point of View." Matt Cohen (see his story "The Sins of Tomas Benares") had published six short-story collections by the time he died in 1999, as well as a volume of collected stories and *Lives of the Mind: Selected Stories* (1994). It was only at the peak of postmodernism in the 1960s and 1970s that Dave Godfrey (1938–) made his contribution to fiction in two short-story collections, among them *Death Goes Better with Coca-Cola* (1968; see his stories "River Two Blind Jacks" and "A New Year's Morning on Bloor Street").

Since the 1980s another writing style has developed in the short story alongside the more prominent modernist-realist tradition, one enriched with hyperrealist, surreal elements, indebted to both realist and postmodernist conventions and fully aware of this double heritage. The vast oeuvre of such authors as Atwood or Gallant displays realist, but also metafictional, postmodernist characteristics in one and the same text, to such an extent that the new "neorealist" variety of the contemporary Canadian short story suggests new labels such as "crossover fiction" (David Lodge). Time will tell whether new, younger talents in short-story writing such as Madeleine Thien (1974–; one collection of short stories to date), Annabel Lyon (1971–; one collection), or Caroline Adderson (1963–; two collections) will eventually make it into the canon of English-Canadian short-story writing. In any case, their stories, too, may serve to demonstrate the impressive development and range of the Canadian short story in the twentieth and early twenty-first century, particularly since the 1960s.

# 25: English-Canadian Poetry from 1967 to the Present

*Nicholas Bradley (University of Victoria)*

THE CENTENNIAL ANNIVERSARY OF Confederation in 1967 serves as a convenient historical event from which to date the beginnings of contemporary English-Canadian poetry. However, the decades-long careers of many notable poets, as well as the sheer quantity and variety of Canadian poetry of the last forty years, suggest that marking a clear division between contemporary poetry and the poetry of the mid-twentieth century is still in many ways an impossible task. Two decades before the centenary, in 1947, the establishment of modern poetry in Canada was signaled by the publication of John Sutherland's *Other Canadians: An Anthology of the New Poetry in Canada 1940–46* and, symbolically, by the death of Duncan Campbell Scott (1862–1947). Irving Layton (1912–2006) — one of the poets in the Montreal circle associated with Sutherland's *First Statement* (1942–1945), a galvanizing journal — published his first book, *Here and Now: Poems*, in 1945. *Periods of the Moon*, the volume he published in 1967, was, astonishingly, his nineteenth. In the centennial year Layton was undeniably one of the leading Canadian poets — *A Red Carpet for the Sun* (1959) alone assured him that position. And in the decades after 1967, Layton's output was still prodigious: By the time of his death in 2006, he had published a further thirty new volumes or selections. To consider him solely as a poet of the modernist moment is therefore to overlook his continuing presence long after his debut as a poet.

Much the same can be said for certain poets who were Layton's contemporaries in Montreal, the epicenter of Canadian poetry in the 1940s. P. K. Page (1916–) published her first book, *As Ten, As Twenty*, in 1946, and her third collection, *Cry Ararat!* (1967), coincided with the centennial. Yet her most recent volume, the autobiographical *Hand Luggage*, was published in 2006. Phyllis Webb (1927–) followed her fourth book, the celebrated *Naked Poems* (1965), with several collections, among them *Wilson's Bowl* (1980) and *Sunday Water* (1982), which newly focused on landscapes of the West coast. Miriam Waddington (1917–2004) and Louis Dudek (1918–2001) also wrote well into the later decades of the twentieth century. Many poets from beyond the Montreal scene — such as Earle Birney, Dorothy Livesay, Wilfrid Watson, George Johnston, and Raymond

Souster — have likewise had long, productive careers which extend from the 1940s and 1950s into the 1980s and 1990s, careers that therefore overlap those of poets born considerably later. Decades after her first book, *Green Pitcher* (1928), Dorothy Livesay (1909–1996) continued to publish new volumes of poetry, including the frank *Unquiet Bed* (1967), *Plainsongs* (1969), and *Phases of Love* (1983). Jay Macpherson's (1931–) *Welcoming Disaster* (1974) extends the mythopoeic style of *The Boatman* (1957). And Birney (1904–1995) wrote "David," the poem on which his reputation is founded, in 1940, thus at around the same time when Margaret Atwood (1939–) and Michael Ondaatje (1943–) were born, to name two of the most accomplished poets of their generation. Ken Babstock, who is currently developing a reputation as a writer of considerable talent, was born sixty-six years after Birney, who by then was writing concrete poems that were very different from his works of the 1940s and 1950s.

Certain poets who made their debuts in the 1960s also had, or have had, long careers that defy strict categorization, as in the cases of Al Purdy, Margaret Avison, and Atwood (although Purdy began his career then only in a figurative sense, having finally discovered his characteristic style and abandoning the derivative mode of his early volumes). Purdy's (1918–2000) *Poems for All the Annettes* (1962) and *The Cariboo Horses* (1965) were succeeded by important and varied collections until his death in 2000. In 1960 Avison (1918–2007) published *Winter Sun*, which received the Governor General's Award. But her later collections, including *Not Yet but Still* (1997) and *Concrete and Wild Carrot* (2002), indicate that her career-making first books are parts of a larger body of work, not the sum thereof, and suggest that to think of Avison only as a poet of the 1960s is to circumscribe her achievement. *Winter Sun* demonstrated Avison's spiritual concerns and her enthusiasm for the elaborate, witty conceits of the Metaphysical poets, but, after her conversion to Christianity in 1963, her poetry assumed an overtly devotional character. *The Dumbfounding* (1966), *sunblue* (1978), and *No Time* (1989) all respond directly, for example, to biblical passages. Her later volumes exhibit more open forms, a further developed sense of humor (Avison is especially fond of puns), and an ecologically sensitive vision. Not least, Atwood's first book, *Double Persephone*, appeared in 1961 and her next collection, *The Circle Game* (1966), won the Governor General's Award; her most recent collection, *The Door*, was published in 2007.

Because Canadian poetry since 1967 has assumed a tremendous variety of forms, generalizations about the writing of the time prove difficult. Poets have held wildly divergent notions of what constitutes poetry, of what it aspires to achieve, of what traditions it should follow (and from which it should depart), and of what its relation to the nation should be. In short, both terms in the designation "Canadian poetry" have been the subject of considerable debate. Certain general claims, however, can be made about the poetry of the last four decades. One of the distinguishing characteristics of English-Canadian poetry since the 1960s is, for instance, the remarkable number of books published. This observation echoes the remarks of various Canadian critics about the writing of their day: In the *Literary History of Canada* (1965), edited by Carl F. Klinck, Munro Beattie wrote that in the 1950s "this country was, by per capita estimate, as well supplied with proficient poets as any country in the world" (785). He further remarked that between 1948 and 1960 there appeared "a greater number of first books by Canadian poets of talent than at any other period in our literary history" (785). In 1973 Peter Stevens wrote, along the same lines, that "the rate of publication of poetry books gained momentum in the 1960s, increasing to such an extent in the late sixties and early seventies that it is not possible to mention in this survey all the books that were published in our period" (245). In the next decade Dennis Lee (1939–) raised the same issue in his introduction to *The New Canadian Poets* (1985), an anthology of writers who published their first books between 1970 and 1985: "Throughout the sixties there had been a gradual but steady escalation in poetic debuts" (xvii). But after 1970, Lee continued, there was a veritable avalanche of books by new poets: "No one can keep accurate count any longer, but one conservative estimate is that from seven hundred to a thousand poets started publishing in book form between 1970 and 1985." Lee predicted that this surge might eventually be regarded "as a temporary anomaly" (l), but the quantity of books published since 1985 and the number of authors writing today indicate that Canadian poetry remains a remarkably large field. Certainly it is no more possible in 2008 than it was in the 1970s or 1980s to survey every published book of poetry; an article in *The Globe and Mail* in 2007 noted that "an estimated 80 volumes of Canadian poetry are set to be published throughout the fall."

Such fruitfulness, coupled with the aesthetic and thematic diversity of Canadian poetry, means that any single narrative account of the contemporary period — the end of the modernist experiment and the rise of postmodernism, for example — would risk neglecting the many poetic strains that diverge from whatever is construed as the principal movement. An overview of a select number of representative figures would, similarly, overstate the extent to which there is critical consensus about which poets are representative (or best, if the criticism is explicitly evaluative). And to describe a sequence of poets in terms of influence and poetic inheritance would fail to acknowledge that some of the most extraordinary poets appear to stand outside any strictly Canadian tradition. Avison and Ondaatje, for example, are highly idiosyncratic figures whose works are not easily placed in a specifically Canadian line in the way that the plainspokenness of Purdy, Alden Nowlan, John Newlove, and Don McKay marks a clear tradition. Canadian writers do not, of course, only read other Canadian writers, so a comprehensive analysis of influence would have to contend with Purdy's long fascination with D. H. Lawrence, with Avison's links to Denise Levertov, with allusions to Wallace Stevens in poems by Ondaatje and Robert Bringhurst, with McKay's admiration of Dylan Thomas and Tomas Tranströmer, with the ambivalence that George Elliott Clarke displays towards the poetry of Ezra Pound, and so on. Despite these qualifications, however, several characteristics of contemporary Canadian poetry can be identified that themselves suggest the degree to which the field is marked by a multiplicity of styles, themes, influences, aesthetic theories, modes of identity, and political stances. In addition, despite the complexities of Canadian poetry as a whole, certain individual poets have set themselves apart by virtue of what Helen Vendler terms a "compelling aesthetic signature."

## Centennial Poetry and Beyond

In certain ways, contemporary Canada began in the years around the centenary, when many of the country's defining social and cultural institutions were established. The Trans-Canada Highway was opened in 1962, national Medicare legislation was passed in 1966, Radio-Québec was created in 1968, the Official Languages Act was passed in 1969, and a federal ministry for multiculturalism was introduced in 1972. Pierre Trudeau became prime minister in 1968 and remained in office, with a brief interruption, until 1984. Following the recommendation of the Massey Report (1951) of the Royal Commission on National Development in the Arts, Letters and Sciences, the Canada Council was created in 1957. The new National Library opened in 1967. And during this time, small literary presses flourished. Two important Toronto-based publishing houses were founded, Coach House Press in 1965 by Stan Bevington and the House of Anansi Press in 1967 by Dave Godfrey and Dennis Lee.

These events, and the centenary itself, at times found themselves mentioned in poems. Earle Birney's "The Mammoth Corridors" (1965) responded directly to the new highway, for example, incorporating phrases from a tourist guide into a narrative account of the drive east from Vancouver. But not all poets saw fit to celebrate the country and its culture (nor did Birney, for that matter). Layton was decidedly less than sanguine about the country's anniversary in his "Confederation Ode," one of the poems in *Periods of the Moon*. "Like an old, nervous and eager cow / my country / is being led up to the bull / of history," he wrote, using the blunt metaphor to convey his sense of Canada's dim prospects. In his foreword to the collection, Layton also attacked the state of Canadian poetry, drawing a distinction between "authentic poetry" and the fad for poetry in the Counter Culture of the 1960s. He dismissed various travesties of true verse and demanded "not a tired anecdote that can just as well be said in prose — indeed much better. Not rant or rhetoric or second-hand sociologizing. Not the stillborn child of the overwrought academic. Not empty words in which there is no risk, no personal involvement. A poem, sweet reader, a poem. The miraculous fusion of sound and sense" (12). The "personal involvement" in Layton's own poetry of the time emerged in his responses to the Holocaust — evident in *Periods of the Moon, The Shattered Plinths* (1968), and *The Whole Bloody Bird* (1969) — and to the break-up of his marriage, the subject of *The Gucci Bag* (1983).

Lee, too, was reluctant to "paint the native maple," as F. R. Scott (1899–1985) had written satirically in "The Canadian Authors Meet" (1927). Lee's *Civil Elegies* (1968; a heavily revised version was published in 1972) presents a gloomy view of the state of the nation. The long poem, subtitled *Pro patria,* has as epigraph quotations from George Grant — whose *Lament for a Nation* (1965) shaped the cultural nationalism of Lee, Atwood, and Purdy — and Saraha, a Buddhist poet who flourished most probably at the end of the first millennium. Lee proposed that Canada was "a nation of / losers and quislings" who were complicit with American imperialism and unwilling to create a polity that reflected the particular historical, cultural, and geographic conditions of Canada. Its extended, prosy lines and the reflexive, tortuous nature of its argument make *Civil Elegies* at once exhortatory and self-castigating. Lee conceived of the poem as a corrective to political rhetoric. Part invective, part confession, *Civil Elegies* is, in many respects, a singular entity in contemporary Canadian poetry. It does, however, establish many of the concerns and techniques that Lee would pursue in later works, including *The Death of Harold Ladoo* (1976), another lament both personal and civic. Lee's *UN* (2003) and *Yesno* (2007) combine ecological concerns — hinted at in *Civil Elegies* — with a radically deconstructive approach to the conventions of the lyric poem.

Atwood's poetry of the era typically concerns constraints imposed on people, especially women, whether by their environment, by social norms, or by interpersonal relationships. *Power Politics* (1971), for example, begins with a violent image, at once sexually suggestive and viscerally grotesque, of the relationship between two people — "you fit into me / like a hook into an eye // a fish hook / an open eye" — and proceeds to examine ways in which power permeates and disrupts romance. "If I love you," Atwood's speaker asks, "is that a fact or a weapon?" The infamous image of the drowned speaker in "This Is a Photograph of Me," from *The Circle Game*, is echoed in "Tricks with Mirrors" (1974), in which the speaker first claims that "Mirrors / are the perfect lovers," then concludes that "Perhaps I am not a mirror. / Perhaps I am a pool." Atwood couples a laconic description of the confinement of an unhappy relationship with the hint of a threat in the poem's last line, "Think about pools." The feminist poems in Atwood's books of the 1970s, which also include *You Are Happy* (1974) — the title is typically ironic — and *Two-Headed Poems* (1978), employ figures of violence, victimization, and emptiness, yet are characterized by a caustic sense of humor. Feminist concerns about identity and agency were also voiced in the poetry of, for example, Pat Lowther (1935–1975) — as in *Milk Stone* (1974) and *A Stone Diary* (posthumous, 1977) — and of Gwendolyn MacEwen (1941–1987) — as in *The Shadow-Maker* (1969) and *Armies of the Moon* (1972). In *The T. E. Lawrence Poems* (1982), MacEwen's psychologically complex, iconographic poems suggest a connection between Lawrence and the poet herself; some critics have drawn parallels between MacEwen's use of the historical Lawrence and Atwood's interest in Canadian colonial history.

Atwood's early poetry commonly juxtaposed past and present. In "Progressive Insanities of a Pioneer," one of the poems in *The Animals in That Country* (1968), the speaker characterizes the oppressive Canadian landscape as "not order / but the absence / of order." In the colonial world that the poem describes, the very "idea of an animal" is terrifying. "Things" in this counter-Edenic realm "refused to name themselves; refused / to let him," the pioneer, "name them." The end of the poem foretells disintegration, the plight of the tormented pioneer and that of the planet itself linked by the image of decay. Atwood's *Journals of Susanna Moodie* (1970) draws on the historical Moodie's *Roughing It in the Bush* (1852), an account of colonial life in Upper Canada, but posits strong connections between that world and the poet's. At the end of the sequence, Moodie emerges from the wilderness of the nineteenth century and appears on a Toronto city bus to utter a warning to the citizens of the present time: "your place is empty." The alienation that Atwood describes in both books applies, Moodie suggests, to the contemporary era as much as to the historical past. The potent critique that Atwood registered had a different target from Lee's in *Civil Elegies*, but it shared Lee's emphasis on the relation of people to their environment. Atwood's literary criticism, principally in the popular and controversial *Survival* (1972; see ch. 22, Rosenthal), similarly asserts a defining connection between place and literature. In later collections, such as *Two-Headed Poems* (1978) and *Interlunar* (1984), Atwood revealed a developing interest in familial relations, although the themes and figures of her earlier works remain prominent.

Atwood has frequently been celebrated as an especially fine poet, but, like many Canadian writers, she has found a much wider audience for her novels (see ch. 23, Kuester). Her first novels — *The Edible Woman* (1969), *Surfacing* (1972), *Lady Oracle* (1976) — were published during the same period as several of her major collections of poetry, a period that culminated in her first *Selected Poems* (1976). Although she continued to publish poetry in the 1970s and early 1980s, her major novels of the 1980s and 1990s — *The Handmaid's Tale* (1985), *Cat's Eye* (1988), *The Robber Bride* (1993), *Alias Grace* (1996) — ensured that popular and critical attention was directed largely (although not exclusively) towards her fiction. Other Canadian poets, including Ondaatje, have also written novels. They are certainly not the first writers, in Canada or elsewhere, to demonstrate proficiency in different genres, but the number of Canadian poets who are also novelists hints at the importance of narrative in contemporary Canadian poetry. In Atwood's case, the thematic continuities in her poetry and prose are especially noteworthy.

In *North of Summer: Poems from Baffin Island* (1967) Al Purdy presented a vision of the country's Far North. The book, which also reproduced a selection of A. Y. Jackson's paintings of Arctic landscapes, was the product of a Canada Council-funded trip that Purdy made to Baffin Island and the Kikastan Islands in the Northwest Territories. The documentary quality of the poems is evident in the opening lines of the book's second poem, "The Turning Point," which establishes the poems' origin in the poet's vivid experience of the Arctic:

> Over northern Canada
> daylight ahead and growing
> behind only darkness
> at 2.30 in the morning
> while the D.C. 4's engines drone

In his "Postscript" Purdy explained to the reader that the poems "seem to me like a set of binoculars thru which you can view the Arctic from several thousand miles away" (83) and that he intended to provide his "own particular kind of optic glass" (84). But as poems such as "Trees at the Arctic Circle" and "The Country of the Young" show, Purdy was not simply recording his observations. He was, instead, writing poems that, at their best, demonstrate an admirable subtlety in revealing the ways in which an environment can confound the observer's expectations. In "Trees at the Arctic Circle" the speaker first mocks the ground willows (*"Salix Cordifolia"*) that he sees "grovelling among the lichens," then comes to admire their persistence:

> And you know it occurs to me
> about 2 feet under
> those roots must touch permafrost
> ice that remains ice forever
> and they use it for their nourishment
> use death to remain alive

The speaker then rebukes himself and ultimately celebrates the trees:

I have been stupid in a poem
I will not alter the poem
but let the stupidity remain permanent
as the trees are
in a poem
the dwarf trees of Baffin Island

The method of *North of Summer* established a template for much of Purdy's later writing, with his numerous trips providing the raw material out of which he would fashion his poems. *Birdwatching at the Equator* (1982), for example, wrestles with an existential dread occasioned by Purdy's observation of the creatures and landscapes of the Galápagos Islands. Conversely, *In Search of Owen Roblin* (1974) firmly establishes the importance of Roblin Lake and Ameliasburg, Ontario, to Purdy's sense of place. Despite his extensive travels, his attachment to "The Country North of Belleville" (the title of a poem in *The Cariboo Horses*) and to Prince Edward County suggests that he was a profoundly regional poet. Like Layton, Purdy was prolific in his later years. *Beyond Remembering: The Collected Poems of Al Purdy* (2000), published posthumously, assembled the poems that Purdy deemed most important and worth preserving — and was the last of nearly thirty books published since *North of Summer*.

Laytonian in spirit if not in output, Leonard Cohen (1934–), another poet from the Montreal scene, released his first album, *Songs of Leonard Cohen*, at the end of 1967 and thus concluded the phase of his career in which he was considered foremost a writer. Having established himself as a poet in the 1950s and 1960s, Cohen achieved phenomenal popular success as a singer and songwriter in the 1970s (*Songs of Love and Hate*, 1971), 1980s (*Various Positions*, 1984; *I'm Your Man*, 1988), and 1990s (*The Future*, 1992). Cohen is undoubtedly one of the most famous Canadian poets, although his popular reputation rests on his music and his persona rather than on his poems. *The Energy of Slaves* (1972), *Book of Mercy* (1984), *Stranger Music* (1993), and *Book of Longing* (2006) are evidence of a commitment to poetry in printed form; these books largely take up the themes and forms of his early works.

In addition to significant collections by Layton, Lee, Atwood, and Purdy, two important anthologies were published around the time of the centennial. Each celebrated the achievement of Canadian poetry and made bold claims for its modernity. In 1966 Contact Press — a small publishing house founded in 1952 by Souster, Dudek, and Layton — issued *New Wave Canada: The New Explosion in Canadian Poetry*, which gathered poems by seventeen young writers, most of them associated with *Tish* (1961–1969), the Black Mountain-influenced magazine from Vancouver, or with Coach House Press. Souster (1921–), the volume's editor, wrote in his preface, with no small measure of bravura, "that within the covers of this anthology is the most exciting, germinative poetry written by young Canadians in the last hundred years of this country's literary history" (vii). Anticipating Canada's imminent anniversary, he announced that "this is Canadian poetry after one hundred years of our history, at last vigorous and very sure of where it is going" (ibid.). *New Wave Canada*, as Souster characterized it, both looked to the future and marked a moment of achievement in Canadian poetry, the culmination of the developments of Canadian modernists such as W. W. E. Ross (1894–1966), "the first modern Canadian poet" (iii), to whom the book was dedicated. Among the poets in *New Wave Canada* were Daphne Marlatt (1942–; then known as Daphne Buckle), who coedited *Tish* from 1963 to 1965; Fred Wah (1939–), an associate editor of *Tish*; and bpNichol (1944–1988), who also moved in *Tish* circles and who would publish the first two books of *The Martyrology*, his life-long, endlessly capacious poem, with Coach House in 1972. Marlatt and Wah published numerous works in later years. Marlatt's *Vancouver Poems* (1972) and *Steveston* (1974) encompass ecological and civic histories; Wah's *Breathin' My Name with a Sigh* (1981) and *Waiting for Saskatchewan* (1985) link geography and ethnicity. Marlatt's and Wah's bodies of work connect the formal experimentation of the early 1960s to the avant-garde practices of the 1970s and beyond.

New Wave Canada also contained poems by Ondaatje, whose works appeared as well in *Modern Canadian Verse in English and French* (1967), an anthology edited by A. J. M. Smith (1902–1980), who was, with Ross, unquestionably one of the most influential Canadian modernists. The poets included ranged from E. J. Pratt (1882–1964) to Ondaatje; among the other young poets were George Bowering (1935–), Newlove (1938–2003), and Atwood. In his preface Smith wrote that "modern Canadian poetry . . . has not left nationalism behind but has transcended it. It has developed a sensibility and a language that are international but not rootless — a biculturalism that . . . joins Canada to the world" (xviii). Recent aesthetic developments, Smith asserted, had rescued Canadian poetry from belatedness and assured it a place in contemporary literature: "Canadian poetry in the fifties and sixties has become more like modern poetry in the United States, England, and France, and less like Canadian poetry in the nineteenth century" (ibid.). By placing the works of the younger writers alongside those of Pratt, Ross, and F. R. Scott, Smith suggested that then-contemporary Canadian poetry was closely related to works of the 1920s, 1930s, and 1940s — as represented, for instance, by Pratt's *Newfoundland Verse* (1923) and *The Titanic* (1935), and Scott's *New Provinces* anthology (1936).

Despite their contrasting emphases on innovation and continuity, the two anthologies appeared to agree on the importance of Michael Ondaatje, the youngest of those heralded as Canada's new poets. *New Wave Canada* included thirteen of his poems, of which ten would appear in his first collection, *The Dainty Monsters* (1967). Six of these in turn were preserved in the selection *There's a Trick with a Knife I'm Learning to Do* (1979). Poems such as "Henri Rousseau and Friends" and "A House Divided" demonstrated that Ondaatje, although still in his early twenties, was already an unusually accomplished poet. As Sam Solecki wrote, *The Dainty Monsters* revealed "a technically adroit new voice with a supple range, an often violent verbal expressiveness, and a fully realized imaginative world" (25). Ondaatje's poetry was also included in *Poets of Contemporary Canada* (1972), an anthology edited by Eli Mandel (1922–1992), along with poems by Purdy, Milton Acorn, Joe Rosenblatt, Leonard Cohen, Bowering, Newlove, Atwood, bill bissett, and MacEwen. Ondaatje's later books provide ample confirmation of the promise of his poetic debut. In *Secular Love* (1984) he adapted the surrealistic language of his early works to the confessional mode of Anne Sexton and, especially, Robert Lowell, whose *For Lizzie and Harriet* and *The Dolphin* (both 1973) described the collapse of a marriage, as *Secular Love* charted the failures of Ondaatje's own marriage. In *Handwriting* (1998) Ondaatje employed a more lyrical style and wrote primarily about his family and his Sri Lankan heritage. The distinctiveness of his voice provides one way of aligning him with Layton, Purdy, and Atwood, each of whom made a characteristic speaking voice central to their poems: Layton's frank and belligerent, yet capable of great sensitivity; Purdy's by design that of a Canadian Everyman, albeit an acutely perceptive one; Atwood's cool and detached. And although Ondaatje does not have obvious imitators, his affiliations with experimental poets in the 1970s offer a means of measuring his influence, much as Purdy's influence can be detected in the works of the poets he included in two anthologies, *Storm Warning* (1971) and *Storm Warning 2* (1976), and in the collections he edited for Acorn (1923–1986; *I've Tasted My Blood*, 1969, and *Dig Up My Heart*, 1983) and in those of Andrew Suknaski (1942–; *Wood Mountain Poems*, 1976).

# Experimental Forms

Ondaatje's poetic career coincides with two major developments in Canadian poetry since the late 1960s: The first was a fascination with extended, nonlyric, multigeneric forms, as represented by, for instance, Ondaatje's *The Collected Works of Billy the Kid* (1970). The second development, discussed at greater length below, was a pronounced interest in questions of origin, ethnicity, immigration, citizenship, and place, as exemplified by Ondaatje's *Handwriting* and poems such as "The Cinnamon Peeler" (1982). The powerful allure of the American projectivist poets — Charles Olson, Robert Creeley, Robert Duncan, Denise Levertov — on the young Vancouver writers associated with *Tish* in the early 1960s continued to exert a shaping force on Canadian poetry in the 1970s and beyond, especially as Bowering, Frank Davey, Marlatt, and Wah became established as writers and critics. Postmodern poetry in Canada also drew on the examples of the disjunctive poetics associated with the American journals *This* and *L=A=N=G=U=A=G=E* and with Ron Silliman's anthology *In the American Tree* (1986). Steve McCaffery (1947–) collaborated with Silliman, Charles Bernstein, and other American poets, as well as with Nichol.

The *Collected Works of Billy the Kid*, subtitled *Left Handed Poems*, is a nonpareil account of the life of Henry McCarty, alias Billy the Kid, the American outlaw of the nineteenth-century Wild West. As with many of Ondaatje's works, there is little that is identifiably or stereotypically Canadian about *Billy the Kid*. Formally, however, the book — which juxtaposes lyric poetry with photographs, narrative prose, historical accounts (often manipulated), and biographical details — links Ondaatje to the poets whose long poems he assembled in *The Long Poem Anthology* (1979): Robin Blaser, Roy Kiyooka, Robert Kroetsch, Stuart MacKinnon, Marlatt, McKay, Davey, Bowering, and Nichol. In his introduction Ondaatje claimed that "our best poetry . . . is involved with process and perspective" (11), as opposed to the self-expression and formal emphasis on coherence that one might associate with lyric convention. Kiyooka's (1926–1994) long poems, such as *The Fontainebleau Dream Machine* (1977) and *Pear Tree Pomes* (1987), suggest correspondences between poetry and painting — Kiyooka was an accomplished abstract expressionist. His *Wheels* (1969–1985) also has an overtly political dimension, referring specifically to the relocation of Japanese Canadians during the Second World War. In the poem, based on his travels in Japan in 1969, Kiyooka remarks sardonically that "i never saw the 'yellow peril' in myself." The distinction between life and art in Kiyooka's poem is blurred, as it is for many long poems in this mode.

The serial poem, in Robert Kroetsch's (1927–) conception, could continue even beyond a single poet's life, as the author's note in *Seed Catalogue* (1977) suggests with playful humor: "'Seed Catalogue' and 'How I Joined the Seal Herd' are Parts 2 and 3 of a continuing poem, *Field Notes* . . . Readers are invited to compose further sections" (6). The desire to compose a "poem as long as a life" and "as big as a continent" — to take two phrases from Kroetsch's statement of poetics in *The Long Poem Anthology* — led Kroetsch and other poets to eschew finite notions of form, theme, duration, and even authorship. Some of Kroetsch's poetry is obviously documentary. The sequence of poems called *Advice to My Friends* (1985), for instance, mentions by name other poets (including Wah, Ondaatje, Mandel, Nichol, and Bowering) as well as friends and family members. The poems do not attempt to disguise the biographical events on which they are based, even if the reader may reasonably assume that some transformation always occurs when a lived experience is rendered into a poem. *The Ledger* (1975), *Stone Hammer Poems* (1975), and *Seed Catalogue* (1977) all concern Kroetsch's family history, his youth on the family farm near Heisler, Alberta, and his struggle to relate the circumstances of his early life to the world beyond the prairies. *Seed Catalogue* incorporates descriptions of seed varieties found in farming catalogues (collage is one of Kroetsch's techniques). It makes evident the division of labor along gender lines: Farming is masculine work while gardening is feminine. Kroetsch — who as a child suffered from allergies to grain — is alienated in the poem from the traditionally male world and linked instead to the female realm of the garden. Gardening is therefore one of the poem's central tropes. "*How do you grow a poet?*" is a plaintive refrain and a question that the poem seeks to answer. Kroetsch notes "the absence of both Sartre and Heidegger" and "the absence of clay and wattles (whatever the hell / they are)," the allusions to continental philosophers and to W. B. Yeats's "The Lake Isle of Innisfree" suggesting both the isolation of Kroetsch's home and the poet's gruff refusal to allow this isolation to impede the development of a poetic sensibility.

*The New Long Poem Anthology* (1991, second edition 2001), edited by Sharon Thesen (1946–), features poets from Ondaatje's original anthology but also adds long poems by, among others, Lola Lemire Tostevin, Diana Hartog, Dionne Brand, Anne Carson, Erin Mouré, Lisa Robertson, and Phyllis Webb. Thesen thus demonstrated that long poems written by women form a notable part of the genre. Writing in Thesen's anthology about *Debbie: An Epic* (1997), Robertson (1961–) alludes to the feminist, deconstructive elements evident in her poems: "How might the rhetoric of foundations be scattered as temporary pleasures, rather than incursions of authority? How might a girl be invited to participate in these pleasures?" (487).

Apart from the long poem, Canadian poets have found other forms and approaches that can be considered — or that announce themselves to be — experimental or innovative. In the lipogrammatic *Eunoia* (2001), for instance, Christian Bök (1966–) looked to the techniques of stringent limitation advocated by a group of writers in France known as Oulipo (1960–). In particular, he followed the example of Georges Perec's *La Disparition* (1969), a novel that avoids using the letter "E." The five sections of *Eunoia* each use words that contain only a particular vowel (the first section is restricted to the vowel "A," the second to the vowel "E," and so on). The sound and the meaning of the poem are highly determined by the constraints imposed by the author. Writers associated with the Kootenay School of Writing (1984–) — an artist-run collective based in Vancouver (but originating in Nelson, BC, hence the name) — have typically linked disjunctive poetics, the visual arts, and urban, working-class politics. In *Down Time* (1990), for example, Jeff Derksen (1958–)

responded to the language and politics of consumerism. And Lisa Robertson, in *XEclogue* (1993) and *Debbie: An Epic*, parodied classical models. These book-length poems, very different from those of Kroetsch and Kiyooka, reveal the influences of Gertrude Stein and a range of feminist and literary theorists. In *XEclogue*'s prologue, "How Pastoral," Robertson proposes that "Nature, like femininity, is obsolete" (np). The poem itself, ironic and allusive, critiques social constructions of the categories "female" and "natural."

The simple opposition of conventional lyric forms on the one hand and the experimental forms of disjunctive poetics and of the long poem on the other hand overlooks, however, the extent to which certain poets may combine aspects of multiple modes — as in Mouré's (1955–) *Sheep's Vigil by a Fervent Person* (2001), which consists of a series of witty, postmodern urban pastorals derived from the Portuguese poet Fernando Pessoa's *O Guardador de Rebanhos* (1914). Ostensibly conventional poetry may also be extremely challenging, both intellectually and formally, as in the versions of Sophocles and Sappho that Anne Carson (1950–) offers in, respectively, *Electra* (2001) and *If Not, Winter: Fragments of Sappho* (2002). Anne Michaels's (1958–) lyric poems also defy easy description: *The Weight of Oranges* (1986) and *Miner's Pond* (1991) are highly complex and make exacting interpretative demands despite the venerable tradition to which they belong. Don McKay's (1942–) inclusion in Ondaatje's anthology further illustrates the difficulty of classifying poets exclusively according to movements or groups. Although the historiographic poems *Long Sault* (1975) and *Lependu* (1978) exhibited characteristics of other long poems of the time, McKay's poetry later took a very different shape. Beginning with *Birding, or Desire* (1983), it became, in some ways, more conventional: McKay tended to work in shorter, lyric forms, and his subject matter identified him as a writer of "nature poetry" — a category rivaled for alleged banality only by "love poetry." Yet his approach to form and subject — ironic, comic, allusive, self-conscious, wildly metaphorical — reinvigorates the lyric mode, even as they link him inextricably to the English Romantic poets.

Stephen Heighton (1961–) likewise writes distinctively and perceptively while drawing on traditional modes and models. He is a subtle observer who is highly aware of the political implications of travel — as were Purdy, for instance, and Gary Geddes (1940–). Geddes's *The Terracotta Army* (1984) stems from a trip to China and assigns personalities and voices to figures based on the funerary statues from the Qin dynasty that were unearthed near Xi'an in 1974. Heighton's *Foreign Ghosts* (1989) originates in travels in Asia (and the return home) and alludes to Bashō, Han Shan, and Shohaku. *Short Journey Upriver toward Oishida* (2004) by Roo Borson (1952–) similarly draws on a Buddhist poetic tradition. Heighton's *The Address Book* (2004) includes "Approximations" of

Baudelaire, Sappho, Dante, Catullus, Rilke, Rimbaud, the Quebec poet Émile Nelligan (see ch. 10, Kirsch), and other poets from various languages and traditions. In the title poem of *The Ecstasy of Skeptics* (1994), written in the *carpe diem* manner, the speaker claims, with an echo of Layton, that the poet-lover's tongue "must learn / to turn the grit of old books / into hydrogen, and burn." Heighton's lyric-elegiac poems, finely tuned, reflective, and poignant, are ignited by their encounters with literary history.

# Poetry of Place and Identity

Purdy objected on nationalist grounds to the adoption of American models by Canadian poets and had little enthusiasm for the experimental poetry of the *Tish* group. His lengthy correspondence with Birney shows that both poets sought to find distinctively Canadian styles and subjects in their poetry. Many other poets have depicted Canadian landscapes — urban as well as rural, suburban as well as wild — as a means of indicating a strong attachment to place, whether national, regional, or local. Indeed, English-Canadian poetry can be understood, to some extent, as an assemblage of regional poetries, although poets such as Purdy and McKay, who write convincingly about various parts of Canada, demonstrate that writers who are intrigued by geography do not always focus solely on a single place.

In the poems of Peter Trower (1930–) the relation of the individual to place is understood in terms of labor, as his poetry stems from his experiences in the logging industry in British Columbia. His colloquial voice links his poems to Purdy's — "The Last Spar-Tree on Elphinstone Mountain" is dedicated to Purdy — and he exploits the technical vocabulary of logging to great effect. His poetry is acutely aware of the fine line that separates necessary industry from environmental destruction: It is at times Wordsworthian in its reverence for nature and often deeply ambivalent about Trower's own involvement in an industry that is vital to the local and provincial economies. The relation to place can also be based on travel, as in Purdy's *North of Summer* or in various poems by P. K. Page, who spent roughly a decade abroad and whose travels provided material for paintings as well as poems. Page's writing about Brazil, in particular, ties her to the American poet Elizabeth Bishop, another expatriate; *Hologram: A Book of Glosas* (1994), a collection of encomiastic poems, refers directly to Bishop, as well as to T. S. Eliot, Wallace Stevens, W. H. Auden, and Dylan Thomas. Page's writing demonstrates that attitudes to place can be expressed through allusion and the acknowledgment of literary influence, as well as in the description of landscapes. Page's later poetry demonstrates an increasingly ecological focus, as the title of *Planet Earth: Poems Selected and New*

(2002) suggests. A fascination with the numinous and her perceptive observations indicate that her poetry is fundamentally important to an understanding of Canadian writing's conception of the natural world.

Regionalism can also be highly politicized. In the early 1960s, through *Tish* and the Vancouver Poetry Conference (1963), the West coast became associated with radical poetics. To an extent that remained the case in subsequent decades. Bowering and Marlatt continued to write from and about the West coast. Bowering's *Kerrisdale Elegies* (1984) adapts Rilke's *Duino Elegies* to a contemporary Vancouver setting; a new poem in the third edition of Marlatt's *Steveston* (2001) is set at the mouth of the Fraser River. But in the eyes of Robin Skelton (1925–1997) and Charles Lillard (1944–1997), who announced a "West Coast Renaissance" in *The Malahat Review* in 1978, then-contemporary West Coast writing was characterized primarily by its attentiveness to both the superhuman world and the landscapes of the region. In *Ikons of the Hunt* (1978), for example, Theresa Kishkan (1955–) looked to Robinson Jeffers and Theodore Roethke (both poets of the American Pacific) as she mythologized places in British Columbia: "Nausikaa, Vancouver Island" brings local geography into the orbit of classical mythology (or vice versa). George Woodcock (1912–1995) began his poetic career in England in the 1930s but later poems, such as "November Day on Howe Sound" (1978), give a sense of his adopted home and of his attempt to engage the indigenous cultures of the place, "the world of / the Gitksan," as he wrote in "The Skeena" (1978). Various works by J. Michael Yates (1938–) also pay careful attention to place, although they do so in surrealistic, philosophical ways. *The Great Bear Lake Meditations* (1970), *The Qualicum Physics* (1975), and *Insel: The Queen Charlotte Islands Meditations* (1983) are regional works that have something in common with the cartographic function of Purdy's poems. They are equally demanding, abstruse reflections that move well away from conventions of the lyric poem.

The literature of a single region, in short, can include multifarious understandings and representations of the place itself. Although the long poem, for example, has been associated with the poetry of the prairies, Kroetsch, Newlove, Suknaski, Mandel, Dennis Cooley, and Lorna Crozier, among others, have also written about the prairies in other poetic forms. Region is perhaps more closely tied to individual identity and perspective than to matters of form: Sid Marty (1944–), like Birney a mountaineer poet, describes the vertical landscapes of the Rocky Mountains in works such as *Headwaters* (1973); Bronwen Wallace (1945–89) centers her world on Kingston, Ontario (see *Marrying into the Family*, 1980); Alden Nowlan's (1933–1983) poetry suggests that the landscapes of rural Nova Scotia and New Brunswick have defined his view of the world; in *Hard Light* (1998) Michael Crummey (1965–) examines the history of Newfoundland and of his own family; and in works such as *Saltwater*

*Spirituals and Deeper Blues* (1983) and *Execution Poems* (2001) George Elliott Clarke (1960–) associates Atlantic Canada with his own ethnic and cultural identity. Clarke's poetry is, in his own coinage, Africadian: It depicts and is informed by the African-Canadian community in Nova Scotia. "I read Irving Layton through the lens of Jean Toomer," he wrote in *Black* (2006), yoking together Canadian modernism and the Harlem Renaissance. He frequently plays on the opposition of Black and White, the latter term not only denoting a racial identity but also carrying associations of Canada, the country of winter. Clarke declared in "Black Power," the preface to *Black*, that "the blackness of my English be that of ice" (7), the apparent paradox calling attention to his African-Canadian, as distinct from African-American, identity. Clarke's exuberant, indeed Laytonian writing is often highly autobiographical, as in "A Discourse on My Name": "First, it is thoroughly British: / *George* is English, *Elliott* Scottish, and *Clarke* Irish. / Of course, this fact makes it a misnomer, / For I am an Africadian" (126). His poetry is also highly allusive, using literary tradition as a lens through which to observe local matters. For example, *Beatrice Chancy*, first a libretto then a verse drama (1999), is based on Shelley's *The Cenci.*

As these examples indicate, questions of identity, variously understood, shaped the poetics of many Canadian writers of the contemporary period. The nationalist concerns that Atwood, Purdy, and Lee addressed in the 1960s were supplanted by an emphasis on ethnicity and community in the works of poets from all parts of the country and from many distinct backgrounds: Difference itself became a major theme. Many First Nations and Métis poets emerged in the 1960s and afterwards. The important anthology *I Am an Indian* (1969), edited by Kent Gooderham, included poems as well as stories and songs. Native Canadian poets have written in various forms and addressed a broad spectrum of subjects, from the political to the introspective. Native poetry often draws on the resources of languages other than English, as in Rita Joe's (1932–) *Poems of Rita Joe* (1978), a bilingual edition in English and Mi'kmaq. Joe's writing is unadorned, highly biographical, and overtly spiritual; her poems are written, Joe explains, with the ambition of instilling pride in her community. Significant collections by individual Native Canadian poets include *Delicate Bodies* (1980) by Daniel David Moses, *Breath Tracks* (1991) by Jeannette Armstrong, *The Gathering: Stones for the Medicine Wheel* (1993) by Gregory Scofield, *Bear Bones and Feathers* (1994) and *Blue Marrow* (1998) by Louise Halfe, *A Really Good Brown Girl* (1996) by Marilyn Dumont, and *Taking the Names Down from the Hill* (2003) by Philip Kevin Paul. A signal anthology, *Native Poetry in Canada*, edited by Armstrong and Lally Grauer, was published in 2001.

Poetry written by immigrants and the descendants of immigrants has likewise taken up the subject of ethnic identity. The identity in question is often European Canadian. Suknaski's poetry offers an example of Ukrainian-Canadian writing; Kristjana Gunnars (1948–) wrote about her Icelandic heritage in *Settlement Poems* (1980); and Patrick Friesen (1946–) made a Mennonite community the subject of *The Shunning* (1980). Poets from other diasporic communities have also made their relation to Canada a central topic. Like Ondaatje, Rienzi Crusz (1925–) was born in Sri Lanka (then Ceylon); he came to Canada in 1965. His poetry, beginning with *Flesh and Thorn* (1975), deals with exile and belonging, but attempts to avoid portraying themes of immigration in binary terms. "Conversations with God about My Present Whereabouts," a poem from *Elephant and Ice* (1980), draws contrasts between tropical heat and Canadian cold, but its hesitancy and nuance suggest the complexities that belie the simple opposition of "here" and "there." "I have almost forgotten / the terraced symmetries / of the rice-paddy lands," the speaker claims; "I now walk / without the lumbering skill / of the elephant." The poem concludes on an ambivalent note, suggesting both an enthusiasm for a new world and an awareness of difference: The speaker has become "A brown laughing face / in the snow," having escaped "Ceylon's deadly sun." Crusz's poetry has been highly praised — by Layton and Birney, for example — and his treatment of nationalism, ancestry, and tradition has been compared by Chelva Kanaganayakam to postcolonial strategies employed by Derek Walcott.

Dionne Brand (1953–) was born in Trinidad and came to Canada in 1970. Her poetry typically examines immigrant identity, with rootlessness a recurring motif, and draws on her own experiences as a Black lesbian feminist. *No Language Is Neutral* (1990) — the title is taken from Walcott's *Midsummer* — and *Land to Light On* (1997) are politically charged collections that also draw on conventions of landscape poetry and romantic lyricism. Canada, for Brand, is a place that threatens to consume the newcomer and the outsider — "I have to think again what it means that I am here," the speaker says in *Land to Light On* — and she therefore rejects what she perceives as the clichés of Canadian literature: "I did not want to write poems / about stacking cords of wood, as if the world / is that simple." In *Thirsty* (2002), a book-length poem about Toronto, Brand makes her adopted city, not the country, the locus of individual identity. Like Brand's poetry, Marlene NourbeSe Philip's (1947–) works frequently confront racism in Canada. In her essays, especially (see *Frontiers: Essays and Writings on Racism and Culture*, 1992), Philip, born in Tobago, has attacked what she views as the limitations of state-sanctioned policies of multiculturalism. Her poetry also seeks to expose the racism that she finds embedded in the English language. Her third book, *She Tries Her Tongue, Her Silence Softly Breaks* (1988), a long, deconstructive poem that begins with a reinterpretation of the myth of Persephone, suggests that the conventions of English enact racism — and therefore must be refused. Yet as George Elliott Clarke has noted, works by Brand,

Philip, and Claire Harris (born 1937 in Trinidad; see *Fables from the Women's Quarters,* 1984) emerge from a particularly Canadian context, although they are deeply influenced by immigration and its effects: "It is not enough to acclaim them as poets of exodus; no, not when Brand writes about Toronto and northern Ontario, not when Harris centers her writing career in Alberta, not when Philip identifies with *Anne of Green Gables*" (*Odysseys,* 266).

Themes of inclusion and exclusion continue to be taken up by younger poets, such as Carmine Starnino (1970–), whose *The New World* (1997), *Credo* (2000), and *With English Subtitles* (2004) draw on his experiences as a child of Italian immigrants. In a sequence in *The New World,* Starnino also seeks to establish literary connections between Italy and Canada by rendering in English works by the Italian poets Clemente Rebora, Corrado Govoni, Aldo Palazzeschi, Eugenio Montale, and Umberto Saba. The particular cultural context of Starnino's poems link them to those of Pier Giorgio di Cicco (born 1949 in Arezzo), whose *Roman Candles* (1978) collected works by Italian-Canadian poets, and Mary di Michele (born 1949 in Lanciano), whose early works, especially, are concerned with immigration and family history, frequently from a feminist perspective. Di Michele's volume of selected poems, *Stranger in You* (1995), charts the increasingly politicized nature of her poetry. Starnino is also a notable poet-critic who fiercely expresses his distaste for what he perceives as the unaccomplished poetry of Purdy, Patrick Lane, and other poets who write vernacular lyrics. Among the poets Starnino opposes to this mode are Richard Outram, David Solway, Al Moritz, and Robyn Sarah.

# Recent Developments: Younger Poets, Ecological Poetics

Two anthologies, edited by Crozier and Lane and modeled on Purdy's *Storm Warning* volumes, have suggested which poets might become the most significant writers of the generation born since the mid-1960s — that is, born at or since the beginning of the period surveyed in this chapter. The second of these books, *Breathing Fire 2* (2004), gathers works by thirty-three poets born between 1970 and 1980, the period in which the poets in Lee's *New Canadian Poets* were publishing their first volumes. Crozier and Lane write that the poets in question "are the inheritors of Purdy, Nowlan, MacEwen, Ondaatje, Newlove, Wallace and Atwood, the inheritors of McKay, [Jan] Zwicky, Mouré, Brand, [Susan] Musgrave and [Tim] Lilburn, but also the inheritors of Babstock, [Karen] Solie, [Stephanie] Bolster, [Tim] Bowling and [Sue] Goyette" (13). The latter five poets are included in the first *Breathing Fire* (1995), along with Scofield, Starnino, Paul, Crummey, and others. Identifying which young poets of any time will have particularly notable careers is, of course, a guessing game. But of those poets from the first anthology, Bolster, Solie, and Babstock have proven especially successful so far. Bolster (1969–) won the Governor General's Award for her first collection, *White Stone: The Alice Poems* (1998). Solie's (1966–) *Short Haul Engine* (2001) was a finalist for the Griffin Poetry Prize, as was Babstock's (1970–) *Airstream Land Yacht* (2006). In *Modern and Normal* (2005) Solie begins with an etymological account of the word "dwell," then reflects upon the theme of dwelling, using language drawn from the natural and physical sciences, ordinary speech, and an assortment of found texts (from a gun catalogue, a set of emergency procedures, a conversation overheard in a bar, an ornithological guide). In tone, Solie's book adapts McKay and Purdy; in form, it incorporates into the lyric mode aspects of the avant-garde poetics of Ondaatje and Kroetsch. Babstock's earlier books, *Mean* (1999) and *Days into Flatspin* (2001), reveal the influence of English poet Ted Hughes, especially in their strong consonance and dense sound patterns, while *Airstream Land Yacht* reflects a new preoccupation with the philosophy of consciousness.

In the 1990s and afterwards an increasing number of poets began to contend with the aesthetic and philosophical ramifications of ecology and environmentalism. McKay, Jan Zwicky, Tim Lilburn, and Robert Bringhurst are the principal figures concerned. Two collections of essays on poetics, both edited by Lilburn, have established the grounds from which these poets write: *Poetry and Knowing* (1995) and *Thinking and Singing: Poetry and the Practice of Philosophy* (2002). Several other poets similarly place ecological considerations and metaphors at the center of their poetics, including Lee, Borson, M. Travis Lane, Di Brandt, and Anne Simpson. In *Birding, or Desire* McKay was concerned with the metaphorical relations between bird-watching and forms of longing. Subsequent volumes — including *Sanding Down This Rocking Chair on a Windy Night* (1987), *Night Field* (1991), *Apparatus* (1997), and *Another Gravity* (2000) — likewise demonstrate McKay's fascination with birds, but they also reveal the metaphorical significance of a host of other motifs, including musical instruments, tools, flight, and gravity. In *Strike/Slip* (2006) McKay takes up geological subjects and themes of "oblivion" and "remembrance" ("Some Last Requests"). In all of his works he explores the symbiotic relations between ideas of wilderness and conceptions of home. His influence can be detected in the works of younger poets not only because of the following that his poetry enjoys but also because of his work as an editor for several Canadian presses, principally Brick Books in London, Ontario.

Jan Zwicky's (1955–) poetry draws heavily on her knowledge of philosophy, as the title of *Wittgenstein Elegies* (1986) suggests. Her two books of philosophy and poetics, *Lyric Philosophy* (1992) and *Wisdom and*

*Metaphor* (2003), examine ethics, ontology, and epistemology in relation to poetry. Her poems themselves, in *Songs for Relinquishing the Earth* (1998) and *Robinson's Crossing* (2004), frequently employ musical metaphors, depict the landscapes of northern Alberta, and describe moments of epiphany that arise from keen attention to the natural world. Levertov's poetry provides an illuminating point of comparison, while Federico García Lorca's influence can be detected in Zwicky's *Thirty-seven Small Songs and Thirteen Silences* (2005). Lilburn's (1950–) poetry, like Zwicky's, combines interests in philosophy and ecology; his poems, often expressly religious, are frequently rooted in Saskatchewan landscapes, as in *Kill-site* (2003). The works of McKay, Zwicky, Lilburn, Bringhurst, and others continue a long tradition of nature poetry. Something of the Wordsworthian mode lingers in their poems, although less so in Bringhurst's poetry than in that of the others. But in their adaptation of the conventions of nature poetry, they extend the tradition and redefine it.

Robert Bringhurst's (1946–) varied body of work is particularly difficult to describe. His earlier poems, contained in *Bergschrund* (1975) and *The Beauty of the Weapons* (1982), are typically spare lyrics that reflect upon the nature of existence and on the relation of the poem to the world. Among his later works — such as *The Blue Roofs of Japan* (1986), "New World Suite No. 3" (1995), and *Ursa Major* (2003) — are what Bringhurst terms "polyphonic poems." They are written for several voices — and in several languages, in the case of *Ursa Major* — and thus insist on their being performed, not simply read silently. Bringhurst has also fashioned poems out of translations or reimaginings of texts from the Presocratic philosophers and the Buddhist traditions of India and China. Despite the range of his poetic projects, Bringhurst's style and characteristic themes are among the most distinctive in Canadian poetry.

Bringhurst's other major works constitute one of the most striking developments in contemporary Canadian literature — although, at least in some senses, the poetry in question is neither new nor Canadian. Bringhurst's *A Story as Sharp as a Knife* (1999) is an introduction to the culture and oral poetry of the Haida, the indigenous people of the Queen Charlotte Islands, also known as Haida Gwaii. Bringhurst subsequently published *Nine Visits to the Mythworld* (2000) and *Being in Being* (2001), translations of the oral poetry of, respectively, Ghandl (Walter McGregor, ca. 1851–ca. 1920) and Skaay (John Sky, ca. 1827–ca. 1910). To prepare the three volumes, Bringhurst worked from transcriptions and translations made by John R. Swanton, an American ethnographer who visited Haida Gwaii from 1900 to 1901. Bringhurst retranslated Swanton's prose version into poetry, proposing that the oral performances be understood not as folklore but instead as literature. Although the translations inevitably have something in common with Bringhurst's own poetry, they are essentially unlike anything else in contemporary Canadian poetry. Bringhurst's suggestion that the original versions, along with other oral texts in aboriginal languages, form the classical literature of the place now known as Canada is compelling — and could profoundly change conventional understandings of Canadian literature. The translations suggest that for all its achievement and variety, Canadian poetry written in European languages in fact represents only a very recent development in the long, rich, and complex history of poetry in North America.

# 26: Contemporary English-Canadian Drama and Theater

*Anne Nothof (Athabasca University)*

CONTEMPORARY ENGLISH-CANADIAN playwrights articulate a diversity of voices and give expression to the country's many particular social and psychological spaces. They map its physical and mental terrain by dramatizing specific communities in terms of their histories, internal conflicts, and psychic landscapes. Since the 1960s regional history has continued to stimulate playwriting, providing local stories that inform the life of the community and the nation. These plays often revisit an apparently benign Canadian history from a critical perspective, and expose moral and political travesties. More recently, English-Canadian playwrights have been engaged in mapping specific communities in terms of ethnicity and ideology. Their divergent stories argue against a homogenous Canada and constitute a complex portrait of many colors, perspectives, and lifestyles. Thus contemporary English-Canadian plays often contest the idea of a cohesive national identity; they interrogate Canada's place in the world and its global responsibilities.

## Mapping an Alternative Terrain

From the late 1950s English-Canadian drama has been developed and produced primarily in a network of small "alternative" theaters in cities across the country. These theaters were established in order to create a distinctively local drama as an alternative to the British and American plays which predominated in the larger commercial houses. Their early work was typically collaborative — collective creations by actors, writers, and directors, who imagined the social landscape of a particular community or group. George Luscombe's (1926–1999) Toronto Workshop Productions (TWP), founded in 1959, experimented with a politically engaged dramaturgy that challenged entrenched ideas of class and gender, using a variety of theatrical techniques from Brechtian docudrama to mime and circus. TWP is best known for its collective creation of a documentary on the 1930s Depression in the prairies, based on Barry Broadfoot's "oral history," *Ten Lost Years* (1974).

Toronto's Theatre Passe Muraille (TPM), under the direction of Paul Thompson (1940–), also developed collective productions inspired by local stories. Within one decade of its founding in 1968, the company had produced twenty-two plays and had taken its aesthetic philosophy across the country. For works such as *The Farm Show* (1972), the Passe Muraille ensemble embedded itself in a community to record its oral histories, stories, and songs, and then improvised characters, structure, and dialogue. The collaborative production was typically first presented for the community members, many of whom saw the dramatization of Canadian lives and issues for the first time. *The Farm Show* was revisited by playwright Michael Healey (1963–) in 1999, its genesis providing the basis for *The Drawer Boy*, which maps the early history of Canadian drama at Theatre Passe Muraille. Healey based his play on his own experiences as a young actor with Passe Muraille: His naive protagonist learns from two local bachelor farmers the importance of the dramatic imagination in life as well as in art.

Passe Muraille has inspired or mentored other companies across the country, including the 25th Street Theatre in Saskatoon and Theatre Network in Edmonton. 25th Street Theatre's *Paper Wheat*, a musical piece about the founding of the Wheat Board — a farmer-controlled organization that markets crops — and its impact on prairie life, toured the country in 1979, bringing a uniquely Canadian story to found spaces in small communities as well as to city theaters. These docudramas and collective creations are not polished dramatic literature, but they revived regional traditions and histories, and helped to establish a matrix of indigenous material for individualized dramatic expression.

Passe Muraille also has engaged in mapping the political terrain of Canada. In 1980, Linda Griffiths (1956–) and Paul Thompson created a monologue about the tumultuous relationship of prime minister Pierre Trudeau and his wife Margaret, entitled *Maggie and Pierre*. With Griffiths playing the roles of the conflicted couple and of a choric journalist, the play toured the country. Since then, Griffiths has performed in, written, and co-written several works exploring Canadian issues: *Jessica* (1981), with Maria Campbell (1940–), a visionary enactment of Native spirits in the life of a young Native woman; *Alien Creature: A Visitation from Gwendolyn MacEwen* (1999), a monologue that engages the life of the Canadian poet; and *Chronic* (2000), which likens modern Canadian life to a lingering disease.

Carol Bolt's (1941–2000) *Next Year Country*, a collective creation with music produced by the Globe Theatre in Regina, is a portrait of unemployed people during the Depression and their confrontation with the government. It was revised and produced by Passe Muraille as *Buffalo Jump* (1972). Most of Bolt's other plays have premiered in Toronto's alternative theaters, including *Red Emma* at Toronto Free Theatre (1974) and her most successful play, *One Night Stand*, a sexually charged confrontation between a lonely woman and a bar pickup, at the Tarragon Theatre (1977).

In Edmonton, Alberta, Theatre Network initiated the collective creation of works that targeted the development of the oil sands in Fort McMurray (*Hard Hats and Stolen Hearts: A Tar Sands Myth*, 1977, with Gordon Pengilly) and the proposed construction of the Mackenzie Pipeline in the Yukon (*Kicker*, 1978), tracing the impact of White society on an Inuit family. In St. John's, Newfoundland, the Mummers Troupe also chose topical and controversial subjects, performing in shopping malls, union halls, city buses, and airports. Working with unions and other politicized groups to script their plays, the Mummers produced ten plays between 1972 and 1983. In *Gros Mourn* (1973), they critically examine the relocation of residents of Sally's Cove, a village on the West coast of Newfoundland, which was confiscated by the government for the development of a national park. Other Mummers plays include *Buchans/Company Town* (1974), *Dying Hard* (1975), *IWA Loggers Strike* (1975), *Stars in the Sky Morning* (written by Rhonda Payne, Jane Dingle, and Jan Henderson, about Newfoundland women's experience in the isolated outport of King's Cross, 1978), *What's That Got to Do with the Price of Fish?* (commissioned by an international development agency, 1976), *Silakepat Kissiane/Weather Permitting* (about life in Nain, Labrador, 1977), and finally *They Club Seals, Don't They?*, which toured across Canada in 1978 and incited considerable controversy, since it sympathetically presented the viewpoint of the sealers and was funded by the Newfoundland government.

## Reproducing History

Contemporary English-Canadian drama is preoccupied with history, revisiting the past in order to understand the present. It interrogates received narratives of the peaceful evolution of the nation with a critical focus on specific incidents, and undermines the self-congratulatory proclivities of a nationalistic historiography. There are few heroes in Canadian drama, and often the antiheroes function as iconoclasts. James Reaney's (1926–2008) epic documentary *The Donnellys*, collectively developed in actors' workshops over an eight-year period in the 1970s, imagines a demonized immigrant Irish family as victims of transplanted religious vendettas. Comprising three plays, it maps the tragic story of the "Black Donnellys" in southern Ontario at the end of the nineteenth century, reconstructing the sectarian boundaries and hatreds. The "wild lands" of Canada are cut into concessions and farms; the surveyor's lines are governed not by social considerations but by geography, signified by the intersecting lines of ladders and ropes placed by a chorus of actors as physical metaphors for the confinement of the individual within fixed social parameters. Against the formidable constraints of religion and politics, Reaney pits the strong wills of the Donnelly family to show that the words and actions of a few can inform the life of a whole community. In the first play of the trilogy, *Sticks and Stones* (1973), Reaney constructs a social mythology by establishing the historical and geographic context for the feud and its climax in the murder of the Donnellys; in the following two plays, *The St. Nicholas Hotel* (1974) and *Handcuffs* (1975), he explores the political and religious determinants that ensnare the family in events beyond their control.

John Gray's (1946–) *Billy Bishop Goes to War* (1978) challenges the historical narrative of Canada's coming-of-age as an independent nation through the trauma of the First World War by demythologizing flying ace Billy Bishop. This satirical musical, performed by John Gray on the piano and featuring Eric Peterson in the role of Bishop and all the other characters, shows Bishop to be focused primarily on winning deadly contests with German pilots and experiencing the exhilaration of the kill. He is a problematic antihero, used by British imperialists as propaganda fodder, but exercising his independent inclinations.

Saskatchewan playwright Ken Mitchell (1940–) also explores the possibility of uniquely Canadian heroes in the history of the country, focusing on eccentric and flamboyant individuals: *Davin, the Politician* (1978) probes the life of a controversial western politician; *The Shipbuilder* (1978) enacts the obsessive dream of a Finnish immigrant, who builds a vessel on his prairie homestead in order to sail back to his homeland; *Gone the Burning Sun* (1984) recreates the controversial private and public life of Norman Bethune, who practiced field medicine in both the Spanish Civil War and in revolutionary China.

For forty years, Calgary playwright Sharon Pollock (1936–) has extensively mapped Canada's historical terrain by looking at the consequences of personal and political choices. *Walsh* (1973) reveals how the federal government's decision to starve Sitting Bull out of Canada in the 1870s resulted in the decimation of the Sioux Nation. *The Komagata Maru Incident* (1976) exposes the racial politics inherent in the British Columbia government's refusal to allow the debarkation of Sikhs from the Punjab in Vancouver in 1914. *Generations* (1980) examines the difficult choices made by members of a southern Alberta farming family — whether to stay and struggle for subsistence on the land or to sell out and leave for the city. *Whiskey Six Cadenza* (1983) dramatizes the tragic consequences of smuggling liquor through the Crowsnest Pass in the 1920s, when individual and community ambitions were thwarted by Prohibition. *Fair Liberty's Call* (1993), set in New Brunswick after the American Revolution, shows how a family is torn apart by its conflicting loyalties to Britain and the United States, and deconstructs what Pollock considers the "Canadian identity" — "upholding compromise over compassion, legality over justice" (Pollock 1993). As Pollock points out in an interview, all of her plays are "about an individual who is directed to or compelled to follow a course of action of which he or she begins to examine the morality. Circumstances force a decision, usually the authority (family, society, government) is removed emotionally from the protagonist, and it usually doesn't end very well" (Pollock 1990). Pollock thinks "that is a very Canadian thing . . . that comes from living in Alberta or the Maritimes and feeling that Ottawa never seems to understand what it is that is required in these places. It also has something to do with being a woman. Male society defines appropriate behaviour and action for women" (Pollock 1990).

John Murrell's (1945–) early works map the history of the Canadian West: *Waiting for the Parade* (1979) portrays the very different responses of five Calgary women to the absence of their husbands during the First World War; *Farther West* (1986) — a frontier melodrama featuring brothel-madam May Buchanan — reflects on nation-building, women's identities, and the meaning of "the West." Frank Moher's (1955–) *The Third Ascent* (1988) considers the personal culpability of American Secretary of War Henry Stimson in the decision to drop the first atomic bomb in 1945, by enacting his three attempts to climb a sacred mountain in southern Alberta accompanied by a conflicted Native guide.

Michael Hollingsworth's (1950–) ambitious historical cycle *The History of the Village of the Small Huts* (initiated in 1982 and developed over a fifteen-year period) is a satirical retelling of the nation's history, tracing the evolution of a Canadian "identity" as a comedy of manners in eight parts under the subtitles "New France," "The British," "The Mackenzie-Papineau Rebellion," "Confederation and Riel," "Laurier," "The Great War," "The Life and Times of Mackenzie King," and "World War II." In his preface to the published text, Hollingsworth explains that his historical epic is a Goon Show enacted by ghosts and demons: It refutes the lie that Canadian history is dull. Hollingsworth gleaned his historical characters and plot from *The Dictionary of Canadian Biography*, added visual images from popular culture, and employed the farcical satiric style of Monty Python and the British television puppet show "Spitting Image," combined with improvisation and carnivalesque comic exaggerations. A series sequel entitled *The Global Village* brings the history of Canada to the twenty-first century with four more parts, including "Trudeau and the FLQ" (1997) and finishing with "Life and Time of Brian Mulroney" (1999).

Contemporary Canadian political plays are largely satiric. Michael Healey's *Plan B* (2002) is an urban political allegory in which personal intimacy is paralleled with the relationship between English and French Canada. The title alludes to the federal government's strategy if the Quebec separatists win their referendum for the independence of the province. In Healey's *Generous* (2006) the opening scenario, a farce about a political party just before its fall from power, establishes the themes of ambition and greed, both of which may be served through apparently altruistic deeds. Frank Moher's *Prairie Report* (1988) satirizes the fundamentalist underpinnings of the Alberta conservative regime.

## Mapping Canadian Society

Contemporary English-Canadian plays often depict family dynamics as predicators of national, social, and cultural values. They demonstrate the ways in which the individual is conditioned by the home environment and the significance of staying home, leaving, and returning. Families also enact patterns of misunderstanding and miscommunication, which may be viewed as commentaries on political scenarios in the country.

David French's (1939–) "Mercer" cycle of five plays explores the cultural and social terrain of a Newfoundland family: *Leaving Home* (1972) introduces the stubborn traditionalist patriarch Jacob, his loyal wife Mary, and their conflicted teenaged sons, all recently relocated to Toronto at the end of the 1950s; *Of the Fields, Lately* (1973), set in 1961, dramatizes the fraught relationship between Jacob and his eldest son Ben, whom Mary has summoned home when Jacob suffers a heart attack; *Salt-Water Moon* (1984) is a lyrical portrait of the courtship of the young Jacob and Mary in Newfoundland in 1926; *1949* (1988) shows the extended Mercer family's response to Newfoundland's becoming a Canadian province in 1949 and surrendering its "independent" status as a British colony. In the prequel *Soldier's Heart* (2002) Jacob is sixteen and in the process of leaving home himself when he meets his father Essau on the platform of a railway station and learns about Essau's traumatic experience during the First World War: He has mistakenly shot his own brother in the chaos of trench warfare at the Somme. David French has also mapped Canadian culture in *Jitters* (1979), a comic portrait of the backstage life of a company of actors facing the premiere of a new Canadian play. All of French's plays feature passionate confrontations in which the characters are fighting for their integrity and their beliefs. In his Newfoundland plays he evokes his characters through lyrical speech, presenting a colorful, colloquial idiom based on the passionate ordinary words of people whose imaginations have been nourished by the paucity and hardship of their lives. Their geographical isolation and spiritual resilience are expressed through stories and songs, various anecdotes, and family history, although one of the central ironies of the Mercer plays is that despite being loquacious, the characters rarely communicate: Their words are aborted, deflected, misheard, or misunderstood.

Michael Cook (1933–1994) similarly has considered the ways in which families and individuals survive or perish in a harsh Newfoundland environment that demands initiative, courage, and determination. His characters are larger-than-life eccentrics pounded by the adverse elements of wind and sea into grotesque shapes. Cook saw a unique culture threatened by the encroachment of a "progressive" government that required conformity and integration, effected through resettlement and the relocation of the outports — isolated coastal fishing villages. He also saw a correspondence between the lives of Newfoundlanders and prairie families, both confronted with the enormity of their environment. In *The Head, Guts and Soundbone Dance* (1973), Skipper Pete and his son immerse themselves in the daily routine of work, in defiance of the depleted fish stocks, but the Skipper's resistance to change has tragic consequences. In *Jacob's Wake* (1974), the ghost of the family patriarch wreaks havoc on his descendents, whom he considers spiritually and physically degenerate.

In *Marion Bridge* (1998), Nova Scotia playwright Daniel MacIvor (1962–) also dramatizes family conflict as a consequence of isolation and deprivation. The family history is enacted through the response of three daughters to their dying mother, who has made a deliberate choice to die on her own terms, leaving her daughters to assess their own lives. Montreal-based playwright David Fennario (1947–) tackles the fraught interaction of English and Quebec working-class families in *Balconville* (1979). In *Condoville* (2005) he reconsiders the same terrain twenty years later, as urban renewal displaces the original inhabitants. Conni Massing's (1959–) *Gravel Run* (1988) ironically surveys bizarre family traditions in rural Alberta. Eugene Stickland's (1956–) *Some Assembly Required* (1994) and *A Guide to Mourning* (1998) examine the farcical conundrums of dysfunctional families enduring Christmas and funerals. More recently, Canadian playwrights have examined the lives of an aging population, and the tragedy of Alzheimer's (Aaron Bushkowsky's *Strangers among Us*, 1998; John Mighton's *Half Life*, 2005; Stickland's *Closer and Closer Apart*, 2007).

Joanna McClelland Glass (1936–) grounds most of her plays in memories of her childhood in Saskatchewan. *Canadian Gothic* (1972) portrays the emotionally debilitating consequences of living in isolation on the prairies, and the conflict between a repressive father and his free-spirited wife and daughter. In *Artichoke* (1975), a morally stringent prairie wife has banned her husband to the smokehouse for an infidelity that has resulted in a daughter, and then indulges in an affair herself with an acquaintance from the past, an English professor who specializes in the poetry of Alexander Pope. *If We Are Women* (1993) is set in a beach house in a "shoreline community" in Connecticut. The play tracks the consequences of border-crossing in terms of the relationship of a Canadian woman writer, her illiterate mother from Saskatchewan, her intellectually sophisticated American mother-in-law, and her rebellious teenage daughter. *Yesteryear* (1989) depicts a happy, fictionalized version of the Saskatoon of Glass's childhood, set in 1948 when the province had voted in a socialist government. *Trying* (2004) is based on Glass's working relationship as a young Canadian from the prairies with Francis Biddle, Attorney General under President Franklin D. Roosevelt and a judge during the Nuremberg trials. The play is set in 1967 in the last year of Biddle's life, when he is coming to terms with his death and his legacy, but the focus is on his secretary's growing resolution to become a writer and transcend the limitations of her heredity and environment. Although Glass's plays are rooted in dysfunctional family dynamics, they also enact the intersections of American and Canadian perspectives, and of youth and age.

Connie Gault's (1949–) plays investigate the small details of women's lives in an isolated prairie environment, and the surprising significance of these details, for example, in *The Soft Eclipse* (1989) and *Sky* (1989). Maureen Hunter's (1948–) *Footprints on the Moon* (1989) also considers the limitations and possibilities of women's lives in a small prairie town; and she explores the genesis of important global historical events in *Transit of Venus* (1992) and *Vinci* (2002). Sharon Pollock's *Blood Relations* (1980) and *Doc* (1984) focus on the psychogeography of the family from a woman's perspective: The first is an imaginative recreation of Lizzie Borden's murder of her parents in 1892; the second of Pollock's own relationship with her parents. Three of her more recent plays, *Moving Pictures* (1999), *End Dream* (2000), and *Angel's Trumpet* (2001), portray creative and willful women who struggle to assert their individuality in a patriarchal society.

The plays of Judith Thompson (1954–) constitute Freudian analyses of the social dysfunction of families as indicators of the horror and violence in modern society. She shows the reality of evil, the loss of moral direction, and predatory behavior. The implication of the title of her play, *Lion in the Streets* (taken from Proverbs 26:13) is that we not merely decry evil, but that we take action against it, first by looking for the evil within ourselves. Many of Thompson's characters are neurotics, living precariously on the margins of society, or threatening to disrupt the "normalcy" of a "civilized" society. They act irrationally, unpredictably, driven by strong feelings and fears. But Thompson also believes in the human capacity to withstand these forces of evil — that is, in the power of love and forgiveness, which she expresses through Christian iconography, such as the apotheosis in *Lion in the Streets* (1990), the image of the Madonna and child in *The Crackwalker* (1980), the redemptive birth in *I Am Yours* (1987), and the redemptive death in the radio play *Sugarcane* (1993). In *Sled* (1997), she maps the Canadian North as both a dangerous wilderness and a place of refuge; in *Habitat* (2001), she portrays the consequences of establishing a home for dysfunctional teenagers in an affluent suburb; and in *Capture Me* (2004), she considers the contingency of interpersonal and international violence.

Joan MacLeod's (1954–) works similarly are engaged in mapping the conscience of Canada. In *Amigo's Blue Guitar* (1990) she examines the neocolonizing tendencies of an expatriate American family living on the Gulf Islands, who sponsor a refugee from El Salvador. In her millennium play *2000* (1996) she demonstrates the limitations of optimism and hope in a world characterized by the unpredictable and the unknowable, but she also enacts those values that strengthen human interaction and common-alities, constituting the lineaments of a civilized society. The setting specif-ically locates the action in a precarious space between the knowable and the unknown, evoking a technologized consumer culture that cannot entirely displace the elemental forces of nature — "a suburb of Vancouver built up against the mountains" (*2000*, 11). As in most of her plays, domestic space is both fraught and comforting; despite its conflicts, it forges the values that guide individual actions. In *The Shape of a Girl* (2001), an adolescent girl finds a frightening correspondence between the senseless murder of a teenager by her schoolmates and her own social behavior. But she discov-ers that in speaking out, in testifying, there is a possibility for understand-ing and redemption.

Wendy Lill (1950–) also interrogates the moral issues embedded in social action or inaction. *On the Line* (1982) portrays the consequences of a strike by immigrant women garment workers in Winnipeg. *The Fighting Days* (1983) focuses on the women's suffrage movement in Winnipeg in terms of the life of journalist Francis Benyon, showing the dark edges of racism and xenophobia in the feminist movement during the First World War. *The Occupation of Heather Rose* (1986) is a confessional monologue by a young idealistic nurse recalling her traumatic education in race rela-tions while working alone in a small Native community which she "occu-pies" from a neoimperialist White point of view, but which in the end "occupies" her as an obsessive guilt. *Sisters* (1989) tells an infamous story of a Native residential school in Nova Scotia, which burned to the ground. *All Fall Down* (1993) examines the irrational and hysterical response of a community when a woman daycare worker is accused of sexually abusing a child. *Corker* (2000) scrutinizes society's treatment of the disabled. Lill has also adapted Sheldon Currie's novel *The Glace Bay Miners' Museum* into a radio and stage play (1995). It shows the disastrous consequences of coalmining on a Cape Breton family and the macabre response of a young woman who loses a father, two brothers, and a husband in the mines. *Chimera* (2007) tackles the ethics of stem-cell research and the lim-its of science and biotechnology in terms of a confrontation between a cyn-ical journalist and the new Minister of Justice.

# Mapping the Psyche

Canadian playwrights have explored the geography of the mind in mono-logues such as Daniel MacIvor and Daniel Brooks's (1958–) *Monster*

(1998), which excavates Oedipal revenge fantasies, and *Cul-de-Sac* (2002), in which the protagonist submerges himself in loneliness and despair. In Morris Panych's (1952–) monologue *Earshot* (2001), a man isolates himself in his room to protect himself from the overwhelming noise of the world. In his other works, too, Panych maps the psycho-geography of the urban Canadian male. His black comedies are characterized by existential themes and a style and sensibility that recall the theater of the absurd. They typically set their interrogations of the meaning of life in culturally and nationally neutral locales and pose broad philosophical questions on human interaction and isolation, on the nature of good and evil, and on the relationship between fantasy and reality. In *Vigil* (1996), a solitary young bank employee impatiently awaits the death of a silent, bedridden old woman, whom he believes is his aunt, filling the time with ruminations and recollections and one-liners on mortality. *Lawrence & Holloman* (1998) explores the relationship of two antithetical personalities — one an optimist, the other a pessimist and nihilist. *The Ends of the Earth* (1992) is a more ambitious investigation of the meaning of life in terms of a journey, again by two men with very different outlooks. *Girl in a Goldfish Bowl* (2002) is set in a home on the edge of the West coast, which the unhappy mother continually threatens to leave. Her nihilism is resisted by her optimistic, ingenuous young daughter who imagines that her dead goldfish has metamorphosed into a young man from the sea who will save them all — he does not.

George Walker's (1947–) black comedies explore the psychogeography of dysfunctional families attempting to survive in a hopeless urban environment. In *Better Living* (1986) from his East End trilogy, Walker considers the possibility of operative humanist values, usually through the character of a woman who defies social anarchy and irrationality by adopting specific goals such as digging an underground room as a defense against the threats of the outside world. In the six plays that comprise *Suburban Motel* (1997–1998), Walker's vision is darker, and he rejects the possibility of personal solutions to social and interpersonal disintegration. In each play, the "end of civilization" is enacted in a motel on the outskirts of society, in a room in which life has been reduced to psychic survival. None of the intruders or visitors offers salvation, but only more complications and difficulties.

# Cultural Diversity

The mapmaking of English-Canadian playwrights has always been conditioned by personal and regional perspectives, but it has also been informed by a sense of the country as an imagined entity. These perspectives are becoming increasingly conflicted, as contemporary playwrights engage in interrogating the nature of borders, identities, and communities. Dramatic "maps" are being redrawn and redefined: They are no longer a colonial definition of space, but a way of establishing a sense of place and of cultural belonging. First Nations Canadian playwrights are revisiting postcolonial history through an alternative mapping of the country. Until the 1980s, Native voices were heard in theaters primarily as interpreted by non-Native playwrights — Sitting Bull in Sharon Pollock's *Walsh* (1973), Rita Joe, her father, David Joe, and her lover Jaimie Paul in George Ryga's (1932–1987) *The Ecstasy of Rita Joe* (1967), and the doomed Native women in Gwen Pharis Ringwood's (1910–1984) trilogy Drum Song (1982). With the establishment of the production company Native Earth Performing Arts in Toronto in 1981, however, Native writers were encouraged to explore the implications of cultural censorship, racism, and institutional oppression. The early plays of Native Earth were message-centered collective creations; they functioned as social therapy as well as community entertainment. Tomson Highway (1951–) was artistic director of Native Earth from 1986 to 1992, and his best-known works, *The Rez Sisters* and *Dry Lips Oughta Move to Kapuskasing*, premiered there in 1986 and 1989. In *The Rez Sisters*, seven women from the Wasaychigan Reserve (affectionately shortened to "Wasy") on Manitoulin Island, Lake Superior, take a weekend trip to Toronto in order to win the jackpot of "THE BIGGEST BINGO IN THE WORLD." Each of the women has "demons" to contend with — abuse, poverty, the deaths of loved ones — but their joint effort to achieve something in their lives brings them together as a real sisterhood. Although they do not win the big prize, and one of them dies during the trip back from Toronto, the others are strengthened by their united effort, which is both guided and tested by a male trickster figure. In *Dry Lips* — the "flip side" of *The Rez Sisters* — the cast is all male, with the exception of the trickster, who is now a female. The women on the Reserve, who are not onstage, have formed a hockey team, which the men consider a threat. Their various responses to this challenge have both tragic and comic consequences. Highway's *Ernestine Shuswap Gets Her Trout* (2004) was commissioned by the Western Canadian Theatre in Kamloops, British Columbia, and the Secwepemc Cultural Education Society. It is set in 1910, when the "Big Kahoona of Canada" is paying a visit to the Thompson River Valley. The Native and non-Native worlds collide, as four Native women prepare for prime minister Wilfred Laurier's arrival, and their Native traditions begin to be displaced.

Drew Haydon Taylor (1962–) also explores the comedy and tragedy inherent in Native communities: *Bootlegger Blues* (1990) considers the plight of a teetotaling Native woman left with 143 cases of beer when a church fundraising fails. *AlterNatives* (1999) enacts the relationship of a young urban Native science-fiction writer and a Jewish Native Studies professor, tested by the arrival of dinner guests who include two Native warriors with a mission to disrupt politically correct responses. Ian Ross's

(1968–) *fareWel* (1996) is a dark comedy about reservation life: The Chief is in Las Vegas, the band is in receivership, and the more radical members want to declare self-government.

The four "city plays" of Daniel David Moses (1952–) track the tragic experiences of a Native family, shifting between the supernatural spiritual world of Native tradition and the present urban condition in which Natives struggle to survive. *Coyote City* (1988) begins with a telephone call from a ghost — a trickster who assumes many different guises, and who sends the family on a search in the city for the missing lover he embodies. *Big Buck City* (1991) tells the story of the lovers and the birth of their baby as a farcical Nativity play. *Kyotopolis* (1993) takes the form of science-fiction satire, showing the death and resurrection of "Babe" in the explosion of a space shuttle. In *City of Shadows* (1995), all of the characters from the earlier plays revisit the previous events as ghosts.

In *Princess Pocahontas and the Blue Spots* (1990) Monique Mojica (1954–) subverts colonial stereotypes about Native women to assert diverse ethnic and gendered identities, but also to demonstrate the influence of transculturation on contemporary Native peoples through the characterization of different women in history. Marie Clements's (1962–) *The Unnatural and Accidental Women* (1997) focuses on serial killings in Vancouver's Downtown Eastside between 1965 and 1987, all ruled by the coroner and reported in the press to be "unnatural and accidental." Using a wide range of forms and media, the play critiques state apathy to racial and gendered violence and celebrates the female victims as life-affirming and interconnected, even after death. In Clements's *Burning Vision* (2003), Canada is envisaged as a hybridization of cultures, languages, and communities — Japanese, Dene, Métis, Irish — all connected by their association with the history of the atomic bombs dropped on Hiroshima and Nagasaki. The protagonist Rose, a young Métis woman, learns how her grandfather died of radiation sickness from mining uranium in northern Canada for the manufacture of the atomic bombs in the United States. Rose is a bread-maker and a dreamer and finds in the dough that she kneads an image of herself and her country: "This grain is fine and even, with slightly elongated cells; the flesh of this bread is multi-grained. You never know what you're going to look like" (58).

With the increase in immigration from a diversity of countries, particularly from Southeast Asia, China, and the Caribbean, the Canadian demographic has changed rapidly in the last twenty-five years. The complex ethnic mix has been officially acknowledged in the federal government's multicultural policy of the 1980s and in the emergence of a national mythology of multiculturalism. Several theaters have been founded with a mandate to develop plays that express this cultural diversity: Cahoots and Obsidian in Toronto, and Black Theatre Workshop in Montreal, for example. The development and production history of Cahoots includes Marty

Chan's *Mom, Dad, I'm Living with a White Girl* (1995), Marlene NourbeSe Philip's *Coups and Calypsos* (1999), Betty Quan's *Mother Tongue* (2001), M. J. Kang's *Dreams of Blonde and Blue* (2002), Anosh Irani's *Bombay Black* (2006), and Ahmed Ghazali's *The Sheep and the Whale* (2007). The satirical plays of Cahoots's former artistic director Guillermo Verdecchia (1962–) scrutinize the ways in which Canadians identify themselves, particularly in relation to other societies and cultures: *Fronteras Americanas* (1993) challenges the Latino stereotype; *A Line in the Sand* (1995) examines Canada's "peacekeeping" role; and *The Adventures of Ali & Ali and the Axes of Evil* (2004) exposes the racial-profiling consequences of American policy on Canada after 11 September 2001.

Montreal's Black Theatre Workshop (founded in 1972) has developed and produced plays that map the African-Canadian landscape. Andrew Moodie's (1967–) *Riot* (1998) dissects racism in Canada from the different perspectives of six roommates as they discuss a variety of topics, from Quebec's political aspirations, to who has and has not paid the rent, to the Rodney King riots in California in 1992. Djanet Sears's (1959–) monologue *Afrika Solo* (1989) tells the story of her own journey back to Africa in order to find her roots. *Wade in the Water* (2003) by Nova Scotia playwright George Elroy Boyd (1952–) traces the migration of former slaves across the Canadian border, and then to Sierra Leone. Obsidian Theatre in Toronto has produced Sears's *Harlem Duet* (1998), a contemporary deconstruction of *Othello*, and *The Adventures of a Black Girl in Search of God* (2002), which delineates the turbulent life of a small Black community in southern Ontario from the perspective of a woman doctor who has lost her daughter. Lorena Gale's (1958–) first play *Angélique* (1998) imaginatively reenacts the story of a slave accused of arson in Montreal and hanged in 1734. Before her death, the protagonist envisages a city "swarming with ebony" (Gale 2003, 70). In the monologue *Je me souviens* (2000), the title of which refers to the motto of Quebec, Gale reconstructs her childhood and coming-of-age as an African Canadian in Montreal, coloring the separatist "pure laine" vision of a new Quebec nation.

The extraordinary multilingual, metatheatrical works of Quebec City–based playwright Robert Lepage (1957–) map a global terrain — the collisions and accommodations enacted in disparate cultures: Chinese, French, and English in *The Dragons' Trilogy* (1985–1987), set in three Canadian Chinatowns during three different eras; the intersections of European and North American cultures in *Tectonic Plates* (1988); the relationship of English and French Canada in *Polygraph* (1989); the consequences of the atrocities of Hiroshima and the Holocaust in the seven-hour epic *The Seven Streams of the River Ota* (1994–1996).

Canadian cultural diversity is also reflected in gay and lesbian plays: *Unidentified Human Remains* (1989), *Poor Superman* (1994), *Martin Yesterday* (1997), and *Snake in Fridge* (2000) by Brad Fraser (1959–)

excavate the violent and deviant stories of a marginalized gay community. *Goodnight Desdemona* (*Good Morning Juliet*) (1988) by Ann-Marie MacDonald (1959–) rewrites Shakespeare's plays from a modern Canadian feminist/gay perspective.

Contemporary English-Canadian drama participates in the imaginative deconstruction and revision of a nation. It creates the history, places, people, images, and ideologies as participatory experiences, recognized or contested, that interact in the formation of the diverse national character of a country of immigrants. Regions and borders give rise to alternative sites of meaning, which articulate who Canadians think they are.

# 27: Canons of Diversity in Contemporary English-Canadian Literature

*Georgiana Banita (University of Constance)*

## The Politics of Multiculturalism

BOTH IN THEORY AND IDEALLY also in practice, Canada has adopted a constitutional policy of multiculturalism that comprises the layered, interrelated histories and cultures of all its constituent groups: English Canadians, French Canadians, First Nations, and other ethnic minorities alike. Before the passing of the 1947 Canadian Citizenship Act, all Canadians were counted as British subjects, but over the following two decades, mounting local and international tensions — such as Quebec nationalism, growing demands for compensation from members of the First Nations, and post-Second World War immigration policies — required a revision of the Canadian concept of nation. Canadian identity was thus detached from a community ideal as being homogeneously White (or more precisely, of Anglo-Saxon ethnicity and religion), reflecting the heterogeneous makeup of its changing population. Beyond its significant indigenous population now numbering about one million people, and its settlement by originally two groups, the English and the French, Canada has been an immigrant-receiving country since the early nineteenth century. Whereas Canada brought a relatively small number of Jews to safety during the Nazi regime, the country — as a deliberate atonement for earlier mistakes such as the repression of the Japanese during the Second World War and the Chinese Exclusion Act of 1923 — opened its doors in the early 1950s to hitherto less-preferred immigrant groups, welcoming since 1990 as many as 200,000 immigrants annually. Today, more than one hundred different minority ethnic groups live in Canada, and the foreign-born alone account for about nineteen percent of the overall population.

Often cited as an exemplar for other nations and a model for promoting cultural diversity as an enrichment rather than a problem, Canada is one of the very few countries to have legislated multiculturalism through a set of policies initiated in 1971 by Pierre Trudeau, adopted into Canada's constitution in the Charter of Rights and Freedoms in 1982, and finally enshrined in legislation through the Multiculturalism Act (Bill C-93 of 1988), which ensued from the 1969 report of the Royal Commission on Bilingualism and Biculturalism. The uniqueness of Canada's multicultural politics, which ideally results in the absence of overt ethnic conflict despite an increasingly heterogeneous population, lies in its federal approach to the nationalistic aspirations of its diverse groups (Kymlicka 1998). This approach consists, however, in primarily passive modes of recognition that focus on cultural heritage and the promotion of difference, in keeping with the Canadian multicultural politics of "integration" rather than assimilation. Though visibly superior to other forms of diversity management, this approach has been criticized by, among others, sociologist John Rex, who calls into question what he refers to as the "simplistic model of the support of ethnic minorities on a purely cultural level" (Rex 1997). Neil Bissoondath (1955–), too, arduously engaged with the downside of official multiculturalism in his hotly debated book *Selling Illusions: The Cult of Multiculturalism in Canada* (1994). Although Canadian law guarantees what some refer to as a cultural shopping center, this has not fundamentally upset the Canadian class-and-ethnicity-based hierarchy in social power structures also known as the vertical mosaic (see Hutcheon 1990).

Multiculturalism is under attack from some quarters for being too successful in promoting cultural pluralism, while others accuse it of showcasing only symbolic ethnicity and the unthreatening aspects of cultural otherness. Critics dismiss Canadian multiculturalism policies as a means of pigeonholing immigrants by confining them to their predetermined identities, thus engendering the dissolution of a unified Canadian culture as well as the formation of ghettos and enclaves. The discussion around multiculturalism therefore constitutes an essential lynchpin in the more general debate on what David Taras has called "a passion for identity" throughout Canadian history. Further spaces of distinction arise from the ubiquitous use of hyphenation to mark a person's belonging to an ethnic group, thereby placing ethnicity outside of Canadianness and in a position of priority, which muddies the already complicated question of national identity for ethnic minorities. Intent on fixing and containing static ethnic identities, multiculturalism does little justice to the more transcultural orientation of what Homi K. Bhabha calls "the hybridity of imagined communities" (1994), with the qualities of fluidity and exchange it implies. The processual nature of identity formation and its inherent fragmentariness are more aptly suggested by Janice Kulyk Keefer's revisionist concept of "transculturalism" that favors a notion of identity based on the constant negotiation and compromise of interrelationships, on the dynamic and overlapping network of a pluralistic narrative. "The play of cultural differences engendered by diverse experiences and constructions of race and ethnicity" (Keefer, 87) would thus supersede a philosophy of multiculturalism bent on defending borders rather than crossing them.

Exploration would replace possible essentialism, while the retrogressive practice of equating so-called "ethnic writers" with foreignness and cultural exteriority would give in to a more flexible and less exclusive concept of identity as liminal space of constant evolution and interplay.

The literatures of ethnic minorities in English Canada abundantly display the chasm between the practical management of diversity and the ideal imagining of multiculturalism on the level of discourse. They reflect both the significance and the popularity of the ideology of a multicultural and inclusive nation, but also the economic and social dissatisfactions of ethnic groups chafing at the invisible marginalization enabled by state-sanctioned tolerance. In 1996, with the publication of Smaro Kamboureli's collection *Making a Difference: An Anthology of Canadian Multicultural Literature*, it became obvious through the editor's remarks that representatives of minority literatures were winning some of the most coveted Canadian literary prizes, which conferred on their works a validity that had previously been denied to writers of non-Anglo-Saxon backgrounds. At the first stage of ethnic writers' assimilation into the mainstream, tokenism — the symbolic, limited inclusion of minority writers, usually associated with an overemphasized attention to difference — resulted in a further consolidation of the selected writers' marginal position. However, a shift in focus has occurred as a result of several factors, which include recent patterns of immigration and demographic change (with an increasing percentage of non-White immigrant groups), the impact of American multiculturalist discourse and postcolonial theory, growing concern about fair representation in writers' organizations such as PEN, as well as literary events such as the 1994 conference *Writing Thru Race* (open only for racial minorities), which was dismissed as segregationist and at the same time lauded as a welcome opportunity for debate. Consequently, the mythopoeic or environmentalist tradition of criticism canonized through the works of Northrop Frye, Margaret Atwood, Douglas Jones, Ronald Sutherland, and John Moss proved to be in need of revision.

As a cultural heuristic for the negotiation of identity and collective as well as individual belonging, diversity has left indelible marks on that segment of Canadian literature that emerges from minority groups. Some common preoccupations and themes characterize the output of Canadian writers of ethnic descent, coalescing into a cluster of aesthetic allegories which are by no means exclusive to these authors, but which prove especially useful in retracing the literary impact of diversity as an overarching cultural and political idiom. Within the parameters of these themes, contributors to the literary minority traditions communicate without suspending their differences. Through their poetry, fiction, and critical texts, these authors speak to each other across boundaries imposed by race, ethnic origin, gender, geography, and ideological affiliations, while their thematic concerns and aesthetics illustrate in remarkable ways multicultural literature's paradoxical tendencies towards homogeneity. Certainly, their individual "accents" are not silenced, so when considered together, they invite the reader to reflect on the social, political, and cultural contexts that have made of Canadian literature in general a collage of voices. Also, a recentering of the issue in the larger context of migration and minority literatures seems preferable to a neat categorization of national ethnic groups simply because so many authors participate in more than one cultural tradition: Statistics Canada reports that as many as twenty-eight percent of Canadians are descended from more than one ethnic group. The majority of Canadian minority literature is dominated by the question of cultural identity. It will become clear, however, that it is virtually impossible to isolate personal from collective identity, or to separate self-perception from the apparatus of power that imposes or suggests identificatory patterns to certain ethnic groups, to the point where identities become instable and extremely fluid entities.

# The Immigrant Novel

According to Margaret Atwood (1939–), all Canadian novels (with the exception of those written by Native writers) are in one way or another immigrant fiction, since, as Atwood writes in *The Journals of Susanna Moodie*, "we are all immigrants to this place even if we were born here." Considered more narrowly, the immigrant novel as a genre describes the encounter of the foreign-born with the predominantly Anglo-Saxon culture of Canada, and their struggle with its conventions. In such novels, the immigrant experience often begins in a spirit of wild adventure, as their protagonists dramatically break with past lives and settle in a new country full of promise, though soon enough this country may contract to an urban ghetto where they are thrown into an introverted, claustrophobic self-protectiveness amid their own kind. Tensions ensue between the family and its hostile environment, as well as between the individual and the family. The sensitive child, often the author-surrogate, escapes through education, but once untethered from the emotional grip of the family and its traditions, the protagonist faces loneliness, guilt for leaving those traditions behind, and a new curiosity about what they might conceal. Most of these novels follow the formula of the Künstlerroman, focusing on a single character who grows into a socially isolated artist, a displaced "multicultural" individual who must undertake a solitary struggle to become productive.

The history of this genre in Canada goes back to the beginning of the past century. The daughter of Icelandic immigrant parents, Laura Goodman Salverson (1890–1970) decided early on that she wanted to learn "the greatest language in the whole world" (Salverson 1939) and write in English, a promise she kept by writing the first Canadian ethnic novel in English, *The Viking Heart* (1923). The book is a saga of nation-building inspired by Norse poetic traditions and historical romance that records the mass migration of 1,400 Icelanders to Canada in 1876, as well as the blessings of kinship and kindred love, which can assuage the blows of intolerance. Similar concerns with immigrant dislocation and the vicissitudes of ethnic assimilation run through Salverson's two other novels, *When Sparrows Fall* (1925) and *The Dark Weaver* (1937), as well as her autobiography, *Confessions of an Immigrant's Daughter* (1939), the latter two books having won Salverson the Governor General's Award. Salverson later broke the ethnic thematic continuity of her work by writing novels in the manner of the historical romance, symptomatically receiving less critical attention and acclaim for these works than for her earlier ones.

In more recent immigrant fictions, self-reflexivity blurs the distinctions between autobiography and fiction by employing metafictional gestures which distract from the ethnic content of the texts and sometimes enhance their qualities as liminal genres that reflect the tug between different cultures. Arabian-Canadian novelist and playwright Saad E. A. Elkhadem (1932–2003), for instance, published the avant-garde Flying Egyptian trilogy — consisting of the "micronovels" *Canadian Adventures of the Flying Egyptian* (1990), *Chronicle of the Flying Egyptian in Canada* (1991), and *Crash Landing of the Flying Egyptian* (1992) — which, through an array of self-reflexive devices, attempts to retell both the experience of immigration and that of fiction-writing. Similarly metafictional, Kristjana Gunnars's (1948–) *The Prowler* (1989) is centered on a narrator who must come to terms with her past while deliberately undermining autobiographical claims to convey through a central perspective the impression of a consistent identity. Thus the narrator's desire to write her autobiography is undercut by her simultaneous acknowledgement of the defeat of that intention. The text ultimately foregrounds the process of writing itself through memories and reflections, which are released by way of free association, regardless of chronology and order. Gunnars dismisses traditional autobiography as self-deception, a prescriptive generic convention that assigns order and closure where there is only chaos, a stance that seems all the more compelling in the context of a novel that recreates the atmosphere of exile, the dissolution of linguistic borders, displacement, and suffering. Just as the book precludes any single point of narrative reference, it presents Iceland as a subservient colony to Danish domination — while both Iceland and Denmark are part of Gunnars's own heritage in relation to a Canada that haunts the text — thus raising the question of where a "centered" identity could be established. Other recent immigrant fictions that describe the experiences of migrant families before and after their arrival in Canada have achieved cult status, among them Nino Ricci's

(1939–) trilogy begun with *Lives of the Saints* (1990) — winner of a Governor General's Award and adapted for a TV miniseries starring Sophia Loren — and continued with *In a Glass House* (1993) and *Where She Has Gone* (1997).

## Anthologizing the Immigrant Experience

Contemporary multicultural literature in Canada is community-based. In its development, the anthology has been employed as a political and aesthetic form to draw attention to collective cultural causes and to bridge the separation among writers with similar ethnic backgrounds. As a means of introducing emerging trends into the mainstream and embracing writing in different genres, anthologies gathered resistant voices from all ethnic quarters. Many anthologies of Canadian minority literatures were compiled in response to the hegemonic practices in mainstream Canadian literature anthologies, which patronizingly marginalized or simply ignored minority writings for a time. As a literary form, however, the anthology has its drawbacks, especially in light of the linguistic variety of the communities it sets out to represent. Emerging from the Chinese-Canadian Writers' Workshop (a nonprofit organization with an Emerging Writer's Award established in 1997 and a quarterly magazine called *Rice Paper*), *Inalienable Rice: A Chinese and Japanese Canadian Anthology* (edited by Garrick Chu, Sean Gunn, Paul Yee, Ken Shikaze, Linda Uyehara Hoffman, and Rick Shiomi 1979) did not discuss a bilingual option, while the later collection *Many-Mouthed Birds: Contemporary Writing by Chinese Canadians* (edited by Bennett Lee and Jim Wong-Chu 1991) did invite submissions both in English and Chinese, yet the editors finally decided to avoid the pitfalls of translation and only included writing in English. *Many-Mouthed Birds* foregrounds political injustices against the Chinese-Canadian population, such as head taxes and the 1923 Chinese Exclusion Act, while *Yellow Peril: Reconsidered* (edited by Paul Wong 1990) addresses existing racial stereotypes of Asian Canadians. Targeting historical damage and "institutional forgetfulness" (that is, the tendency to deal with White reactions to the Chinese rather than with the Chinese themselves), these anthologies provided a necessary forum for Chinese-Canadian writers to deal with the community's hundred-year silence. The diverse backgrounds of the contributors to these anthologies (which include, next to Canada, mainland China, Taiwan, Hong Kong, Singapore, Trinidad, and Zimbabwe) emphasize the collectively shared but nonunified Chinese-Canadian identity. One of the main themes in these anthologies is the concern that the English language colonizes non-English speakers' minds through its structures and inherent sensitivities, or, as one essayist and visual artist puts it,

English, with its history of imperialism and colonization of minds, is a syntactical problem. Its writing reinforces its history because it was the only language accepted in its colonies. . . . I am dependent on English to deflate that which itself has created. I am dependent because it has become the native tongue that most of the reading world knows or wants to know. It is the audacious syntax that generates its own meanings and expectations within contexts it knows nothing about. (Laiwan 1990)

The past two decades have witnessed a rapid increase in the number and success of Asian-Canadian literary anthologies. *Swallowing Clouds: An Anthology of Chinese-Canadian Poetry* (edited by Andy Quan and Jim Wong-Chu 2000) adds to its multicultural sweep an impressive thematic range and includes well-known writers such as Fred Wah and Evelyn Lau next to poets publishing in journals or chapbooks (such as Fiona Tinwei Lam) and regular café performers (Jen Lam). *Jin Guo: Voices of Chinese Canadian Women* (edited by Amy Go, Winnie Ng, Dora Nipp, Julia Tao, Terry Woo, and May Yee 1992) adapts the anthology format to the model of feminist "herstory" and historical testimony. Containing diaries, letters, and reminiscences, *Stone Voices: Wartime Writings of Japanese Canadian Issei* (edited by Keibo Oiwa 1991) is similar in scope and tone and offers very accessible, private windows on the Japanese-Canadian experience of detention and resettlement. *Shakti's Words: An Anthology of South Asian Canadian Women's Poetry* (edited by Diane McGifford and Judith Kearns 1990) offers biting examples of the political injustice felt by the doubly marginalized female immigrants. Illuminating insights into the North American lives of Southern Asians are also provided in *Her Mother's Ashes: Stories by South Asian Women in Canada and the United States* (edited by Nurjehan Aziz 1994) and *Her Mother's Ashes 2* (edited by Nurjehan Aziz 1998), which focus on whimsical, epiphanic moments that suggest cultural tension or malaise and inspire empathy.

Anthologies of African-Canadian writing also employ generic eclecticism and aim to transform literature into a politicized platform. When *Voices: Canadian Writers of African Descent* was published in 1992 (edited by Ayanna Black), it offered a forum for a group of emerging writers such as Lawrence Hill and George Elliott Clarke, who joined company with already internationally acclaimed writers such as Austin Clarke. Published two years later, *Fiery Spirits* (edited by Ayanna Black) compiled short stories and poems exploring racism, feminism, belonging, and alienation by up-and-coming writers such as Dionne Brand. In 2000, the two collections were combined in one seminal volume. Especially for productions from marginalized groups even within cultural minorities, authors and editors have had to rely on smaller, alternative presses, some of which developed into influential and groundbreaking publishing houses, among them Toronto's Sister Vision Press. Founded in 1985 by Makeda Silvera and Stephanie Martin (both from Jamaica), Sister Vision published provocative works by Canadian women of color who would otherwise have experienced difficulties in seeing their books in print. Silvera (1955–) herself faced mainstream resistance to the publication of her book *Silenced: Caribbean Domestic Workers Talk with Makeda Silvera*, because its language was considered inaccessible by mainstream publishers. Despite limited funds and reluctance among the Black literary community to support a press run by a lesbian couple, Sister Vision has published important works on traditionally silenced issues such as lesbianism, bisexualism, and racial oppression, among them *Piece of My Heart: A Lesbian of Color Anthology* (1991) and *The Very Inside: An Anthology of Writings by Asian and Pacific Islands Lesbians and Bisexual Women* (1994).

More recent collections (*Making a Difference: Canadian Multicultural Literature*, edited by Smaro Kamboureli 1996; *Other Solitudes: Canadian Multicultural Fictions*, edited by Linda Hutcheon and Marion Richmond 1990) tend to encompass writings by minority authors of various ethnic backgrounds and to engage with the concept of multiculturalism, pointing out its qualities as both valuable ideal and contentious ideology. Such projects stress the function of the hyphen as connection rather than division, "not as slashes in the variegated cloth of Canadianness, but as the very stitches which hold a quilted fabric together" (Keefer 1995).

# Trajectories of Conflict

Canadian minority literatures frequently address crucial issues such as racism and political tensions in a direct, confrontational manner. Some of these conflicts are fictionalized more than others, with the Japanese repression in the 1940s holding a central position, beginning with the work of Joy Kogawa (1935–). Before her landmark novel *Obasan* was published in 1981, Kogawa had already explored her origins in poetry collections that articulate the sentiments she discovered as a Canadian upon visiting Japan (*The Splintered Moon*, 1967; *A Choice of Dreams*, 1974). Based on Kogawa's own experiences as a child born in Vancouver and living there until the Second World War, then uprooted together with her Japanese-Canadian family and relocated to an internment camp in the interior of British Columbia, the novel follows Kogawa's peregrinations from Alberta to Toronto, Vancouver, and back to Toronto in the late 1970s, investigating her double legacy of origins. Much of the impetus in *Obasan* revolves around the first-person narrator, Naomi Nakane, and her maternal aunt Emily. They have different ways of articulating their pain at being labeled "enemy aliens" by their community and of revisiting their past, Naomi embracing the passive silence of her elderly aunt Obasan, Emily obsessively attempting to document the history of racism against Japanese Canadians. Both of these approaches, Kogawa suggests, are inherent in an immigrant's double existence, one articulate and the other subdued. In the process of the intergenerational autobiographical act, Naomi gradually shifts from resistance to acknowledgement of her past, attesting to the fact that the generation problem in ethnic fiction often correlates with the proximity to or distance from an ethnic tradition. The novel played a considerable role in alerting Canadians to past injustices against Japanese immigrants and contributed, along with Kogawa's own activism, to the redress sought by them from the Canadian government. Kogawa's adaptation of the novel for children (*Naomi's Road*, 1986) appeared in Japanese translation and was adopted as a textbook for Japanese junior high schools. A Vancouver opera version of *Naomi's Road* premiered in 2005. Kogawa's other novels also deal with the repercussions of racism and internment, which she sums up in the trenchant sentence: "What this country did to us, it did to itself" (Kogawa 1981). More overtly political than *Obasan*, Kogawa's *Itsuka* (1992) takes its title from the Japanese word for "someday," implying the collective expectation that at some point in time Japanese Canadians would gain compensation from the Canadian government for their confiscated properties. The Redress Movement succeeded in Canada three years prior to the publication of this novel, which indeed recounts Naomi Nakane's reconciliation with Canada as a result of this positive development. On the more private level of personal redress, Kogawa's third novel, *The Rain Ascends* (1995), deals with memories of molestation in early childhood and the importance of mercy, while her most recent poetry collection, *A Song of Lilith* (2001), blends mythology and contemporary culture in rethinking the Christian figure as a strong female role model for all women, regardless of race, religion, or class background.

Another Japanese-Canadian writer who was concerned with racial discrimination in the aftermath of the Pearl Harbor bombing of December 1941 was Muriel Kitagawa (1912–1974), whose posthumous collection *This Is My Own: Letters to Wes & Other Writings on Japanese Canadians 1941–1948* (1985) describes unwarranted detainments, the signs on the roads saying "Japs Keep Out," the humiliating curfews, and the horror of dispossession. At the heart of Terry Watada's (1951–) short-story cycle *Daruma Days: A Collection of Fictionalized Biography* (1997) lies the same history of repression and alienation during the Second World War, as Japanese-Canadian families were separated and evacuated to the interior of British Columbia. Watada recreates the life stories of the "issei" (first generation of immigrants still imbued with Japanese tradition) previous to their internment and the "nisei" (second generation), who wander through a realm that falls between two worlds. The ravages of Japanese-Canadian history on the lives of its victims are also the interest of Kerri Sakamoto's (1959–) prize-winning novel *The Electrical Field* (1998). To a large extent a response to Kogawa's earlier *Obasan*, Sakamoto's novel documents a generation of Japanese Canadians whose lives were devastated by the

Canadian government's violent dispersal during the Second World War: Redress meetings are held which people are too dispirited to attend, characters cannot stand the sight of other Asians, and death in the camps continues to haunt the protagonist to this day in the midst of a community torn by internalized racism. The entire text can be interpreted as an allegory on the extension of physical confinement into psychological seclusion, a transformation that has marked the Japanese-Canadian community up to today. Sakamoto's later novel *One Hundred Million Hearts* (2003) further pursues this interest in the consequences of conflict, but in the context of the Second World War, which she addresses from a new point of view — that of the Japanese sent off to die for the emperor as kamikaze pilots — thereby questioning issues of grief and sacrifice. Published in 2001, Roy Miki's (1942–) book of poetry *Surrender* upsets and disorients official history, again relating to the internment of Japanese Canadians in the 1940s. This subject also holds personal meaning for Miki, who was born in 1942 on a sugar-beet farm where his second-generation Japanese-Canadian parents were forcibly settled. Like other members of his community, Miki also lobbied the federal government for a redress agreement and coauthored the book *Justice in Our Time: The Japanese Canadian Redress Settlement* (1991). His own collection of essays, entitled *Broken Entries: Race, Subjectivity, Writing* (1998), explores similar issues of displacement and exemplifies his dictum that the most passionate kind of literary work comes from writers who have seen themselves as marginalized, beleaguered, or in struggle with the power of dominant society.

## Against Forgetting: Nostalgic Geographies in Diasporic Writing

Frederick Philip Grove (1879–1948), one of the first immigrant authors in Canada, not only sparked controversy around his identity and origins, which he continually reinvented (for instance, in his fictionalized autobiography *In Search of Myself*, 1946), but also gave voice to the New Canadians in a tone that was both ironic and extremely confident. The struggles of early immigrants that Grove wrote about in epic and tragic terms (*Over Prairie Trails*, 1922; *Settlers of the Marsh*, 1925; *The Master of the Mill*, 1944) and the frankness in his descriptions of their living conditions make his writing exemplary of many patterns that characterize the immigrant experience and literary output. One significant topos that his writing glosses over, however, is the immigrants' nostalgia for their origins and their need to align themselves with other members of their ethnic group, feelings that Grove replaces with a spirit of individualism modeled after Rousseau, Emerson, and Thoreau (especially in Grove's *A Search for America*, 1927). Particularly for writers of the Jewish diaspora, who often dramatize the Holocaust experience and recreate the past as a tangible character, memory and memorialization are the preferred means of coming to terms with their history and their personal loss. Both Adele Wiseman's (1928–1992) *The Sacrifice* (1956) and Norman Ravvin's (1963–) *Café des Westens* (1991) delineate a Canadian "here" haunted by the distant Eastern Europe, the site of pogroms and other radical forms of genocide. Whereas in *The Sacrifice* a brutal murder occasions the return to the traumatic "old country" of hopelessness and death, *Café des Westens* revolves around the metaphor of the café itself, its cultural openness and permeability, recreating in the multicultural city of Calgary the atmosphere of a Berlin café during the years of the Weimar Republic. Ravvin's use of the city as both setting and trope for the multilayered narrative suggests an image of the Canadian metropolis as a cultural palimpsest. Also located in the context of contemporary debates about Germany's political past and its brutality, Suzette Mayr's (1967–) *The Widows* (1998) suggests that only a direct confrontation with history can lead to liberation, both on an individual and a national level. Continuing a line of Canadian feminine survival narratives, *The Widows* is an unlikely story about three elderly German ladies turning their lives around and making a statement on their exiled existence by taking off over Niagara Falls in a space-age capsule. The novel stages the personal negotiations between Canadian and German identities, as well as the aftermath of Germany's discourse on nationhood, as the sisters reinvent Germany in a more acceptable guise within the familiar reality of imported delicacies, behind which the alienating Germany of the war begins to fade.

The discourse of memory is also a staple of other minority writings, especially in connection with intergenerational strife and the pursuit of tradition. In the very first collection of poetry by a Chinese Canadian, Jim Wong-Chu (1949–) stresses the phantom-like quality of Chinese-Canadian life in the title of his book *Chinatown Ghosts* (1986), with the secondary implication that White people's historical amnesia and lack of concern for tradition render them immaterial and insubstantial. Other Chinese-Canadian writers foster identity formation through reinvoking or creating heroes and myths. Paul Yee (1956–) and Jim Wong-Chu create community role models reminiscent of the Chinese "bachelors" and "sojourners," in particular of the railway laborers who helped to build Canadian infrastructures. Prose works by Denise Chong and Wayson Choy also pursue a Chinese-Canadian historiography, following a documentary stance and exploring divergent ways of dealing with the intercultural situation. Choy's (1939–) novel *The Jade Peony* (1995) explores this duality through the generational conflicts among its Chinese-Canadian characters, the younger children tending toward assimilation while the older generation remains unable to accept Canadian culture and even decides to go back to "old China" to die, as "bones must come to rest where they most belong."

Choy's later memoir *Paper Shadows: A Chinatown Childhood* (1999) and his recent novel *All That Matters* (2004) reiterate the intergenerational pressures and anxieties that come with the Chinese immigrants' new lives in Vancouver. Similarly divided between China and British Columbia, Denise Chong's bestselling novel *The Concubine's Children* (1994) recounts the tale of Chong's grandmother, illegally brought to Canada as a concubine and teahouse waitress in the 1920s. Chong's biography of Kim Phuc (*Girl in the Picture*, 2000) — the subject of a now-famous photograph and reluctant poster girl for American atrocities as she flees her Vietnamese village, her naked body scorched by napalm — presents an even more radical schism between communist Vietnam and liberating Ontario. This dualistic structure, which isolates the Chinese community from the European-based Canadian majority, is disrupted by the pluralistic works of Larissa Lai (1967–), who rejects the dualism of remembered tradition and oppressive present in favor of a more complex differentiation. In contrast to the work of Sky Lee (1952–), who employs an inventive syncretism by merging Chinese culture with postmodern self-reflexivity, Lai purposely omits community history and its memorialization, focusing instead on the individual identity formation of young Chinese Canadians in Vancouver today, amalgamating traditional Chinese myths with contemporary urban realities. Especially her novel *When Fox Is a Thousand* (1995) confronts the reader with a history of endless metamorphoses of Fox, the Chinese trickster figure, which brings about a constant confusion of cultural codes and calls into question essentialist concepts of identity. Beyond a metaphor against racialization and sexism, the image of "the Fox breathing life into the bodies of the dead is like a brown person trying to breathe life into an assimilated white self as required by the social pressures of white liberalism" (Lai 1998). The Japanese counterpart to this mythological figure is the kappa, a trickster character from Japanese folklore, which Hiromi Goto (1966–) transplants to the landscape of the Canadian prairies in her magic-realist fantasy novel *The Kappa Child* (2001), which shifts between present and past, the real and the fantastic, playing them off against each other. Like the pregnancy caused by the protagonist's encounter with the (paradoxically genderless) kappa, racial belonging cannot be detected or explained in physical or rational terms, but must be either subjectively accepted or rejected as a kind of illusion. Goto's more recent short-story collection *Hopeful Monsters* (2004) uses its title (which alludes to positive evolutionary mutations) and overtly fantastical elements to address otherness and social difference in ways that go far beyond the traditional immigrant narrative. Works such as this challenge the idea of an ethnic sense of nostalgia for a far-away homeland, with its portrayal of an overvalorized past, a type of reification that Neil Bissoondath caustically referred to as "Culture Disneyfied" (Bissoondath, 83).

Other fictions directly address the places from which authors originally came, showing their settings to be layered with stories and recovering from the impact of colonialism and its detrimental effects. One of the most important Hungarian poets in exile, twice nominated for the Nobel Prize for Literature, George Faludy's (1910–2006) prominence was already secured at the time of his arrival in Canada in 1967. After brief sojourns in Europe, Africa, and the United States, documented in his autobiography *My Happy Days in Hell* (1962), Faludy found in Toronto an antidote to the anxiety and consumerism of modern society, and had no qualms in describing Canada as "the most marvelous decent society I have ever lived in" (Faludy 1989). In meditative diary entries, his *Notes from the Rainforest* (1988) record his reflections on, among other things, cultural differences between Canada and the United States. Sometimes, as in the poetry of Sri Lanka-born Rienzi Crusz (1925–), the lush imagery of a preindustrial past, with its comforting sense of nostalgia, gives way to a complex exploration of the tension between nature and modern postindustrial culture, searching for metaphors (such as "The Sun Man") that could amalgamate the two coexisting segments in a meaningful way. Never in his collections of poetry (*Flesh and Thorn*, 1974; *Elephant and Ice*, 1980; *Singing against the Wind*, 1985; *A Time for Loving*, 1986; *Still Close to the Raven*, 1989; *The Rain Doesn't Know Me Any More*, 1992; *Gamboling with the Divine*, 2003) does Crusz lose sight of the intricacies of racial difference from his double perspective as an immigrant and as a Black man. Taking a more explicitly gendered perspective, Aritha van Herk's (1954–) *Places Far from Ellesmere* (1990) theorizes the contact between self and place within the context of a voyage to the Canadian North, to Ellesmere Island, examining the links between geopolitical interests and discursive configurations. A writer of Dutch origins from western Canada, van Herk sees cartography as a form of interpretation rather than transparent rendition of a spatial reality. Her works explore the connections between Canadian geography and identity, as well as the constraints of both fictional and feminine representations, also deconstructing masculine perspectives on the prairie. In *Places Far from Ellesmere*, van Herk sets out to revise nineteenth-century representations of Arctic space (centered on the confrontation of the White man with the sublime North), while *No Fixed Address* (1986) revises the quest genre to produce a feminine picaresque narrative, and remaps Canadian territory hitherto premised on a masculine logocentric worldview. Van Herk's mental map of childhood memories of growing up in the small rural town of Edberg (central Alberta) illustrates her own critical statement that a map is "not a tracing of shape but a means of shaping" (van Herk 1992). There is therefore no fixed point of nostalgic return to her childhood, but a dispersed focus, turning Edberg into an elaborate fabrication rather than a geographical spot; home is thus equated with the very process of signifying space.

An essential ingredient of immigrant writing is the return to the homeland after a period of exile and acclimatization, a visit that is often dramatized by a romantic plot. Eva Stachniak's (1952–) novel *Necessary Lies* (2000), for instance, describes the female protagonist's return to Poland, in a changed, postcommunist Europe, in order to confront her past and probe the depths of personal betrayal and forgiveness, reconsidering the motives that drove her away from home and seeing her own experience through the eyes of those who stayed behind. Forgetting and remembrance also haunt Janice Kulyk Keefer's (1953–) novel *The Green Library* (1996), whose protagonist Eva sets out to solve the mystery of a photograph that sends her sleuthing back in time to her childhood and across the ocean to Ukraine. Ignorant of her own personal history and of the country where it took place, Eva traverses various stages of pain and awareness of the untold stories of all those displaced persons — especially those from Ukraine — who arrived in Canada after the Second World War, leaving their former identities far behind.

The future of such binary geographical oscillations lies perhaps in a total dissolution of their dualism and a more profound engagement with passages and migrations on a truly global scale, as they appear in the works of Indian-born writer Ven Begamudré (1956–). His cosmopolitan characters in *A Planet of Eccentrics* (short stories, 1990) and *The Lightness Which Is Our World Seen from Afar* (poetry, 2006) easily travel back and forth between India, Europe, and North America. Perhaps the most eloquent example of this transculturalism can be found in the work of acclaimed writer Michael Ondaatje (1943–). With a powerful thematic trinity consisting of history, memory, and truth, Ondaatje reflects on the constant conflict and tension between official and unofficial histories. Born in Colombo, Ceylon (now Sri Lanka), Ondaatje was nine years old when he left his birthplace. After studying at the University of Toronto and Queen's University, Kingston, he embarked on an academic career that finally brought him to the faculty of Glendon College at Toronto's York University, with which he was affiliated until 1988. As a poet, novelist, critic, and documentary filmmaker, Ondaatje belongs to a generation of writers that he himself refers to as the first of the real migrant tradition, next to Salman Rushdie, Kazuo Ishiguro, Ben Okri, and Rohinton Mistry — writers who left their homelands and did not return, but carried their country to another place. However, it was not until *Running in the Family* (1982) — a book about his parents that defies generic definition by blending novelistic, autobiographical, poetic, and documentary elements (also described as a "biotext") — that Ondaatje's background found its way into his work. By contrast, through an intensely private and occasionally violent imagery, Ondaatje's poetry collections (among them *The Dainty Monsters*, 1967; *Rat Jelly*, 1973; *There's a Trick with a Knife I'm Learning to Do*, 1979; and *Secular Love*, 1984) focus on the author's family and some of

Canada's rural landscapes. The poetry collection *Handwriting* (2000) gathers nostalgic views of the author's native Sri Lanka. In *The Story* (2006), Ondaatje's poems around his larger themes of memory and exile, both in typeset and in his own handwriting, are paired with illustrations by the celebrated painter David Bolduc. This eclectic form harks back to the publication of Ondaatje's hybrid work *The Collected Works of Billy the Kid* (1970), which initiated Ondaatje's characteristic collage of poetry, prose, and illustration. Multiculturalism as a paradigm and metaphor runs through several of Ondaatje's novels, especially in relation to his pervasive theme of surrogate, extended, or makeshift families, which emerge from the pooling of individual histories and memories. *In the Skin of a Lion* (1987) is set in the Toronto of the late 1920s and 1930s, placing its central character among immigrants, especially Macedonians, in an attempt to represent the unofficial history of Toronto, particularly the events concerning the construction of the Bloor Street Viaduct and the water filtration plant by immigrants. *The English Patient* (1992) brings together four widely contrasting characters in an abandoned northern Italian villa, where they begin to heal each other's war wounds by sharing stories and histories. The ideal of mutual tolerance is, however, shattered, as the Sikh character decides to return to India and adopts a bifurcated view of the world, divided into East and West. Set in Sri Lanka during its gruesome civil war in the mid-1980s, *Anil's Ghost* (2000) follows Anil Tessira as she returns to her native land after a fifteen-year absence in order to investigate reports of mass murders on the island. One factor in the civil war causing these deaths is discrimination among religious factions and tampering with history, so the novel can be read as a plea for a Sri Lankan mosaic and as a warning that multiculturalism can only work if all histories of a nation's people are acknowledged.

The elusive, imaginary character of homelands also emerges from the works of prize-winning author Rohinton Mistry, born in Bombay (now Mumbai) in 1952, who emigrated to Canada in 1975 to study in Toronto and work there as a bank clerk. After leaving his job to become a full-time writer, Mistry published the short-story collection *Tales from Firozsha Baag* (1987) and three novels (*Such a Long Journey*, 1991; *A Fine Balance*, 1996; *Family Matters*, 2002) which were all shortlisted for the Booker Prize for fiction. Unlike Salman Rushdie, whose fiction is also rooted in the streets of Bombay, Mistry focuses on the Parsi community and the poor instead of the Muslim middle classes, and rejects Rushdie's magic realism in favor of an unsparing naturalist perspective. *Tales from Firozsha Baag*, a collection of eleven interrelated stories, details the lives of the residents of a decrepit apartment building in Bombay through miniature sketches that encode questions of belonging, migration, and identity while testing generic boundaries. Set in 1971 during the India-Pakistan war, *Such a Long Journey* retells events that collapse the distinction between private and public worlds, as the hero acknowledges the temporariness of friendship and loyalty in times of political turmoil and intrigue. Like Rushdie's *Midnight's Children*, *A Fine Balance* is set in Bombay during the administration of Indira Ghandi and the state of emergency, following four characters and the impact of this political tension on their lives. Unlike these historical fictions, *Family Matters* depicts the swirl of contemporary Bombay around the still life of an old Parsi with Parkinson's disease, a widower who compares himself to King Lear and recalls the past of the city and the nation as old age places strains on his family relations and even on his — formerly luxurious — living conditions.

Through a documentary realism that seems symptomatic of this author's writing, Mistry's work explores issues of corruption versus integrity, as well as the conflicting demands of duty and religious faith, especially in the context of the family, which is seen as both nurturing and oppressive. Mistry's characters are fascinated with patterns, of the past or of the present, which they need to impose structure on the chaos that dominates their lives. Their mixed ethnic identities, partaking of different cultures, result in a hybrid writing style that combines the clarity of European realism with the dialogic momentum of Eastern storytelling traditions, suggesting an insightful conception of identity as a sense of command over narrative complexity. The symbol of identity as a layered story is the city of Bombay, described as a "story spinning mill" (*A Fine Balance*) that can provide temporary unity to lives inhabiting liminal places in space and time.

# Racialization

One of the most significant issues in multicultural literature is that of racialization, the construction of images of ourselves or of others by relying on the loaded and biased ideological definitions of racial categories. The work of the most prominent Black writer in Canada best instantiates the literary possibilities of negotiating racial politics and art. Austin Clarke, born in Barbados in 1934, did not begin to write until after he arrived in Canada in 1955. His novels *The Survivors of the Crossing* (1964) and *Amongst Thistles and Thorns* (1965), published a decade later, are both set in Barbados and explore the twin evils of colonial self-hatred and Caribbean poverty. Clarke's Toronto trilogy (*The Meeting Point*, 1967; *Storm of Fortune*, 1971; *The Bigger Light*, 1975) remains preoccupied with his place of birth and the psychological implications of immigration and exile, especially loneliness, self-hatred, economic exploitation, and cultural exclusion, but also with the hostility and indifference of White Canada to the West Indian immigrants, who initially embraced their adopted country as the ultimate El Dorado. Like some of the fictional characters in his collection of short stories *When He Was Free and Young and He Used to Wear*

*Silks* (1971), Clarke traces the marginalization of Blacks in Canada back to the legacy of colonialism and the pervasiveness of racism, but also to the inner and outer corruption of communities forced to live under segregating conditions, issues that he also addresses in his memoir *Growing Up Stupid under the Union Jack* (1980). This autobiography, documenting the author's boyhood and adolescence in colonial Barbados, stresses the naivety and stunted self-consciousness of the colonial subject forced to ignore his own ethnicity and to fit into the straitjacket of an alienating colonial culture. Especially interesting in this context is Clarke's emphasis in *The Bigger Light* on a Black man who achieves economic success as a Canadian businessman in the Anglo-Saxon mould, which encourages in him a certain snobbery and marked reserve toward issues of racial identity. However, despite their persistent alienation, Clarke's characters remain acutely aware of their own failures, which they regard without deception or self-pity. It is in fact precisely this sense of defeat and failure of the much-touted ideal of the Canadian mosaic that binds Clarke's diverse Canadians together, especially the middle-aged immigrants plagued by familial, sexual, and socioeconomic anxieties and uncertainties, as well as by the unsettling implications of female emancipation in the short-story collections *When Women Rule* (1985) and *Nine Men Who Laughed* (1986). A fierce social critic of racialization, Clarke used both his literary works and political writings (such as the pamphlet *Public Enemies: Police Violence and Black Youth*, 1992) to call into question governmental policies that perpetuate racial inequalities in Canadian society. Clarke's more recent works, such as the 1997 novel *The Origin of Waves* and *The Question* (1999), are increasingly introspective meditations on the nature of life in a transnational, fractured world, as their protagonists attempt to bridge distances, both in time and space, to explore the contradictions in their lives and the differences between fact and fiction. Straddling two cultures and two linguistic realms, Clarke's Black characters suffer from the consequences of colonialism to the point of self-hatred and self-denial: Some try to gain acceptance by denying their blackness, others direct violence at themselves or their children through suicide or incest, making up a complex social scene where Blacks themselves are racist or cruel. This world rife with despair has to some extent prevented Clarke from achieving widespread critical popularity, but also adumbrates an idealized vision of a more equitable society. As Wayde Compton points out, Black culture often witnesses the transformation of racism into a lightning rod for the definition of self-identity, and in his collection *Bluesprint: An Anthology of Black British Columbian Literature and Orature* (2001) he draws attention to those writers who "seek to dismantle binary and standardizing racialized epistemologies."

Claire Harris's (1937–) self-professed task as a writer is to return Africa to the heart of Western civilization and help compensate for the traumatic loss that Africans have suffered in North America and Europe, to help Africans accept their joint inheritance, and recognize "the scar tissue embroidering it" (Harris 1984). Written in a variety of styles and making experimental use of space, Harris's works mirror the profound disharmony produced by racialization and gender construction, which result in the clash of languages and genres rubbing against each other. Her poetry collections (*Fables from the Women's Quarters*, 1984; *Translation into Fiction*, 1984; *Travelling to Find a Remedy*, 1986; *The Conception of Winter*, 1989; *Drawing Down a Daughter*, 1992) reflect different ways of approaching form through cultural collage. In a note to her poem "Policeman Cleared in Jaywalking Case" (from *Fables from the Women's Quarters*), the first poem she wrote as a conscious response to uncomfortable examples of Canadian racism, Harris points out that "in the black community to signify indicates an act of acknowledgement, of sharing, of identifying with" (Harris 1984). In this context, signification also implies the creation of new language usages and modes of signifying otherwise obliterated by standard English.

Exemplifying his term "faction" as a combination of fact and fiction in African-Canadian literature, Lawrence Hill (1957–) also addresses the issue of a transgenerational identity quest as the protagonist of his novel *Any Known Blood* (1999) loses his job as a government speech writer and embarks on a journey in search of his past as the eldest son of a White mother and prominent Black father. After writing two books on the history of Blacks in Canada and the nonfiction study *Black Berry, Sweet Juice: On Being Black and White in Canada* (2001), Hill in his latest novel (*The Book of Negroes*, 2007) turns to the bleak period of the West African slave trade, in which millions of Africans perished.

George Elliott Clarke (1960–), one of the most influential voices in promoting the works of writers of African descent, first attracted major attention with his novel in verse *Whylah Falls* (1990), the portrait of a Black Nova Scotian community notable for its rich gallery of characters and the lyrical evocation of their emotions. Clarke has been a spokesman for Black issues, but in contrast to Austin Clarke, for instance, his oeuvre resists overt criticism in favor of representing the richness of his Maritime heritage and Black culture in general, drawing on African-American forms such as blues and gospel, which he blends with intricate allusions to the European literary canon. His particularly successful *Execution Poems* (2000), which relates the tragic destiny of Clarke's own cousins, hanged in 1949 for murdering a taxi driver with a hammer, reveals the author's talent with a defiant, exuberant, and provocative Black idiom, disguising a history of racism and violence. George Elliott Clarke also edited the second volume of *Fire on the Water: An Anthology of Black Nova Scotia Writing* (1990), which includes both literature and artwork, as well as *Eyeing the North Star: Directions in African-Canadian Literature* (1997), another varied and vibrant overview of African-Canadian prose, poetry, and drama.

Concerns about gender in relation to race, ethnicity, and cultural production are also circulating and intensifying in recent literary texts. The question of how gender is constructed and how its representation impinges upon desire, sexuality, and ethnic awareness (and the other way around) are addressed in various ways by writers concerned with ethnic corporeality and gender difference. As early as 1954, with the publication of Vera Lysenko's (1910–1975) first novel *Yellow Boots* — a fable-like, ethnographic document against assimilation — the legacy of ethnic origins seems to depend to a large extent on its female mediation through storytelling, songs, and folkloric customs, which finds expression despite patriarchal resistance. Lysenko's female characters thus oppose the old order of oppressive fatherhood while at the same time preserving what they value about their ethnic origins. As a protofeminist writer with a strong ethnic consciousness, Lysenko also undertook the first history of Ukrainian Canadians (*Men in Sheepskin Coats: A Study in Assimilation*, 1947), which stresses the cultural contribution of immigrant groups and argues for the protection of their national identities within the larger entity of Canadian culture. Calcutta-born Bharati Mukherjee (1940–) focuses in her works on the phenomenon of migration and the alienation often experienced by expatriates (especially in *The Tiger's Daughter*, 1972, and *Days and Nights in Calcutta*, 1977, the latter a joint project with her husband Clark Blaise), but also on her own female experience of racism in Canada, which pushed her to the edge of being a "housebound, fearful, aggrieved, obsessive, and unforgiving queen of bitterness" ("The Invisible Woman," 1981). Her novel *Wife* (1975) is centered on a woman who has been oppressed by Indian men and forced to murder her husband and eventually commit suicide. The short stories in *Darkness* (1985) and the novel *Jasmine* (1989) further develop her earlier studies in female migration and propose parallels between First and Third World patterns of treating women as subordinates. *The Holder of the World* (1993) and *Leave It to Me* (1997) also center on female protagonists in their political and emotional investigations into the conflict between Eastern and Western worlds.

# The Descent of Language, the Language of Dissent

That language in its multiple guises is central to literary discussions of race and ethnicity is highlighted by many minority writers' insistence on language as a catalyst for excursions into history and culture, memory and identity. It is equally central to postcolonial debates that stress the workings of language from a political position asking who is speaking and from what place. For many writers, the use of language as a means of control is a point of entry into a critique of colonialism. The different kinds of discourse that Marlene NourbeSe Philip (1947–) uses in her poetry reveal that tracing the genealogy of the self also involves uncovering the evolution of language. It took Philip two years and twenty-five rejections before the manuscript of *She Tries Her Tongue, Her Silence Softly Breaks* (1989) was finally published, a book that resists the logic of silencing and deconstructs standard English — the language in which the discourses of power are written (see the poem "Discourse on the Logic of Language"). Philip intends to subvert the tradition of poetry itself, which she perceived in the Caribbean as another form of colonization and oppression. "Discourse on the Logic of Language" defies those prescriptions of literary tradition that demand that a poem be separate from its history and easy to identify with. Philip deliberately embeds the poem in its historical context, that of African slaves being prohibited from speaking their mother tongues and having their tongues removed as punishment for breach of this command, finally drawing on the colonizing experience to redefine the lineage of English as a father (rather than mother) tongue — the language imposed by the White male colonizer. While *She Tries Her Tongue* indicts Western culture for the silencing of the African race, *Looking for Livingstone* (1991) reverses Philip's lament for the loss of language, presenting silence as a positive value and potential strength. Traditionally described as "the dark continent," Africa is explored as a land of timeless silence, which forces the narrator into confronting her own silence and advising the use of both silence and speech in poetic patterns of meaning. Throughout her work, Philips consciously challenges the conventional usage of the English language, using dialect or demotic speech and concentrating on the minute connotations of words and phrases.

Language not as a mere instrument of communication but as a medium of self-articulation and for the construction of otherness is a recurring concern for many multicultural writers. The title of Dionne Brand's (1953–) poetry collection *No Language Is Neutral* (1998) makes it clear that any neutrality attached to language only helps to conceal the various gestures of elision by which representation operates. Stranded between nostalgia and longing, the immigrant has only her belief in the power of words to sustain her, whereby the relation between speech and body comes prominently to the fore: "What I say in any language is told in faultless / knowledge of skin, in drunkenness and weeping, / told as a woman without matches and tinder, not in / words and in words and in words learned by heart." Being itself structured like a language, history contains and prescribes a "grammar" of experience that bears the unmistakable signs of repression and enslavement. As the pregnant, Black, Trinidadian narrator living in Canada in Claire Harris's *Drawing Down a Daughter* says to her unborn child, "all I have to give / is English which hates / fears your / black skin." In *Winter Epigrams and Epigrams to Ernesto Cardenal in Defense of Claudia* (1983), Brand meditates on the limited linguistic resources available to women poets, countered by the author's own social and political lexicon. *Chronicles of the Hostile Sun* (1984), which revolves around the American invasion of Grenada, uses the dirge-like repetition of the names of the dead to question whether words can convey the tragedy of the invasion. Brand's other fictions *Sans Souci* (1988) and *In Another Place, Not Here* (1996) are also concerned with language as the means of reinvention, as a site of hybridity registering the tensions and elisions of subjective in-betweenness, but also as a wedge to split European traditions and aesthetics. Such discourses are de-scribed by writing the body and interrogating the otherness of femininity in representation and language. Brand's most recent novel *What We All Long For* (1995) immerses its characters in the Toronto cityscape (also prominent in the poetry collection *Thirsty*, 2002), powerfully evoked through the lens of migrant longing: "Have you ever smelled this city at the beginning of spring? Dead winter circling still, it smells of eagerness and embarrassment and, most of all, longing." Rich in ethnic diversity yet constrained by its Anglo-Saxon heritage, the city provides not only the underlying rhythm of the book, but also an urban poetics which the author felt she needed to bestow on the Canadian metropolis after "reading" New York, London, and Paris.

Hong Kong-born, Vancouver-based writer Jamila Ismail proposes the metaphor of itchy language scars to describe the ways in which contemporary feminist poets with experiences of linguistic displacement make creative use of translation and multilingualism as transgressive tools for exposing the systemic violations of andocentric, colonial, and heteronormative economies, paving the way for a cultural healing of historical wounds. Translation as a metaphor of complex transition also guides the work of Polish-Jewish-Canadian writer Helen Weinzweig (1925–), whose first novel *Passing Ceremony* (1973) epitomizes the tense logic of ambiguity and paradox resulting from the author's reading of books in English translation. "If a writer's literary experience has been in another language," Weinzweig explains, "she must think in that language and 'translate' it into English" (quoted in Kamboureli 1996, 55). Beyond the incorporation of speech color and cultural idiosyncrasy, translation is important in Weinzweig's work as a metaphor for difference in its many guises (in issues of gender, desire, and realism versus fantasy), as her second novel *Basic Black with Pearls* (1980) abundantly illustrates. Josef Škvorecký (1924–), a Toronto-based Czech writer of international standing whose novel *The Engineer of Human Souls* (1984) was the first translation to win the Governor General's Award for Fiction, uses what he calls "American or Canadian Czech" for his novels, which further complicates the linguistic categories of native and acquired tongues.

Hiromi Goto's novel *Chorus of Mushrooms* (1994) is concerned with issues of ethnicity as performance and the process of cultural masquerade — a grotesque mimicry of mainstream culture caused by internalized racism. Moreover, it enacts what Sneja Gunew refers to as the trope of infantilization in migrants: "When they enter a new culture they are repositioned as children renegotiating language and the entry into the symbolic" (Gunew 1985). Simultaneously, the novel weaves Japanese words into the English text, without romanization or translation, marking the author's refusal to cater to those who form the majority, as well as delineating the liminal territory for her readers. As Goto herself explains in her essay "Translating the Self: Moving between Cultures" (1996), "I wanted to highlight that difference exists, all cannot be understood, language could and can be a barrier." Moreover, the novel's acknowledgements contain Japanese constructions that could be considered poor English, proving that she chooses to shape language and culture to her own ends.

Fred Wah (1939–), the author of seventeen volumes of poetry (among them *Lardeau*, 1965; *Waiting for Saskatchewan*, 1985; *So Far*, 1991; *Alley Alley Home Free*, 1992; *Snap*, 1993), has been at the forefront of poetic innovation in Canada. Under the influence of Charles Olson's projective-verse theory, Wah tries "to make language operate as a nonaligned and unpredictable material, not so much intentionally difficult as simply needing little complication" (quoted in Kamboureli 1996, 158). Wah's synesthetic desire to touch the haptic orality of the letter and its calligraphic texture, to understand how language inhabits his body, is a desire that reflects the individual's passage through what Wah refers to as the language of time. In his study *Faking It: Poetics and Hybridity* (2001), which contains essays, reviews, interviews, journals, notes, and poetic improvisations, Wah elaborates on the transnational poetics of China and North America, especially in his minute and particular attention to poetic language. Lien Chao's (1950–) poetry collection *More Than Skin Deep* (2004) illustrates this assumption of a transnational poetics by confronting the two very different languages — Chinese and English — with each other, using this confrontation as a metaphor for cultural adaptation and conflict in Canada. In an earlier bilingual collection (*Maples and Stream*, 1999), Chao juxtaposes parallel stories written in two languages side by side, mirroring each other and signifying the confusion inherent in the immigrant existence. As Linda Hutcheon has put it, "doubleness is the essence of the immigrant experience. Caught between two worlds, the immigrant negotiates a new social space; caught between two cultures and often languages, the writer negotiates a new literary space" (Hutcheon 1990, 9).

Other representatives of minority writing opt for a switch from the linguistic aspects of creating in a foreign language toward the visuality of writing itself, which mirrors their own status as "visible minorities." A cultural autodidact and multidisciplinary artist, Roy Kiyooka (1926–1994), born of immigrant Japanese parents (nisei), resisted the demands and conventions of the mainstream art world and focused on the interface between painting and language and how the two inform each other. Most of Kiyooka's writing engages visual form, content, or design in an effort to record the process of experience both within and beyond language. *transcanada letters* (1975), for instance, gathers lyrical correspondence and snapshots to document years of traveling across the author's adopted country, a style that ultimately inspired Kiyooka to venture into self-publishing under the Blue Mule imprint, printing and binding limited editions of such works as *Hieronymus Bosch's Heretical April Fool Diverti-mementos & Other Protestations* (1986). The final section of Kiyooka's poetry collection *Pear Tree Pomes* (1987) depicts an aging son and his frail mother poring over old photographs, in an interesting variation on Roland Barthes's *Camera Lucida*, the account of a son mourning his mother embedded in a meditation on photography.

# The Myth of Cultural Authenticity

The multifarious notions of self and belonging put forward in Canada's multicultural literatures reinforce the suspicion that the inherited concept of a unified Canadian identity has only imaginative coherence. As a strategy, this coherence is employed not only by mainstream societies but, as Sky Lee's (1952–) first book *Disappearing Moon Café* (1990) suggests, may also reflect how a community might internalize the racism that determines its position as Other to the dominant society. Kae, the novel's narrator, breaks through the family secrecy concealing the knowledge that their Chinese patriarch had a male child with a Native woman — a blemish on the family traditions the Chinese brought to Canada and also a danger in light of the pressures they experience in Vancouver. Cultural heritage thus proves to be not homogeneous but contingent on hidden histories or, as Stuart Hall has put it, a matter of becoming as well as of being. Many writings by Canadian minority authors counteract the rigid image of a unified and uniform experience of interculturalism. Fred Wah's fictitious family chronicle *Diamond Grill* (1996), an emotional and culinary journey into his own and his family's past, presents the reader with a dissolution of pure cultural forms by illuminating his Chinese-Swedish-Scottish-Canadian background and criticizing the Canadian policy of multiculturalism, which does not acknowledge people of multiple ethnic backgrounds like himself. Perhaps the most telling example of multicultural hybridity can be found in the life and works of Cyril Dabydeen (1945–). From his roots as an Asian whose great-grandparents migrated as indentured laborers from nineteenth-century India to the Caribbean, from his experiences as a Guyanese growing up during a period of intense national ferment, and from his life as an adult in Canada where he studied the works of such canonical writers as Sylvia Plath, Dabydeen makes a virtue of heterogeneity in fiction (*Berbice Crossing and Other Stories*, 1996; *Dark Swirl*, 1988; *Drums of My Flesh*, 2005; *Jogging in Havana*, 1992; *My Brahmin Days and Other Stories*, 2000; *North of the Equator*, 2001) and poetry (*Born in Amazonia*, 1995; *Discussing Columbus*, 1997). His works show the rich possibilities of combining immigrant and diasporic selves, redefining migrant self-perception as the far corners of the world draw closer.

Identities being so fluid and malleable, representations of minorities that do not correspond to one's own received ethnic profile raise ethical questions and threaten to undermine an otherwise well-intended act of empathy. Rudy Wiebe's (1934–) first novels *Peace Shall Destroy Many* (1962) and *First and Vital Candle* (1966) deal with the religious and cultural history of the Mennonites who settled in Western Canada, and *The Blue Mountains of China* (1970) documents the experiences of diasporic Mennonite communities in an epic style typical of his later work, all of which thematically resonates with his own background. Yet Wiebe has often found himself involved in controversies around the question of the appropriation of voice, a major focus of multicultural contestation. Not only does he reject the imperial concept of history as it expresses itself in Canada, but in the novels *The Temptations of Big Bear* (1973), *The Scorched-wood People* (1977), and *A Discovery of Strangers* (1994), as well as in the aptly titled short-fiction collection *Where Is the Voice Coming From?* (1974), he challenges especially the hegemonic views of history that deal with First Nations peoples, feeling that their suppression is as repulsive to him as it is to a Native Canadian. Appropriation of voice is closely linked to the notion of cultural appropriation and implies that it might be immoral for a writer from a politically comfortable ethnicity to profit by representing a disadvantaged group, thereby repackaging ethnic heritage into self-promoting ideologies. The implication is that minorities' constructions of their own cultures lack the power to compete in cultural marketplaces with majority representations of those cultures: W. P. Kinsella's (1935–) portrayals of First Nations life, for example, would sell better, both commercially and ideologically, than those of Jeannette Armstrong (1948–) or Thomas King (1943–), or perhaps even than those of Rudy Wiebe, himself a member of a minority group. In his works, Wiebe continually tests the foundations of religious and historical certainty. Not only does he examine the encroachments of White society on traditional Native Canadian, Inuit, and Métis lifestyles, but all his works are imbued with his radical Mennonite faith, challenged from without and exposed to internal pressures. It is this articulation of Mennonite religious values in the process of recounting history from indigenous perspectives that has attracted accusations of cultural appropriation.

It is also important to recognize that not all Canadian minority writers feel committed to telling the story of their origins. Their hyphenization often results not only in an intermingling of different realities, but also sinks them into the realm of a social and cultural limbo, as the autobiographical productions of Chinese-Canadian writer Evelyn Lau (1970–) have shown. After running away from her Chinese family at the age of fourteen and taking to the streets, Lau became a drug addict and a prostitute, an existence that she documented in a journal, later edited and published as the bestseller *Runaway: Diary of a Street Kid* (1989). Although the initial problems that propelled her into this dreary situation are caused by her failure to live up to her Chinese family's expectations, demanding that she compensate for their marginalization by overachievement, once she is on the street Lau completely dissociates from her ethnic background. In the absence of familial guidance, Lau finds no other discourse to frame or narrate her experience, so the text stumbles forward without a narrative drive just as her own life slides from one incident to the next without the coherence of group belonging. After the break with Chinese tradition, Canadian society does not materialize for Lau beyond its debased forms, so that in the end she becomes the very hyphen that divides her double experience. In her later texts, such as her poetry collections *You Are Not Who You Claim* (1990), *Oedipal Dreams* (1992), and *In the House of Slaves* (1994), as well as the short-story collection *Fresh Girls & Other Stories* (1993) and the 1995 novel *Other Women*, Lau offers further insight into the tangled minds of prostitutes and other marginalized women, their self-defeating and disorienting obsessions, suggesting, however, that their uprootedness and lack of direction is not caused by their dysfunctional ethnic background, but is in fact a basic condition of the modern mind. For this reason, Lau herself is seldom coupled with a specific tradition. One exhaustive study of Chinese-Canadian writing goes so far as to explicitly exclude her from its analysis (see Hilf 2000). Lau's non-adherence to a legible script of ethnicity, for which she has been taken to task, does not necessarily mean that her cultural heritage is absent from her writing, since it transpires in the difficulty of locating a coherent site from which to project her voice, as well as in her rather violent encounter with social hegemony. Also, her ethnicity emerges, rather paradoxically, in Lau's highly mediatized persona as the representative of an erased community voice, which has been quickly assimilated by mainstream literature where it sparked debate as to the ethical responsibilities of ethnic authors.

The unified image of Canadian identity has always exhibited fissures and shown itself to be fragile, full of anxiety to maintain, and redefine, its elusive essence. Not surprisingly, then, this increasing diversity influences the way in which Canadian literature is written and perceived. A number of critical and theoretical issues have arisen — pertaining to transcultural identity formation and the writing of literature through the language barrier — that are being absorbed into a critical scene that also reflects the challenges of feminism, postcolonialism, and deconstruction, all of which tie in with ethnic minority writing on a deeper level than its perceived marginality might suggest. Contemporary multicultural literature in Canada certainly raises questions about modern formations of subjectivity through writing, about collective and individual memory, but also about communities, about how they are imagined and how they are experienced or lived, about how the meaning of community itself differs according to "who is doing the imagining" (Bannerji 1996).

# 28: Literature of the First Nations, Inuit, and Métis

*Eva Gruber (University of Constance)*

BEFORE THE 1960s, published writing by Aboriginal authors in Canada was sparse and virtually unknown. The English and French missionaries had introduced writing into the numerous originally oral Aboriginal cultures, and Aboriginal-authored written histories, travel accounts, and autobiographies by authors such as George Copway (1818–1869) and Peter Jones (1802–1856; both Ojibway) exist from the nineteenth century onwards. Yet with the notable exception of Mohawk-English poet and performer E. Pauline Johnson (1861–1913; Tekahionwake), whose work received widespread attention at the end of the nineteenth and beginning of the twentieth century and continues to inspire contemporary Aboriginal writers such as Joan Crate and Beth Brant, what was perceived as Aboriginal literature in Canada were mostly Aboriginal stories collected and published by non-Aboriginal ethnographers as "folklore," "myths," and tales. Okanagan author Jeannette Armstrong recounts a telling childhood experience from as late as a "day in 1965 when a cousin of mine pointed to the road from our one-room school on the reserve and said, 'There's the Indian guy who wrote a book!' All of us rushed to the window to look at him, awestruck. . . . That experience exemplifies how remote the idea of a real live 'Native' person writing a 'book' was at that time" (Armstrong 2001, xv). While there were indeed few Aboriginal writers at the time, the scarcity of Aboriginal writing available in print was also the result of Aboriginal authors being excluded from the Canadian publishing industry and book market, a situation that was to change only slowly in the decades to come.

## Beginnings: Aboriginal Writing in Canada 1967–1990

It was the increasingly organized political resistance referred to as the Red Power or Indian Movement which in the 1960s and 1970s provided the ferment for an Aboriginal literature to grow. In a country whose policy it had been to either assimilate or ignore its Aboriginal population, previously silenced Aboriginal voices began to make themselves heard. Accordingly, the beginnings of Aboriginal writing in the 1960s were dominated by political concerns, most importantly by the struggle for Aboriginal rights and the attempt to reclaim an Aboriginal identity. Starting in the mid-1960s, Native papers, news bulletins, and periodicals emerged (for instance, *The National Indian, Nesika, Indian Record, Akwesasne Notes*, and *Indian World*), providing venues for resistance poetry as well as journalistic reports, essays, and speeches, often subsumed under the term "protest writing." Criticizing the dominant society in a frank and often angry or bitter manner, such writing was frequently more interested in conveying a political message than in literary subtlety. The publication of the 1969 White Paper — officially entitled "Statement of the Government of Canada on Indian Policy," issued by the Trudeau government, with Jean Chrétien as the head of the Department of Indian Affairs — which recommended the termination of special status and the mainstreaming of services for Canada's Aboriginal people elicited a wave of Aboriginal cultural nationalism and Aboriginal writing which lasted far into the 1970s. In response to Trudeau's vision of Canada as "a just society," Harold Cardinal (Cree) in *The Unjust Society: The Tragedy of Canadian Indians* (1969) angrily denounced Canadian Indian policy and accused the government of "extermination through assimilation" (1). Similar denouncements and requests for redress were put forth in Métis writer and activist Howard Adams's *Prison of Grass: Canada from the Native Point of View* (1975), Harold Cardinal's subsequent volume, *The Rebirth of Canada's Indians* (1977), as well as in collections such as *For Every North American Indian Who Begins to Disappear, I Also Disappear* (1971, edited by Wilf Peltier) and texts by Duke Redbird, Émile Pelletier, and George Manuel.

The energy released by these developments not only resulted in confrontational journalistic and essayistic texts but also sparked an outburst in creative writing. Also gaining momentum through the emergence of a new generation of college- and university-trained Aboriginal authors and the sudden interest of the publishing industry in Aboriginal writing, the 1970s saw the publication of a wide range of traditional and personal narratives, autobiographies, poetry, drama, and prose fiction. Among the earliest publications are Nuuchah'nulth author and artist George Clutesi's (1905–1988) works *Son of Raven, Son of Deer* (1967), which recounts traditional Nootka narratives, and *Potlatch* (1969), whose fictionalized narrative follows the events of a traditional Potlatch ceremony over its one-month duration. The publication of traditional narratives and tales continued over the following decades, examples being *Tales of Nokomis* (1970) by Patronella Johnston, Inuit author Mark Kalluak's *How Kabloonat Became and Other Inuit Legends* (1974), *Tales of the Mohawks* (1975) by

Alma Greene (Forbidden Voice), *Medicine Boy and Other Cree Tales* (1978) by Eleanor Brass, *Tales the Elders Told* (1981) by Ojibway author Basil H. Johnston, and Alexander Wolfe's *Earth Elder Stories: The Penayzitt Path* (1988). These and similar volumes, often richly illustrated, preserve cultural heritage and continue the traditions of oral storytelling in written form, an aspect especially visible in two books arising from the collaboration of ethnomusicologist Wendy Wickwire and Okanagan storyteller Harry Robinson (1900–1990; *Write It on Your Heart*, 1989; *Nature Power*, 1992), which transpose Robinson's oral rhythm and idiosyncratic syntax on the page.

Much of the early poetry published in the 1960s and 1970s comprised social protest or resistance poetry. These poems, which because of their frequently polemical style are often referred to as "Indian lament," deplore the consequences of continued colonial oppression on Aboriginal cultures and identities, and voice the pain over loss and the outrage at the injustices and racism experienced at the hands of the dominant society. Many of the texts found only a limited readership, being published in small and often short-lived magazines or newsletters. Others, however, such as Squamish writer and actor Chief Dan George's (1889–1981) often quoted oration "A Lament for Confederation" (1967), delivered at the centennial celebration of the Canadian confederacy in Vancouver to an audience of 35,000, garnered wide attention: "How long have I known you, Oh Canada? A hundred years? Yes, and many, many *seelanum* more. And today, when you celebrate your hundred years, Oh Canada, I am sad for all Indian people throughout the land." Over the following decades, both focus and style of Aboriginal writings changed. The frustration and the struggle to make Aboriginal voices heard, which characterize many early texts, gave way to a wider range of issues, where, however, Aboriginal identity and a concern with history still figure centrally. This shift was stylistically accompanied by a turn to more experimental forms.

Next to two volumes of poetry by Chief Dan George (*My Heart Soars*, 1974; *My Spirit Soars*, 1982), notable publications include Shoshone-Cree-Salish writer Sarain Stump's richly illustrated volume *There Is My People Sleeping* (1970), Ojibway poet George Kenny's *Indians Don't Cry* (1977), Micmac writer Rita Joe's volumes *Poems of Rita Joe* (1978) and *Song of Eskasoni* (1988), Delaware poet and playwright Daniel David Moses's *Delicate Bodies* (1980) and *The White Line* (1990), Mohawk writer Peter Blue Cloud's *White Corn Sister* (1979) and *Sketches in Winter, with Crows* (1981), Ojibway-Irish poet Duke Redbird's *Loveshine and Red Wine* (1981), Cree poet Beth Cuthand's *Horse Dance to Emerald Mountain* (1987) and *Voices in the Waterfall* (1989), as well as Joan Crate's *Pale as Real Ladies: Poems for Pauline Johnson* (1989) and Ojibway poet Marie Annharte Baker's *Being on the Moon* (1990). *Sweetgrass: A Modern Anthology of Indian Poetry* (1971) contains the works of the

Cree-Shoshone-Salish brothers Orville, Wayne, and Ronald Keon, whereas *Seventh Generation: Contemporary Native Writing* (1989), an anthology edited by Heather Hodgson, and *Many Voices: Contemporary Indian Poetry* (1977), edited by Marilyn Bowering and David Day, contain texts of Aboriginal poets from all over Canada, among them such well-known names as Jeannette Armstrong, Lenore Keeshig-Tobias (Ojibway), and Emma LaRocque (Cree-Métis). The latter, together with Daniel David Moses and Tomson Highway, founded the "Committee to Re-Establish the Trickster" in Toronto, whose magazine *Trickster* also published poetry by Aboriginal writers.

The publication of Aboriginal life narratives and autobiographies clearly had its peak in the 1970s. Frequently arising from collaborations with non-Aboriginal writers, ethnologists, and editors — that is, partly still following the as-told-to format — these texts also contribute to the preservation of a traditional heritage and the increasingly vocal assertion of Aboriginal cultural identity. Such cultural grounding as an act of self-definition becomes especially apparent in those texts in which episodic personal narratives blend in with tribal mythologies and histories, as, for instance, in Alma Greene's (1896–1984) *Forbidden Voice: Reflections of a Mohawk Indian* (1971), which combines her family and early personal history with the history and tales of the Mohawk of the Six Nations Reserve on the Grand River, or Dan Kennedy's (ca. 1875–1973) *Recollections of an Assiniboine Chief* (1972, edited by James R. Stevens), which interweaves Kennedy's personal memories with the history and traditions of his people.

Early as-told-to Inuit autobiographies such as Bob Cockney's *I, Nuligak* (1966, recorded by the missionary Maurice Metayer) and the richly illustrated collaborative autobiographies of artist Pitseolak Ashoona (*Pictures out of My Life*, 1971) and photographer Peter Pitseolak (*People from Our Side*, 1975), both prepared from recordings by the ethnologist Dorothy Eber, were followed by volumes such as *Thrasher, Skid Row Eskimo* (1976) — put together by Anthony Apakark Thrasher with the help of Gerard Deagle and Alan Mettrick while serving a prison sentence and detailing his life on Edmonton's skid row — and Minnie Aodla Freeman's *Life among the Quallunaat* (1978). In addition to their autobiographical aspects, both of the latter constitute indictments of Canadian society, an aspect which also characterizes the best-known autobiographical texts of the decade, Maria Campbell's *Halfbreed* (1973) and Lee Maracle's *Bobbi Lee: Indian Rebel — Struggles of a Native Canadian Woman* (1975, recorded and edited by Don Barnett and Rick Sterling). Presenting their personal and community history, these and other Aboriginal life narratives of the 1970s and 1980s confront and engage readers on a personal level while pointing to the discrimination, racism, ignorance, and neglect that Canada's First Nations, Inuit, and Métis were faced with. Thus the Métis writer and activist Campbell (1940–) in her introduction to *Halfbreed* explains that she wants to show readers "what it is like to be a halfbreed woman in our country. I want to tell you about the joys and sorrows, the oppressing poverty, the frustrations, and the dreams" (8). The text recounts the disruption of Campbell's Métis family through welfare authorities after the death of her mother, her descent into and struggle to escape from an inhuman life dominated by alcohol, drugs, and prostitution in the city, as well as her eventual development into a politically and socially conscious Métis woman. Throughout, Campbell draws spiritual strength from happy memories of her childhood in a close-knit and wittily defiant northern Saskatchewan Métis community and of her Cree grandmother, her beloved Cheechum. Like Maracle's (Sto:loh-Métis) more confrontational *Bobbi Lee*, which traces a partly similar life story, Campbell's text constitutes a classic among the works of Canada's Aboriginal literature. Yet the publication history of both texts also points to the problems Aboriginal life writing faced at the time: Campbell's manuscript was substantially shortened by the publisher, and Maracle's text first appeared under the name of interviewer and editor Don Barnett and was later dismissed as "mere protest writing." While many collaborations were productive rather than problematic — as, for instance, that of Wilfred Pelletier (1927–2000) with his non-Aboriginal friend Ted Poole for *No Foreign Land: The Biography of a North American Indian* (1974), which closely follows Poole's recordings of Pelletier's original narrative — in other cases power struggles, misunderstandings, and the risk of appropriation, exploitation, and the relegation of the Aboriginal author to the position of an informant marred the authorial/editorial process. This risk still looms large in Maria Campbell and actress/playwright Linda Griffith's (1956–) *The Book of Jessica* (1989), detailing their conflict-ridden collaboration on *Jessica* (1989), a play based on Campbell's *Halfbreed*, while Lee Maracle's partly autobiographical *I Am Woman: A Native Perspective on Sociology and Feminism* (1988) documents her process of emancipation.

In contrast to the great output in nonfictional prose, there was but little prose fiction by Aboriginal writers in Canada in the 1970s and 1980s. While several anthologies of texts by Aboriginal writers saw publication during the 1970s, they comprise poetry, essays, and traditional or autobiographical texts rather than fiction. Basil Johnston's (1929–) *Moose Meat and Wild Rice* (1978), a collection of twenty-two stories centering on the life of Aboriginal people on the fictitious "Moose Meat Point Indian Reserve" near "Blunder Bay," and Beth Brant's (1941–) collection *Mohawk Trail* (1985) stand out as exceptions. They were followed by the publication of such landmark anthologies of Aboriginal fiction as *Achimoona* (1985), edited by Maria Campbell, *Our Bit of Truth: An Anthology of Canadian Native Literature* (1990), edited by Agnes Grant, and *All My Relations* (1990), edited by Thomas King and based mostly on a special "Native Fiction" issue of *Canadian Fiction Magazine* (1987).

The first Aboriginal author to tackle the novel was Métis writer Beatrice Culleton (1949–), who published *In Search of April Raintree* in 1983. Written after the suicides of both of her sisters, the novel is clearly inspired by Culleton's personal experiences. It follows the life of two Métis sisters, April and Cheryl, who, neglected after their parents succumbed to alcoholism, are left in the care of inconsiderate social workers and grow up in different foster homes. Cheryl's foster family respects her heritage and she grows up to embrace her Métis identity; yet after attempts to help her people as a social worker she becomes disillusioned, gives in to a life consumed by alcohol, drugs, and prostitution, and thus sadly turns what the social workers called the "Native girl syndrome" into a self-fulfilling prophecy. April, in contrast, is taught to be ashamed of her background, and consequently denies her Métis identity — only to be confronted with it all the more painfully in the form of her mother-in-law's blatant racism and a racially motivated rape she suffers after being mistaken for Cheryl. These experiences and Cheryl's suicide finally force April to come to terms with her heritage and to claim her Métis identity. Simple and unpretentious in style, the novel's unclichéd and sometimes shocking honesty — the text was revised for use in schools in 1984 — makes it a moving and highly effective testimony.

Culleton's novel was followed by Jeannette Armstrong's (1948–) *Slash* (1985), which in a realistic mode traces the development of its young Okanagan protagonist Thomas Kelasket through his traditional childhood and troubled adolescence, and his involvement in the Red Power Movement. Growing from Armstrong's need to introduce her students to the events of that important era, the text is both Bildungsroman and fictionalized history, yet exceeds purely didactic or documentary purposes. Slash's realization that for his culture to survive, he himself has to live and pass on his own Okanagan heritage is paralleled by Armstrong's own approach, which she has been following in her own work as a writer, cultural worker, and especially educator. The trained artist from the Penticton Indian Band in British Columbia acted as a cofounder of the En'owkin Centre, a cultural, educational, and creative arts institution in Penticton, BC, which since 1989 also houses the En'owkin International School of Writing, the only degree-granting two-year program in Aboriginal writing in North America, with Armstrong as director. Being one of the most active and most vocal representatives of Canada's Aboriginal literary scene, Armstrong has also published numerous essays, stories, and children's literature.

Other first novels to appear in the 1980s were Ojibway writer Ruby (Farrell) Slipperjack's (1952–) *Honour the Sun* (1987), in which the young protagonist "the Owl" relates through her diary events in an isolated community on the Canadian National Railway (CNR) in northern Ontario, as her initially happy family and community life disintegrate because of alcoholism and abuse while she clings to and draws strength from the traditional teachings of her grandmother; Cree-Ojibway-Irish writer Jordan Wheeler's (1964–) *Brothers in Arms* (1989), a collection of three novellas which all focus on the relationships between brothers, yet just as deeply and sensitively explore in varying contexts what it means to be Aboriginal in contemporary Canada; Joan Crate's (1953–; Cree) *Breathing Water* (1990), following its protagonist, the young mother Dione, on her quest for independence, meaning, and healing; and Thomas King's (1943–) *Medicine River* (1989), which like Crate's novel is episodic in structure, deeply humorous, though less openly confrontational and more concerned with literary aspects, pointing towards a new (postmodern) direction in Canada's Aboriginal literature. Arguably Canada's best-known Aboriginal writer today, King is of Greek-German-Cherokee descent and grew up in California before coming to Canada in the 1980s, where he taught Native Studies at the University of Lethbridge; he received his PhD in literature from the University of Utah in 1986 and currently teaches English and Creative Writing at the University of Guelph, continuing his career as a prolific writer, critic, and filmmaker.

The 1970s also saw the beginnings of Aboriginal drama, which, because of its performative aspects, can in many ways be seen as the genre closest to Aboriginal oral traditions. In contrast to the United States, where the novel proved to be the decisive genre for the Native American Renaissance and where Native drama production has remained minor until today, in Canada theater influenced Aboriginal literature right from the start (also because of the support which Canada's theater scene receives from the Canada Council). Nora Benedict's one-act play *The Dress* (1970), Duke Redbird's *Wasawkachak* (first produced in 1974), George Kenny's *October Stranger* (1977), Minnie Aodla Freeman's *Survival in the South* (1980), Assiniboine-Dakota playwright William S. Yellow Robe's *The Independence of Eddie Rose* (1986), and the anthology *A Land Called Morning* (1986), edited by Caroline Heath, all testify to this early vitality, as does the formation of numerous Aboriginal performing groups in the 1980s, such as Native Earth Performing Arts in Toronto, Spirit Song in Vancouver, or De-Bah-Jeh-Mu-Jig Theatre on Manitoulin Island. Yet the popularity of Aboriginal theater exploded on a national (and subsequently international) scale only in 1987 with the production of Cree playwright Tomson Highway's (1951–) hugely successful *The Rez Sisters*, a darkly humorous portrayal of the lives of seven women on the fictional Wasaychigan Hill reserve on Manitoulin Island who — always accompanied by the Ojibway trickster Nanabush — set out to play the biggest bingo in the world which is coming to Toronto. Its sequel (or rather counterpart) *Dry Lips Oughta Move to Kapuskasing* (1989) features seven male characters faced with their women's plans to form a hockey team, with Nanabush taking the form of a comical goddess. Both plays clearly reflect

Highway's traditional Cree background, but also his education in a Western university system (he is also a trained pianist). In their combination of English and Cree (Highway's only language until age six), deft and lyrical language, the spiritual, sacred, and serious as well as the blatantly profane and slapstick, these rich tableaux blend contemporary Aboriginal realities on the reserve with magical aspects derived from traditional mythology. With several other plays to his credit — among them *Aria* (first performed in 1987), a series of twenty-two monologues, and *The Sage, the Dancer, and the Fool* (first performed in 1989), which presents a young Aboriginal character's views on his day in downtown Toronto from various perspectives — Highway today is Canada's most celebrated Aboriginal playwright.

## After Oka: Aboriginal Literature Coming into Its Own

While the body of writing discussed above might suggest differently, the initial wave of publications triggered by the Red Power Movement of the 1960s and 1970s did not, as Greg Young-Ing points out, "manage to carve a respectable, ongoing niche for Aboriginal literature in the Canadian publishing industry." Quite to the contrary, "in the late 1970s and 1980s the frequency of books published by Aboriginal people tapered off dramatically" (1996, 163). Over twenty years after the 1969 White Paper, it was another political event that directed Canada's attention to its First Nations once again: In the summer of 1990, plans for the expansion of a golf course onto Mohawk sacred sites near Oka in Quebec precipitated an extended and at times violent confrontation between provincial police, and later also the army, and Mohawk protesters who had barricaded the location. After casualties on both sides, the standoff — commonly referred to as the Oka Crisis — ended with the peaceful walk out and subsequent arrest of the Mohawk occupants, yet its impact was to be felt long afterwards. The events, extensively covered by the media, not only saw an outburst of solidarity and support among Canada's First Nations but also made the Canadian public painfully aware of its own continued role as a colonizer and the fact that First Nations claims could no longer be ignored. Exacerbated by the Ojibway-Cree member of the Manitoba legislature Elijah Harper's single-handed veto of the Meech Lake Accord in the same year, the events triggered a huge upsurge in interest in Aboriginal cultures and opened a whole range of new publishing opportunities for Aboriginal writing. This development gained momentum through the strongly increased academic interest in the field, with universities establishing Native Studies programs and offering Native literature courses. As van Toorn points out, the events of Oka feature prominently in several texts by Aboriginal authors, for example, in Lee Maracle's novel *Sundogs* (1992), in Jeannette Armstrong's poem "Indian Summer," and in a newly added part to Beth Cuthand's dramatic monologue series "Seven Songs for Uncle Louis" (1985, 1990). "After Oka — How Has Canada Changed?" is the question Lenore Keeshig-Tobias raises in her essay of the same title, and while politically this question may still be subject to debate two decades after the events, the Aboriginal literary scene certainly has changed for the better, with a range of Aboriginal authors now firmly established in the canon of Canadian literature.

Aboriginal drama has continued its success story since the late 1980s. Established voices such as Tomson Highway and Daniel David Moses produce new plays, of which Highway's *Ernestine Shuswap Gets Her Trout: A "String Quartet" for Four Female Actors* (2005) and Moses's *Coyote City* (1990), *The Indian Medicine Shows* (1995), *Almighty Voice and His Wife* (1992), *Big Buck City* (1998), *Brébeuf's Ghost* (2000), and *City of Shadows: Necropolite!* (2000) were published. Moses's (1952–) highly imaginative and sometimes even dreamlike and slightly bizarre plays are characterized by great intensity and often lyrical beauty, showing his poetic gift. Covering a wide stylistic, generic, and thematic range, Moses, who graduated with a MFA in creative writing from the University of British Columbia, explores such widely diverging subjects as the historical encounters between Canada's Aboriginal people and the European colonizers (*Brébeuf's Ghost; Almighty Voice and His Wife*) and the lives of Aboriginal people in a contemporary urban environment (*Coyote City*).

New voices in Aboriginal drama include Ian Ross, whose play *fareWel* won the Governor General's Award in 1997, Floyd Favel, whose play *Lady of Silences* is included in the seminal collection *Staging Coyote's Dream: An Anthology of First Nations Drama in English*, edited by Monique Mojica and Ric Knowles in 2003, Alanis King Odjig, Yvette Nolan, and performers and playwrights Marie Clements, Margo Kane, Shirley Cheechoo, and Monique Mojica. This strong new female presence among Canada's Aboriginal playwrights productively expands the scope of Aboriginal theater to include aspects of gender in the exploration of Aboriginal existence and intercultural contact, be it in exposing the violence perpetrated against Aboriginal women, as in Nolan's plays (for instance, *Annie Mae's Movement* [2006], about the death of Aboriginal activist Anna Mae Aquash) or in Marie Clements's (1962–) complex and multilayered *The Unnatural and Accidental Women* (included in Mojica and Knowles 2003 and also adapted for the screen in 2006); or in undermining stereotypical perceptions of Aboriginal women as princesses or squaws, as in Mojica's (1954–) hilarious and bitingly satirical *Princess Pocahontas and the Blue Spots* (1991), which follows such racist and sexist depictions through the history of Aboriginal-White contact.

Clichéd ideas of "the Indian" are also deconstructed in prolific Ojibway playwright Drew Hayden Taylor's (1962–) numerous plays (eleven of which have appeared in print to date), focusing on Aboriginal personal and community life both on the reserve (*The Bootlegger Blues*, 1991) and in the city (*AlterNatives*, 2000) as well as on the past, present, and future of Aboriginal cultures (as in *Toronto at Dreamer's Rock*, 1991). While not all of Taylor's plays are comedies, many of them are characterized by an unflinching openness and a strongly humorous take, a feature also prevalent in Taylor's work as a columnist and essayist (collected in four volumes to date, entitled *Funny, You Don't Look like One* I–IV, 1996–2004) and as a filmmaker. Moreover, Taylor explored the phenomenon of Aboriginal humor in collaboration with writers, performers, and comedians in his anthology *Me Funny* (2005) and his documentary *Redskins, Tricksters, and Puppy Stew* (2000). While drama already constitutes the liveliest and most interactive genre of Aboriginal literature, reaching its audience both in urban areas and on reserves (where Aboriginal theater groups attract many young people), Taylor, like many of his colleagues, extended the scope of his work to include the media. Shirley Cheechoo (1952–), too, works as a film director, while Thomas King with *The Dead Dog Café Comedy Hour* (1996–2000) and Ian Ross (1968–) with *Joe from Winnipeg* produced widely successful radio programs for CBC Radio, and both Taylor and King have been active as scriptwriters for film and television. Addressing a wide Aboriginal as well as non-Aboriginal audience, Aboriginal playwrights and filmmakers thus open up what Thomas King has referred to as "new worlds of imagination" (King 1992, xi). They strengthen Aboriginal cultural identity, defying the tradition of being conceptualized exclusively from a non-Aboriginal perspective, and also help to build bridges of understanding between cultures by requiring what Ojibway critic Christine Lenze has called "response-ability" (in Knowles and Mojica 2003, v), a willingness to accept the possibly unfamiliar paradigms and underlying concepts of Aboriginal theater and film.

In the 1990s and 2000s, the stylistic and thematic diversification and partial recourse to traditional forms that had characterized the development of Aboriginal poetry in the 1980s continued. Jeannette Armstrong's acclaimed collection *Breath Tracks* (1991) was followed by Marie Annharte Baker's second volume of poetry, *Coyote Columbus Café* (1994), Rita Joe's *We Are the Dreamers: Recent and Early Poetry* (1999), and Joan Crate's *Foreign Homes* (2002). In addition to his work as a dramatist, Daniel David Moses brought out two more volumes of poetry, *The White Line* (1990) and *Sixteen Jesuses* (2000), while Cree-Métis poet Duncan Mercredi published four volumes of poetry in the span of six years, starting with *Spirit of the Wolf: Raise Your Voice* in 1991. In 2000, Lee Maracle's first collection of poetry, *Bent Box*, saw publication, and a whole range of exciting new work in poetry came from writers such as Armand

Garnet Ruffo (*Opening in the Sky,* 1994; *At Geronimo's Grave,* 2001), Connie Fife (*Beneath the Naked Sun,* 1992; *Speaking through Jagged Rock,* 1999), Rasunah Marsden, Randy Lundy, and Kateri Akiwenzie Damm (*My Heart Is a Stray Bullet,* 1993), who also served as the editor of *Skins: Contempory Indigenous Writing* (2001), an anthology combining texts by Aboriginal authors from Canada, Australia, and New Zealand.

Many contemporary poets, notably Cree poets Louise Bernice Halfe and Greg Scofield (who published four volumes of poetry, among them *Sakihtowin-maskihkiy ekwa peaykamonwin/Love Medicine and One Song,* 1997), and Métis writer Marilyn Dumont, make use of code-switching or indigenized "Rez" English. By inserting Cree expressions into their texts and by resorting to demotic language, they reassert an Aboriginal voice and undermine the alleged superiority of standard English, an aspect also scrutinized in Dumont's (1955–) poem "The Devil's Language" (*A Really Good Brown Girl,* 1996):

> My father doesn't read or write
> the King's English says he's
> dumb but he speaks Cree
> how many of you speak Cree? . . .
> is there a Received Pronunciation of Cree, is there
> a Modern Cree Usage?
> the Chief's Cree, not the King's English (55–56)

Louise Bernice Halfe's (1953–) use of a demotic idiom results in subversive double meanings, for instance, when an Aboriginal woman addresses her letters to the "Der Poop" (dear pope), apologizing for her "ignorance" by explaining that she "don't have you drainin / from doze schools" (in *Bear Bones and Feathers,* 1994, to be followed by *Blue Marrow* in 1998) — at once denouncing the churches' detrimental role in the process of colonization and forced conversion (also the subject of Dumont's "Still Unsaved Soul") and the devastating impact of the residential school system. As part of Canada's Indian policy aiming at assimilation, until the middle of the twentieth century Aboriginal children were taken from their families in order to be educated within a Western framework — that is, deprived of their cultural heritage. The traumatic experiences and cultural disruption caused by this policy are also the subject of stories by Beth Brant ("A Long Story"), Maria Campbell ("Good Dog Bob"), and Jordan Wheeler ("Exposure"), of Shirley Cheechoo's play *Path with No Moccasins* (1991), and of Jane Willis's memoir *Geniesh: An Indian Girlhood* (1973), as well as Shirley Sterling's autobiographical account *My Name Is Seepeetza* (1992). Less confrontational than Aboriginal writing of the 1970s, contemporary works by First Nations writers in Canada thus cannot ignore the impact of a traumatic history and the ongoing effects of colonization, as these examples show. The approaches may have changed, with irony and subversive humor frequently replacing angry denouncement (see Gruber 2008); yet the concerns they address still remain, and many writers conceive of their work as a responsibility towards their communities and a contribution to the process of decolonization by reaffirming Aboriginal presence and cultural identity. This is also borne out in *Native Poetry in Canada: A Contemporary Anthology*, edited by Jeannette Armstrong and Lally Grauer in 2001, which presents the work of the above-mentioned and further poets. The collection not only demonstrates the sheer mass, immense range, and high quality of contemporary Aboriginal poetry, it also testifies to the developmental stages of Aboriginal poetry which Armstrong roughly sketches in her introduction — from a protest era in the 1960s and 1970s, through a decade of experimentation in the 1980s, to an era of literary proliferation and the celebration of Aboriginal cultural diversity starting in the 1990s.

In similar fashion, the output in Aboriginal prose fiction after its hesitant beginnings in the 1980s experienced a huge upsurge in the 1990s and 2000s. Among those already established in the preceding decades, Jeannette Armstrong published *Whispering in Shadows* (2000), a complex and formally innovative artist novel. Centering on the experiences of its protagonist Penny, a single mother and creative artist faced with the conflicting demands and desires of her family and her identity as an artist, her adherence to Okanagan traditions, and her work as an activist, the novel incorporates poems, letters, and Penny's diary to form a multilayered, nonlinear narrative. Beatrice (Culleton) Mosionier's second novel, *In the Shadow of Evil* (2000), deals with the sexual abuse of children, while her first, *In Search of April Raintree* (1983), was republished in 1999 as a critical edition edited by Cheryl Suzack, in which the novel is complemented by Mosionier's essay "The Special Time" and critical articles on the novel. Ruby Slipperjack followed her novel *Honour the Sun* (1987) with *Silent Words* (1992), *Weesquachak and the Lost Ones* (2000), and *Little Voice* (2002), a novel for young readers. Writer, educator, and activist Lee Maracle (1950–), whose autobiography *Bobbi Lee* had been among the first books by Aboriginal authors to be published in the 1970s and who, like Armstrong, is among the founders of the En'owkin International School of Writing, published her first novel *Sundogs* in 1991, to be followed by *Ravensong* in 1993. Focusing on the life of a small Aboriginal community on the Pacific Northwest Coast in the early 1950s, the novel sensitively describes the seventeen-year-old protagonist Stacey's struggle to negotiate an identity between two cultures separated by the bridge she crosses daily to go to school in the Whites' world, and her attempt to cope with tragedy as an influenza epidemic hits the community. Next to two further novels, *Daughters Are Forever* (2002) and *Will's Garden* (2002), Maracle, whose texts are widely anthologized and who can clearly be counted among

Canada's foremost Aboriginal voices, also brought out the short-story collection *Sojourner's Truth and Other Stories* in 1990.

Whereas in the previous decades short stories by Aboriginal writers were mainly published in magazines or anthologies, from the 1990s more collections by individual writers began to appear, as Beth Brant followed *Mohawk Trail* (1985) with *Food and Spirits* (1991), Thomas King published *One Good Story, That One* (1993) and *A Short History of Indians in Canada* (2005), and Drew Hayden Taylor probed the genre with *Fearless Warriors* (1998). Stunning debuts were made by young Haisla author Eden Robinson (1968–) in her story collection *Traplines* (1998) and by Métis writer Warren Cariou (1966–) in the novellas included in *The Exalted Company of Roadside Martyrs* (1999), to be followed by Cariou's award-winning memoir *Lake of the Prairies* in 2002. In many cases, this contemporary Aboriginal "storytelling" clearly ties in with the oral tradition, be it in the oral mode that Thomas King creates through his unusual syntax, use of demotic language, and cyclical structure, which follows the narrative mode of Okanagan storyteller Harry Robinson; or in the conversational history Maria Campbell establishes through the eight Métis narratives entrusted to her, which she collects in *Stories of the Road Allowance People* (1995), following the diction of the English spoken among the Métis. *Arctic Dreams and Nightmares* (1993) by Alootook Ipellie (1951–2007), arguably Canada's best-known Inuit writer, like its earliest predecessor, Markoosie's (1942–) critically acclaimed and widely translated novella *Harpoon of the Hunter* (1970), combines writing and imagery as well as traditional Inuit storytelling and contemporary aspects in its twenty stories. In recent decades, Inuit writing has experienced a real upsurge, with texts appearing in bi- and trilingual editions in English, Inuktitut, and French. Inuit periodicals, papers, and magazines such as *Inuit Today, Inuvialuit, Up Here, Inuktitut,* and *Kivioq: Inuit Fiction Magazine,* which arose from the Baffin Island Writer's Project with Ipellie as editor, now achieve wide circulation, while Penny Petrone's anthology *Northern Voices: Inuit Writing in English* (1988) further helped to establish Inuit writing as an integral part of Canada's Aboriginal literatures.

*Green Grass, Running Water* (1993), Thomas King's celebrated second novel, widely surpasses *Medicine River* (1989) in scope and technique. Rich with historical and intertextual allusions to numerous canonical narratives by such authors as Melville, Defoe, and Cooper, to Canadian literary theory, Hollywood movies, and the Bible, this multilayered narrative interweaves various strands involving contemporary First Nations characters, figures from Aboriginal origin stories, and protagonists of literary texts to result in a panoramic postmodern puzzle. Through its witty humor and unexpected juxtapositions, this complex novel is not only skillfully intellectual, testifying to King's own broad academic background, but also highly entertaining. Deriving its narrative technique from the oral tradition, the

text in its use of metafictional devices and various perspectives and narrators —
among them the omnipresent trickster Coyote — and through its discursive
setup destabilizes the notion of one authoritative voice or Truth. Instead, it
playfully deconstructs stereotypical notions of "the Indian" and undercuts
established hierarchies such as that between Western historiography and
Aboriginal story or the Christian master narrative and Aboriginal myths.
*Truth and Bright Water* (1999), King's subsequent novel, returns to a less
complex structure, yet also partly relies on the magical realism that marked
its predecessor. Set in two border towns, the eponymous Truth in the
United States and Bright Water in Canada, it explores the impact of the
border on a Blackfoot community spread on either side (a topic already
dealt with in King's much-anthologized short story "Borders"). It follows
the life of young protagonist Tecumseh, whose limited and partly naive perspective gives the text an occasionally cryptic quality by raising more questions than it answers. Under the pseudonym Hartley GoodWeather, King
has also started to write detective novels, two of which have appeared so far
(2003, 2006), featuring the Aboriginal sleuth Thumps Dreadful Water.

Until recently, King's internationally acclaimed texts were among the
very few to appear with a major publisher (HarperCollins), while most
Aboriginal literature came out with Aboriginal publishers such as Theytus
Books (Penticton, associated with the En'owkin Centre), Pemmican Press
(Winnipeg), Kegedonce Press, Gabriel Dumont Institute Press, or other
small independent presses such as Fifth House (Saskatoon), Women's Press
(Toronto), Seventh Generation (Toronto), Press Gang (Vancouver), or
Coteau Books (Regina). Slowly, however, Aboriginal writing has reached
mainstream publishing: Eden Robinson's two novels *Monkey Beach* (2000)
and *Blood Sports* (2006) appeared with Knopf, and Ojibway writer Richard
Wagamese's novels *Keeper 'n Me* (1994), *A Quality of Light* (2002), *Dream
Wheels* (2006), and *Ragged Company* (2008) were published by Doubleday,
also the publisher of dramatist Tomson Highway's widely acclaimed postmodern autobiographical novel *Kiss of the Fur Queen* (1998). *The Lesser
Blessed* (1996), the first novel of young Dogrib author Richard van Camp
— a graduate from En'owkin International School of Writing — appeared
with Douglas & McIntyre (while his second, *Angel Wing Splash Pattern*,
appeared with Kegedonce Press in 2002), and Robert Alexie's novels
*Porcupines and China Dolls* (2002) and *Pale Indian* (2005) were published
by Penguin. Moreover, the comprehensive *An Anthology of Canadian
Native Literature in English*, edited by Daniel David Moses and Terry
Goldie and first published by Oxford University Press in 1992, went to a
third edition in 2005. For "minority" literatures it has always been difficult to strike a balance between the need for protected spaces on the one
hand — special anthologies or journals, such as the En'owkin Centre's
*Gatherings* for Aboriginal writing — and the danger of ghettoization and
continued separation from the "mainstream" on the other. The vibrant

field of Aboriginal literature in Canada has negotiated this task admirably, taking giant steps towards making itself both an integral part of Canadian literature yet never giving up its idiosyncratic characteristics and traditional origins.

# Developing a Critical Framework for Aboriginal Literature

While initially Aboriginal literature in Canada was sometimes subsumed under the category of "children's literature" (for instance, in the first and second editions of Carl F. Klinck's *Literary History of Canada*, 1965 and 1976) or dismissed as mere protest writing, in recent decades it has come to receive the recognition it deserves. Aboriginal writing today is among the most innovative and exciting fields of Canadian literature, and its study has now been firmly established in academia, aided by the postcolonial turn and its increased interest in the literatures of previously marginalized groups. Native Studies as a discipline and the study of Aboriginal literature do not always fit into the academic discourse smoothly, though, as they tend to question and challenge established Western frameworks and standards of analysis and cross the boundaries of the academy (see Kulchyski 2000). On the other hand, critics (among them Lutz) have warned against the dangers of tokenism or the preferential treatment of authors whose works lend themselves well to academic analysis (such as Thomas King's postmodern novels or Tomson Highway's playfully complex dramas), while other voices in this heterogeneous field tend to be neglected.

Such tendencies also resulted from the fact that early critical responses came mostly from non-Aboriginal critics and arose from within European (or at times even clearly Eurocentric) frameworks and literary and aesthetic standards. "Until recently, in special 'Native Writing' issues of major literary journals, Aboriginal writers usually supplied the stories and poems, while non-Aboriginal critical essays erected the frameworks for understanding them" (van Toorn 2004, 43). The situation has changed over time, however: More culturally appropriate approaches emerged as Aboriginal critics and scholars (among them many writers) entered the field of literary and cultural criticism and intervened in the academic discourse on Aboriginal literature, and non-Aboriginal critics, sensitized to the issue, have been striving to practice what Renate Eigenbrod called "responsible criticism" (1996). Speaking out against a literary establishment that had relegated Aboriginal literature to the margins, Aboriginal writers such as Lee Maracle (*Oratory Coming to Theory*, 1990), Lenore Keeshig-Tobias, Jeannette Armstrong (who together with Douglas Cardinal published *The Native Creative Process* in 1991), and others have tried to conceive of different frameworks for discussing Aboriginal writing.

Their efforts are collected in volumes such as *Give Back: First Nations Perspectives on Cultural Practice* (1992), the groundbreaking *Looking at the Words of Our People: First Nations Analysis of Literature* (1993), edited by Jeannette Armstrong, and *(Ad)dressing Our Words: Aboriginal Perspectives on Aboriginal Literatures* (2001), edited by Armand Garnet Ruffo and Greg Young-Ing.

For a period in the 1990s, heated discussions on the problematic issue of cultural appropriation dominated the discourse on Aboriginal literature. Non-Aboriginal authors such as Anne Cameron, Lynn Andrews, W. P. Kinsella, and others who made use of Aboriginal materials or even claimed to have been "initiated" into Aboriginal traditions and to be able to speak for or with an Aboriginal voice were urged to "stop stealing Native stories." The conflict has since lost much of its explosiveness, opening the way for such productive collaborations as that between Jo-Ann Episkenew and Renate Eigenbrod, who brought together Aboriginal and non-Aboriginal critics in their coedited volume *Creating Community: A Roundtable on Canadian Aboriginal Literature* (2002), an approach also taken by *Aboriginal Drama and Theatre* (2005), edited by Rob Appleford.

In 2003, Thomas King was invited to be the first Massey lecturer of Aboriginal descent, joining ranks with such luminaries as Northrop Frye, Doris Lessing, and Charles Taylor. Each of his lectures, collected in *The Truth about Stories: A Native Narrative* (2003), ends with a similar admonishment to the audience to take the story: "It's yours. Do with it what you will. . . . But don't say in the years to come that you would have lived your life differently if only you had heard this story. You've heard it now" (King 2003, 29). Similarly, Canadian literature today has clearly heard its Aboriginal authors' "stories." Within a literary tradition in which "Indians" mere decades ago were but subjects in the texts of non-Aboriginal writers, Aboriginal literature is now an irrevocable presence, impressively enriching the Canadian canon.

# 29: The Quebec Novel

*Doris G. Eibl (University of Innsbruck)*

## Identity and Difference in the Quebec Novel after 1967

IN QUEBEC, the massive sociopolitical and cultural changes of the 1960s and the consolidation of the liberal État-providence in the 1970s saw a great overlap of culture and politics. The linkage was, in fact, so significant that in the 1980s, after the failure of the referendum for independence, many intellectuals and writers would reflect nostalgically on the previous two decades. They detected a general disengagement in the literature of the 1980s. The literary critic Gilles Marcotte even spoke of a "génération en deuil de ce qui la précède et de ce qui ne pourra pas advenir," a "génération qui refuse une conscience historique ou un horizon," and he criticized its "bonne humeur tranquille dans le malheur même, dans le dénuement, dans l'absence de raisons." It is, however, only partially true that the literature of the 1960s and early 1970s was an all-embracing testimony of solidarity, the mouthpiece of an emancipating "nous québécois," liberating itself from outdated moral concepts and striving for independence. Literary criticism has often overemphasized the idea of the collective in the literature dedicated to the spirit of the Révolution tranquille, and has tended to neglect those texts that focus on the individual. Particularly with respect to fiction, it is necessary to highlight the impressive breadth of themes and forms in which the individual regains importance.

In comparison with the relative continuity in the development of the novel from the 1960s to the 1970s, the break that took place in the early 1980s was drastic and based less on a different choice of topics than on the manner in which the authors addressed the issue of collective and individual identity and how they positioned the individual in society. The literature of the Révolution tranquille had understood Quebec's lack of cultural identity predominantly as a consequence of colonialism, and the literature of the 1970s had projected its quest for liberation and social change onto master narratives such as Marxism, feminism, or the independence of Quebec. After the failure of the referendum in May 1980, writers saw themselves confronted with the fragility of these models. Consequently, they turned to experimenting with new identities, emphasizing the inconsistency of society and the individual. Identity was no longer presented as an absolute cultural entity, but rather as indeterminable, multiple. While for historians the late 1960s mark the end of the Révolution tranquille, from a literary perspective the social problems that were characteristic of the 1960s continued to influence the Quebec novel until at least the mid-1970s. This is evident in the deliberate and also very creative use of *joual* in the works of Victor-Lévy Beaulieu, Michel Tremblay, Claude Jasmin, and Gilbert La Rocque. The critical analysis of traditional society, family, and religion was still present in numerous works that particularly focus on the decades before the Révolution tranquille. In these depictions of the impoverished and exploited French Canadians, anglophones and francophones were portrayed as polar opposites. In addition to the October Crisis of 1970 — as portrayed in works by La Rocque (*Corridors*, 1971), Jacques Ferron (*Les confitures de coing*, 1971), and Yves Beauchemin (*L'enfirouapé*, 1974) — the vision of an independent Quebec also became an omnipresent literary topos.

The majority of works depicted the province and its people from a historical, socio-critical, and politically motivated perspective. In contrast, texts that committed themselves to literary innovation and formal experimentation were discussed in rather positive terms but were nevertheless excluded from the canon, such as the work of Jean-Marie Poupart (*Ma tite vache a mal aux pattes*, 1970; *C'est pas donné à tout le monde d'avoir une belle mort*, 1974), Louis Gauthier (*Les aventures de Sivis Pacem et de Para Bellum: Tome I*, 1970), Yvon Paré (*Anna-Belle*, 1972), and André Carpentier (*Axel et Nicholas*, 1973). This is also true for the novels of Emmanuel Cocke (*Louve story*, 1973; *Sexe pour le sang*, 1974) and Claude Robitaille (*Le corps bissextile*, 1977), which are all representative of the Counter Culture movement.

Victor-Lévy Beaulieu (1945–), whose oeuvre includes not only novels but also numerous plays and essays, is one of the most impressive and productive literary personalities of the 1970s and 1980s. Until the mid-1980s he committed himself to a truly epic project that was mainly dedicated to the spirit of the Révolution tranquille. In his early novels (*Race de monde*, 1969; *Jos Connaissant*, 1970; *Les grands-pères*, 1971) the author concentrated both on the problem of Quebec's incapacitation and its apparent lack of history as well as on the impact of collective self-estrangement on the individual's destiny. In the course of the 1970s he increasingly focused on the topic of writing, as in *Oh, Miami, Miami* (1973) or in *Don Quichotte de la démanche* (1974), which reinforced the discussion of the author's and the intellectual's role in Quebec. Of the twelve Beauchemin children introduced in *Race de monde*, Jos, Steven, and Abel develop into central figures in the cycles La vraie saga des Beauchemin and Voyageries, and each of them occupies a specific position in a declining society. Jos, in whom Beaulieu's first protagonist Satan Belhumeur (*Mémoires d'outre-tonneau*, 1968) resurfaces, incarnates the disgusted and enraged Québécois, who finally takes refuge in esoteric visions of salvation and loses his grip on reality. The novelist Abel finds Steven, the poet, the only one capable of transcending past, present, and future misery through a poetic foundational act. Abel, in *Don Quichotte de la démanche*, is a critic of society but remains caught within society and in his own paranoia. Missing a national literary tradition, he resorts to foreign authors to overcome his writer's block. Consequently, James Joyce becomes a central figure in Steven's writings, with Steven preparing a critical edition of Joyce's *Ulysses*. In his subsequent novels Beaulieu increasingly stylized the writer into a literary messiah, the writing process into a Passion, and literature into an almost religious authority. *Monsieur Melville*, which is considered his masterpiece and was published in three volumes in 1978 (*Dans les aveilles de Moby Dick*, *Lorsque souffle la baleine*, *L'après Moby Dick ou La souveraine poésie*), testifies to the author's desire for the absolute, which he projects into the creative act of writing. In *Monsieur Melville*, however, Beaulieu also notes that this desire entails the writer's own loneliness: "Malheureusement, Monsieur Melville ne m'a pas attendu pour partir. . . . il fallait que je fasse le voyage moi-même, que je comprenne la grande baleine blanche tout fin seul au fond de mon incompétence." In a demanding blend of various genres (autobiography, biofiction, historiography, travelogue, and novel), Herman Melville becomes the imaginary double of the first-person narrator Abel. However, Melville accomplishes what Abel himself never does, namely, "tout dire dans un livre définitif."

The majority of Michel Tremblay's (1942–) *Chroniques du Plateau Mont-Royal* was written during the 1980s, focusing, as do Beaulieu's novels, on the Québécois before the Révolution tranquille. Among other things, they tell the story of the development of a child into a writer. For his prose oeuvre Tremblay revisited both the characters and the topics of his plays written from the late 1960s onwards (see ch. 33, Scholl). It was especially important to him to depict the dramatic characters within the dynamics of their genealogy. He does so not in the form of a broad overview of the development of a single *dramatis persona*, however, but instead concentrates on snapshots and central moments of social interaction. The first volume of the *Chroniques* with the title *La grosse femme d'à côté est enceinte* (1978) deals with one day (2 May 1942) in the life of the seventy-five-year-old grandmother Victoire, her three children Édouard, Albertine, and Gabriel, as well as her grandchildren, the dog Godbout, and the cat Duplessis. Their difficult coexistence under one roof and the uncertain economic situation of the inhabitants of the Plateau Mont-Royal still permits moments of happiness and understanding, thanks to Gabriel's pregnant wife, "la grosse femme." Not only do the other women confide in her, in *La duchesse et le roturier* (1982), the third volume of the *Chroniques*, she also becomes the confidante of Édouard, who tells her about his homosexuality and dedicates his travel diary to her when he goes to Paris after the death of his mother Victoire in *Des nouvelles d'Édouard* (1984), the fourth volume. Tremblay's novels repeatedly focus on children (*Thérèse et Pierrette à l'école des Saints-Anges*, 1980; *Le premier quartier de la lune*, 1989), whose growing up during the years between 1942 and 1952 is always seen in connection with the social changes in Quebec. This is particularly obvious in the case of Albertine's son Marcel and his nameless cousin, a descendant of "la grosse femme" and Gabriel. While Marcel is unable to cope with the demands of reality owing to his physical disability, his cousin stands for a future of possibilities and social advancement; in him the reader is in fact led to recognize the author himself. The great success of the *Chroniques* was due, on the one hand, to the public's familiarity with Tremblay's plays, and, on the other, to the author's differentiated treatment of his topics. Besides the recurrent criticism of religious and secular institutions and their abuse of authority, the author convinced with well-observed descriptions of social outcasts, prostitutes, homosexuals, transvestites, and artists and their ways of breaking taboos.

Roch Carrier's (1937–) novels, like Beaulieu's and Tremblay's, focus on the analysis of social milieus. Typical for the Révolution tranquille, they deal with the Québécois's alienation, his/her emancipation from immaturity, and liberation from self-destruction. Carrier's first novel, *La guerre, yes sir!* (1968), appeared in an English translation in 1970 and was very successful in English Canada. It was followed in 1969 by *Floralie, où es-tu?* and in 1970 by *Il est par là, le soleil*. In 1981 these novels were republished as a trilogy entitled "Trilogie de l'âge sombre." The title of the trilogy doubtlessly refers to the precarious situation of the characters in the novels, particularly in *La guerre, yes sir!*, where Carrier ridicules stereotypes such as the French-Canadian mother, the obedient francophone soldier, and especially representatives of the church. The partially vulgar language and the carnivalesque descriptions of a jolly funeral feast for Corriveau — a soldier who died in the Second World War and is brought back to his hometown by anglophone soldiers — pick up all those clichés that had determined the self-perception and outsider's view of the francophones at least since the Durham Report of 1839 (which had proclaimed the nonexistence of a francophone culture; see ch. 8, Scholl). The stiff anglophone soldiers are contrasted with the francophone farmers, whose wake ends in a frolicsome party and who are, in the eyes of the anglophones, "moins civilisés que les Sauvages." The tension between the two parties finally leads to a bloody confrontation. The end has often been interpreted by literary critics as an act of francophone insurgency against anglophone dominance, a topic which Carrier also addressed in *Il n'y a pas de pays sans grand-père* (1977), here against the historical backdrop of the demonstrations during the Queen's visit to Quebec.

Similar to Carrier in *La guerre, yes sir!*, Louis Caron's (1942–) first novel *L'emmitouflé* (1977) — which was originally published in several installments in the newspaper *Le Nouvelliste* (23 August–6 December 1976) — deals with the topic of forced conscription. Whereas in Carrier's novel the conscripted help themselves by going into hiding or prefer self-mutilation to the front (the character Joseph saws off his own hand), Nazaire in *L'emmitouflé* escapes to Vermont during the First World War. The narrator Jean-François, Nazaire's nephew, is struck by a similar fate decades later, when he is forced to flee to Montreal to avoid conscription for the Vietnam War. The contrast between francophones and anglophones, already apparent in *L'emmitouflé*, is taken to extremes in Caron's trilogy "Les fils de la liberté." This is not unproblematic insofar as the author, in the prefaces to *Le canard de bois* (1981), *La corne de brume* (1982), and *Le coup de poing* (1990), claims that his fiction is historically true. The novels themselves, however, lack any differentiated depiction of the characters' psychological and ideological development. The story of the Bellerose family stylizes the francophones as pugnacious heroes of liberation and sees the root of all evil in the illegitimate presence of the anglophones. The story of the family begins with Hyacinthe Bellerose and his commitment to the Patriots in the years 1837–1838, then describes the economic rise and fall of his adopted son Tim in the second half of the nineteenth century. This is followed by the story of Bruno Bellerose, a typical Quebec farmer in the first half of the twentieth century. The trilogy ends with the terrorist activities of young Jean-Michel Bellerose in the Front de Libération du Québec (FLQ), the militant liberation movement. Despite the narrative talent of the author, the novels do not convince precisely because of their excessively inscribed ideological assumptions.

Anne Hébert and Antonine Maillet occupy an exceptional position in the history of the Quebec novel of the 1970s. Since the publication of her second novel, *Kamouraska* (1970), Hébert (1916–2000) has been regarded as one of Quebec's most dazzling literary personalities. About one hundred thousand copies of *Kamouraska* were sold in the first year of its publication, before it was translated into twelve other languages — internationally, Hébert's novel is one of the best-received works of Quebec literature. In contrast to many of her colleagues, the author distanced herself from the aesthetics of the Révolution tranquille. In the works published from the 1970s onwards, she created idiosyncratic, claustrophobic worlds in which the individual is involved in intrigues that sometimes border on the fantastic. The closed room — in its real and symbolic dimension — already plays a central role in her first novel, *Les chambres de bois* (1958), which is reminiscent of Jean Cocteaus's *Les enfants terribles* (1929). In *Kamouraska,* the topic of the closed room is illustrated by the fate of the protagonist Élisabeth d'Aulnières, whose symbolic imprisonment comes to stand for a whole society caught up in self-referentiality, self-righteousness, and values that do not leave enough space for the individual to develop. Set in the early nineteenth century and based on a true story, the novel's narrative point of view switches between the perspectives of the omniscient narrator and that of the protagonist, who is watching over the sickbed of her second husband. It relates the circumstances that had led to the murder of her first husband Antoine: In a series of flashbacks, reminiscent of soliloquies, the now aging mother of eleven children sums up her lonely first marriage, her husband's affairs, and his excessive abuse of alcohol. The novel recalls Élisabeth's love relationship with George Nelson, the doctor who murders Antoine, George's escape to the United States, the ensuing lawsuit, in which she herself is accused of murdering her husband, and her rehabilitation through her marriage to Jérôme Rolland. The unique effect of Hébert's novel is based, on the one hand, on the convincing way in which it gives insight into the inner world of Élisabeth, a woman trapped in a restrictive and hostile social corset. On the other hand, the text works with the exceptionally suggestive power of natural symbols, which are particularly effective in the description of the winter landscape: It is the snow that simultaneously covers and, in its purity, reveals everything. In *Les enfants du sabbat* (1975) Hébert, just as in *Kamouraska*, continues to work with the contrast between closed and open spaces. To escape the dark events in her parents' house — the illegal distilling of spirits, prostitution, rape, black masses, orgies, and abortions — the protagonist enters a convent. This allows her remain loyal to her brother, who is disgusted by his mother's incestuous advances and therefore enlists. When, however, she feels betrayed by her brother, who marries an English woman and has a child with her, the bad family spirits in the novice flare up again and she uses magic to bring about the death of her sister-in-law and the child. In *Kamouraska* the destructive passion of the protagonist had been fueled by the restricted space of the house to which Élisabeth is confined. Similarly, in *Les enfants du sabbat* the convent's walls ban corporeality and lust and conjure up dark forces. In *Les fous de Bassan* (1982), which was awarded the French Prix Médicis, it is the barely restrained violence and the latent irresponsibility of the inhabitants of the remote village Griffin Creek that lead to the murder of the cousins Olivia and Nora Atkins on 31 August 1936. In her novels, Hébert repeatedly and from varying perspectives depicts the individual's fight against the stranglehold of a milieu (*Le premier jardin*, 1988; *L'enfant chargé de songes*, 1992; *Est-ce que je te dérange?*, 1999), which she juxtaposes with the absoluteness of life and death.

Even though Antonine Maillet (1929–), who was born in Bactouche, New Brunswick, soon moved to Montreal, her novels are with one exception (*Madame Perfecta*, 2001) all set in Acadia or places relevant to Acadia's history. The fact that Acadian writing is recognized in Canada and abroad as an autonomous literature is doubtlessly due to the great success of Maillet's works, which link the rich oral tradition of the Acadians with the complex portrayal of a social microcosm and the staging of impressive female figures. The oeuvre of the author, who likes to describe herself as the last "conteuse" and the first "romancière" of the Acadians, not only marks the transition from a predominantly oral to a written literature, but also highlights the distance between collective memory and institutionalized historiography (*Cent ans dans les bois*, 1981), between the polyphonic voice of the Acadian people and the reduced abstraction of official depictions. Maillet's preference for Rabelais, for carnivalesque situations and exaggerated figures, is evident in the three autobiographical novels *On a mangé la dune* (1962), *Le chemin Saint-Jacques* (1996), and *Le temps me dure* (2003), and particularly in *Mariaagélas* (1973), *Les Cordes-de-bois* (1977), and in the Prix Goncourt-awarded novel *Pélagie-la-Charrette* (1979). In the latter novel Maillet tries to correct the glorifying romantic myth which has been constructed around Acadia since the success of Henry Wadsworth Longfellow's *Evangeline* (1847). In 1770 Pélagie LeBlanc (called Pélagie-la-Charrette) decides to end the exile of those deported in 1755 and leads her people back to Acadia. The many stories and anecdotes that decorate the portrayal of the long and troublesome journey home take into account all aspects of the "Longue Marche" — celebrations, weddings, and births, as well as deprivations, sicknesses, disputes, and deaths. The novel also distinguishes itself by addressing lesser-known aspects of the Grand Dérangement, for example, the contact of the deported with American resistance fighters and with Black slaves in the southern United States. The fact that the novel was initially not as well received in Quebec as in France may have something to do with its traditional structure and also with its epic dimension, which did not correspond with the critical ideological standards of Quebec literature of the late 1970s.

Also off the literary mainstream, but less well known and hardly noticed by literary criticism, were two novels that were published in the second half of the 1970s and that revived the topos of the North, although in very different ways. Jean-Yves Soucy's (1945–) *Un dieu chasseur* (1976) tackles the myth of masculinity embodied by the protagonist Mathieu Bouchard, who takes on exceedingly archaic and animalistic characteristics. The trapper Bouchard, who lives in the solitude of the woods, retains a symbiotic relationship with nature — a relationship that, from the perspective of the reader, borders on the perverted, for example, when he copulates with a female bear he has killed. When a woman, Marguerite Robitaille, follows him into the woods, the traditional conflict between the "sédentaire" and the "nomade" breaks out, and the trapper feels the energy of his animalistic manliness vanish. Bouchard, who repeatedly tries to elude Marguerite's influence, follows an Indian further north after her suicide. The contrast between the sedentary and nomadic way of life, as well as the linear narration (whose structure is determined by the succession of the seasons) is reminiscent of the great farm novels of the first half of the twentieth century.

Denys Chabot's (1945–) *L'eldorado dans les glaces* (1978), more demanding than Soucy's novel, relates the story of Oberlin, who is describing his life to the narrator on board the Vaisseau d'or. The allusion to Émile Nelligan's poem "Vaisseau d'or" promises a poetic-magical journey through a narrative labyrinth, which consists of the reports of five additional characters whom Oberlin questions in order to recover his own past. The title of the novel refers, on the one hand, to the setting of the story in northern Abitibi, the mythical place of Quebec gold diggers. On the other hand, it denotes a place of lust, namely the brothel that a certain Faustin has opened amid the sparse northern landscape on the Île aux radeaux. It also refers to Oberlin's search for his lover Julie, who knows how to consistently elude him in his eternal quest for fulfillment and happiness. In a game of masks, costumes, and deceptions the author draws illusive figures embedded in the cosmic myths of perpetual ice, great ice melt, and destructive fire, which makes them reminiscent of magic realism.

## Feminism and the *écriture au féminin*

Quebec's feminist movement came to occupy an explorative role in the 1970s, even more so than in other francophone countries. According to literary critic Sherry Simon, it paved the way for the historical and conceptual study of all types of differences within society (Simon 1991). In a social and literary context that attempted to overcome historical incapacitation and alienation by constructing a modern and proactive self-image — as epitomized by the "nous québécois" of the 1960s and 1970s — feminist discourse challenged the conceptual authority of homogeneity. While in the years of the Révolution tranquille and at the beginning of the 1970s feminism in Quebec had identified itself with national commitment, the women's movement was increasingly confronted with the fact that its concerns were secondary to a linguistically, culturally, and politically independent Quebec. Therefore, the movement tried not only to voice women's specific demands — "Pas de Québec libre sans libération des femmes! Pas de femmes libres sans libération du Québec!" was the main slogan of the Front de Libération des Femmes (FLF) — but also to account for the differences within the movement.

The years 1975 and 1976 played a key role in the development and institutionalization of women's literature. During the international women's year of 1975 the Éditions de la Pleine Lune were founded in Montreal, the magazine *La Barre du jour* dedicated an issue to the topic of "Femme et langage," and the Rencontre québécoise internationale des écrivains focused on "La Femme et l'écriture." In 1976 another feminist publishing house was established (Éditions du remue-ménage), the first issue of the feminist magazine *Les têtes de pioche* was released, and Louky

Bersianik (alias Lucile Durand) published *L'Euguélionne*, a representative example of radical feminist prose literature (see below). The fact that about forty percent of the novels published between 1975 and 1980 were written by women shows that Quebec women writers knew how to secure their place in the literary scene. The majority of these novels remained committed to the psychological genre and examined the fate of women, their daily life, and their confrontation with the other sex, such as *Un sens à ma vie* (1975) and *J'elle* (1987) by Hélène Rioux (1949–), as well as *Le plat de lentilles* (1978) by Madeleine Ouellette-Michalska (1930–). The very traditional trilogy Les Pierrefendre (1972, 1975, and 1977) by Yvette Naubert (1918–1982) depicts the story of two generations of women, without avoiding taboos such as abortion and menopause. Several authors — among them Claudette Charbonneau-Tissot (1947–; *La chaise au fond de l'oeil*, 1979) and Germaine Beaulieu (1949–; *Sortie d'elle(s) mutante*, 1980) — deal with women who live in psychiatric wards and mental hospitals. Although not explicitly feminist, these novels all contributed to shedding a different light on women's lives and to expressing, as in Renée Larche's (1946–) *Les naissances de larves* (1975), their urge for freedom as well as intellectual and physical self-determination.

From the early 1970s onwards, and especially from the middle of the decade, explicitly feminist writing practices were developing, practices whose roots can be found in the formalistic verse of the second half of the 1960s. These mainly experimental writing practices were summed up in Quebec under the generic term *écriture au féminin*. Authors such as Nicole Brossard, Louky Bersianik, Madeleine Gagnon, and France Théoret were chiefly influenced by French philosophers such as Roland Barthes and Jacques Derrida, by *Tel Quel*, and the French *écriture féminine*. Furthermore, these authors, by trying to create a literary language that withstands everyday life and the usual logic of identity, revolutionized the understanding of the linguistic signifier. In contrast to their male colleagues who were committed to formalism, however, they were less concerned with neutralizing the subject or the sense of a text. They rather concentrated on infiltrating or permeating the symbolic order of language by undermining the phallocentric codes that negate the feminine, the female body, and its specific desires.

This becomes especially clear in the work of Nicole Brossard (1943–). While in her first novel *Un livre* (1970) the author focuses on the *écriture* and the staging of the writing process, her third novel *French Kiss: Étreinte/exploration* (1974) can already be attributed to the *écriture au féminin*. When Brossard writes that the "langues" — in both senses of the word (language and tongue) — "tournent et se retournent dans la bouche comme des moulins à vent joyeux dans leur élan," she sums up the experimental quality of the text and at the same time refers to woman's liberating discovery of her own body via the body of another woman in a long, passionate "French kiss." The city of Montreal also gets "kissed," as the characters Camomille, Lucy, and Marielle, in the ecstasy of the novel's fractured syntax, scour through the city: Life pulsates in its arteries, as does the lust in the "re-awakened" female body. *L'amèr ou Le chapitre effrité* (1977), which is much more explicit when it comes to its feminist commitment, also deals with the female body. Starting from the programmatic sentence "J'ai tué le ventre et je l'écris," Brossard denounces the historical reduction of women to child-bearing and to ideologically maimed bodies. Following the credo "La vie privée est politique," Brossard's main concern becomes to demonstrate the political dimension of women's private lives. She juxtaposes the patriarchal "réproductrice" with the figure of the Amazon, showing how the latter eludes the male gaze and the pornographic interpretation of her body and lives and writes "herstory" in a community of women, who all read and inspire each other. *Le désert mauve* (1987) also engages with mutual reading, especially with reading as a creative act, and hence attracted a great deal of attention from feminist and deconstructive literary criticism. It consists of three parts: The first part corresponds with the fictitious novel *Le désert mauve* by a certain Laure Angstelle, which, as the reader learns in the second part, the francophone Maude Laures had found in a second-hand bookstore. The second part relates the reflections of the reader Maude, who decides to translate the novel into French and to explore its appeal to her. The third part reproduces this translation, called *Mauve l'horizon*. Brossard thereby underlines the fact that any choice of words can change a text, that reading is a translation, and that each act of writing is also one of rewriting, permeated with the fears, phantasms, hopes, and visions of the reader-translator. Situated in the desert of Arizona, which is used for nuclear tests and is synonymous with a male worldview concentrated on violence and destruction, Brossard's novel-in-a-novel depicts a social microcosm, in which the author once again juxtaposes the brutalization of North American culture with lesbian love as the positive vision of hope.

Louky Bersianik's (1930–) novels *L'Euguélionne* (1976) and *Le pique-nique sur l'Acropole* (1979) were well received by readers and critics, particularly in the golden age of feminism at the end of the 1970s and in the early 1980s. These novels distinguish themselves by emphasizing comedy and irony, in spite of their tragic and serious content. *L'Euguélionne* tells the story of a female alien who lands on earth, befriends some women, studies their social life and their relationship with the other sex, and with sharp intelligence comments on all this from the outsider's perspective. Euguélionne not only criticizes occidental philosophy and psychoanalysis, the Canadian government, and misogynous legislation, but also the inherent sexism of the French language, which is revealed in numerous and exceptionally innovative word-plays. *Le pique-nique sur l'Acropole* is a parody of Plato's *Symposium* and describes seven women having a picnic on the Acropolis. It takes up the topics from the first novel — deepening, for instance, the criticism of philosophy and psychoanalysis — and ends with woman's symbolic rebirth when the Caryatids (columns in the shape of women) of the Erechtheion come to life in the fourth section of the text. Bersianik thus juxtaposes a genealogy of female philosophizing with the dominant male tradition of reasoning. Similarly, Madeleine Gagnon (1938–) with *Lueur: Roman archéologique* (1979) and France Théoret (1942–) with *Nous parlerons comme on écrit* (1982) aim at reconstructing the female voices of earlier generations.

Feminist literary criticism as well as authors committed to the *écriture au féminin* frequently addressed the question of the specificity of female writing and its strategies. Like Brossard, they came to the conclusion that in addition to its irony, humor, and ambivalence, female writing excels in its formal audacity and makes genre hybridity, parody, and intertextuality its dominant form of composition. Further, Suzanne Lamy (1929–1987) emphasizes in *D'elles* (1979) that the cliché of female talkativeness can also be used as a formal element. This "bavardage" also marks the tone and rhythm of Yolande Villemaire's (1949–) *La vie en prose* (1980). Its anarchistic texture demands a lot of concentration on the part of the reader and presumes a profound knowledge of the literary scene in the 1970s and of Villemaire's other texts in order to understand the numerous quotations and allusions. Particularly from the mid-1980s onwards there were also voices who turned against the feminist dogmas that seemed increasingly to determine the development of women's literature. Carole Massé (1949–), for instance, whose novels *Dieu* (1979), *Existence* (1983), and *Nobody* (1986) belong to the feminist *écriture au féminin*, stressed that although she identified with the concerns of the feminist movement, she objected to the increasingly established feminist correctness, which restricted the individual writer's liberty. The 1980s largely renounced the premises of the *écriture au féminin* of the 1970s, and feminist women's literature distinguished itself more and more by distancing itself from didactic assumptions and language experiments. This development can be observed even in the groundbreaking works of Brossard and Théoret. Brossard's *Le désert mauve*, *Baroque d'aube* (1995), and *Hier* (2001) particularly are characterized by their readability and thus accessibility. This is also true of Théoret's *L'homme qui peignait Staline* (1989) and even more so of *Laurence* (1996) and *Huis clos entre jeunes filles* (2000), which are, like Brossard's novels, quite obviously feminist but do not represent the explicit feminist discourse characteristic of their author's earlier work.

## Staging the Writer and Her/His "Américanité"

One special characteristic of the Quebec novels from the 1960s onwards is the regular staging of the writer or author as a character in the novel. The writer and her or his work became the pivot of existential and social questions, for instance, in André Major's *Le cabochon* (1964), Hubert Aquin's *Prochain épisode* (1965), Marie-Claire Blais's *Une saison dans la vie d'Emmanuel* (1965), Jacques Godbout's *Salut Galarneau!* (1967), and in Victor-Lévy Beaulieu's and Michel Tremblay's novels, as well as in the works of the *écriture au féminin*. The novelist and translator Jacques Poulin (1937–), who has been living in Paris since the mid-1980s, shows writers in different situations, in their obsession with skillful execution and narrative ingenuity, in their loneliness and marginality, and in their vulnerability and consuming dedication to accuracy and precision. What the character Grande Sauterelle/Pitsémine, the enthralled reader and companion to the writer Jack Waterman, says in *Volkswagen blues* (1984) about books is valid for all of Poulin's works:

> Il ne faut pas juger les livres un par un. Je veux dire: il ne faut pas les voir comme des choses indépendantes. Un livre n'est jamais complet en lui-même; si on veut le comprendre, il faut le mettre en rapport avec d'autres livres, non seulement avec les livres du même auteur, mais aussi avec les livres écrits par d'autres personnes. Ce que l'on croit être un livre n'est la plupart du temps qu'une partie d'un autre livre plus vaste auquel plusieurs auteurs ont collaboré sans le savoir.

All of Poulin's novels since *Mon cheval pour un royaume* (1967) form a net of literary references that indicate the author's enthusiasm for American literature — especially Ernest Hemingway, J. D. Salinger, Jack Kerouac, Kurt Vonnegut, and Raymond Carver — but also for French-Canadian and French authors such as Gabrielle Roy, Anne Hébert, and Boris Vian. Names of authors, titles of novels, and direct or indirect quotes stand side by side with the staging of a passion that is downright destructive for the figure of the author. This is the case in *Jimmy* (1969), where the father of the eleven-year-old first-person narrator dedicates all his time and energy to a study on Hemingway and therefore neglects not only his marriage but also his son and himself. The novels *La tournée d'automne* (1993) and *Les yeux bleus de Mistassini* (2002) can also be read as an homage to literature. *La tournée d'automne* tells the story of the driver of a "bibliobus," a minivan with a built-in library, in which he travels from Quebec to the Côte-Nord three times a year. *Les yeux bleus de Mistassini* depicts the encounter of the writer Jack Waterman (who has aged since *Volkswagen blues*) with the adult Jimmy in Jack's bookstore in Vieux-Québec. Poulin's oeuvre, however, is not only a passionate and concise conglomeration of references, particularly to North American literature — the author sees himself as an "écrivain d'Amérique qui écrit en langue française" — it also forms a highly original and cohesive scenario based on the variation of constantly recurring characters, themes, and motifs. In contrast to many of his contemporaries Poulin excludes direct socio-critical aspects from his work.

He concentrates instead on the individual's search for happiness, a happiness that his writer-protagonists continuously find in friendly encounters with androgynous female figures who lead them out of their existential dead ends. These female figures are all talented readers and have a sharp and critical gaze regarding the writer's work. *Les grandes marées* (1978) depicts Teddy Bear, a character who has retreated to a lonely island to dedicate himself completely to the translation of comics. Poulin creates a social microcosm around Teddy and critically illuminates its inner dynamics.

In literary criticism the name Jacques Poulin stands predominantly for the increasing interest of the Québécois in his "américanité." In addition to the topics of migration, exile, multiculturalism, and transculturalism — which are discussed by authors such as Marco Micone, Régine Robin, Dany Laferrière, and Ying Chen (see ch. 34, Dupuis) — Quebec literature since the early 1980s also confronted the question of the Québécois's belonging to a specifically North American culture. Numerous novelists of the 1980s and 1990s turned away from the standardized concept of identity that for more than two decades had shown the Québécois predominantly in their national insecurity and had understood their identity deficit to be the result of economic exploitation as well as of political and intellectual incapacitation. To point out the inconsistency of national and personal self-images, authors had their protagonists travel the North American continent and contrast the myth of the "Terre Québec" with the myth of America. To what extent the latter corresponds to a kind of transformational myth — being connected with the idea of a rebirth of humanity and a new start of the "aventure humaine" — is shown in Poulin's *Volkswagen blues*. The trip from Gaspé to San Francisco leads the two protagonists, Jack Waterman and the "métisse" Grande Sauterelle, from one sacred site to the next and from museum to museum, so that their road trip becomes a passage of initiation into the history of North America. It also leads to a new understanding of history and identity, which, through the dialectics of Jack's glorifying vision of the frontier hero and Grande Sauterelle's representation of the indigenous population, results in a constructive existence in the present.

Similarly to Poulin, Pierre Turgeon (*La première personne*, 1980), Gilles Archambault (*Voyageur distrait*, 1981), Jacques Marchand (*Premier mouvement*, 1987), and Alain Poissant (*Vendredi-Friday*, 1988) also depict journeys to the United States as a destabilizing act or as a dislocation of self-perception. They often suggest a fascination with the figure of the trapper, who embodies the freedom that the vast continent promises. Moreover, direct links to Jack Kerouac's *On the Road* (1957) can be found in, for example, the works of Archambault and Poissant. Next to *Volkswagen blues*, the second important "America novel" of the 1980s is Jacques Godbout's (1933–) *Une histoire américaine* (1986), whose protagonist Grégory Francoeur makes his way to California after the failed referendum of 1980 in order to leave his private, professional, and political failure behind him: "On ne peut pas passer sa vie en érection nationaliste, vivre de promesses, de futurs qui n'arrivent jamais." At the end of the novel the disappointed nationalist mutates into a convinced "planétariste," whose aim it is to account for the ethnic diversity of the North American continent and its "culture métissée." In his study *Le voleur de parcours: Identité et cosmopolitisme dans la littérature québécoise* (1989) Simon Harel notes an important detail that can be found in both *Volkswagen blues* and *Une histoire américaine*: The protagonists revise their self-images through the encounter with the Other and recognize the concept of "métissage" as a significant aspect of "américanité." However, the problem of the "métissage culturel" is relocated in an, as Harel describes it, "ailleurs géographique fortement idéalisé," that is, outside of Quebec.

It was only in 2001, with the publication of Suzanne Jacob's (1943–) *Rouge, mère et fils* (2001), that the "métissage" returned to the "belle province" and was dealt with in a historical dimension. Since the late 1970s, Jacob's female figures have questioned the social status quo and have resisted social conventions (*Flore Cocon*, 1978; *Laura Laur*, 1984; *La passion selon Galatée*, 1987; *L'obéissance*, 1991; *Fugueuses*, 2005). In *Rouge, mère et fils* the novelist, essayist, and poet Jacob constructs the plot around the negation of two central aspects of French-Canadian history in contemporary Quebec: that of its "métissage" of autochthon and European cultures and that of its Catholic heritage. In a society in which excessive trips to shopping malls ("grandes surfaces") and supermarkets replace the physical and psychological experience of the "grandes surfaces" of the American continent and its stories, Luc, the son, remains trapped in an existential vacuum until he meets Jean Saint-Onge, who introduces himself as "Le Trickster." The name and nickname of the latter refer to the cultural duality he unites within himself, that is, his "identité métissée" comprising autochthon and Christian roots. The trickster, in the legends of the indigenous peoples, not only represents the possibility of change, but also a transgressive energy that confronts all conventions and norms (see ch. 1, Gruber). Jacob uses this figure to point to the repression of the "métissage" in the official historiography of the "Terre Québec." Thus, she not only creates a new image of the past, liberated from ideological ballast, but also indicates a possible future for the young Québécois Luc. *Rouge, mère et fils* addresses the question of transmission of cultural knowledge, including the awareness of "métissage" and Christian tradition, which the parents' generation, suffering from distrust and cynicism, had refused to pass on to their children, thus inducing a cultural amnesia.

The question of transmission, albeit in a different way, also plays a central role in Monique LaRue's (1948–) novel *La gloire de Cassiodore* (2002), which was awarded the Governor General's Award. The novel takes a satirical look at the milieu of the Cégep (collège d'éducation générale et professionnelle), the Quebec school system in general, its pedagogic premises, and the relationship between the generations. At the same time it is a profound reflection on education and knowledge in the francophone province. As in her other novels, the author's aim is not to deliver a portrait of society but to cast doubt on and to destabilize different dogmas and "truths." In *La cohorte fictive* (1979), for instance, she criticizes feminist truisms of the 1970s, such as the equation of motherhood with submission to patriarchy. In *Les faux fuyants* (1982) the author places two teenagers, Klaus and Élodie, at the center of a fight for life when they become victims of their parents' narcissism. The siblings, who remain silent because they are not able to articulate their injuries, start out on an aimless journey into an uncertain future; Klaus, accompanied by Clarisse, finally ends up in the United States: "C'est dans le présent qu'ils déambulant, . . . figures minimales dont l'ombre se projette sur le réel des autoroutes." LaRue's most important and probably most widely known novel is *Copies conformes* (1989), which is set in San Francisco against the backdrop of Dashiell Hammett's *The Maltese Falcon* (1930). The misogynous undertone of Hammett's detective story is juxtaposed with LaRue's female first-person narrator Claire Dubé. Dubé, despite her traditional social status of wife and mother, acts as an autonomous person and does not lose her individuality in a world of artificiality, quite in contrast to Brigid O'Doorsey — a reference to Hammett's Miss Wonderly, alias Brigid O'Shaughnessy — who, as a result of plastic surgery, has become a frozen mask. The novel addresses the autonomy and individuality of the female body as well as the question of original and copy in the broadest sense. During his six-month stay in California, Claire's husband develops a translation program. As they search for the lost disc which contains the results of his research, the distinction between reality and fiction, between original and simulacrum gets blurred for Claire. While the linguistic code of modern technology creates the illusion of homogeneity and exact congruence between original and copy, Claire's experience contradicts the equation of sign and meaning and stresses language's inherent ambivalence as a consequence of each speaker's individual and social experiences. LaRue argues against the illusion of unambiguity and also against the definability of individual and collective identity, which Claire, through her linguistic and social exile in California, recognizes as a construct.

As implied by the title, Madeleine Monette (1951–) dedicates her novel *Le double suspect* (1980) to the topic of doubling, copying, and rewriting. When Manon is killed in an accident on her way from Rome to Munich, Anne reads her friend's diary, recognizes the alleged accident as a planned suicide, and enters an identification process: She becomes Manon's double, not only wearing her dead friend's clothes and adopting her habits, but also starting to think like her and continuing her diary. Finally, the rewriting of the diary in the form of a novel allows Anne to weave herself into her friend's text, to become aware of her suppressed homosexual desires, and, via the confrontation with the other woman, to accept the ambiguity within herself. As in *Petites violences* (1982) the question of reality plays a central role in *Le double suspect*. Whereas in Monette's first novel, paradoxically, it is fiction that enables the narrator to experience reality, in *Petites violences* it is the city of New York that serves as a metaphor for the abolition of the boundaries between fiction and reality. In the monstrously violent and simultaneously regenerating urban spectacle that is the "Big Apple," the protagonist Martine gains a new perspective on reality. This perspective is characterized by ambivalence and vagueness and results from Martine's experience of herself in a foreign language: "J'aime la façon dont on dit les choses en anglais, la façon dont je m'y retrouve sans m'y reconnaître tout à fait."

The question of "américanité," addressed by various authors from different perspectives, in many ways transcended the discussion about Quebec's cultural roots in the North American continent and took on an epistemological dimension by pointing to the problem of reality. Showing that not only human but also social reality is always characterized by a fundamental antagonism that defies complete symbolization, the authors exposed the political, ideological, and personal master narratives as phantasms, as scenarios which try to cover up the basic inconsistency of human beings and society, particularly that of Quebec society. This did not exclude the desire for wholeness and authenticity, as the above discussion of selected novels has shown. However, authors did not continue to yield to utopias any more but rather faced the condition of foreignness, which was understood as a positive and stimulating condition of existence.

# The Popular Novel

Commercially successful in the last two decades of the twentieth century were not novels that discussed the ambivalence, insecurity, and the uncanny nature of human existence, but rather those that offered clearly outlined images of society: Milieu studies paying homage to a new realism, family sagas, chronicles, and historical novels conquered the Quebec book market and introduced a new era of readability or "texte du plaisir." It conceded the pleasure of recognition to the reader and did not jolt historical, cultural, or psychosocial "truths," even if it sometimes depicted groups from the social margin and thus provided alternative views. In literary criticism this development has often been referred to as the beginning of a "littérature populaire de qualité," to which belong, among others, Michel Tremblay's *Chroniques du Plateau Mont-Royal*, Yves Beauchemin's novels *Le matou* (1981) and *Juliette Pomerleau* (1989), and Francine Noël's *Maryse* (1983), *Myriam première* (1987), and *La conjuration des bâtards* (1999).

Beauchemin's (1941–) *L'enfirouapé* (1974) still circles around the alienation and exploitation of the Québécois — as indicated by the title, which uses a term derived from the English phrase "wrapped in fur," meaning "to be deceived or outwitted" in Québécois. In *Le matou* Beauchemin adopts a new path regarding both content and narration. Set in the 1970s, it is the story of the ambitious francophone Florent Boissonneault, who, after several ups and downs and despite numerous intrigues with respect to the ownership of a "binerie" in the Avenue du Mont-Royal, is victorious at the end of the novel. *Le matou* is reminiscent of the discourse of the farm novel because of its ideologically colored, simple dichotomies. With a lot of humor and nostalgic kitsch the author constructs a strictly linear story and typified figures who lack psychological depth and therefore provide ideal projection surfaces for time-honored truisms. The quality of the novel is based on Beauchemin's intriguing portrayal of small details of everyday life, a talent he also uses in *Juliette Pomerleau*.

The first part of Francine Noël's (1945–) triptych, *Maryse*, owes its success mainly to its topic. Just as linearly structured as Beauchemin's novels, but much more differentiated in the treatment of its subject, the novel tells the story of the working-class woman Maryse in the years between 1968 and 1975, and her development from a "speechless" woman to a writer. By depicting different milieus — the intellectual bohème as well as the francophone bourgeoisie of Outremont and the Hispanic immigrants of the Boulevard Saint-Laurent — the novel highlights the contradictions of the era. The plot of *Myriam première* is set in the postreferendum Montreal of 1983 and continues the story of the friends Maryse, Marité, and Marie-Lyre from *Maryse*, showing them in their private and professional environments. The numerous flashbacks to the grandmother's past and the story of her own family, which Maryse tells Marité's children Myriam and Gabriel, give the novel a narrative complexity that is absent in *Maryse*. With her voluminous novels the author succeeds in writing a female chronicle with a feminist claim, thereby participating in a development in female prose that the literary critic Lori Saint-Martin has called "métaféministe." Unlike the radical feminist novels of the 1970s, the "écrits métaféministes" exclude anything explicitly didactic, are less hermetic, and refuse to be implemented as ideological instruments. Thus, in novels such as *Laura Laur* (1983) and *L'obéissance* (1991) by Suzanne Jacob, *Les images* (1985) by Louise Bouchard, *La maison du remous* (1986) by Nicole Houde, and *Le bruit des choses vivantes* (1991) by Élise Turcotte, the theoretical-fictional treatment of women's issues is replaced by a new narrative, which leaves behind the polarized thinking of the *écriture au féminin*, relativizes the aggressor/man and victim/woman dichotomy, and makes the feminist issue a question of general social relevance.

The success story of the contemporary popular historical novel in Quebec began with the publication of Louis Caron's *Le canard de bois* (1981) and

Francine Ouellette's (1947–) *Au nom du père et du fils* (1984) and continues until the present day. Historical novels by female writers, especially, have flooded the Quebec book market and reached editions of 100,000 to 150,000 copies. Bestsellers in this genre were Arlette Cousture's *Les filles de Caleb* (vol. 1: *Le chant du coq*, 1985; vol. 2: *Le cri de l'oie blanche*, 1986; vol. 3: *L'abandon de la mésange*, 2003), Chrystine Brouillet's trilogy *Marie Laflamme* (vol. 1: *Maria Laflamme*, 1991; vol. 2: *Nouvelle-France*, 1992; vol. 3: *La renarde*, 1993), and Micheline Lachance's *Le roman de Julie Papineau* (vol. 1: *La tourmente*, 1995; vol. 2: *L'exil*, 1998). All of these works focus on the lives of women and create, in narrative simplicity, a history of private life. Cousture's (1948–) *Les filles de Caleb*, for instance, relates the everyday life of the young teacher Émilie in the rural Quebec of the late nineteenth and early twentieth century, her marriage, and an existence marked by austerity, sickness, and death.

Parallel to the popular historical novel, other historical texts emerged, which, like Claire de Lamirande's (1929–) *Papineau ou L'épée à double tranchant* (1980), use irony to reveal the ambivalence of national heroes, or, as is the case in François Barcelo's (1941–) *La tribu* (1981), humorously deconstruct mythical moments of Quebec history in a magical-fantastic ambience. Madeleine Ouellette-Michalska's (1930–) *La maison Trestler ou Le 8e jour d'Amérique* (1984) can be described as "historiographic metafiction," a term coined by Linda Hutcheon (see ch. 22, Rosenthal). The nameless narrator, who questions the objectivity of official historiography, comes to the conclusion that the "Histoire avec un grand H" is but a literary genre that uses a specific style, specific rules, and specific editorial processes: "C'était, de toutes les histoires possibles, celle que l'on choisissait à des fins qui ne se révélaient que plus tard." Given the absence of women in official historiography and the first-person narrator's nearly fruitless search for historical evidence, the narrator uses empathy and, as she calls it, "mémoire corporelle," to reconstruct the story of Catherine Trestler from the nineteenth century. The author juxtaposes the narrator's reflections on her present life with a *mise en abyme*, in which the childhood memories of the narrator are intermingled with episodes from Catherine's life, alternately rendered from the first- and from the third-person perspective. The identification of the narrator with the protagonist of her historical fiction is so intense that present and past overlap in several passages, and the narrator tells her own story via that of Catherine Trestler.

## Homosexuality and Gender Trouble

With the increasing importance of the feminist movement since the 1970s, female homosexuality has become a topic not only in Nicole Brossard's and Louky Bersianik's work but also in the texts of many other authors.

Writers such as Marie-Claire Blais (*Le loup*, 1972; *Les nuits de l'Underground*, 1978; *L'ange de la solitude*, 1989), Jovette Marchessault (*Comme une enfant de la terre*, 1975; *La mère des herbes*, 1980; *Des cailloux blancs pour les forêts obscures*, 1987), Josée Yvon (*Travesties-kamikaze*, 1980; *Danseuses-mamelouk*, 1982; *Maîtresses-Cherokees*, 1986), and Suzanne Jacob (*Flore Cocon*, 1978) deal with homosexuality from different perspectives. Male homosexuality, even though repeatedly put forward as a topic in the 1960s — as, for example, in Jean Basile's (1932–1992) *Le Grand Khan* (1967) — had its true "coming out" only in the 1980s. Robert Lalonde's (1947–) *Le dernier été des Indiens* (1981) places the sexual initiation of the teenager Michel by the Indian Kanak in the time before the Révolution tranquille. It joins the revitalizing experience of same-sex love with the denunciation of a paralyzed francophone society which negates the encounter with the Other/the Indian. Homosexuality is also the central topic in Michel Tremblay's novels *La duchesse et le roturier* (1982) and *Des nouvelles d'Édouard* (1984), which depict Édouard's experiences as the transvestite Duchesse de Langeais in Montreal's homosexual and cabaret scene. In the less glamorous ambience of his novels *Le coeur découvert* (1986) and *Le coeur éclaté* (1993) Tremblay again picks up this topic. Homosexuality is also reworked in Stephen Schecter's (1946–) *T'es beau en écoeurant* (1984), using the example of a love relationship between an anglophone Jew and a French Canadian. In François Brunet's (1950–) *L'acte de folie* (1993) the story of a gay relationship is set against the backdrop of the fight against AIDS.

By challenging the normative status of heterosexuality and by depicting alternative relationships, the problem of sexual identity found its way into literature, predominantly since the late 1980s. Using the example of the transsexual character Marie-Pierre (previously Pierre-Henri), a successful microbiologist, husband of a renowned lawyer, and father of a daughter, Monique Proulx (1952–) in her partially satirical novel *Le sexe des étoiles* (1987) reveals sexual identity as a social construct. Sexual identity is staged here as an experience of continuous estrangement that the characters make in interaction with themselves and others. Biological sex does not have any essential meaning because the human being, man or woman, is understood as heterogeneous. Marie-Pierre, whose greatest wish is to be a woman, soon realizes the discrepancy between her romantic notions and the reality of women's social role, which she refuses to subject herself to. Representing ambiguity even after her sex change — she unites traces of Pierre-Henri's male facial features with the staged elegance of her now female body — she acts with conviction and resolute pride; she thus helps her daughter Camille to accept herself as being different, as a highly gifted adolescent and daughter of a transsexual: "Il faut pas être comme tout le monde. Il faut marcher toute seule à la tête, pis essayer de trouver un chemin que personne d'autre a pris avant."

Gaétan Soucy (1958–) casts an original and unquestioning glance at the question of sexual identity in *La petite fille qui aimait trop les allumettes* (1998), which enjoyed great international success. Only after six chapters does the reader realize that the first-person narrator, who was raised in complete seclusion with his brother and one morning finds his father dead, is in fact a girl. The narrator herself only becomes aware of this after her father's death when she is forced to go to the next village. Her appearance is met with surprise, and finally someone asks: "Pourquoi parles-tu toujours de toi comme si tu étais un garçon? . . . Tu ne sais donc pas que tu es une fille?" The narrator only slowly learns to let go of the notion of being a boy, and even when she recognizes her body as being female on a cognitive level, she remains her father's son and her brother's brother ("Papa me considérait comme la plus intelligente de ses fils"). Against the backdrop of a family tragedy Soucy demonstrates the arbitrariness of the assumption that biological sex and sexual identity (gender) are necessarily congruent and thereby exposes, just as Proulx, sexual difference as a cultural construct of identity.

## Social Criticism in the *roman de la désespérance*

In the late 1980s and during the 1990s a generation of writers came to the fore who, to a certain extent, represented the children of the baby boomers and who could either be associated with the "bof generation" (Jean-Yves Dupuis, *Bof génération*, 1987) or the "génération vamp" (Christian Mistral, *Vamp*, 1988). The literary critic Aurélien Boivin classifies their novels as "romans de la désespérance," referring to the numerous characters whose existence is characterized by insecurity, unemployment, depression, alcohol, drugs, violence, and a general disorientation. In Mistral's (1964–) novels this human condition culminates in an individualism that celebrates excess and marginality. In the works of Hélène Monette (1960–; *Unless*, 1995) and Lise Tremblay (1957–; *L'hiver de pluie*, 1997) the same individualism is now characterized by solitude. The *romans de la désespérance*, particularly those by Dupuis, Mistral, or Louis Hamelin (*La rage*, 1989), also frequently feature an autofictional dimension, which the authors do not attempt to conceal — Dupuis (1955–) and Mistral even use their own names for the protagonists. Also typical is a certain hyperrealism in descriptions of everyday scenes as well as on the linguistic level, for instance, by precisely reproducing colloquial language. Mistral's novel *Vamp*, the first volume of the cycle "Vortex violet" (*Vautour*, 1990; *Valium*, 2000; *Vacuum*, 2003), was much more successful than Dupuis's *Bof génération*. This has to do, on the one hand, with Mistral's linguistic virtuosity, and, on the other, with his characters' boundless vitality despite their precarious situations. Whereas Dupuis's protagonist resorts to indifference and says of himself "j'ai toujours trouvé que j'étais un type qui n'avait rien à dire," Mistral's protagonists and their friends throw themselves — drunk, stoned, and cynical — into the *laissez-faire* of their time:

> Montréal vivait le déclin du nationalisme et s'inscrivait chaque jour un peu plus dans le corps de l'Amérique, et ses enfants les plus turbulents, entre l'alcool, la baise et la littérature, dévoilaient la face cachée du continent vertueux, aperçue du fond des ruelles, des poubelles, des bouteilles et des matelas. C'était la génération vamp, née de la Haute Technologie, qui dormait sur un futon, cultivait des bonsaïs, n'allait pas à la messe et se torchait une poésie du laid, du bas et du sale parce que sa pauvreté n'entraînait pas qu'elle soit insensible.

As the title already indicates, Hamelin's (1959–) first publication, *La rage*, is a linguistic distillate of rage: rage towards a disintegrating society that reveres new technologies, deprives its members of livelihoods, and abandons its children to poverty. The protagonist Édouard Malarmé's rage results in an act of violent revolt when he attacks the tower of the airport in Mirabel, a symbol of technology's triumph over humankind. Hamelin's *La rage*, winner of the Governor General's Award, is in every respect a successful "exercice de style," which captivates the reader through elaborate vocabulary and original metaphors. Hamelin's second novel, *Cowboy* (1992), also voices social criticism. However, this time the focus is on northern Quebec and on the confrontation between Whites and Indians in everyday life, characterized as it is by alcohol and drug addiction. Through the depiction of some eccentric dropouts' propensity to violence, Hamelin deconstructs the myths of the Noble Savage as well as that of the White adventurer in the Canadian North. Be it in his first two novels or in *Betsi Larousse ou L'ineffable eccéité de la loutre* (1994), *Le soleil des gouffres* (1996), or *Le joueur de flûte* (2001), Hamlin manages in all his texts to depict disastrous experiences of the contemporary world and its central cultural, social, economical, and political questions.

The development of the Quebec novel from the Révolution tranquille to the turn of the century testifies to a paradigmatic change in the understanding of identity, which the literary scholar Pierre Nepveu noted in his 1988 monograph *L'écologie du réel: Mort et naissance de la littérature québécoise contemporaine*. Nepveu assumes the end of the "littérature québécoise" and indicates that the phantasm of national unity (as a cultural and linguistic unity) will possibly be overcome. In this sense the development of the Quebec novel stands for an impressive diversity that can only be touched upon here. Using very different literary techniques, the contemporary Quebec novel narrates a specific cultural space and represents a multitude of lifestyles and points of view.

# 30: The French-Canadian Short Prose Narrative

*Doris G. Eibl (University of Innsbruck)*

FOR A LONG TIME Quebec short fiction did not rank highly in the hierarchy of genres. In the 1980s and 1990s, however, it experienced a boom in popularity, with the number of publications steadily rising: In the early 1970s only about ten short-story volumes had been published per annum, whereas the 1990s saw an average of thirty to thirty-five volumes published per year, not to mention publications in numerous journals and weekly as well as daily newspapers. From the mid-1970s onwards a great thematic and formal diversity could be found in French-Canadian short stories. This diversity, characterized by a seemingly unlimited eagerness to experiment, heralded the golden age of the short story in Quebec, as literary critics often call the last two decades of the twentieth century.

The short stories of the early 1970s did not differ greatly from those of the previous decades. There are some exceptions, such as Claude Robitaille's volumes *Rachel-du-hasard* (1971) and *Le temps parle et rien ne se passe* (1974), Louis-Philippe Hébert's *Le cinéma de petite-rivière* (1974), *Textes extraits de vanille* (1974), and *Textes d'accompagnement* (1975), and Albert-G. Paquette's *Quand les québécoisiers en fleurs . . .* (1973), which were all written in a progressive style, renouncing traditional narrative linearity. Most authors, however, remained committed to socio-critical and psychological realism, used folkloristic elements of the oral narrative, or dealt with previous times in autobiographical short stories. Often short-story volumes were produced by already established novelists or critics such as Gilles Archambault (*Enfances lointaines*, 1972), Jean Éthier-Blais (*Le manteau de Rubén Dario*, 1974), Adrienne Choquette (*Le temps des villages*, 1975), or Yves Thériault (*Oeuvre de chair*, 1975). However, in the end it was lesser-known authors such as André Berthiaume and Claudette Charbonneau-Tissot (the latter using the pseudonym Aude from 1983 onwards) whose fantastic stories indicated the direction in which the Quebec short story would develop. Rather than by Berthiaume's (1938–) realistic and lengthy title story about an author stranded in France, readers were charmed by the fantastic dimension of the stories in *Contretemps* (1971). In his later publications (*Le mot pour vivre*, 1978; *Incidents de frontiers*,

1984; *Presqu'îles dans la ville*, 1991) Berthiaume continued to play with elements of the fantastic, focusing on humor and the paring down of external action, and he flirted with the narrative techniques of Argentine writers Jorge Luis Borges and Julio Cortázar. In Charbonneau-Tissot's (1947–) eight *Contes pour hydrocéphales adultes* (1974) the female first-person narrators lead the reader into the Kafkaesque world of confined spaces, which are juxtaposed with the vastness of the narrators' inner worlds. Even though Charbonneau-Tissot abstains from syntactic and semantic experimentation, which were characteristic of the feminist writings of the 1970s, there are still some similarities between her work and the *écriture au féminin*. This is the case, for example, in *La contrainte* (1976), in which writing is the place where new ideas are created and where the female subject can take off the mask of patriarchal conventions. The fantastic uncanny of Charbonneau-Tissot's short stories often serves as a mere pretense for the philosophical examination of reality. Masquerade and masks (*Cet imperceptible mouvement*, 1997) function as metaphors for the problematic longing for authenticity and allow the author to point out the phantasmatic dimension of each and every search for identity.

The influence of the fantastic on Quebec short prose became particularly evident from the 1980s onwards. A clear boundary has to be drawn to distinguish it from the classic fantastic story: Fantastic elements of the oppressive uncanny can be found in numerous modern and postmodern narrations and appear as a natural consequence of the refusal of mimetic narrative, while fantasy is a narration closed in itself. It takes place in a different, impossible world, but retains traditional patterns of action and emotion. Sometimes it also depicts a reality corresponding with the experience of the reader, albeit using dehumanized figures as characters. As of the mid-1970s, extremely active fantastic and fantasy fandoms developed in Quebec, which also influenced short prose. The founding of magazines such as *Requiem* (1974), renamed *Solaris* in 1979, or *Imagine . . .* (1979), as well as several fanzines (*Samizdat, Temps Tôt, CSF, Proxima*) gave new impulses to the genre of fantasy and science fiction. In 1979 the magazine *La Nouvelle Barre du Jour* dedicated a whole issue to science fiction, another one to fantasy in 1980, and since 1984 *L'Année de la science-fiction et du fantastique québécois* has been published annually. The second half of the 1980s also saw the publication of several important anthologies which either focus on the early history of the fantastic genre or chart its developments during the twentieth century. The latter include Maurice Édmond's *Anthologie de la nouvelle et du conte fantastiques québécois au XXᵉ siècle* (1987) and Michel Lord's *Anthologie de la science-fiction québécoise contemporaine* (1988). The most important representatives of the genre are Jean-Pierre April, René Beaulieu, Michel Bélil, Alain Bergeron, Jacques Brossard, Yves Meynard, Esther Rochon, Daniel Sernine, and Elisabeth Vonarburg.

These authors are also well known for their novels, and their works include texts across the genre ranging from "hard SF" to "heroic fantasy," from "space opera" to uchronias and utopias.

While science fiction and fantasy short prose usually remained true to the parameters of traditional narration and particularly focused on story-telling as such, most short stories in the 1980s and 1990s were character-ized by a pronounced awareness of form. At the beginning of the 1980s the authors of the generation of the Révolution tranquille such as Gérard Bessette (1920–2005; *La garden-party de Christophine*, 1980) or André Major (1942–; *La folle d'Elvis*, 1981) still wrote in the vein of the realistic aesthetics of the 1960s and 1970s or modeled their texts on the oral nar-rative. The younger literary generation, in contrast, relied on radical mod-ern and postmodern narrative techniques, and with the foundation of journals dedicated exclusively to the short story such as *XYZ, La revue de la nouvelle,* and *STOP* in 1985, they found an adequate platform for pub-lication. *XYZ* appears three times a year and offers its readers — besides short stories and author interviews — theoretical and critical texts and also includes a chronicle of current publications, always taking international developments into account. The journal *STOP,* which ceased publication in the late 1990s, annually awarded a prize "STOP Concours de nou-velles" and thus enabled the emergence of a new generation of authors, among them Christian Mistral (1964–) and Stanley Péan (1966–). Equally important was the foundation of the publishing house L'Instant même in 1985: Until the late 1990s it published exclusively short prose and dedi-cated itself especially to the promotion of young authors.

The new emphasis on form was certainly linked to the fact that many of the authors originated from the academic milieu — professors and their students — and were well acquainted with the prevalent literary theories. Hence, the theoretical knowledge of linguistic operational mechanisms, that is, their deconstruction and playful staging, influenced their creative work. The endeavor to structure short-story volumes with respect to their content, thus avoiding random combinations of texts, was especially strik-ing. But this striving for thematic and/or formal unity had probably less to do with literary theoretical considerations than with the dynamics of the book market, which preferred the coherent narration of the novel. Consequently, from the mid-1980s to the mid-1990s works appeared that were, on the one hand, collective publications, such as *Nouvelles de Montréal* (1992), edited by Micheline La France, and, on the other, inde-pendent works whose homogeneity was based on one recurring character (Anne Dandurand, *Petites âmes sous ultimatum,* 1991; Élise Turcotte, *Caravane,* 1994). This practice often blurred the generic boundaries of the novel, as is the case in Suzanne Jacob's (1943–) *Les aventures de Pomme Douly* (1988), Pierre Yergeau's (1957–) *Tu attends la neige, Léonard* (1992), and Anne Legault's (1958–) *Récits de Médihault* (1994).

Formal coherence was also established by carefully arranging a short-story volume's macrostructure, as, for example, in Gilles Archambault's (1933–) *Tu ne me dis jamais que je suis belle* (1994), in which twelve longer texts alternate with just as many short texts, and in Hélène Rioux's (1949–) *Pense à mon rendez-vous* (1994), where the individual stories are linked through dialogues with Death.

Genre hybridity became typical in the last two decades of the twentieth century. There were short stories written in the form of letters (Danielle Dussault, *Ça n'a jamais été toi*, 1996), diary entries (Anne Dandurand, *Petites âmes sous ultimatum*, 1991), pamphlets (Gabrielle Gourdeau, *L'âge dur*, 1996), and sociological reports (Suzanne Jacob, *Ah!...*, 1996); others include elements of literary criticism (Gilles Pellerin, *Je reviens avec la nuit*, 1992) or of the essay (Pierre Ouellet, *L'attrait*, 1994) and are reminiscent, as in the case of Pierre Ouellet's work, of the French "conte philosophique." In addition, many works feature intertextual references, as in Hugues Corriveau's *Autour des gares* (1991), where Marcel Proust is quoted in each of the one hundred stories of the volume, in Pierre Karch's *Jeux de patience* (1991), which refers to Homer and the *Arabian Nights*, and in Robert Lalonde's *Des nouvelles d'amis très chers* (1999), an homage to nine authors — Jean Giono, Colette, Gabriel García Márquez, Gabrielle Roy, and Michel Tremblay, among others — or, as Lalonde writes himself, a "piratage par amour." Authors also experimented with self-references and *mises en abyme* (André Carpentier, *Carnet sur la fin possible du monde*, 1992; Francine D'Amour, *Écrire comme un chat*, 1994) and with reflections on the reception process (Gilles Pellerin, *Principe d'extorsion*, 1991), thus making short prose the postmodern writing laboratory par excellence.

Gaétan Brulotte and Monique Proulx are the most prominent representatives of the burgeoning genre of the short story in Quebec in the early 1980s. The literary scholar, journalist, and editor Brulotte (1945–) made his debut as a novelist (*L'emprise*, 1979) and published his first volume of short stories in 1982 (*Le surveillant*), for which he was awarded the Prix Adrienne Choquette (a prize that was awarded for the first time in 1980 and that is very prestigious today). This first collection of ten stories already illustrated that the author was highly interested in linguistic experiments. In *Le surveillant* Brulotte describes the banality of everyday life, in which human beings are victims of oppressive mechanisms in a disconcerting world. As in his later publications (*Ce qui nous tient*, 1988; *Épreuves*, 1999; *La vie de biais*, 2002), it is the hyperrealist style, supported by concise ellipses and short, unembellished sentences, that exposes the absurdity of prevalent modes of discourse. This exposure is effectively staged in the so-called "textes hapistes," in which everyday texts such as police protocols, parking tickets, advertising brochures, instruction manuals, recipes, or resumés are parodied. Brulotte understands the "haptisme" as a new form of mimetic writing, which deprives nonliterary texts of their traditional context of meaning.

The screenwriter and novelist Monique Proulx (1952–) produced a national bestseller with her second volume of short stories, *Les aurores montréales* (1996), which continued the success of her novels *Le sexe des étoiles* (1987) and *L'homme invisible à la fenêtre* (1993). In her first volume of short stories, *Sans coeur et sans reproche* (1983), she designs a "comédie humaine" in fifteen stories, carefully examining the ups and downs of human existence between birth and death. While in her short-story debut Proulx uses the characters Françoise and Benoît to illustrate general human experiences, in *Les aurores montréales* it is the metropolis of Montreal that serves as a backdrop for a postmodern human mosaic at the end of the twentieth century. The juxtaposition of poverty and wealth, youth and age, rootedness and migration is conveyed by Proulx with a note of irony, which is accentuated by the perfectly controlled montage of scenes from everyday life in each of the stories.

Despite their humor and irony, Brulotte's and Proulx's depictions of society are rather gloomy. They mirror a general tendency to depict relationships and family bonds that suffer from a basic fragility and fall victim to various obsessions, ending in emotional and physical violence (Élise Turcotte, *Caravane*, 1994; Hugues Corriveau, *Le ramasseur de souffle*, 1999). Mothers and fathers fail to fulfill their responsibilities (Danielle Dussault, *L'alcool froid*, 1994), children become violent (Sylvie Massicotte, *Le cri des coquillages*, 2000; Diane-Monique Daviau, *La vie passe comme une étoile filante: Faites un voeu*, 1993) or turn their destructive instincts against themselves (Bertrand Bergeron, *Transits*, 1990). The longing for permanent intimacy remains just as unfulfilled as the hope of finding comfort in superficial encounters. The latter correspond with the "non-places" in which they take place: People meet and uncommittedly scan each other in all sorts of places of transition, such as motels, bars, airports, train stations, boats, and underground trains. Very rarely does the aura of some exceptional human being create enough erotic intensity to generate actual love, as for instance in Anne Dandurand's (1953–) *Petites âmes sous ultimatum* (1991). Many characters do not act out of love, conviction, or willpower, but drift in and out of the events while being constantly reminded of the limitedness of human existence. Facing the agonizing certainty of death, they turn into marionettes of their own fear.

The increasing academic attention that the Quebec short story has received since the 1980s is seen by many critics as a mere trend that disguises the difficult relationship between the French-Canadian reading public and short prose. Despite the high standing of short stories in English-speaking cultures, above all in the United States, in Quebec the novel has always overshadowed the short story. One reason for the slow reception of the short story by francophone readers might lie in the difficult aesthetics of numerous authors who concentrated on form and, according to Michel Lord, thus turned short prose into a "genre plutôt pour *happy few*." However, thanks to this exploration of formal possibilities, short prose has developed into an eminently politicized genre, distinguished by substantial and well-researched social criticism.

# 31: French-Canadian Poetry
from 1967 to the Present

*Ursula Mathis-Moser (University of Innsbruck)*

THE YEAR 1967 — WHEN the Expo was held in Montreal and Charles de
Gaulle proclaimed his notorious "Vive le Québec libre" — is seldom
looked upon as a turning point in French-Canadian literature. The end of
the 1960s did, however, demarcate a significant threshold of the coming-
of-age of this literature: 1968 was not only the year in which the magazine
*Les Herbes rouges* was founded and Michel Tremblay's (1942–) *Les belles-
soeurs* premiered, it was also the year of important publications by avant-
garde poets like Nicole Brossard (*L'écho bouge beau*) and Denis Vanier
(*Pornographic Delicatessen*). Gaston Miron (1928–1996) even described
the year 1970 as the end of an era. 1970 saw Montreal's legendary Nuit
de la poésie and the (re)publication of "classic" authors such as Jean-
Aubert Loranger, Hector de Saint-Denys Garneau, Anne Hébert, and
Rina Lasnier. At the same time, Miron's *L'homme rapaillé* and an abundance of radically new poetry volumes were published — among them
Brossard's *Suite logique* and *Le centre blanc*, Michel Beaulieu's *Charmes de
la fureur*, Roger Des Roches's *Corps accessoires*, and Raoul Duguay's
*Manifeste de l'infonie*. In addition, Luc Racine, Pierre Morency, Marie-
Francine Hébert, Marie Laberge, Suzanne Paradis, Hélène Rioux, and
Cécile Cloutier launched their debut volumes. To sum up, the late 1960s
and early 1970s saw a remarkable range of extremely divergent and often
conflicting literary productions.

This rich literary activity coincided with a number of political events.
The Parti Québécois (PQ) was founded in 1968 and acted as a catalyst for
renewed nationalism, at first aiming at the establishment of an associated
state, later with the goal of full sovereignty and independence for Quebec.
At the same time, the Liberal Party's focus on cultural autonomy — as
opposed to political autonomy — and Quebec federalism led to the
Liberals' victory in the 1970 provincial elections. However, the October
Crisis of the same year — with the terrorist activities of the Front de
Libération du Québec (FLQ), the intervention by the federal government
of liberal prime minister Pierre E. Trudeau, and the arrest of more than 450
trade unionists and intellectuals — left a deep psychological wound. The
threat of terror was averted, but the desire for social change became more

urgent than ever before. This desire expressed itself in the flourishing of small Marxist-Leninist groups and the emergence of the Counter Culture youth movement. Intellectuals played a central role, devoting their writing to the concerns of Quebec and its people; university educated, well versed in contemporary cultural theory — structuralism, semiology, psychoanalysis, and Marxism — and backed by the new cultural politics of the province, they produced theoretical ideas, however, that were far removed from everyday reality. Jean Royer rightly labeled the period from 1968 to 1983 a "discursive age." The monolithic "poésie du pays" of the 1960s gave way to the polyvocal "poésie sans pays" (Mailhot and Nepveu 1980), which redefined the relationship between reality and language as well as the position of the artist in Quebec society. Nevertheless, "national poetry" was still influential in the 1970s: Michèle Lalonde's (1937–) poster poem "Speak White" (1970/1974), which the poet herself performed during the Nuit de la poésie, captures succinctly and very emotionally the French-Canadian resentment of English-Canadian cultural assimilation.

## America and Counter Culture

The new orientation of poetry implied a new positioning in North America and a clear distancing from national poetry. As in the 1930s (Robert Choquette), America was perceived as an urban world, with a focus on everyday life and decay and with New York, Los Angeles, and San Francisco as mythical places. It was also the stage for the cultural revolution of the Counter Culture, a radical protest movement of the young generation against the rigid moral norms and codes of an affluent and success-oriented consumer society. Spontaneity, eccentricity, sexual permissiveness and pleasure, jazz, rock and beat, hallucinogenic drugs, and esoteric and pacifistic-oriental ideas were propagated as alternatives. Poetry was supposed to change human consciousness and with it the world. It played with orality, hybridity, an abundance of images reminiscent of surrealism and Quebec automatism, and often interacted with music. It broke all taboos, being ironic, aggressive, multilingual, and international — at a time when the debates on the French language and on language legislation created serious controversy. Counter Culture poetry and ideas finally found their way into (mostly short-lived) avant-garde magazines such as *Mainmise* (1970), *Hobo/Québec* (1973), and *Cul-Q* (1973).

The parallels and references to U.S. American culture were unmistakable. Many Beat Generation artists from Quebec had lived in the United States for years and had witnessed the psychedelic movement. In preambles, dedications, and intertextual references they referred to personalities, book publications, and locations of the American scene. At the same time, Montreal opened its doors to the world with the Expo in 1967. A few years later, in 1975, Allen Ginsberg, William Burroughs, Ed Sanders, and others appeared at the Rencontre internationale de la contre-culture in Montreal. The most radical representative of the new generation, however, was Denis Vanier (1949–2000): With *Lesbiennes d'acid* (1972) he passed, in Patrick Straram's words, one of the "beautiful death sentences on bourgeois aesthetics and social realism." It was followed by *Le clitoris de la fée des étoiles* (1974) and other texts that broke every taboo in order to shock the self-corroding and nihilistic established world. Vulgarity, black humor, obscene images, references to revolutionary movements (FLQ) and to hated symbols of conservatism (L'Hexagone, Code pénal), themes such as drugs, violence, music, and abnormal sexual practices were used as means of provocation and at the same time to express disgust. Underneath all this was a desire for the kind of total liberation that dadaism, surrealism, and automatism had striven for ever since Rimbaud. Thus it was not without reason that Vanier's "texte/terrorisme" (Straram) referred back to Rimbaud's "dérèglement de tous les sens," that the influence of Claude Gauvreau (1925–1971) was omnipresent, and that Straram saw his graffiti/folk-rock as a contribution to a "permanent state of protest." Ready to take up a Marxist fight against imperialism and capitalism, Straram, in the foreword to *Irish coffees au No Name Bar & vin rouge Valley of the Moon* (1972), saw his poetic work and bizarre humor at the service of the " 'révolution' canadienne française pour un Québec libre et socialiste." Even more so than Vanier, who combined prose, free verse, and extensive quotations, Straram (1934–1988) used the technique of collage to merge text, quotation, reference, and biographical detail into a sort of inner monologue, capturing the myths of everyday life in a kind of "psychedelic encyclopaedia" (Lucien Francoeur). Francoeur (1948–) himself, a member and lyricist of the rock band Aut'Chose (1974), also played an important role in the Counter Culture movement with his *Minibrixes réactés* and other texts, composed around 1970 and appearing between 1972 and 1975. Their multiple references to popular culture, myths, and utopias clearly strike a highly masculine tone. In a similar fashion, Louis Geoffroy's (1947–1977) prolific oeuvre reveals a fascination with the America of the 1960s. Sexuality, music, alcohol, and drugs function as catalysts of liberation, but Geoffroy also strikes a political note, for instance, when he incorporates musical structures, themes, and personalities from Black jazz into the texts of *Empire State Coca Blues: Triptyque lyrique 1963–1966* (1971). Geoffroy also referred to May 1968 in his work, as did Paul Chamberland (1939–) in *Éclats de la pierre noire d'où rejaillit ma vie* (1971), his first text inspired by the Counter Culture after a long commitment to the "poésie du pays." With *Manifeste des enfants libres du Kébek* (1971) and *Demain les dieux naîtront* (1974) — and in spite of his rock-culture background — Chamberland finally discovered a new spirituality. Last but not least, performance artists Claude Péloquin (1942–) and Raoul Duguay (1939–) also showed their close affinity with the Counter Culture, the former with his *Manifeste infra* (1967), the latter as the author of *Manifeste de l'infonie* (1970) and the "pyramid poem" *Lapokalipsô* (1971).

## Formalism, Experimentation, and *écriture féminine*

The Counter Culture movement cannot always be clearly distinguished from formalism, which also emerged in the late 1960s as a reaction to Quebec's "poésie du pays" and whose first literary expression, in itself radically new, was Brossard's *L'écho bouge beau* (1968). Around 1971, the creative response to structuralism, semiotics, and the work of the French group Tel Quel led to its belated recognition. As was the case with Counter Culture, avant-garde magazines — *La Barre du Jour* (1965; since 1977 *La Nouvelle Barre du Jour*), *Les Herbes rouges* (1968) — again formed the backbone of the movement. Poetry was meant to focus on the materiality of language and on the self-referentiality of the text, refusing to mirror subjectivity or to pretend a mimetic representation of reality. The denial of truth, meaning, and message put a high demand on the creativity of the reader, who was expected to follow the polysemic traces in the text in a sort of "echo-reading." Consequently, writing and reading became synonymous with "text labor," the transgression of codes, ideologies, and rules, and with playful experimentation. More than in France, theory and fiction went hand in hand and allowed a sense of "jouissance," which Roland Barthes had opposed to radical formalism.

One of the adherents of the new literary mode was Roger Des Roches (1950–), who, as early as 1968, had set the course for an "écriture de la jouissance." His texts from the 1970s were published as *Tous, corps accessoires* (1979). Short, partly in English, and with an eye-catching typography, they deal almost exclusively with the human body. They refer to Franz Kafka, Tristan Tzara, and Philippe Sollers, thwart every intention of meaning, and present themselves as "word-sound-puzzles" (see, for example, the expression "son t(ailé)phone"). Seldom does Des Roches adhere to the rules of syntax or allow for referentiality. Instead, his work reminds the reader of surrealism and automatism, with an added touch of humor. Another representative of formalism affiliated with *Les Herbes rouges* is André Roy (1944–) (*N'importe quelle page*, 1974). Roy remained loyal to formalism up to the late 1970s before he, like others, turned to urban topics, America, and a new "legibility." Like Roy, Normand de Bellefeuille (1949–) believed in the close relationship between body and language, a phenomenon that Claude Beausoleil (1948–) — another formalist poet — formulated succinctly: "J'écris mon corps traversé d'écritures, j'écris des mots qui m'écrivent." Early in his career, Beausoleil broke with tradition and conceived of writing as an investigation and an experiment with linguistic material (*Motilité*, 1975). After surrealist and automatist beginnings, he allowed a new sensibility to emerge in *Au milieu du corps l'attraction s'insinue* (1980), which blends elements from everyday and urban life, body, text, music, and the fine arts and prepares the "return of the subject." Finally, the work of François Charron (1952–) also proved to be multifaceted. Well known for his foreword to Des Roches's *L'enfance d'yeux* (1972), Charron was at the forefront of Quebec literary modernity. *Littérature/Obscénité* (1973) and other texts were directed against bourgeois culture and literary tradition. With works such as *Interventions politiques* (1974) and *Propagande* (1977), Charron revealed himself a committed Marxist, while *Feu* (1978) speaks of the pleasures of formalist experimentation. The latter tendency finally culminated in the award-winning *Blessures* (1978), which already anticipated the metaphysical "poet of interiority." For many of the innumerable adepts of the *nouvelle écriture* — a postmodern modernity, in a way — formalism thus represented a very essential experience. Even if some of these poets subsequently went different ways, they remained open to formalist innovations. This aspiration particularly applied to authors like Michel Beaulieu, the founder of the publishing house Estérel, who was close to formalism in his beginnings. In his search for some transient meaning (*Desseins: Poèmes 1961–1966*, 1980) he increasingly explored mental spaces and returned to legibility. At the same time he extended the materiality of language through the actual materiality of the "object," which resulted in his experimental "book-object" *Le flying dutchman* (1976). Eight years before, Geoffroy had already ventured a similar experiment (*Graffiti*, 1968), but it was only with the famous "book objects" created by the Éditions de l'oeuf and Roger Soublière's (1942–) "text-object" *Anti-can* (1969) that this new poetic approach gained public recognition.

The key figure of Quebec's new generation was Nicole Brossard (1943–). Fascinated by the possibilities of language at an early age, her main concerns were transgression, subversion, investigation, and pleasure. "Fed up with poems talking about landscape, snow, mountains, and the tormented rhetoric of love and solitude" (Brossard in Koski 1993) and wary of the literary establishment, the symbols of Canadian federalism, and the repression by the church, she contributed to experimental magazines such as *La Barre du Jour*. This commitment helped her find her own abstract poetic style in the late 1960s. In *Suite logique* and *Le centre blanc* — written between 1965 and 1973 and published in 1978 under the title *Le centre blanc* — she initially presents herself as a representative of formalism and as an intellectual who experiences alienation not as a woman but "as a Quebecer." Motherhood and the discovery of her lesbian identity then made her into the most significant and enduring voice of Quebec feminism, to whom *La Nouvelle Barre du Jour* dedicated a symposium as early as 1982.

With their persistent deconstruction of syntax, their self-referentiality and ambiguity, Brossard's formalist texts are highly demanding. Her textual experiments give voice to the unspoken, and the absence of explicit meaning — or, the excess of possible meanings — explains to a certain extent the enigmatic title *Le centre blanc*. Brossard's literary discourse changed with the last texts of the 1978 collection, when new metaphors announced a lyrical I who fuses the female body and the text in a "cortex exubérant." As Hélène Cixous suggests with her concept of "voler" ("to steal" and "to fly"), Brossard "steals" from male discourse, perverts it, and liberates herself through "flying." Female creativity in Brossard's poetics articulates itself through the erotic flow of language, creative energy, rhythm, and imagery. "J'ai tué le ventre," she writes aggressively in *L'amèr* (1977), a prose text which, by playing with orthography and sound ("la mère," "la mer," "amère," "a-"), evokes the silenced "woman-mother," the "un-mother," the "bitter mother," and finally water and the sea. In doing so her language expresses a decidedly gender-specific note. Equally remarkable is the deconstruction of literary genres, her predilection for "théorie-fictions," and the image of the spiral as a movement constantly getting out of control and cutting through any surface meaning. The image of the spiral reappears in *Amantes* (1980), where, for the first time, and in a more intimate language, a female subjectivity shines through. Thus, the texts of the 1980s try to rediscover the reader. Subsequently, Brossard also wrote novels, which, although they do not respect traditional genre conventions, reinvent her imaginary world in a city (Montreal) and on a continent (North America). Finally, evocations of places, impressions, reflections, and a female lyrical I determine the world of *Je m'en vais à Trieste* (2003), in which a moving simplicity replaces the excesses of linguistic experimentation.

Brossard's "feminist awakening" coincided with a new collective awareness of the situation of women in the mid-1970s. Irritated by inequitable power structures and women's unsatisfactory social status in postrevolutionary Quebec, women increasingly started to speak out, just as they did in Europe after the student revolts of May 1968. The call for "female decolonization" — reinforced by feminists in France and the United States — resulted in a number of initiatives. The founding of the Front de libération des femmes du Québec (1969) and the Centre des femmes (1972) was followed by women's initiatives in publishing and journalism and the organization of international symposia such as the Rencontre québécoise internationale des écrivains 1975 (focusing on "La femme et l'écriture"). Along with Brossard, France Théoret (1942–) — cofounder of the radical feminist magazine *Les Têtes de pioche* (1976–1979) — and Madeleine Gagnon (1938–) were among the fighters of the first hour. Both considered the oscillating boundaries between self-sufficient formalism, feminism, and Marxist socio-critical discourse to be problematic. "Je ne suis pas contre l'algèbre mais l'algèbre que je sache n'a jamais prétendu à la révolution," commented Gagnon laconically (*Pour les femmes et tous les autres*, 1974). After collaborating on *La nef des sorcières* (1976), Théoret mainly wrote short texts of poetic prose reminiscent of inner monologues, such as *Bloody Mary* (1977), *Vertiges* (1979), and *Nécessairement putain* (1980). In these texts language does not strive for formalist experimentation, but explores the traces of a female subjectivity: Rhythm, musicality, and *vertiges* are paired with a very articulate feminist intention and feminist reflections on the spoken and written word. In *Une voix pour Odile* (1978) the narrator admonishes that her text is not pure spontaneity, but consists of "fragments entre la fiction et la théorie tant je suis occupée par le flux, le passage, l'existence, le refoulé, l'impensé, la négativité, l'en-deça du monde." Like Théoret, Gagnon, too, signed collective works (*La venue à l'écriture* with Hélène Cixous and Annie Leclerc, 1976; *Retailles* with Denise Boucher, 1977) before she dove, with *Antre* (1978), into the depths of female consciousness — that place and time "entre les riens, les lieux entre les trous, interstices d'où l'on aurait bien pu ne jamais revenir et n'en jamais parler." As did Gagnon, Yolande Villemaire (1949–) and Josée Yvon (1950–1994) also aspired to reconquer that same place, that is, the discursive confluence of body and identity. Along with Louky Bersianik (1930–), they belong to the first generation of poets who represented the new *écriture féminine*. In *Maternative* (1980) Bersianik assembled her poetry published between 1977 and 1980, characterized by typical features of "female writing," such as hybridity, the accentuation of semiotic elements, the inscription of the body and of tactile sensations as opposed to male myths, logo- and phallocentrism. Villemaire (*Machine-t-elle*, 1974; *Que du stage blood*, 1977) and Yvon (*Filles-commandos bandées*, 1976), for their part, embraced the merging of body, script, and Counter Culture in their writing. Similar to them, but as early as 1970, Marie-Francine Hébert (1943–) had borrowed from calligraphy and articulated female desire in her provocative "erotic suite" *Slurch*.

## The 1980s and 1990s: "Female Writing," Interiority, and Existential Unrest

French-Canadian poetry of the 1980s continued in many ways what had begun in the late 1970s, although the political background had changed fundamentally with the unsuccessful referendum for independence (1980), the reelection of the Parti Québécois (1981), and years of recession in which classical liberalism reappeared. On the federal level, Quebec found itself in an awkward offside position (Repatriation of the Constitution, Charlottetown). Nevertheless, publishing and, in particular, the production of poetry seemed untouched by politics and flourished with an average of 150 volumes of poetry per year as compared to one hundred per year during the 1970s (Dumont 1999). Theoretical debates had abated for the most part, and differences between the first and the second generation of authors became less prominent. Never before, however, had Quebec seen so many female authors as in this particular decade.

Among the voices of the first generation of female writing, Denise Desautels, Geneviève Amyot, Carole Massé, and Germaine Beaulieu seamlessly continued the *écriture féminine* of the 1970s. At the same time, Anne-Marie Alonzo, Louise Dupré, Jocelyne Felx, and others reinterpreted pre-feminist experiences from a new feminist point of view. They launched cultural initiatives such as *Arcade* (founded by Claudine Bertrand in 1981) and *Spirale* (founded by France Théoret and Gail Scott in 1981) and received awards and prizes, which brought them to the attention of publishers. The second generation of the 1980s, with Hélène Dorion, Élise Turcotte, and Louise Warren, included women writers whom Nicole Brossard and Lisette Girouard characterized as "poets of the intimate," relating to an alter ego and a lyrical "you." "Plus de grands débordements, de colères, d'emportements utopiques," Brossard observes, "seulement une douce inquiétude, une étrange quiétude où l'on s'étudie et s'observe dans la mise en scène amoureuse et existentielle, frôlant ici le quotidien, frôlant là l'enfance, la mort et le réel hyperréel." In fact, this is also true to a large extent for Denise Desautels (1945–), who published innumerable volumes of poetry, many of them illustrated. In her texts Desautels follows the hidden paths of female sensitivity, registering even the most unspectacular gestures. She inscribes the memory of the past and the presence of death in an idiosyncratic poetic language, located somewhere between verse and prose. Her poem "Le 6 décembre 1989" (*Leçons de Venise*, 1990) became widely known after the assassination of some female students from the École polytechnique de Montréal at the end of the 1980s, as did her powerfully eloquent evocation of "le degré zéro" of sensation and caress in *Cimetières: La rage muette* (1995). Similarly, Carole Massé's (1949–) poetry collection *Je vous aime* (1986) strikes an extremely sensitive note. Here, intimacy rests in the evocation of a face, a gesture, an encounter — with the loving I again addressing an invisible "you." Anne-Marie Alonzo (1951–2005) is a "voice from outside," like other poets before and with her, such as Michel van Schendel, Philippe Haeck, Alain Horic, Alexis Lefrançois, and Juan García. In *Geste* (1979) she painfully focuses on the healing of the body destroyed in an accident. Her language draws its inspiration from formalism and tries to describe the gestures of everyday life, as she retrieves the memory of her body and her motherland (Egypt) in *Bleus de mine* (1985). Like Alonzo, Jocelyne Felx (1949–) saw poetry as the creative confrontation with her own intimate world, a confrontation that gives a solid material form to the transitoriness of daily life and presents the reader with "la matière-émotion." Louise Warren (1956–), for her part, integrated a narrative element into her sensual poetry, which also echoes everyday life (*L'amant gris*, 1984). Her poems are sustained by a lyrical I, whereas in Élise Turcotte's (1957–) *La voix de Carla* (1987) the lyrical I hides behind a more neutral medium. Finally, Hélène Dorion (1958–), who in *Hors champ* (1985) celebrates inner exile, blends introspection with metaphysical concern (*Un visage appuyé contre le monde*, 1990).

These individual traits in the work of specific women writers also describe the poetic practice of the 1980s in general. After its dismissal in formalist writing and its tentative rediscovery in the texts of *écriture féminine*, the subject eventually returned, now sexually defined. It is not an effusive lyrical I but rather a calm presence, a glance, a voice approaching reality. It need not be identical with the poet, despite the fact that autobiographical details sometimes shine through. It opens the door to the private and intimate sphere. It tells its own personal story, sometimes invoking a "you," but stubbornly ignoring the collective "we." It explores daily life in its concreteness and banality, the present, and the urban world, and reinvests poetic language with at least some ephemeral sense of referentiality. At the same time, poetry again articulates basic human needs and existential questions, such as love and death. In terms of poetic form, the 1980s showed a preference for narrative structures or fragmented compositions: Many titles play with allusions to the human voice or refer to literary genres such as the diary or the journal, and more often than not, poets also ventured into the domain of the novelist.

These general observations notwithstanding, the poetic landscape of the 1980s remains difficult to describe. Its keyword is diversity — diversity with regard to those who had already written before formalism (for example, Michel van Schendel, Gérald Godin, and Philippe Haeck) and with regard to those who had relaunched their poetic careers in the late 1970s (for example, Alexis Lefrançois, Suzanne Paradis, and Marie Laberge). Lyricism, intimism, and references to reality thereby took on different designs: Van Schendel, for instance, whose poems, composed between 1956 and 1976, were collected in *De l'oeil et de l'écoute* (1980) — followed by *Autres, autrement* (1983), *Extrême livre des voyages* (1987), and other volumes — represented the socially committed writer who saw reality as an inexhaustible source of poetry. This means neither that the artistic imitation of reality is unambiguous nor that it excludes allusions to the poet's intimate sphere. Joseph Melançon (1877–1956) aimed for a "poésie immédiate des êtres et des choses, hors tout filet syntaxique, toute capture grammaticale, tout assujettissement à l'habitude." *Ils ne demandaient qu'à brûler* (1987), the 1960–1986 retrospective of Gérald Godin's work, strikes a different note again; it shows the efforts of the famous "poète-député" to combine lyricism with the photographic representation of lived reality, "automatic writing," and musical elements, and at the same time prepares the touching portrayal of a reconvalescence in *Poèmes de route* (1988). In the case of Philippe Haeck, the lyrical I, in his everyday surroundings, embodies the counterpart to hermetic and formalist abstraction, which results in a very personal, almost activist tone. After the collection *Polyphonie: Roman d'apprentissage* (1978) this tone blends with the auto-fictional "poème-vie" of *L'orielle rouge* (2001). In the work of Claude Beausoleil, formalism eventually flirts with a perceiving subject, whereas André Roy, Yolande Villemaire, and Jean-Paul Daoust attempted to capture the atmosphere of such big cities as Montreal or New York in their works (Daoust, *Poèmes de Babylone*, 1982; *Taxi*, 1984). Iridescent impressions, crude shreds of reality, and ordinary life create a new kind of hyper-realism which can also be found in contemporary novels. Finally, Cécile Cloutier (1930–) opted for still another way of approaching reality: In her collection *L'écouté: Poèmes 1960–1983* (1986) she presented text miniatures based on an emotion, an image, or an object, a technique that revealed her to be a master of poetic minimalism.

Another facet of poetry in the 1980s, which also had its origins in the rediscovery of the subject, was the fascination with love, death, and the fragility of human existence. Apart from Rina Lasnier, Jacques Brault (*Moments fragiles*, 1984), François Charron, and André Roy (in particular his late work), "metaphysical" poets like Fernand Ouellette worked side by side with new voices such as those of Pierre Nepveu, Pierre Morency, and Jean Royer. Ouellette (1930–), an advocate of intermediality and inter-art relationships, has written poetry since 1955 (*Ici, ailleurs, la lumière*, 1977; *En la nuit, la mer*, 1981). His prolific oeuvre constantly refers to a precise place or experience and the perennial presence of death. This is particularly true for *Les heures* (1988), in which he evoked his father's agony. The theme of death is also present in the poetic work of other representatives of the "older generation" like Alphonse Piché (1917–1998; *Sursis*, 1987) and in that of younger ones like Robert Yergeau (1956–; *Le tombeau d'Adélina Albert*, 1987). On the other hand, the "vitalist" poet Pierre Morency (1942–) reclaimed largely positive aspects of human existence and did so in a familiar North American landscape; these elements as well as the dynamics of intimacy became intensified and individualized in *Effets personnels* (1986). Along with Pierre Nepveu, a prominent literary critic, Jean Royer (1938–), for his part, concentrated his poetic efforts on that "chaud désir du monde" that love alone can bring about (*Faim souveraine*, 1980; *Depuis l'amour*, 1987). Nepveu (1946–), on the other hand, focused on the reserved and hesitant scrutiny of everyday existence in a contemporary world: In *Couleur chair* (1980) and *Mahler et autres matières* (1984) he charts a lost reality, identity, and history through fragments of lived experience.

The trends and developments of the 1980s continued into the 1990s, with poetry reflecting on the conditions of human existence. Nevertheless, specific problems like unemployment, environmental issues, urbanism, and media and technology gradually and increasingly came to the fore. The lyrical I began to rediscover its social surroundings and, in the case of (im)migrant writers, its multiple identities (Marco Micone, "Speak What," 1989). As in the 1970s and 1980s, female poets were omnipresent and now straddled several generations: Young authors (Hélène Monette, Kim Doré) stood side by side with leading figures like Brossard and other important writers such as Louise Dupré, Carole David, and Danielle Fournier, whose oeuvres had matured over the years. Exploring female subjectivity (*Bonheur*, 1988; *Tout près*, 1998) with the help of "re-mem-ber-ing," the body, and the imagination, Louise Dupré (1949–) arrived at the pulse of human existence and its elevation through art — "oui, poème, liberté, minuscule consolation" (1988). Danielle Fournier (1955–) con-centrated on the deep discomfort of the female lyrical I and tried to fathom the depths of its intimate (linguistic) spaces (*Langue éternelle*, 1998). In response to the undermined freedom of the female subject, she struck an astonishingly aggressive tone. At the same time, her collection *Poèmes per-dus en Hongrie* (2002) is an impressive hymn to sensuality and bodily love of exceptional linguistic power. In general, although formalist experiments and intertextuality seemed to be banished from the literary scene, giving way to lighter, more legible texts, the reinterpretation of a formalist writ-ing experience continued to be an option. Publishing houses flourished as never before, and big festivals like that of Trois-Rivières guaranteed that poetry stayed alive. The general refusal of collective adventure and socio-political writing in the 1990s eventually came to an end with Robert Fortin's (1946–) *Les nouveaux poètes d'Amérique* (1998), which has been celebrated as a poetic manifesto: "/L/a forêt se meurt / et par ses blessures / le poète s'invente / une autre Amérique / NOUS / étrangers à la mort."

## Poetry in French outside Quebec

The predominance and range of Quebec literature have for a long time overshadowed the literary efforts of other francophone regions in Canada. Acadia, Ontario, and Western Canada had their own poetic traditions, which also articulated collective concerns, although they less frequently used the collective "we." The more or less conventional and folklorist pro-duction of "poésie canadienne-française" (Dionne), which up to the 1960s was characterized by religious or patriotic undertones, diversified under the pressure of Quebec's sovereignty movement and the symbolic with-drawal from the Canadian alliance. With the province of Quebec concen-trating on its own literary awakening, the federal government and the respective provincial Arts Councils had to intervene and lend assistance to local artistic production. Despite the fact that the general demographic, institutional, economic, and linguistic framework of the three francophone regions was not comparable to that of Quebec, the latter remained their main point of reference as they developed their own nationalist movements and regional "renaissances." The new nationalism subsequently resulted in the flourishing of literature in Acadia, Ontario, and the West. Not unlike what had happened in Quebec, these new regional literatures, in the 1960s and 1970s, focused on self-assertion and resistance and, to a certain extent, even became institutionalized. In the 1980s, again similar to Quebec, they began to replace the committed lyrical I with an ideologically neutral one. As a reaction to the forces of globalization they eventually turned to questions of universal concern, while at the same time facing the growing threat of linguistic and cultural assimilation by English Canada. As in Quebec, however, poetry always had its finger on the pulse of the times and reflected changes of identity and self-perception.

This development particularly applied to Acadian literature and, perhaps to a lesser extent, to the West coast of Newfoundland, where in the 1970s cultural historians engaged in the collection and preservation of traditional French songs and tales. The so-called Acadian Renaissance of the 1960s coincided with the introduction of two official languages in New Brunswick (1969), the founding of a francophone university (Moncton 1963) and several publishing houses (Éditions d'Acadie in 1972, Perce-Neige in 1980). The Acadian Renaissance served as a background not only to the oeuvre of Antonine Maillet (1929–), but also to the explosion of poetry in this region. Very much in the tradition of Quebec's "poésie du pays," the problem of identity "cries out" in Raymond Guy LeBlanc's (1945–) *Cri de terre* (1972), in which the Acadian is depicted as "multiplié fourré dispersé acheté aliéné vendu révolté" and as "déchiré vers l'avenir." It also marks Herménégilde Chiasson's (1946–) *Mourir à Scoudouc* (1974) and Guy Arsenault's (1954–) *Acadie Rock* (1973), which takes the reader to the backyard of history, to the world of linguistic humiliation symbolized by *chiac* (a blend of English and French, regarded as an expression of social inferiority and lack of education). In his preface to Gérald Leblanc's early poems (*L'extrême frontière*, 1988) Chiasson reflected on Moncton and the atmosphere of awakening in the 1970s: "Nous ne pouvions que clamer notre révolte, notre détresse. Nous n'avions que notre corps, le désir, la musique, le sentiment diffus et parfois obscène de notre inaliénable besoin d'écrire." Chiasson here also suggested the Acadians' predilection for orality and the performing arts, which, similar to Quebec, found its expression in so-called Nuits de la poésie. Moreover, the Acadians' prediction for orality explains why poets like Calixte Duguay and Gérald Leblanc have also figured among the great names of the Acadian chanson. Leblanc (1945–2005) undoubtedly was and still is one of the key figures in poetry. His texts speak of the aspiration for identity, the appeal of Counter Culture, urbanism, everyday life, homosexuality, and American identity. In the 1980s Leblanc's texts questioned existential experiences (*Complaintes du continent*, 1993), using concise observations and fugitive impressions devoid of any illusion. The following generation finally bore witness to the vitality of Acadian poetry with such names as Rose Després, France Daigle, and Louis Comeau, with late vocations like Roméo Savoie, very young voices such as Dyane Léger and Serge Patrice Thibodeau, and voices of migration like Gérard Étienne.

Although the initial situation was different from that in Acadia, the francophone community of Ontario (the biggest one outside Quebec) also experienced a secondary cultural consolidation in the 1970s. It was boosted by the founding of the bilingual Laurentian University in Sudbury (1960) and supported by publishing houses like Prise de parole in Sudbury (1973) and Le Nordir (1988), Vermillon (1982), L'Interligne (1981), and David (1993) in Ottawa. As a response to Quebec nationalism, a group of poets, reminiscent of L'Hexagone, emerged in the north of the province, shedding light on linguistic realities and on the general sense of inferiority experienced by the francophone minority in Ontario (Jean-Marc Dalpé). Their attempt to reconquer the past gave new life to popular songs and legends and to the traditions of folklore, while at the same time franco-phone writers and artists continued to leave for Quebec (Patrice Desbiens) and Ottawa. Consequently, Ottawa became the center of a new generation of poets, who in the 1990s abandoned the quest for collective identity and rediscovered the individual as their subject. Among them were Andrée Lacelle, Stefan Psenak, Andrée Christensen, and Magaret Michèle Cook (Olscamp), while authors like Hédi Bouraoui and Micheline St-Cyr chose the multicultural city of Toronto as their home.

In Western Canada a strong folkloric song tradition had existed since the early nineteenth century, and the Métis — among them Louis Riel (1844–1885) — had long expressed the threat of linguistic alienation, while colonial immigrants created texts of religious and moral inspiration. The preservation of French language and culture was incumbent on both older institutions such as the Collège Saint-Boniface (Manitoba 1871) and the Cercle Molière (Winnipeg 1925) and newer ones like the Faculté Saint-Jean (Edmonton 1960). Despite these efforts, the assimilation and increasing fragmentation of the francophone linguistic and cultural sphere presented a serious problem, which became even more poignant with the self-discovery of Quebec in the 1970s. Not unlike Acadia, Ontario, or even Quebec, the first reaction of Western Canada to the acute linguistic threat was the foundation of remarkably successful publishing houses (Éditions du Blé in 1974, Éditions des Plaines in 1979). Once the exotic "ailleurs" of European and Quebec novelists, later a well-mapped place in French-Canadian literature thanks to Gabrielle Roy's (1909–1983) oeuvre, the West brought about a small but prominent group of poets prepared to ana-lyze their own creative space, as did Paul Savoie (1946–) in *Salamandre* (1974) and *À la façon d'un charpentier* (1984). In the last third of the twentieth century, the francophone poets of the Canadian West eventually turned to the typical topics that shaped the international scene: J. Roger Léveillé (1945–), for instance, evoked the metropolitan face of Montreal, New York, Paris, and Winnipeg in *Montréal poésie* (1987); Janick Belleau (1946–) revealed herself as a feminist and sensual writer in *L'en-dehors du désir* (1988); and Louise Fiset (1955–) in *404 BCA — driver tout l'été* (1989) explored the female body and expressed her revolt in a graffiti-like style and by using *joual* (Léveillé 1996). Here, the conquest of a territory and an identity has become obsolete; the affiliation and involvement with the international scene is guaranteed. However, the question of how these fragile "littératures de l'exiguité" can survive remains: "Les littératures de l'exiguité n'ont, pour richesse ultime, que le mot *peut-être*" (Paré 1992).

# 32: Orality and the French-Canadian Chanson

*Ursula Mathis-Moser (University of Innsbruck)*

## "La pensée se fait dans la bouche"
## (Tristan Tzara)

ORALITÉS-POLYPHONIX 16, a festival and symposium that took place in Quebec in June 1991, explored fundamental aspects of orality, its forms and functions as well as its specific Québécois character. Orality can operate both in a printed text and in the act of performing, whose most popular manifestation — next to theater and dance — is the chanson. One of the many facets of orality is the euphonic experiment with linguistic material, which has already been touched upon in connection with surrealist and postsurrealist sound effects and language practices (see ch. 17, Mathis-Moser), and which is especially prominent in the works of, for instance, Claude Gauvreau (1925–1971), the poet, composer, and performer Raoul Duguay (1939–), the "automatists," and the representatives of Counter Culture. In many cases this particular form of orality was combined with visual experiments that further hybridized genre borders. Thus Duguay created "visible" rhythms in his texts, rhythms that are visually perceivable through their affinity with the score of a composition; and the almost cosmic vision of his "stéréo-poème-audio-visuel" (Bayard) mixes calligraphy and "lettrism" with effects of sonority and multimedia experiments.

While such games may appear elitist, the chanson has been extremely popular with a wider audience. As a genuinely Quebec genre that does not exist in the rest of Canada in comparable abundance and variety, it deserves particular attention. It is difficult, however, to clearly distinguish the chanson from the *monologue québécois*, another genre typical of Quebec. In both chanson and monologue the two fundamental modes of expression, *chanter* and *dire* (singing and speaking), coexist. At the beginning of the 1970s the chanson, the monologue, and live performances or "recitals" of poetry stood side by side and converged in several enormously popular public events, in which art became an instrument of nationalist politics, and in which orality constituted a privileged place for self-discovery. In some cases (Miron), orality even expressed the poets' refusal to be published within or with the help of contested political and cultural hierarchies.

Monologue and chanson resemble each other in many ways. Both are hybrid forms of art: The monologue combines narrative, dramatic, and poetic elements; the chanson combines text, music, and interpretation. They find their ultimate expression and reception in performance. They have enormous thematic variety and flourished in times of political upheaval: the monologue in the interwar years and during the Second World War and the Révolution tranquille; the chanson at the time of the Patriots (1837–1838) and in the 1970s. They are both passed on orally, and their original forms (that is, the folksong) can be traced back to popular beginnings. Thus, sociologists claim that the reruralization of Quebec, which took place between 1760 and the end of the nineteenth century, was responsible for the emergence of a "folk-society" (Rioux and Martin 1971), which relied on the oral transfer of knowledge. This tradition is still evident today in Quebec's fascination with performative forms of art, in which orality is the central medium. Ultimately, both the monologue and the chanson are inextricably connected with French-Canadian self-perception and sense of self, which have gone through fundamental changes in the course of history. The less formalized monologue, however, more strongly reflects local color than the chanson, the latter having become increasingly international.

In the monologue, a naive, socially marginalized, and inferior lyrical I, alone on the stage and interpreted by the author himself in an authentic Quebec diction, relates the tragicomic events of his or her life and thereby invites the (less naive) audience to identify with the artist and at the same time to laugh in comic relief. This interaction between artist and audience reinforces what is, in fact, *not* said and thus inevitably encourages the audience to question the unsaid. First attempts to play with this form of interaction can be traced back to the beginnings of the twentieth century and were followed by the outstanding performances of later monologuists: Jean Narrache (1893–1970; alias Émile Coderre) played the figure of the unemployed Québécois of the 1929 economic crisis, Gratien Gélinas (1909–1999) created Fridolin at the end of the 1930s (*Les Fridolinades*, first published 1980; see ch. 20, Scholl), Marc Favreau (1929–2005) personified the poetic and humorous clown Sol in the 1960s ("Comment la grande noire soeur devint la belle trop mince à cause de l'excentricité," 1978), and Yvon Deschamps (1935–) embodied a simple "gars ben ordinaire" in the 1970s (*Monologues*, 1973). In all these examples, an average hero with a natural talent for spinning tales holds up a mirror to the sympathetic audience. This also applies to the female monologue and its most prominent representative, Clémence DesRochers (1933–; "L'art d'être femme," 1969), whose creative work clearly demonstrates that the monologue contributed to the discovery of not only national but also female identity. After a period of stagnation in the 1980s the Quebec monologue became extremely popular again in the following decade and continues to live on in the annual "Festival du rire" in Montreal.

## "La chanson": From Folksong to Popular Song

Almost all the artists mentioned above were also involved in the popular song, "la chanson," a genre that has known a long and complex history in Quebec. Starting as an orally transmitted folksong tradition of anonymous origin — subject to constant modifications through the practice of singing — it passed on traditional songs from the (South-)West of France, which were then adapted to the new geographic surroundings and social realities ("métissage," profession of the "canotiers," who transport goods on canoes). The chanson absorbed "foreign" — Irish-Scottish, that is, Celtic — rhythms and techniques; sometimes new lyrics were added to existing melodies for special occasions. The genre also included a number of authentic Canadian creations like "Marie Calumet." It gradually transformed from a "chanson folklorique française" into a "chanson traditionnelle canadienne-française." Before long nonanonymous songs were created, such as "Un canadien errant" (Antoine Gérin-Lajoie, 1842), "Le drapeau de Carillon" (Octave Crémazie and Charles W. Sabatier, 1858), and the later national anthem "O Canada" (Adolphe-Basile Routhier and Calixa Lavallée, 1880). The turn of the nineteenth century prepared the ground for a multitude of collecting activities (see ch. 8, Scholl), which culminated in the establishment of the Archives de Folklore and in the "mise en spectacle" of traditional songs in the famous Soirées du bon vieux temps (Édouard-Zotique Massicotte, Marius Barbeau) and the Veillées du bon vieux temps (Conrad Gauthier). The traditional chanson, which celebrates the "French-Canadian soul," finally gave its own distinctive touch to Abbé Gadbois's radio program "La Bonne Chanson" (starting in 1939).

The radio — ever since the first French broadcast in 1922 — also ushered in the era of a new type of "popular" music. The latter was based on a mass-oriented and technically steered production, diffusion, and (passive) appropriation of music, and presupposed a new lifestyle, which clearly distinguished leisure time from working hours, responding to the increased need for entertainment. Its authorship, as a rule, was explicitly declared. In the years after 1920 Quebec's population primarily listened to French-American sounds that — along with the first "author-composer-interpreter" (ACI) Mary Travers (1894–1941; alias La Bolduc) and a group of microphone-wielding "chanteurs de charme" — dominated the airwaves. They were sharply criticized by Robert L'Herbier and Fernand Robidoux, who subsequently founded and edited professional music magazines and initiated a song contest as a counterbalance (Concours de la chanson canadienne, 1957). In doing so they prepared the ground for the new generation of Quebec "authors-composers-interpreters" and "chansonniers" who — like their counterparts in France — particularly cherished the poetic dimension of their texts.

This new wave of popular music, however, did not break radically with the folk-music tradition. It uses a number of the latter's practices in the sense of a gradual professionalization of folk music on the one hand, and a popularization of highbrow music on the other. Moreover, folk, rock, and pop, the dominant trends in today's popular music, and chanson in Quebec rarely appear in pure form, but tend to combine in highly diverse manners.

# Folk, Rock, and Time and Again Pop

Two phenomena of Quebec's popular music scene can be subsumed under the term "folk" in the widest sense of the word: first, the famous chansonniers (ACIs), reminiscent of the French tradition, and second, the American tradition of Country and Western music. The latter, ever since the 1940s, has enjoyed great popularity in Quebec, thanks to the voices of "soldat Lebrun" (Roland Lebrun), Willie Lamothe, Marcel Martel, and contemporary singers like Claude Dubois and Roch Voisine, who experiment with Country music elements. Yet it is especially the chansonniers — Gilles Vigneault, Jean-Pierre Ferland, Claude Léveillée, Pauline Julien, and Claude Gauthier — who contributed to Quebec's self-perception and identity. They must be credited with having given an authentic and poetic expression to the social reality of the province and the visions of its population, thus creating an authentic chanson "made in Quebec." If in the 1930s La Bolduc's humorous and populist texts about everyday life still combined traditional forms of popular music with local urban identity and popular diction, the early "exports" Félix Leclerc (1914–1988) and Raymond Lévesque (1928–) enjoyed a huge success in Saint-Germain-des-Prés (Paris) and helped prepare the chansonniers' movement at the end of the 1950s, with Montreal's "boîtes à chansons" and the group of Bozos. In the 1960s and early 1970s this movement virtually exploded: Closely linked to the *poètes du pays*, whose political concerns they shared (see ch. 17, Mathis-Moser), this generation of ACIs committed themselves to a new future and the creation of a new collective identity, which they celebrated in their songs long before the Parti Québécois was founded in 1968.

1968 also marked a turning point with regard to music. Assisted by Mouffe (Claudine Monfette), Louise Forestier, Claude Péloquin, Yvon Deschamps, and the Ensemble du Jazz libre du Québec, Robert Charlebois (1944–) presented his famous music show Osstidcho (1968), whose title and contents shocked the audience: For the first time spoken

French and American rhythms blended into a new form. Folk(lore), rock, poetry, and beat were fused to create a new and authentically North American chanson. With this new form of popular music, Charlebois set free his generation's pent-up energies after innumerable yéyé groups had flooded the market since 1964. Charlebois was a rocker, a "crooner," a pop star, and a chansonnier (Le Blanc 1997) all in one. He rapped and even screamed his texts composed in *joual*, thus becoming the founder of an extremely prolific rock tradition in French, long before the same development occurred in France. While similar to the early chansonniers, Charlebois and other "rock poets" (Dubois, Plume, Offenbach, Desjardins) paid particular attention to the text, other artists prioritized musical experimentation (Harmonium, Octobre) and multiethnic inspiration (Les Colocs, French B, Jean Leloup). Their fundamental questioning of outdated political and cultural values, however, remained comparable to the tenor of the earlier chansonniers, although they committed themselves more to ecological questions and minority causes (such as those of the indigenous people) rather than to national concerns. The extremely multifaceted Quebec chanson — be it reminiscent of ACIs like George Brassens (1921–1981) or affiliated with rock music — represented one of the most important voices of the Révolution tranquille (Aubé 1990). From the 1960s onwards political charity concerts (Poèmes et chants de la résistance) and public events like the Nuits de la poésie (1970) have born witness to this fact, as did such spectacles as Superfrancofête (1974; taken up by Jean-Louis Foulquier's Francofolies of La Rochelle), Une fois cinq (1975), and the Fêtes de la Saint-Jean (1976). Charlebois's Osstidcho had obviously provoked an outburst of vitality and diversity in the Quebec chanson that would not exhaust itself until 1976, when voices of political commitment became temporarily silenced.

Among the hundreds of chansons and ACIs that made the history of the Quebec chanson and, in a way, also that of the province itself, only the most prominent examples can be mentioned here. Most ACIs traditionally operated within the professional field of the performing arts and the media, and their style clearly changed over the years. Leclerc, for instance, celebrated nature and the countryside ("Moi, mes souliers," 1951; "Le train du nord," 1951) before he committed himself with poignant irony to the ideology of separatism in "L'alouette en colère" (1972) and "Le tour de l'île" (1975). Lévesque's artistic career followed a similar pattern: After sentimental songs like "Quand les hommes vivront d'amour" (1956), he co-founded the group Les Bozos and addressed national concerns in his song "Bozo-les-culottes" (1967) by paying homage to the simple man of the street who becomes an assassin through circumstances. Léveillée (1932–), another Bozo, showed great musical talent ("Les vieux pianos," 1959), as did Ferland (1934–), who after early successes like "Avant de m'assagir" (1966), "Je reviens chez nous" (1968), and "God Is American" (1970) revived the chanson of the 1990s (*Écoute pas ça*, 1995). Among the female voices — alongside DesRochers — Pauline Julien (1928–1998) fascinated as an excellent interpreter of foreign texts (among others, by Vigneault and Boris Vian) and later of her own songs ("Eille," 1971), which in many cases celebrate female self-determination ("La moitié du monde est une femme," 1975). With Claude Gauthier's (1939–) "Le plus beau voyage" (1972), Julien — who is also known as the "passionaria" of the Quebec chanson — created an unforgettable hymn to a new Quebec that is aware of its roots, but at the same time predestined for a better future in "l'an deux mille." Finally, Vigneault (1928–), the "grand seigneur" of the chanson, gave voice to his love of nature, his sense of community, and the practice of singing and dancing so typical of his hometown Natashquan. In addition to his early portraits ("Jos Monferrand," 1957; "Jack Monoloy," 1960) Quebec is indebted to him for such lively songs as "La danse à Saint-Dilon" (1959), such tender ones as "J'ai pour toi un lac" (1961), and such inconspicuously subversive ones as "Les gens de mon pays" (1965), "Gens du pays" (1975), "Il me reste un pays" (1973), and above all the famous "Mon pays" (1964). When in "Mon pays" Vigneault sings about a "land that waits to be created," it becomes clear why the song was banned during the October Crisis of 1970. Vigneault continues to be present on the national and international scene (Salon du Livre, Paris, 1999). In 1990 he eventually delivered a much noticed collection of 101 songs, subtly alluding to the language Bill 101 (*1960–90: Chemin faisant*), while at the same time innumerable interpreters and composers took up and dedicated artistic creations of their own to Vigneault's heritage.

One of them was Charlebois, whose chanson "Mon pays ce n'est pas un pays c'est un job" (1970, with Réjean Ducharme) can be seen as an explicit response to Vigneault and the changes in lifestyle and production conditions: He alludes to the urban lifestyle and conditions, the working class, *joual*, mass production, and the culture industry; he plays with different electric rhythms and interacts with diverse musical traditions. With "Lindberg" (1968, with Péloquin), "Ordinaire" (1970, with Mouffe), and "Que-Can blues" (1975) he not only conquered Quebec but also Paris, where he was celebrated as one of the first francophone stars to come out of Canada, anticipating famous names such as Luc Plamondon (*Starmania*, 1979), Diane Dufresne, Fabienne Thibeault, Diane Tell, Daniel Lavoie, and Roch Voisine. At the end of the 1970s Charlebois returned to a more conventional style with hits like "Je reviendrai à Montréal" (1976). Regardless of Charlebois's personal evolution, Quebec rock music — more diverse than ever — continued to boom throughout the 1970s, although the critical potential of the texts tended to diminish and to give way to the musical event as such. The groups Offenbach ("Câline de blues," 1971), Aut'chose, and Octobre ("La maudite machine," 1973), their soloists Gerry Boulet, Lucien Francoeur ("Ch' t'aime pis ch' t'en veux," 1975), and Pierre Flynn experimented with rock, jazz, blues, and underground. At the same time folk-rock was influenced by the spiritual and the mystical, with its representatives interested in nature, pacifism, and the indigenous peoples. Among them were the groups Harmonium (*L'heptade*, 1976) with Serge Fiori and Beau Dommage ("Harmonie du soir à Châteauguay," 1974), with Michel Rivard ("La complainte du phoque en Alaska," 1974), as well as Richard and Marie-Claire Séguin. Since the 1970s even poets like Raoul Duguay turned to the chanson ("La bittt à tibi," 1975), accompanied by the multimedia group Infonie. Paul Piché (1953–) managed to make his breakthrough with "Heureux d'un printemps" (1977), whereas Plume Latraverse (1946–; "Les pauvres," 1978) — the satirical and clownesque Counter Culture laureate of the Prix pop-rock — attempted to restore the text to its rightful place with *Métamorphoses I* (1982) and his subsequent CDs. All in all, from the mid-1970s onwards the categories pop (Dufresne, Tell, Thibeault, but also Plamondon and Charlebois), rock, and folk (such as the band La Bottine souriante) became irrevocably blurred.

Irrespective of this development, the years after the referendum of 1980 marked a significant change. They are characterized by a new individualism, the decrease of francophone broadcast ratings (from sixty-five percent in 1974 to ten percent in the postreferendum years), a crisis in the music industry, and another wave of Anglo-American pop music. Only few authentic and original voices retained the audience's interest. Among them were Richard Séguin (1952–), in a new "pose" (*Double vie*, 1985; *Journée d'Amérique*, 1988), Piché (*Sur le chemin des incendies*, 1988), the interpreter and ACI Dubois (1947–; *Sortie Dubois*, 1982), and the Manitoban songwriter Lavoie (1949–; *Tension attention*, 1983). They were followed by new talents such as Luc de Larochellière (1966–; *Amère America*, 1988) and Jean Leloup (1961–; *L'amour est sans pitié*, 1990). The 1990s saw yet another turn: French broadcast ratings rose again, text and musicality made a comeback, and the chanson once more addressed the topics of the self-image and identity of the province, the role of French, racism, and "Americanness." Along with established artists like Michel Rivard (1951–), who was awarded double platinum (1991) for the quality of the texts in *Un trou dans les nuages* (1987), and such popular singers as Daniel Bélanger (1962–), who captured the mood of the 1990s in various and divergent musical traditions, Laurence Jalbert, Joe Bocan, and Lynda Lemay emerged as the new trendsetting female voices. The songs of the group Kashtin, performed in Inuktitut, expressed the latent interest in indigenous peoples, while Michel Faubert (1959–) rediscovered Quebec's oral tradition. It was Richard Desjardins (1948–), however, who became the emblematical figure of the young generation. He combined the critical vision of the topics mentioned above with musical resourcefulness and stylistic accuracy ("Les Yankees," 1988; "Tu m'aimes-tu," 1990), and followed a long tradition by exploring — together with René Lussier (1957–; *Le trésor de la langue*, 1990) — the boundaries of sonority. Les Colocs and French B, on the other hand, impressed audiences with their brilliant and humorous postmodern collages of rap, while Céline Dion (1968–), the world-famous pop diva, has rushed from success to success without betraying the legacy of her native province: *D'elles* (2007) exclusively features texts by French and French-Canadian female poets. Through her career Dion ultimately has realized her country(wo)men's long-held dreams of harmonizing past realities and future possibilities, French roots, and the American way of life. Thanks to her art, Quebec has become an equal voice beside "the rest of Canada," France, and the United States, even if she has partly adopted English as a means of expression.

Outside of Quebec, the French-Canadian song has also enjoyed great popularity across the centuries. In fact, poetry and the chanson supported the local renaissances of French-Canadian cultures in Canada. Angèle Arsenault, Édith Butler, Calixte Duguay, and Georges Langford celebrated their Acadian home, Zachary Richard commemorated his Cajun Louisiana, Robert Paquette and Paul Demers dedicated their songs to francophone Ontario, and Lavoie devoted his early texts to Manitoba. At the same time, numerous names were and still are connected with the neofolk movement (Beausoleil-Broussard, 1755, Garolou, Cano), and there is no doubt that the francophone regions outside of Quebec have also produced famous international stars like Marie-Jo Thério, Roch Voisine, and recently, Natasha St. Pier. All in all, the French-Canadian song convinces through its vitality. Not only has it always "disturbed charmingly" (Chamberland 1992), it has also successfully built bridges for a worldwide "francophonie."

# 33: Drama and Theater from the Révolution tranquille to the Present

*Dorothee Scholl (University of Kiel)*

## Drama and Theater in the 1960s and 1970s

THE 1960S AND 1970S WERE A TIME OF radical cultural, ideological, and political change for French Canada. In 1960 the liberal politician Jean Lesage became prime minister of Quebec. With the slogan "Maîtres chez nous" French Canadians claimed their cultural and economic independence from English-Canadian and American dominance. Authorities that had gone unchallenged for centuries were now questioned: Women began to emancipate themselves from patriarchal power structures, and society freed itself from the clerical system of education. The year 1968 saw the founding of the Parti Québécois, which stood for a policy of sovereignty or rather separatism of Quebec from the rest of Canada, and which came to provincial power in 1976. These far-reaching changes and reforms of the 1960s and 1970s have gone down in history as the Révolution tranquille.

Theater at the time was increasingly used for ideological purposes, which was reflected, in institutions as well as in publishing, by the preference for themes connected with Quebec's volatile situation. This new "national" orientation was by no means unanimously welcomed: In 1971 Paul Toupin, for example, explained the rejection of his plays with their irreconcilability with nationalist expectations, "car le nationalisme en art a, au Canada, préséance sur l'art même." A year later, Pierre Dagenais also expressed this sentiment: "Pourquoi faudrait-il qu'on ne traite que des sujets qui ont rapport avec la situation du Québec? . . . Un écrivain n'écrit que pour les Québécois? Il doit écrire pour le monde entier." Theater became a forum for the representation of the province as a "closed society," thus tying in with Quebec's efforts towards independence. Since the 1970s the term "nation québécoise" had replaced "nation canadienne française," and people referred to their language as "québécois" rather than "français canadien." The theater scene was clearly in tune with the times. Authors like Françoise Loranger, Claude Levac, and Jean-Claude Germain made use of the collective symbols of French-Canadian society for the production of a unifying "Québécité," which also set the province apart from other French-Canadian groups (for instance, the French Canadians of Manitoba). Levac wrote in the prologue to his play *Le Chemin du Roy* (1969): "Quand les dramaturges québécois auront trouvé une armature, une structure théâtrale qui nous soit propre, à l'égale de notre épine dorsale collective, nous aurons non seulement une dramaturgie authentique et nôtre, mais aussi un pays." Félix Leclerc's (1914–1988) *Qui est le père* (1977) deals with the question of the parentage of the new Quebec: Jean-Baptiste (the Québécois) realizes that Uncle Sam (the American) and John Bull (the Englishman) have robbed him of his country; when his son, the "new Québec," is born, he comes into conflict with the other two, who also claim fatherhood. Based on the principle of delimiting and excluding the "foreign" or the "Other," this form of allegorization has a long tradition in French-Canadian literature and forms a significant contribution to the definition of French-Canadian identity. Somewhat analogous to the process of decolonization in the Third World, Quebec attempted to free itself from the colonial past, to overcome its collective estrangement and inferiority complex (that is, the internalized gaze of the Other), and to define itself and its destiny with new self-confidence. In this respect, theater as an art form that uses the spoken word as well as nonverbal communication to affect the audience directly and immediately took on an important function. The decolonization of the theater became particularly apparent in the emphasis on a "national" language and "national" plays over an international repertoire.

Although vernacular language had already forged its way into the theater before the Révolution tranquille, the premiere of Michel Tremblay's *Les belles-soeurs* (1968) is generally considered to be the beginning of a new era in drama, presumably also because the use of *joual* as a sign of difference had become a political issue by the time. The term "joual," a variant of French "cheval" (horse), designates the sociolect of a group whose speakers belong to an uneducated urban lower class. The vocabulary and syntax of *joual* include anglicisms, Americanisms, Canadianisms, and archaisms. Many took this linguistic phenomenon to be the expression of a fundamental alienation; others, however, considered the *joual* — in contrast to standard French — a playful, lively, and down-to-earth language close to people's hearts and minds, and therefore an apt symbol of the Révolution tranquille in the sense of a "national" language. This inherent ambivalence is reflected in Tremblay's theater, which on the one hand stigmatizes *joual* as an "inadequate" language and an indication of "mental laziness," but elsewhere shows it to be lyrical, passionate, and romantic. After 1968, a progressive "joualization" of the theater took place, with a concomitant tendency towards vulgarity, carnivalization, and anticlerical and religious satire. Still, the "Triomphalisme Joualeux" (Michèle Lalonde) also led to self-isolation since outside Quebec *joual* is not readily understood, and in the context of international francophony it is considered exotic and often belittled as (merely) comical. Through the 1980s, however, many authors achieved great regional success with this "realistic" strategy, and *joual* is still being used by contemporary authors to reach a high level of dramatic expression (for example, by Michel Ouellette in *French Town*, 1994). On both the level of content and the level of theme the "joualized" theater took up impulses from earlier authors (for example, Gratien Gélinas and Marcel Dubé); in fact, numerous elements that were marketed as innovative had been on the stage even before the Révolution tranquille. Correspondingly, conflicts of the younger generation with domineering father or mother figures were central motives, although the feminist and homosexual theater of the 1970s and 1980s shifted the focus from collective emancipation to the search for individual identity. The depiction of the "colonized mentality" — that is, frustrated, humiliated, or insulted characters with no chance of escape from their existence — also remained significant. English-Canadian dominance, the orientation towards American models, and the growing influence of consumerism on society also came under attack.

On 24 July 1967, two centuries after the conquest of Nouvelle-France by the English and one hundred years after Confederation, French president Charles de Gaulle visited Quebec. De Gaulle's speeches on the Chemin du Roy, the road between Quebec City and Montreal, praised the cultural and economic upturn in the province. His appearance on the balcony of the Montreal city hall culminated in his notorious rallying cry: "Vive le Québec libre!" This "theatrical" event bolstered the separatists and was repeatedly treated in literature, as well as in the chanson. A year after de Gaulle's speech, Robert Gurik (1932–) produced his play *Hamlet, Prince de Québec*. In this Shakespeare adaptation the king appears as an allegory of the secular anglophone power, the queen as the embodiment of the Catholic Church, Hamlet as an allegory of Quebec ("to be or not to be, that is the question"), and de Gaulle as the ghost urging Hamlet from the balcony of the Montreal city hall: "Venge un meurtre horrible . . . le plus horrible commis depuis les jours d'Abraham" ("les jours d'Abraham" refer to the defeat of the French on the Plaines d'Abraham in 1759, which led to the cession of New France to Great Britain). Yet indecisive Hamlet, divided in his role as the son of the Catholic Church and the "Anglo-American spirit of capitalism," does not know what to do: "Être ou ne pas être *libre*!" He accuses his mother of having conspired with his father and ends as a victim and martyr with the words: "Il faut que ma mort serve aux autres. Il faut . . . que vive . . . un. . . Qué. . . bec . . . libre."

A year after Gurik's *Hamlet*, Loranger and Levac put on their "comédie patriotique" *Le Chemin du Roy*. This spectacular play is conceived as a turbulent hockey game between Quebec and Ottawa. Among others, the politicians Pearson and Johnson ("eux") play against Lévesque and Lesage ("nous"). They fight verbally and physically over the meaning of de Gaulle's visit, whose gigantic statue forms the center of events. Parallel to the politicians' dispute and underscored by their goals in the hockey match, a confusion of bilingual commentary from the press and radio coverage of the game conveys the enthusiasm of the masses, who followed de Gaulle's historic "triumphal procession" on the streets and squares along the Chemin du Roy. Advertisements, stadium music, and extracts from radio news reports, sports scores, and de Gaulle's speeches add to the dramatic effect. With the goals multiplying on the Quebec side the general rejoicing increases: "C'est à notre tour d'avoir du *fun*! (rire) Pis en français pour une fois!" De Gaulle is declared "King of Québec" without further ado, and his performance in Montreal gets enshrined as a monument in the collective memory. The victory of Quebec over Ottawa is finally celebrated with the singing of a new French version of the African-American hymn "We Shall Overcome": "Nous serons nous-même / Nous serons nous-même / Nous serons nous-même toujours / Le Québec est à faire, nous le faisons / Nous serons nous-même toujours."

*Le Chemin du Roy* demonstrates the growing importance of collective dramaturgy, also in that Loranger and Levac wanted their text to be understood as a "canvas" which should enable a joint improvisation by the participants and the recipients. Theater is in and of itself a place of collective creation — in the 1960s and 1970s theater in Quebec was also used as a collective party and a means of expression for spontaneous populist agitation, with the lines between author, director, actor, and audience dissolving and participants improvising with or without a script. Spectacular operetta-style productions, sung poetry recitals, and theatrical performances by chansonniers (such as the Nuit de la poésie in 1970) fostered an emergent feeling of collective identity. Improvisation groups were generally self-managed, which led to the dismantling of hierarchies and the redistribution of responsibilities. The director became an "animateur," and through the art of improvisation the actor was promoted to the rank of author. Since a lot depended on the creative imagination of the actors, there was always the risk, however, that time pressure or the pressure to succeed would result in the reproduction of clichés; in this way, improvisation could also become the spontaneous expression of collective fears, fantasies, and wishful thinking.

In 1969 Jean-Claude Germain (1939–) founded the Théâtre du Même Nom (TMN) in opposition to the Théâtre du Nouveau Monde (TNM). Germain advocated an improvisational theater of minimalist equipment. The metadramatic play *Un pays dont la devise est je m'oublie* (1976; the title is an ironic play on the motto of Quebec, "Je me souviens") is full of tropes referring to French-Canadian history; the two actors assume various roles of celebrities from history and legend, with time and space mixing in the sense of a postmodern "transhistorical party"

(Brian McHale) — Jacques Cartier, for example, appears with an Air France suitcase. Like Jacques Ferron (1921–1985) in *Les grands soleils* (1968) and Jean-Robert Rémillard (1928–) in *Cérémonial funèbre sur le corps de Jean-Olivier Chénier* (1974), Germain's transhistorical spectacles also allude to figures from history, as in the collective creation *Les enfants de Chénier dans un autre grand spectacle d'adieu* (1969), which polemically takes leave of the "great theater" of the Western tradition, featuring a boxing match between the French and the (triumphant) French Canadians. Germain's use of the French language is playful: Names and traditions are parodied, and the titles allude to a programmatic difference (*Rodéo et Juliette*, 1970; *Les hauts et les bas dla vie d'une diva: Sarah Ménard par eux-mêmes*, 1974; *La garde montée ou Un épisode dans la vie canadienne de Don Quickshot*, 1975; *A Canadian Play/Une plaie canadienne*, 1979). This game with language and traditions through ambiguity — to the point of trivialization and chaos — gave expression to Quebec's intensive search for identity. In his separatist play *A Canadian Play/Une plaie canadienne* Germain presents the defeat of 1759 and Lord Durham's politics of assimilation as an incurable wound, repeatedly bleeding afresh. *Le miroir aux tartuffes — Un charivari québécois* (1998) accuses the clergy of having hindered French Canadians' quest for identity through its criticism of the theater. A further notable contribution to French-Canadian theater was Germain's staging of his radio play *Le feuilleton de Montréal, un bal-à-gueule* (1993–1994).

Other groups also used improvisational theater as a means of producing "Québécité." Le Grand Cirque Ordinaire (1969–1976), a traveling troupe led by Raymond Cloutier, created a circus atmosphere (in the style of the Vermont-based Bread and Puppet Theater) by means of sketches, improvisations, dance and song numbers, acrobatic tricks, and travesty numbers — an atmosphere that was meant to give expression to the "conscience populaire." The play *T'es pas tannée, Jeanne d'Arc?* (1969), performed almost two hundred times all over the province, was inspired by Jerzy Grotowski, Konstantin Stanislavski, the Living Theatre, the Open Theatre, and by Bertolt Brecht. Joan of Arc becomes the symbol of the Quebec people; her death at the stake stands for French Canada's defeat by the English. Allegorical figures (the church, Justice, the "Intruder") take the stage with giant masks reminiscent of carnival parades. When the Parti Québécois came to power in 1976, the collective intervention-theater as represented by Le Grand Cirque Ordinaire lost its explosive force in the political sphere. The Ligue Nationale d'Improvisation (LNI), founded in 1977 by Robert Gravel and Yvon Leduc, performed its improvisational plays in a simulated ice rink, humorously joining political issues to Canada's favorite national sport. It also incorporated folk elements, music, and songs as well as audience participation into its productions. The traditions of improvisational theater and collective creations continue in the productions of experimental theaters and numerous ensembles, and today are practiced in almost all schools in Quebec.

In order to construct a "national" identity or a "Québécité," dramatists also looked at the marginal groups of society, that is, homosexuals, outlaws, and figures who were outsiders owing to their poor capacity for verbal expression or their low intellectual or social status. In their grotesque deformity these figures from the margins became sources of identification, their blatant otherness a symbol of the collective situation of French Canadians. This somewhat offensive and self-critical representation of identity had its roots in earlier socially critical theater (see, for example, Dubé, Gélinas, Jacques Languirand) and is still recognizable in contemporary authors like Michel Tremblay or Jean Barbeau.

With the scandal of the premiere of Tremblay's (1942–) *Les belles-soeurs*, directed by André Brassard on 28 August 1968 in the Théâtre du Rideau Vert in Montreal, *joual* became a literary language. The play is set in a working-class milieu; the scene is the kitchen of Germaine Lauzon, who has won a million coupons in a competition run by a department store called "Gold Star." In order to claim the prize in the form of goods, she has to glue the coupons into booklets. She invites fourteen other women from her family, friends, and neighbors to a "party de collage de timbres." The other women are jealous of Germaine because her winnings promise an escape from her miserable existence. In the course of the party, the dark sides of the women come to light, as they show themselves to be trapped in stereotypical clichés, with trivial prejudices towards foreigners and particularly members of other religious groups. Infected by Germaine's capitalistic consumer mentality, their friendship and kinship prove to be corruptible by low feelings of jealousy, envy, and hate. At the end, the women take Germaine's booklets with the coupons for themselves, and a wild brawl ensues in which it rains booklets and coupons. When "their work" has been done, the women sing the national anthem "O Canada." Tremblay's play — in a parodic allusion to the chorus of ancient Greek tragedy — is punctuated by the complaints of the frustrated women: "Chus tannée de mener une maudite vie plate! Une maudite vie plate! Une maudite vie plate!" The play provoked the audience not only because of the use of *joual*, but also because of the ironic treatment of respectable themes like work, family, patriotism, and the church. The audience found the grotesque behavior of the women embarrassing and demeaning; people recognized in the play's stereotypical characters the representatives of a society who for political, psychological, moral, and social reasons are unable to escape a marginal existence and alienation. In his metadramatic play *Le vrai monde?* (1989) Tremblay deals with the issues of reality and identity in the form of a *mise en abyme*: Claude, an author and "angry young man," writes a play that is intended to expose the repressed complexes of his family. In *L'impromptu d'Outremont* (1980) and in metadramatic passages of other plays, too,

Tremblay reflects on his conception of theater: Most of his plays show lonely, alienated people in inescapable everyday situations and circle around problems of gender relationships, religion, and identity. Tremblay, whose dramatic oeuvre encompasses over thirty titles, is counted among the most popular contemporary authors in Quebec.

Something similar could be claimed for Antonine Maillet (1929–) in respect to the Acadian people, the majority of whom live in New Brunswick and in Louisiana, U.S.A. Maillet is committed to promoting the Acadian language, history, and culture. She tries to redefine an Acadian identity fragmented by anglophone influences and to establish a collective awareness of the Acadian francophone community. In her dissertation *Rabelais et les traditions populaires en Acadie* (1971) she examined the folk traditions and figures of speech of her people, whose roots extend back into Rabelais's time. Her carnivalesque play *Les drolatiques, horrifiques et épouvantables aventures de Panurge, ami de Pantagruel* (1983) is also based on Rabelais. Like her narrative work, Maillet's dramas contain elements from legend, utopia, fable, fairy tale, and traditional oral culture; they evoke a poetic atmosphere that explains the Acadian people and at the same time transfigures them. Jacques Ferron directed her first play, *Les crasseux* (1968), in which the Acadian language is pitted against standard French. Maillet's *La Sagouine, pièce pour une femme seule* (1971) also enjoyed international success. Written in Acadian French, which unlike *joual* shares some common features with the dialect spoken in French Normandy, the text places high demands on the actress who plays Sagouine, an obedient old servant from a fishing village, who in long monologues bemoans her homelessness and insists upon social as well as political justice and recognition for the Acadians:

> Les Canadiens français, c'est du monde qui vit à Québec. . . . Ben comment c'est que je pouvons être des Québécois si je vivons point à Québec? . . . Pour l'amour de Djeu, où c'est que je vivons . . . ?

> . . . En Acadie, qu'ils nous avont dit, et je sons des Acadjens. . . . je crois qu'ils nous avont placés parmi les Sauvages. . . . Ben moi, je dirai au gouvarnement: je sais pus rien, j'appartchens pus rien, je suis peut-être pus rien, non plus.

The pluralization of the singular ("je vivons") is an old grammatical form in which the first person singular and plural have merged — but it also expresses an existential condition: Sagouine's monologue is the collective voice of the isolated and dispersed Acadian people. The question of an Acadian identity also dominates Maillet's other plays, in which "La Sagouine" reappears as a "collective" figure. *Don l'Original* (1972) takes up the theme of *Les crasseux*, namely the stereotypical division of society into the rich upper classes and "les crasseux," the poor, exploited lower classes. Allusions to the deportation of the Acadians by the English (1755) link the past with the present. In her epic and human dimensions Sagouine is conceived as a parodic contrast figure to Henry Wadsworth Longfellow's *Evangeline* (1847), as is the heroine in *Évangéline Deusse* (1976).

With her texts, Maillet seeks to convey the "cri du pays" and to call to mind her people and their past. While the literary figure Sagouine raises her voice in courageous protest and transcends her marginality to achieve the dimensions of an epic heroine, the protagonists of Jean Barbeau's (1945–) dramas are broken existences, for whom the possibility of revolt is excluded from the outset. In 1969 Barbeau founded the Théâtre Quotidien de Québec with the aim of displaying scenes from everyday life in both their tragic and comic dimensions. With an oeuvre of over thirty plays, he ranks with Tremblay as the most frequently performed author in Quebec. His characters are usually disadvantaged by life, express themselves in a vulgar idiom, and are unable to free themselves from their underdog positions. They are reminiscent of Samuel Beckett's antiheroes in that they passively wait for a change and long for a better future. In the satire *Ben-Ur* (1969), for instance, the protagonist Benoît-Urbain Téberge dreams of becoming a national hero (like Dubé's Tarzan in *Zone*, 1953; see ch. 20, Scholl). The two-man play *Goglu* (1970) is clearly modeled on Beckett's *En attendant Godot* (1952): The taxi driver Godbout and his friend Goglu sit on the bank of the St. Lawrence River and demonstrate in their monologue-like replies two possible ways of dealing with a monotonous and mediocre existence from which there is no escape. Goglu sees life as hell or as a god-given punishment, and dreams of salvation by love or suicide. Godbout, in contrast, tries to strengthen his friend's self-confidence and make him face reality. In Barbeau's monologue *Solange* (1970) a former nun falls in love with a revolutionary in whom she sees Christ returned. In *Le chemin de Lacroix* (1971) the profane also appears in the light of Christian ideas: Alluding to Christ's passion the play outlines the thirteen "stations of the cross" of the unemployed Rodolphe Lacroix. Arrested by the police although innocent, he is subject to interrogation and torture and finally — victim of his milieu and also of his language, *joual* — has to succumb to the authority of the state (the political context is the October Crisis of 1970). With the comedy *Manon Lastcall* (1972; the title is a play on Abbé Prévost's *Manon Lescault* of 1731) Barbeau focuses on the relationship between art and life: A museum guard hires the charming Manon as a guide, upon which the number of visitors rapidly increases. *Joualez-moi d'amour* (1972; an allusion to the famous chanson "Parlez-moi d'amour") is also a comedy in the boulevard style: A young man is unable to perform the sexual act with a prostitute just because she is French; not until she speaks in *joual* can he overcome his impotence. The drama *Citrouille* (1974) is a harsh examination of the battle of the sexes: Three women take a man (they call him "superman") prisoner in order to humiliate him and finally rape him.

The Révolution tranquille also signaled a change in women's self-understanding. Particularly since the mid-1970s, women became increasingly active as authors and directors and challenged traditional gender roles, such as the patriarchal father and the submissive mother. While several male authors declared their solidarity with the cause of female emancipation and drew analogies between the phenomenon of the repressed woman and the situation of a colonized people, others felt threatened and reacted with feelings of fear (as expressed in horror scenarios like Barbeau's *Citrouille*); in fact, at the time feminism did occasionally take militant forms. In 1973, Carole Fréchette, Solange Collin, and Véronique O'Leary founded the Marxist Théâtre des Cuisines to shake up and mobilize society with productions like *Nous aurons les enfants que nous voulons* (1974) and *Môman travaille pas, a trop d'ouvrage!* (1975). The premiere of the collective work *La nef des sorcières* in the Théâtre du Nouveau Monde on 5 March 1976 was a great success (the title is an allusion to Sebastian Brant's late-medieval moral satire *Das Narrenschiff*, as well as to the term "witch," as feminists at the time were sometimes abusively called). The play begins with the preparations for a performance of Molière's *L'école des femmes* (1662). In monologues written by well-known female authors (Nicole Brossard, France Théoret, Marthe Blackburn, Marie-Claire Blais, Odette Gagnon, Luce Guilbeault, Pol Pelletier), "modern" female types are presented (for example, the actress, the working mother, and the woman who demands her right to sexual fulfillment). The monologue format offered the authors and actresses a chance to dramatize the isolation of woman in society — also in relation to other women — to articulate the female sense of her body, and to speak about issues that had been repressed or unvoiced. *La nef des sorcières* was an important stage in the feminist struggle, which was increasingly supported by publishing houses and series that specifically concentrated on literature written by female authors. Denise Boucher (1935–) achieved a similar success with *Les fées ont soif* (1978), which revoked female stereotypes of a patriarchal religious and literary culture and propagated the utopia of a "female imagination."

The concept of a specifically feminine style of writing (*écriture féminine*) — also advocated by European and American feminism — led in its extreme form to the complete subversion or destruction of traditional forms of expression. Under the premise that an Aristotelian dramatic structure propagated male dominance, female writers produced plays without exposition, plot, or resolution (see Desrochers in Lafon). Like the surreal automatists who inspired the literary experiments of French-Canadian feminists, *écriture féminine* was accused of confusion and a lack of transparency by its critics. Since the 1980s, however, a critical reassessment has taken place, and *écriture féminine* is now considered a significant contribution to postmodern literary aesthetics.

Over the course of the Révolution tranquille many authors tried not only to free themselves from clerical, colonial, and patriarchal authorities, but also from the authority of canonical works of world literature. They implicitly or explicitly stated that the international orientation of literature encumbered the search for a French-Canadian identity. Frequently connections to other literatures were denied or concealed; when canonical texts from world literature were translated into French or *joual*, they were regionalized or even trivialized in terms of their content. The theater used this process of linguistic and cultural assimilation in translation or parody (which has been examined by Annie Brisset) to construct, produce, and propagate a collective identity. For instance, Éloi de Grandmont (1921–1970) changed the setting of his *Pygmalion* adaptation (1968) to Montreal and the London cockney into *joual*. Germain even went so far as to translate texts originally written in French or Canadian French into *québécois* or *joual*. With *Les faux brillants de Félix-Gabriel Marchand* (1977) he rewrote a play by the former prime minister of the same name, who for his part had written an imitation of Molière's *Le bourgeois gentilhomme* (1671) under the title *Les faux brillants* (1885). The Acadian author Maillet also adapted Molière's comedy to a French-Canadian context: In her play *Le bourgeois gentleman* (1978) Molière's Turk — as the incarnation of the foreign — is replaced by the enemy figure of the Englishman, and Molière's citizen M. Jourdain, who imitates the conventions of the nobility, is replaced by "M. Bourgeois," who emulates the customs of the English in a laughable fashion. Another form of canon adaptation can be seen in Réjean Ducharme's (1941–) *Le Cid maghané* (1968), which uses Corneille's *Cid* (1637) to unmask the workings of the yellow press and to critically question Corneille's text (see Brisset).

Michel Garneau (1939–), who produced over forty plays in a short span of time, also translated classical texts into *québécois* (for example, Shakespeare's *Macbeth* of 1606). Not all of these "tradaptations" subjugate the models to Quebec's collective interest, however. Garneau's adaptation of the Gilgamesh epic (*Gilgamesh*, 1976) retains the central motifs of the Sumerian original, although in Garneau's version stereotypical, misogynist ideas like the impurity of woman are emphasized more strongly. In his own plays Garneau continues the tradition of the "théâtre populaire" under the conditions of a multimedial society. *La chanson d'amour de cul* (1974) reproduces sexual fantasies created by the media. Garneau makes use of stereotypes from the fields of advertisement, female and male sexuality, religion, ethnic affiliation, and art.

Robert Gurik also produced "tradaptations." For instance, he adapted Shakespeare to make the "condition québécoise" salient (*Hamlet, Prince de Québec*, 1968). His other plays draw on current political issues and critically as well as satirically reflect the way they are conveyed by the media, which also take on an important function as signs within the theater. In the tradition of Brecht and radical American theater (Saul Gottlieb, Rony Davis), Gurik's "théâtre d'anarchie et de confusion" defamiliarizes political events through irony, satire, utopia, and the grotesque, as well as through film techniques — to the point that it becomes meaningful for a contemporary audience. *Api 2967* (1971) presents the vision of a future posthumanist era; *Le Louis d'or* (1966) is a Pirandello-esque game with theater genres and identities. *Le chant du poète* (1963), *Le pendu* (1970), *À coeur ouvert* (1969), and *Le procès de Jean-Baptiste M.* (1972) contain grotesque and macabre scenes with surreal elements, and by means of Brecht's distancing techniques voice criticism of political repression and social injustice. *Le tabernacle à trois étages* (1972) begins with the national anthem "O Canada" and contains further song and dance sequences. The protagonists Pierre and Robert are modeled on the politicians Pierre Trudeau and Robert Bourassa, whose phrases unmask their true colors: "Mais oui . . . l'important c'est de garder les gens en bas en leur donnant l'impression qu'ils sont en haut." The virtuoso (partially parallel and simultaneous) plot construction is set to rhythm through leitmotif-style questions: "Est-ce ainsi que les hommes aiment? . . . Est-ce ainsi que les hommes meurent?" Gurik wants his audience to ask these questions themselves. The nonverbal signs of the grotesque-macabre scenes also point in this direction: Characters in uniform appear in cheerful mood, praise commercial products with songs in the style of American music-hall revues, and finally, through the use of brutal violence, force the other characters to buy them. The alienation and degradation of people in a media-driven consumer society also become clear through the technique of contrast, for example, when the down-and-out actress Baptiste, dressed as a clown, recites long passages from Racine's *Phèdre* (1677), but is forced to recognize that she is unable to portray a tragic figure. Here tragedy is replaced by the grotesque, which Jan Kott sees as the tragedy of modern man. In *Vingt ans* (1985) Gurik poses the question of what theater will have to say in the year 2000. In *La griffe* (1999) he deals with the theme of fashion in the homosexual milieu and reflects on the fictionality of the theater and of simulated reality. Through his critical use of technology and audiovisual media and with his concept of the grotesque as the legacy of tragedy as well as the juncture of heterogeneous elements, Gurik can be considered the forerunner of directors and scenographers like Robert Lepage and Jean-Pierre Ronfard.

# "De-collectivization," "De-allegorization," and Postmodernization: Developments in Theater since 1980

Creating a distance between their country and the rest of the world, Quebec authors sought to construct a Québécois identity, an identity that became obsolete with the referendum of 1980, however, when the majority of the Quebec people voted against independence. After 1980, many authors who had used the stage as a platform for the demonstration of an identity-forming difference left the theater or turned to other genres such as film or the novel. With the de-politicization and "de-collectivization" of the theater (and of the audience) came a structural change in the conception of the text, the author, and the director. Improvisational theater and happenings, like the propagandist collective productions, lost their political and social relevance, and new forms of the "theater of community" arose (see Wajdi Mouawad, Dominic Champagne). First, however, a re-literarization of the text took place, with borders between genres being crossed and theater conventions (such as the chronological-linear plot line or the creation of illusion) being abandoned.

While the identity issue had taken up the foreground as a collective problem in the 1970s, theater and its conventions — further challenged by the growing importance of audiovisual media — were called into question after the referenda of 1980 and 1995. This development was reflected on the level of dramaturgy in an increasing amount of "drama within the drama," in the practice of *mise en abyme*, and in the fact that many plays featured a poet or dramatist as a figure: The theater was now increasingly becoming a metatheater with a heavy emphasis on the performance character (Michel Marc Bouchard, Normand Chaurette, René-Daniel Dubois, Ducharme, Germain, Tremblay, Ronfard, for example). This led to a "de-allegorization" not only of conceptions of the theater but also of interpretations by theater critics. The interest was transferred to the individual identity of the author (as a homosexual, as a writer, as a woman) or, as in the case of Ronfard, to the conception of a "cultural identity." In this way theater became either a stage for the individual or it opened itself with a curious gaze to the Other. This was also reflected in the rediscovery of an international repertoire. Numerous festivals contributed to widening horizons, because as the setting of an international encounter they were ideally suited to founding a new form of community.

Marie Laberge's (1950–) plays continued in the realistic-popular vein and used the stage for the production of a female identity. Written in *québécois*, they are psychological dramas with simple plots, in which the focus is on isolated individuals, and individualism is defended as a moral value and political demand against the collective pressure of the group (see Smith). Laberge focuses primarily on problems of women in conflict with their environments. In this context, *C'était avant la guerre à l'Anse à Gilles* (1982) demonstrates the possibilities of emancipation: The protagonist Marianne argues at the end of the play against the traditional Quebec society and its conservative ideology (polemically referring to the intertext *Maria Chapdelaine* by Louis Hémon from 1914; see ch. 10, Kirsch):

HONORÉ: Au pays du Québec rien ne doit mourir et rien ne doit changer.

MARIANNE: Vous trouvez? Pa moè! Chus tannée du passé, Honoré, chus tannée de t'nir le flambeau pis de trimer pour des croyances que j'ai pas; j'pense que quelque chose meure . . . j'pense que nous aut' les femmes, on meurt dans l'silence.

In many of her dramas Laberge brings the self-imposed silence or the silence provoked by the Other to the stage. In *Avec l'hiver qui s'en vient* (1980) Maurice, who is mourning his childhood and the death of his aunt Félicie, refuses all communication. In *L'homme gris* (1989) the protagonist closes herself off to communication with her father, who is fixated on his daughter's physical beauty and remains unaware of her inner life. Laberge's female figures are characterized by a foregrounded inner life and self-reflexivity and are generally unhappy and unable to define their own (emotional) lives in the face of the pressure put on them from outside. In the 1990s Laberge turned away from the theater and devoted herself to the novel.

In Maryse Pelletier's (1947–) plays women and their love lives also form the central theme: *À qui le p'tit coeur après neuf heures et demie* (1984) deals with the mentality and sentimentality of women from different generations. *Du poil aux pattes comme les CWACS* (1983) presents various female figures who enter the army during the Second World War. Pelletier's best-known play, *Duo pour voix obstinées* (1984), is a psychodrama in the style of Tennessee Williams. The metadrama *Haï-záaa* (1985) produces a confrontation between actors and members of the audience. Pelletier's writing style is partly realistic, partly ironic and grotesque, as in *Un samouraï amoureux* (1989), for example, in which a dog named Victor, taken for a walk by the protagonist Victorine, is played by a man. *Blanc sur noir* (1986) is an analytical play that explains the development of racism in South Africa and its consequences, relating them to racism in Quebec.

Pol Pelletier (1947–), whose feminist theater has been extremely successful with the public, has also been active in the fight against social and political repression: "J'étais brûlante d'urgence. Tout transformer, il le faut. Et persuadée, je l'étais, que le mouvement des femmes — ou la compréhension profonde de ce qu'était l'oppression des femmes — allait mettre fin à toute oppression, à toute laideur, à toute injustice," she writes in a brief self-characterization in the appendix to her play *La lumière blanche* (1989). Involved in collective productions like *La nef des sorcières* and *À ma mère, à ma mère, à ma mère, à ma voisine* (1980) as an actress and co-author, she had already initiated the Théâtre Expérimental des Femmes (T.E.F.) in 1979 with the aim of creating a cultural center of and for women. In 1988 she founded the theatrical troupe Degré Zéro and a training center for actors ("Dojo pour acteurs"). As the author and actress of her own plays she portrays ecstatic conditions and attempts to convey these to the audience through direct address. Pelletier is interested in changing actors and audience in an "energetic" sense, to reach them through the magic of the expressive body in its psychosomatic totality, that is, through both spirit and body. The mutual goal is the "we," as she explains in *Joie* (1995), a recapitulation of feminist theater and her personal career. In *Océan* (1996), which is even more autobiographical, she deals with the death of her mother and the spiritual experiences of a trip to India. *Or* (1997) takes as its theme the "alchemic" transforming power of the actress who produces a transformation in herself and the audience through her art and, for her part, is influenced in her performance by the atmosphere during the play.

The female search for identity also plays a primary role in the theater of Jovette Marchessault (1938–). While her *Tryptique lesbien* (1980) had originally shared the militant and self-affirmative tendency of feminist theater, she later turned toward analytical texts and attempted to create a specifically feminine world of images, taking inspiration from historical and contemporary texts by female authors such as Violette Leduc and Anaïs Nin. In *La saga des poules mouillées* (1989) she presents a conversation between four female authors who have had a significant influence on the literary culture in Quebec — Laure Conan, Anne Hébert, Gabrielle Roy, and Germaine Guèvremont — and brings their texts into a dialogic relationship with one another. In the rest of her work she is also interested in the women's movement and a genuinely female culture. She brings forgotten female figures and stories to light and rewrites history in the sense of a "historiographic metafiction" (Linda Hutcheon; see ch. 22, Rosenthal). In doing so, she gives the imaginary precedence over "reality."

A similar process takes place in Michel Marc Bouchard's (1958–) dramas, which construct the history of homosexuality or the homosexual identity by means of intertextuality. *La contre-nature de Chrysippe Tanguay, écologiste*, directed in 1983 by André Brassard, is a psychodrama about the traumatized homosexual couple Jean and Louis, who want to adopt a child and who suffer discrimination at the hands of women. As in Chaurette's *Provincetown Playhouse* (see below), artistic work is evoked on a meta- and intertextual level as man's substitute for the birth of a child. The "play within a play" *Les Feluettes ou La répétition d'un drame romantique* (1987), made into a movie the same year it was written, also portrays the homosexual search for identity in conflict with repressive tendencies in small-town society and connects with various intertexts. *Les muses orphelines* (1988) deals with social and identity-related conflicts from the perspective of four children as they feel neglected by their mother, who is in thrall to her Latin lover. With these plays Bouchard created a contrast to the radical feminist theater in which the male gender was the subject of criticism.

René-Daniel Dubois (1955–), too, casts a critical gaze on traditional stereotypes of identity. In *L'ange et le lutin* (1997), a short story told in monologue form, his theme is the homosexual scene, but this time in the urban context of Montreal. His *Le printemps, monsieur Deslauriers* (1987) deals with the generational conflict surrounding a father who determines not to leave his children any inheritance in order to sustain their joy for life. Conceived as a "pièce nationale," the play strives to portray Quebec society in the period after the referendum (1995) — although Dubois was a proponent of independence, he warned in an article in *Le Monde* of the possible negative results of nationalism in Quebec. In *26 bis, impasse Colonel Foisy* (1983) he views himself from an ironic perspective, similar to Luigi Pirandello or Eugène Ionesco: He lets his own character, a woman played by a man with a Slavic accent, criticize his style of writing and his dramatic conception; the woman/character even refers to Dubois's private life and to earlier productions like *Adieu, docteur Münch* (1982). The dissolution of the border between the audience and the actors on the stage goes so far in this play that the actress invites a member of the audience to come to her dressing room after the play. Dubois's style is self-reflexive, playful, and full of inter- and metatextual references. The play *Ne blâmez pas les bédouins* (1984) demonstrates a virtuoso use of various idiolects. Dubois has performed this challenging drama also as a solo version, playing all the parts himself. In Chaurette's *Provincetown Playhouse*, he also interpreted all four roles himself (in the Centre culturel canadien of Paris in 1982).

Normand Chaurette (1954–), too, broke with traditional theater conventions by encapsulating his plots in a complicated fashion, splitting them into pieces, or — like Beckett in Lucky's monologue in *En attendant Godot* — letting language glide into the absurd and robbing it of its communicative function. The cleverly constructed metadramatic *Provincetown Playhouse, juillet 1919, j'avais 19 ans* (1981) brings the problematic division between fiction and reality to the stage and circles around the artistic consciousness torn by reality and delusion. The protagonist Charles Charles is a dramaturge who, on a July evening in 1919, wants to perform a play with the title *L'immolation de la beauté*, which ends with the murder of a child. When he discovers that his lover is betraying him, he turns his fiction into cruel reality out of revenge — theater illusion and brutal reality merge. Chaurette takes up classical traditions (the murder of Astyanax, the Sacrifice of Isaac), but conceals them in the interest of a "métissage" of texts. *Rêve d'une nuit d'hôpital* (1980) evokes the traumatic universe of the poet Émile Nelligan (1879–1941) and reflects on the individual artist at the border between genius and madness. *Les reines* (1991), set in the London of the year 1483, presents in somber colors the tragic extreme situation of the royal family in mortal danger. It contains numerous allusions to English history and, on a linguistic level, achieves the dimension of the absurd found in Ionesco's dramas. *La société de Métis* (1983) is a Pirandello-esque treatment of the role of the artist as related to his art and his audience. Set in Métis-sur-mer in Gaspésie in the summer of 1954, the play initially shows figures like portraits in a museum, who then come to life in order to observe their creator, the painter Hector Joyeux, who, like God, is "à la fois partout et nulle part." *Je vous écris du Caire* (1994) deals with the opera world around Giuseppe Verdi. Chaurette's theater continuously questions the conditions for artistic creation in the various arts.

In an increasingly multimedial environment questions surrounding the artistic subject, the material, and the realistic content of artistic representation as well as the informative function of theater become especially important. After the "téléthéâtres" were replaced by the soap-opera genre ("roman-savon" or "soap-opéra") for commercial reasons, the theater faded from public awareness. Faced with a public schooled in the multimedia world with its changed habits of perception and reception, the director's role as a mediator gained importance with respect to both classical and avant-garde plays. This function is expressed, for example, when collages of selected plays by individual authors are produced with the goal of making the authors known to the public. This anthological form of a reworking through condensation and concentration also offers a means of updating the plays and may lead — depending on the artistic and intellectual ability of the director — to a shallower or deeper version than the original texts. Productions that update the classical repertoire also have two sides: They can trivialize, sensationalize, brutalize, or make pornography of the text, but on the other hand they can also draw attention to aspects of classical texts that had received little attention or had been blocked by receptive norms and habits. Recently, numerous dramaturges and directors have come up with a plethora of individual creations, creative productions, and innovative adaptations. Many of them, by means of their creative way of handling model texts by contemporary authors, have even inspired the latter to revise their texts.

The productions of André Brassard (1946–), to whom Tremblay's plays owe part of their penetrating effect, are characterized by a grotesque realism through both distancing effects and means that destroy illusions. Brassard sees the director as a personality who positions him- or herself between an author's text and the audience and can convey a message beyond the message of the text itself. Jean-Pierre Ronfard (1929–2003) also had a decisive influence on the theater scene in Quebec. Together with Robert Gravel (1945–1996) and others, he founded the Théâtre Expérimental de Montréal, which became the Nouveau Théâtre Expérimental after the dissolution of the group in 1979, when Pol Pelletier founded the Théâtre Expérimental des Femmes. Ronfard's varied experiments extended as far as the conception of a play without actors (*Les objets parlent*, 1986).

Reflection on nonverbal signs, language, and the phenomenon of the voice are leitmotifs in his work. Ronfard was married to the author Marie Cardinal (1929–2001) and directed her Euripides adaptation *La Médée d'Euripide* (1986), which contains a long feminist prologue; as early as 1970 he had adapted the Medea myth himself (*Médée*). In working with literary traditions he once characterized himself as "pillard, plagiaire, dévoreur et restitueur de vieilles affaires, vandale, barbare." Productions like *Lear* (1977; based on Shakespeare's *King Lear*), *La mandragore* (1982; based on Machiavelli's *Mandragola*), *Les mille et une nuits* (1985; based on *Thousand and One Nights*), *Le Titanic* (1986; after Hans-Magnus Enzensberger), *Autour de Phèdre* (1988), *La voix d'Orphée* (1990), and *Hitler* (2000) refer in this manner to classical and modern material, motifs, and myths. In *La leçon de musique 1644* (1986) the music of Monteverdi appears in dramatic contrast to the traditional autochthonous music of Native Canadians. In the gigantic drama cycle *Vie et mort du roi boiteux* (1981–1982), to which Gravel also contributed and which consists of six plays with a total of fifteen hours of performance, Ronfard parodies Western traditions with his "limping king" as the sum of various historical and fictive kings. Here the grotesque — the aesthetic of combining the high with the low, the everyday with the exotic, the old with the new, the sacred with the profane, the sublime with the ridiculous — is the mode through which the past can be made current and the clash of worlds and cultures is produced. Bertolt Brecht sings a duet with Aristotle, God ponders linguistic phenomena with Joan of Arc and Mata Hari, and icons of the twentieth century such as Marilyn Monroe appear together with historical and mythological figures. The theater becomes the site of a metadramatic analysis of its own medium and with its neobaroque and carnivalesque aesthetics follows postmodern tendencies (see Féral). With its multilayered fabric of intertextuality and intermediality, Ronfard's "barbaric" *theatrum mundi* is both palimpsest and métissage. The source texts or scenes are drawn from tradition and are hidden under various modern layers. Some of the original texts are written over to the point of unrecognizability; some appear in authentic freshness.

Robert Lepage's (1957–) productions of his own and other writers' works are also multiculturally and transculturally oriented. The motif of the journey, whether real or imaginary, continental or intercontinental, plays an important role in many of his productions. The play becomes a journey of discovery (*Circulations*, 1984; *La trilogie des dragons*, 1985). Lepage developed his films *Nô* (1998), *Le polygraphe* (1996), and the English version *Possible Worlds* (2000) from parts of his play *Les sept branches de la rivière Ota* (1994). For Lepage, theater is the art of transformation as well as a process; as a starting point and an impulse he generally takes an object — a painting, music, a map, or a text (see Vigeant). What is familiar and comforting to the audience — this can be the technological multimedial environment, but also (multi-)cultural icons such as Leonardo da Vinci, Frédéric Chopin, George Sand, or Miles Davis — forms the frame of reference that Lepage requires as the cultural prerequisite for the communication between the play and the audience. What is conventional, however, will be transformed and transfigured over the course of the play. Through juxtaposition or fragmentation of the individual elements a total work of art with varied connections is produced, a work of art that is consciously left incomplete because Lepage relies on the audience's creative imagination.

Gilles Maheu (1948–) goes beyond the "théâtre d'images" by producing not only images but visions. In 1975, Maheu founded the street and improvisational theater troupe Les Enfants du Paradis, from which the Carbone 14 theater in 1980 was born. Maheu, with his subversive aesthetics, was influenced by Antonin Artaud and Heiner Müller, several of whose plays he directed with great success. Maheu's performance style is decidedly multimedial in its orientation — his means are expressive gesture and strong emotion, surprising and sometimes shocking images, subversion of visual, linguistic, and auditory clichés, ecstatic dance theater, and symbolic decoration, as in *Le rail* (1983; inspired by D. M. Thomas and Jack Henry Abbott), in *Hamlet-Machine* (1987; based on Heiner Müller's *Die Hamletmaschine* of 1978), or in *La forêt* (1994). Maheu's productions are "transtheatrical" because he sees the theater as one means among many of expressing the totality of humanity and because his theater seeks to transcend itself. His visionary productions emphasize the timelessness of archetypes, myths, and ideologies, questioning the ideological, social, and historical prerequisites for subjectivity under the conditions of the actual present day (see Krysinski). With his visionary theater Maheu creates a mysterious and dreamlike atmosphere and presents intense scenarios that are autobiographically inspired, as in *L'homme rouge* (1982) or in *Le dortoir* (1988). In *La bibliothèque ou ma mort était mon enfance* (2003) he counters the noise and oversaturation by the mass media with a "production of quiet," taking the saving power of literature as his theme.

Denis Marleau's (1954–) productions are also characterized by an unmistakably individual style. In 1982, he founded the Théâtre UBU in Montreal, in which he performed condensed montages of Alfred Jarry's Ubu variations: *Ubu cycle* (1989) and *Les Ubs* (1991). He thus updated Jarry's theater through the elimination of its retrograde characteristics and the accentuation of its avant-garde qualities. His innovative productions of avant-garde authors and artists such as Jarry, Kurt Schwitters, Beckett, Ionesco, Pablo Picasso, and authors of the Oulipo brought Marleau international fame. In *Les trois derniers jours de Fernando Pessoa* (1997; after Antonio Tabucchi) he used screens to reflect and multiply Pessoa's various projected identities. In his productions he cultivates the text and the spoken word, which forms the starting point for parody, puns, irony, and satire and exhausts the various everyday possibilities for the use of language. Instead of a theater of sensational emotions, stereotypical or exaggerated gesture, or psychological interpretations he offers a restrained and thus more effective game played by the actors. Instead of spontaneous improvisation he chooses cultural penetration in the service of the play being performed. Using collage and an acting style that accents the absurd, he succeeds in bringing out dimensions of the absurd in earlier plays as well, as in Georg Büchner's *Woyzeck* (1836). His directing style, with its avantgarde influences, is impressive in its intensity, musicality, extreme stylization and sublimation, precision, and clarity.

The rediscovery of texts from the international repertoire and their convincing and original scenic presentation has been a general characteristic of production in Quebec since the 1980s and 1990s. Métissage, collage, pastiche, paraphrase, and intertextuality are used as means of updating old texts, domesticizing "foreign" texts, or conveying them in a new way. This intercultural orientation helped to develop a variety of original texts. Along with André Brassard, Gilles Maheu, Denis Marleau, Robert Lepage, Pol Pelletier, Carole Fréchette, Denise Boucher, Robert Gravel, and Jean-Pierre Ronfard, personalities such as Alice Ronfard, Jean Asselin, Brigitte Haentjens, Lorraine Pintal, Claude Poissant, René-Richard Cyr, and Théo Spychalski have also provided decisive impulses for francophone theater, and Quebec today is an important and innovative center of dramatic culture with a pluralist spectrum of expressive possibilities.

# 34: Transculturalism and *écritures migrantes*

*Gilles Dupuis (Université de Montréal)*

THE CONCEPT OF *ÉCRITURES MIGRANTES*, or migrant literature, first appeared in Quebec during the 1980s. The expression was and continues to be used today to refer to the literary production of writers who, after immigrating to Canada, decided to settle in Quebec — the only Canadian province with a francophone majority — and to write or at least publish within the framework of the province's literary institutions. The criteria for classifying a work as migrant literature vary from one source to another. For Daniel Chartier, author of the *Dictionnaire des écrivains émigrés au Québec 1800–1999* (2003), language is not a determining factor. According to him, a work can be written in any of the two official languages of Canada, French or English, or, for that matter, in any idiom of a distinct linguistic minority (Italian, Spanish, Yiddish, etc.) that chooses to express itself in its mother tongue, and still be identified as migrant or, closer to the author's perspective, immigrant literature. On the other hand, the *Dictionnaire des oeuvres littéraires du Québec* (seven volumes published to date, encompassing the vast period from 1534 to 1985) still considers language as a discriminating factor, or even as the only valid criterion for distinguishing between Québécois and non-Québécois literary works. To be acknowledged as a "genuine" oeuvre from Quebec, the authors of the dictionary implicitly assume that the work must be written in French, considered not only the official language of Quebec, but also the only idiom in which a "true" Québécois (the former French Canadian as opposed to the English Canadian) expresses him- or herself. Historical and political implications make linguistic identity an almost unavoidable ideological issue whenever Quebec's literature and culture are discussed. However biased it may seem, though, this aspect of the province's "national" identity within the nation-state cannot be readily discarded since it remains an essential part of what a majority of Québécois consider to be their distinctive heritage, if not the only surviving element of their remote, yet inextinguishable, French origin. Nevertheless, with the passing of time, and after the fervent nationalistic period of the 1960s and 1970s, Quebec will certainly no longer be able to ignore the literary production of the so-called Anglo-Québécois (not to be confused with "Quebecers," often used by English Canadians to designate the French Canadians of Quebec) and their original contribution to the province's cultural life. The publication of a new and long-awaited literary history of Quebec is a clear sign of this. Indeed, in their *Histoire de la littérature québécoise* (2007) Élisabeth Nardout-Lafarge, François Dumont, and Michel Biron do not hesitate to include writers born in Montreal who wrote in English, such as short-story writer Mavis Gallant (1922–), author of *Home Truths* (1956); prolific novelist Mordecai Richler (1931–2001), author of *The Apprenticeship of Duddy Kravitz* (1959), *St. Urbain's Horseman* (1971), *Joshua Then and Now* (1980), *Solomon Gursky Was Here* (1989), and *Barney's Version* (1997); and celebrated poet and musician Leonard Cohen (1934–), author of *Let Us Compare Mythologies* (1956), *The Favourite Game* (1963), *Beautiful Losers* (1966), *Stranger Music* (1993), and *Book of Longing* (2006). Paradoxically, this belated recognition, which the myth of the "two solitudes" had made difficult to achieve, is partly due to the success that immigrant — foremost among them migrant — writers have encountered in the 1980s and 1990s.

With the relative decline (or at least momentary lapse) of the nationalist movement in Quebec following the bitter defeat of the first referendum in 1980, and with the arrival of a new generation of immigrant writers on the literary scene, the conditions were ripe for the emergence of a distinct migrant corpus within the literary canon. The expression "littérature migrante" is rarely used by literary critics and theoreticians when addressing this specific body of works, some preferring the singular "écriture migrante" (Moisan and Hildebrand, Chartier), while others opt for the plural "écritures migrantes" (Berrouët-Oriol, Nepveu). The former view this phenomenon as merely one particular literary movement within the general framework of Quebec literature (hence the singular), while for the latter, it marks a more profound shift in the development of the literary canon by questioning the very concept of national literature (ergo the plural as opposed to a single literature). Depending on the perspective adopted, either 1983 or 1986 can be chosen as the "date of birth" of migrant literature: In 1983 Régine Robin published her renowned novel *La Québécoite* and the first issue of the transcultural magazine *Vice versa* was released, while 1986 witnessed the "official" coinage of the expression "écritures migrantes" — and its corollary "voix métisses" — by Haitian-born poet Robert Berrouët-Oriol (1951–). In fact, the history of the term can be traced back at least to the writings of another Haitian author, Émile Ollivier (1940–2002; see Ollivier 1984). However, because many authoritative critics have regarded it as originating with Berrouët-Oriol — including Pierre Nepveu, to whom we owe the academic recognition of migrant writers within the institution of Quebec literature, mainly because he used the expression "écritures migrantes" for the first time in an essay devoted to contemporary Québécois literature (see Nepveu 1989, ch. 12) — the year 1986 is still considered by many as a turning point in the history of migrant writing. For instance, in their *Histoire de l'écriture migrante au Québec (1937–1997)*, published in 2001, the first literary history devoted entirely to migrant literature, Clément Moisan and Renate Hildebrand consider the period 1975–1986, which they label "the intercultural phase," as corresponding to the practice of immigrant writing, while the following period, 1986–1997, dubbed "the transcultural phase," is specifically reserved for the phenomenon of *écritures migrantes*. The border between immigrant and migrant writing is difficult to trace and becomes even more blurred if one takes into account the underlying distinction between the discourses of interculturalism and transculturalism.

Prior to the period from 1983 to 1986, writers who immigrated to Canada and decided to settle in Quebec tended to subscribe to the province's literary canon of the time, which was dominated by a national discourse dating back to the Révolution tranquille. Writers such as Monique Bosco (1927–2007), Jean Basile (1932–1992), and Robert Gurik dealt with topics and adopted practices of writing similar to those of their French-Canadian colleagues with whom they shared the same language, either as mother tongue or acquired idiom, often after a prolonged stay in Paris. Gurik's (1932–) parodic play *Hamlet, Prince de Québec* (1968; see ch. 33, Scholl), for instance, is written much in the same vein as the patriotic plays of his French-Canadian counterpart, Françoise Loranger (1913–1995), author of *Le Chemin du Roy* (1969), *Double jeu* (1969), and *Médium saignant* (1970). In the general context of decolonization, which prevailed in the 1960s, both playwrights reverted to parody as a literary device in order to expose and criticize the colonial status of the francophone province within English-dominated Canada. Many immigrant writers who published their works in that period espoused the political views of their French-Canadian colleagues. Another interesting — if not paradoxical — parallel can be found in Leonard Cohen's novel *Beautiful Losers* (1966), in which the English-Jewish main character supports the French Canadians in their striving for independence, echoing the struggle of the narrator in Hubert Aquin's (1929–1977) celebrated novel *Prochain épisode* (1965; see ch. 18, Eibl) to achieve political sovereignty. These writers acted somewhat like foreign artists and filmmakers, who, upon immigrating to the United States, would adopt among other traits the English vernacular in order to blend in with the cultural fabric of that country. One could say that in the 1960s and 1970s the immigrant writers of Quebec reverted to the American model of the "melting pot," while adapting it to their new French-Canadian environment, whereas the following generations, the self-dubbed migrant writers of the 1980s and to a lesser degree the "no name" writers of the 1990s, preferred the Canadian alternative of the "multicultural mosaic," but again applied to the specific French-Canadian context. However, there are various local exceptions: Neil Bissoondath's (1955–) pungent critique of Canadian multiculturalism is one example of the resistance of migrant writers to both the model of the melting pot and that of the cultural mosaic (see Bissoondath 1994). Nowadays, most of the writers identified with the phenomenon of *écritures migrantes* — many of whom refuse the label "migrant" attributed to them — strive to belong to the literary canon of the country in which they reside, while maintaining the right to express and assert their difference. An ulterior complication in Quebec stems from the fact that it is not a country in the political sense of a nation-state, while being considered as forming a nation within the state — historically so by the provincial government and the majority of its population, who often refer to it as "le pays du Québec," and very recently by the federal government itself.

In order to understand how the expression "écritures migrantes" imposed itself historically, in contradistinction to immigrant writings of the past, the theoretical background that triggered the passage from immigrant to migrant literature, namely the critical debate concerning the notions of interculturalism and transculturalism, has to be considered. It may be argued that interculturalism, as discourse, occurs whenever two cultures are present and engage in dialogue together. The purpose of this exchange is the attempt to understand the Other represented by each culture and to be reciprocally recognized as "one." In the exchange, which might fail or only partly succeed, each cultural exponent engaged in the dialogue remains more or less the same, the ultimate goal of this engagement being mutual acceptance, as opposed to being changed by the exchange itself. In some way, Otherness is what is not negotiable in this form of encounter, which one might regard as being of the second type. The intercultural review *Dérives*, founded in 1975 by Québécois and Haitian writers in exile, was a forum where such an exchange took place. The idea was to create a bridge between two cultural groups that were at odds in order to reconcile their differences.

The discourse of transculturalism, by contrast, does not limit itself to two cultures facing each other, trying to work out what they assume to be their intrinsic discrepancies. Transculturalism takes place when at least two — and sometimes three or more — cultures are not only engaged in dialogue, but partake in a more profound and often contradictory process, in which enlightenment, misunderstanding, and continuous reassessment of identity are at play. The ultimate aim is to transform each other's identity through a long, arduous, and sometimes painful negotiation of Otherness. What the Italian-Québécois intellectuals who in 1983 founded and animated the trilingual transcultural magazine *Vice versa* designated as "la traversée des cultures" — the act of traversing cultures, often referred to as "openness to the Other" — is very much akin to a close encounter of the third kind, that is, an encounter of the radical Otherness that lies repressed (or at least unnoticed) in every individual or cultural subject, but that the experience of transcultural contact is liable to release or reactivate. It is never clear what will come out of such a venture, if not the sense of adventure itself.

Comparing *Dérives* — published between 1975 and 1987, as the first manifestation of literary interculturalism in Quebec — and *Vice versa* — published between 1983 and 1996, as the first literary manifestation of transculturalism — it is clear that the two discourses overlap rather than follow each other. Transculturalism did not simply succeed interculturalism in accordance with a "progressive" vision of history (as certain critics would argue). Rather, transculturalism appeared when interculturalism was still very much in vogue in Quebec, if only as discourse. One might even argue that the discourse of interculturalism, which dates back at least to 1975 in the field of Quebec literature, did not produce "intercultural" fiction as such before the 1980s — the so-called *écritures migrantes* — and that the discourse of transculturalism, which started officially in 1983, produced "transcultural" writings only a decade later (hence the "no name" used previously to designate the "migrant" writers of the 1990s). Thus, the practice of immigrant writing would be contemporaneous with the discourse of interculturalism, while that of *écritures migrantes* would have to wait until transculturalism took over as theory. Still, this model is not altogether satisfactory, not only because it also presupposes a form of evolution, this time from theory to practice (as if fiction could not anticipate its own theorization), but because it fails to take into account possible exceptions, such as Régine Robin (1939–), who is both a theoretician of transculturalism and a practitioner of immigrant and migrant writing at the same time. In *La Québécoite* (1983), for example, Robin tells the odyssey of a French-Jewish woman with a vague Eastern European background who, after immigrating to Canada and settling in Quebec, drifts among three distinct neighborhoods of Montreal — multicultural Snowdon, where English is still predominant, chic francophone Outremont, and the cosmopolitan Marché Jean-Talon in Little Italy. In each of these "ghettoes," the anonymous narrator, that is to say "la Québécoite" — literally the nonspeaking Québécoise ("coite" meaning "to be or remain quiet") — experiences, in various degrees, a sense of estrangement, a feeling of being exiled in her mother tongue. She does, however, manage to feel somewhat at home around Jean-Talon's marketplace, a crossroads of languages and identities that escapes Montreal's definition as the embodiment of the two solitudes. In that respect, the first two parts of the novel espouse the immigrant and intercultural perspective, while the third part opens up a space for transcultural contact and the emergence of a migrant voice.

Today, the discourses of both transculturalism and *écritures migrantes* — *a fortiori* both practices — are contemporary, which makes the differences between them if not obsolete, then at least less pertinent than they appeared in the recent past. Nevertheless, if only for the sake of clarity, one can still roughly distinguish between two "generations" of migrant writers in Quebec. The first wave of *écritures migrantes* can be traced back to the 1980s, or even further back if one considers early writers such as Naïm Kattan (1928–), Anthony Phelps (1928–), Gérard Étienne (1936–), and Émile Ollivier as forerunners of what Pierre Nepveu calls the "migrant text" (Nepveu 1988, 234, n. 3). The emergence of migrant writings as constituting a distinct corpus within the body of immigrant writings was made possible by two concomitant factors: The promulgation of Bill 101 by the Parti Québécois in 1977, which established French as the only official language of Quebec (forcing children of immigrant parents to attend French instead of English schools), and the unequivocal defeat of the first referendum on sovereignty-association in 1980 (see L'Hérault 2003). The reinforcement of the linguistic identity of Quebec, followed by a climate of political moroseness and uncertainty that put a temporary damper on nationalist fervor, helped a generation of migrant writers to make themselves heard on the literary scene. It is important to stress that most of these writers already had French as either their first or second language imposed by the former context of colonization in their country of origin. Such is the case, for example, for Haitian writers in exile and authors who emigrated from the former French protectorates in the Middle East and in North Africa (notably Lebanon and the Maghreb). Compared to the immigrant writers of the 1960s and 1970s, fewer writers originally from these countries came from Europe or lived in Paris before immigrating to Canada. This first wave includes most authors listed by Nepveu in chapter 12 of *L'écologie du réel*, namely Anne-Marie Alonzo (1951–2005), Robert Berrouët-Oriol, Pan Bouyoucas, Fulvio Caccia, Antonio D'Alfonso, Joël Des Rosiers (1951–), Nadia Ghalem (1941–), Jean Jonassaint (1950–), Dany Laferrière, Mona Latif-Ghattas (1946–), Marilú Mallet (1945–), Marco Micone, and Régine Robin.

The case of the Italo-Québécois writers is somewhat different than that of other immigrant writers in Quebec. Apart from being intellectuals very much involved in the cultural debates of the province, they were paramount among their contemporaries in promoting the concept of transculturalism. The transcultural magazine *Vice versa* was, in fact, founded by two notable exponents of the Italian community, philosopher Lamberto Tassinari and writer Fulvio Caccia (1952–). Poet (*Irpinia*, 1983; *Scirocco*, 1985; *Aknos*, 1994; *Lilas*, 1998), novelist (*Golden Eighties*, 1994; *La ligne gothique*, 2004; *La coïncidence*, 2005; *Le secret*, 2006), and essayist (*Cybersexe*, 1995; *La république Métis*, 1997), Caccia also published a collection of encounters and interviews with fifteen Italo-Québécois artists and writers (*Sous le signe du Phénix*, 1985) and, along with his fellow countryman Antonio D'Alfonso (1953–), an important anthology of texts written by eighteen Italo-Québécois authors (*Quêtes*, 1983), which helped to establish migrant writings as a distinct body of works in the field of immigrant writing.

Antonio D'Alfonso, a poet (*L'autre rivage*, 1987; *L'amour panique*, 1987; *L'apostrophe qui me scinde*, 1998; *Comment ça se passe*, 2001; *Un homme de trop*, 2005), a novelist (*Avril ou L'anti-passion*, 1990; *Un vendredi du mois d'août*, 2004), and a filmwriter and -maker, although born in Quebec, can still be considered a migrant writer. After founding his publishing house Guernica in Montreal in 1978, he moved to Toronto, where he started to publish essays in English (*In Italics*, 1996; *Duologue*, 1998) as well as works written by English-Italian authors of Ontario. In his first novel, *Avril ou L'anti-passion*, D'Alfonso recounts through the eye of his semi-autobiographical narrator, Fabrizio Notte, the story of three generations of Italian immigrants, each of them embodying a different attitude toward the phenomenon of emigration. Symbolizing fidelity to the homeland, Fabrizio's maternal grandparents, although poor, refuse to emigrate, while his paternal ancestors, out of necessity, reluctantly accept to join their son's family in Montreal, where the Notte have decided to settle after a brief sojourn in Halifax. If both parents remain faithful to their Italian heritage, their offspring, on the other hand, adapt easily to their new environment, even though the children's attachment to their new home is not devoid of ambiguity. Fabrizio's sister Lucia eventually marries an anglophone, the "Other" Québécois, while he himself engages in numerous relationships with his francophone neighbors and a female lover of Hungarian origin. He is by far the most complex and ambivalent character of the novel, not knowing exactly what his true identity is or where his real allegiances lie. In that respect, he is very close to the "Québécoite" in Régine Robin's eponymous novel.

Another preeminent writer stemming from the Italian community of Quebec is Marco Micone (1945–). More renowned as a playwright, he is the author of a famous trilogy on immigration (*Gens du silence*, 1982; *Addolorata*, 1984; *Déjà l'agonie*, 1988), which he continues to rewrite and adapt in various idioms (*Trilogia*, 1996; *Silences*, 2004; *Migrances*, 2005), as well as the author of a curious novel, half essay, half autobiography (*Le figuier enchanté*, 1992), and of an "infamous" parody, "Speak What," first published in 1989 in political reaction to Michèle Lalonde's (1937–) notorious poem, "Speak White" (1970; see ch. 31, Mathis-Moser). In all of his works, Micone shows himself deeply concerned with the economic and social implications of immigration for the poorer classes of society, the peasants ("contadini") and the workers ("operai"). He is also the only intellectual figure of his community to openly advocate Quebec's independence.

Among the Haitian community, very present and active in Quebec since at least the 1970s, a new voice was clearly heard on the literary scene during the following decade, distinguishing its author, Dany Laferrière (1953–), as the best writer of his generation to come out of Haiti. In his witty and provocative novel, *Comment faire l'amour avec un Nègre sans se fatiguer* (1985), Laferrière tells the story of a young Black immigrant, ironically called Vieux, who lives in a miserable flat on Saint-Denis Street in Montreal, along with his philosophical friend Bouba. They listen to jazz, discuss the works of Freud and Mao Zedong, as Vieux, between numerous encounters with White females who fantasize about his Black manliness, wrestles to write his first novel inspired by great Afro-American writers and the Beat Generation. This *mise en abyme* of writing in the text, along with the resemblance between the author and his main character, gives the novel a strong autobiographical flavor. The key to its success, though, lies in the satirical portrait it offers of Quebec's modern society, where the clichés of "positive" racism, "exotic" eroticism, "excessive" feminism, and the literary "jet set" of Montreal are depicted as ludicrous, as well as in the lucid account it makes of the life of poorer Black immigrants in a White wealthy country. Influenced by the theories of decolonization, Laferrière's first novel is also representative of postmodern writing in Quebec.

The second wave of *écritures migrantes* to hit Quebec manifested itself in the 1990s. Along with francophone authors Abla Farhoud (1945–) and Serge Ouaknine (1943–), it consisted of a new generation of writers who did not have French as their first or second language at home, but who had either studied it at school or learned it abroad. Many acquired it later in life, sometimes without completely mastering its complexities. What is noteworthy, though, is that most of them chose French as the medium in which to express themselves as writers. However difficult the task may have been, which might explain why some waited a certain time before becoming writers, they had their "coming out" in literature, or what Hélène Cixous calls "la venue à l'écriture," in the language of the majority. Interestingly enough, it is this generation of migrant writers, who achieved considerable success on the Quebec literary scene, that is now hostile to the very label that made them prominent in the first place. This second wave includes authors such as Sergio Kokis, Aki Shimazaki, Philippe Poloni (1958–), Elena Botchorichvilli (1960–), Ying Chen, Aline Apostolska (1961–), Nadine Ltaif (1961–), Ook Chung, Stanley Péan (1966–), and Mauricio Segura.

Sergio Kokis's (1944–) novels are mostly concerned with his country of origin, Brazil, which permeates all of his writings, both fictional and nonfictional, as well as his paintings, since he his both a prolific writer and a gifted painter. After the resounding success of his first novel, *Le pavillon des miroirs* (1994), which dealt with obsessive childhood memories, he went on writing novels at a steady pace, producing a new work of fiction every year. Of all of these, *Errances* (1996) is perhaps the most representative of the precarious condition of the migrant writer within his own country of origin, that is, prior to immigration. In contrast to Kokis, Ying Chen (1961–) moved quickly away from her homeland China — which is still very present in her first novel, *La mémoire de l'eau* (1992), which fictionally relates the life of her grandmother — in order to write fiction that is not clearly grounded in reality, avoiding both the land of origin and the country of immigration as cultural referents. *Les lettres chinoises* (1993, 1998) remains her only novel in which cultural shock engendered by immigration is central to the plot. Somewhere between Kokis and Chen, Abla Farhoud is the epitome of the migrant author who writes both from the immigrant and the emigrant perspective. In her best novel, *Le bonheur a la queue glissante* (1998), she portrays the saga of a Lebanese family which immigrates twice to Canada, returning once to Lebanon before deciding to settle definitively in Montreal. Culture shock is not only confined to the new country of residence in this novel, it also includes the country of origin as it becomes more and more "foreign" with each migration of the family.

Another trait worth mentioning is the diversity of origins of these second-wave writers compared to their predecessors. In the general context of globalization and generalized immigration, of economic unrest and political upheaval, more and more writers are emigrating from geocultural areas of the world previously unfamiliar to Quebec's literary milieu, such as Asia, India, Africa, South America, and Eastern Europe. To this tableau one must add at least two anglophone writers who participate actively in the cultural life of the French-speaking province, namely Neil Bissoondath and David Homel (1952–). On the other hand, authors living or writing in provinces where English is predominant, such as Michael Ondaatje (1943–), Nino Ricci (1959–), or Kerri Sakamoto (1959), are usually not considered "migrant" writers. It is true that two of these writers, Ricci and Sakamoto, were born in Canada, but that is also the case with Antonio D'Alfonso, who is originally from Montreal and is nevertheless considered a significant exponent of *écritures migrantes* in Quebec. As Pierre Nepveu notes, it is important not to confuse "immigrant" with "migrant" (Nepveu 1988, 233, note 2), the latter term being less restrictive than the former. What one conceives of as his or her "original" identity — or even identities, since many of the writers associated with migrant writings have in fact a double origin — does not necessarily pertain to the country of birth or, for that matter, of origin. Another reason that might explain the gap between French and English Canada concerning the definition of migrant literature has to do with the fact that the very notion of *écritures migrantes* (as the expression in French suggests), along with the related concepts of inter- and transculturalism, never really caught on in the rest of Canada, which is polarized instead by the discourses of multiculturalism and postcolonialism, scarcely diffused in Quebec. Nevertheless, a close parallel can be drawn between the two traditions since they both address, albeit in different terms, the same phenomenon, as the case of Hédi Bouraoui (1932–), a Tunisian-born, Toronto-based francophone writer, exemplifies. What he himself calls the "third solitude" (Bouraoui 1980) — that is, the solitude of the migrant writer with respect to French- and English-Canadian writers — is, in fact, a crossroads where all solitudes can intersect within the incessant crisscrossing of literary migration.

Understandingly enough, exile (both interior and exterior), culture shock (and the ensuing sensation of estrangement), the loss of identity (often accompanied by nostalgia), and the reworking of individual and collective memory (as compensation for loss and longing) are the main themes addressed by writers who have left, more often than not unwillingly, a country they cherished to settle in an unknown, sometimes indifferent, environment. Some of these writers, such as Régine Robin, Jean Basile, and Antonio D'Alfonso, have been critical of the Quebec nationalist discourse, which might explain a certain resistance to their literary endeavors on the part of French-Canadian readers. However, they were foremost among their contemporaries in experimenting with new forms of writing promoted by the discourse of transculturalism such as linguistic métissage, cultural hybridization, and autofiction, thus contributing in an original way to the renewal of literary practice in Quebec. Robin's notion of "la parole immigrante" (*La Québécoite*), later on spelled "(im)migrante" to stress the close affinities of immigrant and migrant voices, and Berrouët-Oriol's concept of "voix migrantes et métisses" ("L'effet d'exil") both insist on the inscription of the oral dimension of exile within the written language of fiction and the possibility of transmitting that experience through a process of hybridization with the culture of immersion (see also Simon 2007). For this reason, the "transcultural experience" can be seen as subversive in relation to the established literary canon.

Since the 1990s, three contrasting attitudes toward the canon and the institutionalization of *écritures migrantes* among (im)migrant writers can be distinguished. There were those whose main source of inspiration remained the lost country of origin, the homeland left behind, for example, Brazil for Sergio Kokis in *Negão et Doralice* (1995), *L'art du maquillage* (1997), *Un sourire blindé* (1998), *Le maître de jeu* (1999), *Saltimbanques* (2000), *Kaléidoscope brisé* (2001), *Le magicien* (2002), and *Les amants de l'Alfama* (2003), or Japan for Aki Shimazaki (1955–) in *Tsubaki* (1999), *Hamaguri* (2000), *Tsubame* (2001), *Wasurenagusa* (2003), and *Hotaru* (2004). Despite the fact that they rejected the term as ghettoizing, these writers can still be considered "migrant," akin in that respect to the 1980s generation that preceded them. Others tried to immerse themselves in Quebec's culture by referring to local traditions, customs, and cultural traits, as, for example, in the plays and novels of Abla Farhoud and Pan Bouyoucas (1946–), which use Montreal as their background. These writers were usually the most critical of the given expression *écritures migrantes*, which they regarded as a reductive trademark rather than an open concept, as it was theorized in *Vice versa* a decade earlier. They preferred to refer to themselves as Quebec writers, affirming their desire to become fully part of the province's literary canon. Finally, there were a few authors who shunned both the "migrant" and the "Québécois" label, as they strove to become "universal" writers. Critical of every form of assigned identity, and confronting the very notions of identity and origin, they tended to cultivate a more neutral style of writing that was advocated, in France, by Roland Barthes's concept of "écriture blanche" and typified by the style of Marguerite Duras. Writers such as Ying Chen in *L'ingratitude* (1995), *Immobile* (1998), *Le champ dans la mer* (2001), *Querelle d'un squelette avec son double* (2003), and *Le mangeur* (2006), and to a lesser degree Ook Chung (1963–) in his short-story collections, *Nouvelles orientales et désorientées* (1994) and *Contes Butô* (2003), or Abla Farhoud in her later novels, *Splendide solitude* (2001) and *Le fou d'Omar* (2005), can be seen as representative of this tendency. The reference to France is no coincidence here, since the classical idea of a universal literature is still rooted in that nation's concepts of literature and literary history. By refusing both the "migrant" and "Québécois" labels, the aforementioned writers in a way adhere to the French model, consciously or not, referring to it as their literary legacy, just as many French-Canadian writers did before them.

In the end, considering a writer migrant, local, national, or universal does not really matter, since from a modern or, better still, a postmodern and postcolonial perspective, all writers nowadays belong to what Anglo-Saxon critics call "World Literature," a much broader and more inclusive concept than Goethe's Weltliteratur, which served as the prototype for a universal conception of culture where exclusion was, in fact, the norm. What does matter, at least for the future of literature in Quebec and Canada, is what the so-called migrant writers have achieved as art and how they have contributed not only to the mere remapping, but also the reshaping of the literary canon. Renowned writers such as Régine Robin, Neil Bissoondath, Sergio Kokis, Michael Ondaatje, Ying Chen, David Homel, Kerri Sakamoto, and Aki Shimazaki are proof enough of the valuable vitality and diversity of migrant writing in both French and English Canada. Aside from winning prestigious awards — in Quebec alone, Sergio Kokis received four prizes for *Le pavillon des miroirs* (Prix Molson de l'Académie des lettres du Québec, Grand Prix du livre de Montréal, Prix Québec-Paris, Prix Desjardins du Salon du livre de Québec), while Ying Chen's *L'ingratitude* was honored with the Prix Québec-Paris and the Grand Prix des Lectrices de Elle Québec — many of these writers have seen their works translated into numerous languages and thus widely diffused abroad.

As far as French-Canadian literature is concerned, the official recognition of migrant writers in the 1990s can be acknowledged as owing to the fact that native writers were encouraged to seek their inspiration outside the national boundaries, with some going so far as to let themselves be permeated by the direct influence of *écritures migrantes*. Such is the case, for example, with Guy Parent's novel *L'enfant chinois* (1998), which recalls many traits (both cultural and stylistic) of Ying Chen's writings, mainly *Les lettres chinoises* and *L'ingratitude*, or with Pierre Samson's "Brazilian Trilogy" — *Le Messie de Belém* (1996), *Un garçon de compagnie* (1997), *Il était une fois une ville* (1999) — written after the first novels of Sergio Kokis were published. Perhaps more significantly, migrant writers often accused of indifference toward French-Canadian culture nowadays show openness toward Quebec's literature. One case in point is Abla Farhoud, who wrote her first play, *Les filles du 5–10–15¢* (1993), in the manner of Michel Tremblay and whose first novel, *Le bonheur a la queue glissante*, is reminiscent (not only in the title) of Gabrielle Roy's classic *Bonheur d'oc-casion* (1945). Mauricio Segura's (1969–) *Côte-des-Nègres* (1998) can also be read as a parodic rewriting of Alice Parizeau's *Côte-des-Neiges* (1983), while Monique Proulx's *Les aurores montréales* (1996) offers more respect-ful pastiches of some of the better-known migrant writers, including Ying Chen, Marco Micone, and Dany Laferrière.

Most of these works were published after 1995, following the very narrow defeat of Quebec's second referendum on sovereignty-association, which prompted an embittered Jacques Parizeau, then premier of the province, to blame the ethnic vote as part of the cause that stopped Quebec from achieving its dream of independence. Coincidence or not, *Vice versa* ceased publication soon after, preparing the way for the critical revision of the transculturalism it had strived to promote, as can be seen in the recent works of Simon Harel (Harel 2005 and 2006), once a convinc-ing defender of *écritures migrantes*. It is hard to say if these political and social factors helped to create new bridges between immigrant and native writing, links that were absent a decade earlier despite the efforts of the Haitian and the Italian writers to bridge the gap between the two main currents of French-Canadian literature. What is certain, though, is that what can now be called the phenomenon of *écritures transmigrantes* — that is, the transmigration of identities from one literary "corpus" to the other, from the "migrant" text to the "national" canon (and vice versa) — manifested itself in the wake of yet another controversial milestone in Quebec's turbulent history.

# 35: The Institutionalization of Literature in Quebec

*Andrea Oberhuber (Université de Montréal)*

## From the Institutionalization of Literature to Literary Institutions

IT SEEMS IMPOSSIBLE TODAY to discuss Quebec literature without consider-ing its institutions and, in particular, its institutionalization over the past century. This predicament explains Gilles Marcotte's (1925–) remarks on "Institution et courants d'air" (1989), in which he observes that "the liter-ary institution is not a new topic in Quebec literature. On the contrary, it is our *oldest idea*. Just as God exists before creation, the institution predates the works" (26). The narrator of Catherine Mavrikakis's (1961–) novel *Deuils cannibales et mélancoliques* (2000) makes a similar statement: "In Quebec, there are more literary prizes than books published. . . . It's all about build-ing the institution, whatever the cost" (150). Marcotte's critical analysis of the inverted chronology of institution and production in Quebec's literary landscape and business has become commonplace; and although in the case of Mavrikakis's narrator the comment may sound rather cynical, the obser-vations of Marcotte and Mavrikakis illuminate the crux of the problem: Both criticize literature as an apparatus that has become a matter of course.

The institutionalization of Quebec literature after the Révolution tran-quille opens a vast field of inquiry: In what ways and to what extent have critics, universities with their respective curricula, journals, publishers, and organizations awarding literary prizes participated in this institutionaliza-tion? What has been the role of literary histories, anthologies, essays, new media, and funding agencies in the process of determining an autonomous Quebec literature, independent of the former motherland France? If, as Marcotte claims, it is true that the institution precedes literary production and that it has generated itself in relative autonomy — arguably becoming more important than the works themselves — then Quebec's institutions can be said to be highly protectionist. Or, to quote Lucie Robert on the paradoxical relationship between literature as an artistic product on the one hand and as a system of autonomous organizations on the other: "Si le littéraire n'existe pas sans ses organizations, celles-ci en revanche existent parfois sans lui sur une base autonome" (Robert 1989, 18). While from a historical perspective the inscription of literature in institutionalized forms implies a process, from a sociological standpoint it is understood as an interface of ideologically determined objects, structures, instruments, persons, and apparatuses of power, which Pierre Bourdieu referred to as the "market of symbolic goods." Like any such institution, the literary institution is caught up in the dominant sociocultural system with its advocates and critics. In the case of literature, this system consists of reading and writing practices — which are either acknowledged or marginalized by diverse actors such as publishers, writers, and readers, who, for their part, are often involved in either governmental or private organizations (Andrès 1985, 94–95). It is the work of literary criticism — disseminated by magazines and journals, publishing houses, etc. — which, as part of the larger system, makes the institution function, to the extent that the institution establishes the norms and codes for literary criticism and determines strategies of orientation and recognition.

Quebec's literary institutions are situated at the crossroads of two traditions: French literature and British literature. In the 1960s a more nationalistic consciousness and the idea(l) of a national literature began to emerge. In hardly any other country is the interplay of a literary, social, and national project as dynamic as it is in Quebec. Literature, according to Marcotte (1989), makes the country, and the country makes the literature. The process of the nationalization of literature formed the basis for its institutionalization, because it triggered the formation of Quebec's own cultural institutions, which should no longer be defined by French traditions. The call for a "national" — as opposed to "regional" — literature gained more and more prominence in intellectual circles in the 1960s, and it is still widespread today. What seemed to Octave Crémazie (1827–1879) an overwhelming challenge has since proved an undoubted success, especially in view of the growing prestige of Quebec literature abroad (in some countries, such as France, Germany, and Austria, it is the second most studied francophone national literature after French literature). Quebec literature has finally outgrown its exclusively local reception and, consequently, its regional character as well. What sets Quebec literature apart from other "minority" francophone literatures (for instance, Belgian, Swiss, Maghrebian, Caribbean, or African literature) is precisely its highly institutional character, entrenched as it is in autonomous institutions that are for the most part free from the influence of the dominant French literary establishment (Michon 1985).

An additional factor in the institutionalization of Quebec literature and its striving for autonomy lies in the increasing number of works published by authors who, unlike the autodidacts and amateurs of the first half of the twentieth century, make literature and/or literary scholarship their primary occupation. The number of scholars in the field of Quebec Studies has grown in proportion to the new interest in the historical variant of Quebec literature, "la littérature canadienne-française." Anthologies, literary histories, and studies testify to this refueled consciousness of literary autonomy, while at the same time they consider the historical roots of both colonizing peoples. The publication of numerous encyclopedias and anthologies such as *Anthologie de la littérature québécoise*, vol. I–IV (1978–1980), *Dictionnaire des oeuvres littéraires du Québec* (1980–2003), *La poésie québécoise, des origines à nos jours: Anthologie* (1986, 1996), or *Literatur in Québec, eine Anthologie/Littérature québécoise, une anthologie: 1960–2000* (2005) certainly acknowledges the existence of Quebec literature and confirms it as an institution. According to François Ricard (1981), the primary role of these works is more that of inventory and archive than of selection and assessment, because for the most part they aim at completeness.

Yet Marcotte's observations on the precarious state of Quebec literature as an institution are still valid today. From the outside it looks strong, but from within it appears chronically fragile. It is ideologically solid and, thanks to a functioning apparatus of production and consumption, relatively autonomous, yet modesty and self-doubt often cause it to react in an insecure and even aggressive manner to criticism from abroad (and especially from France). The fact that in the past thirty years the situation has stabilized and in many ways improved is due in no small part to the work of literary criticism, which, besides encouraging institutionalization, has developed a suitable literary discourse.

## Literary Criticism

In the 1960s, which marked the change from a clerically dominated to a secular society, Quebec literature increasingly became the object of study and critical analysis at French-Canadian universities. Along with that went the development of a specific literary or scholarly discourse, especially through scholarly journals launched by individual departments. The aim was to define Quebec literature as a self-sufficient cultural product and at the same time to find an adequate critical discourse for it. Marcotte's collection of essays *Une littérature qui se fait* (1962) gives expression to the simultaneous emergence of these two branches, as does Laurent Mailhot's contribution "Une critique qui se fait" (1966). Quebec literature can be said to have come into its own at the point where its texts become the object of other discourses. During these years of "discoursivization" the term *Québécité* appears time and again in literary criticism, pointing to a self-definition based on the search for typical texts, topics, and leitmotifs, and generating a high degree of self-referentiality. In addition, critics were also concerned with a methodical approach to literature in order to inscribe it into historicity, and, ultimately, into the collective memory. *Voix et images*, a journal founded in 1967 (until 1975 the title still included the patriotic genitive *du pays*, typical of the ideological climate of the 1960s), has made these three principles the basis of its discursive credo. Situating contemporary literature in a Quebec tradition in literary histories unearths continuities and ruptures that find their beginnings in the texts of New France. This example of a more historical approach, as illustrated by *Voix et images* and other journals, clearly shows that the broadening of the term "literature" — within philology as a whole — required a new discourse, begging the question of what literature is, whether only "aesthetically valuable" texts should be included in the canon, and what constitutes aesthetic value in the first place. At that time, new methods brought new impulses for literary criticism: From the perspectives of the sociology of institutions and of socio-criticism, both of which flourish in Quebec, the literariness of the text is not situated within the discursive site of its production, but is coupled with legitimating bodies such as schools, curricula, critics, and publishing houses. All these contribute to the legitimization and appreciation of texts by motivating rereading and calling forth a literary metadiscourse. As Marc Angenot has argued (1988, 82–98), it is not simply as social constructions but also as discursive ones that these models of representation contribute to the transmission of knowledge about texts and to the latters' specific strategies of argumentation. With the burgeoning and diversification of discourses about literature in a relatively short time, a good deal has been accomplished towards constituting a historical and scholarly Quebec literature and its corresponding literary history (Fortin 1991).

## University and School Curricula

The most solid basis for literature as an institution is constituted by its integration in curricula in general and in higher education in particular. The coexistence of French and Quebec literature in the same curriculum, although rarely with equal representation, is an unmistakable expression of the official status of Quebec literature. Literary business benefits from the representation of Quebec literature in curricula from the sales of the texts and an accompanying increase in the secondary literature associated with them. Even more than in universities, Quebec literature is firmly anchored in the Cégep curricula (Collège d'enseignement général et professionnel, a junior college), at times to the detriment of long-dominant French literature, as can be seen in the pedagogical journal *Québéc français* (Marcotte 1984). The intensive efforts of those involved in the institutionalization of Quebec and French-Canadian literature as well as its literary criticism also illuminate the obstacles that have impeded the implantation of texts from Quebec since the 1960s, and their teaching since the 1970s. In fact, the birth of the humanities in Lower Canada was the result of the initiative of a few individuals. For a long time such activity had been the private preoccupation of a limited number of civil servants, teachers, and journalists, who for the most part published their research in France or in the bulletins of the Société royale du Canada. The implantation of French-Canadian literature can be credited to the untiring commitment of Monsignore Camille Roy, a French-trained literature professor and author of the *Histoire de la littérature canadienne de langue française* (1904), a work in which he candidly expounds his vision of the "nationalization of Canadian literature." In 1906 French-Canadian literature was officially integrated into the curriculum for the first time at Laval University. From his position at Laval, Camille Roy presided over French-Canadian literary criticism in the interwar years. In Montreal Élie-J. Auclair and Émile Chartier played a similar role. In both cases, at Laval and in Montreal, the choice of texts depended more on the nationalistic orientation of the author than on primarily aesthetic criteria (Robert 1989).

Since the 1960s Quebec literature and the corresponding francophone literatures in other parts of Canada — Franco-Ontarian in Sudbury and Ottawa or Acadian in New Brunswick — have increasingly gained credibility in nearly all French literature departments. This is also true for Montreal's English-language universities McGill and Concordia, as well as for the officially bilingual Université d'Ottawa/University of Ottawa, Queen's University in Kingston, and York University in Toronto, and also for the universities in Western Canada. Understandably, however, the historical centers of literary studies continue to be Laval and Montreal (where at the Université de Montréal the Département d'études françaises — since 2006 called Département des littératures de langue française — was established after the dissolution of the Faculty of Letters in 1961; at the Université du Québec à Montréal the comparatist Département d'études littéraires deals with Quebec, foreign, and popular literature). Until quite recently there were Quebec-focused research centers at Laval University and the Université de Montréal — the Centre de recherche en littérature québécoise (CRÉLIQ) at Laval and the Centre d'études québécoises (CÉTUQ) at the Université de Montréal — which during the wave of mergers encouraged by funding agencies were consolidated in 2003–2004 in a large bipartite center, the Centre de recherche interuniversitaire sur la littérature et la culture québécoises (CRILCQ). Since the amalgamation, the online Infocentre littéraire des écrivains (L'ÎLE) has created over 360 clipping files on about 950 authors made available to researchers worldwide.

# Journals

In addition to school and university organizations and curricula, literary journals are undoubtedly among the most important instances of the legitimization of a (national) literature. The 1960s represented a turning point in this field as well. During the Révolution tranquille and the reform of education, the dominant religious journals lost their impact, while at the same time the newly-founded secular scholarly journals of Quebec literature increasingly established themselves. Two factors were largely responsible for this change: On the one hand, the contributors to the secular journals were mainly teachers at the Cégeps, which were formed in 1967; on the other, from 1969 onwards the Quebec government built up the Université du Québec network of regional campuses (at Montreal, Trois-Rivières, Chicoutimi, Quebec City, Rimouski, and in the Outaouais). Thus a new class of intellectuals with new positions and discourses came into being (Michon 1985). The new journals were often founded by university professors: *Études françaises* (1965) in the Département d'études françaises (Université de Montréal), *Voix et images* (1965) in the Département d'études littéraires (Université du Québec à Montréal), *Études littéraires* (1968) in the Département d'études littéraires (Laval), and *Littératures* (1988) in the Département de langue et littérature françaises (McGill). *Ellipse*, *Présence francophone*, and *Incidences* are other important journals on the literary landscape. While *Voix et images* is distinctly and exclusively concerned with Quebec literature, the other scholarly journals also integrate French, francophone, and foreign (non-French-speaking) literatures. Each of these publications, according to their editorial objectives, ensures the advancement of Quebec literature, its legitimization, and, ultimately, its consecration. With different emphases, they all contribute to the symbolic appreciation of the "national" literary production.

The new division of labor between different scholarly reviews within the literary domain enabled newly established avant-garde magazines to concentrate on experimental literature (in 1981, however, Pierre Nepveu also noted a theoretical and ideological muddle lacking any coherent critical agenda). This second category of journals has been concerned with literary production (usually designated *création* in francophone countries) and has focused on reflection and discourses about writing. On the whole, the founding of avant-garde magazines was an important step in the constitution of an intellectual group on its way to gaining more symbolic influence. A few examples readily show the rapid growth in editorial ventures since the late 1950s. First came *Liberté* (1959), featuring fiction, essays, and criticism; then *La Barre du Jour* (1965) and *La Nouvelle Barre du Jour* (1978), with a clear formalist-structuralist orientation as well as a feminist agenda; *Les Herbes rouges* (1968), an avowed subculture magazine with a poetic vision of writing against death; *Dérives*, with its interest in relations between Quebec and the Third World; and finally *Hobo/Québec* (1972) and *Cul-Q* (1973), two genuine underground magazines. Recently their ranks have been swelled by *L'inconvénient* and *Contre-jour*, both ambitious projects trying to stake out new ground in the colorful landscape of literary magazines and journals. Many of these publications maintain close ties with publishing houses; such is the case of *La Nouvelle Relève*, launched by Éditons de l'Arbre, and *Liberté*, which cultivates a symbiotic relationship with L'Hexagone. Magazines focusing on contemporary literature constitute the third and final category of periodicals: *Lettres québécoises* (1976), a literary journal, and its interdisciplinary counterpart *Spirale* (1979) clearly dominate this market segment. A common characteristic of these journals, especially when compared to other countries, is their extreme longevity, above all in the case of avant-garde publications. This can in part be explained by the policy of subsidies in Canada and particularly in Quebec. The two most important funding agencies — the SSHRC (Social Sciences and Humanities Research Council) and the FQRSC (Fonds québécois pour la recherche en sciences humaines) act as liberal states within the state by encouraging competition. Quite apart from the political and socio-cultural act always implicated in the founding of a review or a magazine, the longevity of most of these journals and magazines, whether in Quebec or elsewhere in Canada, is ultimately a question of financing.

# Publishing

A publishing sector had already emerged in the decades between 1900 and 1940. It accompanied the new cultural dynamism expressed in the opening of the Montreal Museum of Fine Arts and the founding of the daily newspaper *Le Devoir*, the scholarly organization Association française pour le savoir (ACFAS), and the National Film Board. In the late 1950s and early 1960s the Canadian government developed an independent cultural policy. The Canada Council for the Arts (1957) at the federal level and the Quebec Ministère des affaires culturelles (1961) at the provincial level were given the role of cultural vice-regents. Both developed special support programs for publishing (Jonassaint 1985). Before the Révolution tranquille, publishing houses were often closely associated with political, religious, business, and administrative interests. The Révolution tranquille thus also proved a watershed for the field of publishing by creating a new cultural elite, a reading public better educated, wealthier, and more interested in literature than ever before. It not only supported this development but accelerated it, so that Montreal quickly became the undisputed center of publishing. Following Fides (1937) were L'Hexagone (1953), Leméac (1957), Éditions de l'Homme (1958), Hurtubise HMH (1960), Éditions du jour (1961), Boréal Express (1963; changed to Boréal in 1987), Stanké (1975), VLB éditeur (1976), and La Courte Échelle (1978) for children's literature, to name but a few.

Despite the existence of a number of regional, ideological, and militant small and medium-sized publishers (for example, Asticou and Vents d'Ouest in the Outaouais region, Bien public in Mauricie, feminist presses such as Remue-ménage and Pleine lune, and presses such as L'Homeureux, which concentrate on gay topics), publishers usually consider and aim at Quebec as a whole, that is, as a national market. At the same time, Quebec nationalism has often set in motion national or regional consciousness-raising in other provinces: French-Canadian writers from other provinces also find publishers for their books, for the most part. With an increasing number of publishing houses on the scene, a further paradox of Quebec's literary institution can be detected: "Many works published in Quebec are not published by virtue of their intrinsic worth or market value, but rather to nourish a proliferating publishing apparatus that serves an ideological imperative founded on the values of community" (Marcotte 1989). It should be noted, however, that such paradoxical situations can often be found in connection with emerging and minority literatures and hold equally true for other countries. It remains nonetheless true that in Quebec, an author in search of a publisher will always find one, if not in the metropolis of Montreal, then in the outlying regions. This is a consequence of the fact that Quebec publishers mostly publish the work of Quebec authors. Jonassaint (1985) shows in his statistical survey that in 1980 ninety-seven percent of the literary manuscripts sent to Quebec publishers were by Quebec authors on a topic related to Quebec. The exceptions were Naaman in Sherbrooke and Nouvelle Optique, both of which have a Third-World orientation.

Within the world of publishing one finds subdivisions and trends according to market segments and target groups: On the one hand, there are the university presses — PUL (Presses de l'Université Laval), PUM (Presses de l'Université de Montréal), PUO (Presses de l'Université d'Ottawa), etc. — which target the market for scholarly publications but are only seldom awarded prizes as a sign of recognition. On the other hand, there are the commercial publishers. According to Jonassaint (1985), some of them are oriented toward a cultivated audience (for example, L'Hexagone, VLB, and Le Noroît), while others are more ideological (Partis pris, Boréal, Fides, Bellarmin, and Paulines), or are targeted toward a wider audience (Aurore, Leméac, HMH, Naaman, Quinze, Éditions de l'Homme, Stanké, La Presse, Héritage, Québec/Amérique, and Beauchemin).

From a historical perspective, it should be noted that the form of Catholicism prevailing in French Canada favored oral culture over literature, whereas the Protestant provinces developed a culture of book learning. This explains the relative time lag in the development of publishing in Quebec: After the end of the Duplessis era and clericalism, Quebec was faced with a huge handicap. This in turn may explain the massive financial support given to publishers by the provincial government, although this support is increasingly subordinated to commercial concerns. The larger the publishing house and the more it publishes, the more it becomes an industry rather than a domain that fosters quality literature. The same could be said about other countries, however, and may be a general tendency accounted for by globalization.

## Literary Prizes

Like the value of a currency on the exchange, literary prizes determine a book's market value. They act as guarantors of the "worth," that is, the aesthetic value of a publication. In the early 1980s, René Lapierre (1981) and Jacques Godbout (1981) came to a similar conclusion regarding the policy of subsidies, in fact claiming that Quebec literary institutions award more distinctions than can be justified, which deflates the symbolic value of such prizes. According to Lapierre and Godbout, prizes confirm the existence of the institutional framework they have created in their self-referentiality rather than contribute to the evaluation of literary worth. Robert Yergeau (1956–) comments in the same vein in his polemical work *À tout prix* (1994). Drawing on Bourdieu's and Dubois's theories of artistic and literary institutions, Yergeau, a professor of literature, publisher, and poet, critically engages with the mechanisms of literary prizes in Quebec and explains the different liaisons between journals, publishers, and media by what he calls a "network effect." His main thesis is that literary prizes are subject to the closed-circuit principle that characterizes the literary discourse surrounding the granting of prizes: A book is valuable because it was awarded a prize; and because it has been awarded a prize, it must be an important publication. Within this discursive logic, Yergeau argues, the ideological implication of the selection remains unquestioned. Yet it is of course always interesting to ask when a certain author was awarded a certain prize — the awarding of distinctions is also a question of the transparency of criteria, jury members, ideological implications, and sociocultural premises.

The most prestigious literary prize in Canada is unquestionably the Governor General's Award, comparable to the Prix Goncourt in France and the Booker and Pulitzer Prizes in Great Britain and the United States. The Governor General's Award, given annually in the categories of fiction, poetry, nonfiction, children's literature (text and illustration), and translation (in both official national languages), is awarded under the patronage of the Canada Council for the Arts. As for Quebec literary awards, there are too many to list them all. The Prix Athanase-David, conferred for the first time in 1922 in a literary and scholarly competition, represented an important step in cultural development: Since 1967 it is awarded for a Quebec author's entire oeuvre, marking Quebec's highest literary distinction. In 1993 the organizers of the Salon du livre de Québec, together with the Association des librairies du Québec, decided to honor the best novel of the year with the Prix des libraries du Québec. The Prix Jean-Éthier Blais was awarded for the first time in 1997 in honor of the former McGill professor and literary critic of *Le Devoir*. It awards the author of a work of literary scholarship published in Quebec. The children's literature category has its own award, the Prix Cécile-Gagnon, named for the children's book author Cécile Gagnon and awarded since 1997 by the Association des écrivaines et écrivains québécois pour la jeunesse (AEQJ).

The question of literary awards reverts to the quote above by Catherine Mavrikakis. How to explain such hyperbole with regard to literary prizes, if not by the paucity of French-Canadian and Quebec literature from the early beginning until the end of the twentieth century? The lacuna in Quebec literature and literary studies was to be filled not only by a boom in creation and creativity, but also by concerted efforts in building a foundation that, in the long run, would safeguard once and for all the institutionalization of literature.

## Conclusion

Quebec literature has now firmly established itself on native grounds: For instance, one of the most prestigious Quebec publishers, Boréal, published the *Histoire de la littérature québécoise* in summer 2007, the first comprehensive history of Quebec literature in forty years, a synthesis of about five hundred years of literary works, contexts, and authors. But signs of success and recognition also come from outside, as the present international undertaking demonstrates. The Book Fair in Guadalajara, Mexico, which took place in 2003 and highlighted Quebec literature and culture at the beginning of the new millennium, is another striking example of the symbolic value of Quebec writers and artists abroad. Media reports agreed that the presence of official representatives of the government, publishers, authors, and creators was a huge success for Quebec literature and the business of literature. At the same time it was a continuation of Quebec's presence at the Paris Book Fair in the spring of 2002, where Quebec literature was also featured. Does the official recognition of this literature at home and abroad indicate that the intensive institutionalization has finally reached its apogee? Is it possible that at the beginning of the twenty-first century the literary institution as such and its constituent parts must be conceptualized anew? These questions, like others connected with the topic of the institutionalization of Quebec literature, suggest that the view from outside is likely to be quite different from the view from within.

# Further Reading

## I. Beginnings

### Aboriginal Oral Traditions

Allen, Paula Gunn. "The Sacred Hoop: A Contemporary Perspective." In *Studies in American Indian Literature: Critical Essays and Course Designs*, ed. Paula Gunn Allen. New York: MLA, 1983. 3–22.

Baker, Marie Annharte. "Medicine Lines: The Doctoring of Story and Self." *Canadian Woman Studies/Les Cahiers de la Femme* 14.2 (1994): 114–18.

Cruikshank, Julie. "Oral Tradition and Oral History: Reviewing Some Issues." *Canadian Historical Review* 75.3 (1994): 403–18.

Einhorn, Lois J. *The Native American Oral Tradition: Voices of the Spirit and Soul*. Westport, CT: Praeger, 2000.

Gingell, Susan. " 'One Small Medicine': An Interview with Maria Campbell." *Essays on Canadian Writing* 83 (Fall 2004): 188–205.

Jahner, Elaine. "A Critical Approach to American Indian Literature." In *Studies in American Indian Literature: Critical Essays and Course Designs*, ed. Paula Gunn Allen. New York: MLA, 1983. 211–24.

Johnston, Basil. "One Generation from Extinction." In *An Anthology of Canadian Native Literature in English*, ed. Daniel David Moses and Terry Goldie. 2nd ed. Toronto: Oxford University Press, 1998. 99–104.

King, Thomas. *The Truth about Stories: A Native Narrative*. Minneapolis: University of Minnesota Press, 2005.

Kroeber, Karl, ed. *Native American Storytelling: A Reader of Myths and Legends*. Oxford: Blackwell, 2004.

McLeod, Neal. "Coming Home through Stories." *International Journal of Canadian Studies* 18 (1998): 51–66.

Ong, Walter J. *Orality and Literacy: The Technologizing of the Word*. New York: Routledge, 1982.

Petrone, Penny. *Native Literature in Canada: From the Oral Tradition to the Present*. Toronto: Oxford University Press, 1990.

Van Toorn, Penny. "Aboriginal Writing." In *The Cambridge Companion to Canadian Literature*, ed. Eva-Marie Kröller. Cambridge: Cambridge University Press, 2004. 22–48.

Young-Ing, Greg. "An Overview of Aboriginal Literature and Publishing in Canada." *Australian-Canadian Studies* 14.1/2 (1996): 156–71.

## The Whites Arrive: White Writing before Canada, 1000–1600

Blacker, Irwin R., ed. *The Portable Hakluyt's Voyages.* New York: Viking, 1965.

Brebner, John Bartlet. *The Explorers of North America, 1492–1806.* 1933. Rpt. New York: Doubleday, 1955.

Cartier, Jacques. *Relations,* ed. Michel Bideaux. Montreal: Les Presses de l'Université de Montréal, 1986.

———. *The Voyages of Jacques Cartier,* ed. Ramsay Cook. Toronto: University of Toronto Press, 1993.

Davis, John. *The Voyages and Works of John Davis,* ed. Albert Hastings Markham. London: Hakluyt Society, 1880.

Fritze, Ronald H. *New Worlds: The Great Voyages of Discovery 1400–1600.* Stroud: Sutton, 2002.

Hayes, Derek. *Historical Atlas of Canada: Canada's History Illustrated with Original Maps.* Vancouver: University of British Columbia Press, 2002.

Jones, Gwyn. *The Norse Atlantic Saga: Being the Norse Voyages of Discovery and Settlement to Iceland, Greenland, and North America.* 2nd ed. Oxford: Oxford University Press, 1986.

Magnusson, Magnus, and Hermann Pálsson, trans. *The Vinland Sagas: The Norse Discovery of America: Graenlendinga Saga and Eirik's Saga.* Harmondsworth: Penguin, 1965.

McGhee, Robert. *Canada Rediscovered.* Hull: Canadian Museum of Civilisation, 1991.

Quinn, David B., and Neil M. Cheshire, eds. and trans. *The New Found Land of Stephen Parmenius: The Life and Writings of a Hungarian Poet, Drowned on a Voyage from Newfoundland, 1583.* Toronto: University of Toronto Press, 1972.

Severin, Tim. *The Brendan Voyage: Sailing to America in a Leather Boat to Prove the Legend of the Irish Sailor Saints.* 1978. Rpt. New York: Random House, 2000.

*The Voyage of Saint Brendan: Representative Versions of the Legend in English Translation,* ed. W. R. J. Barron and Glyn S. Burgess. Exeter: University of Exeter Press, 2004.

Wallace, Birgitta Linderoth. *Westward Vikings: The Saga of L'Anse aux Meadows.* St. John's: Historic Sites Association of Newfoundland and Labrador, 2006.

Warkentin, Germaine, and Carolyn Podruchny, eds. *Decentring the Renaissance: Canada and Europe in Multidisciplinary Perspective, 1500–1700.* Toronto: University of Toronto Press, 2001.

# II. The Literature of New France, 1604–1760

Berthiaume, Pierre. *L'aventure américaine au XVIIIe siècle: Du voyage à l'écriture.* Ottawa: Les Presses de l'Université d'Ottawa, 1990.

Chinard, Gilbert. *L'exotisme américain dans la littérature française au XVIe et au XVIIe et au XVIIIe siècles.* Paris: Hachette, 1911–1934.

Eccles, William J. *France in America.* New York: Harper and Row, 1972.

Émont, Bernard. *"Les Muses de la Nouvelle-France" de Marc Lescarbot.* Paris: L'Harmattan, 2004.

Frisch, Andrea. *The Invention of the Eyewitness: Witnessing and Testimony in Early Modern France.* Chapel Hill: University of North Carolina, Department of Romance Languages, 2004.

Kennedy, John Hopkins. *Jesuit and Savage in New France.* New Haven: Yale University Press, 1950.

LeBlanc, Léopold. *Écrits de la Nouvelle-France (1534–1760).* Montreal: La Presse, 1978.

Lortie, Jeanne d'Arc, ed. *Textes poétiques du Canada français.* Vol. 1, Montreal: Fides, 1987.

Marion, Séraphin. *Relations des voyageurs français en Nouvelle-France au XVIIe siècle.* Paris: Presses universitaires de France, 1923.

Mathieu, Jacques. *La Nouvelle-France: Les Français en Amérique du Nord, XVIe–XVIIIe siècles.* Quebec: Presses de l'Université Laval et Belin, 1991.

O'Callaghan, Edmund Bailey. *Jesuit Relations of Discoveries and Other Occurrences in Canada and the Northern and Western States of the Union, 1632–1672.* New York: Press of the Historical Society, 1847.

Parkman, Francis. *The Jesuits in North America in the Seventeenth Century.* Boston: Little, Brown and Co., 1867.

Roy, Antoine. *Les lettres, les sciences et les arts au Canada sous le Régime français, essai de contribution à l'histoire de la civilisation canadienne.* Paris: Jouve, 1930.

Roy, Pierre-Georges. *Édition et analyse des "Troubles de l'Église du Canada en 1728, poème heroi-comique composé à l'occasion des funérailles de Mgr de Saint-Vallier."* Lévis: Bulletin des recherches historiques, 1897.

Trudel, Marcel. "La vie intellectuelle." In *Initiation à la Nouvelle-France*, ed. Marcel Trudel. Montreal: Holt, Rinehart & Winston, 1968. 279–93.

# III. The Literature of British Canada, 1763–1867

## English-Canadian Colonial Literature

Bentley, D. M. R. *The Gay/Grey Moose: Essays on the Ecologies and Mythologies of Canadian Poetry, 1690–1990.* Ottawa: University of Ottawa Press, 1992.

Blair, Jennifer, Daniel Coleman, Kate Higginson, and Lorraine York, eds. *ReCalling Early Canada: Reading the Political in Literary and Cultural Production*. Edmonton: University of Alberta Press, 2005.

Davies, Gwendolyn. *Studies in Maritime Literary History*. Fredericton: Acadiensis Press, 1991.

Dean, Misao. *Practising Femininity: Domestic Realism and the Performance of Gender in Early Canadian Fiction*. Toronto: University of Toronto Press, 1998.

Fleming, Patricia Lockhart, Gilles Gallichan, and Yvan Lamonde, eds. *History of the Book in Canada*. Vol. 1: Beginnings to 1840. Toronto: University of Toronto Press, 2004.

Gerson, Carole. *A Purer Taste: The Writing and Reading of Fiction in English in Nineteenth-Century Canada*. Toronto: University of Toronto Press, 1989.

Gerson, Carole, and Gwendolyn Davies, eds. *Canadian Poetry from the Beginnings through the First World War*. Toronto: McClelland & Stewart, 1994.

Glickman, Susan. *The Picturesque and the Sublime: A Poetics of the Canadian Landscape*. Montreal and Kingston: McGill-Queen's University Press, 1998.

Henderson, Jennifer. *Settler Feminism and Race Making in Canada*. Toronto: University of Toronto Press, 2003.

Klinck, Carl F., ed. *Literary History of Canada: Canadian Literature in English*. Toronto: University of Toronto Press, 1965.

Lamonde, Yvan, Patricia Lockhart Fleming, and Fiona A. Black, eds. *History of the Book in Canada*. Vol. 2: 1840–1918. Toronto: University of Toronto Press, 2005.

MacMillan, Carrie, Lorraine McMullen, and Elizabeth Waterston. *Silenced Sextet: Six Nineteenth-Century Canadian Women Novelists*. Montreal and Kingston: McGill-Queen's University Press, 1992.

McMullen, Lorraine, ed. *Re(Dis)Covering Our Foremothers: Nineteenth-Century Canadian Women Writers*. Ottawa: University of Ottawa Press, 1990.

Vincent, Thomas B. *Narrative Verse Satire in Maritime Canada: 1779–1814*. Ottawa: Tecumseh Press, 1978.

Warkentin, Germaine, ed. *Canadian Exploration Literature*. Toronto: Oxford University Press, 1993.

## French-Canadian Colonial Literature under the Union Jack

Beaulieu, André, and Jean Hamelin. *La presse québécoise des origines à nos jours*. 10 vols. Quebec: Les Presses de l'Université Laval, 1973–1990.

Bouchard, Gérard. *Genèse des nations et cultures du Nouveau Monde: Essai d'histoire comparée*. Montreal: Boréal, 2001.

*Cahiers de l'ALAQ* [Archéologie du littéraire au Québec], 1993–.

Cambron, Micheline, ed. *Le journal "Le Canadien": Littérature, espace public et utopie, 1836–1845*. Montreal: Fides, 1999.

Dionne, René. *La patrie littéraire, 1760–1895*. Ottawa: La Presse, 1978.

*Études françaises* 30.3 (1994/95): *François-Xavier Garneau et son Histoire*.

Gagnon, Serge. *Le Québec et ses historiens de 1840 à 1920: La Nouvelle-France de Garneau à Groulx*. Quebec: Presses de l'Université Laval, 1978.

Huston, James. *Le répertoire national*. 4 vols. 2nd ed. Montreal: J. M. Valois & Cie, 1893 [1848].

Lemire, Maurice, ed. *Dictionnaire des oeuvres littéraires du Québec*. Vol. 1, Montreal: Fides, 1978.

———. *Les grands thèmes nationalistes du roman historique canadien-français*. Quebec: Les Presses de l'Université Laval, 1970.

———. *La vie littéraire au Québec*. Vols. 1–4, Sainte-Foy: Les Presses de l'Université Laval, 1991–1999.

Lord, Michel. *En quête du roman gothique québécois 1837–1860: Tradition littéraire et imaginaire romanesque*. Montreal: Nuit Blanche, 1994.

Monière, Denis. *Le développement des idéologies au Québec des origines à nos jours*. Montreal: Québec-Amérique, 1977.

Trudel, Marcel. *L'influence de Voltaire au Canada*. 2 vols. Montreal: Les Publications de l'Université Laval, 1945.

Vachon, G.-André, ed. *Une littérature de combat 1778–1810: Les débuts du journalisme canadien-français*. Montreal: Les Presses de l'Université de Montréal, 1969.

# IV. From the Dominion to the Territorial Completion of the Nation, 1867–1918

## English-Canadian Literature, 1867–1918: The Making of a Nation

Ballstadt, Carl, ed. *The Search for English-Canadian Literature*. Toronto: University of Toronto Press, 1975.

Bentley, D. M. R. *The Confederation Group of Canadian Poets, 1880–1897*. Toronto: University of Toronto Press, 2004.

Berger, Carl. *The Sense of Power: Studies in the Ideas of Canadian Imperialism 1867–1914*. Toronto: University of Toronto Press, 1970.

Blair, Jennifer, Daniel Coleman, Kate Higginson, and Lorraine York, eds. *ReCalling Early Canada: Reading the Political in Literary and Cultural Production*. Edmonton: University of Alberta Press, 2005.

Brown, E. K. *On Canadian Poetry*. Ottawa: Tecumseh Press, 1973 [1943, rev. ed. 1944].

Coleman, Daniel. *White Civility: The Literary Project of English Canada*. Toronto: University of Toronto Press, 2006.

Daymond, Douglas, and Leslie Monkman, eds. *Towards a Canadian Literature: Essays, Editorials, and Manifestos*. Vol. 1, Ottawa: Tecumseh Press, 1984.

Dean, Misao, ed. *Early Canadian Short Stories: Short Stories in English before World War I*. Ottawa: Tecumseh Press, 2000.

Gerson, Carole. *A Purer Taste: The Writing and Reading of Fiction in Nineteenth-Century Canada*. Toronto: University of Toronto Press, 1989.

Glickman, Susan. *The Picturesque and the Sublime: A Poetics of the Canadian Landscape*. Montreal and Kingston: McGill-Queen's University Press, 1998.

Kertzer, Jonathan. *Worrying the Nation: Imagining a National Literature in English Canada*. Toronto: University of Toronto Press, 1998.

Mount, Nick. *When Canadian Literature Moved to New York*. Toronto: University of Toronto Press, 2005.

Pacey, Desmond. *Ten Canadian Poets: A Group of Biographical and Critical Essays*. Toronto: Ryerson, 1958.

Parker, George. *The Beginnings of the Book Trade in Canada*. Toronto: University of Toronto Press, 1985.

Ware, Tracy, ed. *A Northern Romanticism: Poets of the Confederation*. Ottawa: Tecumseh Press, 2000.

## French-Canadian Literature from National Solidarity to the École littéraire de Montréal

Beaudoin, Réjean. *Naissance d'une littérature: Essai sur le messianisme et les débuts de la littérature canadienne-française (1850–1890)*. Montreal: Fides, 1989.

Cohen, Matt, and Wayne Grady, eds. *The Quebec Anthology 1830–1990*. Ottawa: University of Ottawa Press, 1996.

De Grandpré, Pierre. *Histoire de la littérature française du Québec*. Vol. 1, Montreal: Beauchemin, 1967; vol. 2, Montreal: Beauchemin, 1968.

Grisé, Yolande, ed. *La poésie québécoise avant Nelligan*. Saint-Laurent: Fides, 1998.

Hébert, Pierre. *Censure et littérature au Québec: Le livre crucifié (1625–1919)*. Montreal: Fides, 1997.

Lemire, Maurice, ed. *Dictionnaire des oeuvres littéraires du Québec*. Vol. 1, Montreal: Fides, 1978; vol. 2, Montreal: Fides, 1980.

———. *Formation de l'imaginaire littéraire québécois (1764–1867)*. Montreal: L'Hexagone, 1993.

———. *Les grands thèmes nationalistes du roman historique canadien-français.* Quebec: Les Presses de l'Université Laval, 1970.

———. *La littérature québécoise en projet au milieu du XIXe siècle.* Montreal: Fides, 1994.

———, ed. *Le romantisme au Canada.* Quebec: Nuit blanche, 1993.

Monière, Denis. *Le développement des idéologies au Québec des origines à nos jours.* Montreal: Québec-Amérique, 1977.

Tougas, Gérard. *History of French-Canadian Literature.* Westport, CT: Greenwood Press, 1976.

Warwick, Jack. *The Long Journey: Literary Themes of French Canada.* Toronto: University of Toronto Press, 1968.

Weiss, Jonathan M., and Jane Moss. *French Canadian Literature.* Washington, DC: Association for Canadian Studies in the United States, 1996.

Wyczynski, Paul, et al., eds. *Archives des lettres canadiennes.* Vols. 1–5, Montreal: Fides, 1961–1976.

# V. The Modern Period, 1918–1967

## Politics and Literature between Nationalism and Internationalism

Blodgett, E. D. *Five-part Invention: A History of Literary History in Canada.* Toronto: University of Toronto Press, 2003.

Corse, Sarah. *Nationalism and Literature: The Politics of Culture in Canada and the United States.* Cambridge: Cambridge University Press, 1997.

Dudek, Louis, and Michael Gnarowski, eds. *The Making of Modern Poetry in Canada: Essential Articles on Contemporary Canadian Poetry in English.* Toronto: Ryerson, 1970 [1967].

Irvine, Dean, ed. *The Canadian Modernists Meet.* Reappraisals: Canadian Writers Series 29. Ottawa: University of Ottawa Press, 2005.

Knister, Raymond. "Canadian Literati." *Journal of Canadian Fiction* 4.2 (1975): 160–68.

———. "Canadian Literature: A General Impression." *Journal of Canadian Fiction* 4.2 (1975): 169–74.

———. "The Canadian Short Story." *The Canadian Bookman* 5 (August 1923): 203–4.

———. "Introduction: The Canadian Short Story." In *Canadian Short Stories*, ed. and introd. Raymond Knister. Toronto: Macmillan, 1928; repr. in Short Story Index Reprint Series. Freeport: Books for Libraries Press, 1971. xi–xix.

Moir, John S., and D. M. L. Farr. *The Canadian Experience.* Toronto: Ryerson, 1969.

Nelles, H. V. *A Little History of Canada*. Oxford: Oxford University Press, 2004.

Norris, Ken. *The Little Magazine in Canada 1925–80: Its Role in the Development of Modernism and Post-Modernism in Canadian Poetry*. Toronto: ECW Press, 1984.

Pacey, Desmond. *Creative Writing in Canada: A Short History of English-Canadian Literature*. Westport, CT: Greenwood, 1976.

Smith, A. J. M. *Towards a View of Canadian Letters: Selected Critical Essays 1928–1971*. Vancouver: University of British Columbia Press, 1973.

Tippett, Maria. *Making Culture: English-Canadian Institutions and the Arts before the Massey Commission*. Toronto: University of Toronto Press, 1990.

Willmott, Glenn. *Unreal Country: Modernity in the Canadian Novel in English*. Montreal and Kingston: McGill-Queen's University Press, 2002.

## English-Canadian Poetry, 1920–1960

Atwood, Margaret, ed. *The New Oxford Book of Canadian Verse*. Oxford: Oxford University Press, 1982.

Doyle, James. *Progressive Heritage: The Evolution of a Politically Radical Literary Tradition in Canada*. Waterloo: Wilfrid Laurier University Press, 2002.

Dudek, Louis, and Michael Gnarowski, eds. *The Making of Modern Poetry in Canada*. Toronto: Ryerson, 1967.

Irvine, Dean, ed. *The Canadian Modernists Meet*. Reappraisals: Canadian Writers Series 29. Ottawa: University of Ottawa Press, 2005.

Kelly, Peggy. "Politics, Gender, and *New Provinces*: Dorothy Livesay and F. R. Scott." *Canadian Poetry: Studies, Documents, Reviews* 53 (2003): 54–70.

Livesay, Dorothy. "The Documentary Poem: A Canadian Genre." In *Contexts of Canadian Criticism*, ed. Eli Mandel. Chicago: University of Chicago Press, 1971. 267–81.

———. *Right Hand, Left Hand: A True Life of the Thirties: Paris, Toronto, Montreal, the West and Vancouver: Love, Politics, the Depression and Feminism*. Erin: Press Porcépic, 1977.

Rao, T. Nageswara. *Inviolable Air: Canadian Poetic Modernism in Perspective*. New Delhi: South Asia Books, 1994.

Sullivan, Rosemary, ed. *Poetry by Canadian Women*. Toronto: Oxford University Press, 1989.

Trehearne, Brian. *Aestheticism and the Canadian Modernists*. Montreal and Kingston: McGill-Queen's University Press, 1989.

———. *The Montreal Forties: Modernist Poetry in Transition*. Toronto: University of Toronto Press, 1999.

## The English-Canadian Novel and the Displacement of the Romance

Dvorak, Marta. *Ernest Buckler: Rediscovery and Reassessment.* Waterloo: Wilfrid Laurier University Press, 2001.

———. "Of Cows and Configurations in Emily Carr's *The Book of Small.*" In *Tropes and Territories: Short Fiction, Postcolonial Readings, Canadian Writings in Context*, ed. Marta Dvorak and W. H. New. Montreal and Kingston: McGill-Queen's University Press, 2007. 134–54.

———, and W. H. New, eds. *Tropes and Territories: Short Fiction, Postcolonial Readings, Canadian Writings in Context.* Montreal and Kingston: McGill-Queen's University Press, 2007.

Frye, Northrop. *The Bush Garden: Essays on the Canadian Imagination*, Toronto: Anansi, 1971.

———. *The Secular Scripture: A Study of the Structure of Romance.* Cambridge, MA: Harvard University Press, 1976.

Keahey, Deborah Lou. *Making It Home: Place in Canadian Prairie Literature.* Winnipeg: University of Manitoba Press, 1998.

Keith, W. J. *Canadian Literature in English.* London: Longman, 1985.

Kerr, D., and D. W. Holdsworth, eds. *The Historical Atlas of Canada.* Vol. 3, Toronto: University of Toronto Press, 1990.

Klinck, Carl F., ed. *Literary History of Canada: Canadian Literature in English.* 3 vols. 2nd ed. Toronto: University of Toronto Press, 1976.

Kreisel, Henry. "The Prairie: A State of Mind." In *Trace: Prairie Writers on Writing*, ed. Birk Sproxton. Winnipeg: Turnstone, 1986.

Kröller, Eva-Marie, ed. *The Cambridge Companion to Canadian Literature.* Cambridge: Cambridge University Press, 2004.

New, W. H., ed. *Encyclopedia of Literature in Canada.* Toronto: University of Toronto Press, 2002.

Omhovère, Claire. *Sensing Space: The Poetics of Geography in Contemporary English-Canadian Writing.* Bern: Peter Lang, 2007.

Ricou, Laurie. *Vertical Man/Horizontal World: Man and Nature in Canadian Prairie Fiction.* Vancouver: University of British Columbia Press, 1973.

Riegel, Christian, and Herb Wyile, eds. *A Sense of Place: Re-Evaluating Regionalism in Canadian and American Writing.* Edmonton: University of Alberta Press, 1977.

## The Modernist English-Canadian Short Story

Arnason, David, ed. *Journal of Canadian Fiction* 4.2 (1975). Special Knister edition.

Bader, Rudolf. "Frederick Philip Grove and Naturalism Reconsidered." In *Gaining Ground: European Critics on Canadian Literature*, ed. Robert Kroetsch and Reingard M. Nischik. Edmonton: NeWest, 1985. 222–33.

Conron, Brandon. "Morley Callaghan as Short Story Writer." *The Journal of Commonwealth Literature* 3 (July 1967): 58–75.

Gadpaille, Michelle. *The Canadian Short Story.* Toronto: Oxford University Press, 1988.

Givens, Imogen. "Raymond Knister — Man or Myth?" *Essays on Canadian Writing* 16 (1979–80): 5–19.

Grove, Frederick Philip. *Tales from the Margin: The Selected Stories of Frederick Philip Grove,* ed. Desmond Pacey. Toronto and New York: Ryerson Press and McGraw-Hill of Canada, 1971.

Knister, Raymond. "The Canadian Short Story." *The Canadian Bookman* 5 (August 1923): 203–4; repr. in Knister, *The First Day of Spring: Stories and Other Prose.* Toronto: University of Toronto Press, 1976. 388–92.

———. "Democracy and the Short Story." *Journal of Canadian Fiction* 4.2 (1975): 146–48.

Legge, Valerie. "Sheila Watson's 'Antigone': Anguished Rituals and Public Disturbances." *Studies in Canadian Literature* 17.2 (1992): 28–46.

May, Charles E., ed. *Critical Survey of Short Fiction.* Vols. 1–7, 2nd rev. ed. Pasadena: Salem Press, 2001.

McMullen, Lorraine. *Sinclair Ross.* Boston: Twayne, 1979.

Neuman, Shirley. "Sheila Watson." In *Profiles in Canadian Literature,* ed. Jeffrey M. Heath. Toronto: Dundurn, 1982. 45–52.

Nischik, Reingard M., ed. *The Canadian Short Story: Interpretations.* Rochester, NY: Camden House, 2007.

Pacey, Desmond. *Ethel Wilson.* New York: Twayne, 1967.

Stuewe, Paul. "Hugh Garner (1913–1973)." In *Canadian Writers and Their Works,* ed. Robert Lecker, Jack David, and Ellen Quigley. Fiction series, vol. 6. Toronto: ECW Press, 1985. 81–127.

### Early English-Canadian Theater and Drama, 1918–1967

Benson, Eugene, and L. W. Conolly. *English-Canadian Theatre.* Toronto: Oxford University Press, 1987.

———, eds. *The Oxford Companion to Canadian Theatre.* Toronto: Oxford University Press, 1989.

Fink, Howard, and John Jackson, eds. *All the Bright Company: Radio Drama Produced by Andrew Allan.* Kingston and Toronto: Quarry Press and CBC Enterprises, 1987.

Lee, Betty. *Love and Whisky: The Story of the Dominion Drama Festival.* Toronto: McClelland & Stewart, 1973.

Massey, Vincent, ed. *Canadian Plays from Hart House Theatre.* 2 vols. Toronto: Macmillan, 1926.

Moore, Mavor. *Reinventing Myself: Memoirs.* Toronto: Stoddart, 1994.

Nash, Knowlton. *The Microphone Wars: A History of Triumph and Betrayal at the CBC.* Toronto: McClelland & Stewart, 1994.

Patterson, Tom, and Allan Gould. *First Stage: The Making of the Stratford Festival.* Toronto: McClelland & Stewart, 1987.

*Report: Royal Commission on National Development in the Arts, Letters and Sciences, 1949–1951.* Ottawa: Edmond Cloutier, 1951.

Rubin, Don, ed. *Canadian Theatre History: Selected Readings.* Toronto: Copp Clark, 1996.

Ryan, Toby Gordon. *Stage Left: Canadian Theatre in the Thirties.* Toronto: CTR Publications, 1981.

Wagner, Anton, ed. *The Developing Mosaic: English-Canadian Drama to Mid-Century.* Canada's Lost Plays, vol. 3. Toronto: CTR Publications, 1980.

Wasserman, Jerry, ed. *Modern Canadian Plays.* Vol. 1, 4th ed. Vancouver: Talonbooks, 2000.

## French Canada from the First World War to 1967: Historical Overview

Hamelin, Jean, and Jean Provencher. *Brève histoire du Québec.* 3rd ed. Montreal: Boréal, 1987.

Linteau, Paul-André. *Brève histoire de Montréal.* Montreal: Boréal, 1992.

———. *Histoire du Canada.* Paris: Presses universitaires de France, 1994.

Tétu de Labsade, Françoise. *Le Québec, un pays, une culture.* Montreal: Boréal, 1990.

## French-Canadian Poetry up to the 1960s

Beausoleil, Claude. *Le motif de l'identité dans la poésie québécoise 1830–1995.* Montreal: Estuaire, 1996.

Blais, Jacques. *Parmi les hasards: Dix études sur la poésie québécoise moderne.* Montreal: Nota bene, 2001.

Cloutier, Cécile, Michel Lord, and Ben-Z. Shek, eds. *Miron ou La marche à l'amour.* Montreal: L'Hexagone, 2002.

Dumont, François. *La poésie québécoise.* Montreal: Boréal, 1999.

———. *Usages de la poésie: Le discours des poètes québécois sur la fonction de la poésie (1945–1970).* Sainte-Foy: Les Presses de l'Université Laval, 1993.

Filteau, Claude. *Poétiques de la modernité 1895–1948.* Montreal: L'Hexagone, 1994.

Gay, Paul. *Notre poésie: Panorama littéraire du Canada français.* Montreal: Hurtubise HMH, 1974.

Giguère, Richard. *Exil, révolte et dissidence: Étude comparée des poésies québécoise et canadienne (1925–1955).* Sainte-Foy: Les Presses de l'Université Laval, 1984.

Gingras, Chantale, and Victor Barbeau. *Un réseau d'influences littéraires.* Montreal: L'Hexagone, 2001.

Lemire, Maurice, ed. *Dictionnaire des oeuvres littéraires du Québec.* Vol. 2: *1900–1939*, Montreal: Fides, 1987; vol. 3: *1940–1959*, Montreal: Fides, 1982; vol. 4: *1960–1969*, Montreal: Fides, 1984.

Mailhot, Laurent, and Pierre Nepveu, eds. *La poésie québécoise des origines à nos jours: Anthologie.* Montreal: L'Hexagone, 1980.

Popovic, Pierre. *La contradiction du poème: Poésie et discours social au Québec de 1948 à 1953.* Candiac: Balzac, 1992.

Royer, Jean. *Introduction à la poésie québécoise: Les poètes et les oeuvres des origines à nos jours.* Quebec: BQ, 1992.

## The French-Canadian Novel between Tradition and Modernism

Allard, Jacques. *Le roman du Québec: Histoire, perspectives, lectures.* Montreal: Québec-Amérique, 2000.

Arguin, Maurice. *Le roman québécois de 1944 à 1965: Symptômes du colonialisme et signe de libération.* Montreal: L'Hexagone, 1989.

Beaudoin, Réjean. *Le roman québécois.* Montreal: Boréal, 1991.

Boivin, Aurélien. *Pour une lecture du roman québécois: De Maria Chapdelaine à Volkswagen blues.* Quebec: Nuit blanche, 1996.

Gallays, François, Sylvain Simard, and Robert Vigneault, eds. *Le roman contemporain au Québec (1960–1985).* Montreal: Fides, 1992.

Gilbert Lewis, Paula. *Traditionalism, Nationalism and Feminism: Women Writers of Quebec.* Westport, CT: Greenwood, 1985.

Green, Mary Jean. *Women and Narrative Identity: Rewriting the Quebec National Text.* Montreal and Kingston: McGill-Queen's University Press, 2001.

Harel, Simon. *Le voleur de parcours: Identité et cosmopolitisme dans la littérature du Québec.* Montreal: XYZ, 1989.

Heidenreich, Rosmarin. *The Postwar Novel in Canada: Narrative Patterns and Reader Response.* Waterloo: Wilfrid Laurier University Press, 1989.

Kwaterko, Józef. *Le roman québécois de 1960 à 1975: Idéologie et représentation littéraire.* Montreal: XYZ, 1989.

Mailhot, Laurent. *La littérature québécoise.* Montreal: L'Hexagone, 1997.

Pont-Humbert, Catherine. *Littérature du Québec.* Paris: Nathan, 1998.

Proulx, Bernard. *Le roman du territoire.* Montreal: UQAM, 1987.

Saint-Martin, Lori, ed. *L'autre lecture: La critique au féminin et les textes québécois.* Vol. 1, Montreal: XYZ, 1992.

Smart, Patricia. *Écrire dans la maison du père: L'émergence du féminin dans la tradition littéraire du Québec.* 2nd ed. Montreal: Québec-Amérique, 1990.

## The French-Canadian Short Story

Carpentier, André. "La nouvelle terroiriste au Québec, 1914–1940: Un imaginaire et une esthétique entravés par l'exaltation de l'idéologie de conservation." In *La nouvelle québécoise au XX^e siècle: De la tradition à l'innovation*, ed. Michel Lord and André Carpentier. Quebec: Nuit blanche, 1997. 17–31.

Demers, Jeanne, and Lise Gauvin. "Contes et nouvelles du Québec." *Stanford French Review* 4.1/2 (1982): 223–41.

Lord, Michel. "D'Antée à Protée: Des glissements de la forme narrative brève au Québec de 1940 à 1990." In *La nouvelle québécoise au XX^e siècle: De la tradition à l'innovation*, ed. Michel Lord and André Carpentier. Quebec: Nuit blanche, 1997. 107–28.

———. "La fragmentation infinie des (im)possibles: La nouvelle fantastiques et de science-fiction québécoise des origines à 1985." In *La nouvelle au Québec*, ed. François Gallays and Robert Vignault. Montreal: Fides, 1996. 53–74.

Lord, Michel, and André Carpentier, eds. *La nouvelle québécoise au XX^e siècle: De la tradition à l'innovation*. Quebec: Nuit blanche, 1997.

Sénécal, Joseph-André. "La nouvelle québécoise avant 1940." In *La nouvelle au Québec*, ed. François Gallays and Robert Vignault. Montreal: Fides, 1996. 37–52.

Telecky, Richard, ed. *The Oxford Book of French-Canadian Short Stories*. Toronto: Oxford University Press, 1983.

Thérrien, Josée. "Bibliographie chronologique de la nouvelle au Québec (1900–1985)." In *La nouvelle au Québec*, ed. François Gallays and Robert Vignault. Montreal: Fides, 1996. 197–264.

Whitfield, Agnès, and Jacques Cotnam, eds. *La nouvelle: Écriture(s) et lecture(s)*. Montreal and Toronto: XYZ and Éditions du GREF, 1993.

## French-Canadian Drama from the 1930s to the Révolution tranquille

Beauchamp, Hélène, Bernard Julien, and Paul Wyczinski, eds. *Le théâtre canadien-français: Évolution — témoignages — bibliographie*. Montreal: Fides, 1976.

Donohoe, Joseph, and Jonathan M. Weiss, eds. *Essays on Modern Quebec Theater*. East Lansing: Michigan State University Press, 1995.

Duchesnay, Lorraine. *Vingt-cinq ans de dramatiques à la télévision de Radio-Canada*. Montreal: Société Radio-Canada, 1978.

Duval, Étienne. *Le jeu de l'histoire et de la société dans le théâtre québécois: 1900–1950*. Trois-Rivières: PUQTR, Théâtre d'hier et d'aujourd'hui, 1983.

Gobin, Pierre. *Le fou et ses doubles: Figures de la dramaturgie québécoise*. Montreal: Les Presses de l'Université de Montreal, 1978.

Godin, Jean-Cléo, and Laurent Mailhot. *Théâtre québécois*. 2 vols. La Salle: Hurtubise HMH, 1988.

Hamblet, Edwin Clifford. *Marcel Dubé and French Canadian Drama.* New York: Exposition Press, 1970.

Houlé, Léopold. *L'histoire du théâtre au Canada.* Montreal: Fides, 1945.

Laflamme, Jean, and Rémi Tourangeau. *L'église et le théâtre au Québec.* Montreal: Fides, 1979.

Lavoie, Pierre. *Pour suivre le théâtre au Québec: Les ressources documentaires.* Quebec: Institut québécois de recherche sur la culture, 1985.

Legris, Renée, Jean-Marc Larru, André-G. Bourassa, and Gilbert David. *Le théâtre au Québec 1825–1980: Repères et perspectives.* Montreal: VLB et al., 1988.

Mailhot, Laurent, and Doris-Michel Montpetit, eds. *Monologues québécois: 1890–1980.* Montreal: Leméac, 1980.

Nardocchio, Elaine F. *Theatre and Politics in Modern Quebec.* Edmonton: University of Alberta Press, 1986.

Rinfret, Édouard-G. *Le théâtre canadien d'expression française: Répertoire analytique des origines à nos jour.* 4 vols. Montreal: Leméac, 1975–1978.

Weiss, Jonathan M. *French Canadian Theatre.* Boston: Twayne, 1986.

# VI. Literature from 1967 to the Present

## Sociopolitical and Cultural Developments from 1967 to the Present

Angus, Ian. *Border Within: National Identity, Cultural Plurality, and Wilderness.* Montreal and Kingston: McGill-Queen's University Press, 1997.

Davey, Frank. *Post-National Arguments: The Politics of the Anglophone-Canadian Novel since 1967.* Toronto: University of Toronto Press, 1993.

Filewood, Alan. *Performing Canada: The Nation Enacted in the Imagined Theatre.* Kamloops, BC: Textual Studies in Canada, 2002.

Francis, Daniel. *National Dreams: Myth, Memory, and Canadian History.* Vancouver: Arsenal Pulp Press, 1997.

Grace, Sherrill. *Canada and the Idea of North.* Montreal and Kingston: McGill-Queen's University Press, 2007 [2002].

Grant, George. *Lament for a Nation: The Defeat of Canadian Nationalism.* Montreal and Kingston: McGill-Queen's University Press, 2005 [1965].

New, William, ed. *Encyclopedia of Literature in Canada.* Toronto: University of Toronto Press, 2002.

———. *Land Sliding: Imagining Space, Presence, and Power in Canadian Writing.* Toronto: University of Toronto Press, 1997.

Rak, Julie, ed. *Autobiography in Canada.* Waterloo: Wilfrid Laurier University Press, 2005.

Wasserman, Jerry, ed. *Modern Canadian Plays.* 2 vols. 4th ed. Vancouver: Talonbooks, 2000–2001.

Wright, Robert. *Virtual Sovereignty: Nationalism, Culture and the Canadian Question.* Toronto: Canadian Scholars' Press, 2004.

Wyile, Herb. *Speculative Fictions: Contemporary Canadian Novelists and the Writing of History.* Montreal and Kingston: McGill-Queen's University Press, 2002.

## English-Canadian Literary Theory and Literary Criticism

Atwood, Margaret. *Survival: A Thematic Guide to Canadian Literature.* Toronto: Anansi, 1972.

Bennett, Donna. "Nation and Its Discontents: Atwood's *Survival* and after." In *Canadística canaria (1991–2000): Ensayos literarios anglocanadienses,* ed. Juan Ignacio Oliva et al. La Laguna: Universidad de La Laguna, 2002. 13–29.

Davey, Frank. *Surviving the Paraphrase.* Winnipeg, Manitoba: Turnstone, 1983.

Edwards, Justin D., and Douglas Ivision, eds. *Downtown Canada: Writing Canadian Cities.* Toronto: University of Toronto Press, 2005.

Frye, Northrop. *The Bush Garden: Essays on the Canadian Imagination.* Toronto: Anansi, 1971.

Grace, Sherrill. *Canada and the Idea of North.* Montreal and Kingston: McGill-Queen's University Press, 2002.

Hutcheon, Linda. *The Canadian Postmodern: A Study of Contemporary English-Canadian Fiction.* Toronto: Oxford University Press, 1988.

Kroetsch, Robert, and Reingard M. Nischik, eds. *Gaining Ground: European Critics on Canadian Literature.* Edmonton: NeWest, 1985.

Lecker, Robert. *Making It Real: The Canonization of English-Canadian Literature.* Concord, ON: Anansi, 1995.

Mandel, Eli. *Contexts of Canadian Criticism.* Chicago: University of Chicago Press, 1971.

McLuhan, Herbert Marshall. "Canada: The Borderline Case." In *The Canadian Imagination: Dimensions of a Literary Culture,* ed. David Staines. Cambridge, MA: Harvard University Press, 1977. 226–48.

Neuman, Shirley, and Smaro Kamboureli, eds. *A Mazing Space: Writing Canadian Women Writing.* Edmonton: Longspoon and NeWest, 1986.

New, William H. *Borderlands: How We Talk about Canada.* Vancouver: University of British Columbia Press, 1998.

———, ed. *Encyclopedia of Literature in Canada.* Toronto: University of Toronto Press, 2002.

Wiebe, Rudy. *Playing Dead: A Contemplation Concerning the Arctic.* Edmonton: NeWest, 1989.

## The English-Canadian Novel from Modernism to Postmodernism

Atwood, Margaret. *Survival: A Thematic Guide to Canadian Literature.* Toronto: Anansi, 1972.

Heidenreich, Rosmarin. *The Postwar Novel in Canada: Narrative Patterns and Reader Response.* Waterloo: Wilfrid Laurier University Press, 1989.

Holzamer, Astrid H. "Zur Rezeption kanadischer Literatur in Deutschland: Vom garstigen Haarball zum süßen Zimtschäler." In *Reflections of Canada: The Reception of Canadian Literature in Germany,* ed. Martin Kuester and Andrea Wolff. Marburg: Universitätsbibliothek, 2000. 10–26.

Howells, Coral Ann, ed. *The Cambridge Companion to Margaret Atwood.* Cambridge: Cambridge University Press, 2006.

Kröller, Eva-Marie, ed. *The Cambridge Companion to Canadian Literature.* Cambridge: Cambridge University Press, 2004.

Kroetsch, Robert. "A Canadian Issue." *Boundary 2* 3.1 (1974): 1.

MacLennan, Hugh. "Boy Meets Girl in Winnipeg and Who Cares?" (1958). In *Hugh MacLennan's Best,* ed. Douglas M. Gibson. Toronto: McClelland and Stewart, 1991. 169.

Moss, John. *A Reader's Guide to the Canadian Novel.* Toronto: McClelland & Stewart, 1981.

New, William H., ed. *A History of Canadian Literature.* 2nd ed. Montreal and Kingston: McGill-Queen's University Press, 2003.

Nischik, Reingard M., ed. *Margaret Atwood: Works and Impact.* Rochester, NY: Camden House, 2000.

Pache, Walter. "Literatur Kanadas: Die andere nordamerikanische Literatur." In *Amerikanische Literaturgeschichte,* ed. Hubert Zapf. 1st ed. Stuttgart: Metzler, 1997. 520–60.

Staines, David. *Beyond the Provinces: Literary Canada at Century's End.* Toronto: University of Toronto Press, 1995.

Vautier, Marie. *New World Myth: Postmodernism and Postcolonialism in Canadian Fiction.* Montreal and Kingston: McGill-Queen's University Press, 1998.

Williams, David. *Confessional Fictions: A Portrait of the Artist in the Canadian Novel.* Toronto: University of Toronto Press, 1991.

Wyile, Herb. *Speculative Fictions: Contemporary Canadian Novelists and the Writing of History.* Montreal and Kingston: McGill-Queen's University Press, 2002.

## The English-Canadian Short Story since 1967: Between (Post)Modernism and (Neo)Realism

Davey, Frank. "Impressionable Realism: The Stories of Clark Blaise." *Open Letter* 3 (1976): 65–74.

Davis, Rocío G. *Transcultural Reinventions: Asian American and Asian Canadian Short-story Cycles.* Toronto: TSAR, 2001.

Gadpaille, Michelle. *The Canadian Short Story.* Toronto: Oxford University Press, 1988.

Hancock, Geoff, ed. *Illusion One: Fables, Fantasies and Metafictions.* Toronto: Aya Press, 1983.

Kruk, Laurie. *The Voice Is the Story: Conversations with Canadian Writers of Short Fictions.* Oakville, ON: Mosaic, 2003.

Nischik, Reingard M., ed. *American and Canadian Short Short Stories.* Paderborn: Schöningh, 1994.

———. *The Canadian Short Story: Interpretations.* Rochester, NY: Camden House, 2007.

———. "The Short Story in Canada: Metcalf and Others Making It New." *Die Neueren Sprachen* 86.3/4 (1987): 232–46.

Owen, Ivon, and Morris Wolfe, eds. *The Best Modern Canadian Short Stories.* Edmonton: Hurtig, 1978.

Rooke, Constance. "Fear of the Open Heart." In *A Mazing Space: Writing Canadian Women Writing,* ed. Shirley Neuman and Smaro Kamboureli. Edmonton: Longspoon and NeWest, 1986. 256–69.

Struthers, J. R. (Tim). *The Montreal Storytellers: Memoirs, Photographs, Critical Essays.* Montreal: Véhicule Press, 1985.

Thomas, Joan. "Introduction." In *Turn of the Story: Canadian Short Fiction on the Eve of the Millennium,* ed. Joan Thomas and Heidi Harms. Toronto: Anansi, 1999. vii–xv.

Wahl, Greg. "An Interview with Clark Blaise." In *Speaking of the Short Story: Interviews with Contemporary Writers,* ed. Farhat Iftekharuddin, Mary Rohrberger, and Maurice Lee. Jackson: University Press of Mississippi, 1997. 45–56.

Weaver, Robert. "Introduction." In *Canadian Short Stories,* selected by Robert Weaver. Toronto: Oxford University Press, 1960. ix–xiii.

## English-Canadian Poetry from 1967 to the Present

Armstrong, Jeannette C., and Lally Grauer, eds. *Native Poetry in Canada: A Contemporary Anthology.* Peterborough: Broadview Press, 2001.

Bowen, Deborah, ed. *Ecocriticism and Contemporary Canadian Poetry.* Special issue of *Canadian Poetry: Studies, Documents, Reviews* 55 (2004).

Bowling, Tim, ed. *Where the Words Come From: Canadian Poets in Conversation.* Roberts Creek, BC: Nightwood, 2002.

Butling, Pauline, ed. *Poets Talk: Conversations with Robert Kroetsch, Daphne Marlatt, Erin Mouré, Dionne Brand, Marie Annharte Baker, Jeff Derksen, and Fred Wah.* Edmonton: University of Alberta Press, 2005.

Butling, Pauline, and Susan Rudy. *Writing in Our Time: Canada's Radical Poetries in English (1957–2003).* Waterloo, ON: Wilfrid Laurier University Press, 2005.

Camlot, Jason, and Todd Swift, eds. *Language Acts: Anglo-Québec Poetry, 1976 to the Twenty-first Century.* Montreal: Véhicule Press, 2007.

Clarke, George Elliott. *Odysseys Home: Mapping African-Canadian Literature.* Toronto: University of Toronto Press, 2002.

Gorjup, Branko. "Margaret Atwood's Poetry and Poetics." In *The Cambridge Companion to Margaret Atwood*, ed. Coral Ann Howells. Cambridge: Cambridge University Press, 2006. 130–44.

Kamboureli, Smaro. *On the Edge of Genre: The Contemporary Canadian Long Poem.* Toronto: University of Toronto Press, 1991.

Kane, Sean. "Skaay on the Cosmos." *Canadian Literature* 192 (2007): 11–29.

Lee, Dennis. "Cadence, Country, Silence: Writing in Colonial Space." *Boundary 2* 3.1 (1974): 151–68.

Quinsey, Katherine M., and David A. Kent, eds. *Margaret Avison.* Special issue of *Canadian Poetry: Studies, Documents, Reviews* 59 (2006).

Rogers, Linda, and Barbara Colebrook Peace, eds. *P. K. Page: Essays on Her Works.* Toronto: Guernica, 2001.

Solecki, Sam. *The Last Canadian Poet: An Essay on Al Purdy.* Toronto: University of Toronto Press, 1999.

———. *Ragas of Longing: The Poetry of Michael Ondaatje.* Toronto: University of Toronto Press, 2003.

## Contemporary English-Canadian Drama and Theater

Ball, John, and Richard Plant, eds. *Bibliography of Theatre History in Canada: The Beginnings through 1989.* Toronto: ECW Press, 1993.

Benson, Eugene, and L. W. Conolly. *English Canadian Theatre.* Toronto: Oxford University Press, 1989.

———, eds. *The Oxford Companion to Canadian Theatre.* Toronto: Oxford University Press, 1989.

Brask, Per, ed. *Contemporary Issues in Canadian Drama.* Winnipeg: Blizzard, 1995.

Canadian Theatre Encyclopedia. http://www.canadiantheatre.com

Filewod, Alan. *Performing Canada: The Nation Enacted in the Imagined Theatre.* Kamloops, BC: University College of Cariboo Press, 2002.

Grace, Sherrill, and Albert-Reiner Glaap, eds. *Performing National Identities: International Perspectives on Contemporary Canadian Theatre.* Vancouver: Talonbooks, 2003.

Knowles, Ric. *The Theatre of Form and the Production of Meaning: Contemporary Canadian Dramaturgies.* Toronto: ECW Press, 1999.

Maufort, Marc, and Franca Bellarsi, eds. *Siting the Other: Re-Visions of Marginality in Australian and English-Canadian Drama.* Brussels: PIE-Peter Lang, 2001.

Much, Rita, ed. *Women on the Canadian Stage: The Legacy of Hrotsvit.* Winnipeg: Blizzard, 1992.

Rudakoff, Judith, and Rita Much, eds. *Fair Play: 12 Women Speak: Conversations with Canadian Playwrights.* Toronto: Simon & Pierre, 1990.

Usmiani, Renate. *Second Stage: The Alternative Theatre Movement in Canada.* Vancouver: University of British Columbia Press, 1983.

Walker, Craig Stewart. *The Buried Astrolabe: Canadian Dramatic Imagination and Western Tradition.* Montreal and Kingston: McGill-Queen's University Press, 2001.

Wallace, Robert. *Producing Marginality: Theatre and Criticism in Canada.* Saskatoon: Fifth House Press, 1990.

Zimmerman, Cynthia. *Playwriting Women: Female Voices in English Canada.* Toronto: Simon & Pierre, 1994.

## Canons of Diversity in Contemporary English-Canadian Literature

Bannerji, Himani, ed. *Returning the Gaze: Essays on Racism, Feminism and Politics.* Toronto: Sister Vision Press, 1993.

Bissoondath, Neil. *Selling Illusions: The Cult of Multiculturalism in Canada.* Toronto: Penguin, 1994.

Chao, Lien. *Beyond Silence: Chinese Canadian Literature in English.* Toronto: TSAR, 1997.

Clarke, George Elliott. *Odysseys Home: Mapping African-Canadian Literature.* Toronto: University of Toronto Press, 2002.

Davis, Rocío D., ed. *Tricks with a Glass: Writing Ethnicity in Canada.* Amsterdam: Rodopi, 2000.

Hutcheon, Linda, and Marion Richmond, eds. *Other Solitudes: Canadian Multicultural Fictions.* Toronto: Oxford University Press, 1990.

Kamboureli, Smaro. *Making a Difference: Canadian Multicultural Literature.* Toronto: Oxford University Press, 1996.

———. *Scandalous Bodies: Diasporic Literature in English Canada.* Don Mills, ON: Oxford University Press, 2000.

Keefer, Janice Kulyk. *Dark Ghost in the Corner: Imagining Ukrainian-Canadian Identity.* Saskatoon: Heritage Press, 2005.

Kymlicka, Will. *Finding Our Way: Rethinking Ethnocultural Relations in Canada.* Toronto: Oxford University Press, 1998.

Mukherjee, Arun. *Toward an Aesthetic of Opposition: Essays on Literature, Criticism and Cultural Imperialism.* Stratford: Williams-Wallace, 1988.

Saul, Joanne. *Writing the Roaming Subject: The Biotext in Canadian Literature.* Toronto: University of Toronto Press, 2006.

Schaub, Danielle, Janice Kulyk Keefer, and Richard E. Sherwin, eds. *Precarious Present/Promising Future? Ethnicity and Identities in Canadian Literature.* Jerusalem: The Magnes Press, 1996.

Taylor, Charles. *Multiculturalism and the Politics of Recognition*. Princeton, NJ: Princeton University Press, 1992.

Verduyn, Christl, ed. *Literary Pluralities*. Peterborough: Broadview Press, 1998.

## Literature of the First Nations, Inuit, and Métis

Appleford, Robert, ed. *Aboriginal Drama and Theatre*. Critical Perspectives on Canadian Theatre 1. Toronto: Playwrights Canada Press, 2005.

Armstrong, Jeannette C. "Four Decades: An Anthology of Canadian Native Poetry from 1960 to 2000." In *Native Poetry in Canada: A Contemporary Anthology*, ed. Jeannette C. Armstrong and Lally Grauer. Peterborough: Broadview Press, 2001. xv–xx.

———, ed. *Looking at the Words of Our People: First Nations Analysis of Literature*. Penticton, BC: Theytus, 1993.

Eigenbrod, Renate, and Jo-Ann Episkenew, eds. *Creating Community: A Roundtable on Canadian Aboriginal Literature*. Penticton, BC: Theytus, 2002.

Gruber, Eva. *Humor in Contemporary Native North American Literature: Reimagining Nativeness*. Rochester, NY: Camden House, 2008.

Hoy, Helen. *How Should I Read These? Native Women Writers in Canada*. Toronto: University of Toronto Press, 2001.

Kulchyski, Peter. "What Is Native Studies?" In *Expressions in Canadian Native Studies*, ed. Ron F. Laliberte et al. Saskatoon: University of Saskatchewan Extension Press, 2000. 13–25.

Lutz, Hartmut. *Approaches: Essays in Native North American Studies and Literatures*. Beiträge zur Kanadistik 11. Augsburg: Wißner, 2002.

McGrath, Robin Gedalof. *Canadian Inuit Literature: The Development of a Tradition*. Ottawa: National Museums of Canada, 1984.

Mojica, Monique, and Ric Knowles. "Introduction." In *Staging Coyote's Dream: An Anthology of First Nations Drama in English*, ed. Monique Mojica and Ric Knowles. Toronto: Playwrights Canada Press, 2003. iii–viii.

Petrone, Penny. *Native Literature in Canada: From the Oral Tradition to the Present*. Toronto: Oxford University Press, 1990.

Rainwater, Catherine. *Dreams of Fiery Stars: The Transformations of Native American Fiction*. Philadelphia: University of Pennsylvania Press, 1999.

Ridington, Robin, and Jilian Ridington. *When You Sing It Now, Just Like New: First Nations Poetics, Voices, and Representations*. Lincoln: University of Nebraska Press, 2006.

Van Toorn, Penny. "Aboriginal Writing." In *The Cambridge Companion to Canadian Literature*, ed. Eva-Marie Kröller. Cambridge: Cambridge University Press, 2004. 22–48.

Young-Ing, Greg. "An Overview of Aboriginal Literature and Publishing in Canada." *Australian-Canadian Studies* 14.1/2 (1996): 156–71.

## The Quebec Novel

Biron, Michel, François Dumont, and Élisabeth Nardout-Lafarge. *Histoire de la littérature québécoise.* Montreal: Boréal, 2007.

Chapman, Rosemary. *Siting the Quebec Novel: The Representation of Space in Francophone Writing.* Bern: Peter Lang, 2000.

Dupré, Louise, Jaap Lintvelt, and Janet M. Peterson, eds. *Sexuation, espace, écriture: La littérature québécoise en transformation.* Quebec: Nota bene, 2002.

Gauvin, Lise, and Franca Marcato-Falzoni, eds. *L'âge de la prose: Romans et récits québécois des années 80.* Montreal and Rome: VLB and Bulzoni, 1992.

Gould, Karen. *Writing in the Feminine: Feminism and Experimental Writing in Québec.* Carbondale: Southern Illinois University Press, 1990.

Hamel, Réginald, ed. *Panorama de la littérature québécoise contemporaine.* Montreal: Guérin, 1997.

Milot, Louise, and Fernand Roy, eds. *Les figures de l'écrit: Relecture de romans québécois, des* Habits rouges *aux* Filles de Caleb. Quebec: Nuit blanche, 1993.

Nepveu, Pierre. *L'écologie du réel: Mort et naissance de la littérature québécoise contemporaine.* Montreal: Boréal, 1988.

Nobel, Peter S. *Beware the Stranger: The Survenant in the Quebec Novel.* Amsterdam: Rodopi, 2002.

Paterson, Janet M. *Postmodernism and the Quebec Novel.* Toronto: University of Toronto Press, 1994.

Purdy, Anthony George. *A Certain Difficulty of Being: Essays on the Quebec Novel.* Montreal and Kingston: McGill-Queen's University Press, 1990.

Saint-Martin, Lori, ed. *L'autre lecture: La critique au féminin et les textes québécois.* Vol. 2, Montreal: XYZ, 1994.

Simon, Sherry, Pierre L'Hérault, Robert Schwartzwald, and Alexis Nouss. *Fictions de l'identitaire au Québec.* Montreal: XYZ, 1991.

## The French-Canadian Short Prose Narrative

Beaulé, Sophie. " 'Décapité, vivant': Espace et personnage dans la nouvelle de SFFQ." *Solaris* 149 (2004): 145–62.

Bordeleau, Francine. "Sur le front de la nouvelle." *Lettres québécoises* 87 (1997): 14–17.

Brulotte, Gaétan. "Bilan de la nouvelle québécoise des dix dernières années du XX$^e$ siècle." *UTQ* 70.3 (2001): 769–800.

———. "Une décennie de nouvelles québécoises 1980–1990." *The French Review* 65.6 (1992): 963–77.

Brulotte, Gaétan. "De l'écriture de la nouvelle." *XYZ* 47 (1996): 65–93.

———. "Formes de la nouvelle québécoise contemporaine." In *L'âge de la prose: Romans et récits québécois des années 80,* ed. Lise Gauvin and Franca Marcato-Falzoni. Montreal and Rome: VLB and Bulzoni, 1992. 67–84.

Dansereau, Estelle. "Réponses plurielles: La nouvelle québécoise au féminin (1980–2000)." *UTQ* 69.4 (2000): 826–48.

Mailhot, Laurent. "Nouvelles, science-fiction, fantastique." In *La littérature québécoise.* Montreal: Typo, 1997. 253–78.

Morin, Lise. *La nouvelle fantastique québécoise de 1960 à 1985: Entre le hasard et la fatalité.* Quebec: Nuit blanche, 1996.

Nadeau, Vincent, and Stanley Péan. "La prose narrative au Québec (La nouvelle) (1960–1996)." In *Panorama de la littérature québécoise contemporaine,* ed. Réginald Hamel. Montreal: Guérin, 1997. 309–51.

### French-Canadian Poetry from 1967 to the Present

Bayard, Caroline. *The New Poetics in Canada and Quebec: From Concretism to Postmodernism.* Toronto: University of Toronto Press, 1989.

Beausoleil, Claude. *Le motif de l'identité dans la poésie québécoise (1830–1995).* Ottawa: Estuaire, 1996.

Brossard, Nicole. "Ludique critique et moderne rebelle/scribelle." *Les discours féminins dans la littérature postmoderne au Québec,* ed. Raija Koski et al. San Francisco: Edwin Mellen Press, 1992. 107–11.

———, and Lisette Girouard, eds. *Anthologie de la poésie des femmes au Québec des origines à nos jours.* Montreal: Les Éditions du remue-ménage, 2003.

Chamberland, Roger. "Les voies/voix multiples de la poésie québécoise contemporaine." *Recherches Sociographiques* 33.2 (1992): 277–98.

Dionne, René. "Trois littératures francophones au Canada." In *Mélanges Marguerite Maillet,* ed. Raoul Boudreau. Moncton: Chaire d'études acadiennes, 1996. 161–80.

Dorion, Gilles, ed. *Dictionnaire des oeuvres littéraires du Québec.* Vol. 6: 1976–1980. Montreal: Fides, 1994.

Dumont, François. *La poésie québécoise.* Montreal: Boréal, 1999.

Gould, Karen. *Writing in the Feminine: Feminism and Experimental Writing in Québec.* Carbondale: Southern Illinois University Press, 1990.

Lemire, Maurice, ed. *Dictionnaire des oeuvres littéraires du Québec.* Vol. 5: 1970–1975. Montreal: Fides, 1987.

Léveillé, J. Roger. "De la politique à la poétique: Deux siècles de poésie franco-manitobaine." In *Poétiques et imaginaire: Francopolyphonie littéraire des Amériques,* ed. Pierre Laurette and Hans-George Ruprecht. Paris: Harmattan, 1995. 109–20.

Magord, André et al., eds. *L'Acadie plurielle: Dynamiques identitaires collectives et développement au sein des réalités acadiennes.* Moncton: Université de Moncton, 2003.

Mailhot, Laurent, and Pierre Nepveu, eds. *La poésie québécoise des origines à nos jours: Anthologie.* Sillery, Québec: Presses de l'Université du Québec, 1981.

Olscamp, Marcel. "Renoncer à l'identitaire: Entretien avec François Paré." *Spirale* 174 (2000): 16–17.

Paré, François. *Les littératures de l'exiguité.* Ottawa: Le Nordir, 2001.

## Orality and the French-Canadian Chanson

Aubé, Jacques. *Chanson et politique au Québec (1960–1980).* Montreal: Triptyque, 1990.

Bayard, Caroline. *The New Poetics in Canada and Quebec: From Concretism to Post-Modernism.* Toronto: University of Toronto Press, 1989.

Chamberland, Roger, and Richard Martel, eds. *Oralités — Polyphonix 16: "La pensée se fait dans la bouche."* Quebec: Intervention, 1992.

Demers, Frédéric. *Céline Dion et l'identité québécoise: "La petite fille de Charlemagne parmi les grands!"* Montreal: VLB, 1999.

Giroux, Robert, Constance Havard, and Rock LaPalme, eds. *Le guide de la chanson québécoise.* Montreal: Syros, 1991.

Kallmann, Helmut, and Gilles Potvin, eds. *Encyclopedia of Music in Canada.* Toronto: University of Toronto Press, 1992.

Laforte, Conrad. *La chanson de tradition orale: Une découverte des écrivains du XIXe siècle (en France et au Québec).* Montreal: Triptyque, 1995.

Lamothe, Maurice. *La chanson populaire ontaroise 1970–1990.* Ottawa: Le Nordir, 1994.

Le Blanc, Benoît. "La chanson québécoise de 1968 à aujourd'hui." In *Panorama de la littérature québécoise contemporaine,* ed. Réginald Hamel. Montreal: Guérin, 1997. 488–517.

Lemieux, Germain. *Chanteurs franco-ontariens et leurs chansons.* Sudbury: Société historique du Nouvel-Ontario, 1964.

Mailhot, Laurent, and Doris-Michel Montpetit, eds. *Monologues québécois 1890–1980.* Montreal: Leméac, 1980.

Mathis, Ursula, ed. *La chanson française contemporaine: Politique, société, médias.* Innsbruck: Institut für Sprachwissenschaften, 1996.

Rens, Jean-Guy, and Raymond Leblanc, eds. *Acadie/Expérience: Choix de textes acadiens: Complaintes, poèmes et chansons.* Montreal: Parti pris, 1977.

Rioux, Marcel, and Yves Martin. *La société canadienne-française.* Montreal: HMH, 1971.

Thérien, Robert, and Isabelle D'Amours. *Dictionnaire de la musique populaire au Québec 1955–1992*. Quebec: Institut québécois de recherche sur la culture, 1992.

## Drama and Theater from the Révolution tranquille to the Present

Beauchamp, Hélène, Bernard Julien, and Paul Wyczinski, eds. *Le théâtre canadien-français: Évolution — témoignages — bibliographie*. Montreal: Fides, 1976.

Brisset, Annie. *A Sociocritique of Translation: Theatre and Alterity in Quebec 1968–1988*. Toronto: University of Toronto Press, 1996.

*Cahiers de théâtre Jeu*. Montreal: Fides, 1976–.

Dargnat, Mathilde. *Quand la parole jette l'encre . . . Le "joual" de Michel Tremblay dans "Les belles-soeurs" ou D'une variante populaire à un style littéraire*. Paris: L'Harmattan, 2002.

David, Gilbert. *Les veilleurs de nuit*. 4 vols. Montreal: Les Herbes rouges, 1988–1992.

David, Gilbert, and Pierre Lavoie, eds. *Le monde de Michel Tremblay*. Montreal: Éditions Jeu/Lansman, 1993.

Féral, Josette. *Mise en scène et jeu de l'acteur. Entretiens*. 2 vols. Montreal: Éditions Jeu/Lansman, 1997 and 1999.

Godin, Jean-Cléo, and Laurent Mailhot. *Théâtre québécois*. 2 vols. Montreal: Bibliothèque québécoise, 1988.

Krysinski, Wladimir. "Section théâtre: Critiques." *Vice Versa* (1986–1997).

Lafon, Dominique, ed. *Le théâtre québécois 1975–1995*. Montreal: Fides, 2001.

Lalonde, Michèle. *Défense et illustration de la langue québécoise;* (suivi de) *Prose & Poèmes*. Paris: Seghers, 1979.

Legris, Renée, Jean-Marc Larrue, André-G. Bourassa, and Gilbert David. *Le théâtre au Québec 1825–1980: Repères et perspectives*. Montreal: VLB et al., 1988.

Smith, André, ed. *Marie Laberge, dramaturge*. Trois-Rivières: VLB, 1989.

Vigeant, Louise. *La lecture du spectacle théâtral*. Quebec: Laval, 1989.

## Transculturalism and *écritures migrantes*

Berrouët-Oriol, Robert. "L'effet d'exil." *Vice versa* 17 (1986–1987): 20–21.

———, and Robert Fournier. "L'émergence des écritures migrantes et métisses au Québec." *Québec Studies* 14 (1992): 7–22.

Biron, Michel, François Dumont, and Élisabeth Nardout-Lafarge. *Histoire de la littérature québécoise*. Montreal: Boréal, 2007.

Bissoondath, Neil. *Selling Illusions: The Cult of Multiculturalism in Canada*. Toronto: Penguin, 1994.

Bouraoui, Hédi. *The Canadian Alternative: Cultural Pluralism and Canadian Unity.* Downsview, ON: ECW Press, 1980.

Chartier, Daniel. *Dictionnaire des écrivains émigrés au Québec 1800–1999.* Quebec: Nota bene, 2003.

———. "Les origines de l'écriture migrante: L'immigration littéraire au Québec au cours des deux derniers siècles." *Voix et images* 80 (2002): 303–16.

Harel, Simon. *Braconnages identitaires: Un Québec palimpseste.* Montreal: VLB, 2006.

———. *Les passages obligés de l'écriture migrante.* Montreal: XYZ, 2005.

L'Hérault, Pierre. "L'intervention italo-québécoise dans la reconfiguration de l'espace identitaire québécois." In *Italies imaginaires du Québec,* ed. Carla Fratta and Élisabeth Nardout-Lafarge. Montreal: Fides, 2003. 179–202.

Moisan, Clément, and Renate Hildebrand. *Ces étrangers du dedans: Une histoire de l'écriture migrante au Québec (1937–1997).* Quebec: Nota bene, 2001.

Nepveu, Pierre. *L'écologie du réel: Mort et naissance de la littérature québécoise contemporaine.* Montreal: Boréal, 1988.

———. "Qu'est-ce que la transculture?" *Paragraphes* 2 (1989): 15–31.

Ollivier, Émile. "Quatre thèses sur la transculturation." *Cahiers de recherches sociologiques* 2.2 (1984): 15–90.

Simon, Sherry. *Translating Montreal: Episodes in the Life of a Divided City.* Montreal and Kingston: McGill-Queen's University Press, 2006.

**The Institutionalization of Literature in Quebec**

Angenot, Marc. "Pour une théorie du discours social: Problématique d'une recherche en cours." *Littérature* 70 (May 1988): 82–98.

Biron, Michel, François Dumont, and Élisabeth Nardout-Lafarge. *Histoire de la littérature québécoise.* Montreal: Boréal, 2007.

Bourdieu, Pierre. "Le marché des biens symboliques." *L'Année sociologique* 22 (1971): 49–126.

Dumont, François, and Frances Fortier, eds. *Littérature québécoise: La recherche en émergence. Actes du deuxième colloque interuniversitaire des jeunes chercheur(e)s en littérature québécoise.* Quebec: Nuit blanche, 1991.

Jonassaint, Jean. "L'édition québécoise actuelle, portrait(s)." In *Trajectoires: Littérature et institutions au Québec et en Belgique francophone,* ed. Lise Gauvin and Jean-Marie Klinkenberg. Brussels: Labor, 1985. 137–60.

Lemire, Maurice, ed. *L'institution littéraire: Actes du colloque.* Quebec: CRELIQ, 1986.

Mailhot, Laurent. "Une critique qui se fait." *Études françaises* 3 (October 1966): 328–47.

Marcotte, Gilles. "Institution et courants d'air." *Liberté* 134 (March/April 1981): 5–14.

———. *Une littérature qui se fait: Essais critiques sur la littérature canadienne-française.* Montreal: HMH, 1962.

Michon, Jacques, ed. *Édition et pouvoirs.* Sainte-Foy: Les Presses de l'Université Laval, 1995.

Robert, Lucie. *L'institution du littéraire au Québec.* Quebec: Les Presses de l'Université Laval, 1989.

Schwartzwald, Robert. "A Literary Quarrel: Publishing in Exile in the 1940s and the Modern Québécois Literary Institution." *Studies in the Humanities* 11.11 (June 1984): 35–43.

———. "Literature and Intellectual Realignments in Quebec." *Quebec Studies* 3 (1985): 32–56.

Yergeau, Robert. *Art, argent, arrangement: Le mécénat d'État.* Ottawa: Les Éditions David, 2004.

———. *À tout prix: Les prix littéraires au Québec.* Montreal: Triptyque, 1994.

# Contributors

GEORGIANA BANITA, MA, is a PhD candidate and lecturer in American Studies at the University of Constance. She has published an article on Janice Kulyk Keefer in *The Canadian Short Story: Interpretations* (ed. Nischik 2007), an analysis of Canadian literary and political theory, translation and cultural politics in *Translating Canada: Charting the Institutions and Influences of Cultural Transfer* (ed. von Flotow and Nischik 2007), and is currently working on a project about terrorism, diaspora, and the Canadian novel. Her most recent articles have appeared in the *M/MLA Journal, Peace Review: A Journal of Social Justice*, and *Parallax*.

DR. NICHOLAS BRADLEY is Assistant Professor of English at the University of Victoria, BC. His recent publications include articles about Robin Skelton (in *The Malahat Review*), Robert Bringhurst (in the *University of Toronto Quarterly*), and Robinson Jeffers (in *Jeffers Studies*).

JULIA BREITBACH, MA, has studied North American Literature, Comparative Literature, and Media Studies at the University of Constance, Yale University, and the University of British Columbia. She has published on the short-story oeuvre of Canadian modernist writer Raymond Knister and the role of photography in Margaret Atwood's poetry, and is currently preparing a PhD thesis on photographic discourses in contemporary American and Canadian novels.

DR. GWENDOLYN DAVIES is Dean of Graduate Studies, Associate Vice President of Research, and Professor of English at the University of New Brunswick. Her publications range from a critical edition of *The Mephibosheth Stepsure Letters* (1990), to the authored *Studies in Maritime Literary History* (1991), to contributions to the three volumes of *The History of the Book in Canada* (2004–2007).

DR. GILLES DUPUIS is Associate Professor at the French Department of the Université de Montréal, where he teaches contemporary French-Canadian literature. He has published several articles on Québécois authors and migrant writers. He is coeditor of *À la carte: Le roman québécois (2000–2005)* (2007) and of a thematic issue of *Voix et images* (2005) titled "Orientalisme et contre-orientalisme dans la littérature québécoise."

Dr. Marta Dvorak is Professor of Canadian and Commonwealth Literatures at the Université Paris 3-Sorbonne Nouvelle. She is former Associate Editor of *The International Journal of Canadian Studies* and current Editor of *Commonwealth Essays and Studies*. She has authored chapters for *The Cambridge Companion to Canadian Literature* and *The Cambridge Companion to Margaret Atwood*. Her most recent books include *Ernest Buckler: Rediscovery and Reassessment* (2001), *Thanks for Listening: Stories and Short Fictions by Ernest Buckler* (2004), *Tropes and Territories: Short Fiction, Postcolonial Readings, Canadian Writings in Context* (coed. with W. H. New 2007), and *Carol Shields and the Extra-Ordinary* (coed. with Manina Jones 2007).

Dr. Doris G. Eibl is Assistant Professor of French and French-Canadian Literatures at the University of Innsbruck. She has recently coedited *Wasser und Raum: Beiträge zu einer Kulturtheorie des Wassers* (2008) and is coeditor (with Caroline Rosenthal) of a volume in preparation, *Space and Gender: Urban and Other Spaces in Canadian Women's Fiction — Espace et genre: Espaces urbains et autres dans la fiction canadienne au féminin*. She has published numerous articles on Quebec women writers (N. Brossard, Y. Chen, S. Jacob, R. Robin) as well as in the domain of cultural transfer and migration literature.

Dr. Sherrill Grace is Professor of English and Distinguished University Scholar at the University of British Columbia in Vancouver. She has published eighteen books and over two hundred chapters and articles on modern literature and Canadian literature and culture. Her most recent books include *Canada and the Idea of North* (2001; 2007), *Inventing Tom Thomson* (2004), *Theatre and AutoBiography* (2006, coed. with Jerry Wasserman), and *Making Theatre: A Life of Sharon Pollock* (2008).

Dr. Eva Gruber is Assistant Professor of American Studies at the University of Constance. Among her publications are *Humor in Native North American Literature: Reimagining Nativeness* (2008) as well as articles on Thomas King's short fiction, on Canadian First Nations literature in translation, and on space and gender in Caribbean-Canadian author Tessa McWatt's writing. Her current research focuses on the question of race in twenty-first-century American novels.

Dr. Iain Macleod Higgins is Associate Professor of English and Director of the Medieval Studies Program at the University of Victoria, BC. His publications include *Writing East: The 'Travels' of Sir John Mandeville* (1997), *Then Again* (poems, 2005), and (as translator) *The Invention of Poetry: Selected Poems of Adam Czerniawski* (2005).

DR. FRITZ PETER KIRSCH teaches French and Francophone Literatures at the University of Vienna. His scholarly interests center on contact and conflict between majority and minority groups. Among his recent publications is *Écrivains au carrefour des cultures: Études de littérature occitane, française et "francophone"* (2000).

DR. MARTIN KUESTER is Professor of English Literature at the University of Marburg and Director of the Marburg Centre for Canadian Studies. Among his publications are *Framing Truths: Parodic Structures in Contemporary English-Canadian Historical Novels* (1992), *Writing Canadians: The Literary Construction of Ethnic Identities* (coed. 2002), and *Reading(s) from a Distance: European Perspectives on Canadian Women's Writing* (coed. 2008).

DR. GUY LAFLÈCHE is Professor of French Literatures at the Université de Montréal. He has worked on the period of New France from his edition of the *Relation de 1634* by Paul Lejeune (1973) to his edition and study of the 1679 Jansenist *Letter of Valentin Leroux* (2003).

DR. ROLF LOHSE teaches French, Italian, and Comparative Literatures at the University of Göttingen. Among his publications are *Postkoloniale Traditionsbildung: Der frankokanadische Roman zwischen Autonomie und Bezugnahme auf die Literatur Frankreichs und der USA* (2005), *Internationality in American Fiction: James, Howells, Faulkner, Morrison* (coed. 2005), and *Renaissancetheater* (ed. 2007).

DR. URSULA MATHIS-MOSER is Professor of French and Spanish Literatures at the University of Innsbruck and Director of the Innsbruck Canadian Studies Centre. She has published several books and numerous articles on French, Francophone, and Comparative Literature. Among her recent publications are the award-winning *Dany Laferrière: La dérive américaine* (2003), *Austria — Canada: Cultural and Knowledge Transfer 1990–2000* (ed. 2003), *Nouveaux regards sur la littérature québécoise* (coed. 2004), and *La littérature 'française' contemporaine: Contact de cultures et créativité* (coed. 2007).

DR. REINGARD M. NISCHIK is Professor of American Literature at the University of Constance. She is former coeditor of the *Zeitschrift für Kanada-Studien* and has published twenty-five books and numerous articles on mainly Canadian, American, and Comparative Literature, recently a chapter in *The Cambridge Companion to Margaret Atwood* (ed. Howells 2006). Among her recent books are the award-winning *Margaret Atwood: Works and Impact* (ed. 2000/2002), *The Canadian Short Story: Interpretations* (ed. 2007), and *Translating Canada: Charting the*

*Institutions and Influence of Cultural Transfer: Canadian Writing in German/y* (coed. with Luise von Flotow 2007).

Dr. Anne Nothof is Professor of English at Athabasca University in Alberta. She has published numerous critical essays and chapters on British and Canadian drama, the most recent of which is "Postcolonial Tragedy in the Crowsnest Pass: Two Rearview Reflections by Sharon Pollock and John Murrell" in *Great Plains Quarterly* (2006). She has edited collections of essays on Pollock and on Alberta theater in the Critical Perspectives series (2008) as well as an anthology of Alberta plays called *The Alberta Advantage* (2008). She is editor of the Canadian Theatre Encyclopedia (www.canadiantheatre.com).

Dr. Andrea Oberhuber is Associate Professor of French and Quebec literature at the Université de Montréal. She specializes in women's writing and text-image topics. She is the coeditor of a thematic issue of *Études françaises* (2004), "Réécrire au féminin: Pratiques, modalités, enjeux," and has recently edited *Claude Cahun: Contexte, posture, filiation: Pour une esthétique de l'entre-deux* (2007). She has published numerous articles in the domain of the French and francophone chanson, intermediality, and cultural transfer.

Dr. Caroline Rosenthal was Assistant Professor of American Literature at the University of Constance until 2008. In the academic year 2008/09, she is Professor of American literature at the University of Heidelberg. Her publications include *Narrative Deconstructions of Gender in Works by Audrey Thomas, Daphne Marlatt, and Louise Erdrich* (2003), "Canonizing Atwood: Her Impact on Teaching in the US, Canada, and Europe" in *Margaret Atwood: Works and Impact* (ed. Nischik 2000/2002), and "Comparing Mythologies: The Canadian North versus the American West" in *Regionalism in the Age of Globalism* (ed. Hönnighausen et al. 2005). Her forthcoming book is entitled *Symbolic Urban Spaces: Contemporary New York and Toronto Fiction*.

Dr. Dorothea Scholl is Assistant Professor at the French and Italian Department of the University of Kiel. Among her recent publications are "Existe-t-il une esthétique franco-canadienne?" in *CANADA: Le rotte della libertà* (ed. Dotoli 2006), *La question du baroque* (ed. 2007), and "La conception d'une littérature canadienne-française nationale et catholique" in *La Croix et la bannière: L'écrivain catholique en francophonie (XVIIe–XXIe siècles)* (ed. Dierkens 2007).

Dr. Tracy Ware is Professor of English at Queen's University, Kingston, Ontario. He has published on Wordsworth, Byron, Shelley, Poe, Trilling, Naipaul, Keneally, and various aspects of Canadian literature.

DR. JERRY WASSERMAN is Professor of English and Theatre at the University of British Columbia in Vancouver. His books include *Spectacle of Empire: Marc Lescarbot's Theatre of Neptune in New France* (2006), *Theatre and AutoBiography: Writing and Performing Lives in Theory and Practice* (coed. with Sherrill Grace 2006), and *Modern Canadian Plays*, 4th ed. (2000/2001).

DR. LORRAINE YORK is Professor of English and Cultural Studies at McMaster University in Hamilton, Ontario. Among her most recent publications are *Literary Celebrity in Canada* (2007), "Biography / Autobiography" in *The Cambridge Companion to Margaret Atwood* (ed. Howells 2006) and " 'First, They're Foreigners': *The Daily Show* with Jon Stewart and the Limits of Dissident Laughter" (coauthored with Michael Ross) in *The Canadian Review of American Studies*.

# Index

Mosionier, Beatrice. *See* Culleton,
Beatrice
Moss, John, 295, 298, 308, 315, 389;
works by: *Enduring Dreams*, 308;
*Patterns of Isolation*, 295
Mouawad, Wajdi, 489
Mouffe (Claudine Monfette), 473,
475; works by: "Ordinaire," 475
Mouré, Erin, 363, 369; works by:
*Sheep's Vigil by a Fervent Person*, 364
Mousseau, Alfred, works by: *Mirage*,
248
Mukherjee, Bharati, 335, 405; works
by: *Darkness*, 405; *Days and Nights
in Calcutta*, 405; *The Holder of the
World*, 405; "The Invisible Woman,"
405; *Jasmine*, 405; *Leave It to Me*,
405; *The Tiger's Daughter*, 405;
*Wife*, 405
multiculturalism, 2 n. 3, 8, 14, 287,
307, 311, 326, 328, 336, 340, 341,
355, 368, 384, 387–90, 394, 401,
409, 441, 499, 505; multicultural
politics/policy, 326, 328, 368, 384,
387–90, 409; multicultural writing,
389, 392, 394, 402, 409, 412. *See
also* interculturalism; transculturalism
Multiculturalism Act, 287, 302, 387
multigeneric forms. *See under* genre
multimedia: multimedia aesthetics in
theater, 209, 220, 271, 272, 277,
487, 493, 495; multimedia in the
chanson, 470, 476. *See also under*
medium
Mummers Troupe, 375; works by:
*Buchans/Company Town*, 375; *Dying
Hard*, 375; *Gros Mourn*, 375; *IWA
Loggers Strike*, 375; *Silakepat
Kissiane/Weather Permitting*, 375;
*Stars in the Sky Morning*, 375; *They
Club Seals, Don't They?*, 375; *What's
That Got to Do with the Price of Fish?*,
375
Munro, Alice, 21, 22, 122, 190, 202,
289, 290, 311, 317, 333, 337–38,
339, 340, 341, 350, 354; works by:
"The Albanian Virgin," 338; *The
Beggar Maid*, 337; "Boys and Girls,"
338; *Dance of the Happy Shades*,
338; "Dulse," 338; "Epilogue,"
338; "Fits," 338; *Hateship,
Friendship, Courtship, Loveship,
Marriage*, 338; *Lives of Girls and
Women*, 337, 338; "Material," 338;
"Miles City, Montana," 338; "The
Moons of Jupiter," 338; *The Moons
of Jupiter*, 338; "The Office," 338;
*Open Secrets*, 338; "The Ottawa
Valley," 338; "The Peace of
Utrecht," 338; *The Progress of Love*,
338; *Something I've Been Meaning to
Tell You*, 338; "What Is
Remembered," 338; "White
Dump," 338; *Who Do You Think
You Are?*, 337
Murrell, John, 377; works by: *Farther
West*, 377; *Waiting for the Parade*,
377
Musgrave, Susan, 369
music: blues, 404, 476; chanson, 3, 3
n. 5, 22, 88, 98, 107, 109, 132,
270, 467, 470–77, 480, 485; folk
music, 101, 104, 108, 109, 132,
229, 473; jazz, 236, 327, 457, 458,
473, 476, 504; musical performance,
30, 31 (*see also* orality; performance);
musical settings of poems, 102, 106,
107, 108; musicality/musical
elements (in texts), 190, 457, 458,
460, 462, 464, 471, 481; as theme,
313, 327, 335, 370, 371, 458, 460,
488, 494; in theater/opera, 209,
213, 219, 275, 277, 278, 286, 374,
376, 482, 488, 494, 496; popular, 3
n. 5, 94, 290, 359, 468, 471,
472–77; rock, 457, 458, 473, 474,
475, 476
mysticism, 118, 233; mystical poem,
191, 233, 240; mystical style, 209,
261, 298, 476
myth: Aboriginal myths, 28, 31, 34,
35, 37, 115, 117, 413, 416, 420,
426; Chinese myths, 397–98;
deconstruction of
myth/demythologizing, 188, 274,
279, 282, 306, 368, 376, 446;